COLLECTIVE DYNAMICS

COLLECTIVE

NEW YORK

DYNAMICS

Kurt Lang & Gladys Engel Lang

QUEENS COLLEGE

Thomas Y. Crowell Company

ESTABLISHED 1834

To Glenna and Kevin

Preface

THE title of this volume departs from traditional usage; the phenomena studied have, since Park and Burgess identified the field in 1922, been grouped together and known as "collective behavior." The change in name, it seems to us, has some merit and is long overdue. "Collective behavior" implies that individual behavior is its opposite. The term defines, as Park recognized, the entire subject matter of sociology, and so it fails to dramatize the main distinction between patterns of interaction characterized by relative spontancity, transitoriness, and volatility and the more clearly articulated, durable, and institutionalized forms with which so much of sociology is concerned. "Collective behavior" may arise outside of a framework of organization or entail its partial breakdown or radical transformation. The focus of this study is on certain dynamic aspects of social and institutional change; hence the term "collective dynamics" to differentiate the patterns that are our concern from those marked by continuity and relative stability.

Like the title, our treatment of the field is somewhat unconventional, yet, we trust, not so unconventional as to obscure the continuity. Our initial point of contact with the field, like that of so many others, was through the writings of Park, Blumer, and Wirth of the Chicago school. The range of subject matter included in this volume derives from this frame of reference. But in our specific formulations we have frequently and consciously parted with tradition.

There has been a persistent fascination among laymen and students with the way men in multitudes exhibit certain peculiar transformations of behavior deducible neither from their characteristics as individuals nor from the group norms which usually guide their actions. Accounts of such transformations have aroused interest among sociologists for another reason: they see in these manifestations of collective agitation the oper-

[v]

ation of social forces on the most elementary level and, hence, a challenge to their discipline. In recent years, the study of collective behavior has somewhat fallen into disrepute among professional sociologists. It is evident that recent research in this field has not kept pace with developments in other fields of sociological inquiry, and for most sociologists impressionistic observations of the bizarre—the crowd, the fad, the hysterical epidemic, witchcraft, etc.—do not represent a legitimate accretion to scientific knowledge. Broadly speaking, the field has suffered a decline; more than being rechristened, it needs to be reborn.

Over the last decade or so, a number of scholars—among them, Robert E. Faris, Anselm Strauss, Ralph H. Turner, Lewis Killian, and Herbert Blumer—have pointed out that new formulations and new concepts are essential if collective behavior is to occupy once more its important position in sociological inquiry. It is toward this task that the authors have directed their modest undertaking. First of all one encounters the inadequacy of the conventionally recognized categories of collective behavior —that is, crowd, mass, public, social movements, etc. The old Continental school of collective psychology lumped together these forms of social action. Then, as critical examination dissected the catch-all category of crowd, *foule,* and *Masse* into many logically discrete sub-categories, they remained grouped together simply because there was no other place for them. But, in the meantime, significant aspects of these phenomena have been studied empirically and analyzed systematically under other headings than collective behavior. For example, the study of public opinion has to a large extent become translated into the study of political socialization, the goal of analysis being the isolation of determinants crucial to the formation of individual opinions. Social movements are most often analyzed as forms of organization with an emphasis on the organized nucleus, the core group. That there remain aspects of social movements, public opinion, mass communication, etc., which cannot be treated as organized phenomena seems evident. There *is* a subject matter peculiar to collective behavior, but an inordinate amount of energy seems to have been devoted merely to differentiating the forms to be included.

We think the subject matter of collective dynamics cannot be entirely defined in terms of certain forms of collective action, that is, the crowd as distinct from an army or the public as distinct from a deliberative body. In our view, what gives unity to the field consists of the *processes* by which the actions and thoughts of persons in collectivities are sometimes rather unexpectedly transformed. These processes of transformation can be observed in many contexts, in organized groups no less than in unorganized multitudes. We have used them as a set of unifying explanatory categories peculiar to our subject and more basic than such accidental factors as size, spatial contiguity, etc., which have most often served as the basis for classification. Guided by a notion of process, we have drawn on an array of propositions taken from research not specifically designed to shed light on aspects of collective behavior. For example, we have drawn on findings from psychological and small-group research whenever these were suggestive.

At the same time, like most writers in this area, we have continued to rely on illustrative materials not based on controlled observation in order to make the subject come alive. But in line with the emphasis on process rather than form, certain subjects are given proportionately less space than is customary. We have especially resisted the tendency to treat crowd behavior as if it were the central element in collective dynamics. Our treatment of social movements, in view of the wide variety and types of social movements in different countries and periods of history, may seem somewhat cursory. To justify this underemphasis we point to the many more specialized and detailed treatments available. Rumor, panic, sectarian associations, fashion, and the polarization of collectivities into leaders, followers, and social objects, on the other hand, are discussed at considerable length because they illustrate and relate so closely to the basic processes.

In writing this book, we had in mind two audiences: our fellow scholars and the students they teach. It is difficult to appeal to both on the same level, and experience alone will tell whether we have succeeded with either. We hope to stir up some interest in our reformulations, trusting that interest will lead to further reformulations. Moreover, the teacher as scholar must feel that he is participating in a developing field if he is to reach, and interest, students. At the same time, the student will more readily find a course in the subject a rewarding experience if he is able to "read" rather than merely "study" the book.

To those interested primarily in a textbook, we point out that the first drafts of the manuscript have been tested on average undergraduates for several years now and that lectures based on them seem to have evoked an encouraging response. The organizational logic is set forth in detail at the end of Chapter 2 and therefore is not repeated here. It has evolved naturally in the course of lecturing. While Chapter 8, dealing with the mechanisms of contagion, belongs logically in Part I, "Introduction," we have found it pedagogically sounder to get as quickly as possible into the substantive materials likely to arouse interest among students. A similar conflict between logic and pedagogy concerns the sequence among Chapters 3, 4, and 5. Some instructors may consider it more appropriate to deal with demoralization and collective defense (Chapters 4 and 5) before illustrating collective redefinition with rumor (Chapter 3). This can be easily done. If the book is too long, Chapter 2, "Approaches to the Study of Collective Behavior," may be skipped without damaging the sequence. The various chapters in Parts IV may or may not be utilized, depending on the interests of the instructor, other course offerings available to the students, and the intent of the course.

Since scientific inquiry is a social rather than an individual endeavor, it is impossible to pay detailed tribute to all of our teachers, fellow graduate students, and present colleagues from whose published work we have benefited or whose ideas, expressed in conversation, have generated ideas contained in these pages. Yet we wish to acknowledge the special influence of Herbert Blumer, both through his writings and as a personal mentor. A very special debt is owed to Tamotsu Shibutani, whose dissertation on rumor was legend among the post-World War II generation of University of Chicago graduate students. Many of us received our introduction to collective behavior through his meticulously prepared course and further benefited from his advanced seminars on the subject. In 1955, Arnold M. Rose's invitation as sociology editor of the Thomas Y. Crowell Company served as a major catalyst. Both he and Ned Polsky, then with the editorial department of Crowell, encouraged us to pitch the text above the lowest common denominator. Among a number of editors who went over the manuscript at various times Charles Partridge and Susan La Farge of Crowell rate special mention—the former's comments on the first four chapters written sustained our incentive; the latter saw the manuscript to the printer. Our thanks also go to John T. Hawes and others on the Crowell staff for their patience as we tried to find niches of free time to complete the work. We are very grateful to Jean and E. Matthew Engel of Brigantine and Atlantic City, New Jersey; for three summers, they cared for their grand-children, our Glenna and Kevin, so that we might write.

Finally, there is always the matter of who is to be held responsible for what. Both authors together wrote and rewrote every chapter, yet each chapter reflects most strongly the viewpoint of the person writing the initial draft. Let the reader play the game of deciding who in each case is to be held to account for major errors.

Kurt and Gladys Lang

Jackson Heights, New York
April, 1961

Contents

[i x]

PART V: *Research in Collective Dynamics*

I

Introduction

I

Introduction

Collective Dynamics & Social Structure

T HE FIELD OF COLLECTIVE DYNAMICS is a subdivision of sociology. Its subject matter includes a variety of transitory social phenomena. In part it is concerned with the formation of crowds, masses, and publics —all of them collectivities in constant flux. Also included for study are the kinds of interaction *within* groups and societies which give rise to flurries of rumors, scapegoating, the selection of victims, the succession of leaders; or which radically transform a group, as in panic. Finally, the field includes some social psychological processes that may unite individuals casually thrown together into more permanent groupings: the gang, the sect, or the active nucleus of a social movement.[1]

Whether the phenomenon to be analyzed consists of some short-lived convergence of individuals' interests and behavior (as in the crowd or a public controversy) or of the disruption of and strain against organized patterns (as in panic) or whether it involves the spontaneous emergence of new group enterprises, in every case it grows out of social interaction: the phenomena are collective. Nevertheless, comparing them with a family, an association, a political party, or a university offers little justification for the designation group behavior with all that the concept of a group and group structure usually implies. It is this lack of structure that sets off the subject matter of collective behavior—or collective dynamics, as it may more properly be called—from the rest of sociology. The term *collective*

1. The sociologist, unlike the psychologist, studies, not individual behavior, but social interaction. Individuals who interact exercise some reciprocal influence on each other. It is possible to take as one's unit of observation an individual's reaction to another, and this is exactly what the social psychologist does. But there is the alternative taken by the sociologist—namely, to focus directly on the situation in which the interaction occurs. In that case one's attention is directed to the characteristic patterns that mark the interchanges between individuals.

[3]

dynamics, in its more technical sense, refers to *those patterns of social action that are spontaneous and unstructured inasmuch as they are not organized and are not reducible to social structure.* This is a formidable definition; to clarify it, one must define social structure.

SOCIAL STRUCTURE

SOCIAL STRUCTURE is a concept, an abstraction, derived from the study of persons within such concrete groupings as tribes and societies, voluntary associations, political parties, intimate family groups, class systems, and economic organizations. Though it is revealed by actual social relationships between persons—by how persons adjust and orient themselves to one another—what is referred to as the social structure is not a set of discrete phenomena which can be observed directly. It is nevertheless possible to pin-point the specific function that this concept plays in the scientific investigation of society.

SOCIAL STRUCTURE AND SCIENTIFIC INQUIRY

The rigorous requirements of scientific investigation can be met through several kinds of inquiry. One of these, perhaps the most important, is the search for scientific laws. By a process of induction, antecedent conditions or "causes" are linked with subsequent observable phenomena or "effects." This gives rise to propositions about events which can in turn be used to make predictions. By checking on whether or not the predictions so derived are confirmed by observation, one tests the accuracy of the general proposition.

Propositions can take two forms: *deterministic* and *probabilistic.* A deterministic proposition would read: given antecedent conditions *a, b, c,* etc., effect *y* will follow; whereas a statement of chance is indispensable to a probabilistic one, for example, given *a, b, c,* etc., the chances are two to one that *y* will follow. Sociologists trying to trace the ramifications of certain antecedent conditions in the social realm employ propositions in the probabilistic form much more frequently than in the deterministic form.

The factors or variables that constitute antecedent conditions may be social influences on individuals (e.g., certain early childhood experiences) or social conditions (e.g., the amount of unemployment). For example, the sociologist may explore the consequences of these factors by determining the degree of race prejudice found among many individuals with similar childhood experiences, or he may observe the degree of racial tension in a community suffering from prolonged unemployment. On the basis of joint occurrences of pairs of antecedent conditions and consequences, he will propose a generalization about certain roots of prejudice or about the precursors of racial tension. A proposition formulated in probabilistic terms would hold that the presence of these antecedent conditions tends to increase the likelihood that prejudice and tension will follow. The same proposition can also be put into deterministic form if one can specify all the conditions that may operate in a concrete situation; for example, high unemployment will increase tension unless the community takes certain positive steps.

Another kind of inquiry is at least equally important in sociology; it is the study of the structure and of the dynamics of a specific social grouping. In this type of inquiry, scientific statements of sociologists seem to be considerably more precise. Researchers seldom undertake the study of a particular political club or bureaucratic organization, for example, in order to predict what is about to happen in that club or bureaucracy; usually they are seeking merely to "explain" an observable trend or behavior pattern. Behavior in the group reveals the existence of some underlying relationships which govern the interaction among the participants. Though its exact nature must be inferred, it is this underlying system of relationships that is called the social structure. The idea of a social structure provides sociology with its unique set of explanatory postulates.

These postulates are applied roughly in this manner: the sociologist studying two families notes that when they are subjected to an objectively similar stress situation, one falls apart; the other remains intact. The explanation is sought in terms of differences in social structure, for instance, in the nature and basis of family solidarity, in flexibility in these relationships in coping with new situations, etc.[2] The analyst's next problem is to find concrete indices by which these differences in structure can be indicated. These indices must be completely independent of the signs of disintegration or survival of the particular family, in order to form the basis for a meaningful interpretation of the difference of the capacity to adjust. The predictive value of these indices can be confirmed only by repeated observation of families under stress. Repeated observation of comparable social situations may confirm the existence of a relationship between the antecedent conditions and the presumed effect. Explanation rests on the assumption of the causal influence of a certain type of social structure. The notion of social structure enables one to tie specific observations into a framework of logically interrelated propositions.

2. Robert C. Angell, *The Family Encounters the Depression* (New York: Charles Scribner's Sons, 1936).

SOCIAL STRUCTURE: WHAT IT IS

Each interaction between two people, any act of what the German sociologist Simmel called "socialization," [3] however specific and fleeting it may be, entails at least a recognition on the part of each participant of the other's presence. Over time, certain general response sequences in the way people recognize, greet, or deliberately take no account of each other can be observed. These and other regularities in the behavior of people toward each other define the relationship between them. It is possible to speak of the relationship as structured if there are mutually recognized expectations which each considers in his behavior toward the other and which he expects the other to consider as well. Social structure in its simplest manifestation is revealed by these patterned interactions between two people.

Most social situations, especially group situations, are considerably more complicated than any relationship merely between two individuals. Every person is enmeshed in a multitude of social relationships which together form a network—society. To view the individual as a person occupying the center of such a network, the center on which all his concrete relationships converge, is to locate his position in society, usually called his *status*. To the extent that social relations are patterned by generalized expectations—that is to say, *structured*—the position a person occupies by virtue of his relationships is a position in *social structure*. *Social structure, then, consists of a set of statuses defined by relatively stable relationships that people in various positions have with each other.* This rather abstract definition will be spelled out and illustrated.

The Importance of Position in Social Structure

Consider, for a moment, an adult male in any society. His age and sex set ascertainable limits on his behavior, the liberties allowed him, and the constraints imposed on him. What others expect of him and, consequently, his behavior in recognition of and in response to these expectations have much to do with the fact that he is a male and of a given age, irrespective of other characteristics. Thus, by virtue of the facts of his birth, he occupies a status or position that in certain respects is similar to that of others who are male and about the same age. Certain implications, though of only a very general kind, can be derived from this elementary fact.

Each adult male is, of course, also involved in a whole series of rela-

3. Kurt H. Wolff (ed.), *The Sociology of Georg Simmel* (Glencoe, Ill.; The Free Press, 1950).

tionships, and these differ from person to person. As a son, each has a very specific relationship to his parents; as a brother, to his siblings; as a husband, to his wife; as a father, to his children. Each of these relationships can be defined in the abstract. Much as they vary from family to family, a certain pattern, at least within certain limits, is pretty much accepted as standard throughout a society, and conformity to it may even be enforced by legal sanction. In a similar way, a person's broader family circle, his social class, his nation, etc., determine his standards and, as one says, structure them. Furthermore, a person assumes obligations and exercises claims that are recognized as valid because of his position in every particular group in which he participates.

SOME CATEGORIES OF SOCIAL STRUCTURE

The assignment of a position to a person on the basis of selected criteria that are not directly instrumental to his performance except insofar as these are viewed as necessary credentials for that performance is called *ascription,* and the position designated in accordance with such criteria is an *ascribed* status. Positions conferred upon a person by virtue of his birth and lineage are the best examples of this: one is born king, and kingship is an ascribed status. But other positions which, in the main, are occupied as a result of individual effort which forces an assessment of the occupant's personal performances are *acquired* statuses.[4] Most occupational positions—though by no means all—are acquired statuses. This distinction between acquisition (performance) and ascription is a basic one in the analysis of social structure.

In general, status is determined by both socially preferred criteria and individual performance. While a person's status as an adult male is fundamentally a matter of ascription, status in most other spheres is assigned on the basis of performance. An individual's position in the occupational world—his status in a business organization—depends on his ability to control and structure a whole series of relationships in an appropriate manner. These include relations with both supervisors and inferiors, with colleagues working on the same level, with persons outside the hierarchy of the business organization (such as clients, members of the same profession, the press, etc.), because they intrude on or affect his position within it. Family connections or connections in the community may give that person an importance within the organization not de-

4. The common terminology, following Ralph Linton, is "ascribed" and "achieved" status. The authors feel that "achieved" tends to confuse status as position with status as prestige. After all, in addition to positions thought of as "success," persons also achieve positions of low prestige. The status of tramp is best thought of as acquired, rather than achieved.

ducible either from his title or from the task he officially performs. Conversely, loss of his occupational status may undermine his position in nonoccupational settings if it adversely affects his performance in this regard; for example, the unemployed head of a family is apt to have his position undermined if he ceases to function as chief breadwinner.[5]

Social position, then, is derived from and determined by a network of relationships that are relevant in a given context. A person's status is not an attribute he possesses. One must recognize that as a person moves from family to occupational world and from there to still other group activities, different sets of relationships become important. Each of these sets defines a particular status.

Status and Role

The behavior incumbent on a person in a given status defines and is defined in turn by his relationships with persons occupying statuses either similar to or different from his own. Each relationship is both subjective and objective. Subjectively, it is defined by the conceptions and implied expectations that people always have of other people's behavior. These subjective orientations have an objective consequence, namely, that within certain broad limits, each contact between two persons who stand in a definite relationship to each other runs true to some form. Each participant in the relationship thus may "count" on certain responses from others and can adjust his own behavior to take account of them. The concept of *role* designates these two aspects in the behavior of two or more persons involved in an interaction.

The particular role a person enacts within a given social position must be viewed as the outcome of his orientations to the expectations of all those other persons deemed significant in the same context. Quite evidently, any single status entails a whole array of role-relationships; but the "generalized" role constitutes some sort of organized whole that lends consistency and unity to the many specific actions that a person occupying any given status is expected to perform.

Social structure explains and "determines" social behavior, because the concept of role permits one to consider that behavior as oriented toward some "objective" norm. To the extent that such a norm is recognized and treated as a valid standard for conduct, the behavior can be considered "structured."

One of the truly remarkable but commonplace observations about social structure, which is the basis for the study of social organizations, is that its forms exist and survive to some extent independently of the individuals occupying the positions. There are traditional (cultural)

5. Angell, *op. cit.*

definitions of status that tend to standardize the interactions with any incumbent. The office of the President of the United States, it is generally acknowledged, is greater than any person occupying it. The occupants have "automatic" prerogatives but also the correlative duties that go with them. Although any individual officeholder may inject his unique temperament into and thus permanently modify the role, some imperatives cannot be left unfulfilled.

The traditional and cultural expectations that one usually associates with an official designation or title constitute the *formal* role. The emergent aspects of the behavior within a position, that is, the aspects neither associated with the specific occupant nor yet given official recognition, make up a residual category. To distinguish them from those formally recognized, they are usually, for lack of a better word, designated as *informal*. Both together form the actual social structure which underlies any organized collectivity and which can be charted after careful study.[6] When behavior ceases to be oriented toward some consistent pattern implicit in an assigned status, new forms of social interaction—forms that are not governed by the prevalent conception of behavior considered appropriate to that status—may emerge with apparent spontaneity. Normally new forms of social interaction do not emerge, because there are a variety of techniques for bringing into adjustment any conflicting and incompatible demands which arise out of the multiplicity of role-relationships.

Sociologists concentrating on the more formal categories of role and status have discovered many examples of how position in social structure determines both behavior and intellectual perspective. Military men of different rank certainly behave differently; they are also apt to view the requirements of military discipline in a different light. Or, in the United States during recent years, the rise of an individual up the income ladder and/or away from ethnic "minority" status has not only changed his standard of living but has also inclined him to vote Republican and to look less favorably on government redress of certain social injustices.

Statistical associations observed between indices of social position and certain kinds of behavior, such as those between vote and income, religion and business success, educational attainment and certain forms of tolerance, etc., are often of a very gross order. Just what they indicate has become clearer by taking into account the subjective orientations of the

6. Robert K. Merton, "The Role-Set: Problems in Sociological Theory," *British Journal of Sociology*, VIII (January, 1957), pp. 106–20. Merton uses the term "role-set" for the complex. The term "role" is restricted to the behavior appropriate to a specific relationship. His usage helps to highlight conflict and tension among the expectations of people who stand in different relationships to the person acting in a situation; traditional usages view role as something giving consistency, "organization," and continuity to the behavior of a person in a given social position.

individual. Since every person is a member of many groups—has many
different statuses and plays many different roles—the possibility of contradictory demands arises. When an individual is confronted with alternatives among several group standards, one speaks of *role conflict* or
of *status dilemma*.[7] In these instances, it is important to know just whose
standard he takes into account. To illustrate, it is easy to see that an
economist who enters government service to gain recognition from his
academic colleagues will behave quite differently from the economist who
sees his future entirely in terms of making his way up within the civil
service.[8]

These subjective orientations have an objective significance as well,
since they refer to standards set by particular groups. The recognition
that behavior within a particular status could be guided by the occupant
of that status in reference to several alternate groups has led sociologists
to differentiate between *reference groups* and *membership groups*. Both
types of group govern the perspectives of persons in given statuses. But
the notion of membership group implies that a person is most likely to
view himself in terms of standards and norms accepted by his peers, that
is, those who occupy a similar status. That this is not always the case is
easily shown. In 1948 most blue-collar workers voted Democratic, and thus
their blue-collar status was a major social determinant of their vote. Those
blue-collar workers, on the other hand, who did not consider themselves
members of the working class voted much less heavily Democratic[9] and,
in this respect, aped the behavior of the higher socioeconomic brackets. It
is likely that these "nonworking-class" workers also took the behavior of
the people in higher statuses as their model in areas other than voting.

The reference group identifies the group to whose standards an individual is oriented, standards that serve him as valid guides of conduct in
any situation. Since it often happens that action is governed by a status
not officially recognized by peers, the reference group and the membership
group are not always the same. The predictive and explanatory value of
concepts is sharpened by taking into account identifications with groups
other than the immediate membership group.

LIMITATIONS OF SOCIAL STRUCTURE AS AN EXPLANATORY CONCEPT

These lines of analysis involving role and status are basically
structural. As such, they are well suited for a rigorous analysis of conduct

7. The reader who wishes to review or introduce himself to such concepts as
"status dilemma," "reference and membership groups," "formal and informal roles"
will find any recent introductory text in sociology adequate.

8. Leonard Reissman, "The Study of Role Conceptions in Bureaucracy," *Social
Forces*, XXVII (March, 1949), pp. 305–10.

9. Bernard R. Berelson, Paul F. Lazarsfeld, and William N. McPhee, *Voting*
(Chicago: University of Chicago Press, 1954).

within a social institution or organization. Though the formal and informal expectations that govern behavior in given statuses do change, they are on the whole sufficiently stable so that, except in periods of rapid social change, their fundamental pattern is altered but gradually. Its perpetuation is ensured by two factors: (1) the control of the interrelations and of the activities of persons in the various statuses by some organized *system* of patterns; and (2) the development out of the sustained interaction of an *esprit de corps* which provides the motive power for the expression of the patterns associated with each individual status.[10]

This search for a collective pattern consisting of integrated roles and sustained by individual motives tends to fix attention on the stability of the "system" rather than on unexpected breaks in it. Likewise, the interest of sociologists as empirical researchers has been directed toward the requirements of stability. They have mainly studied social institutions, namely, those systems by which social action is carried on and by which orderly and managed change occurs. Explanations of change are sought in terms of the relevant categories of social structure.

One can study and understand much of the workings of small groups and larger unities, such as an army or a government, by analyzing their organization and the manner in which the roles performed mesh with each other. Generalizations derived from the study of one group can also be helpful in understanding another one. Yet it is not possible to conduct meaningful investigations of all forms of collective action by reference to social structure. For example, how the stock market functions is more amenable to this kind of structural analysis than how an epidemic of speculation sweeps the country. It is easier to understand how a military establishment functions than to determine how a nation develops a warlike mood. In general, orderly institutionalized adjustments to emergencies are better understood than the spontaneous reorganization that sometimes occurs in the wake of catastrophic disorganization. But the rapidly evolving and therefore unstructured responses are also collective behavior. It is necessary to develop an appropriate set of concepts for these phenomena.

COLLECTIVE DYNAMICS DEFINED

TO RETURN TO THE ORIGINAL DEFINITION: the substance of collective dynamics and mass behavior, the subject matter of this book, consists of those patterns of social action that are spontaneous and unstructured and therefore not reducible to a social structure. These collective patterns, since they emerge out of a more elementary kind of social interaction,

10. Ralph Linton, *The Study of Man* (New York: D. Appleton-Century, 1936), p. 107.

cannot be fully explained on the basis of statuses and roles participants occupy within a given social setting.

Many of the more puzzling and elusive transformations of social life rest on vague rumors, waves of excitement, and sudden conversions in which organized systems play only a very indirect part. Moreover, there are other transient formations, like crowds and fads, which, though clearly collective behavior, hardly ever become integrated into some *system* of patterns.

To understand the dynamics of collective behavior, then, is to understand social action that cuts across social structure and has not yet crystallized into a structure of its own. Such an "unorganized" collective pattern may arise within some group structure, or it may form in areas where there is no organization. The forms of collective behavior that have the characteristics of organization are excluded from the discussion in this book.

Unorganized and transient collective patterns develop spontaneously from some sort of "contagion." When large numbers of people suddenly come to follow new ways often contrary to the structured expectations of the participants, the behavior is sanctioned only by the fact that everyone else is feeling or acting in the same manner, that is, by a collective current. In order to explain phenomena of this order, one needs psychological categories to supplement the categories of social structure. But while the nature of the interaction and the role of events and personalities in these circumstances must be clearly understood, there are still two additional points which stand in need of immediate clarification at this juncture: (1) the seeming paradox of the expression "unorganized collective pattern" and (2) the general relationship between collective dynamics and social structure.

UNORGANIZED COLLECTIVE PATTERNS

What makes a collectivity "organized"? Social structure has been characterized as a system of reference points by which individuals orient themselves in their interaction with others. The internalization of some system of roles, concepts, usages, etc., determines the social perspective from which self-observation and self-evaluation take place. This orientation of behavior in terms of a stable system of expectations prescribes certain norms for judging reality and makes many expressions of emotion unacceptable.

William McDougall, the pioneer social psychologist and student of group behavior, seems to have had just this in mind when he pointed to the advantages of organization in overcoming the inherent tendency of what he called the "group mind" to interfere with rational judgment. He saw the instances of irrationality displayed by persons in the presence of others as the outcome of too direct a "facilitation" among individuals, who reacted to value-laden symbols in a manner that mutually intensified, rather than weakened, the feelings aroused. Organization alone was seen as capable of counteracting the direct emotional impact of one person on another. Group structure, he held, imposed some sort of inhibition on this contagion. It does so in a variety of ways: [11]

1. In every organized group there is some degree of continuity, if not in membership then in some *objectification of positions,* that provide stability even during a turnover of personnel.

2. To be effective, the objective scheme must be understood in some manner by the participants; that is, the mass of the members must share some *idea of the group,* of its nature, composition, functions, and capacities, and of the relations of the individuals to the group. Thus the group takes the form of some collective representation, some symbol, in whose name specific functions are performed.

3. Further, interaction with other groups animated by different ideas contributes to defining the limits of group existence and thereby promotes *self-knowledge and self-sentiment.*

4. *Common traditions, customs, and habits of mind* govern the concrete relations among members.

5. *Set ways of inducting new members* and allocating roles help to assimilate new members to the ways of the group.

6. Finally, the differentiation and specialization of functions among members give rise to a *division of labor.* This enables individuals within the group to act for the group as a whole without requiring the whole group to act under the influence of a similar impulse. For example, an accredited representative or a delegate can speak for the group; the other members need not be present to show their assent.

By contrast, the spontaneous evolution of a collective system of behavior cannot be approached by studying its structure; most of the features above either are lacking or are not determining factors. In these circumstances the interaction between individuals results in no objectification of positions. Collective dynamics deals primarily with action, emotions, and movements where behavior is governed only by the barest elements of tradition or convention. There are no specific goals clearly perceived by all the participants, nor is there any formal division of labor to achieve them. Lines of authority or established ways of recruiting new "members" are similarly lacking. Most of these patterns of behavior are defined as a deviation from an established norm or as the emergence of a new one; hence the characteristic impermanency of these new forms,

11. William McDougall, *The Group Mind* (New York: G. P. Putnam's Sons, 1920), pp. 68–70.

often to the point of immediate dissipation. But once actions are related to objective interests and cease to be a direct response to some collective agitation, even this kind of collective pattern may become a constituent of some social structure. In that case, the agitated crowd metamorphoses into a militia; the revival develops conventionalized forms of worship; the current of public sentiment is made subservient to pressure politics, etc.

Specifically, then:

1. The spontaneously formed collective pattern develops in contrast to patterns that are anchored in social statuses.

2. It presents itself to the participants as the expression of some impulse, hope, or promise not recognized in the social structure.

3. Participation in it is in constant flux, because whoever shares in the agitation, the sentiment, or the behavior is acceptable and contributes to the emergent pattern.

4. Leadership develops only in relation to the immediate needs and demands of the participants.

STRUCTURAL DETERMINANTS OF COLLECTIVE DYNAMICS

THE UNORGANIZED COLLECTIVE PATTERN, as the term is employed here, is a collective psychological phenomenon whose course is governed by impulse, sentiment, and the direct interaction of personalities rather than by an objective structure. Nevertheless, the categories of social position are indispensable and supplement general psychological interpretations even in this context. For, though not reducible to social structure, the emergence of these collective patterns is not entirely independent of it:

1. All persons occupy some position in social structure, and knowledge of what this position is enables one to predict the needs and interests that are likely to appear critical to persons in various positions.

2. An analysis of social structure helps to specify the general social conditions under which widespread and general unrest is likely to lead to a breakdown in pattern and to the emergence of new patterns.

THE DETERMINANTS OF PARTICIPATION

The importance and limits of sociological interpretation for understanding collective dynamics is to be discussed first in relation to the determinants of participation. Susceptibility to direct interpersonal contagion is not evenly distributed throughout a population, and some statuses accurately discriminate between "participants" and nonparticipants. Persons sharing a similar status share similar opportunities and similar deprivations; they tend also, as sociological analysis has repeatedly shown, to be "like-minded" in certain respects. The common plane on which they move shapes their perspective. Therefore, the age, sex, social-class background, institutional positions, etc., of a person permit probabilistic generalizations concerning whether he will be involved in some specific new pattern which is in the process of being accepted by his peers.

In this regard, however, one must keep in mind that sociological categories are most appropriate for explaining the specific response as it is lodged in group affiliations or in a common milieu which people share by virtue of their social position. Therefore, the inclination in research is to deal with the collective pattern in its particularistic aspect; for instance, through what channels *a* fashion diffuses, or what leads to *one* kind of reaction to a shock experienced by many during a disaster, or how *an* opinion is reinforced. The study of fashion may thus become the study of the fashion current at the court of Louis XV, or among the Cliveden set, or among college coeds. Or one focuses, starting with sociological categories, on the *haute couture* of the Paris fashion world as an institution. Both in its operation and in the motives that are satisfied, however, the creation of *a* fashion is quite different from what happens in the world of mass fashion. The behavior of the mass of fashion followers is neither co-ordinated nor oriented toward a specific goal. On the other hand, once a fashion begins to spread, susceptibility to it is influenced by social position, by those influences that make each sensitive to his peers and/or to his reference group.

Similarly, structural determinants operate when one deals with the state of public opinion at a given moment, among a professional group or among a group of friends. Specific group affiliations influence the particular side of an issue people are likely to choose. For example, it has been repeatedly shown that there is a relationship between the voting behavior of blue-collar workers and their occupational status. Conformity in voting is enforced by a whole set of convergent influences from the family, neighborhood, and work environment of blue-collar employees. When these influences are consistent, it is possible to predict which opinion a person will hold. When they operate at cross purposes, such a prediction loses most of its certainty. Still, this observed relationship between social position and political attitude does not explain erratic shifts in public opinion among large masses—such as the swing of blue-collar workers in large numbers to a political party that has traditionally been defined as "antilabor." Such a swing would constitute a break in the social pattern.

Also, it used to be customary to equate *a* mob with *the* mob. To do this is to explain the behavior of crowds as the expression of an uneducated, uncultured, and depressed category of persons. Some crowds indeed are predominantly recruited from among the dregs of society. Yet this equation ignores the kind of interaction in a crowd where the behavior of participants comes to diverge markedly from what one would expect from their customary roles as parents, employees, neighbors, church members, etc. For instance, a *New York Times* correspondent, witnessing a lynching of a prosecution witness in a war crimes trial in Rome in 1944, wrote, "This was no hooligan mob." As explained in Chapter 5, shared experiences under the Fascist regime which had just been toppled accounted for the general hostility toward the victim. But the behavior of the participants in the mob could not be explained solely in terms of these past experiences. Many were respectable "middle class" individuals ordinarily responsive to social authorities and likely to have been horrified at any violence against any witness in a legal proceeding. But temporarily, while in the crowd, inhibitions stemming from their background were not an effective brake on the impulse for revenge.

In all such instances—the new fashion, the public issue—the emotionality of the crowd introduces something to which people respond collectively. The categories of social position, to be sure, are useful insofar as they indicate the social groups among whom these responses are most apt to take a similar direction. But social structure does not explain the emergence of the new pattern itself.

"GAPS" IN THE SOCIAL STRUCTURE

The second major relationship between social structure and collective behavior concerns the discovery of areas of chronic stress which account for the failure of organized expectations to control a situation. In general, such stress occurs at points in the society where there are either no clear norms or no shared expectations, or where the effectiveness of rules has been undermined, that is, where organization is lacking, is ill defined, or has been disrupted. These points may be thought of metaphorically as "gaps." These "gaps" develop to the extent that any one or more of the following four conditions prevail:

1. *Areas of discretion* are left by existing cultural forms—such as custom, convention, folkways, mores, and laws. For no social group, no community imposes standards that allow no leeway for permissible deviance. Not every aspect of behavior is determined by social structure.

An aspect of permissible deviance is the personal idiosyncrasy, which may disappear with its individual carrier. For example, a prominent lady dowager used to turn up each year at the opening of the Metropolitan Opera season in bizarre clothing, engaging in outlandish antics; but the clothing and antics did not "catch" as fad or fashion.

Some deviant patterns which spread do come from the realm of legitimate caprice. "Slanguage" fads, certain word games, some faddish modes of dress, popular hit tunes, a bit of current gossip, though perhaps of only passing popularity, may be disseminated into the focus of interest of large sectors of the society, even to the point of virtual universality. The more widely diffused variations from the dominant cultural motifs come within the purview of collective behavior. On the whole, the pursuit of fashion and fad is a matter of personal discretion, and the whole area of mass "tastes" with its seemingly erratic preferences, the modish shifts in mass attention, the vagaries of public beliefs and sentiment, illustrates this constant, capricious deviation within the limits of official norms in science, in art, in implements, in usages. Some of these shifts become manifest in the differences between generations—shifts that have their roots in the psychological structure as well as in the age composition of society.

2. *The development of internal cleavages* around some issue that concerns personal reputation, politics, standards of propriety, etc., represents another aspect of social life that gives rise to transient collective patterns. Within the broader framework of societal norms, the availability of permissible options (alternatives) allows leeway for individual and collective deviations; however, different definitions of how the norms should apply in a given situation stir up controversy.

For instance, the innovation introduced as *mode* by one segment of society often offends the sensitivities of other segments. As a result, a public issue arises: does the deviation from the habitual forms violate those standards considered binding for all members of the society? The simple dress of the Puritan, the suggestive women's attire criticized by the Church, the black leather jackets and the rock and roll music of teenage circles thus attain the value of identifying symbols around which internal cleavages develop. Many seemingly innocent variations used for the purpose of individuation within a large social collective cease being matters of caprice when they raise problems of this sort. For as soon as some bearers of cultural values begin to take a public stand, the deviations are no longer a matter of personal discretion. The issue that arises calls for some collective decision. Either the norms hitherto accepted uncritically are modified, or they now require conscious rationalization in terms of some interest.

3. In every society some social demands on individuals are not lived up to. This may be due to alternative forms, but it may also be an indication of *tendencies toward alienation. Alienation* refers to an estrangement from social demands to a point where these are no longer viewed as meaningful and valid but, on the contrary, appear to the individual as hostile and alien pressures.

When personality dispositions are the primary basis of alienation, they usually lead to individual deviant behavior. Collective deviation results only on those less frequent occasions when these dispositions are widely shared. Thus it is that the rebellious delinquents, the impatient rioters, the revolutionary agitators, the pernicious rumormongers, and the defectors in flight from danger (when the rest of the army stands firm) together exhibit an analogous alienation from legitimate social authorities. Ordinarily the cleavages within a society are between clearly constituted social strata or between parties whose special interests seek recognition within a broader framework of order. But when the cleavages occur between constituted authority and those who do not accept it, or between those who personify social values and those who feel unable to share in them, one can refer to the condition as one of widespread and general alienation. For example, the sudden acceptance by the participants in an escape mob of behavioral models that are completely at odds with valid norms of behavior is most likely to occur when social authorities are no longer counted on to exercise their protective function. In the same way, the revolutionary movement is directed against forms of authority experienced as unjust, while a distrust of official news sources that fail to provide meaningful information is conducive to the emergence of rumor.

4. The external relations that the members of one social unity have with the members of another often have as their consequence *a blurring of group boundaries* which makes the participants in each susceptible to influence from the other. Partial insulation and intergroup conflict, as developed by William Graham Sumner in his by now classic in-group and out-group dichotomy, act as protective mechanisms by which collectivities define and clarify their collective identities vis-à-vis one another. When intergroup contact takes place within a common framework of norms, it is usually conducted by recognized spokesmen. Hence contact is limited, and the mutually recognized obligations are partial and only involve the participants in clearly defined roles.

However, even the limited contact between groups, whether in peaceful trade relations or open warfare, results in some influence. New cultural patterns "diffuse," and the relations themselves, as illustrated by the shifts in alignment, tend to be volatile. Hence any increase in the amount of intergroup contact, by breaking down the self-enforced normative insulation, constitutes an unsettling influence. The distinction between the in-group and influences introduced from without ceases to be maintained as rigidly as before.

The main factors that may cause an increase in intergroup contact are all forms of geographical and social mobility and, especially in modern times, the revolution in the technology of transport and of communication. In a pluralistic society as well as in the emerging world community, the bearers of diverse traditions are often thrown together. The norms and standards each accepts as valid within his social universe no longer apply.

As the field of vision of individuals expands beyond the horizon set by their own group traditions, there occurs a certain blurring of group boundaries which leads whole groups of individuals to take more and more of their cues from the behavior of unknown others rather than from traditional and folk norms.

Men, women, and even children are becoming increasingly aware of a social environment that extends far beyond regularized face-to-face relations. This uprooting from local moorings is unsettling because it leads to behavior that must always seek to take account of what unknown others do. Thus, the various movements in public taste, the waves of sentiment for or against a public figure, the vagaries of international alignment all testify to the fact that the behavior of individuals who contribute to such a current are shaped at least in part by continuing observation of behavior patterns to which they can only *respond*. Like family and neighborhood, the observations of people outside their group comes to constitute more and more a broader nexus of everyday social participation.

These four "gaps" in social structure are related but conceptually distinct. There is no one-to-one relationship between some specific phenomenon of collective dynamics and a break in pattern due to a particular cause. For example, public issues often emerge in areas that involve options where there are culturally sanctioned alternatives; the function of discussion is to settle on one of them. Similarly, alienation is a factor that influences the nature and direction of internal cleavages. Many social movements have been founded on the hopes of those who, having been "nought," seek to become "all." Finally, the increase in contacts results in a general weakening of traditions. Matters solved by resort to the mores become matters of legitimate caprice; or public issues arise; or there is alienation from the traditional rule of the past.

These gaps suggest special areas in which new forms of collective behavior are most likely to emerge. This does not mean that the participants are dramatically stripped of all the marks that participation in organized groups has left. But in these areas there is nevertheless a weakening of the influence of society.

The next task will be to clarify the explanatory postulates underlying the study of collective dynamics.[12]

12. Chapter 8 reviews what is known about the mechanisms that account for the contagion so evident and so vital for the understanding of unstructured situations. The authors have found it more meaningful first to present materials on rumor, panic, crowd behavior, etc. The reader may wish to turn to that chapter, however, before or after reading Chapter 2.

B I B L I O G R A P H Y

BROWN, ROGER W. "Mass Phenomena," *Handbook of Social Psychology*, II, ed. GARDNER LINDZEY. Cambridge, Mass.: Addison-Wesley Publishing Co., Inc., 1954. A competent and painstaking bibliographic essay by a psychologist.

LINTON, RALPH. *The Study of Man*. New York: D. Appleton-Century Co., Inc., 1936. The now classic formulation, from the anthropological point of view, of status and role.

MERTON, ROBERT K. *Social Theory and Social Structure*. Revised edition. Glencoe, Ill.: The Free Press, 1957. A collection of essays. Merton's formulations shaped the thinking of a large proportion of the post-World War II students of social organization.

NADEL, S. F. *The Theory of Social Structure*. Glencoe, Ill.: The Free Press, 1957. The most recent systematic treatment of roles by a social anthropologist.

PARK, ROBERT E. "Collective Behavior," *Encyclopedia of the Social Sciences*, eds. E. R. A. SELIGMAN and A. JOHNSON. New York: The Macmillan Co., 1937. Park's essay offers a basic concise summary of the field.

SHIBUTANI, TAMOTSU. "Reference Groups as Perspectives," *American Journal of Sociology*, LX (May, 1955), pp. 562–69. A clarification of the concept of reference group.

SPROTT, W. J. H. *Human Groups*. London: Penguin Books, Inc., 1958. A study of social relationships at the "face-to-face" level in structured and unstructured situations.

TURNER, RALPH H., and KILLIAN, LEWIS M. *Collective Behavior*. Englewood Cliffs, N.J.: Prentice-Hall, Inc., 1957. A text with readings, in the tradition of Park, Burgess, and Blumer.

of types of unorganized collectivities and on the description of their life cycles.

These three approaches do not mark distinct schools of thought. Some writers mentioned as typical of one approach have actually, at some point in their interpretations, relied on more than one general postulate. Writers identified with the same point of view may differ considerably in their specific formulations.

What follows is history, but it is not a complete and chronological history of a field. Only certain aspects in each approach are highlighted. Moreover, temporal sequence is disregarded. The origins of all three approaches can be detected in the writings of the late nineteenth and early twentieth centuries; the assumptions of each have been incorporated into contemporary theories. The purpose of the detailed presentation of these formulations is to give the reader a working acquaintance with the major postulates that have guided investigation in the field; to show how these postulates emerged from the intellectual climate of the time and reflect the problems that were—and still are—of concern; to evaluate the postulates and show how this book is indebted to or departs from prior formulations in the use of concepts.

THE PROGRESSIVE APPROACH

NEW COLLECTIVE FORMS that emerge are primarily products of conscious and intelligent adaptation in moments of shifting activity. The impetus for collective transformation comes from changes in life conditions and accidental shifts of activity. As a result new patterns become established or the old structures are given a new and more appropriate meaning. Still, any new collective pattern, whether it arises within or in contradiction to existing social structures, flourishes only in a social milieu favorable to the exercise of critical intelligence. Conflict and crisis lead to progress and "growth of mind" only if they provoke some deliberation. Collective dynamics, then, is concerned primarily with describing how a collective solution to a situation critical for the group (or for a large proportion of its members) arises and is accepted.

The unorganized collective pattern constitutes a spontaneous effort at organization in an area where there has not been any. Under other conditions it represents an effort at reorganization where the patterned ways of the past have proven inadequate. Accordingly, the least organized and most transient forms of collective behavior are elementary efforts, at first groping, from which ultimately a new structure will emerge. They are viewed as the early phases in which collectivities confronted with disruptive forces seek to mobilize their resources to find a new and better basis for rational co-operation.

Approaches to the Study of
Collective Dynamics

THREE BASIC APPROACHES to the study of collective behavior can be isolated. Each formulates the problems for study in its own way and makes use of particular explanatory postulates.

First, there is the approach to collective phenomena as one aspect of man's inevitable *social progress*. Unorganized collective phenomena arise from and are evidence of man's liberation from the constraints of custom. They mark the exercise of critical intelligence and are antecedents to the enlargement of conscious identity. Any irrational tendencies exhibited by crowds and masses are but unfortunate and temporary aberrations from the progressive development.

What appears to be an "era of discussion" for the representatives of this progressive viewpoint is for others an "era of crowds." In this second approach collective dynamics are seen as *pathological regressions*. Crowd and mass behavior, according to this view, reflect the irrational and debasing tendencies to which man is subjected when no longer directed by tradition and supervised by the "select." When these tendencies erupt spontaneously in collectivities, the orderly development of society is set back. Hence the crowd and the mass are regressions to a more primitive stage of collective mental life.

A third viewpoint, designated here as the *natural history* approach, recognizes both the constructive and the pathological characteristics of collective behavior. Whether collective phenomena are viewed as regressive group behavior or progressive reorganization is made to depend on the particular type of collectivity studied. Accordingly, the solution to the problem lies in developing a system of classification that permits this as well as other kinds of distinctions. The emphasis is on the classification

Some clarification of terms is mandatory: The phrase "exercise of critical intelligence" has anthropomorphic overtones; the nature of the "shifts in activity" or "changes in life conditions" that are conducive to its liberation must be specified.

THE LIBERATION OF CRITICAL INTELLIGENCE

The liberation of critical intelligence is manifested (1) in an increasing tendency to question time-honored patterns of thought or of behavior, and (2) in an increase in the possible ideological or behavioral alternatives. There is no question that in modern times wider range is given to choice. This liberation is the result of freedom from the past and freedom to assimilate the values of out-groups. As the authority of the past and the values of "dissident" groups are opened to discussion, the area of individual choice widens. For example, women called in the name of patriotism to work in war factories begin to question whether their place is in the home, while women still in the home, hearing of their sisters' new experiences, begin to question the time-honored subordination of women. And the feminist movement—a collective pattern—is born, or its ranks are replenished.

The explanatory postulate for the development of new collective patterns outside the confines set by in-group tradition is just this extension of consciousness and critical intelligence to new objects. It represents a "growth of mind," an increase in the potentialities for intellectual abstraction. Such a postulate underlies the idea of unilateral social progress, an outlook nineteenth-century social science inherited from the philosophy of history of earlier centuries.[1] The orientation of nineteenth-century social science was, of course, a doctrinaire evolutionism. Mankind and society, it seemed, were impelled along the road of progress by some kind of inexorable law of history, and the main task of social scientists was to discover the underlying psychological and social causes of this progress.

The influence this viewpoint had on the pioneers of sociology and collective behavior is well exemplified by the writings of Charles Horton Cooley. "The central fact of history, from the *psychological* [authors' italics] point of view," he wrote just after the turn of the century, "may be said to be the gradual enlargement of social consciousness and rational cooperation."[2]

In one form or another, the various exponents of the progressive view of collective behavior, such as Walter Bagehot, Graham Wallas, and John Dewey, share this evolutionist orientation. Social evolution, according to them, had led to internal differentiation within ever larger unities. But

1. J. B. Bury, *The Idea of Progress* (New York: The Macmillan Co., 1932).
2. Charles H. Cooley, *Social Organization: A Study of the Larger Mind* (New York: Charles Scribner's Sons, 1909), p. 113.

the consolidation of many individuals from diverse backgrounds within larger societies involved, first of all, a unity of the "mind." The existence of large societies and associations depended on the ability to communicate, and this, in turn, presupposed a shared framework of norms—some common outlook—expressed in a developing consciousness on the part of people that they were participating in and influenced by the larger social universe. Ergo, new forms of collective behavior express a developing sense of conscious identity from states of less abstract self-consciousness in which co-operation was, by contrast, habitual, unreflective, and imitative.

Rational Co-operation as a Unifying Force

Co-operation in primitive, folk societies depends on the existence of similar habits in every individual.[3] The more habitual and automatic the routines of behavior are, the more easily actions that have proved successful in the past can be applied to recurrent crises. As the ways of the group become fixed by repetition, they crystallize into folkways. The body of folkways, initially a product of unthinking repetition, ultimately leads to the emergence of a creed that justifies and supports them. Folkways become transformed into mores once they are deemed essential to the welfare of the entire group. But this transformation has an important consequence: Because they elicit sentiments that involve the entire group, deviations from the creed cease to be a matter of indifference. Every member of the community, by virtue of his conscious identification with the creed, responds to a deviation from the mores as if it were an offense committed against him personally.[4] The mobilization of collective sentiments against deviation is an obstacle to progress. Bagehot is expressing just this idea when he speaks of primitive societies as functioning under the "yoke of custom," [5] and John Dewey evoked the same imagery when he made automatic habits a cornerstone in both his individual and his social psychology.[6]

But once the social universe includes individuals from diverse backgrounds and with different traditions supported by different creeds, identical habits supported by common sentiments cease to provide an adequate basis for co-operation. They work only in collectivities that are internally homogeneous. The social solidarity of a large, complex, and heterogeneous mass society, by contrast to the folk society, rests on ties

3. Emile Durkheim, *The Division of Labor* (Glencoe, Ill.: The Free Press, 1947). One finds various versions of the same theme in Maine, Spencer, Bryce, *et al.*

4. William Graham Sumner, *Folkways* (Boston: Ginn & Company, 1940).

5. Walter Bagehot, *Physics and Politics* (Boston: Beacon Press, Inc., 1956).

6. John Dewey, *Human Nature and Social Conduct* (New York: Modern Library, Inc., 1930).

that are less personalized and consequently more abstract. Deviation is more easily tolerated and innovation more readily accepted because every act is judged not in terms of conformity but by its *utility* to the group. Social evolution toward greater complexity thus mitigates against blind conformity in favor of conscious function because collective sentiments are not immediately mobilized to suppress deviation and innovation. There is more room for choice and for conscious deliberation. While co-operation under the "yoke of custom" rests on unreflective habit, rational co-operation in the mass society depends, above all, on discussion.

The Role of Discussion

In the progressive viewpoint, a basic factor responsible for the rise of more abstract unities out of self-contained communities is the habit of "discussion." Discussion is necessary if the rational co-operation among members of an internally differentiated society is to be substituted for unreflective imitation. It liberates human intelligence from fixed custom and preservative habits. The collective existence, rooted in local and self-contained communities and chained to a past, offered few opportunities for rational deliberation. Small wonder that this formulation appealed most to English and American writers, whose countries had undergone unprecedented expansion and whose parliamentary institutions had not been threatened for many decades. Many scholars who came after Bagehot —like Cooley, Dewey, and McDougall—seem to have agreed with him when he maintained that [7]

> . . . a government by discussion, if it can be borne, at once breaks down the yoke of fixed custom. The idea of the two is inconsistent. As far as it goes, the mere putting up of a subject for discussion, with the object of being guided by that discussion, is a clear admission that that subject is in no degree settled by established rule, and that men are free to choose in it. It is an admission that there is no sacred authority—no one transcendent and divinely appointed man whom in that matter the community is bound to obey. And if a single subject or group of subjects be once admitted to discussion, ere long the habit of discussion comes to be established, the sacred charm of use and wont to be dissolved.

"Discussion," Bagehot went on to say, "gives a premium to intelligence . . . [and] tolerance, too, is learned in discussion." [8]

The effectiveness of discussion, to resort once again to Bagehot's formulations, "as an instrument of elevation depends—other things being

7. Bagehot, *op. cit.*, p. 117f.
8. *Ibid.*, p. 119.

equal—on the greatness or littleness of the things discussed." [9] Many pre-literate peoples place great stock in oratory, but such discussion as takes place rarely touches on fundamentals and is primarily an exercise in rhetoric. The essence of free discussion is that the very truths that so often have been taken for granted and the questions that have been resolved by precedent are put to the test of debate. Most of the major controversies of American society, such as those over slavery, prohibition, government ownership of industry, have questioned fundamental principles. Consequently the common framework within which discussion occurs becomes increasingly abstract and includes a greater diversity of views. Discussion thus presupposes and promotes the emergence of "higher unities of the mind."

CHANGES IN LIFE CONDITIONS

The readaptations that changing life conditions force upon collective life favor the emergence of critical intelligence, provided the change is not so disruptive as to destroy it. These changes are basically of two kinds: (1) calamities and crises brought about by the intrusion of external forces, and (2) the widening of contact among diverse peoples with the quickening of the tempo of communication among them. In fact, it is difficult to differentiate between the two. They often occur together. Both bring about polarization and diversification within a large unity. But in the first case internal divisions are wrought because the disturbing effects do not penetrate evenly into the various subgroups of the society; in the second they arise because homogeneous groups become involved in the larger society. In both cases disorganization necessarily leads to steps toward reorganization, a reorganization not explainable on the basis of habitual routines since these have been disrupted.

Calamity and Crisis

The effects of no calamity or crisis are exactly alike for all members of the society affected. To be sure, the first and immediate consequence of a calamity is always to penetrate and disrupt the many fundamental social and cultural processes. But the specific effects it has are not identical, and indeed are often opposite, for different individuals and groups of the society concerned. These differential effects can be attributed to two factors: (1) individuals differ from one another in their individual and social dispositions; and (2) not all individuals or all subgroups in the society are equally exposed to its impact or equally threatened by its effects. Therefore, Sorokin argues, the reactions that in some parts of the

9. *Ibid.,* p. 120.

society cause destruction as well as mental and moral disintegration are always counterbalanced to some extent by the creative stimulation produced in other sectors. One segment of the populace may be stunned in the face of a disaster like a flood or a typhoon, while the other is moved to excessive energy and zeal to mop up and begin building again. In fact, according to Sorokin, this generation of diverse and opposite reactions is the pre-condition for social survival:

> Otherwise—if the concrete effects of the disaster were all identical, and tended to be entirely negative, many a society would have been irretrievably destroyed by a single major catastrophe. As we have seen, calamities tend to demoralize, brutalize, and disorganize a society mentally, morally, and biologically. . . . [Those which did disintegrate] were precisely those in which the diversity and polarization of effects did not occur to any appreciable extent. In most of the others it sooner or later became the main factor underlying the restoration of the disturbed "social equilibrium" and of a creative cultural life. The counter-reaction to the initial reactions permits a society to preserve a minimum of integrity and, what is still more important, to generate eventually the forces of creative reintegration.[10]

The majority of crises and calamities are not, however, simple reactions to natural catastrophes due to nonsocial factors. Many a "natural" calamity is disastrous only because of its impact on social organization. An earthquake disrupts the food supply by upsetting the transportation system; pestilence may highlight either the deficient standards of the medical profession or a social bias in the meting out of aid; an inundation may cut off outlying areas from a central administration and lead to the establishment of new links with other communities. Indeed, the most far-reaching and frequent disruptions of social organization—especially in modern times are due to war, revolution, and terrorization, at one extreme, or result from the dislocations and tensions that accompany the business cycle, political contests, etc., at the other.

Increase in Frequency and Range of Communication

Some breakdown of the insulating influence exerted by sacred custom is a prerequisite for the emergence of a wider consciousness and of a free spirit of inquiry. New forms usually arise when individuals with different traditions are in sustained interaction with each other. But such contact is greatly circumscribed by the traditions of each group. The tendency is to confine relations to those matters that are purely func-

10. Pitirim A. Sorokin, *Man and Society in Calamity* (New York: E. P. Dutton & Co., Inc., 1942), p. 160.

tional. Such self-enforced insulation, the in-group versus out-group dichotomy, is greatly reinforced by the existence of three types of barriers: ecological, technological, and social.[11] *Ecological barriers* generally have something to do with the spatial distribution of groups and communities; *technological barriers* concern the available techniques of transport and communication; *social barriers* refer largely to those obstacles to communication that inhere in the orientations of people. The destruction of these barriers is not primarily the work of calamity and crisis, except insofar as these indirectly promote intergroup contact—for example, by causing large-scale migration.

Among the ecological barriers geographical isolation is the most significant. Mountain villages, island peoples, inhabitants of deserts and of very cold climates are hard to reach and, even when they are reached, often react with hostility to outsiders. Physical contacts brought about by trade and migration and the interpenetration of cultures through conquest and colonization do more than break down physical isolation. "Culture contact," notwithstanding the temporary disorganization it causes, also promotes tolerance of deviation. It forces a recognition that there are different ways of doing things and that these might be superior. Hence the intermingling of persons from diverse cultures is conducive to creative innovation. It is no accident that the communities founded along trade routes, especially where there were breaks in transportation that made reloading necessary, should have developed into cities in which, because they contained such heterogeneous populations, new attitudes toward freedom first germinated.[12] The city served a hinterland from which it drew the most energetic persons. By concentrating within its walls the diverse influences of the larger world, it also reflected as a microcosm the unity of that world. Metropolitan life incorporated for the first time this unity in diversity.

The revolution in the technology of transport and communication has not only helped to break down physical isolation by making speedier travel possible. It has, above all, created new means of transporting messages that can be "preserved" in their original form. If one thinks of the development of light-weight and inexpensive paper, the invention of printing, the Pony Express, air mail, electronic and wireless means of transmission, the possibilities of transporting messages without reliance on memory become evident. At the basis of the new communication systems are technological means of encoding, storing, and decoding messages so that they can be transported more easily, more accurately, and faster

11. Edward A. Ross, *Social Psychology* (New York: The Macmillan Co., 1908). Chapters 13 and 15 of this pioneer work can still be read with great profit.

12. Charles H. Cooley, "The Theory of Transportation," *Sociological Theory and Social Research* (New York: Henry Holt and Co., Inc., 1930), pp. 17–118.

than by messenger. The emergence of national languages, especially a standardized script and phonetic spelling, creates new possibilities for more intense communication within an expanded universe of discourse. An awareness on the part of people of their participation in a large society and of the existence of that society as a separate unity represented in secondary symbols—such as flags, political maps, etc.—marks the beginning of a larger framework of organization.

Linguistic barriers or, for that matter, technological ones are of course related to social organization. But to set them apart from these others, the term "social barriers" refers only to those obstacles to communication that are due to the internal characteristics of a social system in which the technology for communication is available. In other words, the extent of social contact, though conditioned by ecological and technological factors, is not exclusively dependent on them. For example, familism—a strong in-group consciousness which resists integration into a larger society— tends to be fostered by the presence of rigid age-stratification in which the wisdom of elders is equivalent to the message of sacred oracles. In a literary culture the concentration of knowledge among the scribes and literati, who alone have access to sacred formulae which they jealously guard, also discourages inquiry. Knowledge in their hands is likely to become ritualistic and highly conventionalized. On the other hand, the mobilization of large masses of men—through public education, by improving the means of communication, and by courting their participation in community affairs—quickly cuts through the empty formalism of traditional authority. Similar effects are attributed to an advanced division of labor, which creates wider interdependence at the same time that it increases internal differentiation.

THE TRANSIENT COLLECTIVITY

On the whole, the people activated to conscious participation in the larger society are viewed as agents of progress. They contribute new experiences which revitalize institutions and challenge authorities that are sanctified primarily by the past. The knowledge possessed by elites— by the literati, by a castelike priesthood, by inhabitants of monasteries— is sheltered from many worldly influences and takes no account of the lot faced by the masses. In this sense it is an insulating and parochial influence.

Occasionally the masses act directly even though they are not fully aware of a common goal or of the norms by which individual actions are co-ordinated. Their action appears irrational because all that is needed for the emergence of collective life on this level are "a common object of mental activity, a common mode of feeling with regard to it, and some degree of reciprocal influence between the members of the group." [13]

The unity of such a "group" is founded on the similarity of definitions and/or sentiments generated in the momentary situation; for instance, their confrontation by the same object, and the identical feelings it arouses in each of them. These are then intensified by the interaction. Theoretically any aggregation of individuals may spontaneously engage in some form of collective action as long as the interests and affects of the participants take a similar direction.

It is generally true that crowds, rumors, fads, etc., constitute collective problem-solving activity. The transient collectivity arises out of the agitation or unrest experienced by large numbers of people when the framework within which behavior is oriented becomes too confining. Impulses are released which, ultimately, though they lead to temporary aberrations, also lead to the emergence of new forms. A wildcat strike, for example, appears as a most undisciplined enterprise; yet the product of the spontaneously generated enthusiasm is often a trade-union or a new political party.

In this formulation individual impulse has a constructive function. When on the loose, impulse needs to be brought under conscious direction. In the words of John Dewey:

> Impulse defines the peering, the search, the inquiry. It is 'in the logical language of pragmatism,' the movement into the unknown, not that immense inane of the unknown at large, but into that specific unknown which when it is hit upon restores an ordered, unified action. During this search, old habit supplies content, filling, definite, recognizable, subject-matter. It begins as vague presentiment of what we are going towards. As organized habits are definitely deployed and focused, the confused situation takes on form, it is 'cleared up'—the essential function of intelligence. Processes become objects. Without habit there is only irritation and confused hesitation. With habit along there is a machine-like repetition, a duplicating recurrence of old acts. With conflicts of habits and release of impulse there is conscious search. [14]

In the transformations within collectivities, the development of new modes of collective action, the prime role is likewise assigned to conscious intelligence. But before this intelligent reordering occurs, the impulse not fully channeled into habits causes some disruption and conflict.

---

13. William McDougall, *The Group Mind* (London: G. P. Putnam's Sons, 1920), p. 33.

14. Dewey, *op. cit.*, p. 180.

SUMMARY

The writers characterized as exponents of the "progressive" view of collective behavior place a premium on intelligent adaptation which, in moments of shifting activity, occurs partly by chance and partly as a result of conscious reflection. The capacity of any group or society for adaptation depends on its degree of internal complexity and diversity and on the extent to which its major problems are tackled through discussion. Discussion also breaks down custom. A similar effect is produced by the introduction of novel factors into one's surroundings through calamity and crisis or through a widening of the area within which intense communication occurs. These changes upset traditional routines and create incompatible demands so that a conscious redirection of effort is imperative to preserve the unity of the society.

The chief contribution of the progressive approach is its view of collective dynamics within a broader framework of social change. The unorganized collectivity is symptomatic of social disorganization, but it represents also the incipient phase in a process of reorganization. Still, such a sweeping formulation leaves largely unexplained the inner dynamics by which the new forms develop. In its underlying optimism, it also glosses over too easily the various irrational and regressive tendencies exhibited by the individual not oriented toward an objective framework of norms.

THE PATHOLOGICAL VIEW

IF BAGEHOT AND WALLAS, Cooley and Dewey are the heralds of progress in the "age of discussion," the Frenchman, Gustave Le Bon, followed after World War I by Willfred Trotter, Everett Dean Martin, and Ortega y Gasset are the prophets of doom. They were disturbed especially by the regressive tendencies inherent in what was essentially the "era of crowds." [15] Le Bon, whose influence on the theory of collective behavior was so widespread and persistent, applied the term *foule* (crowd) rather indiscriminately to street mobs, juries, and representative assemblies as well as to political, religious, occupational, and socioeconomic groupings. The "crowd mentality," which he deplored, was not confined to haphazard aggregates brought into shoulder-to-shoulder contact; it influenced and shaped the outlook of participants in the major institutions of the entire society.

15. Gustave Le Bon, *The Crowd: A Study of the Popular Mind* (London: Ernest Benn, Ltd., 1952).

Le Bon, too, recognized that the emergence of the large society meant a weakening of traditional beliefs, which he saw personified by hereditary sovereigns; all social legislation designed to bring about a redistribution of income in the interests of the "masses" was anathema. The true genius of the race, he insisted, was contained not in new legislation but in the conservative institutions of his era. He distinguished between what he considered to be the "unalterable psychological elements" of a race—its great permanent beliefs—and the mobile, changeable elements reflecting transitory and changing opinions, and suggested that "it is easy to imbue the minds of crowds with a passing opinion, but very difficult to implant therein a lasting belief." [16]

Other writers, not necessarily sharing Le Bon's political passions, nevertheless share this image of the "crowd mentality" and of regressive tendencies due to unconscious forces aroused among individuals in the presence of large numbers. "A crowd," wrote a psychiatrist in 1940, "thinks, feels and behaves on a much lower level than the customary levels of the individuals who compose it. The debasement is the deeper as the crowd increases in size." [17]

The effect attributed to increased size is the very opposite of that inferred by theorists stressing the possibilities for rational consensus. The latter see in the formation of ever larger collectivities brought into contact through communication a liberation of conscious intelligence from the yoke of custom. But the crowd pathologists are more in line with the findings of modern psychiatry when they stress the atavistic bases of mass action. Their starting point is the transformation of individuals under the emotional, not the rational, influence of others.

This view that the "crowd" brings pathological elements to the fore is more than an ideological assumption. It has driven home with some force the observation that large unities often act irrationally and under the impact of emotion. "Men, it has been well said, think in herds; it will be seen that they go mad in herds, while they only recover their senses slowly and one by one." [18] There is an incontestable bit of truth in this contention that people in groups are often less rational than individuals on their own. How often are ideas accepted simply because they are the property of a crowd? A jury consisting of highly intelligent men arrives at its judgment on grounds rationally extrinsic to the issue, a fact that every trial lawyer recognizes. Or a commission of experts renders an unintelligible report as the product of compromise. Parliamentary debates,

16. *Ibid.,* p. 17.
17. Edward A. Strecker, *Beyond the Clinical Frontiers* (New York: W. W. Norton & Company, Inc., 1940), p. 61.
18. Charles Mackay, *Memoirs of Extraordinary Popular Delusions* (Boston: L. C. Page & Co., 1932), p. xx.

though the legislators are all well trained, provide evidence of this regression. Their collective judgment falls far short of the accomplishments of the members as individuals.

Observations of this sort impelled the crowd pathologists to see, in the historical changes that brought about a broadening of the horizons of consciousness, a set of consequences directly opposite to those seen by the "progressive" theorists. Changeable and transitory opinions, Le Bon held, now asserted themselves with greater rapidity and in increasing strength. In *The Crowd* he sets himself to explaining their ephemeral nature. The causes are:

1. The weakening of general beliefs: "As the old beliefs are losing their influence to a greater and greater extent, they are ceasing to shape the ephemeral opinions of the moment as they did in the past." [19]

2. The declining opposition to the power of the crowd: its characteristic fickleness in ideas can manifest itself without external hindrance.

3. The development of the modern press: "The most contrary opinions are being continually brought before the attention of crowds. The suggestions that might result from each individual opinion are soon destroyed by suggestions of an opposite character. The consequence is that no opinion succeeds in becoming widespread, and that the existence of all of them is ephemeral." [20]

Hence, the larger consciousness brought about by greater contact, improved communication, and the mobilization of the masses means an extension of the crowd. The panics and psychological fevers, the madness and hysterical eruptions, which had spread in small separate ripples, now were capable of swaying large masses of men all at once. This gives the sum of such agitations the force of a tidal wave, a force they hitherto lacked because the small waves spent themselves in isolated localities.

THE RELEASE OF IMPULSE

A "psychological" (or organized) crowd is said to emerge when the sentiments and ideas of all persons who compose it take one and the same direction. A person comes under the influence of a collective mentality, his conscious personality vanishes. In his actions and thoughts he conforms to the "law of mental unity." Le Bon explains this:

> By the mere fact that he forms part of an organized crowd, a man descends several rungs in the ladder of civilization. Isolated, he may be a cultivated individual; in a crowd, he is a barbarian—that is a creature acting by instinct. He possesses the spontaneity, the violence, the

19. Le Bon, *op. cit.*, p. 149.
20. *Ibid.*

ferocity, and also the enthusiasm and heroism of primitive beings, whom he further tends to resemble by the facility with which he allows himself to be impressed by words and images—which would be entirely without action on each of the isolated individuals composing the crowd—and to be induced to commit acts contrary to his most obvious interest and his best-known habits. . . .

The conclusion to be drawn . . . is, that the crowd is always intellectually inferior to the isolated individual, but that, from the point of view of the acts these feelings provoke, the crowd may, according to circumstances, be better or worse than the individual. All depends on the nature of the suggestion to which the crowd is exposed.[21]

In the framework of crowd pathology, men appear to be of very similar character in the matters of instincts, passions, and feelings, however different their achieved social position and individual intellectual attainments. And since men in collectivities are under the sway of these unconscious sentiments, intelligence, Le Bon contends, will have little influence.

Nowhere in his writings does Le Bon develop an explicit psychology to explain the relationship between unconscious impulses and sentiments and the outbursts of the crowd. He confines himself to pointing out that under the influence of the crowd the situation is redefined, and that under the sway of collective emotion the social environment temporarily allows for the release of unconscious impulse with mutual approval and without fear of sanction. But his general formulation to the effect that there is a transformation has support from clinical findings of modern psychology.[22]

"In the crowd," wrote Martin, elaborating on this viewpoint on the basis of psychoanalytic insight, "the primitive ego achieves its wish by actually gaining the assent and support of a section of society. The immediate social environment is all pulled in the same direction as the unconscious desire." [23] But where Le Bon saw contagion and suggestibility as the primary causes of this redefinition of the situation, Martin held that contagion and suggestibility occur only when the behavior or idea communicated fits in with tendencies the individuals are already disposed to act out by themselves.

---

21. *Ibid.*, p. 32f.

22. Compare also Sighele and Tarde, who drew on cases of *folie à deux* and to whom Le Bon is heavily indebted.

23. Everett D. Martin, *The Behavior of Crowds* (New York: W. W. Norton & Company, Inc., 1920), p. 35.

THE ACCEPTABILITY OF IMPULSE

Four aspects of the crowd situation help to make pathological acts and emotion acceptable: (1) numerical support; (2) decline in individual feelings of responsibility (anonymity); (3) the impression of universality; and (4) the adherence to fictions that disguise the true nature of the impulses released.

THE INFLUENCE OF NUMBERS   Le Bon assigned a pre-eminent importance to the influence of large numbers when he wrote:

> The individual forming part of a crowd acquires solely from numerical considerations, a sentiment of invincible power which allows him to yield to instincts which, had he been alone, he would perforce have kept under restraint.[24]

The principle that expressions of impulses and sentiments are validated by the social support they attract extends to collective expressions generally. The mere fact that an idea is held by a multitude of people tends to give it credence.

ANONYMITY   The feeling of being anonymous sets further limits to the sentiment of responsibility. The individual in the crowd or mass is often unrecognized; hence, there is a partial loss of critical self-control and the inhibitions it places on precipitate action. There is less incentive to adhere to normative standards when it appears to the individual that his behavior is not likely to provoke sanctions against him personally.

THE IMPRESSION OF UNIVERSALITY   In Floyd H. Allport's view, the impression of universality characteristic of the crowd is a result of social projection. "To feel fully the presence of the multitude we must realize an identity between their behavior and ours. The responses which we imagine to be universal are a 'projection' of our own response." [25] In this way the impressions an individual receives from his observation of those around him or by way of the various media of communication are magnified; each person sees himself acting as part of a larger collectivity which, by inference, shares his motives and sentiments and thereby sanctions the collective action. In this sense the crowd is an *excuse* for people all going crazy together.

THE DISGUISE OF IMPULSE   The normally controlling ideas of the immediate and personal environment fail to function in the crowd. This failure is attributed to the concessions that persons who are under the *sway* of unconscious impulses make to each other when these impulses

24. Le Bon, *op. cit.*, p. 30.
25. Floyd H. Allport, *Social Psychology* (Boston: Houghton Mifflin Co., 1924), p. 307.

are disguised as sentiments. Thus, the masked impulses meet with conscious moral approval. This disguise of motives as symbols and abstract ideas, whose unconscious meanings evade recognition, is tantamount to the formation of a collective symptom.

The crowd or even the permanent group acting under strong emotions can be considered as a massive attempt to evade unpleasant or unacceptable realities. The voice of compensatory brotherhood appeals strongly to the crowd-mind, whose pathology is explained by the fact that it stills, temporarily at least, the ego and super-ego of each constituent member.

SUMMARY

This emphasis on pathology is as one-sided as the exclusive concern with the problem-solving aspects of collective behavior. Public controversies, social movements, clandestine communication channels, and crowd behavior have, of course, their pathological aspects, and a great deal can be learned from a study of how social structures are disrupted. Nevertheless, even a destructive mob may be a creative force which helps to topple a stagnant social order by creating an awareness of what every society seeks to avoid recognizing. One need only think of the adoration given to traditional authorities, the cults of mourning that gloss over the facts of death, and the belief in the unchallengeable superiority of a political system, to know that at times the masses may come face to face with facts that the sophisticated mind is able to explain away by "reason."

Whether a collective agitation that disrupts social norms is progressive or regressive depends on how it affects the group's capacity for coping with reality. If the area of conscious co-operation is widened, fictions are destroyed, and adaptability is increased, the effect of the agitation is basically progressive. But it is regressive to the degree that the bond among the participants relies on strong feelings which demand conformity and limit their capacity to assimilate new facts. Every society and group adhere to some beliefs that are held with the tenacity of a "crowd."

THE NATURAL HISTORY APPROACH

THEORISTS whom we take as representing the natural history approach have exhibited a definite inclination toward inductive methods. They appear to have deliberately avoided commitment to a unitary view of collective dynamics. Instead, they seek to arrive at a synthesis that encompasses the many phenomena whose diversity is recognized.

This kind of inquiry divides itself logically into three methods, all of which are employed: observation, description, and classification. First, the relevant facts are ascertained by observation through direct participation, documents, or personal accounts. Next, each phenomenon is reconstructed as accurately as possible in terms of concepts with a precise denotative meaning. The systematization of the descriptions in terms of a general framework is the last step—its aim being a system of classification that permits discrimination among various generic phenomena. An attribute of the method is that its concepts remain highly qualitative, and the propositions derived by it refer to events and sequences that can be observed directly.[26] The classification, too, continues to deal with observed similarities, on the basis of which more theoretical formulations are developed.

CLASSIFICATION

The natural history approach represents the application of "systematic sociology" to collective dynamics. Classification hinges on the nature and character of the interaction out of which the collective forms arise. Each type exhibits its characteristic pattern, which has to be clearly grasped by the observers. Because it eschews concrete postulates, the natural history approach is primarily an orientation. Among its better-known representatives are Robert E. Park and Herbert Blumer, one of Park's students, and the German sociologist Leopold von Wiese.

Their interest in collective behavior stems from a concern with two closely related questions: (1) What is the nature of collective action that is not governed by common rules and understandings? (2) In what ways does spontaneous interaction culminate in new institutional structures and serve as an agent of social change? Hence, the natural first step toward a system of classification is to differentiate as clearly as possible the more transitory instances of collective "regression" from those other spontaneous patterns which result in more permanent reorganizations. If one takes Blumer's schematic summary of the field as a point of departure,[27] it immediately becomes evident that his formulations bear at one and the same time the imprint of Le Bon's stress on crowd pathology and the "progressive" conception that certain forms of interaction lead to the development of new solutions and broaden their participants' outlook.

An initial distinction is that between "elementary" collective behavior and its more "organized" forms. As examples of the first, Blumer cites a

26. F. S. C. Northrop, *The Logic of the Sciences and the Humanities* (New York: The Macmillan Co., 1949), p. 35f.

27. H. Blumer, "Collective Behavior," in A. M. Lee (ed.), *Principles of Sociology* (New York: Barnes & Noble, Inc., 1951), pp. 167–222. His formulations spell out explicitly some of the assumptions contained in less precise form in the early text of R. E. Park and E. W. Burgess, *Introduction to the Science of Sociology* (Chicago: University of Chicago Press, 1924), especially pp. 27–57, 785–952.

highly excited mob, a business panic, a state of war hysteria, or any condition of spontaneously generated social unrest. By contrast, the various kinds of social movement which pretty much represent his other major category, "can be viewed as collective enterprises to establish a new order."[28] The interest in the elementary forms centers on the forms *per se*, whereas interest in the more organized phenomena focuses on how they may evolve into social institutions.

ELEMENTARY COLLECTIVE PHENOMENA

Elementary collective phenomena are divided into three basic categories: the crowd, the mass, and the public. Each kind of collectivity has its distinct characteristics.

Physical proximity, a high degree of emotional rapport and unity, and especially the regressive tendencies postulated by the pathological view are the hallmarks of the *crowd*. It forms when persons who are physically assembled develop a psychological unity as a result of milling. As the crowd develops, the individual is stripped of much of his self-consciousness and falls under the influence of the assemblage acting as one. There are several forms. The crowd may act in some common endeavor or spend its feelings in mere physical movement or expressive activity.

The *mass* is made up of a multitude of anonymous persons physically dispersed and coming from all walks of life. A mass forms when many individuals independently converge in their action or their thoughts upon one and the same object—in that they seek similar goals or pay attention to the same stimulus. The basic difference between the crowd and the mass is in the nature of the interaction between the participants. For example, the mass of people who all watch the same television program and go wild over its star, or the speculators who scramble to obtain an option on a new stock issue do not interact with each other directly and, therefore, do not develop emotional rapport. In fact, they exist as a unity only as a numerical abstraction.[29] Furthermore, they do not react exactly at the same time. Most of them are involved as members of the mass only with regard to some specific occasion and with part of their personalities. Whereas the members of the crowd can act in a concerted fashion, the actions of individuals in the mass merely parallel those of others in the mass.

The *public*, unlike the crowd or the mass, is the product of cleavage.

28. Blumer, *op. cit.*, p. 199.
29. Howard Becker, *Systematic Sociology, on the Basis of the Beziehungslehre und Gebildelehre of Leopold von Wiese* (New York: John Wiley & Sons, Inc., 1932). See von Wiese's distinction between the "abstract mass" and the "concrete mass."

It consists of a group of people confronted by an issue on whose resolution they disagree, and as issues vary, publics vary. Through discussion, some agreement or collective decision is achieved. Because such discussion occurs within a framework of rules, and the discussion appeals both to reason and the *common* interest, it exhibits none of the irrationality of the crowd, nor the shiftiness of the mass. Nevertheless the action of this *public* is elementary. It lacks established understandings, definitions, or rules prescribing what action should be taken. There is no resort to tradition. "Instead of having its activity prescribed, it is engaged in an effort to arrive at an act, and therefore forced to create its action." [30] A person can be a member of as many publics as are dictated by his interests in a decision. However, the premium placed on a reconciliation of interests through a joint decision prevents the precipitate emotional reaction characteristic of the "pathological" crowd.

PROBLEMS OF CLASSIFICATION

Within these major categories posited by the theorists of the natural history approach—crowd, mass, and public—there are many subdivisions. Voodoo dances and public opinion, hero worship and land booms, escape panics and fashion trends, gang formations and voting behavior—and many more phenomena—have to be fitted into the framework. But every refinement of the classificatory scheme raises new problems. What are the limits of the phenomena subsumed in the field of collective behavior? What is to be done with borderline cases, involving a mixture of forms or the transition from one form into another? For example, a public issue is often resolved through the highly structured referendum process: is this collective behavior? Or, should the process by which electoral decisions are made be considered mass behavior (because voting is individual) or public opinion (because debate and discussion precede its resolution)? How should one classify the collective actions of the multitude assembled in response to an event reported over the radio? What about a procession united by sentiments of bereavement which turns into an aggressive mob?

Furthermore, the distinction between elementary collective behavior and the more organized forms cannot be consistently maintained. It is largely a matter of focus. Interest may center on the nature and characteristics of the elementary forms *per se;* to the extent that the individuals who participate in them seem to lose critical awareness, this is attributed to the influence of the interaction, and such a formulation is altogether in agreement with that of the crowd pathologists. But the other major interest, writes Blumer, is "tracing the way in which the elementary and

30. Blumer, *op. cit.,* p. 190.

spontaneous forms develop into organized forms," [31] in effect including under elementary behavior the view of progressive change. Implicit in this linkage between spontaneous interaction and social unrest is an assumption: namely, that their spontaneous character constitutes an elementary effort to bridge some gap in social structure. Elementary forms —like the crowd, the mass panic, or a public sharply at odds over an issue —are symptomatic of at least a partial alienation from custom and tradition. Yet they are also the agents of social change; they culminate in more lasting innovations.

Whether they do or do not does not entirely depend on the nature of the interaction that underlies each form—namely, the awakening of archaic impulses or an appeal to the critical "rationality" of the participants. In the first place, much public discussion addresses itself to prejudices that participants seek to mobilize in the service of the view they represent. Often interaction in the public leads to better rationalizations rather than to greater rationality. The emotionality of the crowd, on the other hand, may give the participants courage to propound eminently reasonable demands that have been ignored. The judgment concerning pathology or growing social consciousness is not easily rendered.

More important, the impact of any elementary collective phenomenon can be known only in context, and this is what the natural history approach by its emphasis on types of collective entities largely ignores. Thus, a mass demonstration may influence public discussion and thereby change policy, or a flurry of rumors may spark a revolution or result in an official legend. A panic may bring about a lasting change in leadership or a juvenile crime wave may undermine educational practices. And when does one know, for example, that a mob action constitutes an incipient revolution? A violent mob is still a collectivity acting out its impulses; it may be the spark that lights the flames of revolution, but it may not have repercussions that are of lasting significance. Fashion, viewed in terms of what is current vogue, is a momentary convergence of individual tastes; it becomes organized collective behavior, not "mass," once one focuses on the movement of style. The crucial variable appears to be the degree of permanency and effectiveness of the action as a result of the spontaneously formed collectivity.

THE STUDY OF CAREERS

The dynamic aspects of collective behavior, the transformations of aggregates casually thrown together and spontaneously formed into more organized patterns, are embodied in what is interchangeably referred to as their *career*, their *sequence pattern*, or their *natural history*. Such a notion was applied to the "crowd" very early. Wrote Le Bon, "it being

31. *Ibid.*, p. 168.

impossible to study here all the successive degrees of *organization* [authors' italics] of crowds, we shall concern ourselves more especially with such crowds as have attained to the phase of complete organization. In this way we shall see what crowds may become, but not what they inevitably are." [32]

Blumer traces the typical "career" of physical-contact groups: their new and special characteristics are built up during the process that begins with (1) *the occurrence of an exciting event,* a crisis, by which tension is established and which brings about conditions conducive to the release of emotions normally held in check; during (2) *the milling stage* people similarly excited develop rapport with one another; (3) the emergence of a common objective is the outcome of interaction under *conditions of rapport;* (4) ultimate crystallization of impulses toward the *common objective* occurs when each individual, under the influence of other members of the crowd, is ready to act. If this fourth stage of development is reached, one speaks of an *acting crowd;* other forms of the crowd, according to Blumer's frequently used typology, do not reach the final phase: the activity of the *expressive crowd* does not crystallize around an objective, but the aroused feelings are spent in "mere expressive actions"; [33] or there is only partial alienation from customary roles and rules, so that heightened emotions are given more or less conventional expression, as in a cheering audience (the *conventional crowd*). *Nevertheless, whatever their degree of development or whatever the context in which they occur, these crowd phenomena are considered essentially "pathological,"* characterized as they are by the rule of impulse and not of reason.

The depiction of sequence patterns has been attempted for other phenomena besides that of crowds. The "anatomy" of collective reactions to disasters, the natural history of a social problem, of revolutions, of social movements, etc., has been laid bare, if not dissected. Among these the category of social movement most demonstrably gives rise to a new social order. The culmination of a social movement encompasses the establishment of parties and churches, changes in conventions and morality, new legislation and new social policies. At the end of their career, the new patterns injected by a social movement become widely accepted and taken for granted. For example, woman suffrage, hard fought over for decades, is beyond dispute in the United States.

EVALUATION OF NATURAL HISTORY APPROACH

The natural history approach must be credited above all with a refinement of the generic forms of mass behavior. But even the most casual observation suggests a number of factors that, in any concrete

32. Le Bon, *op. cit.*, p. 26.
33. Blumer, *op. cit.*, p. 183.

situation, are apt to influence the careers of elementary collective formations:

First, there are external factors, among which the most important appear to be (1) the nature of the precipitating event or events, that is, the "causes" behind unrest, a sudden disaster, etc.; and (2) the available means of communication, whether limited by the distance the human voice carries or supplemented by means of communication that bridges large distances.

Closely related to these two is (3) the size of the aggregate involved. Clearly it makes a difference whether we are dealing with a riot confined to a prison or a series of riots sweeping the country; whether a speaker is addressing a small band of followers, or agitating a mass meeting, or addressing a national audience by means of wireless communication. To this we must add (4) the homogeneity in the predispositions of the people involved: is there a pre-existing tendency to respond in the same way to the same foci of attention?

The life history of any elementary collectivity is further affected by (5) the kind and amount of approval, tolerance, or opposition it encounters, and (6) the effectiveness of the symbols it employs in organizing the underlying motives of participants. Some spontaneous eruptions of unstructured behavior remain diffuse for lack of a suitable object or of suitable means of expression. They are, therefore, less likely to be lasting.

Finally, all the factors outlined above are decisive for (7) the degree of organization these elementary forms are able to achieve. The persistence of collectivities over time, their ability to "commit" participants, the possibility that their consequences will be lasting, all depend upon the establishment of a more or less stable form of organization.

AN APPROACH TO COLLECTIVE BEHAVIOR:
SYNTHESIS

ANY COLLECTIVE TRANSFORMATION must be viewed in relation to some system of norms. A partial disequilibrium results when new elements are being assimilated. The introduction of new elements confronts the collectivity with a problem or crisis that fixed precedent cannot resolve and whose solution consequently necessitates some kind of inquiry. The moral indignation, the delusions, the frantic action which result are, in a sense, efforts to maintain some kind of consistency between impulses and emotions and the prevalent norms.

Viewed in relation to the social order, then, elementary collective phenomena arise when the balance between disruptive and re-integrative tendencies is especially precarious. The new forms of interaction that take shape may be understood as spontaneous responses to a shared danger, as collective attempts to cope with anxiety, as reactions to pressures that threaten the unity of the group, or as incipient movements toward reorganization.

COLLECTIVE PROCESSES

The partial transformations that any social system undergoes in the face of unsettling influences may be subsumed under five basic processes. Each process represents a collective response growing out of spontaneous interaction and not predictable on the basis of prevalent understandings, norms, values, etc.

1. All individuals who participate in a co-operative enterprise share some common definitions. When confronted by unfamiliar objects or events, or when the meaning of an incident or the reputation of a person are in doubt, individuals must arrive at some common idea about the situation before they can act. *Collective definition* is the process by which cognitive assessments are brought in line with one another so that some common and plausible assessment emerges. The least structured way of groping for some common assessment is represented by the rumor mill, the grapevine, and scuttlebutt.

2. But unstructured attempts to arrive at new collective definitions occur only when there is partial *demoralization;* that is to say, when one's routine expectations and one's trust in official sources of information have been partially undermined. All kinds of breakdowns in norms are viewed as indicative of demoralization, since norms and standards of behavior no longer serve as points of orientation. This is particularly true of *panic,* a special manifestation of this process.

3. During periods of stress, furthermore, anxieties are aroused. When these find a common focus and are acted out in behavior that does not threaten the unity of the group, one can speak of a process of *collective defense,* analogous to a compromise symptom by which an individual protects himself against overwhelming anxieties. Hence, certain collective actions can be thought of as group actions which are "symptomatic" of inner group conflict, just as neurotic conflict in the individual results in a symptom. Crowd behavior is a form of collective defense.

4. At certain times large numbers of people appear to change their basic faith. Old goals and old ways are completely abandoned in favor of new ways which catch the collective fancy. *Mass conversion,* the unexpected change of fundamental values under group influence, constitutes the fourth of the basic processes.

5. Out of the spontaneous forms of interaction, new and more permanent forms of organization emerge—social microcosms that articulate and develop the diffuse collective responses. The process by which a crowd develops into an active cell, a hallucination becomes the property of a sect, a political movement forms a party, etc., is called *crystallization*. The sectarian association represents the most elementary form of "permanent" organization crystallizing.

These five processes by which behavior is collectively transformed— *definition, demoralization, defense, conversion*, and *crystallization*—must not, however, be thought of as always following one another in the same order. Their relationships are complex; their sequence varies according to the phenomena studied as well as according to the viewpoint of the observer. For example, one can view the crowd as an emergent defensive operation, sparked by and propelled on by collective definitions (rumors) which have arisen during its milling stage. From that point of view, the gang of rowdies who, once the crowd action is over, swear fraternal loyalty to one another is a product crystallized out of the transient crowd united by emotion. However, one is also justified in viewing many a crowd as the outcome of sectarian agitation. Every crowd has its active nucleus, and its highly charged emotion may be but a response to paranoid tendencies cultivated in a political sect and spread to others. Similarly, a complex set of events, like a political uprising, exhibits at various levels and sometimes concurrently everyone of these processes. Revolutions are often sparked by specific acts which reflect demoralization among the ruling group and, at the same time, give rise to definitions (rumors) which incite the masses and culminate in crowds. Yet, for an uprising to grow and spread, it needs organization. Active cells articulate, direct, and channel the impulses and energies on the loose. The course of such a revolution may well follow some sequence of stages. But what occurs can also be understood as a dynamic balance among the various processes of transformation, whose interplay manifests itself in the uprising.

Each chapter in Part II deals with one of these processes, emphasizing its least organized manifestations. Thus, rumor is considered the prototype of definition; it is the most random (i.e., elementary) manner in which a collectivity finds out what is going on. The chapter on demoralization focuses on what happens to individuals confronted with great danger; it deals with the problem of panic. The crowd is taken as the prototype of collective defense, and the literature on the crowd is reviewed under this heading. The chapter on mass conversion touches on the appeals of political and religious movements as well as on attempts at mass indoctrination. Finally, crystallization is represented by a discussion of the psychology of gang formation and of the religious sect.

Participation and the Participants

Collective pathology, especially, focuses attention on the nature of the interaction between persons not oriented, temporarily at least, toward an objective framework of norms. Under these conditions neither the behavior of participants nor their participation can be fully explained by social position. Both the question of participation and the kind of behavior that evolves require an understanding of the dynamics of individual behavior. All participants are not involved to the same extent or at the same time. They participate together even though they come from widely different backgrounds.

This problem of participation is the unifying theme of Part III of this volume. It relies heavily on findings from psychology. The direct influence that one person exerts on another in collective interaction usually results in the "contagious" spread of an idea, emotion, or behavior. Chapter 8 has to do with the psychological mechanisms that seem to explain contagion.

The chapters that follow examine the problems of differential participation: the emergence of *leadership;* the susceptibility of *followers;* the role of persons who function as *social objects* on whom thoughts and actions converge. In effect, it is through the relations that emerge among different personalities that a collectivity becomes polarized or rearranged into a new triangle of "leader-following-social object" relationships. The leaders may be looked upon as "instigators" acting on a plurality of "susceptibles" by directing their emotions toward "outsiders" not included in the leader-follower relation.

The course of action in which a collectivity engages may be looked upon as *convergence;* that is, all participants tend to move in the same direction and act like each other. At the same time the internal differentiation between leader and follower and between actor and object is a matter of *polarization,* of the way personalities assert themselves.

The emergence of an active leadership is a real problem of collective behavior. Who are the typical instigators of a mob who make up its nucleus? What type of personality is likely to be a revolutionist or a political leader? A second major question is closely related to the issue of leadership, namely, the personalities of the disciples attracted. What factors move a following to be responsive or to remain immune? Finally, the interaction between a collectivity and its "objects" is considered. For instance, the hero is the object of adoration and emulation, whereas the victim or scapegoat is the object of hostility. Both may be outsiders or non-participants in the collective behavior. But, like all social objects, they are integral elements of the psychological situation; the spontaneous action of the collectivity cannot be understood unless the part played by the object is considered as well.

Collective Processes and the Mass Society

The natural history approach removed the notion of a "collective mentality" or "crowd mind" from the realm of ideology. Through careful and continuous case studies and logical analysis, the diverse manifestations of collective behavior were differentiated and conceptualized. Classification also helped isolate factors that accounted for the distinct behavioral pattern of each type. The diversity of subject matter included under collective dynamics was thereby recognized. The main contribution of the natural history approach has been integrative.

At the same time the exponents of the approach eschewed traffic with psychological concepts except on a very abstract level. Distinctions among collective phenomena were made in terms of *formal* characteristics. Each type—the public, the crowd, the mass, the social movement—was viewed as a separate and discrete entity.

The present approach, as already noted, stresses the *processes* of collective change. These manifest themselves not only in interaction at a face-to-face level; they also occur in the society at large where people are not in physical contact. Physical dispersion affects the kind of interaction and, consequently, the form collective action will take. The full significance of the spontaneous patterning of face-to-face phenomena —whether this involves rumor, panic, crowd behavior, etc.—becomes apparent only within the context of the mass society. The predispositions of persons who constitute a particular collective formation are determined, not only by their positions within concrete social groups, but by their position in the larger society.

Part IV of this volume discusses collective processes within the context of the mass society. Chapter 12 has to do with the concept of the mass and the nature of mass behavior. The following chapters deal with: the achievement of popular consent; the influence of the media of mass communication on the behavior of the masses and on public opinion; fashion as the quest of individuals for self-identification and differentiation within a mass society; and the more organized but still spontaneous diversified movements toward social change. All these represent different patterns by which collective problems are solved en masse.

B I B L I O G R A P H Y

BLUMER, HERBERT. "Collective Behavior," *Principles of Sociology,* ed. A. M. LEE. New York: Barnes & Noble, Inc., 1951. This concise summary of the field has for many years been the authoritative and definitive treatment of collective behavior.

COOLEY, CHARLES H. *Social Organization: A Study of the Larger Mind.* New York: Charles Scribner's Sons, 1909. Especially parts II and III develop the significance of communication and the enlargement of consciousness.

GRUENBERG, ERNEST M. "Socially Shared Psychopathology," *Explorations in Social Psychiatry,* eds. A. H. LEIGHTON *et al.* New York: Basic Books, Inc., 1957. Good summary of material on *folie à deux,* dancing mania, etc., from the psychiatric viewpoint.

LASSWELL, HAROLD D., and KAPLAN, ABRAHAM. *Power and Society.* New Haven: Yale University Press, 1950. Includes definitions and brief discussions of a number of categories of collective action.

LE BON, GUSTAVE. *The Crowd: A Study of the Popular Mind.* London: Ernest Benn, Ltd., 1952. A work of great influence, though many of the ideas in it are derived from Gabriel Tarde and Scipio Sighele.

MacIVER, ROBERT M., and PAGE, CHARLES H. *Society: A Textbook of Sociology.* New York: Rinehart & Co., Inc., 1937. Presents a classification of transient collectivities which differs from that of Blumer.

MANNHEIM, KARL. *Man and Society in an Age of Reconstruction.* New York: Harcourt, Brace & Co., 1951. Explains modern manifestations of "crowd pathology" by reference to social, rather than psychological, mechanisms.

MARTIN, EVERETT D. *The Behavior of Crowds.* New York: W. W. Norton & Company, Inc., 1920. An early psychoanalytically oriented treatment of crowd pathology.

NORTHROP, F. S. C. *The Logic of the Sciences and the Humanities.* New York: The Macmillan Co., 1949. Chapter Three discusses the natural history approach as a phase in the development towards an empirically grounded scientific theory.

SOROKIN, PITRIM A. *Man and Society in Calamity.* New York: E. P. Dutton & Co., Inc., 1942. A suggestive survey of how societies have been affected by crises and reorganized to meet them.

WALLAS, GRAHAM. *The Great Society.* New York: The Macmillan Co., 1932. A critique of "crowd psychology" and a formulation of the "progressive" approach.

II

Collective Processes and
Collective Forms

CHAPTER 3

Rumor: The Process
of Collective Definition

In EVERYDAY LIFE rumor is defined and distinguished from other information in terms of accuracy and credibility. News is that which has the ring of truth; rumor is hearsay and apt to be false. To refer to news as rumor is to express skepticism about its veracity. When one is inclined to believe what he hears but fears others may think it foolish, passing the information on as "only a rumor" is a kind of protection.

In connection with collective behavior, we depart from this popular tendency to depreciate rumor as unimportant. Not only may any particular rumor have significant consequences for society, but the dissemination of rumor is a basic aspect of group life. The process by which rumor emerges illustrates the manner in which members of some collectivity arrive together at some common definition.

Furthermore, the importance of rumor as an unstructured collective phenomenon derives from the fact that all that genuinely merits the designation "group life" rests on shared perspective and common definition. The behavior in a group implies the existence of some goal, some explicit scheme, some group way of doing things, which serves as a point of orientation. Students of collective behavior focus on what happens in the absence of such common perspectives and rational rules; their interest centers on those unpredictable developments not explainable in terms of institutional arrangements.

When there are no common definitions and perspectives which can form the basis for common action, how do new definitions and perspectives emerge? In asking this we are inquiring about the nature of the first of the basic processes of collective behavior, namely, collective definition.

The Rumor Process

A PARTICULAR RUMOR is the most elementary manifestation of a shared perspective. The rumor process refers exclusively to those unorganized and fugitive efforts to arrive at definitions when social orientation is necessary, but there are important gaps in the structuring of the relevant cognitive field. Collective definitions arise through the rumor process.

SCUTTLEBUTT AND RUMOR   These collective efforts to find a definition are of two general types. There are those that exist *sub rosa* within organized group structures. These are commonly referred to as the "grapevine," or "scuttlebutt." An army regiment waiting at a port of embarkation provides a good example. According to the rules, notice of destination is handed down through official channels: from field grade officer to junior officer to non-commissioned officer to enlisted man. But speculation about the orders is rife; word jumps from the supply sergeant, who has seen the mosquito netting, to the colonel's orderly, who knows that the medic has stocked atabrine. In their efforts to define their future, soldiers pass their ideas via the grapevine to friends and buddies. Often the information originates with official sources; it is usually attributed to them as it is diverted into the scuttlebutt. These attempts at *sub rosa* definition are meaningful and important only to those within a limited group and at a given time. Being limited to a group, the grapevine often becomes a semiroutine channel of information.

There is at least one other kind of unofficial information, which consists of efforts that go beyond any one structure so that to some degree they become the common property of the larger society in which they lead an underground existence. If, for example, all leaves were canceled for an army company on the coast of southern England in 1943, the soldiers in that company might think they were shipping out, perhaps for special maneuvers. But the rumor that one company was shipping out might easily spread from army post to army post and reach the townspeople. Thus, people all over England might rapidly infer that the invasion of Europe was imminent. Similarly, there are recurrent rumors, specific versions of which, adapted to particular times and settings, become the property of groups everywhere—they are of the ages.

SOURCE AND CHANNEL   Whether they are restricted to organized group structures or go beyond them—and notwithstanding the infinite variety of forms they take—the definitions that emerge out of rumor grow up, so to speak, outside organized channels. Their diffusion and acceptance, the elaborations and crystallization of their content, appear to be undirected and nondeliberate. Usually rumors are not planned; they simply catch, and many a bit of gossip or a story deliberately planted for face-to-face transmission is never relayed because it lacks the quality of contagion.

This approach to rumor places the emphasis on two elements of the process: source and channel. The *source* of the rumor process, the point at which it originates, is always anonymous, no matter how widely and clearly observed are the signs on which the rumored interpretation is based. At the same time the *channels* through which rumor travels may be described as fugitive: the paths seem to elude us as we try to track down a rumor. Even though the rumor content itself becomes public knowledge and displaces or supplants official information, the channels themselves are never public or official.

Information needed for social orientation, then, diffuses by way of the rumor process whenever it emanates from an anonymous source by way of fugitive channels.

Rumor may also be thought of as the most elementary form of organization. This may be briefly explained in this way: All human activity is "functional" in the sense that it serves some purpose and meets some problem. Correspondingly, group behavior may be conceived of as "collective problem solving." In the face of any new situation, the effort to define and clarify is a *prerequisite* for deliberate action. The function of the rumor process is this first step toward group action itself; that is, it is the effort after definition and clarification *ipso facto*. Rumor, thus, not only has the rudiments of group organization in the sense that channels are formed—often to disappear as soon as they are used—but the rumor process is elementary also inasmuch as it involves communication only and not necessarily common action. Though the rumors themselves which are the end product of the process may, especially in times of upheaval, stir men to action, *the process itself exists in and ends with the effort after definition.*

THE SOCIOLOGICAL APPROACH TO RUMOR

The scheme by which rumors are classified often uses criteria of content and deduces from this content certain psychological functions rumor has for the individual. A psychological frame of reference, valid as it may be for certain purposes, obscures the social nexus in which rumor thrives. Accordingly, there are *pipedream* rumors, expressing hope ("A cure for cancer has just been found"); *bogey* rumors, which give substance to fears that are vaguely apprehended (the "yellow peril" of the early 1900's); *wedge-driving* rumors, sowing seeds of distrust and discord among subgroups within the society ("Most Jews manage to get out of the military draft"). Finally, the psychologist has a residual category of rumors, defined not in terms of projective needs expressed in the content, but in *cognitive* terms; in short, some rumors are cognitive efforts after meaning ("I saw a moving van. The people down the street must be leaving.") [1]

This last category, the *cognitive* rumor, does, of course, incorporate the essential character of the rumor process as an effort after definition. But rumor, as a *collective* definition, must be distinguished from an individual conception or hallucination. The rumor process is an effort to understand events that are of public, not merely individual, significance. The sociologist's approach to rumor and his classifications must take into account the relationship between the rumor process, the social context in which it occurs, and the collective action to which it may lead. Rumor is a way of arriving at consensus, a form of orientation around a critical issue. The orientations involved are public; they express group attitudes that may become the basis of orientation for group activity. Sometimes they do indeed express collective pipedreams (millennial hopes), common fears, or intergroup hostility. But it is preferable to begin our more detailed inquiry into the significance of rumor for social action by considering rumor as an effort after technical information.

THE EFFORT AFTER TECHNICAL INFORMATION

Rumor in the modern world may serve, like a primitive omen, as *technical information* whenever more authentic information is lacking and, at the same time, some action is required. Among the Tikopia, for example, the appearance of certain cloud formations is conventionally interpreted to signify an event of social significance. The cloud is an omen giving promise of the imminent arrival of a vessel, which, in turn, signifies a wished-for break of routine. Likewise, a tip on the stock market or a rumor reported in the press, in the absence of more reliable information, serves as a sign that reduces uncertainties concerning whether to buy or sell.

Our interest is chiefly in the explanation of how it is that "rumor"— namely, the products of the rumor process—comes to supplant or stand in lieu of authenticated "technical information." However, the circumstances under which rumor has been investigated have highlighted the *inadequacy* of the technical information that emerges from the process. Much of the pertinent research into the problem was launched in con-

1. For a discussion of the psychological approach to rumor, see Gordon W. Allport and Leo Postman, *The Psychology of Rumor* (New York: Henry Holt & Co., Inc., 1947), especially pp. 36–43.

nection with the rampage of wartime rumors.[2] What stirred the interest of so many people was the observation that some rumors were hampering the war effort, that they persisted with considerable tenacity in the face of official opposition, and that, above all, they could never be considered adequate guides for action. Closely linked to this wartime research were the so-called rumor clinics and related communication efforts which were intended through public refutation—indirect or direct—of rumors to expose and put to rest stories considered harmful. The key to the rumor process was most often sought in those perceptual factors that tend to detract from the accuracy of the content, that is, to distort.

Accuracy and Distortion

Psychological inquiry into the conditions conducive to accurate testimony does help one to understand when verbal reports are most apt to provide accurate technical information. The *Aussage* (testimony) psychologists have asked: When should evidence be accepted? When is it apt to be unreliable? When is it based on mere hearsay? More systematically, the set of problems with which the psychology of testimony was concerned included the pitfalls involved in (*a*) accurate observation (perception and recognition); (*b*) remembering what was observed; and (*c*) accurately retelling this information.[3]

The same three mental functions are involved in the transmission of any message. Observation itself, as has long been known, is already an act of meaningful interpretation. The eye cannot see everything, and the mind strives after organization and meaning. Early experiments on observation by van Gennep and others showed a high frequency of error. While conducting a class in psychology, van Gennep used the participants as subjects. In the middle of one session, ". . . suddenly the door of the hall was thrown open and a clown rushed in madly pursued by a Negro, revolver in hand. They stopped in the middle of the room fighting; the clown fell, the Negro leapt upon him, fired, and then both rushed out of the hall. The whole incident hardly lasted twenty

2. Among the numerous studies, see Floyd H. Allport and Milton Lepkin, "Wartime Rumors of Waste and Special Privilege," *Journal of Abnormal and Social Psychology*, XL (January, 1945), pp. 3–36; Leonard W. Doob, "War Reactions of a Rural Canadian Community," *Journal of Abnormal and Social Psychology*, XXXVI (April, 1941), pp. 200–223; Office of War Information Intelligence Report, *Rumors in Wartime*, 1942.

3. Guy Montrose Whipple, "The Observer as Reporter: A Survey of the Psychology of Testimony," *Psychological Bulletin*, VI (May, 1909), pp. 153–70.

seconds." [4] When students were asked to give their versions of what happened, a quarter of the accounts were found to be highly inaccurate, and very few were without major errors.

The experiments along this line show that: (1) Observation may be inaccurate even where the observation and the reporting of observations are almost simultaneous. Our perceptions differ, each from the other's and in terms of our familiarity with the events observed. (2) With the passage of time, the number of lapses and inaccuracies are apt to increase. (3) Finally, upon relating the incident, the restrictions of language and the need to make the incident intelligible to others lead us to give a more conventional form to the experience. A unique experience, a scene packed with action and laden with fear is assimilated into available language schemata and conventional plots for purposes of effective presentation. The actual experience, the feelings involved, can hardly be recaptured. They can be verbally communicated and shared with others only with great difficulty. Language, with is conventions and stereotypes, can make puzzling events plausible only through their reconstruction in terms of grammatical rules.

"The chief single result of the *Aussage* psychology," Whipple was able to conclude as early as 1909, "is that an errorless report is not the rule, but the exception, even when the report is made by a competent observer under favorable conditions.[5] In all of this, information that comes by way of the rumor channels is no different from any information communicated. But there is an additional source of error; namely, a piece of information or a story changes as it is told and retold.

Certain experiments, though not a precise recapitulation of the rumor process, do indicate the cumulative changes a particular rumor— or what we may call the "rumor-in-process"—may undergo during its career. Rumor transmission was most nearly duplicated experimentally by the method of serial reproduction.[6] This method makes use of chains of reproductions. The starting point for such a chain may consist of folk-stories, of written arguments and descriptions, of picture materials, or of actual happenings directly observed. A reproduction or retelling by A of what he has seen, heard, or experienced is then reproduced by B, to whom it has been communicated and whose version is subsequently dealt with by C, and so on. The experiments in serial reproduction illustrate the laws of perception and how initial errors, judged by a standard of scientific accuracy, tend to be magnified as time and language barriers intervene.

4. Fernand van Langenhove, *Growth of a Legend* (New York: G. P. Putnam's Sons, 1916), p. 122f.

5. Whipple, *op. cit.*, p. 161.

6. Frederic C. Bartlett, *Remembering* (Cambridge: The University Press, 1954).

Some transformation of the initial material, as it is passed along, is likely to occur. These transformations, though conceptually distinct, do not occur in isolation from one another. But, according to the classification, one can analyze the transformation of a particular item of information as it passes along from person to person in terms of (*a*) the deletions that occur (*leveling*); (*b*) the elements that, as a result of deletions, become the dominant theme around which the material is organized into a meaningful whole (*sharpening*); and (*c*) how these reinterpretations relate to individual and cultural biases of the participants within the communication network (*assimilation*).[7] Together they account for the transformation of content.

These experiments in serial reproduction have been used to show the inevitability of distortion in the circulation of rumor. This view must be qualified. For the study of rumor in a natural context indicates that, notwithstanding the pervasive presence of distorting tendencies, the rumor-in-process often emerges more or less intact. Caplow, on the basis of rumors observed in the armed forces during World War II, remarks that the majority of rumors were surprisingly accurate.[8] Certainly the rumor mill often grinds out useful technical information. Schachter and Burdick confirm that ninety-six interviews with the "victims" of a rumor experiment revealed no instances of distortion: "In every case, the planted rumor was repeated to the interviewer in essentially the form in which it was originally planted with no instances of embellishment or variation."[9] Again, in the aftermath of an earthquake in India, which gave rise to a whole series of fantastic rumors, Prasad reports that several of these reached him more than once from separate channels in basically the same form—among them, the prediction, made in mid-January, that on February 28 everybody would change sex.[10]

The question of accuracy, though not unrelated to it, is distinct from the question of distortion. If distortion is not an essential feature of rumor, then there is no basis for an a priori questioning of the accuracy of a rumor. The experimental evidence with regard to the inevitability of distortion is inconclusive for several reasons:

First, the motives that induce individuals to reproduce materials in the laboratory situation are highly artificial. Allport and Postman asked their subjects to note about twenty elements in some picture materials to

7. Allport and Postman, *op. cit.*, p. 80f.
8. Theodore Caplow, "Rumors in War," *Social Forces*, XXV (March, 1947), pp. 298–302.
9. Stanley Schachter and Harvey Burdick, "A Field Experiment in Rumor Transmission and Distortion," *Journal of Abnormal and Social Psychology*, L (May, 1955), pp. 363–71.
10. J. Prasad, "The Psychology of Rumor: A Study Relating to the Great Indian Earthquake of 1934," *British Journal of Psychology*, XXVI (July, 1935), pp. 1–15.

which they were exposed. The ability to retain and repeat these elements is primarily a game in rote memory, whereas in a natural context the rumormonger is apt to repeat only those details that he deems significant. His perceptions and his communicative behavior do not operate in a social vacuum.

Second, the degree to which communications are apt to be reshaped in the transmission process depends on how meaningful their content is to persons who repeat them. If the initial message has high social significance, its recollection and transmission will be correspondingly accurate. On the basis of a more recent replication of the serial transmission experiments, Higham has suggested that a story with an "ego-involved" content will undergo fewer deletions.[11] Bartlett, being cognizant of this possibility, deliberately selected for his pioneering efforts a story in which "the incidents described in some cases had no very manifest interconnection," while Allport and Postman began with picture materials that the subjects themselves had to interpret.

Third, it is recognized that there is a "limit to leveling," and once this limit is reached, further distortion is greatly diminished. Thus, if the information or plant that initiates the rumor process consists of socially meaningful material without unnecessary embellishment, its form need not undergo the conventionalization and simplification that make it suitable for transmission.

Fourth, the fact that rumors travel in circles as well as in chains means that the content is constantly checked against various versions, and this checking keeps the rumor which emerges from departing too far from the original conception.

Rumor need not be distorted or inaccurate. Especially when oral networks serve in lieu of verified technical information, there is a natural tendency to cultivate accurate sources and to exclude from the rumor network those whose past performance has proved unreliable. Thus, face-to-face diffusion of news events plays an important part in disseminating important happenings. But persons interested in "verifying" the information are apt to look for confirmation in newspapers, radio, and other more official sources of information.

RUMOR AND NEWS

UNDER WHAT CONDITIONS is rumor likely to supplant technical information from official sources? First, obviously, when no official in-

11. T. M. Higham, "The Experimental Study of the Transmission of Rumor," *British Journal of Psychology*, XLII (March–May, 1951), pp. 42–55.

formation is accessible and one is forced to rely on fugitive sources of information—for example, in the army, when the battle situation is highly problematic; second, when official sources of information, while accessible, are widely distrusted, as in occupied countries where "official" versions of the enemy's progress are largely discounted; third, when rumors are reported in the newspapers or other mass media, they may be endowed with an "official" sanction so that they appear to be verified.

If rumor may serve as technical information and if, in addition, rumors often make their way into official news media, how is one then to distinguish between "rumor" and "news"? One can differentiate the two as *end products of two fundamentally different processes*. Moreover, an examination of these differences helps to illustrate more clearly what is characteristic and unique about the rumor process as an elementary form of collective behavior.

ANONYMITY AND ACCURACY

Characteristic of the rumor process is the passage of information, whose content is nowhere fixed and verified, through interpersonal channels. It is difficult, well-nigh impossible, for the participants in the rumor network to track down the source of a rumor; rumor is rarely the work of only one person or of a single witness. On the contrary, rumor is a collective product. As Bysow has put it, "the process of news is just the reverse [from that of rumor]. Here we determine the existence of a document or of an authoritative organ, perhaps an eye witness or of traces of the event (e.g., the corpse of the assassination victim). Each person is able to get at it without difficulty. Characteristic for news is therefore the exact determination of its origin." [12] And, conversely, an important corollary to the definition of rumor is: the origin of a message is always obscured in the rumor process, even though it may be imputed to official sources.

This test for the *anonymity* of the source does indeed show the distinction between news and rumor much more clearly than the more common judgment about relative accuracy. Of course, the teller of a rumor can hardly ever remain unidentified. But the anonymity characterizing the rumor process refers less to the participants in the rumor chain than to the relation of every teller to the initial source of information. The anonymity is a matter of accountability.

In communication via the mass media the source is identifiable and hence accountable, whereas the anonymity of the rumormonger lies in

12. L. A. Bysow, "Gerüchte," *Koelner Vierteljahreshefte für Soziologie,* VII (1928–9), p. 422f.

the fact that he himself is directly responsible not for the *veracity* of the content, but merely for its *transmission*. Although he may personally attest to his own firm conviction in the information, he is not held accountable for its accuracy. By contrast, editors and commentators can never extricate themselves from the responsibility for evaluating the news they pass on. Information passed as suitable for dissemination—as being "fit to print"—has the seal of approval of the entire news organization, which must always face the possibility of libel suits and is thus held accountable in a very real sense.

Nevertheless, the attribution of news to an accountable source does not guarantee the accuracy of the information. Newsmen are to a large extent forced to rely on hearsay, meager handouts, and what newsmen and persons "in the know" tell each other. In the light of the finding that distortion is not an essential, though a fairly frequent, consequence of rumor transmission, let us now examine how news in being gathered and processed may be distorted in a manner rather similar to the distortion that sometimes occurs in rumor.

Perspectivistic Slant

How inaccuracies may plague news reporting is neatly illustrated first by an episode reported in *The Quill*.[13] McKenzie, a veteran news correspondent and later head of the School of Journalism at the University of Washington, noted certain discrepancies between an account he had written and accounts by two other journalists about what happened, in September, 1932, the one and only time a Communist presided over the German parliament (Reichstag). The incident reported occurred during its opening session, when the members were met to elect a permanent president. It was customary for the oldest member of the Reichstag, irrespective of party, to preside as temporary chairman until the president could be installed. Clara Zetkin, a German Communist, then the senior member, had been ill in Moscow, but for this occasion the Communists brought her all the way to Berlin. The events covered by the press were thus packed with human drama as well as with political significance—the conduct of the Reichstag in this instance being one of the many episodes the extremist parties, including the Nazis who were soon to rise to power, sought to exploit in order to discredit parliamentary institutions generally.

First, let us compare three accounts of Clara Zetkin's "entrance into the Reichstag":

13. Vernon McKenzie, "We Saw It With Our Own Eyes," *Quill* (December, 1938), cited in Curtis D. MacDougall, *Understanding Public Opinion* (New York: The Macmillan Co., 1952), p. 356f.

Clara Zetkin . . . was carried into the Reichstag on a stretcher and propped up into the president's chair.

Kurt G. W. Ludecke

Clara Zetkin tottered in, supported by Torgler, head of the Communist party. . . . The old lady was assisted to her place.

Lilian T. Maurer

Clara Zetkin entered, supported on each side by a girl Communist member. Her progress was slow and halting. . . . As she mounted the steps to the presidential chair she leaned heavily on her cane.

Vernon McKenzie

Most often divergencies in reporting seem due to incompleteness and deletion rather than sheer inaccuracy. Reporters see much, and their write-ups must necessarily be selective to suit their individual inclinations as well as the space requirements imposed by their editors. This is characteristic of and thus illustrates the leveling process. But in this case the discrepancies, though not crucial, appear to be gross misrepresentations of what went on; certainly one finds it hard to believe that all reports were accurate. Yet the reporting actually represented no deliberate slanting, nor was there a discernible motive for any. The discrepancies can be attributed to what we may call "perspectivistic" sharpening, whereby one phase of an event attains dominance and comes to represent the entire event. McKenzie writes:

> The word "Reichstag" may be used to refer to the building, to the chamber where they held their sessions, or to the body of members itself. When Clara Zetkin entered the Reichstag *building*, Ludecke was in the outer lobby. . . . Mrs. Maurer was seated so that she could see Clara Zetkin as soon as she entered the Reichstag *chamber*. . . . Clara Zetkin did not come into my vision until she had passed *under* the gallery, so that when I caught sight of her (I still believe and contend) she was "supported on each side by a girl Communist member." In reporting the event it was not a case of selection, but a case of reporting that portion of Clara Zetkin's passage from the outer door of the Reichstag lobby to the dais on which she was ultimately seated. Each of us chronicled, quite naturally, that position of her journey which we were so placed physically that we could see. Each of us was right—but incomplete.

The entire episode was reported from each observer's particular position with its resultant perspectivistic slant.

A further, though equally minor, discrepancy showed up in the reporting of a human-interest angle. This human-interest angle escaped Ludecke altogether, an indication that the recording of a news story follows conventionalized interest. The incident occurred when the aged Mrs. Zetkin gave up her chair to the robust Hermann Goering. At this point someone—either Goering or Frick (another prominent Nazi)—quoted a popular ditty,

> It comes but once, Clara,
> It can never happen again.

The discrepancy in the reports involves as minor a point as the word "Clara," inserted by McKenzie but not contained in Mrs. Maurer's report. Explaining his own version, this is what McKenzie writes:

> If someone tells me that I inserted the word "Clara," I won't dispute it. It seemed to me to make the news story clearer for the reader to use the name. I did not actually hear it, but there was so much confusion that I am not sure that it was not used.

It seems to us a clear case of natural, helpful "assimilation" of a story, undertaken in the interest of communicative clarity to suit the predispositions of an inferred audience.

Propagandistic Distortion

That news itself may be "manufactured" to suit popular prejudice is aptly illustrated by Arthur Ponsonby through a series of press clippings—themselves an impressive record of the operation of serial reproduction—about the fall of Antwerp, Belgian military stronghold, to the Germans in November, 1914. The first of the news items appeared in the *Kölnische Zeitung*, a West German newspaper from a heavily Catholic region. What happened as the item was picked up and reprinted successively in France, England, Italy, and again France is shown below.[14]

> When the fall of Antwerp got known, the church bells were rung (meaning Germany).
>
> *Kolnische Zeitung*

> According to the Kolnische Zeitung, the clergy of Antwerp were compelled to ring the church bells when the fortess was taken.
>
> *Le Matin*

14. Arthur Ponsonby, *Falsehood in Wartime* (London: George Allen and Unwin, 1930), p. 161. This example of serial reproduction is incidentally cited by Allport and Postman to illustrate the workings not of newsgathering but of the rumor process. The implications of the different conceptualizations should thus be clear.

According to what Le Matin has heard from Cologne, the Belgian priests who refused to ring the church bells when Antwerp was taken have been driven away from their places.

The Times

According to what the Times has heard from Cologne via Paris, the unfortunate Belgian priests who refused to ring the church bells when Antwerp was taken have been sentenced to hard labor.

Corriera della Sera

According to information to the Corriera della Sera from Cologne via London, it is confirmed that the barbaric conquerors of Antwerp punished the unfortunate Belgian priests for their heroic refusal to ring the church bells by hanging them as living clappers to the bells with their heads down.

Le Matin

Newspapers may express official policies. In war or crisis, it is natural that they seek to single out information reaffirming faith in party or government, faith in victory, or the general conception of the enemy as vile and brutal. Hence propaganda efforts, given official sanction and emanating from an official source, are sometimes reflected in those rumors that become news. The belief in the danger of military Fifth Column activity in World War II arose out of a combination of official announcements and generalized fears and confusion due to Nazi victories.[15]

Summary

The difference between rumor and news lies more in the degree of anonymity than in accuracy. The *source* of a rumor is unofficial and its origin always obscured, even though the transmission may preserve a reference to an official source. Mainly, the "fiction of anonymity" must be preserved by participants in the rumor process. As long as the "source" remains anonymous in the relaying of a rumor, the person passing it on divests himself of responsibility for its accuracy. News is official, and the "teller" always assumes some responsibility for its accuracy or the consequences its dissemination may have. Much as the newsman may resort to his "an unidentified source said today," it is assumed that when there is a demand for identification, the leak "will out"; the source is thus verifiable. The *channels* through which rumors-in-process pass are interpersonal: from a teller to a hearer, who himself becomes a teller.

15. Louis de Jong, *The German Fifth Column in the Second World War* (Chicago: The University of Chicago Press, 1956).

Still, the teller is not held accountable for what hearsay he transmits, only for the transmission itself. He passes the information on as "only a rumor." By contrast, the channels through which news (once it takes form) is disseminated are depersonalized, but the "teller" is accountable for what he tells his audience. Anonymity is thus "guaranteed" to the rumormonger, while the newsman, though remote from his audience, cannot cloak himself and his evidence in complete obscurity.

The many attempts to differentiate between rumor and news have encountered difficulty because they focused only on how the content came to deviate from reliable news as a result of the transmission process. What characterizes news and rumor is the specific manner in which each arises; news comes into being through a different process than does rumor, despite superficial likenesses. Sometimes, as in the illustration on the fall of Antwerp, the way news is distorted shows a certain similarity to the way in which the content of a rumor evolves. Both the errors in news reporting and those in rumor are often oversights. A reporter who fails to check all his information is as likely to share the biases of his generation as the rumormonger is.

Furthermore, rumor can become "news," just as official news is often the grist that feeds the rumor mills. Rumors are accepted as possible cues, either about the popular mind or about what is going on off-stage. Thus, in 1955 the assumption among Washington politicians that President Eisenhower, notwithstanding his recent illness, would run again was an important straw in the wind in the absence of a definite denial by the President.

The essence of the rumor process is its improvisation, its fugitive nature, its spontaneity. News is what emerges from a communication system whose actions are deliberate and to some extent formalized.

THE TRANSMISSION OF RUMOR

THE FACT THAT THE ORIGINATOR of an item of information may have fed it into the rumor mill with the intention of manipulating opinion or behavior might lead one to question whether spontaneity does in fact characterize the rumor process. Consideration of the relationship between the plant and the rumor focuses one's attention on the transmission process and on the conditions under which a rumor diffuses once the process is set in motion. When we call a rumor "just a plant," we are looking at the rumor from its point of origin. We mean that what emerges is an interpretation planted with, or leaked to, some individual or group to begin with. The difference between the plant and the rumor is conceptual rather than substantive. If one focuses on the person who imparts the information, the rumor process may be considered the successful transmission of a plant from which a collective definition emerges. In that case the rumor that diffuses is not just an effort for cognitive clarity.

RECIPIENTS AND TRANSMITTERS

Rumor transmission, it should be noted, involves all participants in two roles instead of only one: they are *recipients of information* and they are also its *transmitters*. A person's interest in the rumor content will not be the same in both roles. For example, as Peterson and Gist put it, believing that one has "inside information bearing on an issue of public concern places a person temporarily in a position of prestige: and the prestige position of the person may be made more secure if the story can be made to sound authentic." [16] A message that consists of relevant information for the receiver may thereafter be transmitted with a partially manipulative intent. But not all those who are likely recipients of a message automatically become active transmitters. Who, we may inquire, is likely to be told a rumor and who will pass it on?

The chances of any person's hearing a rumor are greatly increased if the following three conditions are met: (1) the information must be perceived as *relevant* for the potential recipient, (2) by friends or persons with whom he is in frequent contact, and (3) who are themselves actively interested and involved in the matter the rumor concerns. The third condition, active interest and involvement, seems to determine the chances of anyone's becoming an active *transmitter*. Passing on a rumor involves a desire on the part of the transmitter to affect other people's behavior, to bring their perspectives in line with his own, or, at the very minimum, to share a valuable bit of information.

Even when the rumor process is set in motion as an intentional plant, it conforms to our definition in terms of sources and channel. Accordingly, the initiator evades accountability and lets the diffusion occur spontaneously, so to speak, along unofficial channels. Once information is planted, its diffusion cannot be controlled, since this depends on the availability of likely "recipient-transmitters." Planted information often fails to "catch," a difficulty that has haunted propagandists and stymied efforts to reproduce the rumor process for experimental manipulation in a natural setting.

Many rumors, it is assumed, originate as deliberate plants, but "proof" is usually little more than an inference. For example, one study

16. Warren A. Peterson and Noel P. Gist, "Rumor and Public Opinion," *American Journal of Sociology*, LVII (September, 1951), p. 166.

conducted during World War II concerned rumors (i.e., themes) blared by Axis broadcasts and spread by possible Axis supporters in the United States. A check on their spread revealed that the average rumor had been heard by fewer than seven out of a hundred average Americans in New York and Boston. Moreover, respondents mentioned American newspapers most often as the source of "rumors" that duplicated Axis propaganda themes. Findings of this sort tend to discredit the importance of plants.[17] Again, a World War I story about Joseph P. Tumulty, secretary to President Wilson, having been imprisoned at Fort Leavenworth for espionage activity was widely quoted by the press and even appeared as a headline in one paper; government authorities, according to a report, considered the rumor a German plant, but what evidence they had has never been disclosed.[18]

CONDITIONS OF TRANSMISSION

The conditions under which a particular plant diffuses—or fails to be spread—do not entirely coincide with those under which there is a general flurry of rumors. The motives and conditions for the transmission of rumors are not purely individual; they operate within a framework of social structure.

Most rumors bear the mark of the cultural and intellectual milieu in which they arise. Thus, the rumors, referred to above, connecting Tumulty, an Irish-Catholic, with the Sinn Fein movement (anti-British) naturally "linked" him with the German side. This information was of course enthusiastically picked up by anti-Catholics, anti-Wilson Republicans, and suffragettes disappointed in Wilson's leadership. Similarly, during the years of World War II, the First Lady, Eleanor Roosevelt, was the target of many rumors spread throughout, but not confined to, the South. Among these, the so-called "Eleanor Club" rumors held that Mrs. Eleanor Roosevelt had helped to launch a number of undercover organizations designed to better the Negro's opportunities at the expense of white people. The loyalty of Negroes to the First Lady and her devotion to their cause were the common themes in the stories. According to these rumors, the over-all goals of the undercover "Eleanor Clubs" were that:

White women were to be in the kitchen by Christmas, 1942, or January, 1943. Negro women were to be out of the kitchen. There must be more

17. Floyd L. Ruch and Kimball Young, "Penetration of Axis Propaganda," *Journal of Applied Psychology*, XXVI (August, 1942), pp. 448–55.
18. John M. Blum, "Tumulty and Leavenworth: A Case Study of Rumor," *Journal of Abnormal and Social Psychology*, XLIV (July, 1949), pp. 411–13.

pay, more privileges, less hours. There must be no disparaging remarks about either Mrs. Roosevelt or the President. And Negroes must have equal opportunities with whites.[19]

The origins of these rumors were never tracked down. They drew on the most everyday occurrences. "Whenever you saw a Negro wearing a wide-brimmed hat with a feather in it," a report came from Alabama, "you know he was wearing the sign of the Eleanor Club." These rumors "appeared inspired by those seeking either to cause trouble or to disparage the President and his wife."[20] Behind them were the current demands for an increase in the wage levels of Southern Negroes, which resulted from a general labor scarcity and the migration of Negroes to defense industries, particularly in the North. At the same time Mrs. Roosevelt had been for a long time a favorite target for the scorn and derision that it somehow did not seem proper to aim at the President. But Eleanor Roosevelt's individualistic and unconventional ways made her especially vulnerable.

Furthermore, although each rumor develops its own public (its recipient-transmitters) from among those especially interested and involved, the situations that rumors at variance with official beliefs are to explain do not only concern people in particular statuses. The rumor public cuts across fixed status lines. Rumors flourish among persons in positions where perhaps they should know better. Under conditions of general unrest and excitement, people sometimes are temporarily drawn closer to one another and thus become more communicative.

But many rumors do not enter the public domain. Rumors often circulate among people of widely diverse interests who are friends, because friends often communicate on a wide variety of subjects. Another channel for the communication of a wide variety of subjects has sometimes been located among children. They are often made the scapegoats for carrying gossip in which adults allegedly do not participate. Their active role in word-of-mouth transmission of certain kinds of content derives from the fact that communication by children is not linked to clearly crystallized status positions. Hence they are more "neutral" transmitters; they mingle rather easily, often to the embarrassment of their parents.[21]

Finally, active transmission of rumors takes place only with regard to issues deemed by their transmitters to be of public importance. Expectations or suspicions regarding the consequences of an event for

19. Howard Odum, *Race and Rumors of Race* (Chapel Hill: University of North Carolina, 1943), p. 78.

20. *Ibid.*, pp. 77, 79.

21. Charwomen, doormen, custodial employees, and servants also play an active role in rumor transmission. They are ubiquitous, yet unnoticed and "faceless."

public life must be generally shared for rumors regarding it to spread. What is basic to the rumor process is not so much the individual fears or implied threats or obstacles in the way of cognitive clarity (the pipe-dreams, etc.) but the collective quest after meaning.

Thus, the rumor process, giving rise to a collectivity of rumors, can be seen to refer to a situation in which no one participant can directly observe all that is going on. The bird's-eye view of a social situation is, however, exceptional, and most of the time the public is content to rely on public sources of information. When these sources become generally suspect, unofficial interpretations come to the fore. Leadership itself may become disrupted, no longer having a clear view of the situation with which it is supposed to cope. Rumor, therefore, implies in its very essence a certain disorientation to or reorganization within the regularized ways of doing things we call social structure.

RUMOR AND SOCIAL STRUCTURE

RUMOR, we have said, is always in one way or another fugitive. It involves efforts to arrive at definitions when official structuring of the field in which social orientation is necessary leaves out certain important areas. Rumor is rife when uncertainty, disenchantment, and an air of uneasiness pervade any collectivity. And so rumors, their content revolving about matters of public relevance, also reflect a certain critical orientation to social authorities.

The relation of rumor to social organization and social change can perhaps be understood best by way of the contrast between two broadly similar and yet distinct processes of social definition, which also depend on interpersonal communication: they are gossip; and the products of an oral tradition, such as folk tales, legends, and myth.

GOSSIP

Gossip, unlike rumor, is intimate—not public—writes Bysow.[22] This means that gossip usually remains within the circle in which it starts, whereas rumors are apt to spread farther. The boundaries of gossip are the same as those of an already established group; to have access to gossip means to be on the "inside." Gossip, it is sometimes said, deals with persons, whereas rumor concerns events. But this contrast between rumor and gossip in terms of content leads only to hopeless controversy about when gossip is rumor or rumor is gossip. Certainly, talk about the intimate lives of public figures constitutes rumor, as is so vividly

22. Bysow, *op. cit.*, p. 425f.

portrayed by whispering campaigns which often attend electoral campaigns. The dividing line between gossip and rumor certainly is not clear-cut. In general, however, gossip reflects the existence of a closed and established circle, the persons within which share common definitions and common ways of looking at people and matters.[23] Gossip involves redefinition only within these limits. Whenever gossip goes beyond a closed circle and creates or supports cleavages—when it involves an issue whose truth is disputed—it becomes rumor.

Hence, gossip functions to maintain social control within a group. It conserves the *status quo.* Existing as an everpresent threat, it discourages nonconformity and innovation and tends to keep people in line. One expresses comradeship and solidarity by participating in gossip. The specific content is rather irrelevant for the activity.

Finally, because of its diffuseness, the information transmitted in gossip expresses common interests and mutual sociability. With good humor, we greet our friends with, "Heard any good gossip lately?" Diffuse gossip involves high motivation to tell, and anyone sharing the general orientation of the transmitter is apt to have the information told to him. Gossip therefore relies much more heavily on existing channels than rumor, which tends to create its own network of communication and its own coterie of "believers." In gossip a questioning of the contents or a resort to independent verification on the part of a receiver suggests that that receiver has to some extent already severed himself from his social circle. The petty gossip in which members of a social circle engage usually originates within the circle it travels; it is primarily expressive and functions as a reaffirmation on the part of insiders of their feelings toward one another and toward the ways of the group. The person "who isn't one of us" is the person with whom we do not share our feelings because, presumably, he cannot appreciate them.

Like all distinctions, that between rumor and gossip is sometimes difficult to maintain. What may be gossip within a circle becomes rumor as it reaches a public. Innocent chitchat can easily carry a deliberate plant, and in the course of gossiping people may easily come to take sides. What passes for gossip at an intimate gathering becomes rumor as it circulates at an official cocktail party. The President's golf game, debated by his intimate circle of friends, is gossip; talk about a helicopter's taking him from White House to golf course circulates elsewhere as a rumor. What is gossip in terms of a closed circle will, when viewed in terms of partisan orientations around a divisive issue, appear as the process of arriving at new definitions of a situation—in short, as rumor.

23. Mass-media gossip about celebrities, for example, gives the mass audience the sense of participating in a closed circle.

LORE, LEGEND, AND MYTH

The discussion of gossip brings to mind the characteristics of all knowledge resting on oral tradition. Traditional tales are born and nourished within social groups, and their content undergoes gradual erosion and deposition for no apparent purpose. Indeed, Allport and Postman consider legend but a solidified rumor, an unusually persistent bit of hearsay, which is transmitted from generation to generation. In contrast to rumor, these tales are highly conventionalized expressions of the customary relations between people, which are embodied in the collective heritage and hence reinforced by usage.

The duration or life cycle of an item of information is hardly sufficient for categorizing the various forms and expressions of collective behavior. Doob, for example, considers rumor but an ephemeral fad, which enjoys a brief vogue and fades away.[24] This is not entirely accurate, because many rumors are but variations of similar rumors that have occurred elsewhere or at another time—recurrent themes. Just as we have distinguished between rumor and gossip by reference to their social functions, so can one distinguish between rumor and traditional tales by reference to their social significance rather than to their relative duration.

One kind of tale, the *legend*, usually refers to a historical event, one about heroic exploits by individuals or peoples. These tales testify to the greatness of one's lineage. They enhance prestige and are essentially an expression of pride in one's tradition. For this reason, too, the legendary heroes of one group are often debunked as clay idols by its enemies, or the heroes of one era are degraded by later generations who approach them from new orientations in trying to reform a "world they never made." Historiography is usually concerned with separating legend from fact, and in this sense legend stands in relation to historical truth much as rumor does to verified technical information.

But a very different kind of "motive" lies behind the *folk tale*, or *folklore*, which, as we know it, is primarily an act of sociability. Whatever the popularity derived from their entertainment value, the tellers do not vouch for, nor do the listeners pay tribute to, the veracity of these stories. They are told in traditional settings, and even the role of the storyteller is to some extent formalized. The stranger, especially the wandering minstrel and the troubador, was not only the bearer of news; he was esteemed also as the "owner" of tales which were his special possession. Among the Trobriands, writes Malinowski:

24. Leonard W. Doob, *Social Psychology* (New York: Henry Holt & Co., Inc., 1952), p. 399.

Every story is "owned" by a member of the community. Each story, though known by many, may be recited only by the "owner"; he may, however, present it to someone else by teaching that person and authorizing him to retell it.[25]

Folklore plays its part among moderns as well. Rationally we may not believe that a black cat crossing our path brings bad luck. On occasion, tribute is nevertheless paid to the superstition: we cross the street as our bad luck approaches. There come to mind also such tales as the parable of the proverbial ostrich's burying his head in the sand, a patent misconception to be sure but one that persists as an adage in spite of all evidence.

There is still another kind of tale, handed down from the past: the *myth*. It has a strong supernatural slant. The myth, in contrast to the folk tale, entails a proposition for belief or a promise of fulfillment. Hence it is a collective definition and not just a form of sociability. Yet the supernatural references contained in myth are not simply perceptual distortions added to the initial story in the process of transmission. Myth in primitive society takes on supernatural features because of its function. *Myth legitimates and crystallizes traditional attitudes important to group cohesion, and consequently there is something official about it.* This holds as well for modern myths, like that of manifest destiny or socialist eschatology. For myths constitute ready-made collective representations embedded in group heritage. Therefore these definitions are no longer, like rumor, elementary, spontaneous, and irreducible efforts to grasp something beyond reach. To quote Malinowski again:

Myth is above all a *cultural* force. Myth, as a statement of primeval reality still lives in present day life and as a justification *by precedent*, supplies a retrospective pattern of moral values, sociological order, and magical belief. It is, therefore, neither a mere narrative, nor a form of science, nor a branch of art or history, nor an explanatory tale. It fulfills a function *sui generis* closely connected with the nature of tradition, and the *continuity of culture*, with the relation between age and youth, and with the human attitude toward the past. *The function of myth, briefly, is to strengthen tradition and endow it with a greater value and prestige by tracing it back to a higher, better, more supernatural reality of initial events.*[26] [authors' italics in last sentence]

25. Bronislaw Malinowski, *Magic, Science and Religion and Other Essays* (Garden City, N.Y.: Doubleday Anchor Books, 1954), p. 102.
    26. *Ibid.*, p. 146.

Thus, myths are inclined to maintain certain unities, inasmuch as they "serve to *cover* certain inconsistencies created by historical events, rather than to record these events exactly." [27]

Myth is, however, related to rumor. Among tribes, for example, where witchcraft is widely practiced and therefore a common occurrence, current versions of a broader schematic story are constantly generated. These supernatural stories are somewhat akin to rumor. For instance, among the Navaho, accusations of witchcraft are based on revelations through "divination" and peyote dreams. If a dream or "divination" brings a person under suspicion or the symptoms of an alleged victim correspond to those associated with witchcraft, the "rumor" concerning the person's wizardry is apt to make the rounds. The truth of the accusation is something for which the accusers need take no responsibility. If the original witchcraft is not effective, this is easily explained by counterwitchcraft, which neutralizes the original threat. Moreover, validation of the initial accusation rests on agreement. There is no check on the divination of the accuser, and hence no possible refutation. But the public accusation turns his private dream into a group issue. In modern society also, discarded or ancient myths often form the source for the recurrent rumor, so that what circulates as rumor is but a regenerated myth.

WHY RUMORS ARE BELIEVED AND PERSIST

Certain stories seem to be resurrected again and again. They persist much like myths. Often rumors of this sort go underground and lie dormant for certain periods. But they do not disappear. They are most always revived when the minds of men or the "times" appear conducive to their acceptance.

A list of recurrent or endemic rumors, with varying degrees of specificity, could easily be drawn up. An example of a myth about a minority group is the long-lived myth about the ritual murder of Gentile children required in the annual sacrament of Jews. When Al Smith, a Catholic, ran for President in 1928, all the previous fears about "rum, Romanism, and rebellion"—traditional charges of "Popery" in public office—were openly revived. There are always rumors about the anticipated path of fashion movements, playing on fears of being out of fashion. Resistances toward new products are often cloaked in a host of stories repeating old wives' tales, such as the one that aluminum utensils are poisonous when used in cooking. Market competition sometimes has led to the deliberate use of plants, disseminated by willing retailers pushing brands with higher mark-ups than the dominant name

27. *Ibid.*, p. 125.

brands. The most infamous of these stories, about a leper working in a cigarette factory (or in food processing or in restaurants) is repeatedly encountered; so are rumors that particular corporations, but not their competitors, are in collusion with the "enemy." Still another myth with many specific versions sanctifies the golden past over the drab present. The innocuous myth about the "good old days" is, of course, nothing but a secular revival of the Garden of Eden story, while myths to the effect that stores carry only what the public wants, that mass media cater to popular fancy, and that public housing always results in deterioration are essentially excuses for inactivity.

In sum, the reliability of these stories as an adequate guide for action—that is, their intellectual content—has been pretty well discredited. Their uncanny tendency to persist, given the proper conditions, should therefore be noted. Apparently to label a statement "rumor" does affect belief or disbelief in the statement, but only very little. George Horsley Smith, experimenting under carefully controlled conditions, found that the label "fact" or "rumor," attached to statements whose truth persons are asked to evaluate, tends to reinforce somewhat the inclination to believe or disbelieve the statements. The same statements, when unlabeled, are believed less frequently than when presented as fact and slightly more frequently than when presented as rumor. But beyond that, the "rumor" label is similar to no label at all in that it constitutes an ambiguous stimulus which forces people to make up their minds for themselves. Acceptance in either case is governed by plausibility or, to put it more simply, by the greater readiness to believe what one wants to believe.[28] How an item of information is interpreted depends on (a) the group context, (b) the motives of the rumormonger, (c) the congruity of the situation with reality (as the hearer defines it) or with some official definition of reality, and so forth.

In Smith's experiment, just cited, persons who were asked to judge the "no label" statements wondered whether the items might be part of an information test, an opinion test, whether the subjects were being asked to evaluate "propaganda" statements, or whether this was an effort to ferret out Communists. In another study Allport and Lepkin tried to track down the motives that led people to accept as true wartime rumors of waste and special privilege in high places. The greatest "rumor differential" was between those who considered the rationing program unfair and unnecessary, and those who held contrary views. The rumor itself appears not to have caused this suspicion of waste and privilege. The difference in attitude toward the rationing program held even among those who said they believed the specific rumor but had not actually

28. George Horsley Smith, "Beliefs in Statements Labelled Fact and Rumor," *Journal of Abnormal and Social Psychology,* XLII (January, 1947), p. 89.

heard it before. Apparently the hostility toward the program was helped by the rumor, which gave a justifiable reason for attacking it.[29]

The acceptance of rumor in any natural situation is related to inner needs as well as to the social context in which the rumor occurs. One can say that a rumored statement may answer three kinds of individual need: it relieves tension, and in this sense it is expressive or projective; it justifies actions and beliefs, and in this way serves as a plant to bring others into line; and it explains the fearful and incomprehensible, and, as such, seeks to preserve an individual's integrated scheme of explanation. If in wartime, hostility rumors are more often directed against the in-group than the enemy, in all probability this is because "hostility toward the enemy [is] given complete social sanction and encouragement [and] need not be expressed in rumor."[30] Moreover, such rumors would in all likelihood never receive this opprobious label.

Recurrent Rumors Illustrated

In an ingenious, if not entirely successful, effort to track down certain universal myths in their various disguises, the psychoanalyst Marie Bonaparte divided wartime rumors about the enemy into two kinds, usually existing side by side: tales about the powerless and/or friendly enemy, and tales about the cruel and/or immoral enemy.[31] The tale of the powerless enemy constitutes an obvious attempt to control anxiety by denying there is a threat. In the same vein, rumors about a cruel enemy, who violates all rules of warfare showing neither mercy nor decency, reinforce a group objective by justifying the hatreds which alone enable one to overcome resistance and guilt connected with killing. But such rumors may also lead to terror and disintegration in the face of overwhelming fear.

Perhaps the most interesting of the universal myths collected by Bonaparte is "The Myth of the Doctored Wine."[32] The suspicion on the part of men under arms that an anti-aphrodisiac has been mixed with their food or drink has had currency in mythical as well as in modern times. During World War II various groups of soldiers protested that saltpeter had been put in their food, that they discerned its peculiar taste in the coffee or otherwise experienced its effect. According to

29. Floyd H. Allport and Milton Lepkin, *op. cit.*, pp. 3–36. For another interpretation see Leon Festinger, *A Theory of Cognitive Dissonance* (Evanston, Ill.: Row, Peterson and Company, 1957), chaps. 8, 10.

30. Robert H. Knapp, "The Psychology of Rumor," *Public Opinion Quarterly,* VIII (Spring, 1944), p. 32.

31. Marie Bonaparte, *Myths of War*, trans. John Rodker (London: Image Publishing Co., Ltd., 1947).

32. Bonaparte, *op. cit.*, p. 63.

Bonaparte, who applies her experience with dream analysis to discern the latent meaning of these stories, a temporary decline in sexual potency has been experienced among warriors preparing for battle through the ages. It can be interpreted as an atonement sacrifice in anticipation of victory and as a defense against the anxiety resulting from transgression against the moral law "Thou shalt not kill." Psychologically, the reality of this rumor and of similar stories lies in their suitability for projection of fears and wishes.

Rumor and Humor

The capacity of rumor to act as a relief for tension is further suggested by the kinship between rumor and humor. Where free expression of political ideas is hampered, as in totalitarian states, clandestine humor flourishes. Many a malicious rumor about a public figure does no more than release tension, which might otherwise be channeled into political action. Similarly, political wit facilitates, by means of a partial repression, the expression of an insult disguised as a compliment; self-condemnation for inaction can thus be mitigated, and risk can more readily be avoided. Under certain frustrating circumstances, passing on a rumor (or planting one), like telling a joke, constitutes an escape of impulses otherwise checked, a pleasurable release of tension. Bartlett, too, noted that where strong social tendencies "are subjected to any forcible social control, . . . social remembering is apt to take on a constructive and inventive character, either unwittingly or wittingly." [33]

The psychological essence of rumor, like that of wit, appears to be a partial and temporary abrogation of those ego functions involved in reality testing. This expresses itself in a subordination of the individual to the group, a condition which we may call heightened suggestibility or social contagion. Even many of the people who disbelieve the various wild rumors take care to hide their doubt, thus proclaiming their allegiance to the group orientation. And though on a personal level some people do not really believe rumors, they are unable to withstand the pressure and hunger for information. "Belief in rumor," reports Prasad, "is largely a 'watered' kind of belief which rather expresses the absence of opposition than any strongly entertained conviction." [34] This kind of "suggestibility" also accounts for the rapid succession of rumors during a crisis. Flurries of rumors sometimes begin as individual inventions; they snowball when distortions create new versions. But in a single rumor, transmission involves primarily simplification through deletions and conventionalization.

33. Bartlett, *op. cit.*, p. 267.
34. Prasad, *op. cit.*, p. 14f.

RUMOR AS REORIENTATION

Socially, not psychologically, the basis for belief in rumor lies in consensual validation, in the fact that out of the multitude of rumors, some particular version is apt to gain collective and, ultimately, "official" sanction. Rumor material gains credence through universality. Many definitions compete in the rumor process until a new orientation develops, one that at times moves men to action and at others is expressive of unrecognized moods. Rumor helps also to crystallize differences due to cleavages in the social structure. Just as the emergence of rumor signifies a certain distrust and dissatisfaction with official sources of information, so also the specific path a rumor takes reveals the existence of divisions *within* a social setting. The same rumor is not usually passed on to everyone indiscriminately. The reliance on rumor as well as its content vary in accordance with cleavages.

The relation between rumor and reputation is a case in point. What a person is, his reputation, is still little but the esteem in which he is held, and when that reputation is still emerging, one is apt to encounter different views of the person. In a most diffuse way, friendship reflects such cleavages. One might infer that friends of a person victimized as a result of rumor would be more active transmitters than non-friends; that is, just since they know the person they are most likely to talk about him. This hunch was not born out in a study of rumor in a girls' school. Friends of the rumor victim circulated approximately the same number of rumors as the rest. But when they did circulate a rumor, friends were more inclined to hear and pass on favorable rumors which tended to exonerate the friend from the implied accusation. The difference in the content of rumors was significant.[35] Doob, also, found a definite connection between informal cleavages and the specific rumor transmitted.[36] Cleavages of all kinds seem to account for the proliferation of versions during a flurry of rumors; the proliferation shows that most rumors arise out of various partial perspectives, rather than from an "official" over-all view of the situation.

Another kind of cleavage often exists between an official leadership and their followers. It is likely to be sharpened under conditions of crisis and disaster, when the protective function of a leadership diminishes. But under more normal situations, the degree of reliance on word-of-mouth information depends on degree of access to more trusted sources of information, the amount of access, in turn, being determined by

35. Schachter and Burdick, *op. cit.*, p. 369f.
36. Leonard W. Doob, "War Reactions of a Rural Canadian Community," *Journal of Abnormal and Social Psychology*, XXXVI (April, 1941), pp. 200–223.

social position. In the Soviet Union extensive participation and trust in the unofficial network of communication is greatest among the intelligentsia.

> . . . exposure to official media is for all classes an expression of involvement in the system, whereas exposure to unofficial sources implies involvement only for the upper classes. As one descends the occupational ladder interest and communications decrease, the smaller the proportion of one's word-of-mouth information comes from highly placed people, and what one gets via this medium is more and more the result of passive non-avoidance and less a matter of active seeking.[37]

The reverse is true in the United States. Distrust of official communications and, consequently, greater reliance on word-of-mouth is more widespread among the lower classes.

When there are cleavages, rumor leads to reorientation, and to new definition. Nonetheless, *rumor may support and confirm the existing social structure.* This comes about not only when rumors serve as part of an officially propagated ideology, intended to sustain faith in invincible leaders. The supportive function of rumor will be briefly illustrated in an historical instance where a flurry of rumors resulted in a patently false legend, later discredited. A second instance shows how certain widespread beliefs which, whether or not initially true, ultimately developed into self-fulfilling prophecies gave sanction to deviant behavior.

Rewriting History

The "proof" for a rumor depends in large measure on the kind and number of persons willing to subscribe to the facts alleged. If many rumors about certain kinds of incidents go unchallenged and are widely enough disseminated, they may easily crystallize into a legend. The legend then becomes a public actuality. Van Langenhove was most successful in tracing, through documentary sources, the growth of an interpretation of historical incidents that was practically unsubstantiated by any reliable evidence.[38] The legend in question concerns the exploits of francs-tireurs (partisans) who were said to be harassing German troops during their advance through Belgium in 1914. Van Langenhove was able to show, using German documents, that just about all of the incidents—attacks by civilians, joined and led by members of the Belgian clergy—were totally unconfirmed hearsay. Many had been explicitly refuted by German authorities. Reports about the use of churches as

37. Raymond A. Bauer and David B. Gleicher, "Word of Mouth Communication in the Soviet Union," *Public Opinion Quarterly*, XVII (Fall, 1953), p. 308.
38. van Langenhove, *op. cit.*

military strongholds, of partisans dressed in clerical garb, about priests masterminding guerilla operations, etc., could not stand up under careful scrutiny, even when that scrutiny came from the German side.

How did these tales originate and, above all, how did they come to be believed? First, German troops participating in the "march through Beligum" were evidently surprised by the resistance they encountered. They had been misled by their own official propaganda. Since Belgium had declared itself neutral, no resistance from that quarter was expected—and this despite the fact that Belgium had also, in the name of her neutrality, refused Germany's demand for the free and unmolested passage of its troops.

A second factor was the highly mobile, though sporadic, nature of the Belgian resistance that the German soldiers did encounter. Opposition tactics avoided an open encounter with a superior force and instead concentrated on harassment. This meant that the German soldier, who had just been subjected to the stress and chaos of mobilization, received his "baptism of fire" from a hidden enemy. Given such a situation, it is not difficult to understand how the "imagination figures a mysterious aggressor, and accepting the most improbable hypotheses. welcomes them as an equivalent to certainty." [39] In addition, there were recollections dating back to the 1870 experiences with francs-tireurs in France. To the extent that German soldiers had been led to expect treacherous enterprises on the part of the civilian population, they were apprehensive in regard to them. Dominated by this obsession, they explained every unusual event, every incomprehensible phenomenon, by the intervention of francs-tireurs. Many separate incidents spontaneously arranged themselves in the same special category." [40]

A third aspect of the situation was the context in which these so-called "experiences of German soldiers in Belgium" were reported. As rumors and stories about incidents with francs-tireurs spread and were believed, the soldiers gained collective sympathy and support, and thus they, in turn, became more biased and sensitized to "experiencing" such incidents. "Sometimes a long period elapsed before the facts and the emotions arising from them could be placed on record. During the interval recollection was shaped by novel influences; secondary variations were introduced; . . . a series of convergent influences modelled the incidents according to certain types." [41] The individual experience was thus assimilated to already established belief.

The experiences of the soldiers constituted the seeds planted into a soil in which rumor thrived. Whether the initial accounts were ac-

39. *Ibid.,* p. 125.
40. *Ibid.,* p. 144.
41. *Ibid.,* p. 167.

curate or distorted perceptions is here of little significance, for rumor always draws on some observed reality. Let us briefly trace the process by which unverified and isolated accounts mushroomed into a collective definition.

Personal transmission, mostly oral, supplied the initial material. In this connection we must note that the facts of war are not all of an epic character. Yet the wounded convalescing in public places (as these soldiers were doing) find people ready to listen to whatever facts or epics they are ready to relate. Egged on by questions, they are apt to supply the material desired. But "in their oral form, stories of this kind are not definite, their substance is malleable; they can be modified according to the taste of the narrator; they transform themselves" [42] not always deliberately but because of what is to be proved by means of the "facts."

These individual accounts, personally transmitted, soon were publicly transmitted. And since there was little opportunity for most people to check their veracity, and little motive to question it, these accounts were widely believed. Papers printed letters from the front that fitted in with their ideas of what was going on, and, by being printed, these stories took on a fixed form. Collected in books, the stories then obtained further "consecration." In the words of Van Langenhove, "a simple rumor is transmitted from mouth to mouth and susceptible of many variations, the story becomes crystallized in a written version, it acquires objectivity in a text printed and multiplied by the press; it materializes finally into a book." [43] Lastly, cartoons, photographs, and other pictorial means of transmission are employed to give visual representation to the underlying attitude and to attach it to a tangible symbol.

Official sanction and entry into collective belief results from the fact that, carried by public media, the rumors begin to penetrate everywhere. They become a part of casual conversation; people lecture about them, and they begin to be taught as facts; they become symbols of collective belief. Ultimately, if the development takes extreme form, a "scientific" investigation into "national character traits," backed by official historical doctrine written from selected accounts, may trace the incidents to endemic character traits.

For a rumor with all its individual variations—such as the rumor of Belgian partisan activity against the Germans—to become legendary, it requires acceptance by official spokesmen for a group, party, or community and, in modern society, acceptance by the mass media. In being raised to the status of sanctioned doctrine, permissible prejudice, or partisan ideology, such rumors come to reflect a change in group orienta-

42. *Ibid.,* p. 227.
43. *Ibid.,* p. 245.

tion. But the reorientation that stems from rumor can be even more effective if the rumors from which it derives are self-fulfilling, something clearly not the case with the francs-tireurs legend. *Rumor leads to reorientation not only in that it "rewrites" history, but also by helping to make it.*

The Shaping of History

The term "self-fulfilling prophecy" was first publicized by Robert K. Merton around 1948, but the concept for which it stands is much older.[44] It derives from the observation put forth by W. I. Thomas that "if men define situations as real, they are real in their consequences." Reduced to simplest terms, the self-fulfilling prophecy refers to a premonition that tends to influence future events. For instance, a college examination may be scheduled. A rumor floats about that it is designed to weed out a large number of candidates for a degree or honors. It may then succeed in doing just that. For if students become anxious and worry rather than study, their showing on the examination is apt to be poor. In connection with interracial attitudes and beliefs, Merton has held that the actions of biased individuals confirm their views of minorities; they also perpetuate the underprivileged position of the minorities and thus help to justify the discriminatory practices of the bigots, a process earlier documented by Myrdal in *An American Dilemma.*[45]

History and contemporary affairs offer many illustrations of the self-fulfilling prophecy. The rumor that a candidate cannot win helps to make him a sure loser, as delegates and electors climb on the bandwagon for the "sure winner." Lefebvre in *The Coming of the French Revolution* shows how the belief in a nonexistent "aristocratic plot" became a self-fulfilling prophecy. Belief in the rumored plot crystallized the diverse dissatisfactions of the French peasantry, the rising bourgeoisie, the lower clergy, the Parisian artisans, and the city masses all over France until they were ready to challenge established authority. In turn, this brought about a conspiracy between the first estate and the foreign enemy, the very thing all these groups feared.[46]

Similarly, assumptions about an enemy's intentions during negotiations or open warfare can easily influence their outcome. The sanctification of the doctrine of foreign encirclement by Soviet officials, whatever the bases of their fears, undoubtedly contributed to the actual isolation of their

44. Robert K. Merton, *Social Theory and Social Structure* (revised ed.; Glencoe, Ill.: The Free Press, 1957), Chap. 11.
45. Gunnar Myrdal, *An American Dilemma* (New York: Harper & Brothers, 1944).
46. Georges Lefebrve, *The Coming of the French Revolution* (New York: Vintage Books, 1957).

nation. In economic affairs as well, the fear of inflation and rumors of future scarcity have sometimes set off buying sprees which then brought about the very shortages and price rises that were predicted. Thus, the rumor process, by paving the way toward reorientation, can bring about the situation that confirms the outlook or mood that is anticipated or feared.

Recognition should also be given the proleptic function of rumor. A rumor deliberately launched as a trial balloon, being anonymous and not for attribution, can always be denied. If public reaction is unfavorable, leaders can forsake unpopular political causes and thus avoid disastrous political consequences. The trial balloon tactic—by which a prophecy may, if necessary, be self-defeating rather than self-fulfilling—is indispensable whenever responses cannot be anticipated.

Finally, inferences about matters not definitely known are unavoidable whenever a situation demands immediate action and people cannot wait for absolutely verified information. In these circumstances, even the most reasonable men may differ in their evaluation of clues. But to support an indicated policy or action, leaders are forced to develop a set of cognitive orientations that seem plausible and thus likely to be widely accepted, however little hard data are at hand. On subsequent occasions, these definitions may turn out to be clearly wrong and will be referred back to as rumor, hearsay, or legend. At the time of decision, however, they offered the only viable points of orientation.

The *social function of rumor*, to summarize, is an effort to bring the orientations of others sufficiently in line with one's own to make collective activity possible. These orientations revolve, first, around oneself, as in gossip and reputation by which individuals work out a general perception of members of their circle and, second, around objects towards which the behavior of some plurality is oriented. The transmission of rumor is not, however, entirely a matter of manipulation. It also constitutes an effort to develop through interaction with others orientations toward practices, status divisions, leaders, the future, goals, etc., for which structured and official definitions provide only a questionable guide.

BIBLIOGRAPHY

ALLPORT, GORDON W., and POSTMAN, LEO. *The Psychology of Rumor*. New York: Henry Holt & Co., Inc., 1947. A standard work on rumor from the viewpoint of perception.

BAUER, RAYMOND A., and GLEICHER, DAVID B. "Word of Mouth Communication in the Soviet Union," *Public Opinion Quarterly*, XVII (Fall, 1953), pp. 293–310. Interesting study, based on refugees, of the differential reliance on personal, as opposed to official, news sources.

BONAPARTE, MARIE. *Myths of War*. Translated by JOHN RODKER. London: Image Publishing Co., Ltd., 1947. A study of universal myths and of their latent content from a psychoanalytic point of view.

CHAPLIN, J. P. *Rumor, Fear and the Madness of Crowds*. New York: Ballantine Books, Inc., 1959. This inexpensive paperback edition contains interesting case material on certain more bizarre rumors men have believed in recent American history.

DE FLEUR, MELVIN L., and LARSEN, OTTO N. *The Flow of Information: An Experiment in Mass Communication*. New York: Harper & Brothers, 1958. Study of message diffusion by word-of-mouth.

FESTINGER, LEON, *et al.*, "A Study of Rumor, Its Origin and Spread," *Human Relations*, I (August, 1948), pp. 464–86. A case study of a rumor within a community, with a theoretical interpretation.

FIRTH, RAYMOND A. "Rumor in a Primitive Society," *Journal of Abnormal and Social Psychology*, LIII (July, 1956), pp. 122–32. This evaluation of rumors heard on two field trips to Tikopia in the western Pacific suggests that rumor has certain positive functions.

JACOBSON, DAVID J. *The Affairs of Dame Rumor*. New York: Rinehart and Company, Inc., 1948. Very good, somewhat popularized illustrations of the uncritical acceptance of untested information.

JONG, LOUIS DE, *The German Fifth Column in the Second World War*. Chicago: The University of Chicago Press, 1956. A historical investigation of German sabotage in World War II, which very nicely balances van Langenhove's account of a World War I legend.

JUNG, C. G. *Flying Saucers*. New York: Harcourt, Brace & Co., 1959. This review of reports on objects seen in the sky, with Jung's unique, somewhat mystical interpretation, should be read in conjunction with Marie Bonaparte's book.

MALINOWSKI, BRONISLAW. "Myth in Primitive Psychology," *Magic, Science and Religion and Other Essays*. Garden City, N.Y.: Anchor Books, 1954, pp. 93–148. An anthropological account of the social functions of various tales.

PETERSON, WARREN A., and GIST, NOEL P. "Rumor and Public Opinion," *American Journal of Sociology*, LVII (September, 1951), pp. 159–67. Case study of the diffusion of a rumor in a town.

SMITH, GEORGE HORSLEY. "Beliefs in Statements Labelled Fact and Rumor," *Journal of Abnormal and Social Psychology*, XLII (January, 1947), pp. 80–90. The presentation of fictitious news items to persons holding various attitudes was shown to be affected by the labels of "fact" and "rumor."

Demoralization and Panic

DEMORALIZATION, the second basic process of collective behavior, is represented in almost pure form by panic. Panic, in this frame of reference, may be viewed as a collective retreat from group goals into a state of extreme "privatization." In defining panic as a collective process, attention is thus called to two opposing tendencies which usually exist simultaneously in some state of balance and which affect collective responses to danger. On the one hand, there is the tendency toward privatization; on the other hand, group controls tend to maintain their influence over individual action even under conditions of extreme stress.

PRIVATIZATION   Individual acts—especially in the more extreme forms of panic—have a private, even autistic, orientation. Acts cease to be oriented toward the collectivity. Each person's concern is with his own safety and personal security, whether the danger is physical, psychological, social, or financial. But states of extreme panic are rarely encountered and do not persist for very long. Adaptive and defensive measures usually intercede to affect the direction of an incipient panic before it has run its full course. For example, in the escape panic that often accompanies the disintegration of military units, each combatant seeks support for his individual action in the collective sanction implicit in the general headlong flight, in the fact that everybody else is running.

THE RETREAT FROM GROUP GOALS   Since the complete disintegration of collective effort is extremely rare and, even when it occurs, is only a transitory state, we define panic in terms of an underlying *process of demoralization,* not in terms of specific behavior syndromes. Panic can be considered a collective process only in relation to the group structure it disrupts. The specific form that behavior takes in a situation of extreme stress depends on the defenses at hand. Whether persons yield to anxiety and become terrorized is to some extent determined by their previous experience, their psychological preparedness, their involvement in the group, their faith in leaders. In addition, a number of physical circumstances—such as the nature of the terrorizing event, the time sequence of the impact, the amount of warning, the individual's capacity for free movement, his location in relation to the danger, his amount of vision—undoubtedly have some effect on the direction of responses taken in the state of terror.

Since "group persistence in the pursuit of collective purposes" has long been the distinguishing feature of the sociological idea of morale,[1] it would appear reasonable to characterize this progressive undermining of group purposes, including the disruption of the ability to counter a common danger, as *a process of collective demoralization. Panic is one form that this collective retreat from group goals may take.*

THE PROCESS OF DEMORALIZATION

THE DEMORALIZATION of any collectivity, even a casual congregate or a theater audience, entails a disruption of two elements within any group structure: *cognitive definitions* and *affective ties.*

COGNITIVE DEFINITIONS   There are the patterns of expectations and intellectual schemes by which we all transform nature and society into a meaningful world. We expect the ground under us to remain firm; we trust that seasons, weather, climate, harvest, and so forth follow some predictable pattern. Similarly, we demand that social authorities—city administrations, police, law courts, schools, churches, etc.—discharge their explicit and implicit obligations, just as we count on the affection, esteem, or at least the helping hand of kinsmen, friends, neighbors, or colleagues. Indeed, we count on the fact that human beings will always behave the way we expect human beings to behave. According to the conceptual world in which we live, that which "cannot" happen just does not happen. It is these social definitions and expectations that are upset by a disaster of catastrophic proportions. The development of panic is to some degree independent of actual physical danger, though a subjectively perceived threat is always involved. Any situation giving rise to general alarm brings with it some cognitive disorientation, and therefore rumor as a collective effort to comprehend is a major factor in disasters and other situations that result in panic.

AFFECTIVE TIES   Collective demoralization thus involves a disorientation resulting from the obfuscation or shattering of prior and basic understandings. Still, disorientation due to the unexpected is only one ele-

1. Harold Lasswell, "Morale," in E. R. A. Seligman and A. Johnson (eds.), *Encyclopedia of the Social Sciences* (New York: The Macmillan Co., 1937).

ment of demoralization. For groups are held together not only by shared definitions but also by "moral" bonds. In return for protection and justice, members of organized groups are willing to subordinate their private wishes and goals. They have an emotional stake, a kind of affective investment, in the group. This investment is manifest in *esprit de corps,* pride in belonging, faith in a leader, all of which together describe group morale. Even in the casually assembled street crowd, ordinary courtesy demands a certain sacrifice of self-interest.

When the emotional ties that normally hold a group together are weakened, either because of external danger which cannot be mastered or internal dissension which cannot be resolved, it becomes panic-prone and demoralized. Difficulties that under normal conditions might be treated as a challenge, bringing group members closer to one another, become overwhelming and insuperable obstacles.

Hence, by panic we refer, not to a particular kind of response, but to all the various collective responses that express demoralization.

CONCEPTIONS OF PANIC

THIS CONCEPTION OF PANIC as collective retreat from group goals into privatization is advanced in full awareness that varied forms of behavior have been designated as panic. Quarantelli, Foreman, Wolfenstein, and a number of others have tried to bring some order into the many sociological and psychological approaches to panic.[2] Differences in the conceptions of researchers can be attributed in part to (*a*) the unit of analysis with which they are concerned, and (*b*) their assumptions with regard to the adaptive function of panic behavior.

The first question concerns the unit of analysis: *who or what panics?* Is it the individual who panics? Can a panic occur only in a crowd? Can a nation as a whole panic, or only its leaders?

The second question concerns whether panic behavior is or should be considered nonadaptive by definition; that is, whether only behavior that fails to contribute to a solution of the problem at hand or, indeed, compounds the problem is panic. Can panic behavior be adaptive behavior under some circumstances? For instance, can flight be a perfectly adaptive response?

A brief review of the units of analysis employed and the conceptions

2. Enrico L. Quarantelli, "Nature and Conditions of Panic," *American Journal of Sociology,* LX (November, 1954), pp. 267–75 (includes a bibliography on panic); Paul B. Foreman, "Panic Theory," *Sociology and Social Research,* XXXVII (May–June, 1953), pp. 295–304; Martha Wolfenstein, *Disaster, A Psychological Essay* (Glencoe, Ill.: The Free Press, 1957).

to which they give rise may help us to see the problem of panic in its proper perspective.

TERROR: INDIVIDUALS IN PANIC

As the pattern of response on the *part of an individual,* panic can be viewed as the outcome of unmanageable anxiety. According to this conception, an individual who panics has no faith in his ability to master whatever threatens him. His normal response patterns, being no longer adequate, are replaced with more primitive and impulsive responses. Crying out, random behavior, temporary loss of bowel control are not uncommon. In addition to this overt behavior, the influx of unmanageable fears invokes recollections of earlier shocks and traumas. Thus, the panic response in the face of very real and immediate dangers reactivates childhood fears, fears that do not usually relate to the present environment and its dangers. Adult fear responses—such as paralysis and escape, faith in ritual or in charms, propitiatory gestures—refer to both real and present dangers as well as to imaginary ones. Sullivan views paralysis resulting from inner tension as the most extreme manifestation of panic, with random activity, an exaggerated preoccupation with flight, psychoneurotic and hysterical symptoms as expressions of milder forms of terror.[3]

To distinguish this particular conception of panic, individual disintegration in the face of stress will be labeled as overwhelming "terror." Psychologists, and particularly psychiatrists, are attracted by this definition of panic; some treat even the group expressions of demoralization and panic as if they were nothing but elaborations of individual tensions. For instance, Meerloo, whose writings on panic are well known, has made the individual response to stress the starting point for his analysis of the many patterns in which terror finds expression.[4] Tyhurst, too, has suggested an approach to the study of how *communities* adapt themselves to unexpected stress (bombing attacks, floods, etc.) in terms of how individuals adjust to the events as they develop.[5] From this psychiatric point of view, the natural history of any disaster stresses the behavioral syndromes common to various stages: *impact,* when individuals are directly exposed to the sudden danger; *recoil,* when individuals begin to take defensive action; and *aftermath,* during which individuals begin to find ways to cope with, and gradually adapt themselves to, the shock

3. Harry Stack Sullivan, "Psychiatric Aspects of Morale," *American Journal of Sociology,* XLVII (November, 1941), pp. 277–301.

4. A. M. Joost Meerloo, *Patterns of Panic* (New York: International Universities Press, Inc., 1950).

5. J. S. Tyhurst, "Individual Reactions to Community Disaster: The Natural History of Psychiatric Phenomena," *American Journal of Psychiatry,* CVII (April, 1951), pp. 764–69.

of permanent loss. Popular accounts of well-known disasters—the Johnstown flood of 1889, the sinking of the *Titanic* and the *Andrea Doria,* for example—tend to be accounts of individual reaction to the impact of disaster and its aftermath.[6] Many other group manifestations of panic as well as nationwide hysteria and mass terror can be approached by taking the individual as a starting point.

THE ESCAPE MOB: THE GROUP IN PANIC

Sociologists and social psychologists, influenced by the Continental school of collective psychology, that is, by Le Bon and others, have been most interested in the rout or panic flight. This they have treated as a specific kind of crowd phenomenon, subject to its own regularities and career. A group in panic or what has been called "an escape mob" is a temporary exhibition of crowd pathology.

One sociologist defines panic as:

> an acute fear reaction marked by a loss of self-control which is followed by nonsocial and nonrational flight behavior. Covertly there is an acute fear reaction, i.e., an intense impulse to run from an impending danger. *Panic participants* [our emphasis] are seized by fear of a specific object defined as involving an immediate and extreme physical threat. The most striking overt feature is flight behavior which, while not necessarily nonfunctional or maladaptive, always involves an attempt to remove one's self physically.[7]

This is an image of individuals in terror, that is in a highly agitated, privatized emotional state of acute anxiety. But beyond this the term "panic participants" suggests at least a transient group formation, whose pattern is given by the *common* flight reaction away from a commonly perceived object. Hence *a* panic is always confined to a particular locality; the individuals seek active physical escape.

But if it makes sense to speak of *a* panic as contrasted to *individuals in panic,* then some real consequences must result from this group reaction. The panic rout as an ephemeral form of collective (crowd) behavior is characterized by intensive interaction among the participants. Their effort to escape is not just an individual phenomenon. Foreman, in particular, has highlighted this interaction. What gives the rout its "group"

6. Richard O'Connor, *Johnstown: The Day the Dam Broke* (Philadelphia: J. B. Lippincott Co., 1957); Walter Lord, *A Night to Remember* (New York: Henry Holt & Co., Inc., 1953); Alvin Moscow, *Collision Course* (New York: G. P. Putnam's Sons, 1959).

7. Quarantelli, *op. cit.,* p. 272.

character are (1) the circular and chain reactions and (2) the identity and similarity of escape patterns by which the rout proceeds.[8]

The significance of the interaction is twofold: it channels activities toward escape, and its also gives rise to further fears, a significant aspect sometimes overlooked in recent discussions of escape mobs. Thus, in a group panic an individual acts, at least momentarily, under the influence of others, though to be sure his response is not in terms of organized roles; the group of which he was a member has become disorganized and partially disintegrated. Such collective intensification of fear, in the presence of other persons who exhibit fear, was considered by McDougall to be the essence of panic and, mistakenly, the most elementary expression of the "group mind." [9]

Perhaps influenced by McDougall, disaster research teams set out to study the conditions under which panic rout develops and how it could be prevented. But they found that such panic rout was the exception rather than the rule in natural or military disaster. Led to expect flight and the intensification of emotion, they are inclined to interpret the absence of these symptoms as evidence that panic has been prevented or kept under control. For instance, Martha Wolfenstein, reviewing the literature on disaster, remarks that observers sometimes seem to regard paralysis and other immobile responses to extreme deprivation and danger as reassuring. "The description of disaster victims as 'stunned' and 'dazed' is often accompanied by remarks like: there was no hysteria, no wild excitement. One gets the impression that the observer expected more uncontrolled behavior and emotional expression, and was relieved to find the victims as quiet and well-behaved." [10] It may be more correct to regard the immobility often observed when disaster strikes as a more extreme form of individual response than flight.

MASS PANIC

There is a third way of conceptualizing panic. Panic phenomena are apt to appear in just about any kind of social grouping, assembled or not; panic does not occur only when people are more or less grouped together in a given locality and subjected to the same physical threat. Panic also occurs en masse.

This mass panic, of which the financial panic is probably most frequently mentioned, is often dismissed as being a panic in name only.

8. Foreman, *op. cit.*, pp. 298–99.
9. William McDougall, *The Group Mind* (New York: G. P. Putnam's Sons, 1920), p. 36f.
10. Wolfenstein, *op. cit.*, p. 83.

Nevertheless, such mass panics generally reflect a breakdown of cognitive definitions as well as the abrogation of social responsibility, both characteristic of all organized group activity. Then again, mass panic is more than many unco-ordinated and irrational behavioral reactions; the reactions that occur are due to *shared* psychological conditions, which result in widespread responses to such sources of danger as shocking news, false rumors, terror propaganda, and so forth. Mass panic is something more than individuals everywhere responding individually to real or imagined threat; it constitutes a mass demoralization in the sense that individuals so affected sense a generalized loss of direction and support, an experience they share with others. In this way the psychological structure of a mass panic is akin to that of the escape mob, save that persons affected are not in physical contact, and this gives the mass panic a different quality.

The mass panic is typified by the community-wide demoralization that follows military disaster or a bombing attack, by the demoralization that grips a large segment of the population in response to financial ruin, by the kind of national terror that appears to grip a nation in anticipation of some expected disaster or in the face of a threat imagined but hardly known. A *mass* in panic is made up of individuals who respond not only to their own fears but also to the imagined fears of others. It can be studied as an aggregate by taking the individual and his particular response as the unit of analysis. In that case an understanding of panic is in terms that account for the many individual reactions in the mass.

Hadley Cantril, for example, in his well-known study, *The Invasion from Mars,* has tried to explain how it was that in the autumn of 1938 a radio drama of H. G. Wells's novel *The War Between the Worlds* was able to stir up incidents of panic behavior all over the country.[11] Many individuals not in physical proximity with others contributed to this panic. Hearing a radio drama about an invasion by men from Mars, they fled, fell to the floor in prayer, or sat immobilized, waiting for the inevitable end. One can characterize this as panic, since so many people responded emotionally, rather than rationally, to a highly unusual and completely incomprehensible situation. Furthermore, the response was, from the viewpoint of the situation at hand, functionally useless. People who fled from the "impact area" were running away from an altogether illusory danger, which existed only in the minds of the susceptible radio listeners. But although the danger rested on an illusion, it was experienced as real by many individuals and not just one. The illusions of the many who gave way in panic had their common origin in the radio drama, whose content fitted certain prior experiences: the tense international situation made them

11. Hadley Cantril, *The Invasion From Mars: A Study in the Psychology of Panic* (Princeton: Princeton University Press, 1940).

especially susceptible to taking fright. Among some, defensive reactions set in after the first shock. For instance, some stray characters turned up at recruiting stations and volunteered to fight the supposed foe.

Cantril's study of the "invasion from Mars" focused on individual susceptibility to panic. According to him, no single reason can explain why some who listened to the radio drama became frightened and others did not. The presentation was realistic: "many people who tuned in thought the regular drama program had been interrupted to give special news bulletins. The technique was not new to them after radio reporting of the war crisis in September 1938." [12] The personality characteristics of some people undoubtedly made them especially prone to respond in panic. Besides, the behavior of others present was often the very opposite of reassuring and in some cases promoted inappropriate responses governed by fear.

On the whole, however, it was what Cantril calls the lack of "critical ability" that made radio listeners suggestible and thus led them to panic. People accepted as truth reports of the Martian invasion because the event fitted into a mental context, and those suggestible failed to find ready at hand any contradictory standards against which the accuracy of the radio reports could be evaluated. In other words, a fictitious threat to personal, financial, and group security was interpreted as real and immediate, and many persons fled miles before the night was over. They responded not only to the disaster they heard about but to the fear of war so imminent in 1938. The total effect of the fateful broadcast was one of mass demoralization, which a sizable segment of the listening audience came to share.

This notion of "mass panic," as contrasted to "individual terror" or the "panic rout," corresponds to the use of the term by historians and economists. Writing about nineteenth-century England, with no inkling of how the reporting of "live" news via radio and video might someday compound the problem, Hirst spoke of how news precipitated panic behavior.[13] As he put it, the "newspaper panic" always ended "in the abominable waste of public money" as individuals and governments, threatened by what they read in the newspapers, scrambled to gain "safety."

Newspaper panics include not only financial panics but other mass panics in the form of war jitters, paranoid fears, and collective hallucinations (of flying saucers or witches). For example, the London *Daily Mail* in 1913 initiated the so-called "airship panic" when it wrote:

12. *Ibid.*, p. 79.
13. F. W. Hirst, *The Six Panics and Other Essays* (London: Methuen and Company, Ltd., 1913).

It is now established beyond all question that the airships of some foreign power, presumably German, are making regular and systematic flights over this country. Evidence of the presence of a mysterious airship over Selby, in the West Riding of Yorkshire, on Friday night (February 21), was given on Saturday by a number of responsible persons. No one saw the body of the aircraft, but lights were seen and the noise of the engines was heard.[14]

Near the town of Selby was an army ammunition store. Thereafter reports about mysterious lights seen by observers, who were convinced that they were airplanes, reached London from all over England. The light seen by one observer turned out to be only a "farmer working at night in a field on the hilltop, taking manure about in a creaky wheelbarrow, with a light swung on the top of a broomstick attached to it." [15] Another "airship" from the North Isles, reported in from a ship, was thought by some who observed it to be a flock of birds. Still another of these visions, when viewed through a telescope, turned out to be none other than the planet Venus. Although the craze for seeing airships spread with the newspapers, the coast of Yorkshire, where the panic had started, remained during the few days of scare the main center of disturbance.

The airship panic actually mounted to little more than instances of fright resulting from misperceptions. In speaking of this phenomenon as "panic," we are aware that the behavior of the susceptible individuals differed markedly from those involved in the "Martian invasion." Still, personality disintegration—what we have called *terror*—expresses itself in a variety of ways. The prevalent focus on the description of individual reactions to disaster and loss and the subsequent refinement of types of reactions and types of behavioral sequences are invaluable when description is the goal. But collectively widespread demoralization, whether manifested in fear or in flight reactions, can be treated as mass panic.

We speak of panic as a collective phenomenon primarily in relation to social structure; this is to say, a pattern of individual responses is indicative of collective demoralization insofar as it develops counter to organized group responses. Thus, the pattern of individual responses to the news of enemy airships over Britain indicates collective demoralization insofar as it subverted belief in the power of the country to withstand the enemy and diverted attention from collective defense to privatized fear.

The difficulties of conceptualization, especially the insistence on equating specific behavioral syndromes with collective panic, is revealed in the following passage. Fritz and Marks, summarizing the results of a study of reaction during an Arkansas tornado, said there were

14. *Ibid.*, p. 104.
15. *Ibid.*, p. 111.

very few instances of panic or of *other forms* of uncontrolled behavior [authors' italics]. There was, however, a very considerable amount of confused and uncoordinated activity during and following almost all of the disasters studied by us. . . . Our data indicate that the *immediate* problem in a disaster situation is neither uncontrolled behavior nor intense emotional reaction but deficiencies of coordination and organization, complicated by people acting upon individual (and, often conflicting) definitions of the situation. It is this aspect of disaster behavior which is frequently identified erroneously as "panic." [16]

If the goal is accurate description, such a distinction between collective disorganization and collective panic is most desirable. If our goal is to understand panic as a collective process of demoralization, this kind of distinction may be less important. It does point to the need for some kind of synthesis relating the disruption of group organization to the incidence of individual terror reactions and flight behavior: how far and in what directions under what circumstances must the breakdown of group ties and group definitions proceed before collective fear or collective hallucination gives way to collective immobilization or collective flight?

PANIC: NONADAPTIVE AND ADAPTIVE

A GREAT DEAL OF THE INTEREST IN PANIC on the part of medical authorities, civil defense officials, military specialists, and others derives from a clinical interest in the prevention of "pathological" symptoms. Their approach to the study of panic has a therapeutic goal: they seek the means of effectively inoculating against it. The progressive spread of panic is viewed, irrespective of the level on which it is conceived to operate, as an interference with self-control and as a barrier to rational adaptation. Such interference seems to result from any one or more of five tendencies observable in panic:

1. Paralysis and immobility, which result from contradictory impulses toward action and interfere with accurate perception.

2. Psychoneurotic (conversion and other hysterical) reactions that interfere with self-mastery and efficient bodily and mental functioning.

3. Hyperactivity in the sense of confused, more or less random, precipitate action which is abandoned as soon as obstacles present themselves.

4. Premature and excessive fixation on a particular course of action to the exclusion of consideration of alternatives (especially noticeable in the escape mob or panic rout).

16. Charles E. Fritz and Eli S. Marks, "The NORC Studies of Human Behavior in Disaster," *The Journal of Social Issues*, X (1954), p. 33.

5. Disorganization resulting from the confusion caused by many individuals, each seeking private security from a threat without concern for the security of the larger collectivity.

In any real situation these modes of response do, of course, shade into one another. Immobility in the face of extreme danger may turn into frantic activity or headlong flight. Such frenzy can easily be seen as contributing, in its turn, to general disorganization and confusion. If under such conditions social authorities are prevented from executing measures to control the danger, or from effective rescue operations, further fears arise. Danger becomes exaggerated, generalized, and perceptions may become paranoid. Individuals develop a general "startled pattern"; any minor noise or movement arouses strong anxiety, while this startle pattern produces, on the social level, a tendency to interpret rather familiar events as unusual omens of further disaster.[17] Yet, of the five tendencies outlined above, it is in only the fifth—and, to a lesser degree, in the fourth—that individuals display the kinds of behavior that contribute to the demoralization that underlies a collective panic.

The question of whether panic is nonadaptive must be examined in terms of its value for the individual personality—versus its value for the group as a whole.

INDIVIDUAL SELF-PRESERVATION

Those modes of response that characterize any one person—such as paralysis, the various psychoneurotic reactions, and, to a lesser degree, some of the random and prematurely fixed routes of activity—constitute primarily means of coping with anxiety rather than with danger.[18] To be sure, the anxiety is activated by what is perceived as a threat from outside. Yet these symptoms of individual terror exemplify first and foremost an effort on the part of an individual to master his own anxiety. In this sense, therefore, all activity that serves to decrease anxiety, even if it is completely ineffective in warding off the danger that evoked it in the first place, involves some form of secondary gain: it allows for self-mastery and protects the personality from disintegration.

Many of us are familiar with the loss of consciousness that often accompanies physical pain or shock. This defense against pain is, so to speak, nature's anesthesia. But, while it does not lessen the injury, it inter-

17. This syndrome has been observed in combat units after prolonged exposure (e.g., the "old Sergeant's" syndrome) and following disasters.
18. However widespread their occurrence, in and of themselves, these responses are not group patterns unless they come to be directed toward collective objects. This last possibility suggests a collective defense against panic, a process discussed in Chapter 5.

feres with extricating activity. Similarly, victims of disasters have been observed to respond to the initial shock with apathy, the result of the stunning moral impact. This phenomenon has been noted in various situations. According to Bettelheim, prisoners upon arrival in a Nazi concentration camp acted as if their imprisonment had been a mistake and as if the brutal treatment being meted out was not really happening to themselves.[19] Among Londoners exposed to the aerial blitz of 1940 and after, there were many who refused to take shelter and other ordinary precautions, as if denying the possibility of bomb hits. At the same time many of those who refused to go into a shelter always slept with their clothes on because it apparently made them feel more safe. Ritualistic defenses and personal belief in invulnerability are rather common defenses in any fear-arousing situation.[20] It was such a category of reactions, observed on several occasions in the wake of actual disasters involving loss, that led Wallace to talk about a "disaster syndrome." A common initial reaction to disaster thus consists of a "temporary blocking out of awareness of personal injury or loss, coupled with a great concern for the well-being of family, neighborhood, and community landmarks (such as churches)."[21]

Thus, symptom formation always involves a certain transplantation of affect. In the case of obsessional responses or the reliance on lucky charms —the latter is frequently observed among combat troops or flying personnel—the actual dangers are displaced by other, more symbolic ones. The fear of death while flying, for instance, becomes displaced by the fear of flying without one's lucky piece. This reminds one of the child who, by dragging a blanket with him or clutching his favorite toy as he goes to sleep, assures himself that the world to which he awakens will be the same as that to which he is bidding good night. Moreover, the persistence of familiar objects makes any loss easier to bear. "When objects with which the individual had been identified," writes Wallace, "are threatened, damaged, or destroyed, the individual (not sure of his own capacity to survive unaided) becomes anxious to assure himself that the whole supporting world has not collapsed."[22] This moral support given to the individual, even though it does not actually bestow immunity, is what

19. Bruno Bettelheim, "Individual and Mass Behavior in Extreme Situations," in Eleanor E. Maccoby, T. M. Newcomb, and E. L. Hartley (eds.), *Readings in Social Psychology* (New York: Henry Holt & Co., Inc., 1958), pp. 300–10.

20. Roy R. Grinker and John P. Spiegel, *Men Under Stress* (Philadelphia: The Blakiston Co., 1945), p. 130.

21. Anthony F. C. Wallace, *Human Behavior in Extreme Situations* (Disaster Study No. 1, Publication No. 390), National Research Council, Washington, D.C. See also Wolfenstein, *op. cit.*, pp. 51ff.

22. Wallace, *op. cit.*, p. 20f.

sometimes allows him to face the danger or to bear his losses even though the loss is not lessened.

Responses in panic sometimes have their adaptive value both for the individual and for the group. Janis has argued that, on the basis of published accounts of reactions to the atomic bombing of Hiroshima and Nagasaki, no widespread panic took place.[23] The flight from the area of impact was fundamentally adaptive and occurred without widespread disorder. In much the same vein Quarantelli states that "frequently the flight of panic is the most adaptive course of action that could be undertaken in a particular situation." [24] Nor need the individuals making parallel escapes from fire, the enemy, or falling debris hinder the flight of others. (The exception is the panic rout where, trapped in an enclosed space, persons panic and trample each other in the attempt to get out.)

MacCurdy, too, has argued rather ingeniously that immobility, though a regression to more primitive modes of behavior, is nonetheless an adaptive response with definite survival value.[25] Lack of movement enables many an animal to blend with its surroundings and supplies a sort of natural camouflage. According to his argument, when flight and aggression against danger do not serve as suitable defenses, and when no single directing tendency toward manipulative activity is able to assert itself, an atavistic impulse to escape detection through lack of movement becomes reactivated. Fascinating as this theory of the hereditary origin of paralysis may be, there is now no way to confirm or refute it. But both flight and immobility are in effect withdrawals from facing the danger. The very nature of each, with its inhibition of the higher mental faculties, with the generation of fear over and above a readiness on the part of the organism to respond, indicates that the response is not only to the danger. The orientation and reaction include also an imagined occurrence of actual injury from which there was a narrow escape and against which future defenses might be unavailing.

In fact, some such distinction between fear and anxiety has to be made. *Fear* constitutes a response to a stimulus existing in reality, whereas *anxiety* denotes general apprehensiveness. In the presence of the latter, the ego not only responds to the present danger but initiates at the same time defensive operations to fight off the anxiety. But the natural solution to either external danger or feelings of anxiety is withdrawal, for anxiety is almost always attributed to some real external threat.

23. Irving L. Janis, *Air War and Emotional Stress: Psychological Studies of Bombing and Civilian Defense* (1st ed.; New York: McGraw-Hill Book Co., 1951).

24. Quarantelli, *op. cit.*, p. 270.

25. John T. MacCurdy, *The Structure of Morale* (Cambridge: The University Press, 1943).

GROUP SURVIVAL

What enables persons to persevere, even under conditions that arouse great anxiety, is their involvement in a group. The obligations to their group, their sense of responsibility, or, psychoanalytically, their superego demands that defense be sought in directions other than withdrawal. The group with which a person identifies himself gives him some security. It also returns to him, as long as he lives up to the group ideals, some of the affection he has directed toward it. Writing about air corps combat personnel during World War II, Grinker and Spiegel state that:

> As long as the major portion of the man's interest and affection remain devoted to the welfare of his combat group, he will not develop strong anxiety over the possibility of his own injury or death. His chief concern involves the fate of his group. Then, if the group is strong and successful in combat, he has nothing to fear.[26]

There are, of course, a number of factors that may eventually undermine the investment in, and the protective function of, the group. These result in a reinvestment of emotional and affective ties in the self, and thus they increase the temptation to yield to anxiety and thus to withdraw. Grinker and Spiegel mention a category of men prone to breakdown in combat who have

> little or no sense of loyalty. . . . Although their anxiety is easily stimulated, it is short-lived, since they make an immediate effort to remove themselves from the combat situation which arouses it. . . . The psychological disability lies principally in their behavior toward escape from combat duties, and *in the effect this activity has on the morale* of their units.[27]

Their behavior tends to lessen not only the effectiveness but also the cohesiveness of the unit of which they are a part.

A more general statement of this position has been attempted by Mintz. He explains behavior in panic in terms of people's perception of how others are apt to react. Co-operative behavior has very different results for the individual depending on the behavior of others. As soon as people important in the co-operative effort cease to act in their expected roles, a conflict arises between the needs of the group and those of the individual. Accordingly, "it is chiefly the reward structure of the situation" —the fact that there seem to be no great rewards for sacrificing on behalf

26. Grinker and Spiegel, *op. cit.*, p. 124.
27. *Ibid.*, p. 29.

of the group—that accounts for nonadaptive behavior of groups at theater fires and similar situations.[28]

Another element in disruption of co-operative effort consists in the identification with a subgroup to the point where, unless counterbalanced by individuals who act in the name of the group, it interferes with performances necessary for the attainment of broader goals. "Much of the initial confusion, disorder, and seemingly complete disorganization reported in disaster communities," Killian suggests, "was the result of the rush of individuals to find and rejoin their families."[29] He found that most dilemmas between loyalties to primary groups and loyalties to the community at large or broader responsibilities are resolved in favor of the former.

SYNTHESIS

Consequently, the question of whether panic behavior as a response to threat is nonadaptive must be answered primarily in relation to social structure. For the individual the response may be adaptive in that it wards off overwhelming anxiety or even results in personal survival. But by its very nature, panic is, for the group, nonadaptive. A panic ensues when co-operative defenses become weakened, when the behavior of others is no longer a predictable element in collective action, when lines of communication and faith in the collective ability to handle a danger are destroyed. Hence, panic in its various manifestations is most properly considered the result of a collective process of demoralization.

How then does this view of panic as arising out of and expressing collective demoralization synthesize with those conceptions that treat panic as an individual state of terror or as an escape mob? Freud, in his *Group Psychology and Analysis of the Ego,* opened up a most fruitful line of inquiry, to which our analysis is indebted and which is invaluable for such synthesis. Each individual within a group, Freud postulated, is tied to the leader and to other members of his group by affective (libidinal) ties. "A panic arises if a group . . . becomes disintegrated."[30] Illustrating his notion with the military panic as the prototype, he listed as symptomatic of panic the fact that (1) orders and group directives by leaders go unheeded as (2) each individual seeks personal safety. But this dissolution of group ties has a further consequence: (3) it sets loose in each individual a "dread" over and beyond the external danger, since the security derived

28. Alexander Mintz, "Non-adaptive Group Behavior," *Journal of Abnormal and Social Psychology,* XLVI (April, 1951), p. 191.

29. Lewis M. Killian, "The Significance of Multiple Group Membership," *American Journal of Sociology,* LVII (January, 1952), pp. 309–14.

30. Sigmund Freud, *Group Psychology and Analysis of the Ego* (London: The Hogarth Press, 1949), p. 44.

from the effective operation of mutual obligations has disappeared. The individual cut off from the group feels unloved and thus truly abandoned and forlorn with no one to care for him but himself. Hence, danger cannot be mastered until faith in the group and in the predictability of group rewards has been restored.

STEPS IN DEMORALIZATION

OUR NEXT TASK will be a brief examination of conditions that influence the progressive course of demoralization at each of its stages. The presentation is divided into *impact, privatization, disruption of group norms,* and *mutual facilitation,* but these should not be viewed as clear-cut stages. In any situation antecedent conditions would inevitably be fused with subsequent phases.

THE IMPACT OF DANGER

To reiterate, danger and actual loss stand in some relation to the occurrence of panic, but the response, far from being automatic, is modified by the existence of cohesive forces making for group morale. The evidence for this is clear. First, a group may panic after having mastered similar or even greater dangers many times before. Further, there is a difference between groups: what overwhelms one group may be easily weathered by another. One can actually speak, in the last analysis, of a *panic-proneness* when group discipline and morale have been undermined to a point where even a minor threat causes disintegration.

Factors that make groups panic-prone may be classified as (*a*) predisposing physiological and psychological conditions and (*b*) orientations to the specific danger stimulus.

Predisposing Conditions

Among these conditions are, first of all, those that undermine the physiological stamina to resist; these are the factors most often stressed by military writers on panic. They include extreme fatigue, undernourishment, dehydration, illness, exposure to cold and weather. But there is good reason to believe, on the basis of the differential performance of individuals and groups under conditions of physical stress, that, as Foreman states, such antecedent factors "become causes only as reactions to a crisis are shaped by them (that is, as a stimulus links antecedent tensions with immediate shock)." [31]

31. Foreman, *op. cit.,* p. 297. See also Anselm Strauss, "Literature on Panic," *Journal of Psychology,* XXXIX (July, 1944), pp. 317ff.

These physiological conditions probably affect adversely certain psychological factors, which determine whether or not the members of the group have satisfying emotional identifications: whether they feel surrounded by a psychologically protective group (irrespective of whether this actually affects the chance of survival); whether there is official reassurance as well as any belief in this reassurance. Citing data gathered by the Army research division on World War II morale, Shils advances the hypothesis that morale in combat deteriorated as less scope was given to the protective function of officers.[32] The chief factor breaking down the individual's investment in the group and causing a return to a predominant interest in one's own chance of survival is the loss of men in combat, especially of close friends. It is extremely difficult to transfer the old attachments to newcomers and replacements. At the same time as airmen approached the completion of required combat missions, they began to concentrate more and more on personal survival in the interest of family and home ties.

Orientations to the Danger Stimulus

If "danger mobilizes the emergency resources of an organism," as an analogy from physiology would lead us to believe, it does so only as long as the threat confronting the group is defined as capable of mastery. A stimulus defined as unmanageable—for example, the expectation of a stimulus as panic-producing—may itself induce terror and panic. This was illustrated by the airship panic as well as by the reaction to the radio drama about the invasion of Martians. So, too, Italians at Adawa panicked when they encountered Ethiopian hordes during their 1896 invasion. Though the latter were poorly armed, their reputation as ferocious and cruel warriors did much to instill fear in the Italian troops.

This possibility of a panic response to a stimulus symbolically defined as dangerous raises the broader issue concerning the difference between a sudden, unexpected shock and the arrival of a danger long dreaded but anticipated. According to one line of reasoning, the catastrophic impact is greatest when entirely unexpected and inexplicable, whereas training and preparation against a known danger aid in a socially organized defense. Yet prolonged anxiety may result in the spread of exaggerated rumors and hence increase fear reactions.

Apparently this issue can be resolved by an extremely fruitful hypothesis which suggests that the subjective feeling of vulnerability constitutes a psychological variable intervening between the impact and any possible demoralization. For instance, the panic potential of a group sub-

32. Edward A. Shils, "Primary Groups in the American Army," in R. K. Merton and P. F. Lazarsfeld (eds.), *Continuities in Social Research, The Scope and Method of the American Soldier* (Glencoe, Ill.: The Free Press, 1950), p. 33.

ject to bombing is seen to depend on the numerical relationship between survivors who have been "near misses" and those who have been "remote misses."

> In the near-miss group are those who have been mentally incapacitated by bombing or are, at least, shaken. Their attitude is: "the next one will get me"; or "will the next one get me?" [Among the remote misses, on the other hand,] there is a contrast between the actuality of the destruction of others and one's own scathelessness. . . .

> If the remote-miss person has more courage after a raid than before it, if courage, like fear, is contagious, and if the near-miss group in any community is small, it follows that a light, a "token" bombing must improve morale in that community. Innumerable Home Security reports attest the truth of this conclusion as I have been told.[33]

This hypothesis explains why in some cases continued exposure to danger strengthens morale, yet has the very opposite effect in others. On the one hand, Londoners during World War II showed an increasing ability to adapt to the stress of aerial bombing. Similarly, in Tokyo a light raid had a stimulating effect on morale. Successful mastery of the danger by the majority of the population apparently resulted in greater confidence, though danger had not actually diminished. On the other hand, in American combat units with high casualties, the very evident accumulation of near-miss experiences led to an increase in fear reactions. The U.S. Strategic Bombing Surveys in Germany suggest an even more complicated relationship among damage, losses, and morale. In those cities where bomb destruction did not exceed the 40 per cent mark, saturation raids were followed by a decline in morale, paralleling the amount of bomb damage and, presumably, the amount of near-misses. Where bomb damage was greater, morale improved slightly, presumably because hate of a very real enemy unified the population and partly offset the perception of immediate danger.

Prolonged anxiety with regard to a threat does not necessarily imply preparedness for meeting it. It does indicate the presence of an anticipatory suspense, an apprehension that the danger is directly aimed at the self. Defenses are mobilized against the anxiety, and therefore feelings of acute panic often go together with a total lack of preparedness or even no recognition of the need for protective action. Any impact is therefore responded to as "unexpected and sudden." The sudden emergence of real danger, only vaguely apprehended, highlights the lack of preparedness, just as it unleashes all at once the anxiety previously kept in check. How easily such anxiety becomes generalized is indicated by the very serious

33. MacCurdy, op. cit., pp. 12ff.

deterioration of morale among those who hitherto have heard only the more sensational stories of death and destruction. Anticipation of danger is thereby increased. Unless accompanied by effective countermeasures, guidance by an effective leadership, and group identifications, it will simply result in making the danger seem more overwhelming; that is, it will be defined as unmanageable.

PRIVATIZATION AND REGRESSION

Privatization refers to the undermining of affective primary group ties. It has already been pointed out that any danger stimulus that induces panic does so by reactivating prior traumatic situations, especially those of childish helplessness. Certain aspects of any impact are especially fear-arousing: darkness, which hides the exact nature of the danger and iso-lates the individual from possible help; constriction of free movement, especially the sensation of being choked, emphasizes a lack of mastery; screaming noises reinforce all one's fears. The physiological response to fear will bring with it certain changes in the supply of oxygen, char-acteristic of the foetal state, when the organism was safe and secure as well as in darkness.

Noise, first of all, interferes with group communication; it makes it more difficult to develop a shared definition of the danger. Marshall ob-serves that if ground troops in battle could only talk to one another, group panic might easily be avoided.[34] Noise stimuli are especially overpowering since the child's first concept of social authority was built up out of the many commands he heard—the "don't's" and the "no-no's!" A "screaming" noise continues to be a threatening noise. An interesting use of this principle is given by the Germans' use in World War II of noisy dive-bombers and screaming bombs designed to terrorize military and civilian populaces alike. Initially these forms of attack left their mark. But the gradual discernment of differences in the sounds of missiles facilitated adaptation. People learned not to respond with generalized anxiety, and instead listened carefully to signals of impending danger. Still, until methods of coping with it are learned, terrifying racket lowers the ability to test reality and thus aggravates the emergence of indefinite fears.

How stress lowers the critical threshold of perception has been ex-perimentally investigated by Bruner and Postman.[35] The test situation did not even remotely replicate conditions of real danger. Still, results did indicate that an increase in stress resulted in an increase in perceptual

34. S. L. A. Marshall, *Men Against Fire* (New York: William Morrow & Co., Inc., 1947); copyright 1947 by S. L. A. Marshall.

35. Leo Postman and J. S. Bruner, "Perception Under Stress," *Psychological Review*, LV (September, 1948), pp. 314–23.

errors. These errors can be attributed, according to the experimenters, to a rash "hypothesis formation" on the part of subjects. The structure and meaning of sentences was inferred on the basis of only very scanty recognition of words or syllables.

To be sure, tests of perception and recognition under laboratory conditions cannot withstand uncritical extrapolation to situations of extreme stress. Nevertheless, we find the same process at work under real life conditions. For instance, Prasad concluded from his study of rumors in the wake of an earthquake that rumors have general as well as specific frames of reference. *Specifically,* in relation to the earthquake, rumors contained reports or predictions, often fantastic, of actual or expected damages. *Generally,* the profusion and snowballing of rumors prepared the community for the possibility that practically anything might happen. Rumors about astrological forecasts dealing with the anger of the gods and with major upheavals of the universe were the expression of a generalized fear regarding loss of love by a scolding parent. Such generalized and diffuse fear reactions do not require the injection of deities, though cultural myths often contain them.[36] In both Hiroshima and Nagasaki, rumors expressive of diffuse anxiety concerning the lingering dangers of contamination persisted for some time after the atomic bombing. According to an eyewitness, shortly after the attack "it began to rain. . . . The drops grew abnormally large, and someone shouted, 'The Americans are dropping gasoline. They're going to set fire to us.' "[37]

Specific fears of definable dangers are infinitely preferable to fear of something undefined. Normally "the order [in the universe] is all-comprehensive. Thus a pre-formed scheme specifies our fears and guides our action—whether we are primitive or civilized, animal or man. . . . If under shock of an experience that shatters our scheme of order, we doubt or no longer trust this scheme, the dividing line [between the possible and the impossible] fades and indefinite fear invades the bewildered soul."[38]

Perhaps the most total and at the same time unimaginable fear is the fear of death—that is, of total loss. As Freud pointed out, it is impossible for an individual to imagine his own death except through the eyes of others. Fear of death becomes manageable through one's imagination of immortality in the eyes of others, the other members of one's group.

36. J. Prasad, "The Psychology of Rumor: A Study Relating to the Great Indian Earthquake of 1934," *British Journal of Psychology,* XXVI (July, 1935), pp. 1–15; For another illustration see J. H. Powell, *Bring Out Your Dead: The Great Plague of Yellow Fever in Philadelphia in 1793* (Philadelphia: University of Pennsylvania Press, 1949), especially pp. 104–6.

37. John Hersey, *Hiroshima* (New York: Bantam Books, Inc., 1948), p. 50.

38. Kurt Riezler, "The Social Psychology of Fear," *American Journal of Sociology,* XLIX (May, 1944), pp. 491ff.

Hence, the better integrated the group, the more certain the immortality, and therefore the easier it is to display fearlessness in the face of possible death. What makes the "total terror" characteristic of totalitarianism so unbearable is the futility of sacrifice. Protest and martyrdom lose their meaning, as the historical record is destroyed. A similar but very much less significant shock was experienced by soldiers, inaccurately reported as dead, upon finding on their return to "life" their personal effects divided up among others.

As long as the universe of discourse, the sharing of definitions, protects men from indefinite fear, panic can be mastered. But when demoralization becomes general, the need arises for a person who transforms the general fear into something definite and thus binds it. He reinstitutes a frame of reference, a simple cause-and-effect relationship. Thus, either flight and withdrawal become general, or the generalized anxiety becomes transformed into a specific fear of something or other.

DISRUPTION OF GROUP NORMS

So far we have talked about privatization as the undermining of affective *primary* group ties. However, there is another element to group structure, one we refer to as *secondary*. Such a secondary group structure consists of the more remote and abstract symbols and entities which nevertheless command allegiance. Codes, commands, and formally defined obligations are the cement that holds together the larger unity made up of a multiplicity of smaller cells. Hence, the disruption of group norms is distinct from, though related to, privatization and regression.

Now it has often been maintained that the morale of smaller groups is more easily maintained than that of larger units. Wrote McDougall: "The smaller groups harmonize more effectively than the larger groups the purely egoistic and the purely altruistic motives." [39] The fewer group members, the easier it is for an individual to find concrete rewards, recognition, and affection. Still, MacCurdy presents a contrary viewpoint: the payment for self-abnegation, he argues, lies in the power that accrues to the group.[40] Only group idealism (a sublimination of the herd instinct) can surmount the instinct of self-preservation. Hence, the larger the group, he infers, both in terms of numbers and dispersal, the more worthwhile the individual sacrifice and the greater the potential payment in terms of "immortality."

This opposition of views seems to rest on this fact: in the small group, rewards are immediate, whereas in the large group they are deferred. To what extent primary ties or secondary obligations have precedence

39. McDougall, *op. cit.*, p. 117.
40. MacCurdy, *op. cit.*, p. 80f.

depends on the time perspective under which members of a group operate and on the degree to which these obligations harmonize. We have already noted how, in a disaster, family ties often take precedence over community needs and how, after prolonged exposure in combat, the ties of home begin to reassert themselves against the demands of the military unit.

Consequently, in the assessment of group morale, one must weigh the forces making for cohesion against those that disrupt it, such as the reassertion of primary ties at the expense of support of the larger group.[41] Two factors that govern the cohesiveness of groups in the presence of deprivation and danger are group traditions and leadership. When group traditions—for example, soldierly honor, patriotism, a reputation for selfless service, etc.—are legitimatized by primary group loyalties, efforts to withdraw from danger are likely to be kept to a minimum because the individual stands to lose the immediate gratifications that come from belonging to a group. In the same way, the leader has to make himself acceptable by anticipating dangers and showing his concern and effectiveness in providing for the welfare of the group.

> By making adequate information accessible, the leader transforms "unknown" into "known" danger; he gives, as it were, the danger signal. By actually turning himself against the danger and by thus inviting identification in action, but naturally also by providing outlets for the group's desire to participate in 'protective activity,' the leader prevents the transformation of real danger into imaginary danger. Under his guidance the danger is estimated in reasonable terms.[42]

But these primary group identifications operate within a broader secondary framework. When this broad framework is no longer supporting, when leadership proves inadequate, when the substance of political, religious, and moral ideals conflicts with the formal injunctions, it is no longer in harmony with the primary group structure. Thus, the German army under Hitler, held together by primary group ties supported by secondary symbols, began to be vulnerable, not when the strategic situation deteriorated, but after essential supply and medical services broke

41. The experimental approach to panic has correctly tried to assess the balance between cohesive and disintegrative rewards within small units. What unfortunately has been ignored in experimental manipulation of panic is the fact that these laboratory groups are not real groups and that therefore the reward structures are purely individual definitions, unrelated both to primary ties and to ideological convictions and traditions. Cf. John R. P. French, "An Experimental Approach to Group Panic," *Journal of the Elisha Mitchell Scientific Society*, LVII (December, 1941), pp. 195ff.

42. Ernst Kris, "Danger and Morale," *American Journal of Orthopsychiatry*, XIV (January, 1944), p. 153.

down and units were so disrupted that "being in the army" no longer seemed to guarantee minimal protection, food, and shelter.[43]

Size, measured by number in a group, is crucial to morale, but in an indirect way. The enlargement of a group usually brings with it a dissolution of homogeneity. The hard core is apt to decrease in proportion to a more or less diverse following not adequately integrated and assimilated to the "group" ideals. In the sustaining of morale and the prevention of panic, active cells and clear-cut roles whose occupants have a conscious sense of mission are most important. These facilitate identification and assure that danger can be mastered. Emergency units, soldiers, civil defense officials, firemen, and so forth constitute the disciplined and organized parts of society which are apt to recover social consciousness most quickly. These have been called in various contexts the "disaster protocracy," the "hard core," or the informal "emergent leadership."

It must not be concluded from this, however, that rigid organization can of itself protect against disintegration. It is in the nature of a catastrophic impact that preparation is inadequate, that cultural protections collapse. A reliance on dogmatic faith which makes no allowance for the possibility of disaster may result in extreme vulnerability to the unacknowledged possibilities. Goering's promise that "no enemy airplane will ever reach Germany" became legend among disaffected Germans, whereas Churchill's promise of "blood, sweat, and tears" became the rallying cry of the British, who stood fast before an *acknowledged* danger. Moreover, every social organization has its breaking point, a point at which disruptive influences are reactivated by the loss of protective and affective functions of the group. There is a point beyond which all cultural protections may fail, a point of inflexibility.[44]

CONTAGION AND MUTUAL FACILITATION

In panic there is the question of the mutual intensification of fear and how interaction channels fear into "escape" activities. In disasters people usually tend to interpret the initial signs of danger in terms of their accustomed frame of reference. In a factory where carbon monoxide gas was escaping, each worker at first attributed his growing nausea to some personal illness, such as a hangover, not having eaten any breakfast, etc. Similarly, during an explosion in South Amboy, New Jersey, which

43. Edward A. Shils and Morris Janowitz "Cohesion and Disintegration in the Wehrmact," *Public Opinion Quarterly*, XII (Summer, 1948), pp. 280–315.

44. Fred C. Ikle, "The Social Versus the Physical Effects of Nuclear Bombings," *The Scientific Monthly*, LXXVIII (March, 1955), pp. 182–87. See also F. C. Ikle, *The Social Impact of Bomb Destruction* (Norman, Okla.: University of Oklahoma Press, 1958).

shook houses and shattered windows for many blocks, those affected were inclined to believe that the furnace or the hot water heater in their own house had exploded. The NORC disaster studies conclude that:

> social interaction was of considerable importance in giving warning of the danger. In the case of the carbon monoxide asphyxiation [mentioned above], conversation among the workers and observation of each other's behavior were the principal factors leading to a definition of the situation.[45]

Similarly, persons who heard the sound of an approaching tornado took it to be the noise of an approaching train or some other common event. Those, on the other hand, who discussed among each other what the noise might mean tended to be aware of the tornado more quickly than others.

The real issue is not whether social interaction is characteristic of panic situations, but whether *being in the presence of others* has a re-assuring or an aggravating effect on the anxieties that arise with a recognition of the danger. If a group gives effective succor to individuals exposed to danger, it probably has a reassuring effect. On the other hand, the sight of uncontrolled fear may be quite unnerving.

> Where physical signs and broadcast warnings may have left people quite unaffected, they may begin to be alarmed where they see others taking the potential danger seriously. So, for instance, on the occasion of an oncoming flood, one person says: "I heard the whistles blow (the signal to evacuate), but nobody left so I didn't either." Another in the same situation states: "I didn't believe it (when she heard the flood warnings). Then I saw other people leaving and I got scared." [46]

Thus, although at first people are reassured by others who do not take the warning seriously, when people do become frightened, *their alarm may be intensified precisely because it had been unacknowledged.* The general confusion aggravates imaginations of the danger involved and the fear of possible abandonment. Each person has only a partial view. He senses danger, but he can assess its nature and extent only through the reactions of others. When the *Andrea Doria* began to sink after colliding with another liner, the collision was announced in Italian. This announcement left English-speaking passengers with a general sense of danger but without the specific information needed to take defensive measures. For their interpretation of what was happening, they had to rely on cues from those around them. An investigation of the causes of mass panics during

45. Fritz and Marks, *op. cit.*, p. 36.
46. Wolfenstein, *op. cit.*, p. 46.

World War II describes this process so vividly that we will cite from the general report at length:

> . . . Every large panic starts with some very minor event . . . for the general purposes of control it is more important to have exact knowledge of the small cause than the large effect. . . . I think it can be laid down as a rule that nothing is more likely to collapse a line of infantry in combat than the sight of a few of its number in full and unexplained flight to the rear. Precipitate motion in the wrong direction is an open invitation to disaster. That was how each of [seven incidents studied] got its start. One or two or more men made a sudden run to the rear which others in the vicinity did not understand. But it was the lack of information rather than the sight of running men which was the crux of the danger. For in every case the testimony of all witnesses clearly developed the fact that those who started the run, and thereby spread the fear which started the panic, had a legitimate or at least a reasonable excuse for the action. It was not the sudden motion which of itself did the damage but the fact that the others present were not kept informed.
>
> For example, a sergeant in the First Battalion, 502nd Infantry, was hit through an artery during the Carentan Causeway fight on June 12, 1944. It happened in a flash. One second he was hit and the next he was running for a first-aid station without telling his own squad why he was getting out. They took after him and then the line broke. Others who hadn't seen the sergeant make his dash saw someone else in flight. They too ran. Someone said: "The order is to withdraw." Others picked up the word and cried it along the line: "Withdraw! Withdraw!" It happened just as simply as that.
>
> In one incident in the Pacific (reported in the book *Island Victory*) an artillery observer's party had had its radio drowned out. To continue communication, the observer asked and received permission to withdraw to the company CP so that he could use the radio there. But because there was considerable mortar fire falling along the front, the party withdrew at a run instead of a walk. The men in the infantry line saw these men pass in a rush (it was night) and they got up and ran.[47]

The specific direction and form of panic behavior, as well as the amount of interpersonal contagion, depends on a number of factors. The general conditions conducive to the formation of a panic rout are the limitation of the danger to a specific locality and a scarcity of escape avenues. Coste, studying trench warfare in World War I, also found the density of the group to be a determining factor. When fear builds up among persons crowded closely together in a shelter, one might expect them to flee in a contagious panic. Coste, however, suggested that de-

47. S. L. A. Marshall, *op. cit.*, p. 145f.

moralization under these crowded conditions, when it occurs, is more likely to take the form of paralysis. Dividing a military formation into small units, he also believed, is likely to minimize the spread of privatized behavior since it facilitates official communication and maximizes the influence of the leader; collective flight is not likely to be triggered by the headlong flight of one or a few individuals.[48]

The spread of panic behavior in response to danger is also a function of the integration of a subgroup into a larger framework of organization. In World War II, small groups of German soldiers, once cut off from their units, tended to surrender after only token resistance.[49] Finally, whether individual panic becomes contagious depends on prevailing social definitions. Several hundred American infantrymen holding a sector of the line where chemical attacks were expected all developed similar hysterical symptoms. They attributed these to having been "gassed" but the chemical warfare personnel could find no evidence that an attack had occurred. There was a regular mass evacuation. Yet those who reported themselves as casualties could not be considered deserters from the group.[50]

Shared behavior patterns such as these symptoms allow each individual to withdraw from a dangerous situation without violating group codes. They mark the onset of a collective form of defense against the panic behavior that threatens the group and constitutes collective demoralization. In demoralization, the escape is effected without group sanction. It may be a matter of individual withdrawal, of withdrawal into the shelter of some antagonistic primary group, of psychoneurotic conversion, and so forth. The collectivization of these symptoms into a group response, which integrates the participants at least temporarily, means that we are really dealing with collective defense, the next basic process to be discussed. Thus disaster and danger also give rise to aggressive scapegoating, pietistic hopes, or unrealistic mass euphoria (the post-disaster Utopia to which Wolfenstein refers).

B I B L I O G R A P H Y

Cantril, Hadley. *The Invasion From Mars: A Study in the Psychology of Panic.* Princeton: Princeton University Press, 1940.

48. Charles Coste, *La psychologie du combat* (Nancy: Imprimerie Berger-Levrault, 1928), p. 110.
49. Grinker and Spiegel, *op. cit.*
50. E. A. Strecker, *Beyond the Clinical Frontier* (New York: W. W. Norton & Company, Inc., 1940), pp. 77ff.

An analysis of the reaction to Orson Welles's famous radio drama.

CHAPMAN, DWIGHT W. (ed.). *Human Behavior in Disaster: A New Field of Social Research.* Vol. X, No. 3 of the *Journal of Social Issues,* published by the Society for the Psychological Study of Social Issues, 1954. This issue contains references to and summaries of the research on disaster conducted under the auspices of the National Research Council.

FOREMAN, PAUL B. "Panic Theory," *Sociology and Social Research,* XXXVII (May–June, 1953), pp. 295–304. A theoretical formulation dealing with the escape mob and its natural history.

GRINKER, ROY R., and SPIEGEL, JOHN P. *Men Under Stress.* Philadelphia: The Blackiston Co., 1945. Psychiatric observations on air corps combat performance, with many references to the importance of social relations and group goals.

JANIS, IRVING L. *Psychological Stress: Psychoanalytic and Behavioral Studies of Surgical Patients.* New York: John Wiley & Sons, Inc., 1958. This thorough analysis of reactions to stress includes a number of propositions that may well have relevance to group situations.

KILLIAN, LEWIS M. "The Significance of Multiple Group Membership in Disaster," *American Journal of Sociology,* LVII (January, 1952), 309–14. This study demonstrates that allegiance to subgroups during a disaster may interfere with the effort of the larger community.

MACCURDY, JOHN T. *The Structure of Morale.* Cambridge: The University Press, 1943. The near-miss versus remote-miss hypothesis, together with some other suggestive formulations.

MARSHALL, S. L. A. *Men Against Fire.* New York: William Morrow & Co., Inc., 1947. Based on investigations by the author of panic among United States troops during World War II.

QUARANTELLI, ENRICO L. "Nature and Conditions of Panic," *American Journal of Sociology,* LX (November, 1954), 267–75. A definition of "panic" as the escape mob, including a bibliography on panic.

RIEZLER, KURT. "The Social Psychology of Fear," *American Journal of Sociology,* XLIX (May, 1944), 489–98. Analyzes the social conditions that produce generalized and diffuse fear in the broadest possible framework.

WOLFENSTEIN, MARTHA. *Disaster, A Psychological Essay.* Glencoe, Ill.: The Free Press, 1957. A partial summary and a rather free interpretation based on the disaster studies conducted under the auspices of the National Research Council.

CHAPTER 5

Crowd Behavior

BY "CROWDS" people generally mean a multitude engaged in a lynching, riot, strike violence, or revivalistic orgy. The term "crowd behavior" usually suggests images of destructiveness, looting, violence, and disorder. The crowd is thus associated with bizarre and undesirable conduct. In a society where men stress rationality, control of one's temper, good manners, getting along with the neighbors, any action is censured in which the individual submits to his passions instead of keeping his wits about him. The individual in the crowd appears to do exactly what ordinarily is disallowed.

Theoretical formulations and empirical study have also emphasized the same socially disruptive aspects of crowd behavior, e.g. looting during a disaster and the actions of a revolutionary mob. Individual behavior in the crowd, it is assumed in most of these formulations, is marked by a loss of critical self-consciousness. Each man runs with the pack; he follows the leader; he leaves his conscience behind.

> An individual in a crowd is a grain of sand amid other grains of sand which the wind stirs up at will [Gustave Le Bon wrote in 1897]. Moreover, by the mere fact that he forms part of an organized crowd, a man descends several rungs in the ladder of civilization. Isolated, he may be a cultivated individual; in a crowd, he is a barbarian—that is, a creature acting by instinct. He possesses the spontaneity, the violence, the ferocity, and also the enthusiasm and heroism of primitive beings.[1]

Of three early theorists in this field, Gabriel Tarde and Scipio Sighele approached crowd phenomena from the viewpoint of criminology.[2] The

1. Gustave Le Bon, quoted in R. E. Park and E. W. Burgess, *Introduction to the Science of Sociology* (Chicago: University of Chicago Press, 1924), p. 892.
2. Gabriel Tarde, *L'opinion et la foule* (4th ed.; Paris: Librairie Felix Alcan, 1922), pp. 349–87; Scipio Sighele, *Psychologie des Auflaufs und der Massenverbrechen*, trans. from Italian by Hans Kurello (Leipzig, 1897).

third, Le Bon, generalized largely from impressions of the revolutionary mob during the Paris Commune of 1871. This tradition still survives. Moreover, the very practical concern with crowd control, as well as a natural curiosity about the spectacular and bizarre, have led people to think of the crowd primarily in terms of the disruptions produced.

Nevertheless, the pioneer collective psychologists occasionally pointed to the good that might come of evil. While Le Bon saw the crowd as always *intellectually* inferior to the individual, he thought that *morally* it could be either inferior or superior. Thus, "from the point of view of feelings and of the acts these feelings provoke, the crowd may, according to circumstances, be better or worse than the individual." [3] A crowd might often be criminal; it could also be heroic. But its intellectual inferiority was inevitable according to the law of "mental unity," which holds that all thoughts and impulses turned in the same direction are brought down to the least common denominator.

The stress on the bizarre and evil aspects of crowd activity has lately been questioned, as have many of the other attributes of crowd behavior long taken for granted. Observers have pointed out that there is no uniformity of behavior, no mental unity in the crowd. Some are leaders; some are led. The kind and intensity of participation in crowd activity differs from person to person. Even in mobs, people act without loss of critical self-consciousness; they are not so carried away and so unresponsible for their actions as some theorists have held.[4] It is suggested that behavior in the crowd may be neither very different from behavior in more ordinary circumstances nor inherently inferior, either intellectually or morally.

WHAT IS A CROWD?

A CROWD is often considered a collectivity with certain formal characteristics which are said to account for its unique psychological structure. But scholars seeking a formal definition agree on only a limited number of points:

1. A crowd is, first of all, to be distinguished from the organized group in any of its forms.

2. The crowd is temporary. It may form out of an organized group, or it may give rise to a permanent organization. But the crowd itself never has a permanent structure.

3. Le Bon, *op. cit.*, p. 892.
4. See, for instance, William A. Westley, "Nature and Control of the Hostile Crowd," *Canadian Journal of Economics and Political Science*, XXIII (February, 1957), pp. 33–41.

3. Any assembled aggregate of individuals, given the proper conditions, is capable of transformation into a crowd. Whatever reasons have brought people together or led them to perceive a likeness in one another, the emergence of a crowd looms as a possibility in every street throng, in every assembled audience, or in every category of persons—though not yet in contact—who share a similar concern, such as admiration for the same crooner or opposition to the same government measure.

4. A crowd is forever in process; it is a changeling.

5. A crowd consists of a large number; three do not make a crowd.

These basic and rather general characteristics define a crowd for most sociologists and social psychologists. In addition, there are borderline phenomena which some writers consider a subspecies of crowd and others prefer to treat in an entirely different way.

COMPACT AND DIFFUSE CROWDS

How many people make a crowd? The number of people involved is of importance insofar as it affects the nature of interaction characterizing the crowd. According to the many definitions, *a* crowd may be anywhere from hall-sized to world-wide.

Le Bon, Sighele, Tarde, Ross, and—more recently—Turner and Killian have not considered physical contact an essential attribute of their definition. The compact crowd, assembled at some locality and hence limited in size, is not essentially different from the diffuse crowd;[5] its participants behave in roughly the same manner, except that the interaction that gives rise to the diffuse crowd is more indirect: the community-wide transmission of rumor takes the place of jostling and milling in the localized crowd. All the other characteristic features of the compact crowd, say Turner and Killian, are also present in the diffuse crowd. Accordingly, one would view Americans everywhere, temporarily transformed by the Japanese attack on Pearl Harbor, as a crowd: imaginations were translated into wild rumors; officials tried to outdo each other in spearheading the counterattack; the thoughts of people, irrespective of their prior opinions, were drawn toward the same objective; and whereas Hirohito could be dealt with only in effigy, song, and cartoon, thousands of Americans of Japanese ancestry became direct victims of the passions aroused. In this scheme, diffuse and compact blend. Persons who everywhere follow a fad (e.g., the goldfish-swallowing orgy) together constitute a diffuse crowd as do, for example, the participants in an extended rumor network who have no direct contact with one another.

A special significance accrues to the diffuse crowd: it provides the

5. R. H. Turner and L. M. Killian, *Collective Behavior* (Englewood Cliffs, N.J.: Prentice-Hall, Inc., 1957), Chap. X.

social context out of which the many compact crowds precipitate. Nevertheless, in seeking to define the formal properties of a crowd in being, one should not be distracted by analogous processes in larger collectivities. A revolution breeds crowds but it is also something other than a crowd. The nation-wide rally against the attack on Pearl Harbor did precipitate crowd behavior here and there, but there was deliberate and planned mobilization of group loyalties for the purpose of organizing a collective defense. It is true that the temper of the times and widespread crisis may make crowds ubiquitous and that the formation of one crowd may precipitate the formation of another. A particular crowd, however, depends on physical crowding together.

ACTIVE AND PASSIVE CROWDS

Many writers divide the compact or localized crowd into two major subtypes: the *active* and the *passive*.[6] The crowd in action is sometimes called a *mob,* whereas the examples cited in illustration of the passive crowd include little that cannot be subsumed under the various kinds of audience, such as the casual group of sidewalk superintendents watching an excavation or the more intentional and formal audiences met for entertainment or edification.

The degree of organization is sometimes used to differentiate the active and the passive crowd. The active crowd is said to be lacking altogether in organization. The crowd objectives are seen as developing only out of the interaction *within* the crowd, where behavior is not oriented in terms of prior roles and tradition. The passive crowd or audience, by contrast, occupies the borderland between the active crowd and the organized group. Like the latter, the audience assembles and acts according to certain minimal conventions; unlike the organized group, any particular audience has no past and generally no furture. Since its members guide their behavior in accordance with some fairly general prescriptions, an audience usually has some structure and division of labor: there is a recognized "leader"—a speaker or spokesman. The audience, moreover, usually assembles at an assigned place, and certain behavior is implicitly expected of audience members. When people leave their seats, heckle or maintain respectful silence, applaud speakers, talk among themselves, or stand up, this is usually in accord with long-standing and widely accepted traditions. One shouts "Bravo" at the end of an operatic aria; one stands to applaud the honored dinner speaker. The orators in London's Hyde Park or Chicago's Newberry Square are fair game for hecklers, but one feels impelled to suppress even the slightest cough at a symphony concert. In England the audience cheers the "good show" of the opposing team; in the United States the touchdown scored by the visiting squad is

6. R. E. Park and E. W. Burgess, *op. cit.,* Chap. XIII.

met by groans. Yet everyone knows how the physically assembled audience, when confronted by what it considers undue provocation or stirred to the proper pitch of excitement, may explode into action almost instantaneously and become something quite different. What had been a spirited audience thus becomes an active crowd (or mob).

The audience can therefore be viewed not only as a kind of crowd. Dynamically it constitutes an active crowd at an earlier stage before conventional controls have given way. In the mob the crowd motif has become dominant, while in the audience emotions are still manipulated and subordinate to the goals of the constituted leader, speaker, etc. To say that the audience represents a higher phase of organization means that the active forms of crowd behavior exist only in their incipient forms and have not yet dissolved the conventional norms.

FURTHER CLASSIFICATIONS

The best-known classificatory schemes derive from efforts to systematize and categorize quite different crowd phenomena. Many systems have been proposed—some very detailed—but concerning the various subspecies and how these should be defined there is only limited agreement. One can, however, discern two broad approaches to the problem of classification: (1) according to *forms of interaction* and the *direction* these take and (2) according to the *substance* of the collective action and the *content* of the common moods that characterize the various kinds of crowd. In general, we can speak of *formal* and *substantive* classificatory schemes.

Formal Classification

The nature of formal classification has already been alluded to in relation to such attributes as dispersion and degree of organization. It has been pushed furthest with regard to the crowd "objective" which temporarily unites the crowd participants in concerted action.

First, is the distinction with regard to the crystallization of some definite course of action. Some crowds develop a line of action in relation to some identifiable goal, while others merely mill around in their state of agitation without ever coming to express their feelings in some uniform way; for example, the crowd impatiently waiting for the gates to open is a milling crowd.

Second, the kind of crowd objective that develops and the relationship of the crowd members with regard to it permit further categorization. With regard to the kind of crowd objective, there is the *active-expressive* dimension—not to be confused with the *active-passive* dichotomy based on degree of organization. In the acting crowd the objective is the attainment of some external goal; by contrast, the expressive crowd fulfills its objective simply by acting out its own feelings. For instance, in the dancing crowd, the prototype of the expressive crowd, no external objects toward which the action is directed appear; the individuals spend themselves in their constant and frantic motion.

With regard to the relationship of the crowd members to the crowd objective, another dimension distinguishes between an objective toward whose achievement the members *must* co-operate and the existence of similar objectives that each member accomplishes by parallel, but *not necessarily* co-operative, action. For example, a lynch mob is typed as a *solidaristic* crowd following a unified objective, but the looting crowd would exemplify *individualistic* crowd behavior, since the acquisition of stolen goods carried out under the impulse of collective excitement basically required no concerted effort: crowd members must co-operate to lynch their victim; they loot side by side but not together.

Having accomplished its lynching objective together, the solidaristic crowd may further vent its feelings by sacking the home town of its victim. This shift in crowd objective—from the victim of lynch injustice to looting—constitutes another axis for classification. If the lynch mob disperses upon fulfilling its murderous intentions, it constitutes a *focused crowd*. On the other hand, if it goes on to wanton destructiveness or indiscriminate aggression—attacking cars, beating up passers-by, the kinds of hostility that so often are acted out under the cover of crowd behavior and appear to follow no clear-cut goal—the crowd is marked as highly *volatile*. There are many intermediate types as, for example, when action is directed not against one person or objective but against a class of objectives—for example, violence against zoot suiters.

Various combinations of these types—active-expressive, solidaristic-individualistic, focused-volatile—result in additional subtypes.[7] In practice, however, the maintenance of these formal distinctions between instances of crowd behavior has not always been easy or particularly useful in understanding the dynamics of crowd behavior. The changeling nature of the crowd has contributed to these difficulties.

Substantive Classification

The introduction of substantive categories to distinguish crowd phenomena has also failed to produce clearly delineated types. Examples of types derived on the basis of the content of crowd action are: the *aggressive,* the *acquisitive,* the *escapist,* and the *expressive* crowd.[8] These

7. Turner and Killian, *op. cit.,* pp. 100–101.
8. R. W. Brown, "Mass Phenomena," in Gardner Lindzey (ed.), *Handbook of Social Psychology,* II (Cambridge, Mass.: Addison-Wesley Co., Inc., 1954), p. 840.

terms describe the meaning and substance of the crowd objective and the quality of behavior associated with it. The acquisitive crowd (e.g., a buying stampede) differs from the aggressive crowd: in the latter the object is to do injury; while acquisitive crowd behavior may be ruthlessly selfish, it is not intentionally aggressive. Still we have the problem, inherent in the nature of the crowd, of accounting for transformations—for example, the escapist (fleeing) crowd which, learning it has been tricked, turns against its seducer; the dancing crowd which gets out of hand and turns to looting.

In classificatory schemes, substantive categories may be used in combination with formal ones. Blumer, for example, speaks about four kinds of crowd.[9] The first two, the *casual* and the *conventional,* are essentially passive and thus constitute audiences. The expressive-active distinction between the third and fourth types corresponds to another formal dichotomy. The *expressive* crowd, according to Blumer, fails to develop an objective and thus differs from the *active* crowd. Later effort to refine these categories merely leads to additions, such as the *milling* and the *fleeing* crowds. Because of these difficulties some persons have suggested that the best way of classifying crowds is in terms of the feelings built up within them. Accordingly, one would distinguish between collective anger, collective dread, collective greed, etc., and seek to uncover the processes by which each mood becomes collective.[10]

Limits of Classification

Few scholars who have applied their efforts to classification would argue that their own schema were more than convenient devices for the purpose of guiding future observations and bringing out relationships in their data which might otherwise go unnoticed. Unfortunately for the investigator, the concern with classification has, like ulcers, become an occupational hazard. For it can be said without risk of heresy that there is at present no fully satisfactory classification of crowds. Let the reader recall for a few minutes the behavior of any crowd in which he has participated or about which he has read. A lynching mob is, of course, "aggressive." It may start as a casual crowd. After that it may mill about aimlessly. It also contains, sad to say, large elements of "conventionalized" behavior; in part lynchings follow a conventional pattern, repeated from group to group: there are usually recognized leaders who act as spokesmen. If the classification becomes an end in itself, too much

9. H. Blumer, "Collective Behavior," in A. M. Lee (ed.), *Principles of Sociology* (New York: Barnes and Noble, Inc., 1951).

10. Tamotsu Shibutani suggested this approach in seminars at the University of Chicago in 1950 and 1952.

effort is applied to what are essentially word games. When does a conventional crowd become active? Or does not the notion of "organized" crowd express a paradox? Does not the active crowd have many characteristics in common with the expressive crowd? Crowd behavior, as we shall say, is a compromise solution and thus always contains conventional elements.

The crucial research problem is the development of propositions to explain why in one case the spontaneous interaction culminates in, let us say, unfocused aggressive action, whereas in some other instance conventionalized but highly emotional expressive behavior is the outcome. This requires only some agreement on the essential characteristics of the genus crowd. Its natural history, or career, can then be attributed to specific, situational factors.

THE FORMATION OF A CROWD

A COLLECTIVITY of any kind is capable of transformation into a crowd when it develops a condition loosely referred to as *rapport*—that is, "a mutual responsiveness, such that every member of the group reacts immediately, spontaneously, and sympathetically to the sentiments and attitudes of every other member." [11] To describe how any particular crowd arises, one needs to indicate the steps by which a chance collection of individuals or members of an organized group enter into a condition of rapport and respond to one another's feelings without reference to their usual roles. What follows is a schematic outline.

STEP 1   *A certain number of people must be together in intense interaction.* How many? Theoretically, crowd phenomena range from the sharing of psychopathological symptoms, as in *folie à deux*—when the mental illness of one person thrives on and receives support from another—to the *folie en masse* of an entire nation. But although the phenomena underlying *folie à deux* may be analogous, or even homologous—an issue still to be determined—the two-person group is not a crowd formation. At most it forms a nucleus for a crowd. It is more like a permanent group since the two partners, in supporting each other's symptoms, play definite roles *vis-à-vis* one another. Their relationships follow persistent patterns. At its minimum, as Brown points out, a crowd must be hall-sized, meaning a crowd "too big for a room but small enough to be face-to-face." [12] This is no exact quantitative limit, though it conveys rather well the image of a somewhat confused, milling collection, confined within some area, which has gotten at least a little bit out of hand. And yet it would be interesting

11. R. E. Park and E. W. Burgess, *op. cit.*, p. 893.
12. Brown, *op. cit.*, p. 837.

to see whether the forms of behavior that on occasion arise in hall-sized aggregates do not also manifest themselves in smaller groups—groups of twenty, of twelve, of eight, or even fewer. The smaller the group, the more easily, it seems, is its activity controlled and confined. The participants are less apt to be anonymous, and every one of them is capable of addressing himself to the entire group as in an audience. The form of interaction most typical of the crowd is, by contrast, one that Madison Bentley long ago described as "shoulder-to-shoulder," based on partial anonymity, rather impersonal, and thus contrary to status and role.[13]

The upper limits of size, on the other hand, seem to be set by the opportunities for frequent and direct interaction through which rapport, in the sense of a common emotional reaction, is able to develop. Physical proximity appears to be a prerequisite for this, although with the increase in communication people in different places may engage in behavior that, in its origins and in many of its manifestations, is very much akin to behavior in the crowd. But this constitutes crowd behavior only if the participants ultimately come to act as a unity on the basis of rapport. The numerous small crowds that at the same time but in different localities engage in strikingly similar patterns of behavior had better be called *psychic epidemics*. Everywhere there are sources of tension which, as a result of contagion, lead to the formation of particular crowds. But however similar the behavior and intent of these disparate crowds, together they hardly form *a* single crowd.

STEP 2   *There must be heightening of ordinary feelings as a result of a series of events or possibly of only one extraordinary event.* In general, one expects that the people who form a crowd come together in a state of more than ordinary agitation. Occasionally a collection of apathetic or carefree people may, in response to some triggering incident, be sufficiently aroused to form a crowd; but this is surely the exception rather than the rule. People who, as the sayings go, "couldn't care less" and "aren't mad at anyone" are unlikely to band together in a lynching, though a sudden dramatic threat may create panic. An audience listening to a lecture on cybernetics might act out its fright in case of fire; it is not likely to mob the speaker just because it disagrees with what he is saying. The parade crowd, given the proper musical and visual stimulation, could be aroused to some heights of patriotic ecstasy, thus transforming the nature of the interaction.

STEP 3   *For the assembly of people to form a crowd, the heightened feelings must culminate in a common mood—a mood that is shared.* No doubt the quality of this common mood has a determining influence

13. Madison Bentley, "A Preface to Social Psychology" in *Studies in Social and General Psychology from the University of Illinois*, ed. by M. Bentley, XXI (June, 1916), p. 15.

on the direction and subsequent development of activity. But whatever its quality, the mass intoxication that occurs begins to dissolve ordinary restraints. People soon become abnormally sensitive to others who share their feelings. Under certain conditions, for example, the spectators of a parade, jammed together along narrow pavements, may cease to pay attention to the music and passing floats. Trying to maintain a solid footing, individuals concentrate on shoving those who seem to be deliberately pressing against them. Dirty looks turn into overt accusations. The general exaltation and good feelings take a different turn. There is much individual discomfort and annoyance, which eventually boils over into anger which is shared by everybody. This mood is capable of erupting through the normal controls, until people, ordinarily polite, use their elbows in the most disagreeable fashion.

STEP 4   *For this common mood to be translated into overt action, those in rapport must first begin to redefine the situation.* Under the sway of collective excitement, the situation is transformed into one where it appears that conventional expectations inherent in a person's status can be violated with apparent impunity. This redefinition of the situation is perhaps the most important prerequisite for the formation of a crowd. Most street crowds are made up of people from all walks of life and their anonymity vis-à-vis one another probably promotes a redefinition of the situation as an opportunity for self-indulgence. Concern about the judgments of others who do not join in the collective action (i.e., representatives of established convention and authority), some of whom are in any crowd outburst, thus becomes unimportant. Condemnation from near-by spectators is ineffective because it involves no loss of face, no expulsion, no demotions, no other kinds of sanction. In fact, the passivity of these onlookers signals their acquiescence; if anything, it seems to contribute to the feeling of omnipotence—"no one can stop us"—that people in a mob often have.

But an explanation solely in terms of anonymity is clearly inadequate because it overlooks two things: first, some situations are defined as occasions for collective orgy even though the participants are well known to each other; and, second, in the crowd people, far from being insensitive to others, are, on the contrary, in a state of rapport and thus highly attuned to others. The difference in their action seems attributable to the fact that the voice of reason is under partial sedation. Criminal elements who take deliberate advantage of the confusion to escape detection are an appendage to the crowd; they do not create it. And as far as the active participants who spark the crowd behavior are concerned, the silent and critical nonparticipants exercise no effective restraint.

The mechanisms that dissolve critical self-consciousness cannot as yet be adequately explained. In general terms, one can point to two factors which act in a complementary fashion. The crowd situation offers (1) positive *rewards* which temporarily outweigh any realistic assessment of consequences, (2) as well as a strategy for *guilt evasion*. Even though it may lead to his arrest, the fan who throws the bottle at the umpire enjoys his notoriety more or less consciously.[14] The writhing participant in a revivalistic orgy may expose himself to public ridicule, but he heeds only the rewards of salvation. Besides, the sight of others acting in a proscribed manner without punishment or other disastrous effects suggests to the observer that he can indulge in the same actions without any guilt. The tacit approval that bizarre or forbidden behavior receives in the crowd encourages rather than inhibits similar action. Thus, a college boy who ordinarily would not burglarize steals into the women's dormitory to carry off silk panties. Encouraged by his peers and "brothers," he enters the crowd spirit from which he had probably once considered himself immune. The risk of group punishment only serves to underline his belongingness, and the group action exempts him from personal guilt.

STEP 5   *The temporary definition of the situation culminates in the formation of a specific crowd when a large part—not necessarily all —of those assembled in close proximity begin to respond in a similar fashion.* When a significant proportion of the crowd has redefined the situation as a chance for self-indulgence in which ordinary experience can be evaded, the crowd becomes a psychological unity whose specific outlook is situationally determined. Action and sentiment fall under the influence of the crowd milieu. Persons act without regard to their usual roles because in the crowd they are, at least temporarily, tied to one another by emotional impulses.

The behavior characterizing the crowd at this stage is more than the sum total of individual actions. The individual is temporarily "transformed": he acts differently from the way he would act by himself. Some of the ordinary checks on behavior are cast off, and inhibitions dissolve. In every ordinary choir, people who are ordinarily self-conscious about their ability to carry a tune sing in full voice along with others. In the same way the mood shared in an aggressive, destructive, or orgiastic crowd seems to offer a milieu that protects individuals from self-consciousness and the pangs of anticipatory guilt.

14. Everett D. Martin wrote: "Everybody is perfectly aware of what is being said and done; only the moral significance of the thing is changed . . . what is unconscious is the fact that the social is actually being twisted around into giving approval to the things which it normally forbids." *The Behavior of Crowds* (New York: W. W. Norton & Company, Inc., 1920), pp. 35–6.

CROWD BEHAVIOR AS COLLECTIVE DEFENSE

ANY CROWD SEEMS to provide something like a shield behind which feelings can safely be expressed. As such, it constitutes a form of collective defense against anxiety. Crowd behavior is the process by which shared anxieties come to be discharged and externalized as a common defense against demoralization and disintegration. Collective defense can, however, characterize individuals in a collectivity larger than a shoulder-to-shoulder crowd.

The readiness with which any crowd changes the direction of its activity or the intensity of its feelings suggests that a definition of crowd behavior in terms of process is preferable to one dealing with the forms it assumes. Where one assembly disperses in panic, another finds a collective defense against panic in orgiastic togetherness as hallelujahs fill the hall. Consider a hall packed with jittery individuals. Shout "Fire!" and panic ensues. Then stop people as they flee, and shout "April Fool!" Fear turns to collective anger, and violence may even be directed against the practical joker. Some years ago in Quito, Ecuador, a radio program based on the fictitious invasion from Mars induced the spread of panic.[15] When authorities, seeking to reassure the populace, told them it was fictitious, the panic was transformed into aggressive destruction. A crowd swept down upon the building housing the radio station and, incidentally, the principal newspaper as well. The building was burned, and there were fifteen dead and fifteen injured as a result of the anger unleashed.

Specific crowds are apt to form when the focus around which a group is integrated is threatened. The crowd object offers the group a new focus. The participants act impulsively but always in such a manner that their individual standing in the group and, consequently, group solidarity are not undermined. The sections that follow will clarify further the conception of crowd behavior as collective defense.

THE UBIQUITY OF CROWD BEHAVIOR

Potentially a crowd may emerge out of any conglomeration of people, whether they collect by chance or are assembled intentionally. The crowd mind slumbers everywhere. Since the better educated seem to share the popular notion that crowds are for the most part foreign to the "civilized" country and alien to their class, it seems necessary to call attention to the ubiquity of crowds.

Why, people always ask, are there more riots and hysterical epidemics in Latin and Slavic countries? Why do mobs form so often in the Middle

15. *The New York Times*, February 14, 1939.

and Far East? With a little thought, however, one can recall reading in newspapers, witnessing on television, or hearing from one's parents about mob activity that involved many peoples and many places.

A scholarly journal contains a survey of mob activity in New England before 1765, when "any excitement, such as the use of the whipping post or the pillory, was sufficient to bring together a tough and turbulent audience, often armed with rotten eggs and other repulsive kinds of garbage," and after 1765, beginning with the Stamp Act, when politically manipulated mobs tarred and feathered the objects of their derision and carted them through the towns for the entertainment of the crowd. The Boston Tea Party, "most famous of all Boston's pre-war mobs," was not an isolated or unusual incident.[16]

News items in the early 1930's, a time of world-wide depression, are replete with stories of crowd activity in Western democratic nations. In 1934 Amsterdam saw rioting on quite a large scale against the reduction of government unemployment benefits. As in the United States in 1932, hunger marches in England sometimes erupted in violence. On February 6, 1934, the Chamber of Deputies in France was stormed by a crowd, leading to the fall of the Daladier government the following day.

Neither education nor a full stomach guarantees immunity. Carry A. Nation, former schoolteacher and hatchet-swinging scourge of all saloon-keepers, symbolized the morally indignant mob. Women suffragettes sometimes engaged the police in physical battle. Hardly a football season passes, moreover, in which the enthusiasm of at least some college audience does not spill over into diffuse destructiveness.

To go a step further: Certain forms of crowd behavior are not simply tolerated but fully condoned. The tearing down of the goalposts after the victorious home-coming game, the collective euphoria with which groups everywhere greet the signing of a peace, the excessive enthusiasm with which heroes may be greeted, the traditional throngs welcoming the new year in Times Square—all these are looked upon with favor and even promoted. Certainly not every one of these conventional binges gets completely beyond control.

THE NATURE OF SOCIAL UNREST

That crowd behavior is peculiar to no one class, no one ethnic group, no one country can be demonstrated. Yet the chances that crowd activity will erupt in deviant and unapproved directions *everywhere, any time* are not the same. Under what conditions, then, is crowd activity most likely to erupt in deviant and unapproved directions? Theoretical

16. Ronald Longley, "Mob Activities in Revolutionary Massachusetts," *New England Quarterly,* VI (March, 1933), pp. 98–110.

discussions are almost unanimous in their stress on one answer: when a society is characterized by widespread "social unrest."

Social unrest, in the form of general personal anxieties or collectively defined threats, was defined by Park and Burgess in 1922 as perhaps the most elementary form of collective behavior. Personal restlessness, as they saw it, is transformed into social unrest when transmitted from one individual to another by way of *circular response*. In this manner, A communicates his discontent to B, and B's discontent is then reflected back to A. The initially vague manifestations of personal dissatisfaction are reinforced as they become collective property.

Social unrest is probably more typical of a dynamic mass society than of a stable folk community. Generalized social unrest, conducive to the formation of specific crowds, is most often associated with the *disintegration of the social order*. It characterizes periods of crisis, when there are disturbances in the usual forms and routines of living. War, revolution, periods of moral disintegration reflect the transitions from an old order that is breaking down to a new one that has not yet taken its place. Crowds reign because the expectations that once guided conduct have lost some of their validity. They no longer altogether fit the changed social positions, and new definitions of the situation are as yet inadequate, untried, and tenuously held. The ordinary stress and strain of living becomes inordinately complicated.

Yet social unrest may prevail even when there is no apparent upheaval in the form of a military defeat or a social catastrophe. Nor is it a condition entirely confined to modern civilization. In the most stable folk society the conditions of life also entail hardship. On occasion the sacrifice of a scapegoat or an annual orgy, in which restraints are temporarily cast off, bolsters collective defense. But when institutionalized channels for the expression of anxieties and dissatisfactions are lacking, the defense is likely to take an entirely unexpected form. As this lack is more typical of modern society, therefore aggressive rioting, unsanctioned by authorities, against external objects is generally associated with a society in rapid transition. We can speak of social unrest growing out of a *latent and diffuse kind of unrest*, even in the absence of overt crisis.

Four instances of riotous crowds [17] are examined next in some detail

17. Descriptions of these riots were drawn from personal observation of the Shanghai riot, informal interviews, and press stories from *The New York Times,* the New York *Herald Tribune, Time, Life, The China Weekly Review, The China Press, The Ottawa Citizen,* and *Ottawa Journal.* Some of the original newspaper material on the Robeson riot was collected in 1950 by Dr. Jerome Carlin, then a fellow graduate student at the University of Chicago. It has been supplemented by reference to the *Presentment of the October 1949 Grand Jury of Westchester County: The Peekskill Incidents,* White Plains, New York and the report of the American Civil Liberties Union. For materials on the Montreal hockey riot, we have

to illustrate the range of conditions out of which social unrest may develop. In each case the behavior of the crowd developed as a defense against the widespread anxieties and diffuse fears characterizing the specific times and milieus. These same case studies will be used in the rest of the chapter to illustrate other hypotheses concerning crowd behavior.

Riots under Conditions of Widespread Social Disorganization

Rome, Italy, saw in 1944 its first lynching since the latter part of the eighteenth century. The chief prosecution witness in the trial of a Fascist collaborator was dragged from the courtroom by a mob which beat him, threw him into the Tiber River, paddled him to death, and strung his body feet up (as Mussolini's body had hung in Milan) from the bars of a jail window. In 1946 in Shanghai, then still governed by Generalissimo Chiang Kai-shek, a protest demonstration outside a police station grew into city-wide rioting. Before the lawlessness ended, store windows were broken, a printing shop was burned, automobiles were wrecked, a street car was overturned, and bystanders were roughed up.

Both these riots developed in a period of accelerated changes. Rome had just been liberated by Allied armies from years of fascist rule and virtual occupation by the Germans. The old regime was gone; a new governing force recognized by the people had not yet been established. Rome was occupied by armies which until recently had been its enemies. Unemployment was widespread, food scarce. The black market flourished. Morals were low; disillusionment with the authority of the government was prevalent. "Nobody," said Count Sforza at the time, "wants to be in the government."

In the fall of 1946 events in Shanghai seemed no less directly headed toward a crisis. The fascinating metropolis had become a center of great social discontent. Because of the long civil war, which was still being fought in China, prices were rapidly moving upward. The city itself was jammed, its streets literally overflowing with refugees, and new ones arriving daily. A cold wave had swept the city at the end of November. Rumor had it that at least fifty frozen bodies littered the streets every morning. The police had antagonized the population through their arbitrariness and cruelty as well as their incessant attempts at extortion. Just prior to the riot they had issued edicts that put the many street vendors under such restrictions that they would be able to survive only by violating them, and for this they needed police connivance.

The rapid disintegration of the social order meant a number of things

also made use of Sidney Katz, "The Strange Forces Behind the Richard Hockey Riot," *MacLeans's Magazine*, September 17, 1955, pp. 11–15.

to the mass of inhabitants in both Shanghai and Rome. They were confronted with a host of new problems as whatever security they had enjoyed by way of old routines waned altogether. Old norms were not valid, and therefore citizens were fearful. There were new contacts with armies in transit and foreign occupation forces. Migration had contributed to a leveling process, and people from all walks of life found themselves in more frequent contact with each other, often with their positions completely reversed. New hopes, goals, and prospects of improvement found expression in planned agitation, diffuse rumors, bogey stories, promises based on hearsay, and dreams of the "future." The hopes were for a better day, peace, food, a gain in social prestige, political reform, even social revolution. Meanwhile the dissolution of established conventions and social ties, the devaluation of skills formerly of use, and the alienation from authorities indicated the absence or inadequacy of institutional channels of expression. This, then, was the substance of the individual dissatisfaction that had metamorphosed into social unrest in both cities at the time of these riots.

THE ROME LYNCHING / This riot grew out of the trial of Pietro Caruso, Rome's police chief during the final months of the German occupation. He was the first Italian accused of collaboration to be brought before the tribunal for punishment of Fascist crimes. A major charge against him was that he had provided 50 of the 320 hostages whom the Nazis executed at the Ardeatine caves. Relatives of the victims of that atrocity were invited to be spectators at the trial, which was to be held starting September 18, 1944, at the Palazzo di Justizia facing the Tiber River at the foot of the Umberto Bridge.

Thousands of people gathered in front of the palace from the early morning hours on. The police cordons were quickly broken by the mob which pressed on, howling, to the entrance. The big hall on the first floor was already jammed with authorized spectators and newspapermen. At 9:30 A.M., just as the presiding judge was about to enter the courtroom, the mob rioted into it, overturned tables, and surged toward the judges and correspondents. All semblance of order disappeared.

Everybody, including the *carabinieri* (the state police), sought shelter wherever it could be found. Caruso had not yet been brought up from the cellar where he was hidden. The mob, believing him to be in the anteroom, clamored for his appearance. Pollock, British police chief for the American Military Government, and Mario Berlinguer, the Italian official in charge of the prosecution of Fascist crimes, both tried to calm the crowd.

After a half-hour of exhortation from these two officials, the fury of the crowd seemed to abate somewhat. An announcement was made that the trial would be postponed. The crowd might have dispersed then if two women had not pointed out Donato Carretta among the witnesses. Carretta had been the vice-director of the prison in which the hostages were held prior to their execution. He had been one of Caruso's right-hand men, but he was scheduled to be a major prosecution witness. Some young men grabbed and hit him. He was dragged and kicked downstairs into the main entrance hall of the palace. There a few *carabinieri* made a halfhearted attempt to usher Carretta out and away from his attackers. Near the entrance a young man jumped him while his back was turned, knocking him down. Others immediately started kicking and beating him. Carretta got up and ran but was trapped at the end of the courtyard. A lieutenant in the *carabinieri* made two attempts to have Carretta driven away in a car. Both drivers, one American and one British, refused. Herbert Matthews, reporting the incident, states: "When I bitterly kept telling the crowd around me that this was worse than fascism and that Italy would get a black name throughout the world—some shamefacedly admitted this was bad." [18]

By this time Carretta was unconscious. For a while the crowd stood around the body on the street. One young girl—well-dressed and looking like a student, who had been one of the ringleaders—kept kicking Carretta. Finally someone shouted, "Throw him into the Tiber!" The limp body was dragged, not lifted, across the wide street to the bridge, then heaved into the water some thirty feet below. The shock of cold water apparently revived Carretta, who managed to crawl to the bank and hang on, half in the water just below the bridge. Some of the mob got a rowboat, went up to him, and pushed him back into the water. Whenever he tried to make the bank again, they stopped him with their oars.

Hundreds and then thousands of persons crowded the embankments and the Sant' Angelo Bridge, some hundreds of feet away. There were many women. Many of the men as well as the women were middle-class or lower middle-class. "This was no mob of hooligans," said Matthews. Some were horrified. When one woman hysterically protested, she had to be rushed away lest the crowd mob her. Many laughed gleefully as they watched.

Carretta died as he floated under the Sant' Angelo Bridge. Some howling men dragged the body out of the water and along the ground right to the near-by Regina Coeli prison. There they strung

18. *The New York Times,* September 19, 1944.

up the body. By this time the crowd had swelled to an estimated seven thousand. They believed Caruso was inside, but the prison police managed to keep the doors closed and took down Carretta's body. Then the crowd dispersed without any further violence.

It is ironic to note that a rumor quickly spread that Caruso had been killed; many people in the crowd probably did not know who was the actual victim of their lynching.

THE SHANGHAI RIOT / The long lasting Shanghai riot began in the early morning of November 30, 1946, when a number of relatives of street vendors who had been arrested appeared at the police station with food parcels for the prisoners. Altogether six hundred vendors had been picked up for continuing to operate in the Lonza and Whangpoo districts of Shanghai in violation of the recent police decrees. Many of these vendors were refugees driven out of their native villages or off their farms, either by unsatisfactory conditions or by fear of conscription. According to some reports, the police had merely asked relatives to line up in an orderly fashion, but some of them, wearied of their long wait, had begun to protest and to mill around the police desk.

About 8:00 A.M. a crowd, composed of relatives of the prisoners, staged a presumably spontaneous demonstration outside the police station. About five or six hundred people were present. A rumor started that six of the street hawkers had died in prison as a result of beatings and brutal treatment. All morning the crowd milled around the police station. Shortly before noon the crowd grew more clamorous. Bricks, stones, and bottles were heaved at the police. The police responded by arresting several "agitators" in the crowd, whom they pulled, one by one, into the station, beating them as they were being dragged. One young man in an overcoat grabbed a policeman's lapel and took down his number after he had beaten one person. This young man, too, was dragged into the station. A *China Press* reporter followed this man into the building but was ordered out.

By this time the crowd had grown to several thousand. At 2:00 P.M. a fire hose played streams of water against the crowd. The crowd backed away slowly, never ceasing to yell. Every time the water was turned off, the angry crowd closed in upon the police station. This went on for two hours. Once the crowd wrested the nozzle from the firemen and played the water on the policemen, who succeeded in dispersing them.

At 4:45 P.M. three city councilors arrived. One of them told the police not to beat a man while dragging him into the police station.

At 5:20 P.M. K. C. Wu, then mayor of Shanghai, entered the police station amidst sporadic shouts. Members of the crowd entered several near-by buildings. The crowd was finally dispersed by machine-gun fire followed by a police charge, with bayonets and clubs, against the crowd.

Thereafter the crowd began its rampage of Shanghai. It filled the streets, wrecked store windows along the Nanking road, insisting that shops close in sympathy with the rioters. One printing shop was burned to the ground. A subsequent report by the mayor alleged that the demonstrators sent children to ask shopowners to close, and that these children were each rewarded with five-thousand Chinese dollars.

A streetcar was overturned. Automobiles were wrecked. Another crowd formed around the Lonza police station. The wrath of the crowd was not turned against foreigners, but some said they had been struck in the face by ruffians who held up their cars. Some of these attackers were said to have shouted, "Down with Nanking! Chou En-Lai [Chinese Communist leader] is right!"

That evening Wu, in a broadcast, announced the release of all vendors. Rioting nevertheless continued until early morning. The next day rioting was less spontaneous and was organized at particular points. Shops were closed when riot leaders threatened to smash them if they reopened. The police cordoned off the downtown areas. In the afternoon three trucks with demonstrators tried to enter the race course to hold a meeting. This establishment, traditionally closed to Chinese, was guarded by United States military personnel who turned back the trucks.

The rioting seems finally to have stopped after Wu spoke on the radio again that evening. He said nobody had been killed during the riots and that all vendors had been released. A delegation of vendors had come to him with a written declaration disclaiming responsibility for the riot. In all, 221 persons had been arrested. Finally, he said he was ordering the police to shoot to kill anyone creating disturbances or carrying arms without authority.

Riots under Conditions of Diffuse and Generalized Anxiety

In the summer of 1949 occurred what are called "the Peekskill riots." Some thirty miles north of New York City proper, a boisterous demonstration organized by a veterans' group to protest the appearance of Paul Robeson, well-known Negro baritone and Soviet sympathizer, touched off fighting and violence in which many innocent bystanders became victims. In Montreal in 1955 a hockey match turned into an egg-throwing affair on the part of spectators and was abruptly brought to a halt by tear gas. After that an angry and violent crowd ransacked stores in the main business district. What one writer called "the most destructive and frenzied riot in the history of Canadian sports" added up to an estimated thirty-million-dollar loss due to lootings and destruction. Eight police cars were damaged plus some private vehicles, while twelve policemen and some twenty-five citizens were injured.

Both these riots occurred in what appear to be relatively stable times. There was no background of social disorder and upheaval and distress behind the Robeson riot. By 1949 World War II had been over for four years and the Korean War had not yet begun. The country was prosperous. A President of the United States had just begun his second term of office, and partisan politics was at a reasonably low ebb. American troops were not fighting anywhere. Veterans had adjusted to civilian life, were meeting installment plan payments, and were settling down to a routine existence. The country in general had arrived at a new global consciousness.

Nonetheless, awareness of events at a distance produced anxiety. This was a period when the mass media, in reporting and commenting on world events, were focusing on the threat of world destruction in the new atomic age. News revolved around the cold war and the power struggle between the great nations of the world; an overwhelmingly anti-administration press fastened on administration snafus and ineptitude, building up what in 1952 became the case for the Republican campaign, the charges of communism and corruption in government.

The individual was apprised of dangers from everywhere, from communism abroad and at home, from an inept and corrupt government, from bombs and possibly even invasion. The anxiety was real enough, but about the exact nature of the threat—how it might strike and what it might do to him—the individual was in a quandary. The reality of generalized insecurity is nevertheless attested to by a number of diverse symptoms.

This was the period when "flying saucers"—now unidentified flying objects—made headlines. A consultant for the National Association for Mental Health vividly summarized New York's case of "atomic jitters." [19] A stream of iridescent bubbles floating through the window of a sky-scraper, he recalled, appeared to one stenographer to be a chain reaction; she fainted, causing the whole office to panic. A minor explosion in a subway touched off cries of "Bomb!" Several persons were injured in the ensuing stampede. To get away from the "primary target area" thousands of New York families resettled in the surrounding country. Small wonder,

19. George S. Stevenson, "Antidote for Atomic Jitters," *The New York Times Magazine,* May 13, 1951, pp. 13ff.

then, that during a period when some respected leaders were seriously pushing a strategy that called for showering the Soviet Union with A-bombs before their atomic program caught up with ours, some citizens of Peekskill were ready to focus on the one eligible target who had the audacity to show up in their quiet area. The only other suggestions for personal salvation in the public domain at that time were: get interested in civil defense, build yourself a bomb shelter, report suspicious characters to the local FBI office, go to church every Sunday, or get yourself a new hat and cheer up.

While Canada was somewhat less vociferous about aggressive Soviet intentions, Montreal, the largest city in Quebec, was experiencing growing pains. The nation was in the throes of economic growth and of a population boom, and was establishing itself as a "middle power" on the world scene. Quebec was rapidly becoming industrialized. Throughout the province country-reared French-speaking youths were entering an English industrial milieu. Many immigrants to Canada made Montreal, first point of entry, their abode. Migration and contact between groups were bringing rapid changes in old ways. Long-standing (and often officially unacknowledged) French-English antagonisms were aggravated by the new intermingling. Competition between the two groups was reflected in national political life and in many a local squabble, and—as in other cities—teen-age leather-jacketed motorcycle gangs engaged in internecine warfare. The accelerated pace of change in French Canada caused individual restlessness which aggravated, and was aggravated in turn by, ethnic inferiority feelings.

In both Peekskill and Montreal, then, there were pent-up anxieties and hostilities, diffuse in nature, ready to overflow instantaneously and in unexpected directions once events provided a proper target on which, and against whom, they could be focused.

THE PEEKSKILL RIOTS / These riots began with a Robeson concert which was to take place at Lakeland Acres picnic grounds near Peekskill on Saturday, August 27, 1949. Veterans' groups, to demonstrate their opposition to Robeson's left-wing sympathies, decided to stage a protest parade that day. The demonstration reportedly had the backing of the assistant district attorney of Westchester County, who lived in Peekskill. Three-quarters of an hour before the concert was to start, the parade, with its Mohegan Fire Department band and the Veterans of Foreign Wars drum corps, began to move past the picnic grounds. Paraders carried signs such as: DOWN WITH THE COMMUNISTS! COMMUNISTS NOT WANTED! SWEEP OUT THE COMMUNISTS! (the last attached to a big broom). Pickets blocked the entrance to the grounds. They rushed anyone trying to leave or enter, shouting, "There's a Commie!" The parade marshal called for the crowd to disband, but some fighting ensued; about one hundred and fifty concert-goers and five-hundred veterans joined in. The fighting spread from the entrance out along the highway, where a crowd hurled stones at departing cars—several were overturned. At the height of the disturbance, pickets ran into the picnic grounds, mounted the stage, and forced one of the instrumentalists to play "Yankee Doodle Dandy" and "The Star-Spangled Banner." The next group of pickets pulled the platform apart and built a bonfire, which was further fed by the seats. When the fighting spread to the picnic grounds, floodlights were turned on and several fiery crosses blazed on the field. The local police called for help. With the help of a contingent from the state police, which arrived before 10:00 P.M., order was restored by 11:00.

When, only several days later, Mr. Robeson announced plans to return the following Sunday for a second concert at another near-by site, agitation began immediately. Fourteen veterans' posts planned a protest parade and demonstration on the highway. They asked residents to display flags in front of their homes as a sign of their support.

All day Saturday automobiles with signs that read WAKE UP, AMERICA! PEEKSKILL DID cruised through Peekskill. Strain became evident in an unending series of arguments, held in stores and cafés, about this affair. Many summer residents closed their homes and departed.

Starting early Sunday morning, busses from New York, New Jersey, and Westchester County brought in a special guard force of Robeson supporters. Leon Strauss of the Fur Workers (a lieutenant during World War II) set up a "skirmish line" of approximately three thousand highly disciplined men for a quarter of a mile on either side of the only entrance for cars. Many of them were armed with baseball bats, and they maintained strict discipline. While the Peekskill police were busy cutting down effigies of Mr. Robeson, the several cordons of guards prevented anyone but concert-goers from entering.

A steady stream of cars and busses with concert-goers began arriving rather early. Over two hundred state troopers—setting up mobile headquarters, with portable radio station, walkie-talkie sets, etc.—entered the scene a little later. A police helicopter flew overhead.

Veteran leaders, playing "God Bless America," moved their parade down the street near which the concert was being held.

There were fifteen hundred men in line, with approximately two thousand cheering, shouting, and applauding as they passed.

Robeson arrived, and the concert began. Paraders tried to drown out his voice but, because of the loudspeakers, were unsuccessful. A few armed men tried to cross the picket line, and some late arrivals were stoned. The police broke this up. Heckling was continuous.

At the end of the performance, concert-goers were urged to remain until plans for their safe departure had been made. The jeering crowd of men and women began to throw stones. Troopers pushed back the crowd, pleading (rather than ordering) that they disperse. By 4:30 P.M. concert-goers started for the cars lined up on the street outside. Soon rocks went flying at the cars that emerged. People lined the highway. Youths started with pebbles, then began hurling bigger stones. Stoning and violence spread from the concert site all along the road to Yonkers. Men, women, and children standing along the highway, in holiday spirit, were heaving rocks and shouting imprecations at the passing cars and busses. Housewives, boys in their late teens and early twenties, with "Vet" written on their shirts in yellow chalk, participated. One man was reported to have said, "Why should we get sweated up? The kids do a better job and the cops don't run them in!"

Long after the trouble had ended, the crowd loitered in the streets of Peekskill, continuing their scrutiny of passing automobiles. At 11:30 the last of the force of three thousand who had guarded the audience departed.

THE MONTREAL HOCKEY RIOT / This riot really began when Clarence Campbell, president of the National Hockey League, after a full hearing, announced the suspension of French Canadian hockey hero Richard, "The Rocket," for the remainder of the hockey season. The reason: he had engaged in violence against both an opposing player and an official who tried to restrain him.

Canadians take their hockey seriously, and the Montreal club was then leading second-place Detroit by only two points. Quite naturally feelings ran high because Richard, the star player on whom the Montreal Canadians depended, was the cherished idol of all the Montreal fans. Few voices, either English or French Canadian, publicly supported a decision made by an English Canadian against the player whose suspension more than ever made him the champion of French Canada.

Before noon, partisans with placards hailing Richard and condemning Campbell appeared in front of the Forum, where the

Canadians played. The numbers swelled throughout the afternoon, and they obviously received general support. While newspapers and radio stations headlined every new development, the crucial question soon boiled down to this: would Campbell dare to make a public appearance at the game? One Montreal paper reported an attempt to buy up a block of seats near Campbell to be occupied by a special delegation of hecklers. A local radio station, expecting trouble, sent a mobile sound unit to the scene.

Two hours before the game was to start, the demonstration was in full swing. About this time, youngsters wearing black motorcycle jackets began to join in. They were allegedly brought in by trucks. Besides the demonstrators, estimated at about six hundred, thousands were outside the Forum seeking admission to the game. As the Forum loudspeaker announced that there were no more seats, one of the demonstrators shouted, "We don't want seats. We want Campbell," a cry that was enthusiastically taken up.

Campbell, escorted by a police inspector, reached his seat inside the Forum just as Detroit scored a second goal against Montreal. He was immediately recognized and greeted with catcalls. Campbell, rather than the game, became the focus of attention.

Spectators had apparently come prepared. In addition to programs, bottles, and rubber boots, Campbell was showered with eggs, tomatoes, and all sorts of vegetables. Every time Detroit scored a goal—they scored two more during the first period—the crowd vented its anger on him.

The police, especially detailed on this night to protect Campbell, did little to interfere with the crowd. A young man who stepped up to Campbell and struck him was allowed to get away. Another, who squashed a couple of tomatoes against his shirt front, was arrested only after Campbell kept on urging the police to take action. The three hundred or so ushers, policemen, firemen, etc., whose duty it was to maintain order in the Forum were hardly in evidence.

At 9:11 P.M., after the end of the first period, the crowd began to close in on the N.H.L. official. They surrounded his box, and there was no one to restrain them.

The explosion of a tear-gas bomb by a person never identified saved Campbell at that critical moment. People did not know what had happened. They thought it was fire or that the ammonia pipes under the ice had sprung a leak. Panic was prevented only by the police and firemen, who now intervened decisively, keeping all doors open. Fans were turned on to disperse the fumes. In the confusion Campbell and his party escaped into the first-aid center, not far from where he had his seat. The fire department stopped the game, and Campbell ruled it forfeit to Detroit.

Until the frightened and excited fans poured out, the crowd outside had been neither destructive nor in any way out of control. But as soon as their numbers swelled, the mood changed entirely. Demonstrators hurled overshoes, chunks of brick, and whatever ammunition they could find at the Forum. Doors were torn off their hinges. Several people were injured.

The police were reluctant to apply force because of the number of women and children in the crowd. Consequently the corps of rioters, after discharging their ammunition, could always find safety in the crowd.

By 11:00 P.M. the crowd was estimated at more than ten thousand. They first besieged the stadium, but soon began to attack the ground-floor stores of the Forum. Rioters heaved rocks through windows and looted the stores, taking mostly small objects not easily traceable. Along Montreal's main shopping street, some fifty stores were damaged and looted. By the end of the riot there were two hundred and fifty police, including twenty-five radio patrol cars, on the scene. Five hundred policemen attending an employees' association meeting two miles away were never called. The reason, as the Montreal police chief explained later: "more police would only have provoked the crowd."

All the while, Montrealers tuned in to CKVL enjoyed on-the-spot radio coverage. Some time after midnight the radio stations were prevailed upon to cease broadcasting the trouble. By 1:00 A.M. police, forming a solid chain, gradually drove the crowd down St. Catherine Street. The rioting and disorder finally halted about 3:00 A.M. From all evidence, most of the troublemakers were not hockey fans. There were many teen-agers, who, according to one witness, were being egged on by older people.

Conditions of Crowd Proneness

These four case studies illustrate that crowd behavior in its unconventional and disapproved forms occurs during periods of evident disorganization. But it occurs also during periods of gradual change. The conditions giving rise to social unrest are so varied and its sources in the individual so deeply rooted that *a crowd potential can be said to exist at all times and in all places.* Within any complex society some segments are always in a state of unrest. Furthermore, given the proper conditions, the unsocialized potential of most individuals can be mobilized.

Situations which generate strong affects and/or prove the inadequacy of the routine defenses that normally hold them in check are, however, *most* likely to activate this potential. The formation of any specific crowd is thus a function of (*a*) feelings whose expression normally produces anxiety and (*b*) the absence, or at least the breakdown, of routine defenses against anxiety in the form of conventions, techniques, and reliance on authorities. There is an increase in anxiety as well as a search for ways to cope with and channel the affects that precipitate this increase.

Crowds considered in this light constitute a form of collective problem-solving activity.[20] The aggravation of existing problems to a point where they threaten the unity of a group, or the emergence of unfamiliar ones outside the framework in terms of which solutions are normally sought, facilitates the formation of crowds. Specifically, the following three conditions are likely to activate anxieties and to raise unrealistic hopes:

1. *An increase in frustration.* The imposition of social barriers felt to be unjust, new threats, etc., unleash the crowd potential. Hostilities accumulate, and the crowd is a solution insofar as it offers an outlet for resentment.

2. *The widening of intergroup contacts.* Any "frontier" stimulates individual effort. At the same time it plays up conflicts in values and loosens conventional ties. The unity of the crowd is developed against an out-group defined as alien. As the case studies of riots show, it matters little whether the intergroup contacts result from migration, the presence of occupying forces, economic penetration, or the extension of one's world as a result of the development of more rapid and more vivid means of communication.

3. *The development of unrealistic objectives.* Vague promises or concrete goals for whose attainment no specific means seem available indicate a condition of *anomie*. In these circumstances, social restraints on the arousal of appetites or on excessive hopes are not easily accepted. Disappointment with the rate of progress toward unrealistic objectives precipitates various irrational collective outbreaks.

The breakdown of conventionalized defenses against anxiety aroused by an increase in frustration and excessive expectations can be categorized as follows:

1. *The dissolution of conventions.* Routine definitions of action and the use of established channels for the achievement of socially valued goals are no longer accepted as valid. Hence, people in their search for new outlets for emotions tend to form crowds and engage in crowd action.

20. Guy E. Swanson, "Preliminary Laboratory Study of the Acting Crowd," *American Sociological Review*, XVIII (October, 1953), pp. 522–33.

2. *The inadequacy of techniques.* The aggregates out of which crowds form usually lack a background of experience that helps them to deal with the particular problem at hand. The individual participants do not possess the skills that would permit rational co-operation for the achievement of their objective. Consequently the behavior that ensues tends to be precipitous and intemperate and often interferes with the attainment of their actual purpose. (The hockey riot, which ended in the game's being forfeited to the opposing team, is a good example.)

3. *Alienation from authority.* The negative aspect of the ambivalent relation to authority expresses itself in an unwillingness to accept the kind of guidance that one normally heeds. One form of this alienation is moral indignation, which need not be directly vented on the authority but may be diverted to substitute targets.

INDIVIDUAL VULNERABILITY AND COLLECTIVE DEFENSE

THE CONCRETE THESIS to be developed and illustrated here consists of the following propositions: (1) The development of anxiety in the individual is inherent in the nature of socialization. Therefore, (2) individuals, groups, and whole societies build defenses for use in situations likely to arouse anxiety. Whenever (3) these defenses prove inadequate in the face of mounting pressures, the individual "goes to pieces" and becomes susceptible to "crowd influences."

SOURCES OF PERSONAL INSECURITY

Each human wins the right to live in society only after he is "socialized." First to gain the love of his parents, then to gain wider acceptance, the individual has to control some of his impulses. This means giving up some of his "selfish" demands. He submits to restraints by his family just as he later adapts to the groups in which he seeks acceptance.

Socialization, to apply a phrase popularized by L. K. Frank, consists of the "management of tensions" which result from the demands of a social environment. Though each person, in adapting to the group, has acquired techniques that help him to control impulsive expressions of anger, fear, love, etc., an unsocialized potential nevertheless remains. Against its emergence each person in his ego sets up a protective armor. An anxiety reaction sets in almost automatically when these defenses are threatened. Their nature and adequacy will, of course, vary from individual to individual, depending on the specific threats to which the anxiety is a response. Some defenses rely on avoidance; some entail delusions; still others rely on frantic activity. The bully is a bully because he is a coward; the shrew yells because she feels incompetent to deal with a situation; the drunkard may drown his shyness in drink. But a bully thinks he is brave; the shrew becomes sure she can handle all things by herself; the drunkard "just likes to be sociable." In every case the defenses, in promoting self-deception, avoid the despair of what would be unbearable anxiety and guilt.

To some degree these defenses are culturally typed. Thus, the most typical forms vary somewhat from country to country and from class to class within any country. But it can be stated that the capacity of any individual to bear anxiety depends in large part on his unique psychological make-up. Whether or not he succumbs to panic and responds "irrationally" is a measure of the adequacy of his defenses. Should his defenses disintegrate, the acting out by others of the very same impulses without punishment constitutes an irresistible temptation. Similarly, in the more focused riots, the individual is more likely to be drawn into the activity if the object of the aggression provides a satisfactory solution to an inner conflict. While the crowd does not create a *unique* viewpoint, it does offer a clear-cut avenue of action and thus is capable of overcoming traditional reserve.

DEFENSE: THE SUPPORTIVE ENVIRONMENT

It has already been suggested that people in general are more susceptible to the deviant forms of crowd behavior (i.e., collective crimes) in some periods than in others. This observation points to sociological factors. The second part of our thesis holds: (1) In all societies there is a range of options that allows individuals to find socially congenial patterns to support their personal defenses and relieve them from undue pressure. In addition, (2) there are certain "built-in" defenses which, in approving temporary collective expressions in contradiction to social standards, act as safety valves.[21] When the two elements above are ineffective—that is, when social pressure builds up and there are no approved safety valves—collective defenses develop spontaneously in a direction that permits an evasion of accumulated guilt.

Occasions for "escape" always exist. The strictures of society differ not only from time to time; they are apt to vary from position to position within a collectivity. It is possible to escape the strict restraints of the group in rather ordinary circumstances or to "lose oneself" in roles peripheral to the more demanding everyday routines. The compelling routine of a bureaucracy supports compulsive defenses, while off-the-job activities may offer periodic opportunities for escape.

Beyond this, some occasions specifically tolerate a collective lower-

21. This notion is found in H. Schurtz, *Altersklassen und Mannerbunde* (1902), and later in Sigmund Freud, *Totem and Taboo* (1913).

ing of social barriers below rather ordinary limits. This occurs in certain transient collectivities. For example, a man travels to a strange town, sharing a day on the train with strangers whom he will never meet again, or so he supposes. In these circumstances he is not entirely without guidance as to what the others will permit. He follows along, in part because his status of "stranger in town" or "passer-by" is not central to his life career. So, too, various audiences, intentionally assembled but without lasting ties, will permit expressions of enthusiasm by people "on the loose." The old college grad returns to the football game in his raccoon coat, a flask of whisky in his pocket. Once more he is the school-boy and free of the responsibilities of adulthood. He yells raucously; he hugs pretty girls; he staggers down the aisles. The crowd laughs, for for he is as much a part of the football game as the football.

Not only is behavior in violation of convention sometimes tolerated; on some occasions it is actively condoned. Ritualistic orgies among primitive people, though they have the look of a crowd out of hand, are not simply *spontaneous* manifestations of crowd contagion. The be-havior follows predictable conventions. The Yurok, Erikson tells us:

> once a year, having organized themselves for the great engineering feat of bridging the river with a fish dam that yields a winter's food supply [of salmon], indulge in promiscuous license and throw atonement and purification to the winds—whereupon they reach a sobering stage of satiation and reinstate self-restraint and communal measures of securing the divine right to pursue and snare the sacred salmon.
> . . . we suspect that the individual cycle of usurpation and atonement was provoked and exploited as a collective magic means of coercing nature.[22]

In much the same vein, a good many aggregations that one is inclined to consider crowds—enthusiastic parades, theater audiences, mass rallies, or madly dancing crowds in revivalist churches—are for the most part emotional expressions congealed into convention.

CROWD ACTIVITY AS DEFENSE AGAINST ANXIETY

In times of social disorganization, pressures mount and group supports that normally act as a check lose some of their authority. As previously shown, in Rome and Shanghai at the time of the riots, old ties and legitimate symbols no longer held allegiance. New cleavages arose, and there were no authorities to take the place of the established

22. Erik H. Erikson, *Childhood and Society* (New York: W. W. Norton & Company, Inc., 1950), p. 166.

institutions. The individual felt bound only by his internalized sense of duty and morality. Such apparent normlessness in the face of mounting pressures causes tension and even resentment at the lack of clear-cut strictures. The reaction is not merely one of demoralization. If that were the case, one would expect very little beyond general apathy, privatization, and withdrawal, but not aggressive mobs. The greater likelihood that they will go unpunished is not a sufficient explanation for people's turning against law and convention in such a situation; for they act with vengeance and with great persistence. Moreover, as in the lynching of Carretta, the crowd often turns against a substitute object rather than the original source of frustration. Or, as numerous instances of rioting show, the goals of the crowd become diffuse. Or a hungry mob burns down a bakery, an act that hardly helps to alleviate the food shortage. Hovland and Sears showed that reported lynchings between 1882 and 1930 were sparked by economic discontent. They obtained a coefficient of —.67 between the price of cotton and the number of lynchings in the southern United States, showing that, in general, the number of lynchings rose during any year in which the price of cotton fell. But the violence against Negroes did not soften the economic distress.[23]

Crowds do not as a rule form as a result of simple chance. The crowds that form out of street throngs have obscured the relationship between crowd behavior and the social milieu from which it emerges. Crowds evolve out of precipitate group responses or out of some nucleus gathered for specifiable purposes, that is, staging a protest, watching a parade, attending a trial, etc. Even when crowds form unexpectedly, without any apparent background of prior association or group purposes, each person enters the crowd with certain dispositions and social perspectives. Frustrations that people believe themselves to be suffering jointly with others, group identifications, etc., constitute the background against which a casual crowd flares into action.

Acts committed under the sway of collective emotion rarely lead to constructive remedial action, but nevertheless offer symbolic solutions to certain inner conflicts widespread among participants. The crowd action permits the participants, for the moment, to act out certain impulses without risking group censure. The specific direction that the activity and thoughts of a crowd take is partly determined by the dispositions of the individuals and the values of the groups out of which the crowd emerges. The crowd activity is a group disguise of impulses whose open discharge would bring any individual into conflict with the group and thus cause him unbearable anxiety. The collective behavior is symptomatic of a conflict that the participants have in common. It serves

23. C. I. Hovland and R. A. Sears, "Correlation of Lynchings with Economic Index," *Journal of Psychology*, IX (1940), pp. 301–10.

as a collective symptom around which the behavior of individuals whose anxiety is a threat to the group is momentarily integrated.

In this connection, one must note the apparent euphoria often experienced by individuals in crowds. From the perspective of the crowd, the action appears right and just. The occasional bravery, heroism, and foolhardiness people sometimes exhibit is explained by the nature of the crowd as a collective defense that shields the individual from guilt.

How the action of a crowd can be considered a group-sanctioned defense against the activation of impulses that threaten to disrupt the group has been illustrated by Ruth Eissler in her study of riots in a home for delinquent girls. The delinquency of the inmates, ranging in age from twelve to eighteen years, consisted in the main of sexual promiscuity, petty larceny, and running away from home. In large measure, the delinquent behavior was a defensive reaction against latent homosexual strivings. Since these were totally unacceptable to the girls, it was important for each inmate to prove herself heterosexual. The riots took place during a period of administrative turnover when the girls were under unusual tension. Whenever tensions became unbearable, the girls could turn only to each other for comfort. This immediately threatened to reactivate the homosexual strivings which could not be acknowledged. Unable and unwilling to attack the new head of the institution, the girls turned against one of the inmates, accusing her of the very sexual perversions of which they considered themselves guilty. Hence aggression was discharged; the group acted in a unified fashion against the threat that each, within herself, experienced as a danger.[24]

Crowds do not form unless suitable objects are found. These objects are usually perceived as threats to the integrity of the group the crowd members represent. Thus crowd action represents a spontaneous collective defense by which group values are upheld.

THE NATURE OF INDIVIDUAL EXPERIENCE IN THE CROWD

In Le Bon's classic formulation, (a) the crowd results in a lowering of critical self-consciousness and (b) all individuals are swayed by the same impulse. One cannot discuss these two propositions separately. The psychological unity of the crowd stems from the fact that persons lose themselves in it; thus, they divest themselves of their conventional values and act instead on the basis of common feelings. The boundaries of the crowd are defined solely in terms of the individuals participating in the action.

This formulation stressing the integration of individual impulses into

24. See Ruth Eissler, "Riots," *Psychoanalytic Study of the Child* (New York: International Universities Press, 1949), III–IV, pp. 449–60.

a collective pattern appears to apply more adequately to crowds on the small side than to the large-scale rioting of the kind observed on the streets of four separate cities. Concerning the latter, some distinction should be made between the active core of the mob and the much larger number of people on the periphery who contribute little beyond their presence; their presence is, of course, a real contribution.

On the basis of his study of a Texas lynching, Pruden has distinguished among three different degrees of involvement in a crowd.[25] There are:

1. *Intimidated spectators,* who disapprove but dare not intervene.
2. *Tacit supporters,* who are either "neutral" or favor the crowd action but do not actively participate.
3. *The active mob* (i.e., *the core*), who spark and carry the action.

All three make the street mob what it is.

While there is no established division of labor in the crowd, not everyone behaves in the same way. Behavior differs first of all in accordance with the various vantage points. The person at the periphery of the crowd sees what happens differently and acts in a different way from the person right in the middle or near the middle. As the Rome lynching illustrates so well, there are different degrees of participation. Not all "participants" lost critical self-consciousness. Only a small number were active perpetrators of the crime. To be sure, another, somewhat larger group reached a state of emotionality in which they were ready to lynch anyone who protested what was occurring. By far the largest number present were only an "audience" and, according to Matthews, who witnessed the lynching, quite ready to express shame or declare the crowd activity a blemish on the record of Italy. Still, this audience was not courageous; it passively watched the spectacle. Such audiences in other parts of Italy were attending executions of Fascists condemned by partisan courts (illegally, according to military government regulations) without any overt display of excitement. Since only a small number of persons in a mob act out the behavior that characterizes the entire mob, the role of this audience merits attention. There is no evidence that all of these spectators lose critical self-consciousness to a point where they are ready to join in, but their articulate support or even tacit approval suggests that they condone the action and thus help to incite it.

The presence of an active core has suggested that every crowd has a

25. Durward Pruden, "A Sociological Study of a Texas Lynching," in L. Wilson and W. L. Kolb, *Sociological Analysis* (New York: Harcourt, Brace & Co., 1949), pp. 335–43.

nucleus that provokes it.[26] To be sure, agitators and provocateurs, with conscious intent, may stir up and incite a crowd. But the Rome riot, again, demonstrates that some crowds erupt into action quite spontaneously, without any prior organization, to give expression to underlying unrest. Once a crowd is in action, an active core of pace-setters or leaders does emerge. Such emergent leadership is not necessarily identical with the leadership that may have first deliberately stirred up emotions leading to the crowd's formation; indeed, it may displace that leadership. Neither in Rome nor in Shanghai were the leaders in any way recognized prior to the time the crowd went into action. In the Montreal hockey riot some leadership probably existed from the very beginning. Yet as the action of the crowd became volatile and as the original purpose of the demonstration disappeared in the general looting and destructiveness, those who had organized the heckling and torment of Campbell, the hated official, also faded into the background. A similar development occurred in the Robeson riots. The veterans' groups that had organized the protest stayed in the wings as other leaders took the stage. "Why," said some, "should we get sweated up? The kids do a better job and the cops don't run them in." An analyst of the Montreal riot strongly doubted that most of the troublemakers were hockey fans. In the crowd, therefore, leadership may quickly pass from one group to another.

The extent to which individuals actually lose a clear awareness of what they are doing cannot be determined with any degree of finality. Certainly people in a crowd talk to one another. They make assessments of the situation. What they say and do and how they participate depends on how they size up the situation. The distinguishing characteristic of action in the crowd is that it is governed by a short-term perspective which has little regard for future consequences. Though the fact that others act in the crowd manner supports the individual's extraordinary and unusual behavior, he is nevertheless not entirely unaware of what he is doing. Even as he abandons himself to the seductive influence of the crowd, he appears to have at least a dim awareness that he can justify his own transgressions in the name of the crowd. His guilt is theirs, and together they are not guilty. On the other hand, when the member of any crowd is asked to recall what happened, feelings of guilt may be provoked. He blocks these by recalling that "he didn't know what he was doing" or that he was not "himself." The action allegedly occurs without forethought; what happened and the motives behind it are conveniently placed in oblivion.

26. Scipio Sighele, *Psychologie des Sectes* (Paris: M. Giard et Cie., 1898), pp. 42–51; reprinted and translated in Park and Burgess, *op. cit.*, pp. 202–7.

THE NATURAL HISTORY OF A CROWD

ANY SPECIFIC CROWD involves two general phases which are analytically separable. In the first phase the psychological unity characterizing the full-blown crowd is built up. During the second phase the crowd sets the pattern for the dissipation of tensions accumulated during the build-up. Between these two phases is a turning point when anything is likely to happen. In the history of any crowd, then, there are a *build-up* phase, a crowd *poised for action,* and the *denouement.*

More attention has understandably been given to the way a crowd forms and develops than to what happens afterward. A schematic outline has been given of how a typical crowd develops definitions of the situation that permit persons to act out with impunity impulses normally forbidden. Actually the behavior during the build-up phase takes many different forms: unfocused action in the form of milling, taking inventory of a situation, deliberate planning, agitation, or even conventionalized expressions of emotion. Every parade crowd, every audience at a mass rally, the onlookers at an automobile accident (if they start seeking the guilty party) contain a potentially active (as opposed to passive) crowd. While it is not necessarily the prologue to an undisciplined outburst, every casual or conventional assembly may nevertheless be treated as part of the build-up phase, during which the kind of rapport may develop that transforms it into a crowd in action.

An assembly is apt to become active when conventional modes of expression are inadequate and when suitable objects present themselves. For example, on the night of the Montreal hockey riot, the crowd potential was activated by the appearance of the hockey commissioner. His physical presence sufficed to transform the audience, keyed up for the game, into an aggressive mob. In the next section of this chapter another case study will point out why one passive crowd failed to go beyond the build-up phase.

What moves the crowd poised for action seems to depend on the collective mood that develops during the interaction. Is it pity, dread, ecstasy, or what? This mood is determined only within limits by the backgrounds of the participants. Pace-setters, by chance actions, may give an unexpected direction to the behavior of the crowd. Other persons serve as objects: pity may turn to ridicule or fear into anger.

The denouement has to do with the way in which the collective mood is acted out or spent, with *how* the feelings are utilized or expressed.

Little is known about typical cycles and circumstances of crowd development, for explanations of what actually happened are usually reconstructions after the fact and therefore not highly reliable. A look at the Robeson riot at Peekskill illustrates how one crowd led to the formation of quite a different one, which was nonetheless directed at the same objective. The collective anger was not spent in the first riot. In the interval between the first concert and Robeson's second appearance, rumor, gossip, and the mass media kept tension at a high pitch, so that a well-organized crowd with a definite objective was prepared to stage further violence.

But whereas the focus of resentment in Peekskill was a rather vague category of "communists"—people who were attending the concert and of whom the rioters had no clear image—in Rome the crowd knew exactly who its "enemies" were. It is true that most of the Italians had come to watch a trial and not to prevent it. Nevertheless, most of the crowd had very specific grievances against Fascist police activity. Collective resentment and hatred was focused on the perpetrator of the massacre at the Ardeatine caves, but erupted against a man who, though a prosecution witness, symbolized the Fascist regime. Matthews of *The New York Times* insisted that the participants were not hooligans, and the overwhelming weight of evidence indicates that only a small proportion of people were caught up in the fever of the lynching. The majority of spectators did not participate in the lynching, though according to all signs they hardly disapproved. The lust for revenge was satisfied as soon as the body of the victim was cut down from the jail window where it had been hung. Without waiting for the trial, which by then had been officially postponed, the crowd dispersed. Justice had been done and frayed tempers assuaged; there remained no excess of emotions to feed further violence. When it occurred later, the trial ran its uneventful course.

In Shanghai the relatives of the street vendors at first felt frustrated for exactly the same reason—their treatment by the police. But this specific focus of hostility merely symbolized much more diffuse grievances. They were, it appeared, ready to fall on any real or imagined offense as a pretext for venting pent-up hatred against a "regime" deemed responsible for their plight. When water hoses drove them away from the jail, their mounting fury sought new outlets. The crowds—including the people who had initially no connection with the vendors—now turned against many symbols of superiority—namely, shops, goods, autos, Americans, etc. Violence abated only after the mayor, in fully publicized orders, told the police to shoot to kill. The possibility of drastic reprisals stopped the crowd, which by then had lost is psychological unity.

The pattern in Montreal is still different. Public indignation was fanned by the mass media which kept the demonstration in the limelight. What happened inside the Forum was no spontaneous outburst; yet the law enforcement officials seemed surprisingly tolerant of it. The public demonstration against the author of an unpopular decision turned into general violence only after the spectators had fled the Forum in near panic. Forfeit of the game was an additional aggravation. The confusion, it seems, was deliberately exploited by gangs of hoodlums. Because the police force was reluctant to take drastic countermeasures, the milling mob went on a general binge which ran a more or less typical course.

THE CONVENTIONAL CROWD

MANY "CROWDS" appear to have all the prerequisites for a build-up, but the expected excitement never quite comes off. Conventional crowds, for example, like all audiences, act primarily by vowing assent, clapping, jumping, etc., in response to a central person. In others, so-called expressive crowds, tension is dissipated in movement, gestures, and shouts that are more or less conventionalized. The action is not directed against anyone but merely expresses the participants' feelings. What can be learned about crowds from those in which an expected disorder fails to develop?

The celebration welcoming MacArthur to Chicago in April, 1951, offers such an example. The welcome came in the wake of a national furor, stirred up by President Truman's summary dismissal of the general from all his commands. Wrote two contemporary observers within a few months of the event:

> When MacArthur, a week after being notified of his discharge in Tokyo, flew inward from the perimeter of American power, he made a similar journey toward the center of American consciousness. Indeed, it can be maintained that for several strange electric days he was the center of American consciousness. It is doubtful if there has ever been in this country so violent and spontaneous a discharge of political passion as that provoked by the President's dismissal of the General and by the General's dramatic return from his voluntary, patriotic exile.[27]

No crowd in the sense that the term is employed here ever developed in Chicago. Observers found a parade crowd, a spectator crowd, with people acting pretty much as in other ticker-tape welcomes. Only in this instance, many waited so long for so little (a mere glimpse of the General and perhaps not even that) that, in the words of some, had they stayed home and watched television, they might have seen better.

Observers were in agreement that the waiting crowd was quiet,

27. R. H. Rovere and A. M. Schlesinger, Jr., *The General and the President* (New York: Farrar, Strauss, and Young, Inc., 1951), p. 5.

orderly, in "good humor," devoid of signs of great excitement, "passive," persistent in a strange sort of way. When MacArthur passed, all strained to see. There was mild and sporadic cheering, but observers reported no "hysterical" reactions. Normal reserve among the spectators never allowed pro-MacArthur sentiment to develop.

The spectacle was pretty much dissociated from any political undertones. People avoided political conversations. This is graphically illustrated in one report:

> A man—about twenty-five years old—ventured to remark, "Boy, if the Republicans were smart, they would put up MacArthur for president. In fact they should try to have an election right now; he would be sure to get in . . . The people always feel sorry for the underdog, and it wasn't nice the way Truman fired him. I bet he would get elected easily— Don't you think so?" This was said to no one in particular.
>
> A Negro man—about the same age and well-dressed—suggested, "Let's forget about politics and enjoy the parade." Several people—about five—then said, "Yes, forget about politics and enjoy the parade." The man still continued. "I really think he would get in if the Republicans played it right." No one answered him or made any further comment about it. By this time everyone was stretching his neck to see if MacArthur's cars were coming. The people on boxes reported that he was not yet in sight.[28]

Why didn't a crowd develop, especially in view of the anti-Truman provocations continuously printed by at least one Chicago paper? An obvious explanation might be that the police were present in such force. But there was little need to restrain this audience. It showed no taste for violence or disorder. Several other factors help to explain this:

1. People came for the most part as members of groups intent on watching a spectacle. Friends, co-workers, students off from school, joined with each other to see the parade. These associations constituted no incentive to act contrary to their usual roles.

2. The crowd, contrary to what radio and newspapers kept on suggesting, was angry at no one. It was a happy holiday crowd, attracted by curiosity and given an unexpected holiday. The pro-MacArthur members came to pay tribute to their hero. It did not seem a day suitable for revenge in the name of a demolished idol.

3. Whatever resentment lay dormant was given an acceptable outlet. By the unanimous consent of the city council, this was MacArthur's day. Even the President had done everything to assure him a hero's welcome upon his return. This was no unplanned demonstration. People knew what to expect. They knew the general's schedule and that whistles

28. Material from the files of the authors.

would announce his arrival. The parade route was planned, including a wreath-laying ceremony. Everyone was assured of an opportunity to see him, and the television coverage put him in reach of all. Most of what was likely to happen was entirely predictable and true to pattern. Any rumors were confined to expectations concerning the parade—for example, did the motorcycles passing mean that it was about to start?

Though criticism of MacArthur was voiced openly by many people and generally went unheeded, there is no telling what might have happened had the crowd sentiment found an object of hatred. The few anti-MacArthur displays were in quieter suburban areas and caused little stir. After all, the day belonged to MacArthur.

Contrast this for a moment with the resentment of the Montreal fans at the fate of "The Rocket," which found little outlet. There were reports throughout the day that, should Campbell show up at the game, there would be trouble. His appearance at the game from which he had banished the main attraction was something of a provocation. There were the same heightened feelings as in the MacArthur crowd, but the people who showed up were much more unanimous in their views. Second, the game began in an atmosphere fraught with the expectation that "something might happen." These rumors, even "officially" confirmed, attracted many spectators ready to seize what Redl and Wineman have called group situations offering "delinquency support." None would have missed a chance to get in on some reckless or cruel behavior which would go tax-free in the general melee.[29] Finally, the crowd, believing Campbell still in the Forum, had found an object on whom to vent their hostility.

THE CONTROL OF CROWDS

MORE ATTENTION has been given to how crowds are kept under control than to the ways in which crowd behavior unexpectedly shifts.[30] The main factor in controlling a crowd is of course to prevent it from getting out of hand in the first place. To subdue a crowd once it has started on a disruptive course of action is much more difficult. Only the rioting in Shanghai seems to have been brought to an abrupt termination by decisive intervention. The other three crowds dispersed more or less of their own accord, though police action always loomed in the background. It is nevertheless possible to distinguish between the *two*

29. F. Redl and D. Wineman, *The Aggressive Child* (Glencoe, Ill.: The Free Press, 1957), p. 158.

30. Blumer, *op. cit.*; also Joseph D. Lohman, *The Police and Minority Groups: a manual prepared for use in the Chicago Park District Police Training School,* 1947. Gordon W. Allport has also been active in the field of crowd control.

main ways in which crowd activity is terminated: loosening of the internal cohesion of the crowd and *intervention* by outside force.

LOSS OF COHESION

Crowds disintegrate in a "natural" way under one of three conditions.

1. *Achievement of the crowd objective.* This objective is easily established only in a more or less organized mob. The Peekskill riot and the Montreal spectators clearly failed to attain their initial goal. The Peekskill concert was held notwithstanding the demonstration; and not only did Campbell elude the crowd at the Forum, but its action even caused the Canadians to lose the game. In both cases the violence thereafter fed on rather diffuse objects. The situation is less clear in Rome and Shanghai. In the Rome lynching, the immediate objective of the crowd was obviously satisfied, and the crowd dispersed thereafter. This objective, however, was a substitute, and the scheduled trial was only postponed. In Shanghai the vendors were released, but since the mobs had been fed by a host of other resentments, it is difficult to ferret out any particular objective.

2. *Dissipation.* The energy and emotion of a crowd, unless replenished by new recruits, is apt to spend itself in various activities irrespective of whether these are directly related to the initial objective. This can be seen most clearly in the general destructiveness of the Montreal crowd, the indiscriminate rock-throwing along the highways of Westchester County, and the diffuse violence of the Shanghai mobs. Energies can also be dissipated in a crowd that never reaches the active stage. A crowd that mills without any object on which to focus will eventually tire; but it is also apt to be on the lookout for substitute objects.

3. *Shock effect.* Under certain conditions, which cannot be specified with any exactness, the self-indulgence of the crowd reaches a point at which guilt can no longer be evaded: participants may be "shocked" back to reality. Examples of this are the effort of vendors to dissociate themselves from the rioting, the admission by some Roman bystanders of the shame brought on Italy, and occasional acts of atonement by Montreal rioters (such as the return of pilfered goods by mail). The spread of such impulses to the entire crowd is rare and would require organized leadership capable of addressing the crowd as a whole.[31]

Shock effect is very likely to lead to sudden shifts in the direction of crowd activity, as in the spontaneous defense of a scapegoat or the sudden turning of the crowd on new objectives or a change from anger to uncontrolled weeping.

31. Chester I. Barnard, *Organization and Management,* selected papers (Cambridge, Mass.: Harvard University Press, 1948).

INTERVENTION

The best way to communicate to a crowd that responsibility can no longer be safely evaded is by decisive outside intervention, a "show of force." This leads to a consideration of external force as a measure against crowds. One suspects that, notwithstanding all police manuals, open counterviolence is the method most often used to break up crowds. But it is risky. Police, prison officials, and military forces are reluctant to bring criticism on themselves, and stopping a crowd at the price of several victims may not be worth it. The Montreal police held back, first because of possible sympathy with the motives of the rioters, thereafter out of fear of the possible cost. Yet, as in Rome, it is the display of apparently unpunished aggression that gets crowds started. It seems of utmost importance to intervene decisively so as to make clear the consequences of crowd action as well as the possibility of alternative solutions to problems. The Shanghai crowds yielded to superior force; yet they fought back because no alternative redress seemed available and the brutality of the police only justified their efforts for vengeance.

There are three major indirect methods of handling crowds:

1. *To prevent a head-on collision* by redirecting the attention of the crowd, so that it is no longer focused on one object. The psychological unity of the crowd is thereby destroyed.

2. *To prevent the crowd from ever focusing on a single object by "keeping 'em milling."* The idea is to keep the people moving, letting them wear themselves out, until they realize the pointlessness of their behavior, give up, and go home.

3. *To substitute new goals or new methods for achieving these goals.*

These approaches are usable only when the forces of law and order are clearly in evidence. The environment must provide support for orderly behavior in two respects: instead of temporizing with the crowd, the guardians of law and order must make it clear that violence will not be tolerated; and the motives behind the crowd behavior, far from being ignored, must be channeled into new and approved directions—always a tricky business.

B I B L I O G R A P H Y

In this chapter there are many references to classic and general references on crowd behavior. Below are listed some of the few systematic observations of crowd behavior reported by social scientists.

DOUGLASS, JOSEPH H. "The Funeral of 'Sister President,'" *Journal of Abnormal and Social Psychology*, XXXIX (April, 1944), pp. 217–23. A report on the funeral of a church leader in a backwoods town on the Mississippi delta. Often cited to illustrate the nature of an expressive crowd.

EISSLER, RUTH. *Psychoanalytic Study of the Child*. Vols. III/IV. New York: International Universities Press, 1949.

JENNINGS, HUMPHREY, *et al. May the Twelfth: Mass-Observation Day Surveys, 1937*. London: Faber and Faber, Ltd., 1937. One of the first exciting mass observation reports based on reports of Coronation Day sent in by volunteers who kept diaries.

LANG, KURT, and LANG, GLADYS ENGEL. "The Unique Perspective of Television and Its Effect: A Pilot Study," *American Sociological Review*, XVIII (February, 1953), pp. 3–12. The impression of a parade crowd from the point of view of televiewers compared to that of participating observers strategically placed along the route.

————. "Decisions for Christ: Billy Graham in New York City," *Identity and Anxiety: Survival of the Person in a Mass Society*, eds. MAURICE STEIN, ARTHUR J. VIDICH, and DAVID MANNING WHITE. Glencoe, Ill.: The Free Press, 1960. Report on the Madison Square Garden audience of the famous evangelist, based on mass-observation data.

LEE, ALFRED MCCLUNG, and HUMPHREY, NORMAN D. *Race Riot*. New York: The Dryden Press, Inc., 1943. A well-known study of mob behavior in Detroit, based on participant observation and interviews and supplemented by other data.

LEIGHTON, ALEXANDER H. *The Governing of Men*. Princeton: Princeton University Press, 1945. Contains a description and interpretation of a strike and near riot in an internment camp for citizens and other persons of Japanese descent during World War II.

PRUDEN, DURWARD A. "A Sociological Study of a Texas Lynching." Dallas: Southern Methodist University Studies in Sociology, 1936, I, pp. 3–9. An investigation of a lynching in Leeville, Texas; particularly good for analysis of the kinds of participant.

SWANSON, GUY E. "A Preliminary Laboratory Study of the Acting Crowd," *American Sociological Review*, XVIII (1953), pp. 522–33. An attempt to study crowd behavior in the laboratory.

TUMIN, MELVIN M., and FELDMAN, ARNOLD S. "The Miracle at Sabana Grande," *Public Opinion Quarterly*, XIX (Summer, 1955), pp. 125–39. On-the-spot observation by trained researchers of a crowd waiting for the appearance of a virgin saint in Puerto Rico.

CHAPTER 6

Mass Conversion:
Changes in Group Norms

A CONVERSION is (*a*) a complete turnabout (*b*) in central values that is (*c*) fairly permanent. The process of *mass conversion* refers to a change of social norms—a change in a way of life—rather than to a change merely in social judgments. While it does involve a change in judgment, it is a change that undermines the total frame of reference of the groups or individuals involved. Three comments on the definition of conversion may make the precise usage of the term more meaningful; at the same time they serve to distinguish mass conversion as a process from collective definition and collective defense.

1. *Conversion is more than opinion change.* The process of conversion, unlike that of definition, involves a reorientation of basic attitudes in regard to both the person's inner needs and his group identifications. These attitudes differ from those held only as a matter of convenience, which give way as soon as evidence and social pressure move a person in a new direction. In short, conversion is more than redefinition or opinion change. It involves a change in the fundamental attitudes that *determine* perceptions.

Opinions change constantly in response to new perceptions. For instance, a person is persuaded rather easily to think that one brand of lipstick is better than another; a dramatic piece of news quickly forces individuals to adjust their expectations about the imminence of war; a lecture or a book often provides new information impelling a change of view about historical events or the current state of the nation. New perceptions thus induce opinion change; yet views on the fundamental questions of the world and society change only under extraordinary circumstances. So great is the resiliency of a person's basic outlook that he usually defines external events and objects in such a way as to fit it. Only the transformation of the fundamental orientation itself marks a true conversion.

Of course, any conversion is accompanied by redefinitions of the outer world: the convert's image of the world is different from what it was before. The new meanings read into world events are derived from the new points of reference, and his acceptance of them is motivated by strong inner pressures. Redefinitions merely bring the image of the world in line with the new insight.

2. *Conversion is a conscious commitment to a new way of life.* This aspect of conversion highlights the fact that mystical experience and mass hysteria are not essential to conversion. Neither the intensity of excitement nor the abruptness of revelation that heralds a change of heart guarantees that what appears a dramatic change is indeed a change or that, if it is, it will last. It is true, of course, that individual conversions often occur following prolonged moral conflict which the stimulus of collective excitement helps to resolve. But neither the personal anguish evidenced in a moral crisis nor the group hysteria occasionally provoked during a revival or a political meeting should be mistaken for conversion. Confessions and resolutions screamed under the stress of revivalistic preaching or other oratorical harangues are frequently temporary. Given the chance to reconsider, many "converts" slide back into their old habits and into the company of former associates. For a conversion to be more than temporary, a person either must be strongly motivated or must follow his conversion experience by severing completely his earlier associations. At the same time it must be pointed out— and this will be enlarged upon later—that what appears to be a change of heart, made under highly emotional circumstances, is often merely an affirmation of what has always been believed. In that case the mass hysteria, by dramatizing them, serves to uphold existing values.

Genuine conversion is marked, then, by a *conscious* commitment to a new creed. It need not be initiated under the emotional sway of crowd-mindedness, and hence mass conversion is a process different not only from collective redefinition but also from collective defense. For the newly converted, to be sure, the acceptance of new authorities may provide an intrapsychic defense that enables him to resolve moral conflicts. Yet, whatever the individual motives and satisfactions in conversion, any widespread reorientation away from existing norms and their replacement by new group standards is a collective process. The import of many individual conversions taken together is quite different from group symptoms that, in their devious ways, serve to uphold values to which the participants already subscribe.

3. *Conversion can occur in any area of belief or practice that entails*

strong conviction and commitment. Conversion need have no supernatural reference. Many religious sects insist on a specific, conventionalized conversion experience as a qualification for membership. But the sociologist or psychologist seeking to undercover the personal and social significance of that experience is not bound by any particular theological doctrine.

According to William James, it is important, in judging the religious types of regeneration, to recognize that

> they are only one species of a genus that contains other types as well. For example, the new birth may be away from religion into incredulity; or it may be from moral scrupulosity into freedom and license; or it may be produced by the irruption into the individual's life of some new stimulus or passion, such as love, ambition, cupidity, revenge, or patriotic devotion. . . . In these non-religious cases the new man may also be born either gradually or suddenly.[1]

Something approximating a religious conversion experience is common among reformers, participants in certain humanistic cults, and in esoteric and revolutionary sects. This is evidenced by the following passage describing one person's abandonment of rugged individualism for socialism:

> It is quite fair to say that I became a Socialist in a fashion somewhat similar to the way in which the Teutonic pagans became Christians—it was hammered into me. Not only was I not looking for Socialism at the time of my conversion, but I was fighting it. . . .
>
> . . . my joyous individualism was dominated by the orthodox bourgeois ethics. I read the bourgeois papers, listened to the bourgeois preachers, and shouted at the sonorous platitudes of the bourgeois politicians. And I doubt not, if other events had not changed my career, that I should have evolved into a professional strike-breaker . . . and had my head and my earning power irrevocably smashed by a club in the hands of some militant trade-unionist.
>
> Just about this time, returning from a seven months' voyage before the mast, and just turned eighteen, I took it into my head to go tramping. On rods and blind baggages I fought my way from the open West, where man bucked big and the job hunted the man, to the congested labor centres of the East, where men were small potatoes and hunted the job for all they were worth. And on this new *blond-beast* adventure I found myself looking upon life from a new and totally different angle. I had dropped down from the proletariat into what sociologists love to call the

1. William James, *The Varieties of Religious Experience* (New York: New American Library, 1958), p. 147.

"submerged tenth," and I was startled to discover the way in which that submerged tenth was recruited. . . .

The woman of the streets and the man of the gutter drew very close to me. I saw the picture of the Social Pit as vividly as though it were a concrete thing, and at the bottom of the Pit I saw them, myself above them, not far, and hanging on to the slippery wall by main strength and sweat. And I confess a terror seized me. What when my strength failed? when I should be unable to work shoulder to shoulder with the strong men who were as yet babes unborn? And there and then I swore a great oath. It ran something like this: *All my days I have worked hard with my body, and according to the number of days I have worked, by just that much am I nearer the bottom of the Pit. I shall climb out of the Pit, but not by the muscles of my body shall I climb out. I shall do no more hard work, and may God strike me dead if I do another day's hard work with my body more than I absolutely have to do.* And I have been busy ever since running away from hard work. . . .

To return to my conversion, I think it is apparent that my rampant individualism was pretty effectively hammered out of me, and something else as effectively hammered in. But, just as I had been an individualist without knowing it, I was now a Socialist without knowing it, withal, an unscientific one. I had been reborn, but not renamed, and I was running around to find out what manner of thing I was. . . . Since that day I have opened many books, but no economic argument, no lucid demonstration of the logic and inevitableness of Socialism affects me as profoundly and convincingly as I was affected on the day when I first saw the walls of the Social Pit rise around me and felt myself slipping down, down, into the shambles at the bottom.[2]

Autobiographical literature generally contains a rich storehouse of conversion experiences. Revolutionary socialists especially have often employed the term "conversion" to describe their formal commitment to their secular version of the Redemption. For the Italian ex-Communist Silone, joining the Communist Party had meant:

a conversion, a complete dedication . . . breaking with one's parents and not finding a job . . . My own internal world, the "Middle Ages," which I had inherited and which were rooted in my soul, and from which, in the last analysis, I had derived my initial aspiration to revolt, were shaken to their foundations, as though by an earthquake. Everything was thrown into the melting pot, everything became a problem. Life, death, love, good, evil, truth, all changed their meaning or lost it altogether.[3]

2. Jack London, "How I Became a Socialist," *The Comrade*, March, 1903.
3. Richard Crossman (ed.), *The God That Failed* (New York: Bantam Books, Inc., 1952), p. 99.

That the literature on the subject of conversion refers mainly to the religious sphere is due to the value certain religious denominations place on it. In addition, there is the fact that nonreligious matters do not usually stir up emotions and imaginations of equal intensity. Within any era or in any society, nonreligious conversion can occur on any matter important enough to the group. Only changes concerning basic modes of life (e.g., criminality, immorality, etc.) or such fundamental loyalties as national and party ones generally arouse both the inner conflict on the part of the convert and sufficient popular interest in his conversion to permit their being treated on the same plane with purely religious conversions.

Mass conversion refers to collective transformations of the kind we have been discussing. From the viewpoint of society, it represents a widespread and fundamental shift in social norms. It is evidenced either in the wholesale defection of individuals from compliance with the fundamental beliefs of the group or in shifts in the mores of the group itself which cannot be explained adequately in terms of the underlying social structure. Whole categories of people in subscribing to new norms thus disrupt many of their old relations, restructure them, and form new ones. Mass conversion involves basic changes in social structure.

INDIVIDUAL CONVERSION

CONVERSION ALWAYS INVOLVES a change in norms. Logically, all individual conversion experiences could be typified as either: (1) *conformative*, that is, signifying an awakening to or an acceptance of conventional authorities; or (2) *nonconformative* in the sense that one turns away from accepted rules, that is, from conventional authority. In reality, every conversion entails the acceptance of some authority, even if it is at variance with most widely accepted conventions. Conversion thus represents a movement away from one authority to another, which involves also a change in setting.

REGENERATION

The *moment of awakening* is not to be mistaken for the *process of conversion*. As a point of fact, most so-called conversions are nothing more than culminations of normal growth processes. The seeds of religious convictions planted in childhood usually bear their fruits in adolescence, and this blossoming of religious faith in teen-agers has been a major concern of the psychology of religion. G. Stanley Hall, in 1881, was the first to point out that conversion understood in this way was both a natural and typical adolescent phenomenon.[4] The testimony of revivalists as well as numerous statistical studies of varying reliability all indicate that the overwhelming majority of experiences defined as conversion occur between ages twelve and twenty, with most just about in the middle of that period—namely, fifteen, sixteen, or seventeen.[5]

Adolescent Awakening

The reasons why adolescence is the period most characterized by conversion experiences are not difficult to fathom. The preadolescent child is not prepared to grasp the full meaning of a faith or of a cause in which he may have been reared. Until the period of adolescent growth, experiences are pretty much confined to those relating to the child's personal needs. He sees himself at the center of the universe. Adolescence signifies the disruption of this self-centered world. During this period of growth, imaginations begin to cover a much wider area, and it is this reaching out for ideals beyond the family circle that is capable of giving new significance to religious teachings. This awakening signifies the social maturation of an individual as he gains a new self, defined by reference to a wider community of other believers.

At the same time it is no accident that the period of most frequent religious awakening should coincide with the period of sexual maturity. Every person is born twice, first as a physical self and the second time as a social and moral being. The sexual needs of individuals in particular involve relations with others, their ultimate function being the perpetuation of the species. The study of religious conversion experiences from St. Augustine to modern clinical records indicates the frequency with which such crises involve sexual anxieties which must be resolved. The vision of new opportunities that results from the crisis attenuates guilt and allows the sexual impulses to be brought under control. Small wonder, then, that the period of awakening occurs when such problems assert themselves in full force.

The Element of Suddenness and Crisis

Adolescent "conversion" experiences rarely bring a complete turnabout. The documents describing dramatic conversion experiences, so often cited in literature, do not appear to be typical of the process of religious regeneration among most adolescents. On the basis of an inquiry concerning the religious awakening of some two thousand college students

4. G. Stanley Hall, *Adolescence*, (New York: Appleton-Century Company, 1937), II, pp. 281–362 *passim*.

5. *Ibid.* See also Elmer T. Clark, *The Psychology of Religious Awakening* (New York: The Macmillan Co., 1929).

affiliated with a variety of Protestant denominations, E. T. Clark concluded that a crisis involving a dramatic and sudden change was far from typical. In this study, it was found, "a real emotional crisis is reached and passed . . . and a definite change of attitude seems to have taken place" in only 6.7 per cent of the respondents. An additional 27 per cent of the subjects did refer to some event that had served to arouse their religious consciousness. Yet although this event did stand out in their memory, the group reported only very minor emotional upheaval and gave no indication of any marked change either in attitude or in habits of life. For the remaining two-thirds, religious awakening was a gradual and steady process of growth.[6]

Clark's conclusions have been confirmed, even for members of a revivalist church. Members of the Swedish Mission Covenant Youth were asked which among three hypothetical "conversion" experiences described most closely how they themselves had come to embrace the rather ascetic way of life imposed by the morality of their church. "More than two-thirds of the SMCY [Swedish Mission Covenant Youth] in our sample," sums up the author, "talk about a religious conversion dated to a certain day and a certain place but . . . they have all been influenced previously by at least some religious institution and almost all of them have been brought up in religious homes." [7] Acceptance of a moral code that forbade practically all commercially offered entertainment—dancing, secular reading, etc.—came about in the form of a *sudden* change of life attitudes and behavior for only one-sixth of the members. As far as the others were concerned, the "turn" in their lives meant merely a more complete and conscious identification with ways they were already following in practice.

In view of the instances cited, it would be useful to speak of the awakening typical of adolescence as "regeneration" and to reserve the term "conversion," as some theologies do, for experiences that signify a true reversal of a way of life.

It can readily be seen that many so-called conversion experiences are induced by a theology that cultivates them. They are the normal adolescent stirrings, one of which is afterward singled out and reinterpreted as *the* conversion experience; the rest are ignored and largely forgotten. Clark, in his study, observed that, notwithstanding a decrease in the number of crisis awakenings (i.e., sudden regenerative experiences) among the younger generation, persons subjected at home to stern religious training experienced a sudden crisis awakening in about the same proportion as their elders had before them.

Apparently there are many psychical *equivalents* to the regeneration

6. E. T. Clark, *op. cit.*, pp. 47ff.
7. Hans L. Zetterberg, "Religious Conversion as a Change of Social Roles," *Sociology and Social Research*, XXXVI (January, 1952), pp. 159–66.

experiences of adolescence. The forms they take are culturally typed. For example, in the Roman Catholic Church, with its emphasis on the sacraments, any subjective emotion accompanying Communion is incidental; what is stressed is the formal initiation into organized religion. Also, Sir James Frazer in *The Golden Bough* [8] describes initiation rites that subject youths to harrowing experiences or that elicit strong emotions. These rites signal to the youths, and to the entire tribe, their readiness to accept adult responsibility. Some tribes of Indians seek individual visions, while others emphasize conventional *rites de passage*. Then again, Margaret Mead, drawing on her observations in Samoa, has suggested that "the more or less tangible balance of cultural forces" influences the relative calm or storm and stress of adolescent years. If adolescence involves no new revelations, no new restrictions, if the young person is confronted with no new choices, she maintains, the additional problems presented by sexual maturation are not apt to be overwhelming.[9] Thus, there is no need for emotional experiences attendant on physiological change to be singled out as of special social significance in every cultural milieu. If one accepts this interpretation, regeneration experiences are not typical adolescent phenomena but result from special kinds of socialization.

INDIVIDUAL SUSCEPTIBILITY TO CONVERSION

Conversions can occur during any period in life, though quite evidently the conflicts that promote them exist in greatest concentration during the years of youth, when people seek orientation toward a larger world as well as congenial associates.

Research and literature give the impression that conversions that mean a radical departure from standards developed in the family milieu usually occur somewhat later than do regeneration experiences. The latter do not seem to require the stimulus of new experience and the prospect of new fellowship that the radical break signifies. For youngsters away at college, for apprentices new to the world of work, for members of street-corner societies drafted into the army, removal from a familiar milieu means exposure to new political, religious, or moral influences. New tastes are thereby acquired. We know that juvenile delinquents often enter on a new way of life by the age of twenty. The conversions to sectarian cults, likely to take place *after* adolescence, also occur on the basis of new associations. Half of an ex-Communist group mentioned that they had

8. Sir James George Frazer, *The New Golden Bough*, abridged and ed. by T. H. Gaster (New York: Criterion Books, Inc., 1959).

9. Margaret Mead, "Adolescence in Primitive and in Modern Society," *Readings in Social Psychology*, ed. G. E. Swanson, T. M. Newcomb, and E. L. Hartley (2nd ed.; New York: Henry Holt & Co., Inc., 1954), p. 537.

become drawn into radical activity for the first time only *after* the age of eighteen, and a quarter of them had become involved between the ages of nineteen and twenty-two.[10] The drastic break characterizing the first generation of any radical movement or religious sect can only be explained on the basis of new experiences in an unfamiliar setting for which inherited views are completely unsuited.

If the external manifestation of conversion is discontinuous social structure—that is, a passage between groups with little in common—the internal condition is a divided self, torn between contradictory incentives. Whatever the origin of the moral conflict in which the cleavage of conscience expresses itself, the issue may not be at all clear to the person. Characteristic of preconversion experience is a feeling of malaise, from which the conversion usually spells release. Pioneering work in the psychology of religion at the turn of the twentieth century suggested a similarity between the mental states preceding conversion and pathological melancholia, except that preconversion melancholia manifested the sense of sin which, in the Protestant theology, is so essential to the achievement of divine grace.

The feeling of incompleteness experienced by the convert is a vague discontent about nothing in particular. This kind of moral anxiety manifests itself concretely in many different ways. First, there may be a struggle that focuses on something specific, like an addiction or temptations to which a person has submitted in the past—for example, the classic conversion of St. Augustine or the case of an alcoholic. Second, vague but generalized loss of *joie de vivre* suggests that the tendency to be wrapped up in one's self (the concentration of affect on one's self) is being countered by a corresponding denial of emotions. The isolation of affect is a classic defense mechanism, which often produces physical symptoms that are quite real: for instance, a person in his struggle against incipient hypochondria ends by losing all bodily feeling, as if one's body were not his own but belonged to someone else. Third, an individual may reveal an exaggerated concern with the state of the world, often accompanied by world-destructive fantasies foretelling its imminent collapse. To the degree that the candidate for conversion has lost his lust for life, the world has indeed come to an end for him; the individual no longer stands in a meaningful emotional relation to it.

These preconversion states appear to have exact counterparts in other circumstances. The release from a sense of guilt or an unsatisfactory life experience that a person may find in some socialist Utopia is similar to the psychological "uplift" that the convert often mentions as an aftermath of his conversion. This uplift thus constitutes a displacement of his inner

10. Gabriel Almond, *The Appeals of Communism* (Princeton: Princeton University Press, 1954).

conflict: his inner needs are, so to speak, externalized in his newly found views, and emotional support is derived from the circle of believers who share the precious "knowledge." This externalization may focus on religious revelations.

INTEGRATIVE CONVERSION:
THE MENTAL CRISIS OF JOHN STUART MILL

Not every mental crisis leads to the compulsive rejection of the whole body of one's prior beliefs; the externalization of unacknowledged inner conflicts is not the only way out of severe melancholia. The experience of Alcoholics Anonymous shows that crises can be mastered through the integrating of new insights. An example of similar integration is the conversion experience about which John Stuart Mill speaks in his famous *Autobiography:*

> From the winter of 1821 [at the age of not quite fifteen], when I first read Bentham, and especially from the commencement of the Westminster Review, I had what might truly be called an object in life; to be a reformer of the world. My conception of my own happiness was entirely identified with this object. The personal sympathies I wished for were those of fellow labourers in this enterprise. . . .[11]

There are some analogies here with the religious awakening, or regeneration, discussed above. Mill was fully identified with a cause, and he had assimilated the philosophy of his father, the well-known Utilitarian James Mill. Yet:

> The time came when I awakened from this as from a dream. It was the autumn of 1826. I was in . . . the state, I should think, in which the converts of Methodism usually are, when smitten by their "first conviction of sin." In this frame of mind it occurred to me to put the question directly to myself: "Suppose that all your objects in life were realized; that all the changes in institutions and opinions which you are looking forward to, could be completely effected at this very instant: would this be a great joy and happiness to you?" And an irrepressible self-consciousness distinctly answered, "No!" At this my heart sank within me: the whole foundation on which my life was constructed fell down. . . .[12]

He was no longer able to gain enjoyment from pleasures he had hitherto found satisfying. His whole life seemed empty; he was so tired of living that he could not bear to think of how the years would pass.

11. John S. Mill, *Autobiography of John Stuart Mill* (New York: Columbia University Press, 1924), p. 93.
12. *Ibid.,* p. 94.

The turning point came when Mill read Marmontel's *Mémoires,* which stirred him to the point of tears. Afterward the world gradually began to take on new meaning for him. Mill believed the experience during this period had two very marked effects on his opinion and character. Previously, he said, he had depended on working toward a goal that could never be exhausted by attainment, and the object envisioned in its pursuit had been the attainment of pleasure. His new theory of human happiness held that:

> only those are happy . . . who have their minds fixed on some object other than their own happiness; on the happiness of others, on the improvement of mankind, even on some art or pursuit, followed not as a means, but as an ideal end. Aiming thus at something else, they find happiness by the way . . .[13]

The other important change related to his discovery of feeling and of the limitations of a purely intellectual and analytical mode of thought.

> The cultivation of feelings became one of the cardinal points in my ethical and philosophical creed . . . I now began to find meaning in the things which I had read or heard about the importance of poetry and art as instruments of human culture.[14]

These discoveries, moreover, soon meant a separation from those of Mill's habitual companions who had not undergone a similar conversion. More and more he fell into friendly intercourse with those among his former adversaries with whom he was now in sympathy. The adoption of a new philosophy of life also meant a growing estrangement from the father who had taught Mill his first philosophic doctrines but who remained a committed Utilitarian to the end.

The depression into which Mill had fallen typifies a variation of the vague uneasiness and sense of incompleteness referred earlier to as "moral anxiety." Insight brought its resolution. Mill broadened his philosophy to encompass feelings and emotions, and thereby found his "true self."

A conversion like that of Mill is the result of maturation. It is *integrative;* that is, the new insights release conscious desires to expand and be creative. It entails a breakdown of mannerisms and defensive conventionalizations which may have kept one's "true self" hidden and which, at the same time, keep one apart from others. The result of integrative conversion is an expanded feeling of fellowship; the affect, or feeling tone, on which the change is based is derived from love. There is relief from fears since much that could never be admitted is now no longer threatening.

13. *Ibid.,* p. 100.
14. *Ibid.,* p. 101.

REGRESSIVE CONVERSION

On the other hand, there are conversions that are described as pathological, or *regressive* in contrast to the integrative ones. Regressive conversions represent pseudo solutions in the face of disintegrating inner conflict. This type of conversion is most likely to occur in unstable and prepsychotic persons. Emotional pressure predominates over rational insight, and the conversion rests on affect other than love. Strong hatred and resentment plus hostile and destructive impulses toward others mark the preconversion experience, though these feelings are not given full expression. Among such persons, it appears, a conversion—whether religious, political, or esoteric—is potentially capable of warding off a psychosis. The conversion channels hatred into forms acceptable to some "master." [15] A newly found devotion to a god or a political cause or a group experiment in living permits the expression of hostilities toward out-groups. At the same time through his identification the person finds socially affirmed approval while the fear of disapproval, which led to an estrangement from others, is thereby overcome.

Patterns of Regressive Conversion

As early as 1900, Coe published a study on the personal temperaments of seventy-four persons who either had been converted at revivals or had expected a conversion and been disappointed at not experiencing it. Among his sudden converts he found that "sensibility" (suggestibility) was predominant, while an autonomous "will" was much more frequent among those who had failed to be converted. Testing his subjects for hypnotic sensibility, he again found it to be more typical of those who had undergone striking transformations. From this Coe concluded that those susceptible to conversion were passive and those disappointed were rich in spontaneous self-suggestions. Most important, far fewer of the "resisters" had ever experienced "automatisms" (a general designation for all sorts of religious hallucinations, strong affections, and bodily agitations).[16]

15. Leon Salzman, "The Psychology of Religious and Ideological Conversion," *Psychiatry*, XVI (1953), pp. 177–87.
16. George A. Coe, *The Spiritual Life* (New York: Abingdon Press, 1900). See also Edwin D. Starbuck, *The Psychology of Religion* (3rd ed.; New York: Charles Scribner's Sons, 1901); William James, *op. cit.*, lecture 10; H. J. Schou, *Religion and Morbid Mental States* (New York, 1926); and Anton T. Boisen, "Economic Distress and Religious Experience: A Study of the Holy Rollers," *Psychiatry*, II (1939), pp. 185–94.

Revivalist sects place special value on those experiences—typical of regressive conversion—that are provoked by the presence of an "outside" power. The individual is gripped and literally possessed to the extent that he is externally controlled. It is interesting to note that psychiatric combat casualties exhibit the same physical symptoms as these converts.[17] Among the common automatisms of motor actions familiar to students of conversion are the jerks, the bark, and the gift of tongues. The paroxysms that shake and jerk their victims have been observed in many contexts. If the feet are affected first, the victims jump and dance. Such dancing manias were observed throughout Europe after the Black Death; there were several outbreaks in Japan during regimes in which the populace was undergoing special hardship from which there seemed to be no apparent escape. The very same symptoms also appeared in the famous Ghost Dance revival among the American Indians, and research into group hysteria reveals many occasions on which female students were suddenly seized by the "shakes." Such automatisms are thus hardly the sole property of Protestant revivals.

The *gift of tongues*—or, technically, glossolalia—is the automatism that seems to have persisted most generally right down into the present. In glossolalia, speech is entirely divorced from thought. The victim feels himself the medium for another voice which takes possession of him. These voices are taken as a token of conversion. In recollections of religious experiences, it is often a voice that commands and it is the voice that proves the presence of God. But the gift of tongues is truly a crowd phenomenon, which is actively sought by the participants in a revival meeting.

These and other possession phenomena brought about under the influence of collective excitement are also culturally typed. In the *bark* the votaries fall on all fours and lope about until they form groups under a tree. In their yelping, barking, and snapping they simulate dogs. The action always is channeled into pretty much the same pattern, which symbolizes the "treeing" of the devil. Participants play a definite role, though they are apparently unconscious and have no recollection of what was a conventionalized performance. Sargant reports an even more striking example of culturally typed possession among the voodoo cult. The worshipers, under the influence of the drumming, "carry out all the detailed behavior expected of the particular deity by which they believe themselves possessed." Voodoo has numerous deities, or *loa*, which are combinations of African tribal gods and saints about whom the worshipers learned from Catholic priests. These *loa* "are believed to descend and take possession of a person, usually while he or she is dancing to the

17. William Sargant, *Battle for the Mind: A Physiology of Conversion and Brainwashing* (New York: Doubleday & Company, Inc., 1957).

drums. The possessed person then behaves as the particular deity should behave; the different habits of loas being a matter of tradition." [18]

This regressive kind of conversion occurs most frequently in highly authoritarian religions. Its primary regressive feature is the unquestioning submission to an authority that is all-knowing and all-powerful. To hear voices or to be possessed by spirits is to accept divine authority without question. Where conversion experience constitutes a change, this reflects an effort to channel hatred into forms acceptable to the new "master." In a successful solution, the new-found devotion permits the expression of hostilities toward out-groups; yet only by means of a continuous flow of inspiring experiences can the neophyte maintain his devotion at a level of intensity sufficient to contain his feelings. The neophyte who exceeds all others in his zeal is only too familiar a figure; his intolerance of deviation and his crusading stamina testify to the redirection of hostility.

The equivalents of such a conversion are found in other spheres, such as politics. To many a confirmed Marxist an adversary who acts in good faith is just about inconceivable. Furthermore, the doctrinal disputes concerning the correct interpretations of dialectical materialism indicate that many a convert speaks with a voice not his own. It is equally characteristic for the youngster who seeks escape from an arbitrary and unsatisfactory authority to submit to the even more unyielding code imposed by his delinquent gang. In every one of these instances the convert accepts some person or group as a higher authority, and the acceptance gains him at least a temporary peace.

When and if the authority does not, in the eyes of the convert, live up to the faith placed in it, the convert does not simply revert to indifference. He moves with relative ease from one authoritarian faith to another. The appeal of communism in Catholic countries is well known. On the other hand, prominent ex-Communists, breaking with the party, have embraced the Catholic faith, in which they may or may not have been brought up. The proposition that when one authoritarian faith is weakened, a new and equally authoritarian cult moves in to fill the void can be supported with many case histories.[19] Benito Mussolini, Jacques Doriot, and Henry de Man turned from revolutionary socialism to fascism. Count von Stauffenberg, who was in his youth a devotee of the literary esthete Stefan George and later organized Russian prisoners into fighting contingents under the Nazis, came to hate the regime so much that he volunteered to place a bomb meant to kill Hitler. To escape domineering paternal authority, many a person joins a totalitarian movement. Reservoirs of potential converts to totalitarian movements are found among

18. *Ibid.*, pp. 106–7.
19. Eric Hoffer, *The True Believer* (New York: New American Library, 1958), *passim*.

minor bureaucrats freed, in the course of depression or upheaval, from the restraints of organizational discipline. Armies in dissolution are also a likely recruiting ground for authoritarian groups. These subjects literally "escape" into another code of beliefs.

"Typing" Regressive and Integrative Conversions

Not every conversion can be neatly typed as either integrative or regressive. Most contain elements of both types, and the schematic descriptions presented here are intended to represent the "pure" types. As a rule, in sudden conversions, it is the effort to gain relief from ambivalent attitudes provoked by authorities which is predominant, and thus such experiences are closer to the regressive type. Rational insight, on the other hand, usually comes more gradually and rarely results in a complete about-face. Yet a conversion in which integrative elements predominate is not necessarily in the direction of established authority. *Whether or not the conversion leads to the incorporation of or alienation from generally accepted creeds has little to do with the psychological mechanisms involved.* But the kind of psychological mechanism involved does have much to do with whether mass conversions are "gains" for society or pathological outbursts.

ROLE CHANGE

Conversion involves a passage from one group into another, an initiation into a new way of life. Through the conversion experience, the convert validates his full inner acceptance of the role and responsibilities incumbent on a new member. Also, new interests, hitherto submerged, become the basis for new associations.

From the viewpoint of the individual this is *initiation*. From the societal viewpoint, such a movement on the part of large numbers of individuals into new statuses constitutes *assimilation:* whole populations give up their old ways and merge themselves with the new. Assimilation thus can be thought of as mass initiation.

Criminologists, for example, have long been aware that converting criminals to a lawful way of life requires, among other influences, a change of associates. It is a standard rule of parole that parolees must stay away from past accomplices. For Communists to break away meant not only giving up beliefs but breaking old ties and gaining acceptance into a new circle of friends. John Wesley, the Methodist revivalist, was fully aware that lasting effects of his preachings could not be assured unless they were followed up through intimate contact, and so he organized his converts into small prayer groups. In these the neophytes would confess their sins to one another, thereby supplying mutual support against the possibility of backsliding.

A good example of this kind of proselytizing is the rehabilitation work of Alcoholics Anonymous, all of whose members have at one time been compulsive drinkers. In the first place, A.A. members do not consider themselves "reformed drunkards." What unites them is their recognition that all are victims of a very real mental obsession and a physical allergy whose progress they are striving to arrest. Such an admission is the prerequisite to a cure, and in this sense the approaches of A.A., the Salvation Army, and similar groups are alike. In A.A. especially, the alcoholic begins to discuss with fellow members the effects his addiction is having on his domestic, social, and professional lives. New ties are formed around this collective effort, and soon the alcoholic feels ready to do almost anything to overcome his addiction. Only by honestly trying to reform does the person in A.A. begin to move toward full recovery. The transformation is rarely dramatic. Most of the time it is gradual, and advances occur only as the member gains insight into himself. However, in gaining this insight he is aided by the sympathies of fellow sufferers, and when he has mastered his addiction, the convert is impelled to carry his message to others. This not only helps to keep him dry, but it unites him with others in a common enterprise.[20]

Certain much less dramatic changes in character are constant and normal phenomena of everyday life. Any transition from one role to another means the temporary disappearance of certain interests and the acquisition of new ones that replace them. Of course, few people regularly change from Dr. Jekyll into Mr. Hyde. Yet some transformations are absolutely essential. For an undertaker to give way to his normal human compassion while doing business would be "out of character," however compassionate a man he may otherwise be. A leading politician enjoying a vacation not only wants to forget his political cares; he may go to great length to disguise his identity. Naturally the shift from one role to another does not preclude a return to the first role. The commitment is limited and transitory, and the center of the person's energies is left intact. For a conversion to occur, the new role and its interests must become all-absorbing and affect the core of the individual's personality. Once one is so committed to a new role, a return to former ways means backsliding, becoming a despised renegade.

Thus the convert in changing roles is initiated into a new life. In contrast to the normal acceptance of an adult role, the convert's initiation

20. Charles H. Upton, "Alcoholics Anonymous," *Criminology: A Book of Readings,* ed. C. B. Vedder, S. Koenig, and R. E. Clark (New York: The Dryden Press, Inc., 1953), pp. 328–34.

follows a discontinuous pattern, which constitutes a radical break. He changes his attitudes to assimilate views consistent with the new affiliation.

MASS CONVERSION AND SOCIAL STRUCTURE

THE RELATIONSHIP between mass conversion and social structure involves the following:

1. An element of alienation from social structure in the form of rejection of certain ways, or in wholesale defection.

2. The availability of alternative ideologies or action which offer new solutions.

3. An experience that enables individuals to perceive these alternatives, previously not recognized, as viable.

4. A movement of individuals, who accept or submit to a new social authority, from one social milieu to another.

The opportunities for conversion within a society are in direct proportion to the variety of acceptable standards, since conversion involves a change from one standard to another. Where there is only one group standard, conversion and apostasy are identical—unless, of course, the whole group is radically transformed. Mass conversions also occur as a movement within a pluralistic society where many divergent standards exist side by side. For the individual convert the experience is a psychological change, but for a society mass conversion has a broader significance: it leads to basic realignments among groups or to shifts in basic public orientations.

Thus, an increase in mobility should increase the frequency with which conversions occur. The immigrant may change only his residence, but his children enthusiastically accept the ways of their new locale. A host of life experiences undermine and devaluate parental authority. Nor is such a deviation between parental standards and life experience confined to immigrant groups in the United States. A study of ex-Communists from four Western countries, with long tenure in the party, revealed that the majority came from families whose attitudes toward religion could be called pious or observant. They reported that by the time they joined the Communist Party they had become indifferent, if not markedly hostile, toward the religious tradition in which they were reared.[21] Another study indicated that college coeds from a conservative background became more liberal as they approached their senior year. As these students came to identify with the college community, which emphasized an awareness

21. Almond, *op. cit.*

of public issues, they accepted its attitudes, and their formal familial allegiances often served as negative reference points.[22]

MANIPULATION OF THE SOCIAL MILIEU: PERSUASION AND TERRORIZATION

The individual may convert more easily if the social support he derives from his associates facilitates a change. Support for this proposition comes from several kinds of observation.

Persuasion

Efforts at persuasion are likely to be successful if the new view can be justified by a group standard. The National Research Council's Committee on Food Habits, in research carried out in conjunction with the need to combat wartime food shortages, found that group discussions were more successful than lectures in inducing housewives to serve unpopular meats—beef hearts, sweetbreads, kidneys—which were high in nutritive value. Lecturers had argued in favor of these meats with logic and emphasis, but they failed to sway the women, whose deep-seated aversions to them were embedded in individual habit and custom. It is unlikely that the women were deceived by the informal atmosphere of group discussions into thinking that their decision to try the intestinals was entirely autonomous. Rather, one source of resistance to change was seriously weakened: the individual could perceive any change in group standards and thus assure herself that, in using such edibles, she would be doing what others were doing.

This principle also finds practical application in all sorts of group work. The idea behind group therapy among delinquents, alcoholics, etc., is to create an atmosphere conducive to free discussion of individual problems shared by all. It should be stressed, however, that the aim is not the setting up of a new *group* goal. The group setting facilitates decisions about primarily individual goals and matters of outlook.

Whether a message via the mass media—television, press, radio—affects views depends on the kind of social reinforcement it receives. When the mass media are able to change perceptions of the group norms to which specific opinions are anchored, rather striking changes in the latter may sometimes be observed.[23] The classic experiment by Sherif on the autokinetic effect is revealing in this regard. Confronted with a stationary light in an otherwise totally dark room, each group of experi-

22. Theodore M. Newcomb, *Personality and Social Change* (New York: The Dryden Press, Inc., 1943).

23. This issue is the subject of more detailed treatment in Chapter 14.

mental subjects developed its own consensus about how far the light had moved. The group consensus served the individual member as a normative yardstick, even after he had been removed from the group and faced the same problem of judging by himself. In some ways this setting is analogous to a situation in which the mass media are used.[24] Mass media communications per se are capable of converting fundamental loyalties only in pathological cases or if they act in conjunction with local group dispositions.

Terrorization

The systematic application of terror acts to undermine group supports in quite a different way. *Total terror* is not to be confused with the fear-arousing devil and hell preaching of a revivalist or the concrete and worldly fears invoked by an agitator. Its aim is less the manipulation of social norms than their utter destruction. Under a system of total terror, the individual, deprived of normal group support, feels isolated, and his isolation is most potent in inducing compliance and preparing him to accept new beliefs.

Social isolation, whether deliberately induced or a natural accompaniment of a social role, leads to an exaggerated concern with one's own fate, a syndrome similar to the immediate reaction in disaster. As long as primary group ties and social solidarity continue to provide support for the old standards, even extreme terror is ineffective. The Chinese Communists made persistent efforts to destroy all friendships, emotional bonds, group activities, and spontaneous leadership which developed among their American prisoners of the Korean War. The Nazis in their concentration camps began by placing criminals in charge of internal administration. Whereas in group therapy the total environment is meant to be therapeutic, flexible, and permissive, totalitarian systems confront their subjects with demands in such an inflexible and unyielding atmosphere that there can only be acquiescence.

Another element in the social isolation of the individual consists of constant threats and degradations. Mutual spying in order to enforce arbitrary measures breeds an atmosphere of general suspicion. Since no one can be trusted, the individual is left to his own resources at the very time when concern with his fate is uppermost in his mind. The fact that authorities reward compliant behavior provides positive motivations for compliance. The thoughts of the subject, writes one Eastern European refugee from communism, begin to focus on the one "alternative" pre-

24. Muzafer Sherif, "Group Influences on the Formation of Norms and Attitudes," *Readings in Social Psychology*, ed. E. E. Maccoby *et al.* (New York: Henry Holt & Co., Inc., 1958), pp. 219–32.

sented to him.[25] Soon the recognition dawns that "there is no other way." Almost any conviction becomes preferable to the hopelessness that is the plight of the victim of terror, and he is forced into a situation of childlike dependence. According to Bettelheim, a psychologist imprisoned by the Nazis, such regressions were "mass phenomena" in the concentration camp and "would not have taken place if it had not happened in all prisoners." It was enforced by the group as a protective device since individual transgressions threatened not only individuals who erred but the entire group. He noted many indications that concentration camp victims began to accept as their own the values of the Gestapo.[26]

The destruction of group supports operates in still a third way. In a completely manipulated setting, predictions can be *made* to come true. This holds not only for the rewards a captor may be willing to offer but for the threats he is prepared to carry out. A milieu totally controlled and centrally manipulated, through rewards to produce the "right" attitudes and behavior, precludes any opportunity for checking the validity of the "wrong" views. Not all totalitarian settings have achieved total control. An evaluation of the effectiveness of Chinese indoctrination techniques in changing the ideological attitudes of United States prisoners of war concluded that they *converted* only very few, though the views of many may have been affected on some peripheral issues. The failure to convert more is attributed to the fact that the creation of feelings of social and emotional isolation through the destruction of all formal and spontaneous associations was never sufficiently extended to make the prisoners completely dependent on the Chinese.[27]

THE SELF-IMAGE: INDUCEMENT OF GUILT

There has been a good deal of talk in the press about what appears to be a mysterious process known as "brainwashing," and extravagant statements have been made concerning the success with which it has been practiced by totalitarian regimes. No authoritative evidence seems to support these claims. The term seems to have been the invention of an American journalist who translated the Chinese term *hsi nao* in this way. The Chinese themselves apparently refer to "cleansing oneself" or "self-criticism." And the basic elements in the mass indoctrination program by which such regimes induce and enforce adherence to official beliefs are *criticism* and *self-criticism*.

25. Czeslaw Milosz, *The Captive Mind* (New York: Alfred A. Knopf, Inc., 1953).
26. Bruno Bettelheim, "Individual and Mass Behavior in Extreme Situations," in G. E. Swanson *et al., op. cit.*, p. 636.
27. Edgar H. Schein, "The Chinese Indoctrination Program for Prisoners of War: A Study of Attempted Brainwashing," *Psychiatry*, XIX (1956), pp. 149–72.

The practice of criticism as a technique for indoctrination has long been familiar to students of the Soviet Union and of the communist movement. That the Soviet leaders should have set such great stock in eliciting confessions is sometimes attributed to the training so many of the old Bolsheviks received in Russian Orthodox seminaries before embarking on careers as professional revolutionaries. There is something irrational in this insistence on self-castigation, when confessions could be obtained through torture or, failing this, through outright forgery. Such tactics have never been eschewed by the leaders of the Russian Communist movement. Yet their opponents would have found simple confessions without ideological ranting more credible, and ideological converts to communism all over the world would never have doubted what came from official sources. A U.S. Air Force survey insists that false confessions were in fact extorted from Air Force personnel more quickly and economically by North Koreans who apparently had not yet learned the Communist way of doing things.[28] The communist movement shares its irrational insistence on confession and self-criticism with other movements that aim at mass conversion.

No matter how successful and irrevocable any conversion appears, most researchers agree that the older standards are not completely banished—merely buried. Many conversions are maintained by the deliberate inducement of guilt, the only protection against which is the complete transformation of character, including blocking out all vestiges of former beliefs. A comparison between the methods by which Chinese cadres were indoctrinated and the proselytizing techniques of a modern "religious" cult, the Oxford Group, documents the importance of this inducement of guilt. Such a comparison does not suggest that the goals of the two movements are identical or that the Oxford Group backed up its psychological appeals with the coercion at the disposal of the Communists.[29]

Among the Chinese, initial training themes were intended to instill a maximum of disillusionment in the minds of the trainees. The leader

28. Albert D. Biderman has written extensively on the effects of Communist indoctrination attempts. See, for example, *Effects of Communist Indoctrination Attempts: Some Comments Based on an Air Force Prisoner-of-War Study* (Air Force Personnel and Training Research Center Development Report TN-57-119, Lackland Air Force Base, Texas, 1957). *The U.S. Fighting Man's Code* (Office of Armed Forces Information and Education, Department of Defense, 1955) contains a good summary of the studies done on the effects of brainwashing, and a useful bibliography.

29. The following comparisons and quotes are drawn from: Richard L. Walker, *China Under Communism: The First Five Years* (New Haven: Yale University Press, 1955); Allen W. Eister, *Drawing-Room Conversion; A Sociological Account of the Oxford Group Movement* (Durham, N.C.: Duke University Press, 1950); and *The New York Times Magazine*, February 23, 1936, pp. 6ff.

acquainted himself with minute details of the background of each trainee in order to discover the individual's weak spots. "The individual becomes aware that he can have no secrets. His life and his thoughts are to become public property."

On the other hand, the approach to the prospective Oxford Grouper was more indirect. The first problem for the proselytizer was to win his confidence and to arouse in him a sense of sinfulness. The means employed was the house party in which, according to an eye-witness account, "cordiality serves as an anaesthetic under which soul surgery . . . is rendered painless. The surroundings of the house party are so ingratiating, the groupers so considerate in avoiding trespass on the field of religion, unless invited, that the guest feels it is almost an abuse of hospitality not to give them a chance at his soul. He is under an obligation and therefore at a disadvantage."

As talks between the guest and his Grouper confidante went on, the latter might say, "If you were being absolutely honest with yourself, what would you consider the worst thing you've ever done?" The task of converting the "sinner" was facilitated if some specific episode, guilt, or anxiety attributable to his sin was uncovered which could be surrendered in exchange for security. In much the same way the members of a Chinese cadre vie with one another in publicly proclaiming their many real and imagined sins; they are constantly fearful of displaying insufficient enthusiasm.

The Oxford Grouper used to keep a little booklet in which he wrote what God said to him. And to make certain that God's words were not misunderstood and that the communication came from an authentic divine source, this booklet used to be submitted to others in the Group—a practice called "checking guidance." Sometimes, when it was suspected that "error" was passing through a convert's mind, a message could actually be vetoed. Likewise, the Communist trainee was required to keep a diary and to open his autobiography to the scrutiny of others. In the "group struggle" meetings, under the supervision of the Communist cadre, everyone exhibited an eagerness to expose the errors of others.

Ultimately, when this continuous self-castigation and humiliation begin to become unbearable, some course of action must be offered as a way out. Near the conclusion of the indoctrination process, the Chinese trainee apparently reaches a stage where the consistent denunciation of his entire past taxes his conscience heavily. By throwing himself enthusiastically into every task, he is told, his doubts can be resolved. Finally, he cuts his "tails" to the old society—his family, former friends, old beliefs, etc. In the Oxford Group also, the rewards of group guidance and surrendered living were not gained without cost.

The price was the surrender of whatever sin the sinner or the soul surgeon could specify. In order that the change be felt genuine and satisfying, it was necessary that it be preceded by some such recognized form of sin as pride to be humiliated, selfishness to be surrendered, impurity or dishonesty to be confessed and at least partially or symbolically atoned for through restitution . . . . The action, whatever it might be according to guidance, would quite often have to be difficult or "hard" in order to be felt by the sinner himself and by onlookers as genuine and as evidence of effective and complete surrender.

In either case, the convert is committed to new associations. Life-changing practices seldom, if ever, took place apart from some activity sponsored or planned by the Group. After the final convincing, the Communist found release from his guilt and was fired by the need to publicize his new convictions. The enthusiasm thus generated constitutes a partial solution to inner conflict and an escape from social isolation into a new community.

THE ROLE OF CHARISMA

The spontaneous emergence of new faiths depends on charismatic personalities, who by their prophecies inspire a following dedicated to spreading their message. Mass conversions are sparked by a coterie dedicated to a cause, and so the creation of cadres who will carry the faith is most important.

The divinely inspired message usually calls for a return to the "true faith." It parades under the guise of renewal. Where social forms have become ossified, when church and party appear to have deviated from the true faith, the charismatic leader makes his appeal to the outcasts—that is, to those who find the discrepancy between reality and hope the greatest. Individuals in such social positions seem most susceptible to the messianic hopes proclaimed by the voice of God. In many instances the emotional appeals of prophets do foreshadow future developments. Davenport, summing up the achievements of John Wesley, writes:

There was not a practical reform mooted in eighteenth century England which he did not further with his voice and with his pen. He advocated a more equitable system of taxation. His arguments for juster Parliamentary representation were made seventy years before the reform was accomplished, but they were as strong as any that were advanced on the eve of its fruition. He lent active aid to the cause of the prisoner, the lunatic, the debtor, and the slave. In all these matters he was only an evangel. The reforms were demanded by the spirit of the age, and more

potent and active agents than he were directly concerned in their fulfillment. But the spirit of the movement which he inaugurated strongly reinforced the spirit of the age.[30]

Yet there is another way to look at the achievement of charismatic
leaders and the sudden conversions they achieve. The reforms they advocate do come, but only gradually. Temporarily they may succeed in
stirring imaginations to a high pitch of excitement. The men they convert
constitute a social movement, but the movement itself becomes ossified
into an institution.[31] And with the growth of institutionalization the
emergence of new charisma becomes an increasingly rare phenomenon.
With the growth of rationalization, changing life conditions and the problems they bring are dealt with through rational adaptation. Progress itself
becomes routinized, and change occurs according to scientific maxims.

Thus, it is not surprising that the mass conversions that do occur today
are most often the result of mass manipulation by terror (or through the
art of public relations) or through clinical efforts at group therapy.
Spontaneous conversions in response to a charismatic appeal tend to occur
more in peripheral areas of behavior and are more and more associated
with pathology.

B I B L I O G R A P H Y

ACZEL, TAMAS, and MERAY, TIBOR. *Revolt of the Mind.* New
York: Frederick A. Praeger, Inc., 1959. The resistance of intellectuals
behind the Iron Curtain to indoctrination.

ALMOND, GABRIEL. *The Appeals of Communism.* Princeton: Princeton University Press, 1954. A quantitative study based on a sample of
ex-Communists in France, Italy, England, and the United States.

BAUER, RAYMOND A., and SCHEIN, EDGAR H. (eds.) *Brainwashing,* in *The Journal of Social Issues,* XIII [No. 3], 1957. Articles, with
bibliographies, by a number of social psychologists who participated
in studies of American repatriates from China and Korea (including
a review of Kinkead's book).

CROSSMAN, RICHARD. *The God That Failed.* New York: Harper
& Brothers, 1950. Six autobiographical sketches of well-known, former
Communists and Communist sympathizers.

DAVENPORT, F. M. *Primitive Traits in Religious Revivals.* New

30. F. M. Davenport, *Primitive Traits in Religious Revivals* (New York: The
Macmillan Co., 1905).
31. See chapters on social movements.

York: The Macmillan Co., 1905. Excellent and vivid accounts of the Indian Ghost Dance and the Methodist and other revivals.

EISTER, ALLEN W. *Drawing-Room Conversion; A Sociological Account of the Oxford Group Movement.* Durham, N.C.: Duke University Press, 1950. An account of Moral Rearmament and especially of the techniques used to win converts.

JAMES, WILLIAM. *The Varieties of Religious Experience.* New York: The New American Library, 1958. This classic by the great American psychologist-philosopher is available in an inexpensive paperback edition.

KINKEAD, EUGENE. *In Every War But One.* New York: W. W. Norton & Company, Inc., 1958. This book, by a *New Yorker* staff writer, tends to exaggerate the effectiveness of Chinese indoctrination techniques on American prisoners in Korea.

MCLOUGHLIN, WILLIAM G. *Billy Sunday Was His Real Name.* Chicago: The University of Chicago Press, 1955. This fascinating history of Billy Sunday's crusade reveals many similarities with Billy Graham's four decades later.

POWDERMAKER, FLORENCE B., and FRANK, JEROME D. *Group Psychotherapy.* Cambridge, Mass.: Harvard University Press, 1953. The study of social influences in therapeutic groups may provide clues to the understanding of mass conversion.

SARGANT, WILLIAM. *Battle for the Mind: A Physiology of Conversion and Brainwashing.* New York: Doubleday & Company, Inc., 1957. A physiologist's interpretation, with interesting illustrations, of conversion, brainwashing, revivalism, etc., in terms of Pavlovian psychology.

TOCH, HANS H. "Crisis Situations and Ideological Evaluations," *Public Opinion Quarterly,* XIX (Spring, 1955), pp. 53–67. A psychological formulation of how ideologies are adapted or abandoned in crisis situations.

WILLIAM, W. "The Society of Alcoholics Anonymous," *American Journal of Psychiatry,* CVI (1949), pp. 370–75. The psychiatric life history of a converted alcoholic.

CHAPTER 7

Crystallization: The Active Nucleus

I N SOCIETY, as in nature, process and structure are aspects of the same set of events. As the individual repeats and repeats some activity, it congeals into habit; emergencies are "coded" until what was crisis becomes routine. Group routines congeal into group norms and group ritual. So, too, when the spontaneous and nonroutine forms of interaction result in some kind of equilibrium, elements of social structure are at once discernible. Any collective alienation from the existing social structure contains—potentially, at any rate—the seeds of new organization. For instance, panic reflects the unrest out of which emerge crowds as well as stable action groups. Mass conversion may form the basis for social movements.

Crystallization thus designates the process by which alienation from the social order finds expression in an elementary form of organization. Fluid forms of interaction become routinized, and fugitive patterns of behavior are transformed—we say they "crystallize"—into cohesive units with a sense of solidarity and with a more or less definite structure.

The resulting collectivity constitutes a *sectarian association*. The adjective *sectarian* signifies that such an association exists as a secondary phenomenon, which develops as a result of cleavage from an already existing social order. Its members have turned away from the world. The *esprit de corps* that sets off the microcosm from the larger world is often based on hostility.

ELEMENTARY ORGANIZATIONS

THE SECTARIAN GROUP is treated here as the most elementary form of association. It is elementary, however, in a rather unique way—in terms

[179]

of process. What this means will become clearer if some other conceptions of elementary forms are briefly reviewed. Among students of society, the term "most elementary" has been applied to a number of other kinds of grouping. Each writer's definition has been governed by the problem he sought to solve. For some, notably Durkheim, it was a matter of reducing social phenomena to the simple forms they exhibited during their origins. It may also be a matter of analytical reduction to the simplest kind of relationship, as in Simmel. On the other hand, McDougall sought it in the most spontaneous forms of interaction that are without tradition and presuppose no framework of norms apart from the momentary psychological unity produced by the interaction.

"PRIMEVAL" FORMS

Durkheim sought to understand the fundamental cause of some general social phenomena—for instance, religion—by studying their manifestations in their most elementary form.[1] Two criteria were used to select this form: (1) its existence in the simplest and most homogeneous society possible; (2) the closest possible relation to its "origins"—that is, a form which was not traceable to still earlier forms and from which, by inference, later and more complex variations were derived. Thus, Durkheim turned to primitive societies as the source in which he might study the most elementary forms of religious life.

Durkheim's formulation is not suited to the study of most of the phenomena with which collective dynamics is concerned. These are, by their nature, not "original" phenomena but they develop out of, and in contradiction to, existing social patterns. Primitive societies—even the most "simple" and homogeneous—display a marked degree of organization. Both their stability and their high degree of conventionalization make *spontaneous* collective deviations, while not impossible, nevertheless most uncommon.

THE DYAD

Methodologically speaking, wrote Simmel, the simplest form of socialization is that which operates between only two parties.[2] The *dyad* —a collectivity made up of not more than two elements—constitutes a form of group life in its own right. Its simple duality has a determinate impact on the structure of the relationship. Moreover, dyadic relationships constitute the cellular structure out of which complex social organisms

1. Emile Durkheim, *Elementary Forms of the Religious Life* (Glencoe, Ill.: The Free Press, 1947).

2. Georg Simmel, *The Sociology of Georg Simmel* (Glencoe, Ill.: The Free Press, 1950), pp. 122ff.

are compounded. In these organisms the dyad does not exist as an independent entity. It constitutes an active nucleus only by virtue of a concrete social relationship to the larger structure. Hence, the dyad is primary in a methodological or analytical sense, but not necessarily in terms of development.

THE CROWD

McDougall's main interest was in the principles underlying collective mental life rather than in the forms of the relationships. He treated the crowd as an *unorganized* group and hence the most elementary manifestation of the group mind. Many of the features of group life, he assumed, which become increasingly complicated as higher degrees of organization are achieved, can be observed in relative simplicity in the crowd. Unfortunately McDougall's discussion of rudimentary groups— collectivities that are more than crowds but not yet associations or nations —is extremely sketchy. The crowd in his scheme begins to resemble an organized group when all its members are possessed by the same clearly defined purpose. It falls short of being a group nevertheless unless this purpose is transformed into a collective will based on some idea of the group as a whole. Individuals casually thrown together, as in a crowd at a railroad station, sometimes develop such a consciousness. Or an audience, which is oriented to leaders and spokesmen, constitutes a collection of persons with some degree of organization.[3]

This formulation touches on issues important to collective dynamics. It spells out the conditions for social organization. But the problems of how the active nuclei crystallize out of a casual crowd or an audience and develop into permanent forms are ignored. Actually, moreover, crowds as elementary manifestations of collective life do not always flow out of chance collections of persons. The crowd that develops out of an organized group spells the group's partial dissolution, rather than the crystallization of an elementary organization.

THE SECTARIAN ASSOCIATION

It is in the sectarian nucleus that the disaffection that occasionally provokes a crowd to action becomes verbal and definite. This nucleus, too, spells the beginnings of a more permanent association. Unless oriented to some notion of a group, behavior—however rampant it may be—is not social action. Sighele, governed by his interest in collective crimes, pointed to this relation between mass sentiments and organization in a most succinct manner: "The sectarian group [*secte*] is a select [*triée*] and permanent crowd; the crowd is a transient sectarian group which has not yet

3. William McDougall, *The Group Mind* (New York: G. P. Putnam's Sons, 1920).

picked its members. The sectarian group is the chronic form of the crowd; the crowd is the sharpened form of the sect." [4] Because the sectarian group has an internal structure—some permanence, a conscious sense of identity with criteria for inclusion and exclusion, etc.—it exists submerged beneath the surface of the transient crowd and is able to survive it. It consciously sets itself apart from, and in opposition to, society. *Esprit de corps,* a characteristic of all sectarian formations, signifies a compensatory brotherhood of the select, dedicated to an unconventional authority of their own choosing.[5]

In the framework of sociological analysis, the term "sectarian" has other than religious connotations. As long as the population within a society is heterogeneous, schisms may occur over any matter that is sufficiently important to aggravate emotions. Understandably, where religion is the dominant value, any consciousness of difference among sectors of the population is apt to express itself in religious terms. Other kinds of sectarian associations crystallize around any one of many political, intellectual, or cultural interests—provided, of course, that these concerns are *central* and that they arouse in the sectarian the feeling that he is not granted full expression within recognized institutions. The sectarian responds by seceding into new forms of association set up in opposition to the social order. That his secession earns the hostility or contempt of the surrounding world only justifies and reinforces his convictions.

The crucial fact about the sectarian association is that it is cemented as a result of conflict with the "outsiders." All who are not specifically included are thus excluded from the sectarian cells, which seek to subvert the superiority of the outside world. "The sectarians are forced to segregate themselves by a consciousness of unlikeness between themselves and their oppressors and are drawn together by a sense of mental and moral kinship." [6] The associations they form are outside the pale of society, and the sectarian consciously moves on a different plane of understanding from the rest of the population. If anything, he avoids being drawn into communication with them.

The sectarian nucleus is a form of organization because the sectarians who set themselves against constituted authority do so consciously and deliberately, and not merely under the impact of a momentary emotional impulse as they do in the crowd. In a manner of speaking, the sectarians consider themselves the elect. But initially they lack common interest, a concept of the group in its entirety, recognized roles, etc., which char-

4. Scipio Sighele, *Psychologie des Sectes* (Paris: M. Giard et Cie., 1898), p. 46.
5. See, for instance, Silone's statement quoted in Chapter 6, page 156.
6. John L. Gillin, "A Contribution to the Sociology of Sects," *American Journal of Sociology,* XVI (September, 1910), p. 241.

acterize groups generally. What unity they have derives from generalized dissatisfaction and unrest, which in the nucleus crystallize into antagonism. For unlike the crowd, the sectarian nucleus endures. Its initial psychological unity paves the way for a more permanent, usually highly disciplined, structured organization with positive goals.

SECTARIANISM AND SOCIAL STRUCTURE

SECTARIAN NUCLEI that develop a code subversive of official mores do not form by accident or whim. On the contrary, the sectarian's advocacy of counter mores reflects the unfocused quest by some segments of society for a group code responsive to their particular needs. Persons in social positions where they feel effectively shut off from legitimate expression of their needs show an inclination to achieve recognition in sectarian associations.

THE LOWER CLASSES

The persons at the bottom of the pit, the impoverished, the proletariat probably come first to mind. There is, indeed, a relationship between position in the class structure and membership in small and exclusive religious sects. Christianity was about three hundred years old before it developed a significant following among the socially well-to-do. Later it was the poor—whose social and psychological needs were neglected by the conventional religion of the day—who joined the original Protestant sects that split away from the established Church. The Anabaptists, who revolted and sought later to found the kingdom of God in Muenster, had their firmest base among the poor peasants. John Wesley, the original Methodist preacher, stimulated the greatest emotional response among the outcasts of Newgate and Kingsbridge. The movement from church to sect among Southern millworkers was summed up by Liston Pope in this manner:

> The poorest mill workers have afforded the invariable starting point of sects in Gaston County [Texas], but as a new sect passed toward churchly status [i.e., reached out toward influence in and recognition by the community] the percentage of mill workers in its membership has correspondingly decreased; roughly the degree to which any denomination is churchly at a given moment varies inversely with the percentage of its membership composed of mill workers.[7]

7. Liston Pope, *Millhands and Preachers: a Study of Gastonia* (New Haven: Yale University Press, 1942), p. 118.

Using an attitude questionnaire, Dynes found that most of the American Protestants in Ohio who by their attitudes indicated acceptance of a "sect-type" religious organization had a low socioeconomic status rather than a high one. These differences remained significant even among persons with similar denominational affiliations. A typical "sect" response was, for instance, strong agreement with the statement: "I think it is more serious to break God's law than to break man's law." A strong agreement with the statement "I think a person who is not willing to follow *all* the rules of the church should not be allowed to belong" is an example of a "church" response.[8]

The very special need the small religious sect fills among the poor has been summed up by Clark:

> Finding themselves ill at ease in the presence of an effete and prosperous bourgeoisie, their emotional natures unsatisfied by a middle-class complacency, their economic problems disregarded by those who have no such problems to meet, and their naive faith and simple interpretations smiled upon by their more cultured fellows, the poor and ignorant revolt and draw apart into groups which are more congenial. They elevate the necessities of their class—frugality, humility, and industry—into moral virtues and regard as sins the practices they are debarred from embracing. Those pinched by economic circumstances look askance at theatregoing, card playing, and "putting on of gold and costly apparel," but indulge in the same when their early fortunes improve. Their standards of conduct are invented from the simple lives they are impelled at all events to lead and which are congenial to their simplicity.[9]

THE YOUNG

Not all sectarian groups recommend quietism, however. Nor are the moral communities based on the "holy" way of life the only sectarian solutions available to the lower strata. The moral community built around the "tough" way of life represents an entirely different kind of negativism, one that is entirely secular. Being deliberately "ornery" or simulating the tough way of life is a subcultural trait prevalent among boys' gangs in deteriorated urban areas. The delinquent way of life has recently been described as a solution to the "status problem" of these youths.[10] Lack of

8. Russell R. Dynes, "Church-Sect Typology and Socio-Economic Status," *American Sociological Review*, XX (October, 1955), pp. 555–60.

9. Elmer T. Clark, *The Small Sects in America* (rev. ed.; New York: Abingdon Press, 1949), pp. 16ff.

10. Albert K. Cohen, *Delinquent Boys: The Culture of the Gang* (Glencoe, Ill.: The Free Press, 1955). For another approach, see A. R. Crane, "Pre-Adolescent Gangs: a Socio-Psychological Interpretation," *Journal of Genetic Psychology*, LXXXVI (June, 1955), pp. 275–79.

recognition of the lower-class youth by controlling agencies—the school, for example—which personify a middle-class moral code is countered by violent rejection of this code.

The tendency of boys to segregate themselves into exclusive groups is not confined, however, to deteriorated neighborhoods of the city. This is an age-graded phenomenon, peculiar neither to lower-class youth, nor to urban and congested neighborhoods, nor to a society that aggravates the status problem by placing a high premium on social mobility.

FRONTIERS AND SECTARIAN ASSOCIATIONS

Sectarian associations—whether sects, gangs, bands, etc.—are also "frontier" phenomena: they are most likely to form among people who push on against a hostile environment, whether geographic or moral. The American West not only sheltered gangs of marauders who warred against established authorities in the legendary style of Jesse James; it was also the locus of several great religious revivals, which reflected its political and economic cleavage with the comfortably settled East. The religion of the West produced anew, according to Niebuhr:

> many of the characteristics of the faith of the disinherited, for the psychology of the frontier corresponds in many respects to the psychology of the revolutionary poor. This is especially true of the emotional character of religious experience, which seems to be required in the one case as in the other. The isolation of frontier life fostered a craving for companionship, suppressed the gregarious tendency and so subjected the lonely settler to the temptations of crowd suggestion to an unusual degree.[11]

The frontiersman found the respectable religion of the East too tame. He demanded a voluntaristic church in harmony with his democratic and self-reliant way of life.

There is in every metropolitan city what Robert E. Park used to refer to as the *moral frontier*. Here persons from diverse cultural heritages come together. To the immigrant from another milieu such an environment is definitely hostile; he usually enters at the lowest rung of the social ladder and bears the scorn of his self-appointed betters. Most important, he is often forced to adapt to new modes of life without much prior preparation. The organizations among in-migrants are in part a protection against these surroundings. Some religious sects simply defend the migrants against the necessity of making a thoroughgoing readjustment. In-migrants to the North from the rural South have often joined typical

11. H. Richard Niebuhr, *The Social Sources of Denominationalism* (New York: Meridian Books, 1957), p. 141.

secessionist "churches." Other groups, like the infamous Mafia, engage in violent and criminal activities.

MARGINALITY

In minority group status lies still another impetus for sectarian association. This need not always take the form of a return to old cultural traditions. The members of minorities, intent on gaining recognition, may swell the ranks of criminal, political, and esthetic sects. They are naturals for separatist groups, whether on a national, ethnic, or racial basis, as long as their antipathy toward a society that has thwarted their innermost aspirations finds support there. The basis of delinquent gangs and religious sects is often ethnic. Both tend to make use of the same feelings but channel them differently.

Marginality—the lack of full acceptance of persons who move on the margins of several groups—is not confined to minority group status. The "alienated" intellectual, trained to use symbols, often lacks the audience he craves for his product and thus seeks sectarian solutions. Some have joined in secret societies—like the Freemasons of the eighteenth and nineteenth centuries, which had strong religious as well as political overtones. Esthetic and religious sects also abound, and there have been many artistic "secessions." A recent example is the "beat" who joins with others in the desire for "genuine" experience. The cult of the "beat generation" seeks no converts. Instead the "beats" cultivate a special kind of experience inaccessible to "squares" with their deliberate bohemianism. Their jazz, wrote Eugene Burdick about this group in *The Reporter*,

> serves them something of the same function Marxism served the disenchanted intellectual of the 1930's. It is a kind of orderly center on which each can make his own interpretation. The fantastic but deeply felt "interpretations" of Marxism, the antic splinter groups, have their parallel in the views of jazz that the hipsters develop. There is the same angry quest for what "it" means, whether it is Marx's dialectic or the pattern of notes played by Charlie Parker, the short-lived alto-saxist.[12]

When the attention of such cells turns toward politics, they become the catalysts of revolution. Discontented intellectuals formed the Bolsheviks, the purest of all cells, and beer-hall pamphleteers unable to find employment commensurate with their education developed the ideological hodgepodge that justified Hitler's policies. The various political, literary, intellectual, and even mystical sects both express and contribute to the ferment in society.

12. Eugene Burdick, "The Innocent Nihilists Adrift in Squaresville," *The Reporter*, XVIII (April 3, 1958), p. 32.

SUMMARY

Psychologically, then, the majority of sectarians appear to be misfits or outcasts. Frustrated and disappointed in their expectations, they seek fulfillment in some more genuine experience or in devotion to some holy cause. These misfits do not, however, form a social category. But when controlling institutions—family, school, church, government, etc.— fail to function adequately with regard to large segments of the population, they are likely to be experienced as meaningless and, at their worst, as unjust. They become the target of warfare, or some higher power is "called on" to destroy them. Hence, one should expect the tendencies toward sectarian formations to be more pronounced during periods of unrest. Sectarian groups stem from the same—or very similar—objective conditions as the crowds of which they often form the active nuclei.

Those who are most prone to seek sectarian solutions in opposition to conventional modes are: (1) the socially inferior classes who are deprived of their "just" share of social values; (2) the preadolescents and adolescents whose developing adult interests go unrecognized in conventional groups; (3) minority groups and other "marginals" who are not fully accepted; and (4) the rootless intelligentsia frustrated in legitimate employment of their "creative" aspirations. Their readiness for such solutions is further aggravated by an oppressive system of social relationships that stifles the direct expression of deviant tendencies. Thus, despotic regimes, rigid class structure, and extreme conventionality would seem to promote sectarianism.

VARIETIES OF ACTIVE NUCLEI

SINCE THE SECTARIAN ASSOCIATION arises as an effort by some part of a community to integrate itself anew, its protest against the institutional order rarely encounters support from officialdom. But the radical break on the part of the sectarian takes many forms. These may crystallize in two generally opposite directions. One culminates in the formation of a *gang;* the other in the *sect,* taken in its more narrow religious meaning. Between these two extremes are many mixed forms.

1. By comparison with those of the religious sect, the interests of the gang are not only worldly but concerned with the here and now. The gang has no futuristic illusions and, in fact, often avoids concern with anything but the immediate present; whereas some apocalyptic hope, some promise of redemption, appears an indispensable characteristic of

every sect—political as well as religious—although the image of this world is still a potent force.

2. The protest of the religious sect is against prevailing institutions as corruptions of a divine order. The sectarian code seeks to substitute positive rigor where laxness and compromise are the custom. By contrast, the practices of the typical gang are primarily a reversal of order. Instead of rigor, the gang aims to overthrow restraint and substitute license. While the member of the religious sect feels himself superior to secular institutions, the gang followers aspires to remain outside of them. Wach apparently had in mind a distinction between gang and sect along these lines when he wrote: "If the radicalism should be expressed in negative instead of positive forms (antinomianism, licentiousness), we would suggest that such a ground be called a *band,* not a sect." [13]

3. As far as gang formation is concerned, vague dissatisfactions on the part of its members coalesce into a code of active warfare against official norms. *The sect, one may say, is the passive form of the gang.* Moral asceticism marks the sect as a religious elite, whose members have asserted their devotion to the true life by eschewing both worldly rewards and accepted license. Their exclusive concern with personal salvation effectively separates them from the world, but in effect this often amounts to indifference or even tacit acceptance of generalized depravity or worldly injustice.[14] Nevertheless, this passivity implies a definite, but inactive hostility toward the world.

Though at first glance they seem to have little in common, both these forms—gang and sect—spell a definitive defiance of official authority, whose place is usurped by a "superior" and more rigorous code. Notwithstanding its advocacy of license, the hold the gang has on its membership is far more absolute and totalitarian than any claim ever advanced by the world outside. One must not, however, confuse the gang's rigorous discipline, which simulates the absolute fellowship of the sect, with the substantive rigor of the latter's doctrine.

Some religious sects have reacted against outsiders with the utmost violence, and orgiastic behavior is a characteristic of many gangs.[15] In twelfth-century Germany, for example, there was a sect known as the Brethren of the Free Spirit. In accordance with the doctrine of immanence,

13. Joachim Wach, *Sociology of Religion* (Chicago: University of Chicago Press, 1944), p. 199.

14. Ernst Troeltsch, *The Social Teachings of the Christian Churches* (London: George Allen and Unwin, Ltd., 1931).

15. For this reason Park and Burgess' suggestion of a correspondence between the "gang" and the "crowd that acts" and between the "sect" and the "orgiastic (ecstatic) or expressive crowd," though it aims at a similar contrast, seems somewhat overdrawn. It assumes a genetic dependence of the spontaneous expressions on forms of crystallization.

which holds that the ultimate principle of the universe is not to be distinguished from the universe itself, members believed that each "brother" among them was God. They defied conventions and went around naked. They also robbed, raped, killed, and pillaged their neighbors, until they were finally stamped out by force.

The Sons of Freedom, a radical offshoot of the orthodox Doukhobors, made themselves so obnoxious to the natives of British Columbia that the Canadian Government was prepared to pay their way back to the Soviet Union, from which they had fled the czars about 1900. They had refused to send their children to school and engaged in a series of bombings and burnings of homes and barns. As a gesture of defiance, they disrobed in public, thus earning the nickname of "Strip-teasers."

Many a religious sect, inspired by its doctrines, has preyed on outsiders. Perhaps the most notorious were the Thugs, a religious secret society in the northern pale of settled India. Since they felt no allegiance to any other authority, they found in their religious doctrines the justification for waylaying and murdering lone travelers and sometimes even attacking caravans. The victims were defined as infidels and were thus outside the community of the faithful. Since then the term "thug" has become an accepted English synonym for any cutthroat or ruffian.

Whether a gang or a sect will emerge as the predominant form of elementary organization depends on a number of factors, such as the temperaments of the leaders and the following they attract. Furthermore, during periods following decisive political defeat, when there is little hope of either influencing or escaping from one's "fate," protest is apt to be diverted into mysticism and quietism. This occurred in 1908 in Russia after what appeared to the revolutionaries an inexorable setback to an attempt to overthrow the czars. In the Depression decade the downtrodden and homeless poor in the United States turned in large numbers to the Pentecostal churches, while the more active and less enervated embraced Marxism, the Townsend Plan, Technocracy, etc. If, on the other hand, the controlling authorities appear subject to influence or merely ineffective, more active forms of protest are encouraged. The disasters suffered by German cities as a result of Allied bombings thus encouraged marauding by delinquent gangs and bands of foreign laborers. At all times gangs have thrived in the confusion of crowds or in the shelter of "open" spaces. Finally, a passive-resistance movement, a rather unique form of protest in that it combines active political warfare with moral perfectionism and otherworldly holiness usually emerges when it seems that open resistance cannot succeed.

GANGS

There are many different sectarian associations of the gang variety. Not only groups of delinquent boys but also professional criminals banded together in larceny, bands of marauders, politically active seditious cells, etc., can all be considered as types of gang in active war against the social order. Notwithstanding the variety in membership, goals, and values among these diverse types, Thrasher's definition, formulated from his study of 1,313 boys' gangs in Chicago, seems to cover all gangs. Accordingly, "the gang is an interstitial group originally formed spontaneously, and then integrated through conflict." [16]

At one extreme the gang shades off imperceptibly into the *clique,* a loose association within a play, work, or neighborhood group which, with increasing intimacy, develops sympathy and rapport among its members. A clique may be a play group, or it may be formed for some specific common interest—for instance, the poker circle—or it may be a loose faction within some organized setting, as among associates who work together in any kind of association. Opposition to external pressures experienced as hostile sometimes transforms such a clique into a gang, with its characteristic sense of unity and internal structure.

Many gangs hardly pass beyond the phase of a clique. Thrasher calls these rudimentary gangs *diffuse.* The solidarity of such a gang is not assured. Nor can the informal leader count on the loyalty of his following. The morale, the discipline, and the minimum of inner discord that a gang requires for survival develop only as a consequence of many joint experiences and extended conflict. The *solidified* gang is a more tightly knit cell. An interesting gang type of phenomenon has occasionally been observed among twins, who support each other in their antisocial behavior by insulating themselves from a surrounding world. On separation, the support for their antisocial behavior disappears and the "gang" begins to disintegrate. Similarly, after being drafted into the army, gang members are often weaned away from their associates.

At a higher level of organization, the gang may begin to adopt the conventions of a club or of some other, more formal organization. Doc's gang, which Whyte described so vividly in his *Street Corner Society,*[17] engaged in many formal activities around the poolroom and bowling alleys. This street-corner group was definitely alienated from many controlling institutions of the society. The corner boys foreswore social mobility. They made no effort to acquire the accouterments of middle-class

16. Frederick M. Thrasher, *The Gang* (Chicago: University of Chicago Press, 1927), p. 57.

17. William F. Whyte, *Street Corner Society* (Chicago: University of Chicago Press, 1955).

respectability. Yet they were an integral part of the organization of their slum neighborhood, existing on the fringe of the rackets and the political machine.

Highly organized gangs may federate to form a criminal syndicate, a political party, or a secret society. Thus, the revolutionary rabble is transformed into a militia, or the band of hoodlums performs services for a political machine. For this to occur a definite ideology, a clearly envisaged goal, or some tangible reward is necessary. When the gang renders specific services, it is beginning to accommodate itself to some outside group, though not necessarily to the social order against which it wars.

A brief look at the main features of the delinquent culture in American cities reveals the antagonistic relation in which the gang stands to the official world. There is no accommodation. Instead, the gang reacts with deliberate malice against accepted standards for apparently no purpose. But it does so in the name of group autonomy. "The delinquent's conduct is right, by the standards of his subculture, precisely *because* it is wrong by the norms of the larger culture," [18] and the group enforces rigorous compliance on its members. It has been noted, however, that the delinquent gang code serves no long-range purpose. There is an almost compulsive emphasis on short-run hedonism, or "living it up for the moment," and an avoidance of any planning.[19] Of course, the last is a special feature of the juvenile gangs and not characteristic of such gang variants as conspiratorial plotters, for example.

The gang type of sectarian nucleus may contain certain conventional forms of behavior and even conduct some mystical rites. Smut sessions, "talk fests" (the rehearsal of adventure), collective sex orgies, and other kinds of festivity are in the repertoire of most boys' gangs. The Illuminati, a secret society that did much to prepare the groundwork for the French Revolution, had extensive ceremonies. Plans of the most practical nature, aiming at the transformation of society, were discussed by those who had proved themselves worthy of initiation into all its secrets. After the Revolution, many of the semimystical fantasies of the Illuminist cells became conventions of everyday life.[20]

The emphasis of the political cell is on both mysticism and action. One finds the same linkage in the philosophies of Louis Blanqui, mid-nineteenth-century terrorist and mystic, and of the anarchists. The romanticism of the Russian terrorists—political gangs who had a humanitarian ideology and subscribed to a doctrine of direct action—is legion. In their demand for complete dedication to a revolutionary cause, even the "scientific" Bolsheviks exhibited some mysticism; they were altogether too preoc-

18. Cohen, *op. cit.*, p. 28.
19. *Ibid.*
20. Una Birch, *Secret Societies and the French Revolution* (London: John Lane, 1911), p. 60.

cupied with scholastic doctrinal disputes about many impractical and irrelevant issues. The gang type of conflict association shades into the religious sect and into the conspiratorial group.

THE RELIGIOUS SECT

The term "sect" has been applied broadly to include every kind of secessionist tendency, be it with regard to religious, political, scholastic, or esthetic matters. In its popular connotation, a *sect* designates, first, a small group and, second, a transgression of the limits within which all organizational, ideological, or cultural disputes are expected to stay. This popular usage touches on some real sociological distinctions.

In trying to differentiate a religious sect from a church, one should keep in mind that, as a distinct sociological type, the former is defined not by the specific doctrinal "heresy" it commits but by the way it exercises its attraction and hold over its membership. The specifically religious sect, discussed here as the prototype of all sects, does *not* necessarily subsume all variations of what are popularly spoken of as religious sects.

The sect originates as a small primary group restricted to the faithful disciples of a holy man in possession of charisma. When Father Divine first moved to New York in 1915, he still called himself "The Messenger" who brought the word of God. He had with him six or seven devoted followers but nothing in the way of an organization. This small circle settled in a flat which they shared in every way, the disciples turning over their entire wages to Father Divine. The common meals among the Messenger and his Angels have since turned into conventions, and the status of Angel is conveyed in an official investment by the leader of the cult.[21] Yet like many other formalized religions, this one emanated from a sectarian nucleus of disciples who alone recognized the divine inspiration of their leader.

The dynamic relationship between sectarian origins and the church type of religious organization, though denied by Troeltsch, has been traced in many settings. As a religious group moves to cover the whole secular world, it inevitably accommodates itself to secular authorities and accepts the ways of the world. Ethical purity is thus compromised. In seeking continuity, the leaders of the group begin to rely increasingly on the upper classes. Approval comes more easily and stability is assured by this accommodation to the secular world. Thus, if the sect seeks to preserve the principle of election (basic to its very nature), it must eschew universality. Hence the small size of the sect appears to be simply a con-

21. St. Clair McKelway, *True Tales from the Annals of Crime and Rascality* (New York: Random House, 1957), pp. 147–97. See also, Hadley Cantril, *The Psychology of Social Movements* (New York: John Wiley & Sons, Inc., 1941), Chap. 5.

sequence of its beginnings in the fellowship of the elect. Troeltsch counterposes the church as a "natural" community to the sect: the most important point is that people are born into the church but voluntarily join a sect by undergoing a conscious conversion.[22] One sees how this principle was compromised in the Half-Way Covenant of the Congregationalists, a denomination with definite sectarian origins. In this way, baptism was offered to second-generation members who submitted to Congregationalist discipline but were not full members because they lacked the necessary experience of salvation. As more and more people became members by way of their parents, however, the element of voluntary choice declined. The Half-Way Covenant was meant to keep within the fold of the emerging church those whose "election" to grace had not yet been assured by a religious experience.

Analogous processes of accommodation are observable in other denominations as they move to hold a permanent, rather than a select, following. "Birth-right memberships" made their appearance in the Society of Friends. In many Baptist groups the age of "adult baptism" was progressively lowered until in some groups twelve-year-olds were eligible. Finally, in the church that has completed the transition from voluntary society to institution, charisms cease to be a matter of private experience. They are vested in authority legitimatized by tradition and by reception of the sacraments. Thus the charisma of the church inheres in its offices (*Amtscharisma*).[23] By contrast, even the "ministers" in a sect constitute a lay leadership, often without formal training. Their guidance is accepted by their followers solely on evidence of personal *charisma*—that is, the visible signs of subjective holiness in response to a calling that all recognize.

The sect has many characteristics that set it off from established religious groups, which are part of the social order. Two of these are essential: the sect is an association that (1) insists on original experience, a charism, as a criterion for admission and thereby (2) substitutes its own internal fellowship, based on an experience open only to the select, for formal religious authority. These characteristics account for the many other specific ones that differentiate the religious sect from the religious denomination. They also distinguish the sect from other types of religious protest: for example, a monastic order finds a place within the framework of the Church; or, again, many secessionist groups acquire, with or without political aid, the legitimate credentials of a dissenting church (as did the Anglican and Lutheran churches) or of a recognized denomination (for instance, religious groups in a pluralistic society).

The sect "gathers a select group and places it in sharp opposition to

22. Troeltsch, *op. cit.*, Vol. I, pp. 331–36.
23. Term used by Max Weber.

the world," wrote Troeltsch.[24] Hence the sect, like the gang, has some of the marks of a conflict group. Its survival in a hostile world is greatly facilitated by its rigorous demands on morality. Because of its size, the sect is often powerless. It usually lacks men of influence among its following. In the intensity of devotion on the part of its members and in its doctrinal purity, the sect does however seem able to offset partially what it lacks in worldly resources. The opposition from the social milieu fosters *esprit de corps* and heightens the morale of its members.

But the type of conflict in which the sect engages is very different from that of the gang. The strength of the sect, Faris suggests, lies in the fact that its conflict is with a "world" that is a subjective image. Since the members are so certain of ultimate success, it is possible for the sect to survive great disasters.[25] While the avowed attitude of sectarians to the world may range from toleration and indifference to active hostility, the sect's opposition to existing institutions is masked by apocalyptic and messianic hopes. Prophecies of doom and redemption offer ultimate salvation only for the select. The sectarian, regardless of his explicit avowals, has to some extent turned away from the world. "The sects substitute religious status for social status." [26] They are differentiated according to the varying states of grace.

When worldly prophecies are clearly invalidated, the sectarian may turn against the world in active hatred. Herein lies one of the conditions for passive, as opposed to active, response to the world. Edmund Wilson accounts for the different responses of the Essene and the Christian. The former, though belonging to a deviant sect, accepted many of the assumptions of Judaism. Hence, when the Maccabees suffered military defeat at the hands of the Romans, the Essenes had to conclude that it was willed by God. At a later stage, the dissociation between God and Caesar had been accomplished, and the Christian was

> in some ways in a stronger position than the priests who drew up the Essene oath. The Essenes are smarting and sullen—we find their attitudes toward their enemies stated bitterly and in most un-Christian terms in the Manual and in other writing; the Gospels have the heartening ring of audacity and spiritual freedom. Yet it was also, as it now appears, the sectarians that had framed this oath who were preparing, by their precepts and discipline—"to report none of their secrets even though tortured to death"—the resounding moral triumph of Christianity.[27]

24. Troeltsch, *op. cit.*, p. 339.
25. Ellsworth Faris, "The Sect and the Sectarian," *American Journal of Sociology,* LX (May, 1955), pp. 75–89.
26. Pope, *op. cit.*, p. 137.
27. Edmund Wilson, *The Scrolls from the Dead Sea* (New York: Oxford University Press, Inc., 1955), pp. 37ff.

The opposition between the sect and the dominant social order manifests itself in its recruitment from among the culturally disaffected. In addition, the sect tends to isolate itself from the community out of which it has emerged. The names of American settlements founded by sects, often on a communistic basis, are many. For instance, the founding of Providence by Roger Williams, of the Oneida community by John Humphrey Noyes and his followers, and the Mormon trek into Utah were, by virtue of the industry and frugality of the sectarians, among the more successful. The survival of the sect is not guaranteed by physical isolation, for it cuts the sect off from its natural reservoir of recruits among the socially alienated.

When not leading a sheltered communal existence, in which its principles are put into practice, the sect maintains its character by such means as bizarre customs and forms of worship, a special vocabulary and forms of address, insistence on rituals, and full initiation of its new members into secrets only after a period of trial. But the measures designed to insure doctrinal purity also transform the sectarian spirit. Sectarian fervor tends to wane as its doctrine crystallizes. Schisms may develop. More important, like the gang in its terminal phase, these religious sects take on the character of conventional groups—especially for second-generation followers. Religious sects become denominations or, as in the case of political sects or esthetic secession, a political party or school takes shape. These become accommodated to the existing order and may eventually be completely assimilated.

THE FAN CULT

The phenomenon of the fan club illustrates quite well the crystallization of the expressive crowd into permanent form. The behavior that such clubs so studiously cultivate and the collective revelry in which they engage pretty much exhaust their purpose in being. The really enthusiastic devotee of a celebrity is not content to read about his idol in fan magazines or to send him lovelorn letters. To express his feelings adequately, he joins with others. The source from which fan clubs blossom forth is the spontaneous enthusiasm of such devoted admirers.

These clubs are the elementary nuclei of the fan cult. Of course, the image of the idol, usually from the world of entertainment or of sports, is carefully cultivated by publicity agents. Moreover, the initial impetus often comes from persons with a stake in his future and occasionally from deliberate plants. It would nevertheless be an exaggeration to explain the mushrooming of fan clubs only in terms of the engineering of a publicity agent. The overwhelming majority of local clubs form as a spontaneous effort to channel the enthusiasm generated by a public figure. Mass media communications and careful promotion have merely contributed to the massive scale and the faddish way in which these modern cults emerge. Societies and clubs formed in admiration of some actor or literary figure have been common among the elite publics of the theater or literature long before the nickelodeon and the cinema made such idols accessible to almost everybody.[28]

The James Dean cult is of special interest because it highlights one aspect common in the cult of the hero—his immortality. He is endowed with superhuman qualities, which enable real heroes, as well as legendary characters, to survive evidence of mortality. James Dean, a young movie actor, was killed while racing in his Porsche sports car. A rumor that he was still alive was soon printed in several gossip columns. It was immediately seized on by his following. This rumor was superb publicity for two of his movies, which had not yet been released at the time of his death. The same reluctance to accept death appears in legends about "sleeping" heroes—for example, the myth of Barbarossa—in the recurrent rumors that Hitler did not actually die in Berlin, and in the overwhelming public reaction to the death of Rudolph Valentino.

The hero cult practiced by the fan clubs is only a special case of a widespread phenomenon. In sociological literature, a *cult* is generally any collectivity that cultivates a particular kind of personal experience or set of practices among its followers. It entails adherence to some rudimentary ideology, usually reinforced by a legendary image, but there is no unyielding group code of the kind that characterizes the ideal-typical gang or religious sect. The experience for which people strive may be salvation, and to this extent the cult borders on the sect. It may involve healing or the belief in the efficacy of a set of unorthodox practices. In the main, however, the cult involves not the doctrines themselves but their practical expression. The abstract collectivity of a cult is co-extensive with the spread of practices stemming from its beliefs. As Becker put it, "instead of joining a cult, an act which implies the consent of others, one simply chooses to believe in particular theories or follow certain practices, and the consent of other members of the cult is not necessary." [29] In the special case of the fan cult, the participants seek the psychological uplift that stems from their shared admiration of a hero.

Still, the abstract collectivity of believer-practitioners does not exist apart from a particular group context. In the elementary nucleus of the fan club, the fans are drawn together as they begin to communicate with

28. Richard Moody, *The Astor Place Riot* (Bloomington, Ind.: Indiana University Press, 1958) provides a good example.

29. Leopold von Wiese and Howard Becker, *Systematic Sociology* (New York: John Wiley & Sons, Inc., 1932), p. 627.

one another. This appears to be true of every cult.[30] In these local groups, the cult members develop a special set of symbols based largely on the imitation of characteristic phrases, gestures, ways of dress, etc., of their model. There is a high premium on knowledge about his public performances and the nonpublic aspects of his "private" life. In the fan clubs, the cultists try to outdo each other; high status depends on successful imitation and on acquisitions which establish a fan's closeness to the idol. By creating an apparently intimate relation between himself and a person actually separated by great social distance, the fan actually shares in the esteem due the star.

The fan club also cultivates styles that are somewhat deviant or are, at least, exaggerated versions of those currently accepted. While the gang stands in a special relationship with the crowd and the sect with religious revival, the fan club's main significance is its relation with fashion. Marlon Brando and James Dean became the special heroes of black-leather-jacketed motorcycle enthusiasts—roles they had played on the screen. One sixteen-year-old president of a Jimmy Dean club admitted that "a lot of boys I know don't like Jimmy. But they respect him. He's so different from the boys in high school. He did what he wanted to do. If he didn't want to do something, he didn't. Nobody bossed him." One of the more recent idols of adolescent alienation has been Elvis Presley, whose imitators have at times been sent home from school because of their conspicuous sideburns and later, pushing their identification still farther, for wearing draftee Presley's "dog tags."

The sociological category of gang or sect often shades over into that of fan following. The disaffected have always sought special heroes. Gangs, for example, have the wrong heroes to admire. Members of delinquent gangs are most frequently drawn to heroes from the world of sports, especially prizefighting. The apparent invincibility of Al Capone, gangster of the Prohibition era, made him a special hero of gangs at one time. Other figures, like Huey Long, represented the underdog. While there are many heroic roles that represent national or "universal" models, the excessive and extreme devotion of the fans usually involves some deviance in their choice.

If the fans develop a sense of identity with each other—*esprit de corps* —they begin to differentiate themselves more clearly from those who do not share their admiration. The cult of jazz, for example, identifies not only the "beats" of San Francisco's Co-existence Bagel Shop. In Eastern

30. Eister, for example, who defines Moral Rearmament as a cult—as opposed to a sect—nevertheless insists that its "life-changing practices" seldom if ever took place apart from some group-planned or group-sponsored situation such as the houseparty of the traveling team. Other examples would be witchcraft cults, nudism, etc.

Europe this taste has become fraught with political significance, since it represents a protest against the standardized art conveying a socially important message. Likewise, a fan club may develop into a definite pressure group. In Ramseur, North Carolina, the Bing Crosby club, which represented 40 per cent of the town's population, was a power to be reckoned with. It forced the city fathers to rename one of the main drags Crosby Street.[31] Similarly, the abstract following of saints, fashion leaders, or even political figures may crystallize into a definite organization in support of specific aims. Consequently the cultivation of a legend may provide the basis for sectarian interest groups. In general, however, these legends and behavior only express sentiments that have been somewhat submerged; they transform the commonplace into the "profound" and fill with some vitality an otherwise drab existence.

THE SECRET SOCIETY

To protect their association and to cement unity among the membership, many a sectarian group takes on some characteristics of a secret society with an elaborate ritual from which nonmembers are barred; the neophyte qualifies only after a period of trial and gradual initiation. Unlike the sectarian association, out of which it arises, the secret society is hardly the result of spontaneous interaction. On the contrary, its structure is largely a matter of conscious design, in which nothing is left to chance. The common possession of a secret in itself binds the members together in a pledge of nonbetrayal. In the way the secret represents a unity against outsiders, the secret society has much in common with the other types of sectarian nucleus.

The pledge of silence effectively protects the association from external influence: sometimes by concealing its very existence, as in a revolutionary conspiracy or a criminal band; sometimes by merely preventing the diffusion of knowledge to outsiders about its membership and practices, as in certain fraternal associations. The shared secrets, from which outsiders are excluded, inevitably strengthen internal bonds, because everyone must have explicit confidence in the psychological capacity and honor of those sworn to secrecy.

The protest that differentiates gang from sect is a substantive distinction, but the category of secret society is a formal one. Thus, secrecy has a role in the development of a religious sect, where admission is also made contingent on passing a series of "tests." Access to the secret always marks the initiates as an elite, from which those not yet proved worthy are excluded. In this exclusiveness one observes the foundation of an

31. Mentioned by M. F. Thorp, *America at the Movies* (New Haven: Yale University Press, 1939).

aristocratic principle. Because secrecy is able to reinforce the superiority of the religiously elect, the natural inclination of the isolated sect is to move in the direction of the secret society.

Gangs also tend to become secret societies. Naturally gangs of assassins, like the Thugs or the Mafia, have employed secrecy to avoid detection, while secret codes and hiding places fascinate even the most innocent of boys' gangs. Thrasher's study revealed that gangs may develop the features of a secret society for two reasons: (1) because secrecy, initiation, ritual, passwords, codes, etc., serve a real function or (2) because the knowledge of secret societies inspires imitation.[32] A document describing Itschkie's Black Hand Society, a gang of about fifteen boys, twelve to fifteen years old, illustrates these functions.

> The real gang is a small, compact, select body around which there forms a wide fringe of more or less harmless would-be gang boys who remain on "probation," so to speak, and serve as protection for the central nucleus of the group. The real gang is a close, secret organization, operating on a business basis. Meetings are held in secret; plans and campaigns are formulated; tasks are assigned to members especially trained by their leaders for their particular jobs; signals are worked out: and finally—the deed accomplished—the proceeds are pooled . . .
>
> New members are chosen with great care and must often serve long periods of probation. . . . The prospective Black Hander must also be compatible: he must go through a grilling by every member of the group, in order to make sure that he is "game for anything," that he is sufficiently tough—for on these two points the members greatly pride themselves. Finally, once a gang boy, he remains, save in exceptional cases, under the complete domination of the group, pledged to tell no secrets and to divulge no plans.
>
> It is around the leader . . . that the gang crystallizes . . . On the fringe of the gang are many younger boys who would like to be gang boys but who are not yet quick enough at the trade to make their gang membership pay, or who are not yet old enough to appreciate the necessity of keeping still . . . Itschkie's gang, carrying out a series of delinquent enterprises in the face of police and neighborhood opposition, evolved secret signs and other devices for the purpose of mutual protection . . . strong opposition necessities centralized control and severe discipline. Thus, in Itschkie's group there developed a compact body in the gang, differentiated from mere fringers and hangers-on, who could not be trusted or initiated into the gang's secrets.[33]

32. Thrasher, *op. cit.*, p. 68.
33. *Ibid.*, pp. 310–24.

Conventionalization may in time make the preservation of the secret membership, ritual, usages, formula, and doctrines a primary and conscious purpose of the association. Hutton Webster has explained the rise of secret societies among preliterate peoples as an outgrowth of initiation ceremonies. Societies among the men of a tribe like the Hopi exists for the more effective domination of uninitiated outsiders. Such domination becomes impossible once knowledge of the true nature of the kachinas that are used to frighten recalcitrants is diffused.

Notwithstanding this process of conventionalization into a hardened structure, the secret society, because of its relation to outsiders, can be included among the sectarian cells. Its development presupposes the existence of a society in opposition to which it has formed. "Within the larger circle" of this society, wrote Simmel, "it opposes a narrower one; whatever the purpose of the society, their opposition has, at any rate, the sense of exclusion." [34]

Perhaps its sectarian character can be seen more clearly if we contrast the secret society with a typical interest group. The latter exhorts individuals to join in pursuit of some particular purpose. Apart from its relevance to his contribution to the attainment of the goal, the personality of the member remains "anonymous." He participates only in a segmented role. His commitment to the group is limited. Consequently a multitude of special interest groups, to any number of which each person may be committed, exist as an integral part of the social order. By contrast, commitment to the secret society is more total. Anything that may diminish the ability of a member to keep his lips sealed matters to a group that considers separation from the rest of society—however temporary—essential to its purposes.

Because of its secrecy, the clandestine association enjoys a measure of license. It can transgress normal conventions. In this respect it matters little whether the association harbors a political conspiracy or rebels against the law by engaging in collective crimes. Secret orgies or unorthodox forms of worship (the infamous black mass) may also be substantive motives. Or the association may usurp for itself the right to take the law into its own hands—for example, the twelfth-century Vendicosi, the German Vehmgericht (resurrected in modern form by nationalists following the German surrender after World War I), or the Ku Klux Klan. The essence of the secret society is at least a partial autonomy from the social order from which it segregates itself.

But this autonomy, as Simmel cautions, may easily lead to anarchy. Therefore, the coercive, seemingly senseless, and highly conventionalized practices of the secret society have a definite function: to answer the need for some normative order.

34. Simmel, *op. cit.*, p. 362.

In the secret society the nature of ritual . . . is by no means inconsistent with group freedom which resembles anarchy, with severance from the norms of the inclusive society. On the contrary, just as the widespread diffusion of secret societies is usually proof of public unfreedom, of a tendency toward police regimentation and of political oppression, in short, just as it is a reaction stemming from the need for freedom—so, conversely, the internal, ritual regimentation of a secret society reflects a measure of freedom and severance from society at large which entails the counter-norm of this very schematism, in order to restore the equilibrium of human nature.[35]

The cells of social movements, especially under despotic regimes, thus germinate in the shelter of secrecy.

THE MECHANISMS OF ELEMENTARY ASSOCIATION

The variety of forms in which alienation from the social order finds elementary expression, the variety of forms which provide shelter in which new norms mature should not obscure their underlying similarities. The following propositions outlining the natural history by which these nuclei come into being summarize the general pattern and need to be modified in relation to the specific forms that they take.

1. Sectarian associations form at the fringes of the social order in response to needs unrecognized by established organizations.

2. The subjective origins of the sectarian association lie in the spontaneous interaction among persons drawn together by some vague disaffection.

3. The opposition that the divergent nucleus excites from its environment solidifies the loose affinities into an association with a group consciousness. Its solidarity, morale, esprit de corps, its conventional practices, and the rudiments of its ideology are promoted by the clash with hostile forces.

4. During its early phases, the internal structure evolves as the direct response to each individual's participation in the common activity.

5. The sectarian association, because of its opposition to the larger society, demands more complete commitment and greater devotion than more segmented organizations. There are few areas in which discretion vis-à-vis fellow members is to be allowed.

6. Two courses appear to be open to the sectarian association that would preserve its integrity in the face of opposition: conventionalization as a clandestine sect or underground organization—a secret society; or accommodation to the dominant society so that it may operate openly as

35. *Ibid.*, p. 361.

part of it. The readiness with which the sectarian association is able to gain acceptance seems to determine which of the two courses it follows.

SIGNIFICANCE OF THE ALIENATED NUCLEUS

THE SECTARIAN ASSOCIATION would hardly be considered more than an incidental rubric under collective dynamics were it not for the fact that it marks the transition from elementary and unorganized social patterns into the more organized ones. Thus, the significance of such a group goes beyond the activities of its participants; it constitutes more than a whimsical aberration or a temporary pathology. Not only is it symptomatic of general disaffection but the sectarian association forms the fundament for efforts at general social reconstruction. In this respect its significance is threefold: (1) it offers the psychological support requisite for permanence by which doctrines, cultish fads, and other practices in violation of norms are sustained; (2) ideologies and doctrines, in the shelter of the group, are nurtured to the point at which they can be openly presented; and (3) through agitation and proselytizing the message is ultimately carried to a larger following which constitutes a social movement.

PSYCHOLOGICAL VALIDATION

The "group psychological support" that participants render to one another in their counternorm behavior constitutes one of the most important facets of the sectarian's psychology. An association usually develops around a key individual, such as an especially daring delinquent, a person endowed with charisma, or a glamorous Hollywood idol. His personal qualities spark behavior among a following. To the extent that the sectarian group monopolizes the loyalties of its following, it lowers self-consciousness in terms of the norms of the larger world by means of a group code, which provides insurance against conventional values and worldly possessions. The group climate is thus conducive to the free expression of unconventional behavior. In contrast to the transitory redefinition of behavior in the crowd, the influence of the sectarian association appears to operate to some degree even if other members are not physically together.

One encounters this mutual insurance time and again. A band of criminals bears the guilt evoked by their antisocial acts more easily when they have a model who acts free of guilt. Marie Hossenlopp in her study of juvenile thieves gives an excellent description of how they mutually reinforced one another's behavior.[36] For some members of these gangs, participation under a boy much more antisocial than they constitutes a regression toward a form of infantile activity and sociability; in other words, they revert to the irresponsibility of infancy. In the more highly organized gang, such "guilt insurance" comes from the delinquent code that protects them against identification with individuals who threaten the basic allegiance to the sectarian principles. The Youth Board Worker must be accepted by the "group" as no "threat" before he can hope to make contact with the boys. And "the only good cop is a dead one," so nobody makes friends with a cop—even his brother.

MATURATION OF IDEOLOGY

To the degree that the sectarian association evolves some more or less stable group code, there is an insistence on purity and full commitment. This, in turn, facilitates the development of an ideology and a strategy for action, which may ultimately reach full fruition in a larger social movement. Thus, the delinquent gang is often the training ground for initiation into the codes and techniques of professional crime. The Essene, pledged to a code of absolute love for his fellow sectarians, prepared the way for the ultimate victory of Christianity.

The role of the "ideologically pure" sectarian nucleus has sometimes been ignored, at other times exaggerated. Wesley used small prayer groups in which mutual confessors kept watch on each other. Lenin in 1902, during the split among Russian Social Democrats, insisted on complete ideological purity. Each revolutionary was to be a professional and subject to the strict supervision of the party. Persons like Martov and Plekhanov (known as Lenin's teacher), who held "heretical" views, were expelled. While it would be an exaggeration to say that the subsequent revolutions occurred according to blueprint, the general ideology, rationale, and thought patterns were nevertheless developed in these nuclei.

AGITATION AND PROSELYTIZATION

The discipline and rigorousness of the highly developed sectarian association makes it eminently suitable as an instrument for agitation. The contrast between sectarian associations that are "exclusive" and those that are "universalistic" in their aim has probably been overemphasized. Every developing sect seems to have an urge to find a larger following, even if that following is not initiated into its innermost life. As a matter of fact, sectarian exclusiveness and the quest for universal in-

---

36. Marie Hossenlopp, *Essaie psychologique sur les bandes de voleurs jeunes* (Clermont-Ferrand: Imprimerie generale, 1944).

fluence are complementary, rather than antagonistic, principles. The search for influence stems from the imbalance between the divine inspiration of the sectarian group and its rejection by others. The sectarian's total commitment, the conclusion that outsiders are misguided, and the separateness of the sect helps to make the doctrine an effective instrument of persuasion.

Again, it is in political and religious sects that one finds the most active and dedicated proselytizers. The ordinary person is not a *homo politicus*, and his dedication to ideals is only partial. The religious and political ideas that are, as the historians say, always "in the air," are brewed in the sectarian association; to say that ideas are being discussed everywhere is only to say that by one route or another they have entered men's minds. Thus, Trotsky raised the question: Who led the February revolution in Russia which so suddenly led to the abdication of the Czar? He argued against the theory of spontaneous conception: the revolution was not impersonal but merely nameless:

> In every factory, in each guild, in each company, in each tavern, in the military hospital, at the transfer stations, even in the depopulated villages, the molecular network of revolutionary thought was in progress . . . Elements of experience, criticism, initiative, self-sacrifice, seeped down to the mass and created, invisibly to a superficial glance but no less decisively, an inner mechanics of the revolutionary movement as a conscious process.[37]

Conscious and experienced workers educated in the party of Lenin brought the unrest to fruition. But, Trotsky immediately adds, they, while able to guarantee the victory of the insurrection, were "not adequate to . . . transfer immediately into the hands of the proletarian vanguard the leadership of the revolution."[38] Clearly, for that, conscious preparation and planning by an active inner core were required. What gives the sectarian revolt or the unfocused collective crime the name of revolution is its ultimate victory. As the sectarian ideology becomes universally sanctioned, there results the kind of mass conversion that genuinely ushers in a new order.

37. Leon Trotsky, *History of the Russian Revolution* (New York: Simon and Schuster, Inc., 1937), p. 151.
38. *Ibid.*, p. 152.

B I B L I O G R A P H Y

ASBURY, HERBERT. *The Gangs of New York.* New York: Alfred A. Knopf, Inc., 1928. An account of underworld gangs.

CARR, EDWARD H. *The Romantic Exiles.* New York: Frederick A. Stokes Company, 1933. Essays on the major Russian revolutionary figures and circles in the nineteenth century.

CLARK, ELMER T. *The Small Sects in America.* New York: Abingdon Press, 1949 (revised edition). Descriptions of the many small religious groups in the United States.

CRANE, A. R. "Pre-Adolescent Gangs: a Socio-Psychological Interpretation," *Journal of Genetic Psychology,* LXXXVI (June, 1955), pp. 275–79. An explanation of why most preadolescents join non-delinquent gangs.

COHEN, ALBERT K. *Delinquent Boys: The Culture of the Gang.* Glencoe, Ill.: The Free Press, 1955. An explanation of delinquent gangs as a subcultural solution to the status problems of lower-class boys.

HOBSBAWM, E. J. *Social Bandits and Primitive Rebels.* Glencoe, Ill.: The Free Press, 1959. A study of "pre-political" protests and social movements.

NIEBUHR, H. RICHARD. "Sects," *Encyclopedia of Social Sciences,* edited ALVIN W. JOHNSON (Vol. XIII). New York: The Macmillan Co., 1937. A brief but excellent discussion of the sociological concept of sect.

POPE, LISTON. *Millhands and Preachers: a Study of Gastonia.* New Haven: Yale University Press, 1942. A now classic study of the sect type of religious organization in a Southern milltown.

REDL, FRITZ. "The Psychology of Gang Formation and the Treatment of Juvenile Delinquents," *The Psychoanalytic Study of the Child* (Vol. I, pp. 367–77). New York: International Universities Press, 1945. Deals with the various psychological mechanisms by which gang behavior spreads.

SHERIF, MUZAFER, and SHERIF, C. W. *Groups in Harmony and Tension* (chaps. 8–9). New York: Harper & Brothers, 1953. An experimental study in a boys' camp which documents the role of conflict in the development of group cohesion.

SIMMEL, GEORG. *The Sociology of Georg Simmel* (Part IV). Glencoe, Ill.: The Free Press, 1950. A discussion of the role of secrecy and of secret societies.

THRASHER, FREDERICK M. *The Gang*. Chicago: The University of Chicago Press, 1927. Based on data of 1,313 boys' gangs in Chicago, it contains much vivid description and a discussion of the gang and related social phenomena.

WILSON, BRYAN R. "An Analysis of Sect Development," *American Sociological Review*, XXIV (February, 1959), pp. 3–15. A general discussion of the sociology of the sect.

YABLONSKI, LEWIS. "The Delinquent Gang as a Near-Group," *Social Problems*, VII (Fall, 1959), pp. 108–17. A conceptualization of the gang as an elementary collective phenomenon intermediate between the crowd and the organized group.

III

Susceptibility and Polarization

III

The Mechanisms of Contagion

MANY INDIVIDUAL DEVIATIONS from normative patterns do not become collective. But the ones that do are spread because individuals tend to act, think, or feel as they observe others acting, thinking, or feeling. Thus, an individual hallucination becomes a rumor, personal cowardice in the face of danger becomes collective demoralization, private acts of aggression turn into a lynch mob. Likewise, individual innovations flourish into fads or fashions; opinion that at first appears radical begins to attract support from all over. The epidemic aspects of these breaks in the established patterns are often referred to as "social," "mental," or "behavioral" contagion. However vivid a metaphor it is, the concept of contagion does little to explain the actual phenomenon.

THE EXPLANATION OF CONTAGION

CONTAGION has been attributed to a variety of mechanisms, all of which may fall into one of three classes: imitation, circular reaction, and suggestibility. Regardless of the specific usage given these terms by various writers, we define them:

Imitation is the tendency to do the same thing that one observes others doing.

Circular reaction is a process by which the emotions of others elicit the same emotions in oneself, which in turn intensify the emotions of others.

Suggestibility is an abnormal state of hypersensitivity to images, directives, and propositions emanating from others.

The following discussion of these mechanisms of contagion is not a full critical treatment of the writings of the scholars mentioned. The citations are for purposes of illustration only.

IMITATION

WALTER BAGEHOT   Writing under the world-shaking impact of Darwinism and evolution, Bagehot stressed the existence of an irreducible proclivity toward imitation. Such a proclivity, he held, is especially pronounced among primitive peoples and is the foundation of individual habit and custom. In the more advanced stages of civilization, imitation becomes overlaid with rational discussion, but it continues to manifest itself in everyday life.

Men, both grave and frivolous, Bagehot argued, were equally susceptible to imitation. On the money market, he wrote, "you will find one day everyone enterprising, enthusiastic, vigorous, eager to buy, and eager to order: in a week or so you will find almost the whole society depressed, anxious, and wanting to sell. . . . These opinions were formed not by reason, but by mimicry." [1] Literary styles, fashions, political meetings, general opinion, and ultimately national character were used to illustrate this innate propensity. Its operation is often unconscious; yet, according to Bagehot, we respond with great pain if our imitations fail.

GABRIEL TARDE   The assumption "that the propensity of man to imitate what is before him [was] one of the strongest parts of his nature" is hardly the kind of "truth" Bagehot took it to be. But it served him and many others who followed as a postulate to explain the existence of society as well as some of the particular tendencies in a society. Hence, it is in this regard that its explanatory value must be examined. Bagehot himself never explored all the ramifications inherent in his theory; it remained for a French sociologist, Gabriel Tarde, to base a systematic sociology on the conception of an irreducible human instinct of imitation. Just as biology had its substructure in the laws of habit and heredity, astronomy in the laws of gravitation, and physics in the laws of vibration, so, too, according to Tarde, sociology was concerned with the general laws of imitative repetition.[2]

The main difficulty with this postulate is its use to explain both structured *and* spontaneous behavior. Like Tarde, William James deduced man's educability and thus the whole of civilization and social structure from this single trait. The proclivity to imitate was viewed as a fundamentally adaptive response. Later, when Trotter postulated a "herd instinct," imitation was endowed with survival value; from it man

1. Walter Bagehot, *Physics and Politics* (Boston: Beacon Press, Inc., 1956), p. 69f.
2. Gabriel Tarde, *Social Laws* (New York: The Macmillan Co., 1899), p. 61.

derived the unique advantage of homogeneity, so helpful in the struggle for existence.[3]

Tarde's indiscriminate use of the term "imitation" very quickly became a target of criticism. Critics charged, and justifiably, that

> he was not content with treating every case where the sight or hearing of any action results in the performance of similar action as an instance of a general instinct of Imitation but groups under the name of Imitation, acts which are in no sense results of the observation of similar acts. Two men who have never seen each other may walk in much the same way because, being men, they have legs of much the same shape, or they may both use safety matches because they find them the most convenient way of getting fire, and in either case Tarde ascribes their action to Imitation. Even if a woman buys a hat at the same shop where she herself bought one before, she declares that she acts from Memory and that Memory is a kind of Imitation.[4]

Tarde uses the word "imitation" in so many senses, and so runs the various senses into each other, that, notwithstanding their apparent scientific modernity, many formulations contained in his *Lois de l'imitation* are baffling and unsatisfactory.[5]

When its meaning is stretched to explain every instance of human similarity, the concept of imitation becomes nothing but a descriptive label. As an *analytic construct*—a tool for analyzing and understanding what we do not already know—it fails entirely. For example, to explain how innovation "catches," Tarde includes under the concept of imitation the phenomena of *opposition* (the conflict between two imitative streams) and *adaptation* (the reconciliation between them). Thus, his scheme goes as follows: Imitation makes for similarity by imposing what Bagehot calls the yoke of custom. But the very imitation of a strong impulse, a dire need, an innovation, or an invention—a random occurrence—sets up a new current, which is in opposition to the older current of custom. These clashing currents of imitation must be reconciled, or combined through adaptation.

WILLIAM F. OGBURN   Tarde's scheme of analysis has found a broad sociological application in William F. Ogburn's theory of social change.[6] According to Ogburn, innovation occurs most frequently in the

3. W. Trotter, "Herd Instinct," *Sociological Review*, I (1908), pp. 231–42; or *Instincts of The Herd in Peace and War* (London: T. F. Unwin, 1916).

4. Graham Wallas, *The Great Society* (New York: The Macmillan Co., 1932), p. 120.

5. The analogy with photographic processes suggests also that a times Tarde is really dealing with suggestibility.

6. William F. Ogburn, *Social Change* (New York: The Viking Press, Inc., 1922).

realm of technology through "invention." The rate of invention is directly dependent on the number of available elements in the material culture. Each new invention sets off a stream of imitations. Still, the habits required by the new technology tend to clash with the prevailing traditions; the latter change but slowly. In Tarde's terms, this marks the opposition between two currents of imitation. Ogburn points to the existence of a cultural lag, whenever adaptation of old habits—outmoded and no longer useful—to the new technology is blocked by strong sentiments.

Learning Theory

This formulation, however, offers no psychologically adequate explanation of why sometimes it is the past that is tenaciously imitated, while at other times it gives way easily to imitations of new innovations. Under what circumstances is opposition rather than adaptation likely to spread by imitation?

Much social behavior appears to be imitative, but little evidence has been adduced to support Tarde in his postulation of an irreducible imitative tendency. Children do ape their elders, and many of the behavioral forms in crowds, in fashion, as well as in highly conventionalized activity have the outward appearance of imitation. More recent psychological theory has located the sources of imitative behavior in learning.

An explanation of the emergence of imitative tendencies on the basis of learning postulates an organism whose behavior, to begin with, is determined solely by organic tensions. Behavior is unfocused in the sense that it is not directed toward objects in the environment. Among the many "chance" acts that occur, those are strengthened that, although innate tendencies, result in a reduction of tension.

In what circumstances will an act have this "effect"? The answer is given in terms of responses that are "reinforced." As a result of repeated experiences, an organism learns to discriminate among "cues." An object or an event serves as a cue if it "signals" that a specific act (response) will remove the tension that motivated the act. Linkages between responses and the cues eliciting them become established because the "effect" follows the act. Each time the tension is removed, the link between the response and the cue is reinforced.

Children learn rather early in life to make responses that are imitative of the acts of others. As their ability to discriminate among cues is limited and they do not know what responses to make, children turn to the people from whom rewards are generally expected. Confronted with an unfamiliar event, a child turns to its mother. The smile on her face suggests a friendly act and elicits from her infant charge a broad smile expressing comfort. Moreover, when after random exploration a response that duplicates that of another person leads to a removal of tension, the behavior of that other person will become a cue for him in other situations. Thus, imitative behavior follows the laws of social interaction.

Imitation must, however, be viewed as a very specific kind of response. Miller and Dollard differentiate among three apparently similar forms of matched behavior: same behavior, copying, and imitation, or matched-dependent behavior.[7] In *same behavior* "two people perform the same act in response to independent stimulation by the same cue, each having learned by himself to make the response. Two persons, for instance, may take the same bus because each reads the card indicating its destination." [8] In the characteristic case of *copying*, one person learns to model his behavior on that of another, and it is crucial that the copier know when his behavior matches the model's. "Training to copy often begins with an external critic who rewards similarity and punishes dissimilarity; in the end the copier must be able to respond independently to the cues of sameness and difference." [9] Thus, the music teacher sings certain notes, and then punishes the copier for singing off key or rewards him with praise for singing on key.

Matched-dependent behavior occurs when the leader, but not the follower, is able to read the relevant environmental cues. The imitator then is dependent upon the leader, whom he watches for signals about what to do when and where. Since presumably the leader is able to discern the cues and govern his behavior by them, the imitator merely uses the leader as a cue for his responses. But he does not have to expend effort on duplicating exactly the act of the leader: the ability to make the response must have been previously acquired. Acts that are too inconvenient or too complicated will not be matched.[10]

Matched-dependent behavior of this kind tends to occur whenever one person is older, shrewder, or more skilled than another. "What is crucial is that the cue from the leader's behavior is often more stable than other cues provided by the environment." [11] The leader makes his own response to cues in his environment more regularly and discriminatingly than his imitator, who depends on the leader's response. Left to his own devices, the imitator would be at a loss about what to do. For example, children learn to imitate bigger children in a variety of

7. Neal E. Miller and John Dollard, *Social Learning and Imitation* (New Haven: Yale University Press, 1941), p. 92f.
8. *Ibid.*, p. 92.
9. *Ibid.*, p. 92.
10. *Ibid.*, p. 11.
11. *Ibid.*, p. 97.

situations. The child who feels confused by the alternatives facing him in a strange situation may find it easier to follow the older children than to learn how to master the situation by himself. Likewise, the student may find it easier to copy the answers from somebody else's math paper than to work them out himself. The adult lost in the labyrinth of the subway station tends to follow the "crowd."

An imitative response that is learned and strongly reinforced in one situation tends to become generalized to similar leaders and similar situations. It is not, however, generalized toward *every* available model. Individuals learn to think of some persons (or types) as good or bad models depending upon whether or not imitation of them has been rewarding. Whom a person imitates depends principally on whether he perceives an analogy between his own social position and that of the potential model. Whether or not a person imitates depends also on whether or not the behavior observed in a given situation appears to offer a suitable role-model. A person's ability to discern useful or suitable models in the behavior of others determines the extent to which he is likely to imitate.

This mechanism of imitation, conceptualized in terms of learning, thus helps to explain the diffusion of demonstrably useful practices as well as the spread of opinion and fashion.

IMITATION AND UNSTRUCTURED SITUATIONS

In some instances, people seem to imitate indiscriminately. To explain this some psychologists find it necessary to fall back on the assumption that a generalized tendency to imitate was implanted early in life. Thus, in an ill-defined situation, imitation ceases to depend on an assessment of status, and models are chosen with little discrimination. This facilitates the acting out of tendencies normally held in check and leads a temporary dissolution of social norms. Neither of these results can be explained in terms of past learning, unless one accounts for a sudden change in the reward structure of the situation. Analysis indicates that contagion is hardly indiscriminate, but it depends on the meanings people attach to particular acts in particular situations.

Miller and Dollard have applied their theory to a lynch mob.[12] They think that a common stimulus to which most of the participants would have responded individually, even if they had been alone, is essential. (In the case studied, it was the commission of a crime.) Individual responses are then intensified by stimuli from other persons in the crowd. The large numbers signal the assurance of anonymity. Also the individual has learned through past experience that following the crowd is

12. *Ibid.,* Chap. XV ("Analyzing a Lynching").

likely to be rewarding; at least it is a safer bet than going it alone. Consequently, perceiving oneself in the presence of a crowd, all of whom are doing the same thing, reinforces the primary stimulus, around which the crowd formed, and helps to channel and direct the response.

This theory is easily expanded to explain collective phenomena. It offers a useful and consistent explanation, which is, moreover, supported by a wealth of data from learning experiments conducted on animals as well as on humans. But it tends to emphasize the predictable and conventional aspects of crowd behavior and to avoid the problem of unconventional and forbidden behavior.

CIRCULAR REACTION AND EMOTIONAL RAPPORT

Most interpersonal communication involves interpretation of meanings, and we speak of this as *symbolic communication*. Once language in any form has been acquired, people cease to react directly to a vocal gesture, movement, or act; they respond instead to the meaning behind them. To the extent that A is aware what B's action means—that is, he can "read" B's intentions—A reacts to the significance that this action has both for B's future conduct and for his own in relation to B. But if B now takes into account the significance A will read into B's act, and if this significance is the same for both, the meaning of the act is shared by both. By virtue of this, the act becomes a significant symbol, and from now on the behavior of both A and B is oriented to this shared meaning. Language, society, and culture are made up of precisely such symbols whose meanings are shared and thus fixed.

Certain writers consider the direct communication of feeling and affects to be more elementary than symbolic communication. Emotions, they say, are conveyed nonsymbolically; that is, people directly "sense" the feelings behind bodily movements, tone of voice, postural gesture, though—unlike words—these have no precisely fixed meaning. Indeed, these motions, expressions, and intonations are "expressive" and not usually framed by their transmitter with any intent to communicate. On the contrary, the transmitter often tries to control his expressions and to conceal clues to his psychic state.[13] In general, the direct transmission of feelings and emotions through what is often termed "sympathy" is seen to differ from symbolic communication in three ways:

1. The behavior of the person who exhibits the emotion is a direct expression of his inner state and altogether without communicative intent.

2. The response of the receiver is spontaneous and impressive in-

13. Among the writings of Herbert Blumer on nonsymbolic interaction, see "Social Attitudes and Non-Symbolic Interaction," *Journal of Educational Sociology*, IX (1936), pp. 515–23.

asmuch as no specific meaning can be pinned to any particular gesture (in contrast to the specific meaning given words).

3. The communication does not involve interpretation of symbols, but rather something in the way of intuitive understanding, based on a feeling of familiarity with the same emotion in oneself.

This "spontaneous and direct response to the gestures and actions of the individual, without intermediation of any interpretation," as Blumer describes it, is most likely to occur under conditions of extreme emotional agitation. Then, despite attempts at concealment, a person reveals his mood, to which an observer immediately adapts.[14] While *imitation* was used to explain the contagion of behavior, *circular reaction* refers to the spread of like feelings out of which similar behavior develops. Emotional expressions convey a mood, which is relayed from person to person simply by the effect of its visible manifestation. McDougall and, later, Park, Blumer, and others relied on circular reaction to explain the contagion of mood. Rapport, the outcome of circular response, provides the key to crowd behavior:

> In the crowd, then, the expressions of fear of each individual are perceived by his neighbors; and this perception intensifies the fear directly excited in them by the threatening danger. Each man perceives on every hand the symptoms of fear, the blanched distorted faces, the dilated pupils, the high-pitched trembling voices, and the screams of terror of his fellows; and with each such perception his own impulse and his own emotion rise to a higher pitch of intensity, and their expressions become correspondingly accentuated and more difficult to control. So the expressions of each member of the crowd work upon all other members within sight and hearing of them to intensify their excitement; and the accentuated expressions of emotion, so intensified, react upon him to raise his own excitement to a still higher pitch; until in all individuals the instinct is excited in the highest possible degree.[15]

Expressive gestures, it is further held, exert a special claim on attention. A conscious act of decision, some self-justification, and a deliberate exertion of intelligence are required to ignore the feelings and affect implicit in these gestures because their impact is "emotional." Moreover, this kind of interstimulation occurs when emotions have already been aroused and people are excited, and when, as a consequence, their threshold of accessibility is lowered. Therefore, critical judgment is interfered with. Any intensification of excitement by its very nature

14. Erving Goffman, *Presentation of Self in Everyday Life* (New York: Doubleday & Co., Inc., 1959).

15. William McDougall, *The Group Mind* (London: G. P. Putnam's Sons, 1920), p. 36f.

thus takes a "circular form, in which individuals reflect one another's states of feeling and in so doing intensify this feeling." [16]

For Blumer the distinction between interpretative interaction and circular reaction becomes basic in understanding collective behavior. Among human beings who are in association, he writes, responses "are not made directly to the stimulation, but follow, rather, upon interpretation; further, they are likely to be different in nature from the stimulating acts, being essentially adjustments to these acts. Thus interpretative interaction . . . tends, in degree, to make people different; circular reaction tends to make people alike." [17] Consequently circular reaction is the natural mechanism of contagion in elementary collective behavior. The key to the occasional dissolution of societal norms is the heightened affect generated by circular response, which develops "rapport and unreflective responsiveness." This accounts for the conduct one observes in crazes, dancing epidemics, general rioting, and so forth, as well as for the prevailing mood of a population during an epidemic of speculation or a wave of war hysteria.

Circular Reaction as an Explanatory Concept: Critique

The proposition that feelings expressed in emotional gestures are directly conveyed to others in whom they elicit a similar response which in turn intensifies the original feeling must be examined in the light of psychological evidence. Is the contrast between symbolic, or interpretative, interaction and the direct contagion of emotions that results in emotional rapport really as fundamental as it appears? Is the communication of emotion necessarily more effective than words in arousing affect? And does it necessarily elicit a similar response?

1. Even though they appear automatic, responses to visible expressions of emotions, such as anger, fear, or hate, are nevertheless learned. Concerning the observation of signs of fear in others, Allport writes that we have learned to read them "as signs that *there is really something to be afraid of.* It is not fear induced from others that we experience, but our own fear of dangerous situations which has been conditioned by social stimuli." [18] In the discussion of panic, incidents on the battlefield were used to illustrate this point. For a soldier trying to control his own impulse to run away, the sight of his officer running toward the rear signifies an impending withdrawal. Fearing to be alone when

16. Herbert Blumer, "Collective Behavior," in A. M. Lee (ed.), *Principles of Sociology* (New York: Barnes & Noble, Inc., 1951), p. 170.

17. *Ibid.*, p. 170f.

18. Floyd H. Allport, *Social Psychology* (New York: Houghton Mifflin Co., 1924), p. 235.

the enemy attacks, the soldier runs after him. His frantic flight spreads his fear to other soldiers. When they follow him, his response is confirmed; it becomes circular and mushrooms into a full-blown panic rout, until ultimately no one will know the initial reason for running.

2. Even the response to social stimuli that are solely gestures entails some interpretation. A field observation of an admittedly minor stampede during General MacArthur's victory procession in Chicago following his recall from his Far Eastern command in 1951 documents how the excitement spread.

> After MacArthur and the main celebrities had passed my spot most of the people moved east toward Wabash Street, where they turned south *evidently* hoping to get another glimpse of the General. By the time I got to Lake Street, the General had passed there as well, and there was the same standing around as at the other spot. Finally the crowd began to disperse.
>
> But instead of going in the more orderly fashion that had followed the breaking up of the first crowd, these people began to run along Lake Street toward the lake. I estimated that within ten or fifteen minutes, between ten and fifteen thousand passed the spot from which I watched. *I could not figure out where they were going.* I therefore tried to stop some of the people in order to find out. After two failures (the kids were in too much of a hurry to stop), I was able to stop a young man of about twenty-five.
>
> "Where are you running?" I asked.
>
> He replied, "Where they're going."
>
> "Well, where are they going?" I asked.
>
> He looked puzzled and answered, "I don't know, but I'm going to be there."
>
> Stumped for another question . . . I let him continue. I stopped two young high school girls and finally found out that they were going to the Stevens [the hotel where the parade was to end] to see the General. The interesting thing, however, was not that people were running, but that *most of them did not know their destination.* I counted seven different people running along the street and shouting at their friends, "Where are you going?" Only once did I hear someone shout, "The Stevens!" [19]

This observer inferred that those running sought excitement; the number of people running heightened his own expectations and caused excitement in him.

This incident is roughly analogous to what happens in crowd outbursts. For example, an attack on a grain merchant or an owner of a bakery during a bread famine suggests to bystanders that a person re-

19. Report from the files of the authors.

sponsible for the shortage has been found. His anger thus aroused, the bystander joins the others. Their unanimous action documents the guilt of the victim.

3. The interpretation of a particular gesture is no more reliable than one of words. Experiments in the judging of facial expressions definitely show that they do not directly convey their meaning. The strained expression of a track star as his chest cuts the ribbon conveys his feelings accurately only if the context is understood. In evaluating character from photographs, an individual relies heavily on labels and imputes traits consistent with social stereotypes that he values or dislikes. He supplies gestures with a context that may or may not be valid just as he does with spoken or written language; if he supplies the wrong context, however, he is likely to misinterpret them.

> All expressions of an individual, when perceived by another person, *must be interpreted if they are to be understood.* Except for the lack of attribution of intention to statements that are regarded as personal or emotional expression, this process of interpretation in no way differs from that used with consciously formulated messages. Thus, in the process of daily living, emotional expression, ordinary adaptive actions, and gestures are treated in somewhat the same manner. In all three the identification of the context of a statement comes first. Our language has words for these contexts, and such nouns as "breakfast," "wedding," "cocktail party," "shopping," and "waiting," designate the occasions. After the discovery of an appropriate label for a particular situation, the attempt is made to fit the observed statement to the situation as well as to what is known about the individuals concerned. In pursuit of this aim, the identification of *roles,* including one's own, is necessary. . . . If such evaluation were not possible, we would be at a considerable loss in interpreting appropriately . . .[20]

4. Passions are aroused as easily by emotional speeches as by expressive gestures. The rumor circulating in a crowded hall about a fire arouses fear, the blood-and-thunder exhortations at a revival meeting stimulate religious affections, and the harangues of an agitator stir up anger at social authorities. Communication is linguistic. The assumption that the prevailing mood is carried primarily by the gestures of the speaker would seem to deny that words, like gestures and expressions, themselves have autistic connotations of which the listener may not be aware.

5. Bodily signs of emotion, of euphoria or fear, do not invariably produce the same emotion in an observer. This is not in itself incompatible with the theory that facilitation is caused by circular response to

20. J. Ruesch and W. Kies, *Nonverbal Communication* (Berkeley: University of California, 1957), p. 46.

emotional gestures. Circular reaction occurs only when collective excitement interferes with critical self-consciousness. Under calmer circumstances, any tendency to respond with similar feelings is held in check by conscious effort. But the display of emotion often evokes emotion that is the direct opposite of the original one. People derive courage from observing others who are more afraid than they are. Expressions of hate frequently induce fear, exhibitions of manic euphoria, disgust, etc. Collective acting out of impulses does indeed lead to a temporary dissolution of socially reinforced inhibitions. But such a situation is anxiety-producing. Unless it facilitates guilt evasion, the intensification of emotions produces *shock effect,* the very opposite of contagion.[21] The disposition to feel or act out the emotion one perceives must be present independently in the follower. The behavior of the instigator merely triggers the act of the second person because the two are "in rapport."

SUMMARY   This critique of circular reaction has pointed out: (1) that the communication of affect involves interpretative response; (2) that the interstimulation of feelings may be provoked as readily by the communication of words; and (3) that the communication of feelings may provoke responses opposite to the original stimuli.

The Nature of Emotional Rapport

In emotional rapport, the end product of circular response, the riveting of attention excludes disturbing stimuli. Those assembled are attuned to each other and feel as "one." This exclusion of the outside world occurs also in *hypnotic rapport,* explained by Hull as "selective anesthesia." [22] The hypnotic subject appears to act contrary to his normal self. His critical function, it seems, is temporarily held in abeyance. He relies on suggestions from the hypnotist. To be sure, the rapport exists between two persons only; yet the influence of the crowd is often judged to be analogous with hypnotic influence.

But hypnotic influence does not correspond to circular response because its underlying process is asymmetric: hypnotic interaction is controlled by the hypnotist from whom the suggestions emanate. The hypnotist suggests to his subject, either explicitly or implicitly, that the latter will be responsive to him and to him alone. To induce this response, the experimenter must gain the confidence of his subject. He must convince him that there is nothing to be afraid of. But while the hypnotist

21. Fritz Redl, "The Phenomenon of Contagion and 'Shock Effect' in Group Therapy," in K. R. Eissler, *Searchlights on Delinquency* (New York: International Universities Press, 1949), pp. 315–28.

22. Clark L. Hull, *Hypnosis and Suggestibility* (New York: Appleton-Century-Crofts, Inc., 1933).

evokes emotional attitudes of trust, the gestures employed in inducing a trance serve only to divert attention and, according to recent research, can be dispensed with entirely. The responsiveness of the subject depends on explicit verbal instructions and commands. Bramwell has shown that children cannot be hypnotized until after they have learned to speak.[23] Thus, hypnotic rapport, far from being a primitive response, is in part learned by the subject. He learns to behave as commanded by the hypnotist.[24]

The question of whether the emotional rapport characteristic of mass meetings, religious revivals, gold rushes, or outbursts of public sentiment constitutes a form of hypnosis is easily answered when we recognize that interstimulation in such circumstances takes place in two dimensions rather than one: leader-follower and follower-follower. *Rapport* consists of a focusing and narrowing of attention, a mutual sensitivity to feelings and behavior of others, and the exclusion of other stimuli that interfere. In talking of rapport in the group setting, one must differentiate between the two dimensions in which influence operates: the *suggestibility* between the leader who suggests and the follower who accepts; and the *identification* among all the followers. Suggestibility accounts for definitions of the situation accepted from a leader, while identification accounts for mutual facilitation, the process stipulated by emotional rapport theory. Facilitation presupposes some particular affinity among the followers. They become not only sensitive but attuned to each other; they identify with each other. As a result, barriers set by conventional role-models dissolve.

SUGGESTIBILITY

The "leader" exerts his influence by redefining the situation for the follower. The more sensitized the latter is to the former, the more uncritically will he accept his every suggestion. This sensitivity to cues from others constitutes suggestibility. It is a mechanism in contagion. But imitation of a leader follows from his suggestions only under special circumstances; in most instances of suggestion, the responses are not matched.

Normal Suggestibility

The existence of a "normal" suggestibility adds to the difficulty of explaining suggestibility in its contagious form. To accept a suggestion

23. Cited in Bernard Wolfe, *Hypnotism Comes of Age* (Indianapolis: The Bobbs-Merrill Company, Inc., 1948), p. 6.

24. Robert W. White, "A Preface to the Theory of Hypnotism," *Journal of Abnormal and Social Psychology*, XXXVI (October, 1941), p. 483.

does not entail a suspension of all critical judgment. If we begin to wonder whether what we see as green may in actuality be a shade of blue, it is often because others see it as blue. We tend to look to others to confirm our judgments. For instance, in a series of experiments, Asch was able to modify the individual's judgment about which one of three lines was the shortest.[25] An individual confronted with unanimous majorities expressing what he "knew" to be a wrong judgment, nevertheless began to doubt his own perception. Yet the introduction of even one other person supporting his judgment so reassured him that, though still in the minority, he stuck to it. In experiments on ideo-motor suggestion, blindfolded subjects usually responded with a slight forward movement to "suggestion" that elicited thoughts of falling on one's face. A subject with his eyes open and able to rely on his full sense perception would not quite respond in that way.

Not all critical functions are suspended in normal suggestibility. This state implies only a special sensitivity to cues emanating from another person (or persons) who is, speaking objectively, extrinsic to the situation but is nevertheless important to it. The task of testing reality, the judging of "what is," is assigned by the follower to another person or group. This occurs also in moral evaluations, the judging of "what is right." In evaluating a political program, for example, it is "normal" to be guided by the judgments of others. In part, this is an implicit function of generally accepted norms and frames of reference. People have learned through repeated experience to be sensitive to how others react. Sometimes one actually turns for guidance to other persons. In structured situations, everyone knows whose points of view to take into account. Furthermore, the responsiveness to prestige figures or to specific group standards may be stimulated by general symbols, such as Mother, Home, Flag.

The two conditions that are generally mentioned in the literature as conducive to normal suggestibility are: (1) the absence of an adequate mental context for responding to (or interpreting) an observation or an event; or (2) a strong disposition in the subject to fit observations into a pre-existing mental context.

We turn now to "abnormal" suggestibility. The apparent transformation in behavior that occurs during hypnosis may help to explain the dissolution of norms in other contexts.

Hypnotic Suggestibility

Hull, in his book *Hypnosis and Suggestibility*, infers a continuous progression, as well as a very real relationship, between the prestige sug-

25. Solomon E. Asch, *Social Psychology* (Englewood Cliffs, N.J.: Prentice-Hall, Inc., 1952), Chap. 16.

gestion to which persons are prone to respond in the "normal" state and the hypersuggestibility characteristic of the hypnotic trance. He supports this view with evidence that the responses of hypnotic subjects are far from automatic; posthypnotic suggestions are often carried out in highly individual ways. In response to the experimenter, moreover, the hypnotic subject is able to perform both complicated operations and difficult social roles, and although successful hypnosis temporarily drives it into the background, a vestige of critical reserve nevertheless persists. Even a relatively minor mistake—for example, a suggestion that the subject commit an act unacceptable to him—immediately weakens the depth of the spell.[26]

Persons differ in degree of susceptibility to hypnotic suggestion. Many people cannot be hypnotized at all, and even a willing subject often rebels at carrying out suggestions that go against his deeper inclinations. The hypnotic subject enters the situation with preconceptions about both experiment and experimenter. He is not a mere tool upon whom strange effects can be wrought by tapping the right level or in whom "dissociations" can be created by splitting off parts of his consciousness. The assumption that the tendencies a subject brings to the experiment are not completely inoperative during the trance is in line with observations concerning the greater susceptibility of children and the greater resistance of officers, as compared to enlisted men, to hypnosis.

According to one formulation, hypnotic behavior is "meaningful goal-directed striving, its most general goal being to behave like a hypnotized person as this is continuously defined by the operator and understood by the subject."[27] Thus, the role of the hypnotized person must be learned, and in order to want to learn that role the subject must first learn to trust the experimenter. There must be an incentive. Sarbin has depicted the strength of the motivation to become a willing hypnotic subject as influenced by two factors: the person's conception of himself and his perception of the role he is to play at the demand of the hypnotist. If the two are congruent—if, for instance, a passive person expects to play a passive role—and if no contradictions ensue to cause reservations, then the subject may be considered favorably motivated and thus willing.[28]

Data drawn from a number of sources suggest that behavior in response to hypnotic suggestion is culturally typed, that it is never far out of line with what might reasonably be expected. Sarbin cites the con-

26. M. Brenman, M. Gill, and R. P. Knight, "Spontaneous Fluctuations in Depth of Hypnosis and the Implications for Ego-Functions," *International Journal of Psychoanalysis*, XXXIII (1952), pp. 22–33.

27. White, *op. cit.*, p. 483.

28. T. R. Sarbin, "Contributions to Role-Taking Theory I: Hypnotic Behavior," *Psychological Review*, LVII (1950), p. 262.

ventional content of hallucinations. For example, the hallucinations of Plains Indians while under the influence of peyote, a drug, are partly defined by the definitions prevalent in the culture. In the *couvade,* a Melanesian custom, the husband actually experiences labor pains during the birth of his child. Individuals who fall into "ecstatic" trances in group meetings also appear to follow certain patterns.

Psychoanalysts go a step further. The hypnotist's command to sleep is a command to withdraw all interest from the world and to concentrate instead upon the hypnotist. In reactivating latent tendencies,

> the hypnotist awakens in the subject a portion of his archaic inheritance which had also made him compliant toward his parents and which had experienced an individual re-animation in his relation to his father; what is thus awakened is the idea of a paramount and dangerous personality, toward whom only a passive-masochistic attitude is possible, to whom one's will has to be surrendered—while to be alone with him, "to look him in the face," appears a hazardous experience.[29]

As a person gives up some of his normal critical functions, he is all the more amenable to outside influences. Or, to revert again to a behavioristic formulation, by holding some of one's own symbolic (thought) processes in abeyance, the influence of the symbolic actions of others gains ascendancy.

Suggestibility and Group Formation

In the one-way mechanism called suggestibility, the person influenced employs the leader as a standard; for example, the hypnotist is constantly defining standards for the behavior of the subject. This formulation is valuable in understanding group formation; as Freud put it, hypnotic situations have many of the features of two-person groups.[30] All the members of any group evaluate themselves according to the "external" standards of a leader or of a generalized or abstracted group ideal internalized by each. Such self-evaluation constitutes the essence of group formation. Only when the group is highly organized, and thus internally differentiated, do group definitions and standards vary in accordance with the individual's status and role.

The personalized group ideal represents something in which one would like to participate, in whose power one would like to share, by whom one would want to be protected, and on whom it is not dishonorable to become dependent. Being attracted to a leader, a prestige figure, a powerful personality, entails a recognition of the standards he sets

29. Sigmund Freud, *Group Psychology and the Analysis of the Ego* (London: The Hogarth Press, 1949), p. 99.
30. *Ibid.*

and a willingness to govern one's conduct by them. This does not mean that, even in a relatively undifferentiated kind of association, the object represented by the leader or the group ideal is what the follower *is*. One may cherish a movie heroine, a featured singer, an evangelist, or an agitator, who represents what is admired and what is wanted. Yet total emulation is precluded. To become like the leader—except in certain, often superficial externals—is impossible for the mass of followers. The moment the follower considers himself on absolutely equal terms with the leader, he becomes less susceptible to his suggestions, less pliant, and less responsive.

Suggestibility and Identification

The leader indirectly exerts still another kind of influence. When a group of people accept the same standards or are susceptible to suggestions from the same person, they acquire a common identity. Each sees himself as what the other *is*. Mutual identification among followers constitutes the second kind of influence that binds a group together. There is nothing mystical about this mechanism.

Unfortunately the term "identification" has been applied to a variety of object relationships. We reserve the term here to refer to the sharing of the mood of another person or acting as another acts. In this kind of identification one does not merely take another's critical attitudes as standards, but actually appropriates some characteristic or trait. One thereby extends one's self-love to objects that are one's own. For example, the mass of a people commonly react with self-satisfaction to the individual accomplishments of a few compatriots; pride in these others with whom they identify brings pride in themselves.[31]

A *group* can be defined as a plurality of persons who share an ideal or a standard that each has internalized and who, as a result of this internalization, identify with one another. Because the participants in such a group are suggestible to the views of the authority they accept, they tend to see the world in the same way, through the "eyes of the group," and thereby validate their individual observations.

ANALOGIES OF IDENTITY: CONTAGION

WHAT WAS SAID ABOUT IDENTIFICATION above holds for all groups. But what about facilitation in transient collectivities when people seem

---

31. The object in this case constitutes what Freud calls a *narcissistic* object; the "leader" object to whose suggestions the follower is susceptible is an *anaclitic* object. See Sigmund Freud, *op. cit.*, and Otto Fenichel, *Psychoanalytic Theory of Neurosis* (New York: W. W. Norton & Co., 1945).

to follow the actions and act out the emotions of others in an altogether unusual fashion? In such elementary groups individuals appear to act under momentary influences: prohibitions built up over time are temporarily inoperative, as participants are attuned to others who are often scarcely known to them and against whom they may harbor antipathy. Under the influence of such transient groups, participants become responsive to new ideals revealed in the actual behavior of the group. *The essence of behavioral or emotional contagion appears to lie precisely in the externalization of these ideals:* they are externalized by being acted out.

Accordingly, contagion occurs only with regard to behavior that the follower already has a tendency to act out. The example of others acting impulsively temporarily redefines the situation and thus triggers the tendency. Where the inner balance is labile, relatively minor provocations by others suffice to activate behavior that would otherwise be inhibited.

HYSTERICAL CONTAGION

Shared psychopathology constitutes social contagion in its most literal form. The pathological symptoms of two or more persons often depend on and sustain each other. It has long been recognized that hysteria, more than other kinds of psychopathology, is easily spread by social (or mental) contagion. The sight of the outward symptoms of hysteria—convulsions, nausea, imaginary fears—can lead to the same symptoms in the observers. Many documents on the spread of St. Vitus's dance following the Black Death suggest that this was hysteria in one of its worst epidemic forms. The nation-wide spread of hysteria has been observed in many countries during periods of stress.[32]

Local outbreaks in the United States have been investigated by clinically trained psychologists. In some instances outbreaks of "shakes" diagnosed as hysterical have forced schools to close down. This also occurred in a number of cities in Europe around 1900.[33]

Observations about the spread of hysterical symptoms produce the following generalizations: First, the onset of symptoms, such as jerkings and foaming at the mouth, is most often caused by the sight of another person so afflicted. Yet direct observation is not absolutely necessary.

32. See J. F. C. Hecker's pioneering studies on the dancing mania and other psychic epidemics during the Middle Ages; also E. H. Norman, "Mass Hysteria in Japan," *Far Eastern Survey* (January 17, 1945), pp. 65–70. Similar phenomena are described in anthropological literature on the Ghost Dance and "cargo cults."

33. See D. M. Johnson, "The 'Phantom Anaesthetist' of Mattoon: A Field Study of Mass Hysteria," *Journal of Abnormal and Social Psychology*, XL (April, 1945), pp. 175–86 and E. A. Schuler and V. J. Parenton, "A Recent Epidemic of Hysteria in a Louisiana High School," *Journal of Social Psychology*, XVII (May, 1943), pp. 221–35.

Identical symptoms have spread among persons who were only told of such an outbreak or who learned of it through newspapers and radio. Second, drastic and decisive interference with the collective response by persons in authority can halt an outbreak. Third, young girls in their teens and early twenties are the most vulnerable, as documented by psychologists and evangelists alike. For example, John Wesley was keenly aware that young girls of these very ages were most prone to respond with bodily affectations to his preachings.

THE SIGNIFICANT ANALOGY

A recognition of the erotic components of hysterical symptoms is indispensable to an interpretation of the spread of hysteria. The symptom indicates an unresolved inner conflict. A general readiness to accept guilt for some unacknowledged wish or antisocial act or a strong need, experienced by a whole group of persons, to escape from an intolerable situation of danger, depravity, or destitution opens the possibility of identification with a specific symptom that one person's ego has produced as an acceptable solution to tension. When this occurs, hysteria is likely to spread.

The kind of identification that occurs in hysteria, Freud maintains, "may arise with every new perception of a common quality shared with some other person who is not an object of the sexual instinct. The more important this common quality is, the more successful may this partial identification become, and it may thus represent the beginning of a new tie." [34] *The identification does not presuppose any prior emotional or sympathetic relationship; it results directly from the definition of the situation of those exhibiting the behavior as analogous to one's own.* Furthermore, the perceptions may occur with regard to nonpathological behavior. Temporary and transient collective outbreaks arise when new identities are unexpectedly perceived. New patterns of action or thought diffuse directly upon this perception, however odd they appear in relation to the usual objective norms of conduct.

What is meant by the externalization of ideals may be clarified by reference to the distinction between "association" and "mass" made by Waelder.[35] This approximates the distinction between collective behavior based on *normal social influence* and *contagion based on mutual identification.* An *association* exists for limited ends. Persons come together on the basis of individual interests which they share. Commitment is partial, and insofar as the particular interests underlying the as-

34. Freud, *op. cit.*, p. 65f.

35. R. Waelder, *Psychoanalytic Aspects of War and Peace* (Geneva Studies [Geneva: Geneva Research Center, 1939]).

sociation are concerned, the conscience of all members is homogeneous. Beyond soliciting their support in certain prescribed ways for the attainment of the common goal, the association has no claim on its members. The specific definition of interests and obligations minimizes discord between the demands of membership and the individual conscience. The *mass*, on the other hand, arises when some group ideal is not fully integrated into the conscience of the individuals. The mass ideals which symbolize the conflict also permit its externalization. The term "mass" is used by Waelder as a convenient designation for the spontaneous unity with which some transient formations assert certain principles in order to justify deviant forms of behavior.

This mass conscience is effective only when human beings find themselves together with large numbers of others either physically or spiritually. In the crowd they are in physical contact. Similiar identifications arise also whenever individuals feel themselves "spiritually" acting as functionaries or trustees of some mass ideal that appeals to dispositions normally held in check. A mass in this generic sense forms because, when reality is too pressing or when self-evaluations are too severe, there must be some relief. The collective elation people in crowds occasionally experience indicates that in these circumstances the boundary between what one is (the ego) and what one has to live up to (the superego) is blurred. The underlying impulses are always in danger of erupting. When they do, the contagion proceeds in directions either not yet crystallized into social structure or even in direct opposition to it. Crystallization into definite forms implies also a more permanent restructuring of the ego.

MASS CONTAGION

The emergence of a leader who represents the "typical" qualities of his following is the essential feature in the transformation of behavior in the elementary collectivity. To be sure, the leaders in a crowd are often professional agitators, and social movements attract many renegades from the dominant classes. But action is sparked by the man in the streets. Furthermore, masses, in Waelder's sense, subscribe to the myth of action; barriers and incapacities suffered by those who are or feel themselves deprived are to be eliminated. Most social movements, even when not avowedly religious, are eschatological in their ideology. The implicit promise to the "common" man, the temporary lifting of restraints, and the fusion with "mass" ideals mark this kind of collective action as pathological.

The transformation, furthermore, rests on a delusion fostered by this identification with others. Suggestibility is greater in very large collectivities because delusions gain in strength as a result of social projection. The participant can see only those with whom he is in contact. If they are like-minded, he will be able to project an image of the larger unity acting under a common impulse. "The allusion to the 'concern' of large numbers," Allport wrote as an illustration of social projection, "produces unthinking belief in the importance of the statements made. . . . The unscrupulous journalist has scored in securing attention and in controlling a portion of public opinion through social projection and the illusion of universality." [36]

The transformation of behavior in these collectivities appear regressions by comparison with the high degree of individualization most persons have achieved through participation in organized social unities. Individualization depends on a capacity for self-observation from a variety of perspectives, which become increasingly generalized (depersonalized) and organized. To see oneself as others see one means, ultimately, the internalization of some abstract principles, whereas the self-evaluations made on the basis of mutual identification have almost the exact opposite effect.

Mass contagion thus involves (1) a tendency on the part of followers to accept appeals and action that are at variance with their normal social selves but are consonant with their inner needs, and (2) a diminished willingness to appraise one's own behavior in terms of broader standards. It is most likely to occur when the behavior or emotions observed fit in with inner conflicts and thus reduce the capacity for critical self-observation.

SUMMARY   The concept of imitation helps to explain follow-the-leader behavior, when the proper response is in doubt but the goals of leaders are assumed identical with that of followers. Circular reaction draws our attention to the dissolution of norms, when collective excitement builds up a readiness to follow suggestions at variance with normal behavior. To understand the specific direction new forms of behavior take, a dynamic approach that takes account of inner conflicts is needed. Through identification, people become suggestible to propositions that appear highly irrational. Hence, the three approaches supplement each other.

B I B L I O G R A P H Y

ASCH, SOLOMON E. "The Doctrine of Suggestion, Prestige, and Imitation in Social Psychology," *Psychological Review*, LV (1948),

36. F. H. Allport, *op. cit.*, p. 309.

pp. 250–76. A critical analysis of the assumptions behind prestige suggestions, documented with a re-analysis of certain data.

BLUMER, HERBERT. "Social Attitudes and Non-Symbolic Interaction," *Journal of Educational Sociology,* IX (1936), pp. 515–23. An up-dated version, in terms of the social psychology of George Herbert Mead, of McDougall's theory of primitive sympathy.

GROSSER, DANIEL, *et al.* "A Laboratory Study of Behavioral Contagion," *Human Relations,* IV (1951), pp. 115–42. The pick-up of behavior occurs in small groups and depends on social support.

HULL, CLARK L. *Hypnosis and Suggestibility.* New York: Appleton-Century-Crofts, Inc., 1933. A discussion of hypnotic suggestion as ideo-motor suggestion with much, though now dated, experimental evidence.

MILLER, NEAL E., and DOLLARD, JOHN. *Social Learning and Imitation.* New Haven: Yale University Press, 1941. Includes data from numerous learning experiments on rats and human beings as well as an analysis of diffusion and the lynch mob in terms of learning theory.

POLANSKY, NORMAN, *et al.* "An Investigation of Behavioral Contagion in Groups," *Human Relations,* III (1950), pp. 319–48. This study should be read in conjunction with that of Daniel Grosser, *et al.*

Leaders: Initiators and Instigators

WHO IS LIKELY TO BECOME A LEADER? Much time and thought have gone into the effort to define leadership in terms of some specific competence or list of personal attributes—for example, intelligence, self-confidence, sociability, ambition, initiative, or physical and constitutional characteristics such as weight, height, health, energy, and appearance. In the biographies of great men, scholars as well as journalists have sought the key to genius. Sir Francis Galton, on the basis of his investigations, came to the conclusion that genius will triumph: men who attain eminence possess exceptional ability, and really able men become eminent even under adverse circumstances.[1]

These attempts have been almost completely abandoned by psychological research workers. Studies aimed at defining the personality traits of leaders have revealed no consistent pattern of traits that characterize *the* leader. The "born leader" theory has been scientifically abandoned and survives only in the popular imagination where, once a person becomes a leader, all kinds of "proof" can be adduced to show that from the cradle on he gave signs of his ability.

Leadership is now conceived of as an emergent and reciprocal relationship. It exists between a person and a social situation; between an individual and followers whose behavior is in some manner directed or determined by him.[2] Moreover, persons who are leaders in one situation may not necessarily be leaders in others; nor will every situation that seems to "demand" a leader turn one up. This does not deny the importance of the leader's personality in any particular circumstance, but

1. Sir Francis Galton, *Hereditary Genius* (London: The Macmillan Co., 1914).
2. R. M. Stodgill, "Personal Factors Associated with Leadership: A Survey of Literature," *The Journal of Psychology*, XXV (1948), p. 65.

it stresses the interactional quality of all leadership—namely, to be recognized and accepted by the led.

The Elements of Leadership

To DO JUSTICE to the more sophisticated notions of leadership, which stress the interaction between leader and led, it is necessary to inject at least four elements into the definition: (*a*) *role performance,* the (*b*) *influence* of which is (*c*) *central* with regard to (*d*) *collective action.* This is a synthetic definition, and some writers have preferred to place all their emphasis on only two or three of these elements. If leadership is to be distinguished from related phenomena, however, all four must be included.

ROLE PERFORMANCE

Leadership always involves effective action. It is thus distinct from *authority,* which is a potential that need never be exercised. A person may have authority because he has a particular position, or because he is thought of as competent in a given field, or because he is, by virtue of birth and training, a "man of distinction" or a "proper Bostonian." But authority *ipso facto* does not mean leadership. Small and Vincent emphasized this conceptual distinction in the first textbook of sociology, published in 1894. Leadership was viewed as the *active* side of authority; in their scheme authority referred only to the social definition of rights and responsibilities inherent in a position, while leadership had to do with the exercise of these rights.[3] Leadership stems from what the leader does. Where there is *formal* power deriving from the position held, such as the presidency, but little *effective* power is exercised, we speak of formalistic authority and not of leadership.[4]

INFLUENCE

Leadership always involves influence but is not synonymous with it. *Influence* involves the ability to affect the behavior of others. It may, of course, derive not from a leadership role but from institutional authority. When a toll collector on a turnpike greets autoists with a "Good morning!" and sends them on their way with a "Thank you!" the

3. Albion W. Small and George E. Vincent, *An Introduction to the Study of Society* (New York: American Book Company, 1894).

4. Harold D. Lasswell and Abraham Kaplan, *Power and Society* (New Haven: Yale University Press, 1950), p. 152.

motorist may be "influenced" to respond in kind. If the chief executive of a business organization undertakes some charitable enterprise, junior executives may suddenly evince an interest in that charity. But neither the executive nor the toll collector thereby becomes a leader. Actually every person in a social situation exercises some influence on every other person who is aware of him.

The leader does influence the led, for leadership is a matter of social relationships. He initiates action for a "following." But this following is not necessarily co-extensive with some organized group, as leadership usually arouses opposition as well as co-operation. The influence of the leader is thus not always integrative with existing structures. It can split a group into factions. Gouldner has emphasized this point in considering the "leader as any individual whose behavior stimulates the patterning of behavior in some group," which thereby forms his following but is not necessarily the group as previously constituted.

> By emitting some stimuli, he facilitates group action toward a goal or goals, whether the stimuli are verbal, written or gestural. Whether they are rational, nonrational, or irrational in content is also irrelevant in this context. Whether these stimuli pertain to goals or to means, cluster about executive or perceptive operations is a secondary consideration, *so long as they result in the structuring of group behavior.*[5]

CENTRALITY

What the leader exercises, then, is a central influence. The leader occupies a position of centrality in the sense that he is the *focal point* for the activity of his group. The stress on centrality of influence also helps to overcome the common objection that every follower is a bit of a leader; that is, that every follower may have an effect on the activity of the group and that often the leader waits to find where the followers want to be led.[6]

Followers may initiate action, but their influence is not central. A follower may initiate some action that serves as a cue for a leader. Or a follower may initiate some activity that another follower picks up. *But* in groups larger than two, the follower does not originate action for the leader *and* for other followers *at the same time.*[7] Should a follower do so, he would no longer be a follower; he would, indeed, have emerged

5. Alvin W. Gouldner (ed.), *Studies in Leadership* (New York: Harper & Brothers, 1950), p. 16.

6. See, for instance, R. B. Cattell, "New Concepts for Measuring Leadership in Terms of Group Syntality," *Human Relations,* IV (1951), p. 182.

7. William F. Whyte, *Street Corner Society* (Chicago: University of Chicago Press, 1955), p. 262.

as a leader. For the leader serves as a unifying agent, initiating action that affects the behavior of a collectivity who follow him.

There are several kinds of person who are focal points of activity in a collectivity. Some of these are *not* leaders according to our concept; rather, they are *objects* around whom the others may be rallied or who are "used" in some other way as unifying agents. Unlike the leader, they do not initiate action: for instance, the movie star who becomes the social object of a cult, or the political figure who becomes the central person in a nation-wide furore over public corruption. Either one may be a leader of some group for whom he initiates action, but in relation to another collectivity he may simply serve as social object—of mass adulation or of public vilification. Social objects are discussed at length in Chapter 11, when the distinction between the two types of central person—leaders and objects—should become clear.

SYNTHESIS: COLLECTIVE ACTION

Finally, the central influence which the leader exercises must be related to collective action or collective emotions. This last requirement of leadership is exemplified in the proposition that "the rank and file identifies with the leader and adopts his perspectives." [8] It is not sufficient that a person dominate the thoughts of one person or that he influence the behavior of persons here and there in different ways. The central influence is exercised on a collective unit, in which individuals feel closer to each other by virtue of the fact that they are united in a common endeavor under one person. Given leadership, the followers come to act as a collectivity.

Leadership, even in institutions, is always emergent, developing only in the active performance of a role that integrates behavior in the interest of shared goals and objectives. This is well summed in Barnard's general formulation that leadership "refers to the quality of the behavior of individuals whereby they guide people or their activities in organized effort." [9]

On the one side leadership shades off into influence; on the other, into formal authority. Any concrete leadership situation will, of course, involve both emotional suggestibility and dominant authority, but neither alone guarantees it. In studying leadership as an interactionist phenomenon, social scientists have had to avoid the democratic bias that defines leadership in terms of "rational" appeal and assumes that totalitarianism is the antithesis of leadership since it is a one-way relationship based on

8. Lasswell and Kaplan, *op. cit.*, p. 156.
9. Chester I. Barnard, *Organization and Management* (Cambridge, Mass.: Harvard University Press, 1948), p. 84.

discipline and unquestioned authority. For even the most totalitarian of systems has to recognize that there must be consent, however it is engineered.

THE SOURCES OF POWER

ONLY A FEW of all the participants in collective behavior stimulate action that affects the pattern of behavior in the group; that is, only a few are leaders. A leader may direct activity in two ways: he embarks on a course of activity that deliberately evokes group-relevant responses from the followers, or he instigates, rather than directly initiates, action. The *instigator* serves merely as a catalyst. By his mere presence or by certain actions not intentionally directed at the group as a whole, he may be able to get others to initiate action. In this case the actual initiator is only a "front" for the instigator, who may be the real leader—or, in popular parlance, the power behind the throne.

This distinction between leaders who initiate and leaders who instigate is roughly analogous to the more familiar distinction made in institutionalized settings between informal and formal leaders. The instigator in the bureaucracy—the factory or the army—is the unofficially recognized leader among the workers to whom the bosses turn when there is trouble—namely, the *informal* leader. Or the instigator in the political hierarchy may hold an office that fails to reflect his central influence—for example, the chairman of the county committee or the postmaster who is unofficially the party boss. The *formal* leader, or initiator, is the person through whom the power in the organization is officially exercised.

THE QUEST FOR POWER

Consciously or not, the power-seeker displaces his private motives onto public objects. He then rationalizes the choice of objects in terms of some public interest. This sort of rationalization is the distinctive mark of the *homo politicus*.[10]

Only the rare leader would publicly admit that he enjoys "power for the sake of power," that he enjoys influencing the behavior of others for his personal satisfaction. Yet, as Bertrand Russell has stated, "The men who cause social changes are, as a rule, men who strongly desire to do so."[11] One need not subscribe to the great-man theory of history to recognize that there are power-seekers in society and that persons so motivated

10. Harold D. Lasswell, *Psychopathology and Politics* (Chicago: University of Chicago Press, 1930), p. 262.
11. Bertrand Russell, *Power* (London: G. Allen and Unwin, Ltd., 1938), p. 15.

have their place.[12] Do people have to seek power in order to gain it? A Huey Long or a Napoleon admittedly sought power for himself, though always in the "national interest." Other leaders may be quite sincere in denying that they enjoy the exercise and responsibilities of authority. Whatever his "real" motives, every power-seeker portrays himself—to use the language of conversion—as a "vessel" in the service of others. Whether persons *must* seek power in order to secure it cannot be answered here, but most people who have gained power indeed sought it.

Irrespective of his motives, then, the objectives the power-seeker espouses are generally popular in the sense that they are rationalized as expressing the will of the people. But these objectives may be in fact oppressive, unattainable, fantastic, or meant to deceive those whom they are professed to succor. On the one hand, a would-be leader can espouse a cause whose attainment is contrary to his personal self-interest, as when a war veteran has advocated legislative measures that would deprive him of a partial disability payment. On the other, the power-seeker may propose measures in the public interest that actually serve only his private interest; for example, many a legislator has put through bills designed to further his own as well as other vested interests.

The mechanism of rationalizing private motives onto public objects is most obvious in scapegoating, where the would-be leader may displace his hatred of the world onto some minority group, for example. He argues for its destruction as a public menace: its members, he claims, have promoted national depression, conspired to cause war, or sought the destruction of patriotic governments. It must be understood, though, that the democratic leader rationalizes his motives in much the same way. It is his objectives that are different. His need for response from others can inspire him to help them help themselves.

THE LEGITIMATION OF AUTHORITY

Authority, to be effective, must be legitimated. This means that if one is to influence the behavior of others as one wishes, one's authority must be accepted by others. Such acceptance may be tendered on a number of grounds. Max Weber proposed a classification of types of authority according to the ways in which the exercise of power is socially legitimated. Though his classification has been criticized and modified, it remains useful for highlighting the difference between leadership in organized and unorganized collectivities.[13]

12. A. McClung Lee, "Power-Seekers," in Gouldner, *op. cit.*, pp. 667–78.
13. H. H. Gerth and C. W. Mills (eds.), *From Max Weber: Essays in Sociology* (New York: Oxford University Press, Inc., 1946).

In Weber's scheme, there are three types of authority: legal-rational, traditional, and charismatic.

Legal-rational authority "is based upon an *impersonal* bond to the generally defined and functional 'duty of office.'" The *right* to exercise authority is set forth in decrees and regulations. The actual exercise of such power is approved by others because they accept the rules by which the person in power attained his position. Thus, United States citizens accept the authority of a newly elected President regardless of the bitter campaign preceding his election. The limits of the authority they tender him are spelled out in formal statute and informal practice which have grown up over the years.

Traditional authority does not have statutes to back it, but its moral force may be even more binding. This is the authority approved by people because it has always been so and so always shall be. In Weber's words, it stems from a "belief in the everyday routine as an inviolable norm of conduct." It is domination that rests "upon piety for what actually, allegedly, or presumably has always existed." [14] However much his rule may be on the wane, the man of the house is traditionally the head of the house. Traditional authority often is exercised as a birthright.

In *charismatic authority*, the led impute extraordinary personal qualities to the leader whether these are actual, alleged, or presumed. His authority rests in the image that other persons have of him. Whether or not the image is correct is unimportant; what matters is the image he is able to project. Weber's charismatic leader was the bearded prophet with a message, whose authority was not a matter of "rights" but of "righteousness." The term "charisma" has become somewhat watered down. When we say that a man is endowed with charisma, we mean that he has what used to be called "it" in the heyday of flappers and Clara Bow.[15] He is a leader by whom those led are "fascinated." For many, in 1952, Eisenhower was such a figure. Adlai Stevenson received a letter of condolence from a female partisan after he lost the Presidential race that year: "They say, Governor," she wrote, "that General Eisenhower won because the women were so attracted to him. Well, thank God, Mr. Stevenson, you have no sex appeal!" [16]

Over a period of time or at any one time, the authority of a person may reside in all three types of legitimation. The magnetic personality may attain legal office and remain there so long that his authority becomes

14. *Ibid.*, p. 79.
15. An explanation offered by Professor Louis Wirth in his lectures at the University of Chicago.
16. As remembered from a column in the Chicago *Sun-Times* by Irv Kupcinet shortly after the election.

traditional. Thus, Franklin Delano Roosevelt remained long enough in office to become a "traditional" leader to a whole generation who knew no other President. Moreover, the images people have of the kind of a man a President should be surely help to get certain persons elected. Their charismatic appeal may continue to give sanction to their power even while they hold office. Again, Americans like to attribute forceful personalities to military heroes; their authority as peacetime experts is thus legitimated not only by the office which they hold but by the image with which they have been endowed.

LEADERSHIP IN UNORGANIZED COLLECTIVITIES

POWER, THEN, IS LEGITIMATED by position and personality—that is, the image followers have of a man. In stable social situations authority stems chiefly from position—traditional or legal. Leadership is then exercised on the basis of authority inherent in a status. But, as has been pointed out, whether and how that authority is exercised depends in large part on the personalities of those exercising it. An official position gives a magnetic personality a platform from which he can operate. Even where an unusually charismatic personality manages to win power, that power soon finds supplementary legitimation via formal office.

It is in its nature that spontaneous collective behavior should form around persons rather than office.

1. There is, at first, no established leadership, and leadership seems to be won by sheer force of personality. By what other authority than his own dynamism does a man seize hold of and direct a crowd?

2. Elementary collective behavior occurs when there are breaks in routine. Then people everywhere, lacking legitimate authority, are most likely to meet the demands for power by persons lacking power. The charismatic leader typically announces his mission and calls for converts where existing routines no longer suffice to answer pressing social problems. He makes his bid for leadership in the midst of deprivation and frustration, where societies are torn by social strife, where fraternal and communal ties are disrupted, where social unrest is rife.

3. The charismatic leader, rather than be dependent on the existent status system, is likely to smash it and set up his own. Hitler, having dissolved the Reichstag, proclaimed himself Fuehrer and chancellor.

4. Leadership legitimated by personal appeal always evolves additional sources of legitimation. For, though the leader may establish his right to power by virtue of his magnetic personality, the maintenance of his rule usually depends on his ability to re-enforce his authority through more formal channels of command. The creation of some stable form of

organization serves to legitimate his leadership. His authority becomes institutional as he begins to derive his power from an office. Thereafter he has an investment in the continuance of that structure as the source of his power.

THE TRANSFERABILITY OF LEADERSHIP

One is tempted to speak of leadership in collective dynamics as characteristically charismatic, but this is true only if we think in terms of a "winning" or "adaptable" personality who manages to project the proper image in various situations. The mark of the leader in a dynamic situation, as Redl has pointed out in another connection, is not a "strong personality" but an adaptable one.

Thus, *greatness* is more an attribute of a man's image held by people who "need" to worship him than an attribute of a man.[17] What matters is what people perceive, what they imagine to be true of a man. The requirement that the leader be able to project a successful image is particularly important in mass behavior and has received special attention with the advent of television into the world of politics. We hear of the "real" personality that can't come across on television; it is as if the coaxial cable somehow intercepted the charisma and stopped it cold. The successful leader must transmit the proper image to his followers. Whether they perceive him at the end of a hall where he is rousing them to a crusade or through the assistance of electronics is a matter of social insignificance.

In highly dynamic situations new problems and new definitions are constantly arising, and to meet them the effective leader must change the image he projects. To bind his followers and keep their loyalty, he must have a "group psychological flexibility" which "enables a leader to issue integrating psychic stimuli in *varying* situations to a *diversity* of individuals." [18] His leadership must be transferable.

Lasswell took cognizance of the importance of sensitivity to changing situations when he classified political leaders as "specialized"—for example, the Old Testament prophet who was successful only as an agitator —or "composite"—for example, Garrison, who was an agitating orator and an organizer, or Lenin, who combined talents as agitator, theorist, and administrator. Kurt Lewin painted the following picture of such an adaptable leader:

> I had a chance to observe rather closely a young fellow who had been active in the German Youth movement before Hitler. Subsequently he

17. Wilhelm Lange, *The Problem of Genius,* cited by Hans Gerth and C. W. Mills, *Character and Social Structure* (New York: Harcourt, Brace & Co., 1953), p. 412.

18. Fritz Redl, "Group Emotions and Leadership," *Psychiatry,* V (1942), pp. 573–96.

had been taken over by the Nazis and made an assistant to a District Youth leader for a number of years. For one reason or another he had fled the country and become politically anti-Nazi. This individual showed rather marked symptoms of maladjustment such as aggressiveness and egocentrism. Being a clever fellow, he made his way, learned the amenities of the American style, and showed a friendly and smooth surface. After a number of years he gave the appearance of being quite well adjusted and was usually considered a likeable fellow.

Only those who knew him intimately and followed his actions closely for a long time could see that actually his conduct had become more insidious than ever before. Having an exceptionally fine sense for relations of status and power, the fellow would find out immediately who were friends, who enemies, where lay the strength or weakness of everyone, or what ideas were fashionable at the moment. On the basis of this quickly gained intimate knowledge of power relations he would pursue an active egotistic policy with an extreme degree of aggressiveness, using lies without inhibition and figuring out destructive frontal attacks with a cleverness that made people gasp. I could not help but feel that here we had a practically "pure" case of Nazi culture. This aggressiveness did not diminish but rather increased and became more dangerous as the individual became personally secure without changing his basic culture.[19]

The flexible leader, working within the limits of a society congenial to his basic personality structure, sizes up the elements of any situation and contrives to meet it. The man with charisma in the eyes of others is undoubtedly the man with this psychological flexibility. He is the leader who can stir up the people when they are sunk in hopeless apathy, provide them with a program when they are aroused, and then go on to command the social movement he creates as prophet, organizer, and later administrator. Labor leaders like John L. Lewis or Walter Reuther seem to have had this composite kind of charisma.

But leadership is not always transferable from one situation to another. As new crises arise in the formation and development of unorganized collectivities, different persons may suit different phases of development. The personal magnetism of some leaders holds only so long as the situation in which they are successful does not change. Charismatic as they may be for one following at one time in one place, they are not flexible. The leader who successfully harangues and arouses the slumbering crowd gives way in time to the leader who more nearly fits the developing needs of the collectivity. The leader who guides the distraught minority toward

19. Kurt Lewin, *Resolving Social Conflicts* (New York: Harper & Brothers, 1948), p. 48f.

some utopia may be viewed as a fool, a fake, or a knave when he pleads his mission before a hostile audience.

In the discussion that follows our concern is with three types of leader whose power is derived mainly from their personal qualities. Theirs is a leadership peculiarly noninstitutionalized. They make themselves available and come to power under the most spontaneous of circumstances. Their influence is primary in the sense that they get things going; they initiate change or instigate others to initiate it. They are: the *innovator,* the *influential,* and the *agitator.*

THE INNOVATOR

An innovator, in its formal usage, is somebody who introduces a new object or a new idea or who makes a change in something established. "Innovation" has sometimes been used interchangeably with "leadership" or "invention." "Innovator" here identifies a certain type of leader but not one who necessarily "invents" the behavior he initiates or instigates. An innovator is most often an infectious catalyst, an instigator whose suggestion "catches," whether immediately or after some time has elapsed. Sometimes the suggestion is aimed only at a collection of people in close proximity to one another. Or it may be meant to affect the attitudes and behavior of people everywhere over the years. The innovator is a central person whose main contribution is to provide the suggestion that stirs people up or goads them to action. His concern, unlike that of the agitator, is not primarily with the response of people to himself.

The *seducer* is an innovator who works without intent, plan, purpose, premeditation. His is the most elemental form of innovation. He acts as an infectious catalyst simply because he is the "first to start it" or his presence stirs others to action. For instance, Redl offers the illustration of a class of fifteen-year-old children, in high spirits at the end of their morning sessions, waiting for their teacher, a stern leader with a patriarchal tendency. The relationship between teacher and class has been strained of late, but his authority has not been questioned. As the teacher enters, the boys stand at attention.

> Suddenly, one youngster, neither much liked, respected, nor feared by the others, starts yelling aggressively in a much more rebellious manner than anyone would have expected, especially toward this teacher. Before the teacher can react manifestly, they all join in. The whole class is in an uproar, more intensively so than any of them can afterwards "understand." [20]

20. Redl, *op. cit.,* p. 580.

This youngster engages in unusual behavior, and the group follows his suggestion; it changes from class to chaos; the definition of relations between class and teacher is forever altered. The class may never again be so unrestrained, but it will never again be so unquestioning. The social structure has been formidably revised.

There are other instances of such elementary innovation. When Redl portrays the central person as a "bad influence," he gives us a picture of seduction through "magic." This is the crowd model who is more than mere follower: he is an infectious catalyst. Watching any sizable group of unsupervised children at play may reward the reader with the sight of such an innovator performing.

> There are children in many classes who are constantly being accused of being "undesirable elements" by all teachers, parents, and by the other children, too. And yet, they can scarcely be accused of "having an evil" influence. Usually what they are accused of is unclear but it is assumed that their mere presence in the classroom affects the others badly—"brings out the worst in them." And yet it would be embarrassing to say how they do this.[21]

The "bad influence" apparently hasn't the same internal conflicts which others in the group have. This "unconflicted" personality constellation has an infectious influence on the conflicted wherever the two come in contact, a phenomenon that in its dyadic form is *folie à deux* and under other circumstances *folie en masse*. This innovator is not, however, always the bearer of mischief. Such catalysts also serve as good influences and may even emerge as heroes who, by holding their ground, turn the tide and are thereafter much loved and revered. Thus, the man who refuses to join the lynch party and the captain who stands by his ship when it goes down.

Innovators are sometimes unsung heroes of their own generation, saints to the children of their children. The innovator whose innovation catches but slowly is the precursor of whom Gerth and Mills write.[22] This is the man who creates a role but finds no institutional opportunity to play it. He is self-appointed, and his performance as decision-maker is only imaginary. But he goes through much internal preparation for the day when he and his followers will take over. He may be a prophet whose prophecies turn out to be true much beyond his time, and he is without honor in his own day save, perhaps, as the Elijah to a small group who comprise an obscure and perhaps ridiculed sect. Our own time is full of innovators who are now hailed as the first who foresaw the possibilities

21. *Ibid.*, p. 581f.
22. Gerth and Mills, *Character and Social Structure* (New York: Harcourt, Brace & Co.), p. 424.

of some new idea—for instance, Billy Mitchell, the advocate of air warfare, and Hyman Rickover, the admiral who "sold" his atomic submarine
to the public before he "sold" it to the Navy. There are also those who
"first foresaw the dangers" whether as premature anti-fascists in the era
of Nazi conquest or as premature anti-Soviets in the days before the
Cold War.

Lewis Dexter has written a most provocative article on "some
strategic considerations in innovating leadership," in which he attempts
to outline a sociology of innovation.[23] The innovator, like other leaders
in unorganized collectivities, is rarely well adapted to society. Such
people, Dexter writes, "are not likely to be people who conform readily,
graciously, and with ease to the social pressures and directives upon
them." They "invent" a new idea and want to "sell" it to the people but
may be unaware that they must often sell themselves along with their
ideas.

Successful innovators are probably group psychologically flexible.
But they are also planners. One suspects they are students of collective
dynamics and artists at mass manipulation. The unsuccessful (and
typical) innovator fails to recognize that what is customary is sacred, that
the mores make everything right, and that there are spheres in which
custom is king. He has no sympathy with such sentiments, even if he
understands their *raison d'être* intellectually. Change brings sorrow and
suffering to some, and this the successful innovator must recognize.

Unsuccessful innovators—or precursors—frequently suffer, writes Dexter "not because of their *good ideas* [but] because of their *total personalities*." Unorthodoxy in one field may well be accompanied by unorthodoxy
in another. "It is characteristic that several potential donors to a project
for reducing the chances of war were unwilling to give anything when
they observed that the leading advocate of the idea had dirty fingernails.
He himself was not aware of this; he does not care about appearance.
But they could not judge his ideas; they could judge his cleanliness. And
so they refused to support his plan."[24]

THE INFLUENTIAL

A national magazine put on a high-powered campaign to persuade
potential advertisers to make use of its pages. For weeks it titillated newspaper readers with the phrase WHO IS THE INFLUENTIAL? Eager readers
who awaited the answer with bated breath finally learned the secret:
"the influential" was the reader of the magazine. He was an influential

23. Lewis A. Dexter, "Some Strategic Considerations in Innovating Leadership,"
in Gouldner, *op. cit.*, pp. 592–604.
24. *Ibid.*, p. 598.

because, so a survey revealed, he was more likely than readers of other magazines to talk about what he saw and read.

Whether or not people listened to what readers said or, if so, were led to buy is not clear. But the campaign does dramatize a fact we all know: some people seem to be more able than others to influence public opinion and behavior. There are two ways in which public opinion is most commonly determined by opinion researchers. One is to take a random sampling of people's opinions and conclude that the sum of them all represents public opinion. Or, by determining what certain *key persons* think, researchers can anticipate what public opinion will be, on the assumption that they are central influences in the shaping of opinion, fashion, and mass behavior. These persons we shall call "influentials."

Influentials operate at all levels of society, and their importance stems from the prestige which accrues to what they say and do. However, this prestige derives from two totally different sources. In some cases prestige adheres to formal position in society and is explainable in terms of role and status. Thus, the mayor is a leader in his community; the doctor, the minister, and the local schoolteacher may carry some weight in any town meeting because of their positions. These persons are leaders by virtue of their ascribed position or because of their specific accomplishments. Other persons occupy positions of power and prominence in society mainly because of their access to or control over the formal channels of mass communication. The radio commentator has influence because he is able to get his views over to millions of persons—a fact that makes his views, whatever they may be, authoritative. The movie star has influence because she occupies a position in the social structure which, for one reason or another, we reward with high income and much prestige.

But prestige that adheres to formal positions has a way of being transferable. The prestige of a certain position sometimes becomes attached to the *person* occupying that position and puts him in a position of leadership that is not entirely explainable by formal structure. Kate Smith during World War II put on one of the first radio marathons to sell war bonds. As a radio celebrity she had become a familiar voice to millions of listeners; she had popularized the favorite patriotic song "God Bless America." But her success in selling bonds could be attributed to more than her position as radio songstress; her listeners thought of her as sincere; she served them as a model of behavior. Listeners shared her ordeal as she went through the twenty-four-hour stint; they wondered that she could "take it" and they often felt a need to reward her personally and encourage her by buying bonds.[25] Indeed, all during the war, celebrities were recruited to stir the people to invest in the government. During

25. Robert K. Merton, *Mass Persuasion* (New York: Harper & Brothers, 1946).

election campaigns stars of stage and screen as well as celebrities in all walks of life are called on by political parties to lend their prestige.

In the same way persons with access to the formal channels of mass communication may gain such prestige that they are in a position to win followers in whatever sphere they choose to operate. Walter Winchell, known for years as a gossip columnist, became a political prophet widely followed and in a position to make and break political reputations. Robert Montgomery, Tex McCrary, and Rosalind Russell—entertainment personalities all—became leaders of the movement that carried Eisenhower to the Republican nomination in 1952. Military heroes, like Davy Crockett, have employed their prestige to seek political power. And religious leaders, such as Adam Clayton Powell, Congressman from New York City, can use the pulpit in personal political crusades.

There is a second type of influence which does not stem from formal position. This is the influence of what are often called "informal opinion leaders." These are the people in one's immediate circle to whom others turn for advice on what to buy and how to think, the persons who have an effect on the opinions of others. The search for this personal influence received its impetus from a pioneer study of voting behavior in 1940.[26] One purpose of the study was to discover the factors that helped people make up their minds. Among the findings were these: some persons are high mass-media consumers; they pay attention to campaign speeches and to what is communicated via radio and the press concerning issues and candidates. For many others in the community these high consumers are primary sources of information and opinion about the campaign. By relaying what they have perceived and understood, they help to shape opinion. Persons who have not yet made up their mind how to vote and who are indifferent to the campaign may be influenced by what is said to them on election day or even by some casual remark heard near the polling booth.

These people are not greatly different from those they influence. They are not found in any particular occupational or educational stratum, nor can they be distinguished by any formal role. What sets them off is their position of relative prestige among their peers and a greater attentiveness to information that comes from outside and therefore is not known through local experience. In general, this means a greater attentiveness to what the mass media say—whether it is about politics, dress styles, the movies, sports, etc. Even the rumormonger who has become a local oracle, may owe her success to a tip she got from the paper.

Such opinion leaders are usually very sensitive to the needs and desires

26. Paul F. Lazarsfeld, B. Berelson, and H. Gaudet, *The People's Choice* (New York: Duell, Sloan & Pearce, Inc., 1944).

of their peers. They choose information in which their peers are likely to be interested or which they will want to hear. They make use of the fugitive channels through which rumor spreads. For their peers they initiate action and open up new worlds. From the viewpoint of the greater society, they act as carriers of what other influentials have already initiated. In this way they add their own prestige to the activity and help to ensure its acceptance in the local group. Thus they set the tone in controversial discussions. They help to prepare the ground for new ideas and hasten the speed with which they catch on.

It should be clear that, in referring to its readers as influentials, the magazine mentioned above was merely employing the results of social research as an advertising gimmick. Not every reader who tells her husband what she saw in the ads is an influential as we have used the term here. Nor is everybody whose opinion is sought after by somebody else thereby an influential. At any level of society—whether he is widely known or operates within his local milieu or some interest group—a person acts as an influential only when he utilizes the trust others give him to initiate activity that coalesces in collective activity. His is a *central* influence.

THE AGITATOR

Agitation stirs things up. The agitator seeks to arouse people and to get them to do something he wants them to do. He seeks to gain people's attention, to rub salt in their psychological wounds, to shake them up, to throw doubt on their old beliefs and attitudes, and to turn their sentiments and thoughts toward the ideas, promises, and suggestions he offers.

But *the hallmark of the agitator*—that which sets him aside from other leaders—*is the high value he places on the response of the public*.[27] Whatever his ultimate aim, his immediate goal is to set people in motion: this is his forte and his reward for a job well done.

Different situations in which the agitator works may require different talents, and one agitator may achieve success only under certain circumstances. Another who is psychologically more flexible may change his tactics to meet a changed situation. Thus, agitators may be men of few words or many. They may softly suggest and entice people, or they may harangue and implore them. Blumer noted two *principal* kinds of situation in which agitators operate.[28] The first is marked by abuse, unfair

27. Harold D. Lasswell, *Psychopathology and Politics* (Chicago: University of Chicago Press, 1930), p. 78.
28. H. Blumer, "Collective Behavior," in A. M. Lee (ed.), *Principles of Sociology* (New York: Barnes & Noble, Inc., 1951).

discrimination, and injustice, but people don't question their way of life; it is taken for granted. There is general apathy and inertia. "What will be will be." The task of the agitator is to tap the sources of discontent and create social unrest where none exists. Usually the successful operator in this situation is excitable, restless, and aggressive. His energetic behavior and dynamism attract attention; his excitement is infectious.

In the second situation the agitator is calmer, more quiet, and dignified. The people are aroused, and there already is social unrest. But, though disturbed about the *status quo*, they see no way out. Their collective tension has no satisfactory outlet. The task of the agitator is to intensify, release, and direct this tension. He stirs people, not by *how* he addresses them or by his movements and gestures, but by *what* he says. He is caustic, incisive, and biting. He raises questions and makes people aware of just what their position is and what their alternatives are.

What most differentiates one agitator from another is, however, not tactics, which vary according to the situation, the people, and the culture, but *the involvement of the agitator* with what he preaches. As is well known, revolutionary movements, as well as parties in power and other pressure groups, sometimes employ persons to act in such roles. There are what may be called *professional agitators*. Where his employer is an accepted or legally sanctioned authority, the agitator may operate to stir people out of their apathy and to whip up enthusiasm for things as they are. He serves as a salesman or recruiter, as a "disinterested party" who, for instance, reminds people that it is their duty to get out and vote. "It doesn't matter for whom you vote, just vote."

Thus, some agitators, whether professionals or not, have little involvement with the message they try to get across. The goal is response from the people but the agitator may neither feel a special call to spread the gospel or to evoke a feeling of personal loyalty toward himself from those he addresses. He helps those who will follow him to express *their*—not *his* —will by awakening and concretizing their frustration. He renders an important service to them by providing the means—suggestions, ideas, understanding of past hurts—for the assuagement of their common anxieties. Their frustrated drives can be manifested and satisfied openly. Gouldner has dubbed instigation of this sort "secular" in contrast to the methods and purpose of the "sacred" agitator who more nearly duplicates Weber's ideal type of charismatic leader.[29]

Other agitators are very much involved with the message they try to get across, for it is really an extension of themselves—of their own egos. And so we can think of these as *narcissistic* agitators. What this leader tries to do is to sell himself through his cause, though it may appear that he is there only to express somebody else's will. He most keenly requires

29. Gouldner, *op. cit.*, p. 63.

the devotion of others and their obedience to his will. He binds his followers to himself and, usually, through himself to one another. The most studied of this breed is the "fascist agitator" or "prophet of deceit," as Lowenthal and Guterman have so aptly named him. But no less typical are other prophets who set out to recruit followers for their sacred missions.

The Narcissistic Agitator

As a class, according to Lasswell, agitators are strongly narcissistic. Investigation of case histories usually turns up some strong obstacle encountered in early love relationships or some record of overindulgence and admiration in the family circle. Libido, in the psychoanalytic interpretation, is blocked in moving outward toward objects and settles back upon the self. Though the professional agitator may seek and enjoy the excitement of the crowd response, the devotion of a following is not absolutely necessary to him. On the other hand, it is the worship of *his* followers that the truly narcissistic agitator craves. He seeks to arouse emotional responses *which are then reflected back on himself.*

The narcissistic agitator believes—or believes he believes—in the message he preaches, just as he believes in himself as its herald. The techniques he employs to arouse his audience express important underlying drives of his personality and so are more than techniques to move his audience; they are weapons by which he woos the love of others. His message is so involved with himself that he easily infers that anyone who disagrees with him—that is, who does not love him—is in communion with the devil. His opponents always show bad faith or timidity.

This man with a mission has to believe in himself as the right man to carry out that mission. He often sees himself as "born" or "chosen" to lead others, who are bound—for their own good, even if they do not recognize it—to follow him. He is not merely expressing the will of the people; they may be without a will, and he proclaims it for them. He must be an optimist; whither he goes and whosoever follows will surely come into a brighter and better life. What he preaches is inevitable; yet he is needed to bring it to fulfillment. In his quest for power the narcissistic agitator displaces his private motives on public objects and then rationalizes them in terms of the public interest. His ostensible purpose may be democratic or authoritarian.

Portrait of a Pacifist Agitator

Lasswell presents a case history of a socialist-pacifist agitator whom he viewed fundamentally as an agitator and only incidentally as a social radical. What the agitator valued was the response of the public.[30] The causes he had espoused were many. During high-school days he was assigned to act the devil's advocate by defending the unpopular free-trade side in a tariff debate. Though his relatives were high-tariff Republicans, the more he read and thought about it, the more convinced he became that the free-trade position was sound. His "conversion" to free-trade led him to commit heresy: he came out for the Democratic candidate for the Presidency. In college his biology course "converted" him to the theory of evolution, which was not accepted by his family. In divinity school he challenged certain doctrines of the rigid theology and soon got the reputation of being a smart and troublesome upstart of doubtful orthodoxy. He resigned from his first congregation when an uneducated housewife gossiped about the dubious orthodoxy of his beliefs. Then he organized a Law and Order League to harry criminals and the police. In his new pastorate he held raiding parties on gambling establishments and won invitations to lecture on current religious and social problems. During this time he became a socialist and joined the Socialist Party and presently became their Congressional candidate. When World War I broke out in Europe, he denounced it with his "customary ardor" and was finally compelled to resign his pastorate because of the tenacity with which he argued for the pacifist position.

Among the private motives that were displaced and rationalized were these:

1. He suffered from a strongly repressed hatred of his only brother and a sense of guilt for this unfraternal attitude. This conflict he partially resolved by his political concern. Thus his brotherly love for all mankind was the reverse of his anti-brother drive; he denied his feelings toward his brother and displaced his affection upon remote social objects—the downtrodden and humanity.

2. The pacifist-agitator's struggle to maintain his sexual repressions was also displaced on a public object. He elaborated his very elaborate personal prohibitions into generalized prohibitions for all society, and just as he laid down the law against brother hatred, he condemned deviations from the rigid puritanical code by which he lived.

3. His feelings toward the father, a widower, were highly ambivalent. The negative side of the agitator's attitude toward authority came out in the choice of the abstract (remote) objects upon which he vented his hatred. The hostility toward the parental authority, which was denied conscious recognition and direct indulgence, was displaced against substitute symbols, such as the dogma requiring the acceptance by faith of the Scriptures, the capitalistic system, and the militarists.

Still the question is: why this particular type of displacement? Why

30. Lasswell, *op. cit.*, p. 79f.

did this particular person work out his affects by seeking to arouse the public directly? Why didn't he manipulate objective materials or concern himself with the emotional responses of some single person or of a few persons in an intimate circle of his own? The answer, as hypothesized by Lasswell, seems to provide a possible clue to the personalities of many highly involved agitators: since the narcissistic reactions prevent the individual from entering into full and warm emotional relationships with other people, he must seek response from a more impersonal public.

The Prophet of Deceit [31]

The fascist agitator, while exploiting a state of discontent, does not try to define the nature of that discontent rationally. Rather, he increases his audience's disorientation by destroying all rational guideposts and proposing that they adopt modes of behavior for which appropriate models are lacking. The opponents he singles out are vague and without discernible features; elusive and all-pervasive as they are, they are that much more formidable and dangerous.

The fascist agitator emphasizes his predestination as leader; it is the duty of others to follow him. He not only understands the situation better than others but he has suffered more than they have. "The general purpose of his activity, be it conscious or not, is to modify the spontaneous attitudes of his listeners so that they become passively receptive to his personal influence." [32] At the same time he seeks to develop a passionately unquestioning coterie of followers who are personally loyal to him, who report to him and take orders from him even after the movement he leads *may* have otherwise become highly bureaucratized.

Themes of Agitation

The prophet of deceit refers to himself in two ways: as a man "close" to his followers, like them, understanding them, a "great little man"; as a bullet-proof martyr, aloof from the commonplaces of everyday problems and everyday people, who, despite his extraordinary sufferings, is always victorious over his enemies.[33]

He plays constantly on sources of discontent among his followers. The themes a fascist agitator uses depend upon what troubles the people. Lowenthal and Guterman found that neophyte native fascists in the United States in the 1930's and 1940's constantly employed five themes

31. Leo Lowenthal and Norbert Guterman, *Prophets of Deceit: A Study of the Techniques of the American Agitator* (New York: Harper & Brothers, 1949).
32. *Ibid.*, p. 6.
33. *Ibid.*, p. 119.

in their speeches to stir up emotional responses and play up the basic distrust of the world about them common to potential recruits.

THEME 1   *The Eternal Dupes.* Such talk is effective among "people who bear the world a grudge because they feel it has cheated them . . . [The agitator] seems to say, 'Let us be honest, let us admit we are disillusioned, ignorant and cheated.' . . . By reversing the optimistic stereotype of liberal society, the agitator makes the feeling of acknowledged failure seem respectable." Thus, the agitator releases a latent masochism in which his followers are free to wallow in self-pity, secure that he will take care of them.[34]

THEME 2   *Conspiracy.* By stressing the "plotting" against them by a "ruthless enemy" (the foreign scapegoat), the agitator plays upon paranoiac brooding and projection among his potential followers. They can project their hostility upon the conspirators.

THEME 3   *Forbidden Fruit.* The agitator suggests that if the followers "are obedient to him, they will be offered the luxurious sinners as sacrificial prey." [35]

THEME 4   *Disaffection.* "Through these three devices—unseriousness, transformation of values, and negation of universalism—the agitator tries to convince his audience that ideals and values [current in the world around them] are merely misleading advertising slogans, used to defraud the dupes." [36] Nothing is what it seems.

THEME 5   *The Charade of Doom.* The follower "is compensated" for all he has suffered and all he renounces "by a kind of tragic dignity that raises his insignificant personal defeat to the status of an historical event." [37]

Lowenthal and Guterman conjecture that these themes are effective not because the agitator promises to maintain the American standard of living or to provide jobs for all, but because he intimates that he can supply emotional satisfaction denied in the contemporary social and economic setup. "He offers attitudes, not bread." [38] The agitator not only redefines their situation for his followers but provides them with a defense against demoralization. He encourages them to a verbal discharge of emotions—to hit back at those who direct history against them. He does not present universal aims in which all people can share but sets his movement up as "a kind of protection agency which will ward off the enemy." [39]

34. *Ibid.,* p. 23.
35. *Ibid.,* p. 29.
36. *Ibid.,* p. 33.
37. *Ibid.,* p. 39.
38. *Ibid.,* p. 91.
39. *Ibid.,* p. 91.

The themes of the prophet of deceit are not subtle in their motivational appeal, as are those of propaganda. They *directly* reflect the predispositions of the audience. The agitator "does not confront his audience from the outside; he seems rather like someone arising from its midst to express its innermost thoughts. He works, so to speak, from inside the audience, stirring up what lies dormant there." [40]

The New Nativists

The 1950's saw the rise of a new breed of agitator in the United States, who sought to foster open opposition in the South to the Supreme Court decision of May 17, 1954, barring segregation in the public schools. There is good evidence that, despite the quasi-religious fervor with which Southerners hold segregation, their reaction to the decision was originally mild.

The agitators, however, were not long in getting to work. Among the most potent of the movements that sprang up to combat the ruling were the White Citizens Councils. The Council leaders have varied their tactics to meet particular situations. In contrast to the older and now disreputable —in "better" circles—Ku Klux Klan, the Councils often appealed to the "respectable" elements of the community and advocated economic pressure rather than violence. But the Councils have had their extremist fringe listening to and following the more narcissistic agitator.

The most notorious of these agitators was John Kasper, who served a prison term in Tennessee for his part in fomenting violence. Kasper headed a splinter group within the White Citizens Council which openly advocated boycott and violence and directed its appeal to more deprived, less reputable groups in the community. His tactics and strategies are typical of such leaders.

Kasper, a Northerner educated at Temple University, Yankton College in South Dakota, and finally Columbia University, became involved with the Council movement in June, 1956, when he founded a chapter in Washington, D.C., from which Jews were excluded as desegregationists. He first came to national attention in Clinton, a mill town of four thousand persons in east Tennessee. Clinton had made plans to integrate its schools in August, 1955, and on August 20 fifteen Negroes registered for school. There were no incidents, and peaceful integration seemed assured. On August 25 (a Saturday) Kasper arrived in Clinton. By means of a telephone campaign, door-to-door canvassing, and small meetings, he managed to "arouse the populace"—or at least enough persons to stir up trouble. On Monday a picket line appeared around the school. Federal Judge Taylor issued an injunction forbidding interference with the

40. *Ibid.*, p. 5.

school's integration. But Kasper continued to agitate, seeking to shake up those not already "enrolled" in his campaign and to direct the activities of those already in his service. Rioting broke out and had finally to be quelled by National Guard tanks ordered out by the governor.

Kasper was easily the most fiery, extreme, and charismatic of the Council leaders. He told a meeting of the North Alabama Citizens Council, which a group of hooded and robed Klansmen attended, that the Klansmen were welcome. "We need all the rabble rousers we can get. We want trouble and we want it everywhere we can get it." Moreover, he went on, the aim was to *seize* control of local affairs; by "seizing" it: "We will have our martyrs and some will have to die before this is over because the Federal government means death to all of us." He called for "marching bands" or "roving forces of fearless patriots" to converge on any place threatened by desegregation. "Their fight is your fight and you must be willing to leave your home and go where your help is badly needed." [41] Later in Nashville, Kasper's instigation evidently led to the dynamiting of an elementary school and other outrages.

The composition of the mobs that rioted in Clinton testifies to the kind of follower to whom Kasper pitched his appeals and who were likely to respond. There were poor rural people, youths (many of them teenagers), and coal miners from an area which was hard hit by unemployment—the frustrated and the discontented. According to observers other participants were the "criminal element," the psychopaths who feed on every opportunity for excitement and lawlessness. A photographer who was manhandled by the crowd said, "These people weren't just mad at the Negro and integration—they were mad at everybody in the world. Things have been going very badly and they could let off some hate." [42]

Emerging from prison in the summer of 1958, Kasper was met by a small coterie of followers who remained loyal to him. But during his imprisonment the situation in many key points in the South had changed. With the intervention of Arkansas' governor in the notorious Little Rock disorders and with the postponement of desegregation through judicial decree in some areas, open opposition to the Supreme Court's decision had received official sanction and was therefore more "respectable."

Agitators like Kasper, having stirred up people everywhere, gave way to influentials who had a program for deterring desegregation through more "rational" and orderly means. Indeed, the violence the agitators did so much to foment remained a weapon in the hands of influentials in their more organized and legal efforts to maintain the status quo.

41. John Bartlow Martin, *The Deep South Says Never* (New York: Ballantine Books, Inc., 1957), pp. 120–21.
42. David Halberstam, "The White Citizens Councils," *Commentary*, XXII (October, 1956), p. 302.

BIBLIOGRAPHY

BARNETT, H. G. *Innovation*. New York: McGraw-Hill Book Co., 1953. The most systematic presentation of innovation, though mostly in its more organized forms.

BYCHOWSKI, GUSTAV. *Dictators and Disciples from Caesar to Stalin*. New York: International Universities Press, 1948. A psychoanalytic interpretation of history, based on biographical data.

GIBB, CECIL A. "Leadership," *The Handbook of Social Psychology*, ed. Gardner Lindzey Vol. II, pp. 877–920. Cambridge, Mass.: Addison-Wesley Publishing Company, Inc., 1954. A survey of the psychological literature on leadership, especially the personal and situational determinants of leadership.

GOULDNER, ALVIN W. (ed.). *Studies in Leadership*. New York: Harper & Brothers, 1950. Perhaps the best selection of studies on leadership in practically every kind of situation.

KATZ, ELIHU, and LAZARSFELD, PAUL F. *Personal Influence: the Part Played by People in the Flow of Mass Communication*. Glencoe, Ill.: The Free Press, 1955. Demonstrates that personal influence operates on every level of society and varies somewhat in accordance with the area of interest.

LASSWELL, HAROLD D. *Psychopathology and Politics*. Chicago: The University of Chicago Press, 1930. The political leader is treated as the person who displaces private motives onto public objects.

LOWENTHAL, LEO, and GUTERMAN, NORBERT. *Prophets of Deceit: A Study of the Techniques of the American Agitator*. New York: Harper & Brothers, 1949. A portrait of the American nativist agitator and of his appeals in the framework of Lasswell's theories.

WEBER, MAX. *The Theory of Economic and Social Organization*. New York: Oxford University Press, Inc., 1946. Authority depends on being perceived as legitimate, so that the follower is willing to accept influence.

The Susceptibility of Followers

I N HIS ESSAY *Le crime à deux*, Sighele observed that the criminal couple always consists of the *incube*, an initiator who spawns the action and sets its tone, and the *succube*, who succumbs to the influence of the former but in doing so reacts back upon him. What interested Sighele especially was the succube. Often this person seems little more than a vehicle for carrying out a misdeed conceived by another. The succube's violent self-disparagement after the crime documents his claim that he felt dragged by an irresistible force, under whose influence, despite great efforts to free himself, he was led to commit the crime. Analogous forms of this psychological relationship between an incube and a succube, Sighele contends, are present in every couple, whether they are moved by wholesome and normal inclinations or by insane, suicidal, or criminal ones.[1]

Notwithstanding Sighele's formulation and the detailed observations he offered in its support, the question of who is susceptible to contagion in its varied forms attracted little interest until recently. The follower merited study not in his own right but only insofar as his attitudes and behavior shed light on the nature of leadership and on the selection of leaders.

CONFORMITY AND GROUP INFLUENCE

THAT ATTITUDES, interest, behavior, etc., are anchored in the expectations of others is of course a sociological axiom. In one manner or another everyone is continually subject to pressure from the groups to which he belongs, and to a corresponding degree his views are apt to be

1. Scipio Sighele, *Le crime à deux* (Lyons-Paris: 1893), p. 55.

stable and predictable. Anyone can also orient his behavior toward any group whose perspective he wishes to adopt even though he is *not* a member. Indeed, an individual may do so precisely because he seeks acceptance or membership in the group. An individual's conformity to the expectations and norms of any particular group—that is, the degree to which he tries to bring himself into line with others in a *structured situation*—thus varies with two factors: the strength of his *motives* to be accepted by the group and his *assessment of group relevancy*, that is, how applicable are its norms in the specific situation.

In most day-to-day situations the desire for recognition and social acceptance probably governs the strength of the motives to conform. Therefore high valuation of one's membership in a group would lead one to accept most of its views and mannerisms. Since deviance is usually met with implied or actual sanction—in the form of ridicule, censure, avoidance, or even ostracism—social pressure operates most effectively in those groups whose members are most strongly committed. Individuals expecting the greatest psychological rewards from membership will similarly show the greatest sensitivity to group standards. Research evidence generally supports this proposition. People who have many friends in a group, who are often chosen by others as friends, who enjoy high status, who have been members for a long time, and who have no other conflicting group commitments usually display significantly greater resistance to counter-norm influences.

Furthermore, when persons must make judgments for whose validity there are no direct tests, the group judgment itself serves as proof. The individual gains reassurance from the support of others; matters of right and wrong become matters of faith and belief. Such consensual support, moreover, appears to the individual to endow "his" standards and the judgments based on them with a degree of objectivity. Hence, there is an objective necessity, quite apart from the individual's need for security, for such external group standards. If an individual defines a given group perspective to be legitimately relevant in a situation requiring judgment and/or action, this is an indicator of the *group's salience*. When an individual so perceives a group's perspective and norms as salient he is likely to comply with them. There is a body of incontrovertible evidence to support this proposition as well. It is through the internalization of relevant group norms that an individual's attitudes and behavior are patterned.

SUSCEPTIBILITY TO COUNTER-NORM INFLUENCE: CONTAGION

UNDER COUNTER-NORM INFLUENCE the susceptible individual responds directly to subjectively compelling cues from other persons; his "transformation" is not a matter of internalized norms. There is an element of psychological intoxication in this, and the definitions governing the behavior of the susceptible are highly volatile. The kind of influence he submits to is not readily explainable in terms of orientations rooted in social structure—that is, changes in role and status.

THE NATURE OF SUSCEPTIBILITY

If susceptibility to contagion is a definite trait reflecting a non-specific tendency to yield, regardless of the situational context, it follows that a person susceptible in one situation would generally be susceptible in others as well. It should, then, be possible to differentiate between the degrees to which such individuals exhibit this trait and to predict their behavior in a variety of circumstances. On the other hand, if the susceptibility of a follower is specific, hinging on a congruence between a disposition present in him and a particular suggestion, it would not carry over from one context into others.

There are two fundamental difficulties in the way of an empirically grounded answer: one is conceptual, the other methodological.

Difficulties of Conceptualization

Conceptualization in this area is inadequate. There is no agreement on what single trait or response pattern best designates "generalized susceptibility." Among the indices that have been employed in *experimental* study are the following:

1. *A tendency toward conformity with conventional group norms.* This measure was discussed above; tendencies along this line tend to introduce an element of stability into judgment and behavior.

2. *Persuasibility.* This is measured by change in opinion in response to communications directly addressed to the subject and explicitly designed to promote a specific viewpoint.

3. *Suggestibility.* To distinguish it clearly from other measures of interpersonal influence, suggestibility is defined as the effect of manipulated cues on sensory experience or cognitive definition of a stimulus situation. In such experiments the subjects are explicitly instructed to pay attention to only one kind of stimulus—for instance, to the content of a statement or to the figures on an inkblot test. The change or deviation produced by apparently innocent hints about how some prestige figure or one's peers responded to a particular stimulus measures the degree of suggestibility to other persons.

4. *Susceptibility to ideo-motor suggestion.* Susceptibility to verbal suggestions is measured by certain tests involving physical movement,

such as the amount of postural sway produced in a person on being told that he is falling.

5. *Hypnotizability*. This consists of a willingness to define and act out without resistance a situation defined by the hypnotist. Various measures have been employed to measure the depth of trance into which individuals will fall under hypnotic influence.

There is no a priori justification for accepting any of these measures as synonymous with susceptibility to counter-norm contagion in a natural setting. Nor can one definitely say that they are all measures of one underlying trait. Attempts to define a common factor through correlational studies have not resulted in a strikingly convincing finding. To begin with, some people are quite evidently more amenable to accepting suggestions while others are generally negativistic and hostile. Correlational studies support this observation.[2] Second, susceptibility to prestige suggestion seems to be related to the factors that influence persuasibility. These susceptibles, according to experiments, are more responsive to majority opinion and definitely more responsive to arguments expressed in socially accepted forms.[3] Third, ever since Hull first used it, the body-sway test has been used as a reasonably good indicator of hypnotizability. Fourth, while there is every reason to postulate some relationship between conformity to normal group influence and susceptibility to hypnotism, one study by Barry indicated that subjects more susceptible to hypnotism and to direct suggestion in the waking state were not more susceptible to opinion change induced by providing information about majority opinion.[4] Finally, hypnotizability has been related to "as if" behavior, which designates a person's ability to behave as if the situation were different from what it actually is.

Methodological Considerations

A second difficulty in the way of determining the nature of generalized susceptibility derives from methodological considerations. Susceptibility in any of the meanings above can be observed only within a particular situation. It is not easy to decide whether one is justified in viewing an instance of critical change toward an artificially set-up standard as generalized susceptibility, or whether it might be more readily interpreted as the outcome of a particular disposition which happened to be congruent

2. T. W. Richards and Marjorie P. Simons, "The Fels Behavior Scales," *Genetic Psychology Monographs*, XXIV (1941), pp. 259–309.

3. Carl Hovland *et al.*, *Communication and Persuasion* (New Haven: Yale University Press, 1953), chaps. 5 and 6.

4. H. Barry, "A Test for Negativism and Compliance," *Journal of Abnormal and Social Psychology*, XXV (1931), pp. 373–81.

with the proffered stimulus. An empirical answer to this question would require observation of persons exhibiting susceptibility in a variety of situations.

Janis has moved in this direction. He investigated the personality traits associated with persuasibility that may be described as "topic-free." This is interpreted to mean that the subject's acceptance of an argument does not depend on the *content* of the argument used in the experiment. Of course a person's willingness to accept a new view is known to hinge very much on previous knowledge and other related attitudes. Every specific response to arguments is therefore "topic-bound." But if persuasibility in one situation is related to persuasibility in others, one may then speak of it as a general trait.

The subjects used in Janis' experiments were exposed to three communications very different in subject matter, but quite similar in format. A positive—though only moderately significant—tendency for persons influenced by one communication to be influenced by the others was found.[5] He is careful to observe that persuasibility, though partially independent of the *topic,* may nevertheless be bound to *other non-content* factors in the situation. Among these are: the types of argument used, the characteristics of the communicator, the social setting in which exposure occurs. For example, Janis and his associates found some individuals, though not all, more susceptible to emotional than to rational arguments; some demanded an explicit statement of argument conclusions; some responded especially to fear-arousing communications, etc. The variety of possible combinations between dispositional and content elements makes the study of generalized persuasibility a difficult methodological problem.

Whatever measure of susceptibility is employed, some persons display high susceptibility in a greater number of situations than others. Still, because of the conceptual and methodological difficulties, social psychologists have tended more and more to explain their findings in terms of the specific situational context. For instance, Krech and Crutchfield, reviewing the experimental work dealing with suggestibility, conclude that it "has failed to supply unambiguous evidence that suggestibility is a personality trait and that individuals can be differentiated with respect to that trait independently of the situation in which it is presumed to appear. Almost all the data available can be much more readily interpreted to mean that whether or not an individual accepts a suggestion is a function of the total psychological situation." [6] Similarly, the evidence concerning hypnotizability indicates that trust and confidence between

5. Hovland, *op. cit.,* p. 185.

6. David Krech and Richard S. Crutchfield, *Theory and Problems of Social Psychology* (New York: McGraw-Hill Book Co., 1948), p. 337.

hypnotist and subject is the most important factor governing susceptibility to hypnotic influence. It has even been suggested that the somewhat greater susceptibility of women—a persistent finding—may have nothing to do with the feminine personality but has much to do with the fact that most experimenters are male! [7]

CONFORMITY AND SUSCEPTIBILITY: AN INVERSE RELATIONSHIP

We have developed the following principle of the nature of susceptibility: *The clearer and more stable the norms governing a situation* (i.e., a structured situation), *the more susceptibility to interpersonal influence acts to re-enforce the norms and stabilize the situation. But when the norms lose some of their clarity or persons find themselves without guides to conduct* (i.e., an unstructured situation), *this very same susceptibility is likely to operate, not as a stabilizing force, but as counter-norm contagion which disrupts and modifies the ordinarily valid norms of conduct.*[8]

This formulation takes no account of the psychological mechanisms involved. It is even possible that they are the same in both situations, but that they have different implications in situations of collective excitement when structures temporarily disintegrate. The degree of counter-norm susceptibility would appear, then, to vary with two conditions. It increases as (1) the group salience decreases and (2) the motives to conform are for one reason or another weakened. The first of the conditions is a situational variable—namely, an individual's perception, or definition, of a situation as affording gratifications not ordinarily sanctioned and thus conflict-producing or guilt-arousing. The other refers to personality dispositions: a general tendency toward impulsiveness and spontaneity leads a person to seize at once on any situation offering such opportunities. It is also possible that high anxiety is apt to make normally inhibited persons particularly susceptible in situations that promise solutions to their unique inner conflicts.

It is necessary to examine the influence of these two factors separately.

---

7. Cf. Pattie, in Roy M. Dorcus, *Hypnosis and Its Therapeutic Applications* (New York: McGraw-Hill Book Co., Blakiston Division, 1956).

8. See Norman Polansky *et al.*, "An Investigation of Behavioral Contagion in Groups," *Human Relations*, III (1950), p. 337, for evidence that directive influence to which an individual conforms "passively" is inversely related to "active" pickup of behavior when no intent to exert influence is communicated.

DEFINITION OF THE SITUATION

SUSCEPTIBILITY, then, depends in part on how a situation is defined. The follower who in his judgment or behavior deviates from an accepted norm does so in response to certain cues that elicit responses that no longer support the norm. Much depends on what cues are perceived and how important the various alternatives are.

DIFFERENTIAL CONTACT

Sensitivity to the potential of a situation for counter-norm behavior depends, first of all, on differential exposure to—that is, contact and association with—deviant models. The potential follower must be exposed to a new object. The object may be an appeal he is expected to answer, a new definition he is to accept, or a model he is to imitate. Obviously a person cannot pass a rumor along unless the information is first imparted to him. To be sensitive to fashion, to certain views, to criminal gang life means association with others among whom such patterns diffuse.

To some extent, each rumor, each public issue, each innovation has its characteristic "following," built around more or less permanent associations and contacts. Differential exposure is a matter of chance contact as well as association. Occasionally the susceptible is drawn into activities because he came upon the model by chance; but most of the time he seeks out those in whose behavior he expects to find rewarding models.

AWARENESS OF ALTERNATIVES

Exposure and association are hardly sufficient to account for differential susceptibility, for even in the same situation, confronted with the same influence, people display different degrees of involvement. Rejection is easier if the individual perceives genuine alternatives among which the object is only one. An inner compulsion to follow is greatest, on the other hand, when the object appears the *only way*—however contrary to custom and convention that only way is.

If an individual is aware that he can find support for definitions in groups other than that in which he momentarily finds himself, he is less likely to be susceptible. But the limited perspective of the crowd, the judgment of style in a local group, the absolutism of certain mass movements, all urge upon the individual patterns that appear to be universally accepted. This tendency to define as universal the definitions formed from one's own limited observations is called social projection.

To refer once more to the "Martian invaders": In Quito, radio listeners heard that their country was invaded from Mars. Some listeners never doubted the validity of the "news." The situation was defined as "invasion," and those who thus defined it ran. The presence of others also running served to confirm the situation and reinforce their behavior. The flight mob followed one another on a route out of the city. But then officials used loudspeakers and other available means to assure the panic-stricken that no invasion had occurred, and thereby to redefine the situation. At this point many saw in the universal flight evidence that they had been deliberately fooled. Hence, there was *only one way* in which to look at the official reassurance: it is not *we* who have erred in our assessment, but *they* who misled us and who therefore deserve punishment. And the radio station became the target of the crowd wrath.

With like effect, the propagandist monopolizes perceptions in a specific direction so that no alternative definitions can come to the attention of his followers. He aims to make *one* alternative appear the only way. During war, propaganda centers on how best to win, not on the alternatives to winning. Publicizing a movie as a hit and keeping criticism from its potential audience hastens mass interest in it. Likewise, the enthusiasm for many a social movement derives from the fact that its membership never explores alternative possibilities. Hence, the most susceptible followers are those whose attention is fixed on only a single solution and from whom alternatives are effectively excluded.

The possibility that alternatives come to the attention of a public does not hinge altogether on the physical availability of channels of communication. Lack of tolerance, premature fixation on a specific alternative, stereotyped thinking can be as effective in insulating a person from alternatives as can their complete absence. It is our hypothesis that persons who insulate themselves from broader social influences are most prone to seize upon the first definitions that occur to them and adhere to them without further validation. Such people are readily manipulated by appeals to stereotyped beliefs and attitudes. Examples of this are the crowd where, temporarily at least, the individual is shut off from the world of nonparticipants and sees the crowd behavior as the *only way*. It is much the same with the urgings of a charismatic leader whose personal appeal and insight suggest that he is in possession of the only answer. The sectarian formation insulates its following in an exclusive community of true believers. Even when the *only way* appears threatened, its immediate abandonment or compromise is unlikely. Faith can be strengthened either by seeking the validation that comes from winning new converts or by turning away from the world toward a personal solution. Perhaps the truest enthusiasts of mass movements are not the leaders, who are in contact with the world and seek clearly conceived goals, but the followers, who are the least torn by doubt. If presented with a viable alternative, a decline in faith among the following may result in their wholesale conversion to another movement.

In sum, a definition of the situation as lacking alternatives is fostered by: *social projection,* when the individual sees "his" definition as a universal definition; *monopolization of perception,* through which the situation is so structured for the individual that he has no opportunity to weigh an alternative; and *social insulation,* a term for the individual's characteristic perceptual habits which prevent him from perceiving alternatives.

Choice among Alternatives

Effective exclusion of alternatives is more typical of the folk community, bound by tradition and custom, than of modern society. Occasionally modern man escapes into some sectarian microcosm where he shuts out the sounds of a hostile world, but most of the time he is confronted with a profusion of alternatives which make choice necessary.

Increasing heterogeneity in society resulting from the division of labor, as Durkheim has pointed out so incisively, means a weakening of sentiments held in common by all individuals. The social bond, based on similarities among members of a society, is weakened; still, the complex division of labor provides another basis for social solidarity insofar as people, however different from one another, are more dependent on one another. Therefore the number of necessary relations among them are multiplied. Isolation is broken down because communities with different traditions nevertheless become functionally interdependent in supplying each other with necessary commodities and services. Such developments led to what Durkheim called an increase in dynamic or moral density— that is, an increase in the number of different relations as well as in their frequency. The establishment of a rationally conceived system of norms to regulate the relations among persons of diverse traditions and sentiments thus becomes a practical necessity.

Under these conditions the defection from conventional norms and the establishment of new patterns may occur in two manners fundamentally distinct: (1) rational innovation in which the alternatives are weighed in terms of practical group interest; (2) regression to authorities that impel the premature acceptance of a solution as the best alternative.

RATIONAL INNOVATION   The acceptance of a new pattern or the setting up of a new norm after alternatives have been deliberated constitutes rational choice. This implies that as many alternatives as possible have been carefully judged in terms of standards that comprise the broadest conception of the collective interest. It does not imply that the decision rationally reached always is the best one in the light of subsequent experience. The participants in the decision-making process, however rational, do not possess complete knowledge or infinite wisdom. Still, the norms governing discourse forestall the automatic preclusion from consideration of alternatives and make it obligatory for social authorities to take into account the partial perspective of each subgroup, each special interest, and each deviant view. In essence, this constitutes the establishment of a new norm by public opinion in a democracy.

REGRESSION: PRIVATIZATION AND APATHY   On the other hand, the complexity and internal differentiation of a mass society reduces cognitive clarity on matters of public concern among its citizens. Traditional standards cannot always be easily transposed to new situations. Many individuals are at a loss to grasp the implications deriving from alternative courses of action. The profusion of competing understandings and the disruption of normative expectations often lead to what some writers have called "cultural confusion." In quick succession an individual may define a situation in one way and then in several other ways. Lacking information or an adequate frame of reference for the complex judgments requisite for participation in public life, individuals become susceptible to a collective form of regression called "privatization," or mass apathy. They concern themselves exclusively with their private needs and do nothing beyond satisfying them.

To such do-nothingness there are, however, two apparently contradictory aspects. On the one hand, this apathy may constitute a withdrawal from collective life inasmuch as matters are deemed too complicated or too nebulous to do anything about. Not capable of understanding their meaning, the individual reacts with distrust to social authorities. For instance, politics is viewed as corrupt. The individual, believing his views count hardly at all, sees no reason to participate. Public moods, stemming from followers with this outlook, are apt to persist even in the face of facts that should call for a redefinition of the situation. For example, in the spring of 1958 a kind of mass pessimism was reflected in strong consumer resistance. Even following an upswing in business activity, the pessimism prevailed. Many consumers could not understand the many signs to which they were daily subjected and, unable to arrive at a judgment on the economic future, they "played safe" by not buying.

On the other hand, do-nothingness may result in a positive "solution." The withdrawal from participation in public life is often the counterpart to an acceptance of some "higher" authority which offers security and support for private motives. An example is the delinquent who has rejected prevailing norms and institutions. He is highly susceptible to contagion and, to borrow Lindner's apt phrase, he is a "rebel for somebody else's cause," [9] as long as this offers opportunities for guiltless indulgence in the forbidden. The delinquent's adulation of certain men from the sports world or entertainment field constitutes a cultivation of delinquency-prone ego ideals:

> One of the best tricks of the delinquent ego who has defected from the publicly accepted norms of behavior is to deny the desire for actual delinquent exploits but to hang on to an ego-ideal of a person whose image is secondarily encouraging the delinquent fun. Movies, radio, television, and the comics offer ample stereotypes for those whose creativity doesn't quite enable them to fabricate their ego-ideals out of their own ingenuity.[10]

Political movements also gratify private needs. G. M. Gilbert suggests that, under conditions of rapid ideological change, collective authoritarian regression is likely to result when individuals flee toward the security of conventional authority. This "escape from freedom" Erich Fromm saw as a psychological explanation for the totalitarian solution. It is an escape from a world that appears so disorganized, with means-end relationships so unpredictable, that the individual feels it impossible to take any practical steps to satisfy his life goals.[11] The individual escapes from the confusion of freedom to the safety of command.

Whether persons, perceiving alternatives, seek rationally for solutions or seize on the first, safest, or easiest answer depends on their individual capacities and the pressure of their motives. The next two sections deal with intellectual and motive factors in an individual's susceptibility to counter-norm influences.

INTELLECTUAL FACTORS

A PERSON'S INTELLECTUAL CAPACITIES are often assumed to determine vulnerability to various forms of contagion, because knowledge and critical ability are believed to be the best defense against premature foreclosure of alternatives. Hence, the idea that most mobs are riffraff and that only the uneducated can be victimized by the charlatan. Evidence does not support this folklore.

9. See Robert Lindner, *Rebel Without a Cause* (New York: Grove Press, Inc., 1946).

10. Redl and Wineman, *The Aggressive Child* (Glencoe, Ill.: The Free Press, 1957), p. 149f.

11. G. M. Gilbert, *The Psychology of Dictatorship* (New York: The Ronald Press Company, 1950); Erich Fromm, *Escape from Freedom* (New York: Farrar and Rinehart, 1941).

At an extreme, the mentally defective are undoubtedly more susceptible to irrational influence. Social conformity does require an adequate internationalization of the perspectives shared by others. Congenitally incapable in this regard, the mental defective is occasionally subjected to deliberate influence by others unscrupulously bent on exploiting his deficient intellectual powers. More often he ends up isolated from his fellow men; his private world is impenetrable by others and cannot be shared.

For the normal range of personalities there is little indication of an invariant relation between immunity to counter-norm influence and intellectual capacity, whether the latter is measured by standard intelligence tests, educational achievement, etc. The once popular notion that hypnotizability and low intelligence went hand in hand is also scientifically unsupportable. On the contrary, the indications are that some intellectual capacity to reason abstractly is a positive asset. Highly susceptible subjects have scored high on the D/w ratio of responses on the Rorschach, for example.

The long-held notion, hardly supported by laboratory experiments,[12] that intellectual ability meant immunity to propaganda and manipulation via mass media must likewise be discarded, even though it appears to gain some support from Cantril's study of reactions to the radio drama, *War of the Worlds,* a survey of responses in a natural setting. The "suggestibles" (susceptibles), in contrast to others who recognized the broadcast as a fiction, took at face value the bulletins on the Martians' landing and their military advance. This difference in response is attributed to the suggestibles' partial loss of "critical faculty"; that is, they did not make adequate checks to ascertain the authenticity of the broadcast. Persons whose education was limited to grade school were found more suggestible than those with more formal schooling. For the former, casual exposure to the broadcast was sufficient evidence of an actual Martian invasion. They failed to "hear" the announcement that this was a dramatization or to wonder that events moved with incredible rapidity. If they conducted checks, it was against data external to the broadcast which generally validated what they already believed: if there were few cars on the street, this meant the roads were blocked; if there were many cars, this meant everybody was fleeing the enemy's advance. It is Cantril's interpretation that the suggestibles lacked a frame of reference for evaluating such novel situations, being deficient in both information and formal training concerning matters outside their own milieu. Hence, education is a factor likely to differentiate those governed by critical faculty from those deficient in it.

12. G. Murphy, L. B. Murphy, and T. M. Newcomb, *Experimental Social Psychology* (New York: Harper & Brothers, 1937), p. 930.

CRITICAL ABILITY AND SUSCEPTIBILITY

The inference that educational achievement reduces suggestibility to communications from the mass media is not all warranted by evidence. Critical judgment about such communications is exercised in two ways: (1) whether the content is consistent with external facts, either known to or ascertainable by the subject; and (2) whether the communication is internally consistent in that the inferences are valid, all questions dealt with, and the motives of the communicator considered trustworthy. In view of this, critical ability, which is associated with education, promotes susceptibility to some communications for the same reason that it is a barrier to the acceptance of others.

Formal schooling is not just a measure of critical ability, but relates to social habits as much as to intellectual capacity, the two being difficult to disentangle. Among those with less formal schooling faith in the authenticity of radio and television, as opposed to print, is generally greater. They have fewer alternate sources of information about world affairs, and most of what they know is not sought out but comes to them casually, in the form of newscasts and special bulletins interspersed with regular programs. Moreover, as Cantril clearly indicates, the institutions of formal education cultivate the capacity for judging information by reference to the impersonal and abstract standards of the cosmopolitan community. Persons less well trained to use print and lacking an abstract frame of reference are more prone to check an unusual newscast in terms of experiences directly accessible to them and to look to other persons for guidance. The educated thus apply the test of external and internal consistency more often.

The research of Hovland and his associates on the relationship between susceptibility to persuasive communications and the factor of critical ability is especially illuminating on this point.[13] In one study, they compared the effects of a taped presentation deliberately designed to offer only supporting evidence for its conclusion with another version that dealt also with opposing arguments. Both versions were intended to impress upon soldiers the magnitude of the effort required to defeat the Axis. Soldiers who at the time they were tested thought the war would be won within two years or less were considered "unfavorably" predisposed to the communication. The prospect of a prolonged war was held by the majority of military experts. Such a view was also conducive to high morale and serious military effort. The two-sided version, it turned out,

13. Carl Hovland *et al.*, *Communication and Persuasion* (New Haven: Yale University Press, 1953).

was generally more effective in inducing high-school graduates to be less optimistic about the duration of the war, while the one-sided version was more likely to have this effect on those who had failed to complete high school. The broad conclusion drawn from this and similar studies is that intellectual capacity influences the kind of communication to which persons will be most responsive.[14] Persons with high intelligence, mainly because of their ability to draw valid inferences, will most likely be influenced by persuasive communications that rely on impressive logical arguments. But, mainly because of their superior critical ability, they tend to be less influenced than those with low intelligence by persuasive communications that rely primarily on unsupported generalities or on false, illogical, or irrelevant argument.

The irony is this: since the Axis was decisively defeated some six months after the study, the logical arguments influenced those of high intelligence to accept a view that proved to be patently false. Critical ability is no assurance of a valid judgment when adequate facts are not available or when deductions are based on premises subsequently not borne out. The effectiveness of the two-sided version can be related also to the utilization of "facts" the educated were prone to accept and of "authoritative" military sources they credited with expertise. The question of susceptibility cannot be judged by whether or not the views or images accepted are correct. But the educated, quite naturally, are more responsive to sources of information that they esteem.

Consequently, the operation of critical ability must be viewed in relation to prevailing norms. For example, in the Soviet Union alienated members of the elite, distrusting official sources, relied more heavily on the grapevine than did their subordinates; the Italian mob subjecting Carretta to postwar lynch justice was definitely not a lower-class rabble. The year 1960 saw widespread rioting by students in countries as different as Korea and Turkey, paralleling earlier student riots in Hungary. Furthermore, those most susceptible to literary vogues, fashions in interior decorating, the latest political view or psychological theory, etc., are often exceptionally adept in sensing the latest shift in the collective current. Far from being defective in critical ability, they exhibit an unusual sensitivity to cues that encourage deviation from norms. Much the same can be said for members of antisocial formations. Redl and Wineman introduced the concept of the "delinquent ego" into their studies of the antisocial behavior of children. This ego is bent on defending impulse gratification at any cost. Instead of looking for a synthesis between desires, reality demands, and social values (i.e. norms), their critical ability at certain moments operates totally on the side of impulsivity, helping them to get away with things. Many of these children show an adequate knowledge

14. *Ibid.*, p. 183.

of norms, and the voice of their conscience will be heard. Yet they possess an uncanny ability for finding in a situation those elements that permit guilt-free indulgence of impulses otherwise proscribed.

MOTIVATIONAL PRESSURES

FOR A LONG TIME, how a person assessed a situation was viewed solely as the outcome of rational-cognitive processes, as an effort after meaning. Other determinants were not considered. Of course, some congruence must exist between opinions and attitudes and their objects, but an attitude is hardly determined solely by an object. Appraisal is often as much a function of the inner dynamics of the personality and of its anchorage in relationships to other persons. Recognition of this has led to the distinction among three separate functions of opinions and attitudes: (1) object appraisal; (2) instrumental adaptation to goals; (3) ego defense.[15]

THE FUNCTIONS OF BELIEF

Attitudes and opinions serve in the *appraisal of objects*. By giving meaning and apparent certainty to a mass of disorganized impressions and disparate bits of information, they involve rational-cognitive functions. The rational-cognitive approach requires a person to fit observations into a preexisting mental context by considering alternatives as well as their implications. He asks himself, in effect, though rarely explicitly: "In view of the possibilities, what can logically be expected to follow if I accept such and such a view or act in such and such a way?"

Since knowledge of probable consequence is usually incomplete, attitudes serving in object appraisal can be influenced by logical persuasion and new information. The "facts" presented in an appeal must be true in the light of what people know and be logically consistent with the conclusion. A person, who wishes to lead, failing to persuade potential followers by "true" statements, must distort the facts.

No one is, of course, governed entirely by reason, and individuals differ greatly in their capacity to make dispassionate appraisals of information. Propagandists, advertisers, symbol manipulators, and those

15. The analysis in this section followed from a suggestion by Alex L. George, "Comment on Opinions, Personality, and Political Behavior," *American Political Science Review*, LII (March, 1958), pp. 18–26, that Smith *et al.*'s work on opinions might be useful for a typology of followership. The pertinent works here are: M. Brewster Smith, J. S. Bruner, R. W. White *et al.*, *Opinions and Personality* (New York: John Wiley & Sons, Inc., 1956), and Daniel Katz *et al.*, "Ego-defense and Attitude Change," *Human Relations*, IX (1956), pp. 27–45.

bent on managing the masses have, with increasing sophistication, sought out the chinks in the rational armor of men everywhere, chinks that every person has. These consist of those attitudes by which people seek to impress or keep up with the Joneses and those which bolster their sagging egos. The positive (or negative) attitude toward some objects is hardly a matter of information but has strong emotional underpinnings.

Attitudes and opinions have a second function as *instrumental means for attaining individual goals*. Confronted by a new situation, individuals whose attitudes serve primarily this instrumental function are apt to validate their views by reference to other persons whose censure is feared or from whom social acceptance is desired. The crucial question is: "Who are the important people likely to assess me? How will I look to them?"

In the light of this, an individual will check his opinions against the possible effect they will have upon his relationships. His susceptibility can thus be expected to increase, not when objective appraisal commends it, but when the pressure to conform is greatest. Thus he yields when confronted by unanimous majorities or when he can expect some gain from following. Prestige models and high-status leaders will influence him most. In general, his susceptibility appears governed by his hopes for social recognition and reward, his apprehensions of punishment and ostracism.

Attitudes and opinions have still a third function, *protection of the ego*. They serve as defenses that permit expression of an unacceptable impulse in a way that nevertheless prevents a full recognition of the motives involved. Smith and his associates label this function *externalization;* the attitude adopted toward an object or an event is colored by an unresolved inner difficulty. Persons whose assessment of objects and situations is typically governed by the need for ego support are not likely to change their views under the impact of irrefutable evidence, but they are most prone to accept evaluations that allay fears, anxieties, and guilt. When a change does occur, moreover, it is likely to take the form of an explosive externalization (a sudden conversion, the unreasoned acceptance of a new faith) which meets their inner needs. It has little to do with reasoned argument.

It must be said at once that these are not functions of specific attitudes. The same attitude may serve individuals in different ways; the same attitude may be held out of rather different motives. For example, when the development of Salk vaccine was first publicly announced, many persons opposed the desirability of mass inoculation against polio. Some scientists were skeptical: they argued that there was not yet conclusive proof of the vaccine's providing lifelong immunity against all kinds of polio; that many people had already developed a lasting immunity; that there was always the risk of mishaps, of triggering an outbreak in a person already exposed. Having critically appraised the situation, they urged utmost caution. A second group of people had no firm evidence on which to base their opinion against vaccination. Still, they refused to go along because none of their friends seemed to think it worth the trouble to get a vaccination. Still other persons clamored against mass inoculations on the assumption that this was a plot—on the part of Roosevelt supporters active in the anti-polio drive or of profit-greedy laboratories or of the Russians—to push Americans into accepting a risky policy. They may further have expressed generalized distrust of authority and of medical authority in particular.

Typologies

These attitudes toward the polio vaccine reflect characteristic individual modes of dealing with situations. For analytic purposes, one can differentiate among personality types whose attitudes *predominantly* serve them in one way more than another. Some persons have a high capacity for objective appraisal, and their beliefs are largely the result of rational inquiry. By contrast, the *instrumentalist* believes and supports primarily what appears as advantageous. Third, the person with strong defensive needs, the *high ego-defender* or externalizer, will inject these into his assessments of situations and many of his beliefs will be traceable to unconscious anxieties displaced from their original source.

It is also possible to use these modes of orientation to distinguish among situations. In that case, one considers the motives around which a particular collective action crystallizes. This can be illustrated by a strike situation. First, a collective decision to strike may be taken because business conditions are favorable and the workers appear to be entitled to an increase which the union's economic advisors know the company can well afford. The collective decision is thus taken after critical appraisal of the facts. Second, the strike may be called as a defensive measure on the part of the union to counter deteriorating solidarity or to counter the claims of a wildcat leadership. In that case, a vote for the strike is likely to be a vote in support of the union, having little to do with the economic demands. Third, the decision to strike sometimes expresses primarily resentment, serving to bolster the injured self-respect of workers out of work who attribute their employment to malicious intent on the part of management. They may or may not be correct in the evaluation of management, but the point is that critical appraisal of the facts does not enter into the decision to strike. Thus, the decision to strike can be characterized as either rational or instrumental or defensive. The basic motivational structure that governs any concrete situation would have to be abstracted both from the content of the attitudes expressed and the personalities of the individuals who hold them.

It should be possible to depict the *social psychological texture* of every instance of elementary collective behavior by studying not only the attitudes held by individuals involved (particularly the followers) but also their motives for holding them. On this basis, one may arrive at some idea of what kind of follower is most likely to be most susceptible to particular objects and forms of contagion. A typology of susceptibility is proposed at the end of this chapter after a consideration of the characteristics of two kinds of "believers": those who are insecure and low in self-esteem and whose relationships with other persons seem constantly threatened (the *instrumentalists*); and the *high ego-defenders*.

INSTRUMENTAL ADAPTATION: THE SOCIALLY INADEQUATE

SUSCEPTIBILITY to others depends in part on whether a person is sufficiently self-confident to go his own way or whether he requires immediate reassurance and reward. The degree of confidence a person has in himself derives from the appraisals of himself that he imputes to others. These imagined appraisals raise or lower self-evaluation. Security in this regard seems a function of both personality and situation. It is manifest in an individual's general inclinations to feel socially adequate and subjectively competent. But the momentary strength of these feelings varies in relation to a person's objective status; positive judgments from others are apt to counter and compensate for underlying feelings of social inadequacy.

Feelings of social adequacy are probably a consequence of early experiences basic in the socialization process. Where these have been generally reassuring, confidence in dealing with social situations is likely to result. The internalized evaluations generated by others' opinions constitute the basis of a person's self-esteem. They enable him to withstand temporary frustration. Given a high frustration tolerance, a person can afford to be critically independent, even when no rewards appear forthcoming or in the absence of social support and in the face of unanimous opposition. His need for reassurance is not so overriding that it prevents him from taking a long-range perspective or from engaging in objective appraisals on the basis of norms long internalized. A self-image of personal worth, securely anchored in positive identifications with significant others and reassuring experiences with them, is relatively invulnerable to immediate pressure.

At the other extreme, the person generally lacking in feelings of social competence needs constant reassurance from others as tangible evidence of his acceptability. Hence, he is forever seeking the positive appraisal of his associates. His indiscriminate need for affiliation can be viewed as basically ego-alien. Acceptance of a view or conformity in behavior is hardly a matter of inner conviction and, for that very reason, requires outside support and reward. The highest value is placed, not on independence and autonomy, but on immediate acceptance from associates and authorities. What combination of circumstances brings with it an exaggerated and generalized need for affiliation is not too well understood. It can be suggested, however, that it reflects (*a*) a lack of opportunity for real independence, (*b*) fear of rejection; and (*c*) a reaction against hostility toward the parent, which has become generalized to include the norms of any group that temporarily seems important.

1. The reasoning above suggests that *persons lacking in self-confidence in interpersonal relations will display above-average susceptibility to most forms of direct social influence.* Janis found this to be true of the group of subjects he exposed to a series of three persuasive communications dealing with the likely occurrence of future events.[16] Those with low self-esteem most frequently adapted their opinions to the views expressed in the communications, and this tendency was independent of the specific content of the argument. Feelings of social inadequacy were measured by nine items, such as social inhibition, shyness, uneasiness in social gatherings, etc.; inhibition of aggression, by six items, such as rarely criticizing others, lack of oppositional feelings toward "bossy" people, etc.; and depressive affect, by response to three items concerning whether the subject often felt "blue," "unhappy," or "discouraged." Asch has demonstrated rather conclusively that the perceptual judgments of low-confidence subjects can actually be distorted by group influence even where an objective standard exists.[17] A control group confronted with the task of estimating which among three lines was the shortest solved it without major error. But many of the experimental subjects, when confronted by group evaluations that were clearly wrong became doubt-ridden and disoriented, exhibiting a strong impulse to revise their judgment to conform with that of the majority. The most susceptible third, the "yielding" subjects, sometimes lost confidence in their own perceptions, or distrusted their own judgments of what they saw, or at the very least lacked the fortitude to oppose openly their private judgment to that of a peer group unanimously arrayed against them. In much the same vein, Berkowitz and Lundy [18] have shown that

16. Hovland, *op. cit.*, chap. 6.

17. Solomon E. Asch, *Social Psychology* (Englewood Cliffs, N.J.: Prentice-Hall, 1952), chap. 16.

18. Leonard Berkowitz and R. M. Lundy, "Personality Characteristics Related to Susceptibility to Influence by Peers or Authority Figures," *Journal of Personality*, XXV (1957), pp. 306–16.

persons low in interpersonal confidence are most susceptible to statements, irrespective of whether the opinion in them is attributed to peer or authority figures. Finally, Brenman and Reichard's finding that free-floating anxiety (determined by Rorschach responses) is associated with susceptibility to hypnotic influence supports the idea that yielding may be a generalized adaptive response.[19]

2. *The confidence with which a person may oppose a group is also a function of his objective position within the group.* As pointed out in the discussion of group salience, high status and prestige within a group provide concrete rewards, and group support constitutes a partial validation of one's views. Consequently one may assume that high status and popularity constitute a solid basis for interpersonal confidence. Thus, the high-status individual who is aware of his actual position in the group is likely to experience greater freedom in his interpersonal relations. He is also likely to set a higher value on a membership that offers security. In extreme circumstances his ambition for high status reflects a quest to make up with esteem from others for a lack of inner security. But while the high-status group member enjoys a certain tolerance because of this status, the valuation of his position encourages sensitivity to the needs of his associates and discourages the deviation he is permitted.

3. *Active susceptibility occurs when the action raises the prospect of support from surroundings and from important individuals, who are expected to give their approval and/or to follow along.* This generalization is supported by findings on behavioral contagion within organized groups. In these instances new ideas and ways of acting seem to travel down the status hierarchy, but the *lower* a person's prestige position in the group, the less likely is he to pick up behavior initiated by other members.[20] At the same time a "strong belongingness need" also seems to interfere with contagion susceptibility. From these two observations it can be inferred that persons who do not define position in the group as secure but who place a high value on being accepted lack the psychological freedom necessary for spontaneous imitation. On the other hand, these same individuals were found to be highly susceptible when the group as a whole or high-status persons within the group attempted to influence them directly—that is, when their suggestions and directives were unambiguous. Ambiguity about what behavior is acceptable to the group is minimized under two conditions: (1) when it is near unanimous in its judgment, so that standing apart threatens isolation, and (2) when

19. M. Brenman and S. Reichard, "Use of the Rorschach Test in the Prediction of Hypnotizability," *Bulletin of the Menninger Clinic,* VII (1943), pp. 183–87.

20. Norman Polansky, Ronald Lippitt, and Fritz Redl, "An Investigation of Behavioral Contagion in Groups," *Human Relations,* III (1950), pp. 319–48.

high-status individuals or authorities clearly express the appropriate standard.

4. *Following along for the sake of reward may operate in relation to reference groups, in which an individual is not a member but in which he aspires to be accepted by adopting their ways.* Thus the middle classes are the conformists vis-à-vis the fashions initiated by the more well-to-do. They accept fashions in dress, for instance, less as an expression of individuality than as a means of identification. Slavish adherence to group standards also distinguishes the parvenu or the neophyte; his actual position is insecure and he feels he must demonstrate that he is worthy of acceptance.

EXTERNALIZATION AND THE HIGH EGO-DEFENDER

CONFORMITY may take compulsively defensive forms manifested in a susceptibility to join deviant or antisocial formations. In this case ego integrity and self-esteem are maintained only by a rigid adherence to certain conventions. Inner conflicts are displaced to secondary symbols— a cause, a special group which can be hated—and the defensive pattern is itself made acceptable through conventionalization. Unlike the "instrumentalist" who is susceptible to momentary pressures and enthusiasms, the high ego-defender, once he has displaced and attached his affects to a suitable object, is not likely to abandon his faith just because the climate of opinion tells him it would be the rewarding thing to do. His rigidity precludes easy and spontaneous adaptation in new situations.

The susceptibility of the high ego-defender resides in his psychopathological inclinations. One recognizes here the crowd pathology viewpoint which has come down to us from Le Bon via Freud and Lasswell. According to this formulation, the high ego-defender is the mainstay of the "crowd mind"; he is the devoted sectarian, the True Believer. This justifies the earlier treatment of crowd behavior, sectarian formation, and the appeal of mass movements as collective defense. They offer microcosms that protect from overwhelming anxiety and through whose actions a more attractive rewarding universe can be created. Counter-norm contagion occurs only when the model corresponds to an individual's inner defenses, or when the rigid defenses threaten to collapse and new safety valves are needed. Usually the high ego-defender's anxieties are not directly expressed, but his susceptibility is apt to assert itself in explosive externalizations directed against objects deemed acceptable. Thus, the paradox that rigid conformity may, under suitable conditions, be transformed into the most extreme form of counter-norm contagion.

CHARACTERISTICS OF THE HIGH EGO-DEFENDER

A number of socio-psychological studies have shown a relationship between a lack of persuasibility and personality traits typical of the high ego-defender. Janis found students resistant to views presented in persuasive communication ranked high on a set of items covering various symptoms of neurotic anxiety—(such as hypochondriac complaints, morbid fears, insomnia, nightmares, excessive perspiration, and chronic concern about bodily injury). Obsessional traits were also indicated by answers to a set of two items: (1) inability to get rid of some unimportant idea "which comes to mind over and over again" and (2) constant need to make up rules of self-control so as to be sure to do the right thing at the right time.

High resistance to group influence in a natural setting—a woman's college noted for its "progressive" atmosphere—was found to be related to being stubborn or resistant, negativism, general aloofness, and a low capacity for social relationships. Students such as these continued to rely on their parents as reference points for political attitudes. Other correlational studies suggest that among preschool children low conformity to social demands goes together with a lack of emotional control, excitability, quarrelsomeness, and cruelty.[21] Obsessional tendencies also seem to make for immunity to new influence. Especially where such inclinations meet with group support, resistance to anything new is heightened.

Studies of hypnosis show that persons with strong ego defenses, especially those marked by an abnormal degree of rigidity, do not enter as heavy a trance as others. At different times a strong need for autonomy, hostility, and aggressiveness have been shown to be incompatible with acceptance of suggestions from a hypnotist. For example, when students were subjected to a jigsaw puzzle experiment, some were found to react with increasing irritability to difficulties; others took them in their stride, remaining good-natured and optimistic or finding some alibi for their troubles. Those in the latter group were found to be generally better hypnotic subjects.

The high ego-defender, because he feels vulnerable, needs rigid defenses against unacceptable aspects of his personality. His rigidity, in binding anxiety to specific objects, is his defense. Under ordinary circumstances, he exhibits high conformity to conventional norms and hangs

21. See T. W. Richards and M. P. Simons, "The Fels Behavior Scales," *Genetic Psychology Monographs*, XXIV (1941), pp. 259–309, for a study of nursery-school children.

rigidly onto his views. Since his defenses are forever in danger of being breached, he exhibits deficient powers of adaptation. To make him amenable to social (and hypnotic) influence, it is first necessary to have him relax his guard. He is a susceptible follower only in situations that minimize anxiety and promise security. Counter-norm influence is accepted if it bolsters defenses and offers a solution to inner conflict.

The susceptibility of the high ego-defender is not general but highly specific, and he is apt to be immune to contagion in most areas. This can be formulated as follows:

1. The motive patterns of high ego-defenders, especially their unconscious needs, are an extremely important determinant in many instances of elementary collective behavior.

2. This very defensiveness implies that the attraction exercised by a model (as incorporated in an ideology, an attitude, a social movement, etc.) derives primarily from its analogy with unconscious dispositions. Only those patterns that represent suitable externalizations of inner conflict are accepted.

3. Social support from others for "solutions" helps to win high ego-defenders.

4. Specific models, modes of life, ideologies, appeals, etc., that receive social support are accepted with startling alacrity by persons otherwise resistant.

The life histories of political and religious fanatics offer support for an interpretation that a socially supported ideology or set of beliefs may spell a solution to inner conflict. Lasswell, as illustrated in Chapter 9, has presented life histories to document the defensive function of political ideology and to establish the relationship between psychopathology and belief. Boisen, a minister once committed to a mental institution, has sought to demonstrate an affinity between mental illness and susceptibility to religious quickening. He has stressed the therapeutic value of the Holy Roller type of religion during the Great Depression. Unless a person can adjust his inner requirements to take account of others, Boisen holds, he is likely to withdraw into a tiny world of his own. We recognize the resolution of a mental crisis as "religious" only if it deals with socially validated experience. Otherwise it would be considered a "mental disorder." [22]

The high ego-defender (externalizer) is thus to be distinguished from the socially inadequate (instrumentalist) by the specificity of his susceptibility. Once committed, the former is apt to hold on to his defenses unless anxiety can be minimized.

22. Anton Boisen, *Religion in Crisis and Custom* (New York: Harper & Brothers, 1955), pp. 67–69.

AUTHORITARIANISM

Best known of the studies investigating the relationship between followership and rigid defensiveness are those using the authoritarian-democratic dimension. Not very long ago, fascist ideology, despite its many contradictions, was widely accepted and could not, it seemed, be countered by rational argument. Practical requirements of wartime and postwar operations heightened interest in the problem. It was necessary to understand the foundations of German morale, and for this purpose German prisoners of war and political internees provided accessible subjects. At the same time there was concern over the fascist potential in the United States. It was natural that interest should center on such questions as: Who is likely to be an anti-Semite or a racial bigot? What dispositions characterize the fascist agitator? Who would become an active Nazi? To cite from the introduction to the best known of these studies, *The Authoritarian Personality:* "If there should be a marked increase in anti-democratic propaganda, we should expect some people to accept it and repeat it at once, others when it seemed that everybody believed it, and still others not at all. In other words, individuals differ in their *susceptibility* to anti-democratic propaganda, in their readiness to exhibit anti-democratic tendencies." [23]

The California Study

The authoritarian-democratic dimension has been used in a variety of contexts since it was first developed in the California study. California researchers began by developing a series of attitude scales. An anti-Semitism scale was made up of items covering the several forms that prejudice and persecution of Jews might take. The various parts of this scale were found to be intercorrelated. Persons with strongly negative opinions of Jews, it was found, also felt hostility toward them and were able to find moral justifications for their attitudes. Thus anti-Semitism seemed to refer less to a specific opinion than to a broad pattern of views—an ideology.

Anti-Semitic ideology, the researchers then reasoned, does not exist as a separate and discrete syndrome unrelated to other attitude clusters that exhibit a broad similarity with anti-Semitism—namely, self-differentiation from Negroes, from minority groups in general (other than Jews and Negroes), and patriotism in the sense of viewing America as an in-group and all other nations as out-groups. A general ethnocentrism

23. Theodor W. Adorno *et al., The Authoritarian Personality* (New York: Harper & Brothers, 1950).

scale, constructed around these assumptions, revealed the existence of just such a broad cluster of out-group rejection combined with in-group submission and idealization.[24]

An attitude scale to measure patterns of belief symptomatic of a general receptivity to fascism was also developed. The items out of which it was constructed covered such areas as attitudes toward self, family, people in general, sex, personal values, etc. The resulting *F-scale* was to be an indirect test of ethnocentric attitudes, without touching on specific beliefs concerning minorities and foreigners. Therefore, items were screened out or modified until scores on it correlated highly with those on the ethnocentrism scale.

The theory underlying the construction of the F-scale held that ethnocentrism was a particular version of a general pattern of defensiveness called "authoritarianism." As fascist ideology was seen as another version of this underlying syndrome, the F-Scale is assumed to measure the fascist potential. But there is no direct test of this assumption, apart from the observed positive correlations between F-scale scores and other attitude scales dealing with ethnocentrism and between the F-scale and certain items in the radical-conservative scale indicative of a pseudo-conservatism, as opposed to traditional laissez-faire conservatism.

The nine areas covered by the measure of authoritarianism are generally indicative of a pattern of defensiveness that usually goes together with high outward conformity.

The most typical feature of the authoritarian's relationship to the moral aspects of life is the lack of integration between the precepts by which he lives and the rest of his personality. This is expressed by (1) *conventionalism,* the rigid adherence to middle-class values; (2) *authoritarian submission,* a submissive, uncritical attitude toward idealized authorities of the in-group; (3) *authoritarian aggression,* the tendency to be on the lookout for and to condemn, reject, and punish people who violate the conventional values. These three are indicative of the authoritarian's failure to build up a set of enduring values. Values continue to be conceived as imperatives demanding strict adherence and backed by external force and compulsion, because they have not been sufficiently internalized.

Another aspect of the authoritarian syndrome is ego weakness. The defensiveness of the authoritarian follows from the fact that unacknowledged impulses constantly threaten to breach ego defenses and become conscious. Since the authoritarian tends to shift all responsibility to external agents and forces, it is unlikely that he can be influenced by ap-

24. Answers on the various kinds of items were related rather than independent. Some relationship, though not a very close one, was found between ethnocentrism and political conservatism ($r = .5$).

peals to self-insight. That would constitute an admission of weakness. Ultimately questions of right and wrong come to be reduced to what is reassuring. His defensiveness results in a constriction of the self, for which he compensates by joining in a higher and more powerful cause. This is expressed in: (4) *anti-intraception,* opposition to the subjective, imaginative, the tender-minded; (5) *superstition and stereotypy,* belief in mystical determinants of the individual's fate, and a disposition to think in rigid categories; (6) *power and "toughness,"* preoccupation with the dominance-submission, strong-weak, leader-follower dimensions, over-emphasis on the conventionalized attitudes of the ego, and exaggerated assertions of strength and toughness.

Since self-insight is alien to the authoritarian, his evaluation of the world around him is colored by his inner conflicts which are, so to speak, externalized. This manifests itself in (7) *destructiveness and cynicism,* generalized hostility, and vilification of the human; (8) *projectivity,* the disposition to believe that wild and dangerous things go on in the world, and the projection outward of unconscious emotional impulses; (9) exaggerated concern with *sexual* "goings-on." Aggressiveness and weakness, when they are expressed, are channeled so as to avoid the likelihood of moral censure. They are attributed to others, and when members of the out-group become threatening, the authoritarian will turn against them with explosive violence. His authoritarian aggression is a defense of standards tenuously held.

To summarize, then, the *authoritarian personality*—the individual with a high F-score—seems prone to accept the existing authority structure in society, comfortably receiving orders from above and giving them to those below. With respect to ideology, he is apt to be religious, politically conservative, socially conforming, somewhat superstitious, and hard-headedly "practical" in the sense of being opposed to "idealistic" schemes. Yet he refrains from voting. His authoritarianism helps to organize and give meaning to *surface* attitudes, values, and opinions.

But certain contradictions in his beliefs suggest that deeper personality traits may run diametrically contrary to those consciously expressed. He expresses an exaggerated need to adhere to and defend conventional ideologies because he is so dependent on them as norms. His rigidity, his inability to tolerate ambiguity, leads him to react with great hostility to any perceived threat, and therefore he is apt to be highly susceptible to ideologies whose appeal is in harmony with inner dispositions. For example, to direct aggression against his own family may be inconceivable to the authoritarian; yet, during war he believes that extermination of the enemy population is a commendable policy. Likewise, a profession of beliefs in the very tenets of traditional conservatism is combined with a readiness for violent change which would, in effect, abolish the very institutions with which the individual appears to identify himself. The veneer of morality is poorly integrated with other aspects of the personality and merely masks the underlying anticonventionalism, based on repressed hostility against both family and in-group. He is inclined to do the very things he so rigorously and punitively opposes in others, yet always in a devious and unclearly recognized manner.[25]

Authoritarianism and Susceptibility

How does the authoritarian character structure of followers affect the nature of the collective behavior in which they participate?

1. When acting in a group setting, the follower has an influence on the social atmosphere that even the personality of the leader cannot counter. The experimental evidence, based on studies of small groups, indicates that leadership behavior depends more on the F-scale scores of the followers than on the personality of the leader.[26] While a great deal more evidence is needed to establish in just what ways and how the authoritarian followers affect collective behavior, a number of social scientists have come to believe that the typical rank-and-file Nazi came much closer to the authoritarian model than did the active leaders of the movements.[27]

2. When acting in an unorganized setting, followers will spawn leaders to suit their own image; [28] that is to say, in the more fluid and real life situations the influence of the follower will reveal itself in the

25. These inferences from the scale were fairly well supported by clinical interviews and projective tests conducted on smaller groups of extreme high and low scorers. But some of the very same trends found in high scorers, such as hostility and dependency, were also found among low scorers. When observed among low scorers, however, they usually appeared more ego-integrated, that is tied in with other trends of the personality. Thus the inner life of the "lows," though richer, was perhaps more troubled. They were more able to see faults in themselves, while the prejudiced group engaged in more self-idealization. Thus, the F-scale can be taken as a rough measure of defensiveness, and the ideology of high scorers as an externalization of inner conflicts and unacknowledged shortcomings.

26. William Haythorne, "The Effects of Varying Combinations of Authoritarian and Equalitarian Leaders and Followers," in E. E. Maccoby, T. M. Newcomb, and E. L. Hartley, *Readings in Sociol Psychology* (3d ed.; New York: Henry Holt & Co., Inc., 1958), pp. 511–22.

27. G. M. Gilbert, *op. cit.;* also Paul Kecskemeti and Nathan Leites, "Some Psychological Hypotheses on Nazi Germany," *Journal of Social Psychology,* XXVI (1947), pp. 141–83, and XXVII (1948), pp. 91–117 and 241–70.

28. Fillmore H. Sanford, "The Follower's Role in Leadership Phenomena" in G. E. Swanson *et al., Readings in Social Psychology* (Rev. ed.; New York: Henry Holt & Co., Inc., 1952), pp. 328–40.

personalities elevated to leadership, as they cannot in experimental studies in which group leaders are appointed.

Equalitarians display no inherent need for a strong leader but will accept one if the situation so demands. The leaders they are most apt to choose will be sensitive to others, prone to make their suggestions for action subject to group sanction, and therefore less inclined than other leaders to give direct orders to their followers. Satisfaction with the leader depends mostly on his competence in "human relations." Functional competence in relation to group goals is much less important.

By contrast, authoritarians prefer status-laden leadership, strong authority, and definite direction on the part of a "boss." A leader must above all contribute to the attainment of group goals and satisfy individual demands. Personal warmth and understanding count for very little. Authoritarians display open hostility toward a leader who appears weak, and therefore, whether by personality disposition or not, he is impelled to carve out for himself vis-à-vis his following a directive and authoritarian role. Moreover, authoritarians appear more susceptible to directive influence from an authoritarian leader. In small groups studied by Haythorne, morale appeared higher when both leaders and followers were homogeneously either authoritarian or nonauthoritarian. In the heterogeneously constituted groups, conflict between leader and group members was much more frequent. Confronted with a rigidly directive leader, a group of equalitarians may become demoralized, whereas authoritarians tend to become restive and uncomfortable when leadership is nondirective and fails to provide security. In general, authoritarians are more sensitive to views expressed by their peers if these are attributed to authority figures.[29]

3. Authoritarians, dependent on protective-directive leadership, seem more prone to demoralization when the supportive institutional milieu threatens to disintegrate. The authoritarian is heteronomously oriented in that he relies on group support to counter his passive dependency needs or the tender components of his personality. Under an ineffective leadership, concern for his own safety gains the upper hand, and guilt over his own weakness tends to be displaced on the leadership now charged with betrayal.

4. The authoritarian appears prone to the explosive hostility sometimes characteristic of the crowd. This usually occurs in the name of some moral cause or authority and again reflects his tendency toward projectivity. Furthermore, since the authoritarian wants to lose his self to a higher principle, thus alleviating feelings of inadequacy and resolving all ambiguity, he seems an eminently susceptible convert to various forms of mass movement that hold out high promise. In this connection, Hoffer

29. Berkowitz and Lundy, *op. cit.*

in *The True Believer* has even suggested that, as long as they answer the fundamental psychological needs of the authoritarian, such movements are "interchangeable." The substantive ideology of the movement itself matters very little. It permits the collective expression of hostility against victims perceived as members of an out-group, representing counter mores, to whom most of the ills of the world can be attributed. The susceptibility of the authoritarian operates primarily in those collective situations that afford the fullest expression to these inner motives without thereby threatening ego integrity.

PERSONALITY AND FOLLOWERSHIP

ACCORDING TO STUDIES of the authoritarian personality, the triumph of Nazism depended primarily on the existence of what we recognize as compulsive character. We contend that the *content* of an ideology cannot be adequately deduced from the personality characteristics of followers, and that any personality may be served by different ideologies in much the same way. Studies of Nazi followers bear on this point.

IDEOLOGY AND PERSONALITY

The high ego-defender holds to his views with great rigidity, and authoritarian ideology is well suited to his personal needs. Nevertheless, adherence by authoritarians to fascist ideology occurs only under certain facilitating conditions. There has to be a marked increase in fascist propaganda themes. The ideology has to be supported by some social authorities. The significance of high defensiveness as a source of particular opinions can be judged only in relation to the information environment and to the broader framework of values and institutions with which these individuals are continually in contact. This reservation is clearly stated in the introduction to *The Authoritarian Personality* but seems often forgotten in the quest to understand the personality characteristics of the Nazi supporter.

Studies of Nazi prisoners of war, though emphasizing how acceptance of the National Socialist creed was sustained by personality tendencies deeply rooted in the individual life history, have shown how it was also the product of the broader sociocultural context. For instance, Dicks found that POW's who held Nazi or near-Nazi beliefs and ideology with conviction and fanaticism had a personality structure that conformed closely to the authoritarian model.[30] The vast majority of the remainder,

30. Henry V. Dicks, "Personality Traits and National Socialist Ideology," *Human Relations*, III (June, 1950), pp. 111–54.

though submissive and apolitical, had also assimilated many facets of Nazi ideology with its inner contradictions. Like the fanatics, they tended to subordinate themselves to strong authorities; unlike them, they lacked the aggressive paranoiac activism.[31] Their acceptance of an authoritarian ideology was more a response to a homogeneous environment. Their submission to Nazi models was a function, principally, of the near universality with which Nazi beliefs were preached and accepted. It had little similarity to the vicious scapegoating of the high ego-defenders.

Certain observations drawn from the study of German prisoners also show that authoritarianism expressed itself in different ideological beliefs than it did among Americans. In Germany conventional religious affiliation or religious indifference (as contrasted with the acceptance of the Nazi version of deism, or atheism) supplied a partial immunity to Nazi ideology. In the United States, on the other hand, conventional religiosity and authoritarianism tended to go together, because their claims did not compete. The Germans had as a rule taken over the religious values of their mothers, and "mother cathexis," the form of religious values which, Dicks contends, is less likely to be transferred to male groups. But American religiosity bears the imprint of its milieu; it is strongly puritanical and ascetic, as opposed to a religion emphasizing sentimental and moral values—that is, maternal values. Hence these contrasts do not necessarily contradict the psychodynamic interpretations made in a specific sociocultural context. They show, however, how the correlations between personality characteristics and ideology in one situation often differ from those in others.

The bearing of the sociocultural milieu on the relationship between personality and ideology has been especially emphasized by Hyman and Sheatsley in their methodological critique of the California study. They cite some, at the time unpublished, evidence to show that the positive association between authoritarianism and prejudice does not characterize even all segments of the United States population to the same degree.[32] A clustering of prejudice and authoritarianism (and thus, by implication, defensiveness) may be most typical of the educated who are amply exposed to contrary information, whereas certain unscientific beliefs about personal differences continue to have an effective hold among the less educated. The California findings are affected by the fact that the sample was heavily loaded with the better-educated groups.

Finally, in the POW study, real rejection of Nazi ideology was char-

31. *Ibid.*, p. 152.
32. Herbert Hyman and Paul Sheatsley, "The Authoritarian Personality: A Methodological Critique," in Richard Christie and Marie Jahoda (eds.), *Studies in the Scope and Method of The Authoritarian Personality* (Glencoe, Ill.: The Free Press, 1954), pp. 50–122.

acteristic of only a small group—"usually because they had cathected some other system," such as Catholicism or Marxism.[33] The stanch resistance of Jehovah's Witnesses in German concentration camps makes another important case in point. Several writers have pointed to an "authoritarianism of the left," equally rigid and xenophobic as that of the right, the main difference being the leftist tendencies to identify with the underdog, to suspect plots, and to differentiate themselves from and distrust not "out-groups" but the established power elite. To which ideology a high ego-defender succumbs, it is hypothesized, is greatly influenced by what permissible targets of hostility are offered him by his immediate environment. Among certain groups the expression of hostility toward entrenched and traditional interests is widely accepted and consequently safe. Politically this constitutes the syndrome of the "protester," who identifies with the underdog. This syndrome is described briefly in one of the more speculative chapters of *The Authoritarian Personality*. On still other occasions one may discern compulsive tendencies to identify with anti-authoritarian patterns so typical of the delinquent personality and the psychopath. The various anti-authoritarian ideologies can express defensive needs no less than the rigid in-group conventionality of the authoritarian.[34]

The ability to deviate from official authoritarian patterns may be founded on two different needs: (1) rigid and intolerant need to preserve individual autonomy at any price (the characteristic of the defensive personality), or (2) the development of autonomy based on insight. In connection with the latter, broadening experiences act as an insulator from the influence of a persuasive authoritarian ideology.

THRESHOLD HYPOTHESIS

Perhaps all the literature on the authoritarian syndrome and its relationship to susceptibility adds up to this: there is no one-to-one relationship between personality needs and followership behavior. Broadly similar kinds of personality can be found among Nazis and non-Nazis, the prejudiced and unprejudiced, Republicans and Democrats, etc.— though they may not, of course, be distributed in exactly similar propor-

33. Dicks, *op. cit.*, p. 152.

34. Edgar H. Schein and three associates found similarities in the personalities of both active resisters and active collaborators among American soldiers in Chinese prison camps—similarities that differentiated the two groups together from the large uncommitted middle group. It is possible that the various authoritarian measures merely indicate the degree of active commitment to a set of alternate ideologies. See E. H. Schein *et al.*, "Distinguishing Characteristics of Collaborators and Resisters Among American Prisoners of War," *Journal of Abnormal and Social Psychology*, LV (September, 1957), pp. 197–201.

tions. Personality differences cannot therefore be viewed as a sufficient cause for emergent collective behavior. The impact of personality is mediated by a number of supporting or neutralizing factors. Hence, susceptibility depends in part on how well an ideology or emergent activity answers pre-existing personality tendencies. It depends equally on how the situation in which exposure occurs is assessed and defined. In one era youth is politically radical; in another, they engage in individual and futile protest, while the older members of society, psychologically freer from its taboos, can afford radicalism.

Followership in general is channeled along lines of prestige and status and in conformity with some group traditions and expectations. In general, the crowd mind that raises nondebatable demands and brooks no dissent asserts itself most frequently in the realm of things political, moral, and religious, when strong feelings and sacred issues are at stake and deviation is not tolerated.

The "outsider" is the object of contagion. When the environment is permissive, persons enjoy a certain degree of freedom to deviate; they can indulge in what they are inclined to think of as their "individuality." Debate is possible, and fads and fashions flourish. But in times of crisis, when there is no prior organization to govern action nor a tradition to guide the acceptance of opinions, the personalities of followers are apt to exert a more independent influence.

Regardless of the situation, however, susceptibility to counter-norm contagion presupposes the existence of some area of conflict in the follower. Either the situation is confused, or the balance between internal controls and impulses and interests that seek expression is precarious. Internalized group standards thus lose some of their effectiveness. But if there were complete freedom, the follower would not require an initiatory act by another but would simply follow his own whims. The suggestion from another person is effective because it points to a path the follower is already disposed to follow. The chronically anxious are probably the most susceptible to panic, since they have no faith in their own judgment anyway. The explosive externalizer is prepared to be extrapunitive. The presence of a need in the follower can alone explain his susceptibility. If the impulses to be held in check are weak, internalized controls could be upset only by a very strong external pressure. The amount of social support a person requires in order to be sucked into some specific counter-norm activity thus depends on the amount of inner resistance to be overcome.

A person whose internalized controls can be upset very easily may be considered to have a very low threshold of susceptibility. Again the analysis of the relationship between personality and susceptibility suggests that a person's threshold varies greatly according to the situation. An individual who is highly volatile in one regard may be a stanch resister in many others. *There is no reason to suppose that susceptibility exists as a generalized trait; what is needed is a description of situations and the kinds of rewards they offer to the potential followers.*

One of the most useful approaches is to look for the point at which an individual becomes involved in a collective current. The motive patterns among followers probably vary according to the phase at which they join in. A social movement, for example, is apt to attract followers for whom the ideology and membership fulfill different functions during the various phases of its career. The Communist Party, during the popular front period (1939–1941), attracted a much higher proportion of followers not fully aware of the exoteric aims of the movement. The individual needs it served were largely self-related. Consequently their tenure was relatively short; as the movement changed its character, these same needs could be better met in other ways. Likewise, the early members of the Nazi movement probably were most often anti-democratic personalities to whose extrapunitive disposition the movement appealed. The insecure and opportunistic coat-tail riders teamed up when membership promised realization of personal goals. But by that time the movement had begun to change its character, and some of the early Nazis became dissatisfied. Ultimately some "equalitarians" might be induced to join certain aspects of the movement, but for quite different reasons: because they wanted to remain effective or because they lacked information with which to counter all the claims of Nazi propaganda.

The same thing seems to apply to other forms of elementary collective behavior. A political demonstration, after turning into a riot, attracts all kinds of riffraff without knowledge or interest in the grievances that formed it. Or when a "selling panic" sweeps a white neighborhood in response to rumors that houses are being sold to Negroes, important psychological dispositions probably determine who will flee first, who will hold out but then get frightened and join the sellers, and who will actively resist as a matter of principle. In this last example, too, knowledge of how such panics are manufactured by real-estate operators and the adherence to group standards that place a high value on racial integration operate as mediating and neutralizing influences.

A TYPOLOGY OF SUSCEPTIBLES

One must then look for supporting and inhibitory influences that govern an individual's threshold of participation in situations entailing the potential gratification of some alienative need disposition. The following typology is based on the assumption of labile balance between personal disposition, valid norms, and the possibilities inherent in the situation for gratifying these dispositions.

1. *Members of deviant subcultures or antisocial groups.* These have the lowest threshold for participation in counter-norm activity supported by their deviant codes. Such activity is in harmony with their way of life. The counter-norm activity is raised to a norm among the alienated nucleus in which it is cultivated. There is some doubt, however, that such sectarian associations have been able to divorce themselves completely from conventional standards, and thus the formations of which they are members can be considered a contagious influence that constantly enables them to avoid guilt or censure.

2. *The impulsive.* This category of persons has an extremely labile internal balance. While normally they may be socially conforming, their susceptibility to contagion inheres in the resonance the object of contagion finds in compelling inner dispositions. Their impulsiveness is a function both of failure to internalize effectively the norms and of failure to master techniques by which tension can be dissipated.

3. *The suggestibles.* Loss of responsibility through anonymity implies that responsibility is displaced on external agents and that the individual can once more enjoy being unaccountable. Moral compunction will not be stilled entirely, but it appears that the formation of a collective situation bestows a partial immunity from forces one is ordinarily required to consider. The suggestibles tend to respond to cues in their immediate surroundings.

4. *The opportunistic yielders.* This category of persons can be observed to follow a movement or to hold an opinion when it appears to become dominant. This may mean either that it is being followed or about to be accepted by important persons. Through social projection it becomes the "only way." A subvariant of this is *the impostor*, a type described by Hecker in the dancing mania, who went around inciting others for personal benefit.

5. *Passive supporters.* This category of people promotes impressions of universal support. The passive supporters do not actually participate in a mob, hold an opinion, etc. But they do nothing to counter it, so that their silent presence at a mass meeting with a few active shouters is apt to suggest that the latter speak in their name. They cannot be stampeded into active participation, but nevertheless participate vicariously.

6. *The resistant.* Persons who have internalized standards and norms directly opposed to the object of contagion constitute the resisters. This group may be large or small. When a community is after a lynch victim or a revolutionary movement on the way to power is guilty of excesses,

their number is apt to be very small. For an action carried by a very large nucleus will attract many opportunists, while the passive supporters make it seem that support for the action is unanimous. Hence, the resistant runs considerable risk, for he threatens to spoil the appearance of near unanimity. On other occasions there may be a sufficient number of resisters to dissuade the opportunistic yielders from joining. Then the passive supporters appear to be on the side of the resisters, and outbreaks of contagion can thus be effectively quarantined.

B I B L I O G R A P H Y

ADORNO, THEODOR W., *et al. The Authoritarian Personality.* New York: Harper & Brothers, 1950. The most ambitious attempt to pin down the hypothesis that susceptibility to fascism is a function of personality dynamics.

DICKS, HENRY V. "Personality Traits and National Socialist Ideology," *Human Relations,* III (June, 1950), pp. 111–54. An empirical study of German prisoners of war that interprets susceptibility as a displacement of mother cathexis.

GILBERT, G. M. *The Psychology of Dictatorship.* New York: The Ronald Press Company, 1950. Contains studies of Nazi leaders and some interesting observations of their relations to the personality of followers.

HOFFER, ERIC. *The True Believer.* New York: The New American Library, 1958. General observations on the appeals of mass movements lead to the hypothesis that the specific ideology matters little.

HOVLAND, CARL I., *et al. Communication and Persuasion.* New Haven: Yale University Press, 1953. Chapters 5 and 6 assemble relevant evidence on susceptibility to persuasive communication.

SARNOFF, IRVING, *et al.* "The Motivational Basis of Attitude Change," *Journal of Abnormal and Social Psychology,* XLIX (January, 1954), pp. 115–24. A discussion of the implication of perceptual, learning, and dynamic approaches to personality for affecting attitudes.

SIGHELE, SCIPIO. *Le crime à deux.* Lyons-Paris, 1893. Sighele shows that in the criminal pair, the suicidal pact, and *folie à deux,* one person always acts out an intention originating in the other.

SMITH, M. BREWSTER, BRUNER, J. S., WHITE, R. W., *et al. Opinions and Personality.* New York: John Wiley & Sons, Inc., 1956.

CHAPTER 11

The Emergence of Social Objects: Victims and Rallying Points

Polarization occurs between leader and followers and also between participant-followers and central persons who are the *social objects* of their behavior. Those who are social objects occupy a central position without being leaders. They differ from leaders in two important ways: first, they neither instigate nor initiate action for a following; second, they do not participate in the action or share in the collective mood of which they are the focus. The category of social objects thus includes such diverse roles as victim, villain, martyr, idol, hero, and fool.

Not all objects in the focus of collective behavior are persons. The object may be a symbolic representation of a collective goal—a totem, a flag, or sacraments. Similarly, collective attention may be preoccupied with a rumor, a news item, or a social problem concerning which the participants take sides. Or a spontaneous demonstration may have no object beyond a visible display of the solidarity needed to reinforce demands. The expression of solidarity, as in ritual and ceremony, may even be its own end.[1] But persons constitute a special kind of object among the many possible focuses of collective action.

Types of Social Object

The person cast in the role of social object can be looked at in two ways: (1) what is objectively done to him; and (2) what emotions focus upon him. A person may, on the one hand, constitute a target

1. Cf. Emile Durkheim, *Elementary Forms of the Religious Life* (Glencoe, Ill.: The Free Press, 1954).

against whom collective action is directed. Thus, the milling mob or the angry demonstrators vent their common hatred on whoever is an accessible target. His presence crystallizes the diffuse feelings and individual expressive acts around a specific objective. Thereby the behavior becomes truly collective, and the central person may be its *victim*.

By contrast, the person considered as a *rallying point* is the center of group formative and group integrative processes. The development of common emotions toward an *idol* or a *bête noire* helps to define the boundaries of fellowship. A suitable object becomes the starting point of the whole affair. Therefore the crucial thing about the rallying point is not how he is objectively treated or whether he accepts that treatment willingly. He serves as a point of reference in relation to which common identifications come to be perceived.

THE VICTIM   A victim in the narrow sense is a target of collective aggression, which has as its central purpose his destruction, his expulsion from the group, injury to his social reputation, or the infliction of bodily harm. Yet one is also a victim of gossip or of adulation that is not wanted, or the butt of collective jokes. The victim always emerges in opposition to a body of molesters who view him as an outsider. In some ways the victim is as effective a unifying agent as a leader. But he initiates no action to be followed, whereas the solidarity of the molesters operates against his person. Hence, the victim's function in collective action is almost the direct opposite from that of the leader, who initiates and directs action for his following. The leader's action is positive, whereas the victim operates as a negative pole. Unlike the victim (even the victim of undesired adulation), the leader is never the objective of group action he initiates.

RALLYING POINTS: IDOLS AND VILLAINS   The other major category of collective object is the persons who spontaneously emerge as centers of common emotion. It is possible to differentiate among rallying points in terms of the specific sentiments they elicit. Though there are undoubtedly many (and more subtle) ways of making distinctions, collective objects emerge out of four basically different moods: *admiration, compassion, ridicule,* and *vilification.* In the first two the object is elevated in status, and, more important, he is the center of emotions that are basically positive. Ridicule and vilification, on the other hand, degrade the person toward whom they are directed; the tenor of the feelings aroused is more or less negative.

All the rallying points for positive emotions are here called *idols;* those for negative emotions *villains.* The corresponding processes of polarization are *idolization* and *vilification.*

Both leader and victim are also the objects of group emotions. But the role of leader and idol are by no means identical. As an object of worship the leader need not lead; instead he is idolized. Likewise, the person serving as a negative reference point is not always attacked or destroyed. Sometimes this villain is carefully nurtured so as to assure his availability for condescension or blame. More important, idols and villains cannot be distinguished by their own acts or by their objective consequences. A person who is the idol of one group is a villain for another. The late Senator Joseph McCarthy of Wisconsin was a hero for many but the chief villain of those who identified with his victims. One of these, the Secretary of State under Truman, Dean Acheson, was hanged in effigy in many parts of the country but was elevated to martyrdom in others.

The lines between idolization and vilification are easy to cross as issues change and the public realigns itself. Today's fool is tomorrow's prophet and, when proven wrong, may become a villain. Thus Charles A. Lindbergh was first a "flying fool," next a "hero" (Lucky Lindy), and again for those arrayed against him a "villain" when, before 1941, as an America-Firster he opposed United States aid in any form to the Allied fight against Hitler. All this happened within the span of a dozen years.[2]

Collective idolization can take many forms. Some persons gain public admiration for their extraordinary accomplishments or, at least, are credited with such accomplishments. Collective adulation defines the hero. It also encompasses the saint, who symbolizes virtues rather than achievement. Another kind of idol is the tragic hero, so defined by compassion he arouses. The typical tragic hero of drama, to cite Aristotle, invites general pity and sympathy because he is "a man not preeminently virtuous and just, whose misfortune, however, is brought upon him not by vice and depravity but by some error of judgment, of the number of those in the enjoyment of great reputation and prosperity."[3] His defeat is brought about by the kind of circumstance that everyone can imagine himself experiencing. How easily a hero may become an object of ridicule, a fallen idol (or vice versa), will be illustrated. A victim who suffers in the name of a cause and to whom, therefore, superior virtue and fortitude are attributed may also be idolized. These collective sentiments, not his acts, transform such a victim into a martyr.

The villain is most typically a *bête noire*. He represents and is represented as a most unworthy and despicable character around whom negative emotions easily crystallize. What defines the fool are collective ridicule and derision. The fool is made to look not so much morally inferior as grotesque. The denigration is thus more indirect than in the

2. Kenneth Davis, *The Hero; Charles A. Lindbergh and the American Dream* (New York: Doubleday & Company, Inc., 1959).

3. See Aristotle, *Poetics* (New York: Everyman's Library, No. 901), p. 1453a.

case of the *bête noire*. If a villain is hated too much, he is apt to become a person who must be destroyed—that is, a victim. Often the villain is *not* a particular individual; he is as likely to be pictured as the representative of some, however vaguely defined, "accursed" group, whose power is unduly magnified. To members of such groups the public imagination imputes the most sinister motives. If, on the other hand, his universal human qualities are recognized, the villain will arouse pity. It is possible to make an entire group the object of vilification, as in the case of minority groups, while individual members known personally are exempted from the collective curse.

A person can be both an idol and a villain at the same time but for different people, depending on the cleavages that already exist within a society. Hence, the rallying point emerges vis-à-vis a *public*. Ultimately the people tend to agree on whether the person deserves to be worshiped or scorned. Legend then stabilizes the image, and the appropriate emotion becomes crystallized into a cult.

SUMMARY A person's behavior as leader or his suffering as victim are the objective consequence of what he does or what is done to him. Both leadership and victimization involve collective acts, whereas the selection of rallying points concerns changing identifications. Thus, the leader or the victim may each be transformed into traditional idols or villains. Emotions are volatile and subject to change. As the rallying point for a cause, the victim of collective aggression may become the point of positive identification. After the execution of Sacco and Vanzetti, for example, the two victims, believed innocent, were elevated to martyrdom and thus idolized. Most victims remain villains until they are forgotten, and the memory of leaders is often kept alive by institutionalized commemoration, a form of idolization.

MAJOR QUESTIONS This typology is only tentative. Its purpose is to make clear the various ways in which a person can exert a central influence on a collectivity without being a leader. In analyzing the collective dynamics of participant-object relations, three kinds of question need to be kept in mind:

1. What does the social object contribute? Why should one person be selected rather than another? In other words, what traits bring him to attention and make him suitable for the role? Does his subsequent behavior confirm these expectations?

2. What functions do the various kinds of social object have for the participants in the collective action? These functions involve psychological satisfactions as well as group-related needs.

3. What are the conditions under which the emotions toward an object undergo a reversal? Specifically, when are victims and villains likely to become idols, and when do victims and idols become villains?

What the Object Contributes

Like the follower whose active disposition contributes to his susceptibility, the social object is hardly ever a completely passive sufferer on whom violence, scorn, admiration, etc., are bestowed. Even if the victim of the mob does not volunteer for that role, he may inadvertently be inviting his executioners. Or the self-effacing saint, idolized for his legendary modesty, is hardly ever propelled into fame without some ostentation on his part. In every case the personal dispositions, the behavior, the characteristics, or the associates of the persons selected as objects contribute to their "fate," however unwillingly it is borne and in spite of all public disclaimers. Neither the protestations of innocence nor the violence with which the victim defends his person, his privacy, or his reputation constitute proof that he himself is not one of the most important contributory factors in his selection.

Persons contribute in varying degrees to their becoming the object of a cult, of revulsion, of a joke, etc. But the willingness with which a person lends himself to the part is only one of the factors that determines his objective contribution. Willingness depends on the congruence between what a person considers the prerogatives and obligations of his institutionalized status and the way people in the collectivity behave toward him. The victim who identifies with the morality that his tormentors represent is more likely to cooperate. Furthermore, when there are precedents for the behavior, reluctance is further reduced. For example, it is easy for the man who has accomplishments to his credit to accept a hero's welcome, because the manner of paying homage is largely governed by conventions. But if he is mobbed, he may not play his part with the requisite dignity; excess admiration easily becomes repulsive.

A person must therefore learn to play the part in which he is cast. Being the center of collective emotions becomes painful when they undermine rather than support a person's self-conception. A person chosen as an idol may be asked to reveal his private habits; his reluctance to do so may cut short the period of idolization. The part of hero is often borne as reluctantly as that of victim or villain. As an artist's talents are recognized, he gains admiration, which is compatible with his status as performer. But he also becomes the center of emotions that are hardly compatible with his formal position.

> We have only to think of the troop of women and girls, all of them in love in an enthusiastically sentimental way, who crowd around a singer or pianist after his performance. It would be easy for each of them to be jealous of the rest; but, in the face of their numbers and the consequent

impossibility of their reaching the aim of their love, they renounce it, and, instead of pulling out one another's hair, they act as a united group, do homage to the hero of the occasion with their common actions, and would probably be glad to have a share of his flowing locks.[4]

Quite different roles may be thrust on the artist as well. He may become the object of scorn, of revulsion, or of hostility. Dos Passos wrote about the controversial Isadora Duncan at the beginning of World War I:

> In her own city of San Francisco the politicians wouldn't let her dance in the Greek Theater they'd built under her influence. Wherever she went she gave offense to the philistines. When the war broke out she danced the *Marseillaise,* but it didn't seem quite respectable and she gave offense by refusing to give up Wagner or to show the proper respectable feelings of satisfaction at the butchery.[5]

The artist can also lend himself as the public fool. The oversize nose ("schnozzola") of Jimmy Durante became his personal trade mark on which his special form of comedy rested. He identified with others' views of his own shortcomings and thus turned them to his advantage. Self-depreciation is a playful exercise. It takes the bite out of the joke, and hence there is no true victim. All can join in the laughter since its derisive nature is disguised. By contrast, all the other Jimmy Durantes who find their noses a source of self-regret are not gladly made fools. Unless the butt of the joke willingly cooperates, joking about a physical defect is too openly aggressive and malicious. Similarly, when a statement of faith in the name of a group with which one identifies is proclaimed as heresy; or when some personal failing turns the object into a fool, a rallying point becomes an unwilling victim.

VICTIMIZATION

THE SELECTION OF A COLLECTIVE VICTIM turns a member of the community, who has enjoyed all the rights of membership, into an internal enemy. By turning against him the collectivity deprives him of its protection. The victim is cast out or degraded. He becomes public property.

Victims contribute to their own victimization in varying degrees. "In a sense the victim," as von Hentig has pointed out in connection with

4. Sigmund Freud, *Group Psychology and The Analysis of the Ego* (London: The Hogarth Press, 1949), p. 87.

5. John Dos Passos, *The Big Money,* Part III of *U.S.A.* (New York: Modern Library, 1930), p. 159.

the individual criminal act, "shapes and moulds the criminal. The poor and ignorant immigrant has bred a peculiar kind of fraud. Depressions and wars are responsible for new forms of crime because new types of potential victims are brought into being." [6] Individuals become more vulnerable if they are easy and rewarding targets; that is, if they expose themselves, and if an offense against them promises gain.

The victims of collective crimes are not arbitrarily chosen either. But not every person defined under the law as suffering criminal harm is a collective victim in our sense. For example, the objects of a swindle perpetrated on a massive scale, though contributory agents, are not collective objects. Those duped by the South Sea Bubble of the early eighteenth century or by the Florida land boom of the 1920's are the susceptible followers on whom a hoax is perpetrated. They participate in a parallel collective action, whereas the collective victim is, to repeat, a central person on whom that action is focused.

All collective victims are the targets of aggression or resentment that is normally controlled in the interest of group solidarity but finds a suitable outlet in them. To a greater or lesser degree all victims are "scapegoats of society"; [7] whether or not they actually committed any wrong is totally irrelevant. The personal characteristics that determine the choice of a scapegoat often have but an indirect bearing on the cause for which he is sacrificed. He is offered because others cast upon him, quite irrespective of his own life, sins and failings for which he is not fully responsible.

The victim may accept his role voluntarily. If he subjectively identifies with the cause in whose name he is sacrificed, he is a *martyr* rather than a scapegoat. Some martyrs have volunteered as victims; more often the martyr for a deviant cause has renounced the chance for escape. Still, the typical scapegoat sees no justification for his destruction. From his viewpoint, the suffering to which he is exposed and the harm done to him are unrelated to any cause with which he identifies. Hence, in the last analysis, the sacrifice of the martyr is a self-sacrifice, while the fate of the scapegoat is suffered innocently.

Between these two extremes there are many degrees to which the victim identifies with the action brought against him. Some persons unconsciously want to be victimized. Observation of delinquents has shown the skill with which children ferret out types whose pathology supplements their own and thus supports their delinquency. Not only do they

6. Hans von Hentig, "The Victim and the Criminal," in C. E. Vedder, S. Koenig, and R. Clark, *Criminology: A Book of Readings* (New York: The Dryden Press, Inc., 1953), p. 77f.

7. Ruth Eissler's term. See "Scapegoats of Society," in Kurt R. Eissler (ed.), *Searchlights on Delinquency* (New York: International Universities Press, 1949), pp. 288–305.

find friends with similar dispositions, but the youngster with strong sadistic trends can be relied upon to spot the potentially willing masochistic partner in no time at all even when their personalities show compatability on no other grounds. The victim thus may tempt his persecutor.[8] An adult's apparent indifference to conventions may make him the object of action he does not consciously want to bring upon himself.

There are also the heretics, who advocate their teachings in the name of the community. But heretics are made by a community that insists there be no rival doctrine to those officially sanctioned. If a person upholds his heresy in the face of pressures, he thereby contributes to his victimization in the name of a cause with which he identifies and for whose sake he is willing to take the consequences. Hence, any boundaries between the heretic, elevated to martyrdom by his followers, and the dissident victim or between the unwilling scapegoat and the unwitting tempter are somewhat arbitrary. Still, the degree of subjective identification with the goal to be achieved by the sacrifice entails an important distinction.

The change of status that transforms an accepted member of the group into an outcast or victim comes about in three main ways: (1) Group interest (as perceived) may require sacrifice of a member either for ceremonial purposes or to achieve some collective goal. Insofar as the behavior is highly organized and conventionalized, this possibility need concern us little. (2) The victim, by his behavior, may appear remiss in his obligation to the group. (3) Criteria of group membership in the community may be redefined in such a way as to place whole categories of persons into the status of outcasts to whom normal obligations and the privileges of membership no longer extend. A person is often hunted down because of his characteristics, but any person who falls into a given category becomes, by that fact alone, available.

THE SACRIFICIAL SCAPEGOAT

Almost every society has had its scapegoats. In many primitive societies, according to Sir James Frazer, ritual sacrifices were periodically employed to clear the air of evil and to make amends. During the ritual, "evil influences are embodied in visible form or are least supposed to be loaded upon a material medium, which acts as a vehicle to draw them off from the people, village, or town." [9] The vehicle, though often a wagon or a boat or other form of transport, can be an animal or some symbolic object. Occasionally it is a human being.

8. Von Hentig, *op. cit.*; F. Redl and D. Wineman, *The Aggressive Child* (Glencoe, Ill.: The Free Press, 1957), p. 156f.

9. Sir James G. Frazer, *The New Golden Bough* (New York: Criterion Books, Inc., 1959), p. 514.

The fundamental fact about "scapegoating" in primitive societies is that the object, whether a material artifact, an animal, or a person, is destroyed for the benefit of others. It serves principally to ward off physical harm and natural disaster. When a person is sacrificed, he protects those who destroy him from their enemies—demoniacal, heavenly, or merely human.

The death of the scapegoat protects the others because he makes them powerful. This occurs in a number of ways. In the first place, by removing guilt, the ceremonies preserve the group from the consequences of giving way to their impulses. Frazer tells us that the periodic expulsion of devils through the public ceremony of scapegoating may be preceded or followed by a period of general license, during which the ordinary restraints of society are thrown aside, and all offenses, short of the gravest, are allowed to pass unpunished. The ceremony frees men's minds from "the oppressive sense, under which they generally labour, of an atmosphere surcharged with devils; and in the first revulsion of joy they overleap the limits commonly imposed by custom and morality." [10] Someone has died for their sins, and thus they may rejoice at their own escape. Such revels are soon halted as normal restraint is reimposed.

Sacrificial ceremonies also permit periodic escape into self-indulgence. Because absolution is expected through the scapegoat, license is encouraged. Sometimes it is the victim of the ceremony who is permitted to indulge himself at will for a period before his slaughter. He actually acts out the forbidden impulses which the others vicariously enjoy. Since he is thereafter punished, his persecutors likewise punish themselves vicariously through his sacrifice. It means an escape from guilt for the entire group.

Scapegoating is a projective device. Guilty thoughts and wishes are cast onto an alter ego in the same way that small children may impute their "bad" thoughts and forbidden games to an imaginary playmate. Johnny hasn't spilled the milk you see on the kitchen floor; his "playmate" knocked the glass out of his hand. And in the most prevalent form of this defense, adults are prone to gloat over the petty faults and peculiar quirks of their neighbors and acquaintances.[11] Symbolically, the latter too serve as scapegoats.

The *scapegoat motif* then represents forms of individual and collective self-punishment. Its function is revealed by what happens to the person who endeavors to rescue a scapegoat. Western society has not yet welcomed with any mass enthusiasm reformers' crusades on behalf of unmarried mothers or reformed prostitutes. The disgrace of these "fallen"

10. *Ibid.*, pp. 529–45.
11. J. C. Flugel, *Man, Morals and Society* (London and Baltimore: Penguin Books, Inc., 1945), p. 206.

women has been sharply contrasted with the virtue of marriage; the former continue at various times and places to be subjected to almost every kind of persecution and indignity. Similar uneasiness has been manifested in the past concerning efforts to do away with punishment and pain in various spheres. The first introduction of anesthetics was greeted with a chorus of disapproval and alarm from clerical, lay, and even medical quarters. Evidently it was felt that men (and still more, women) in trying to evade pain would call divine displeasure down upon all humanity.[12]

Selection of. Scapegoats

The following is an inventory of circumstances and traits that help to focus collective action on a particular victim.[13]

1. *Accessibility.* The first and most general condition is that the victim be physically available. To victimize an inaccessible person is impossible, although he may symbolize a victim and thus become the object of scorn and other negative emotions. He would, in the terminology used above, serve as a rallying point, a villain. The victim becomes accessible by being near by and inadequately protected. A crowd searching for a particular person will often select substitute victims with similar characteristics if the latter are more accessible. In vendettas, kinsmen are substituted for original criminals as objects of revenge. Immediately after the attack on Pearl Harbor, the "collective indignation" and fears of Americans resulted in the mass relocation and internment of many American-born Japanese and long-time residents of Japanese ancestry.

2. *High visibility.* Next in order of generality is the presence of some distinguishing characteristic that identifies a person as a potential victim. These characteristics are often physical traits. According to information gathered by Frazer some half-century ago, the king in Uganda, having been warned by the gods that his enemies were working magic to bring disease or other calamities to the people, would choose a human scapegoat whose sacrifice would stave off disaster. "The scapegoat consisted of either a man and a boy or a woman and her child, chosen because of some mark or bodily defect, which the gods had noted and by which the victims were to be recognized." [14] The victims would be sent to the frontier of the land of the king's enemies, where their limbs would be broken. Too crippled to crawl back to Uganda, they were left to die a lingering death in the country of the enemy. The disease or plague, thus transferred to the scape-

12. *Ibid.,* p. 212.
13. Cf. the pamphlet *ABC's of Scapegoating* (Central Y.M.C.A. College, 19 La-Salle St., Chicago, Ill.), foreword by Gordon W. Allport. The term "psychologically available" is from Everett C. Hughes.
14. Frazer, *op. cit.,* p. 565.

goats, was carried back by them to the land from which it had been sent.

There are many characteristics by which scapegoats may be selected. Sometimes the sacrificial role falls upon the first-born son, the aged, or those broken down by debauchery. In a heterogeneous mass society, individuals are of course often identified by their racial characteristics. But customs, modes of dress, and behavior at variance with the majority may also serve as criteria of ascription. An American soldier in uniform, taking photographs with his camera, is an identifiable target in an Oriental city torn by unrest. Or the victim may be a person just passing through town. His appearance and mannerisms may not differ much from local ones, but as a stranger he constitutes a target readily visible in the community.

3. *Psychological availability.* The victim must in some way be considered expendable by the persecuting collectivity. In Siam, for example, it used to be the custom on one day of the year to single out a woman broken down by debauchery, and carry her on a litter through all the streets to the music of drums and hautboys. She was insulted and pelted with dirt. After having been carried through the whole city, she was then thrown on a dunghill or a hedge of thorns outside the ramparts and forbidden ever to enter again the walls of the city. The persecutors "believed that the woman thus drew upon herself all the malign influences of the air and of evil spirits." [15] The old woman could be sacrificed to the evil spirits without disruption or economic loss to the community. It is unlikely that she was the object of much pity or sympathy on the part of the offerers.

A person becomes psychologically available when, because of some specific act or, simply, because he is not useful in society, some stigma is attached to him. He is now expendable. Also, the suitability of victims may hinge on little more than a past history of stigmatization. Stigmatization, which initially hinged on some external or extrinsic trait, thus becomes self-confirming, since doing away with the victim will ultimately be viewed as a collective benefit to the community.

4. *Personification of the forbidden.* The sacrifice of a scapegoat is both a propitiatory gesture and an act of atonement. In propitiation, assurance of future indulgences is sought, while atonement is for sins already committed, though perhaps not acknowledged. But the scapegoat, while personifying the forbidden, need not actually transgress the moral norms of the society. It suffices that he should appear to do so. For "the existence of those whose super-egos are less burdensome is an outrage to our sense of justice (why should we bear this burden and they be free from it?) and a menace to our own obedience to our superego. For both these reasons we resent the heretic, the freethinker (religious and political), and the moral nonconformist, and in consequence we persecute them and

15. *Ibid.,* p. 534.

turn them into scapegoats." [16] Any visible behavior that suggests deviance in this sense identifies the sinner. Thus, butchers who become victims during food riots are frequently accused of passing off for other cuts of meat the genitals of animals or other "profane" ingredients.

5. *The resister.* A most likely candidate for attack is the person who questions the legitimacy of the collective action. The repentant sinner who admits his sins and thus—by implication—the justness of the action against him stands a chance of being saved. But the unrepentant sinner is doomed. For the same reason, the scoffers who refuse to join in the exercise of collective righteousness are often linked with victims and become the targets of aggression.

6. *Vulnerability.* Not only the powerless but also powerful individuals, provided they are accessible, may become the victims of collective vengeance. One need only think of revolutionary mobs attacking the hated symbols of authority. But this happens only when the social order disintegrates and powerful figures have lost their authority. Consequently persons normally in a position to retaliate, instead of "weak" persons, are chosen only after a community has become demoralized. Thus, under "normal" conditions, the choice of victims (as illustrated by lynch justice) is likely to follow the lines of convention. It is directed against persons of minority status or, as in the old West, as an illegal, though generally accepted, way of law enforcement. In periods of rapid social change and of great unrest, former heroes and divinely established authorities may be destroyed in an act of collective vengeance.

WITCHES AS VICTIMS

While nowadays most people scoff at the idea of witches, they were very real to people living some centuries ago. The superstitious belief in disembodied spirits revisiting the world led to a deluge of blood and horror. For a period of two centuries and a half Europeans shuddered over men who could summon evil spirits to spite or harm their fellow beings. Mackay described the period of witchcraft heresy hunting as "an epidemic terror [which] seized upon the nations; no man thought himself secure, either in his person or possessions, from the machinations of the devil and his agents." [17] Witchcraft was blamed for all sorts of personal ills and public misfortunes. Through witchcraft men sought to account for the destruction of barns by storm, the death of diseased cattle, the illness of loved ones. Also drought, famine, and pestilence, once considered the unexplicable will of Providence, now became known as the work of some

16. Flugel, *op. cit.,* p. 242.
17. Charles Mackay, *Extraordinary Popular Delusions and the Madness of Crowds* (New York: Farrar, Straus, 1932), p. 462.

neighboring hag. Such persons had to be destroyed; their pact with the devil was apt to bring down upon the community the rightful wrath of God. Witches were psychologically available, if they could be identified.

The turning of hostility against "outsiders," in whatever form, is always indicative of social dislocations. Defection and deviance always flourish under conditions of unrest. At the same time many who are suffering but compliant seek explanations that will not undermine their traditional beliefs. An image of community solidarity, otherwise threatened, can thus be projected. At this point the self-interest of some elements in the community, not necessarily the dominant group, inclines them to exploit these feelings to further their own ends. By offering the "deviants" as victims to an aroused populace, they provide them with an explanation for their misfortune and yet manage to achieve private goals.

The witch mania that rocked the Massachusetts Bay Colony late in the seventeenth century is one of the best-chronicled collective orgies in search of victims. It illustrates not so much the causes of witch hunts but how victims are chosen. Before the mania had spent itself, twenty witches were executed and many more were imprisoned.[18]

> The witch mania began with a certain "children's affliction." In what would now appear to us a bit of childish disobedience, a group of girls secretly listened to tales of witchcraft told by an illiterate slave who had been brought as a child to Salem from Barbados. For this they would certainly have been punished if discovered. But they were not. The youngest of the girls, plagued by guilt, fell into convulsions, babbled, screamed, and sometimes ran around on all fours, barking, braying, screaming, as if she were suffering the tortures of the damned. The "possession" (a familiar bit of adolescent hysteria) soon caught on; one after another the girls were seized. Their behavior was so startling that soon they became the center of attraction for circles of awed spectators. Though their affliction apparently was real enough, the girls "at this point were having a wonderful time. Their . . . notoriety was infinitely rewarding to childish natures beset by infantile cravings for attention. Hitherto snubbed and disregarded, they were now cosseted and made much of. They could hardly have attracted more notice if among them they had married the king and all his court." [19]

18. There are various versions of the Salem witch hunt. Most of the quotations used here are drawn from the vivid account by Marion Starkey, *The Devil in Massachusetts* (New York: Alfred A. Knopf, Inc., 1946). But the facts have been checked against other published sources. Arthur Miller's play *The Crucible* (The Viking Press, 1953) treats the Salem mania in detail.

19. Starkey, *op. cit.*, p. 30.

Onlookers, trying to understand their behavior, first got the idea that the girls were bewitched. The girls on first being asked: "Who afflicts you?" were simply dumbfounded; they did not understand the question. They were, it appears, just a "pack of bobby-soxers," teen-aged girls," inflamed by the terrors of Calvinism as they understood it, depressed by the lack of legitimate outlet for their natural high spirits [who] found relief for their tensions in an emotional orgy." [20] Egged on by the community, the first victims were soon publicly "cried out" by them.

FIRST VICTIMS, VISIBLE AND AVAILABLE   The first victims were "natural" choices; they were visible and easily fingered. Besides, their marginal status in the community made them psychologically available and thus very vulnerable.

> The first witch arrested was the Negro slave who had entertained the girls with fragments of voodoo which she remembered from her West Indian childhood. There were few slaves in Salem, and her color was visible to those in search of a scapegoat.
>
> The connection of the first victim with the girls' sins was obvious, but for the second victim no such connection was apparent. She was an old crone, a nuisance in the community. She was shrewish, idle, slovenly, something of a tramp, in the habit of begging from door to door. Moreover, she smoked a pipe. Her hair was matted. Already, during an earlier epidemic, she had been accused of spreading smallpox as a result of her negligence. She was poor, and the Puritans had little pity or patience with the poor, since poverty was willed by God and considered a mark of guilt.
>
> The third of the witches cried out was a person once moderately well-to-do, who had lost caste. She was the target of much gossip and rumor to which she showed a certain indifference. She had on her husband's death taken an overseer into her home and was said to be living in sin with him. Provoked by the village gossip, she had become remiss in church attendance, hardly in line with Puritan morality, and was thereby compounding her sin.

MORE VICTIMS: "THREATS"   From here on, the circle of victims widened. The ones cried out in the next phase fell into one of two categories: (1) villagers who were objects of envy or who, as a result of neighborhood squabbles, had become generally unpopular; and (2) all persons who openly scoffed at the witchcraft charges, thereby incurring the particular enmity of the girls. The first category of persons was evi-

20. *Ibid.*

dently available. Their victimization was not apt to stir up much protest. Persons in the second category, on the other hand, posed a clear-cut threat to the collective mania in which the community was indulging itself.

Typical of the second batch of victims was one "witch" who, after her execution, was proclaimed innocent. Rebecca Nurse was one of the folk martyrs of this collective delusion. The large and closely knit family of which she was the matriarch, though not born to "gentry," was acquiring a large estate by their diligence. "Though no one could deny that the Nurses were decent, God-fearing people, their conspicuous prosperity had something questionable about it; their cheerful self-sufficiency could be and was resented." [21] There had been several disputes over land with neighbors who were "old gentry." Rebecca herself was well loved and an almost saintly woman; but she had a temper, which she once let loose on a neighbor whose hog got into her garden. The neighbor died shortly afterward, and the neighbor's wife never ceased to talk about the coincidence. Yet the superstitious gossip of her neighbor and the specific offense she had given were only contributory factors in her victimization and hardly suffice to explain it. On grounds such as these, almost anyone could have been named as a witch.

She was the first of a whole string of older matrons and dowagers, most of them hard-working countrywomen, named by the teen-agers. Says Marion Starkey, "These young girls, still on the threshold of the biological experience that these matrons knew so lustily and well or else, as seems probable from the later record of some of them, getting furtively and sinfully what their elders enjoyed lawfully, shrank from the pitilessly realistic appraisal" that the stalwart countrywomen made of them.[22] They appraised the antics of the girls as the natural stuff of adolescence. By their remarks, they incurred the uncompromising enmity of the girls.

These matrons were opinionated and outspoken. In this instance, to their own misfortune, they turned out often to have been right. One of the victims, cried out during the second phase, was so skeptical of the genuineness of the girls' affliction that it bordered on downright heresy. Named as sinner, she accused the girls in return. Similarly, the first man to be accused of wizardry had voiced some very strong and very public remarks about the girls. In the court of Salem he stood by his accused wife and protected her. He said common sense was abdicating before the crazed fantasies of wenches in their teens wanting attention. Right there in the court

21. *Ibid.*, p. 52.
22. *Ibid.*

the girls thus provoked went into their mediumistic trance and pronounced him a "most dreadful wizard."

EVERYONE A POTENTIAL VICTIM   Little by little those singled out as victims were no longer the most visible or expendable or even the deviants of the community. Accusations began to fasten on the skeptics who questioned the girls' exhorbitant charges and thereby posed a threat to their newly acquired importance. Often the witches named were relatives of those already denounced who, in defending the accused, impugned the innocence of the afflicted children and therefore had to be eliminated themselves. In other words, the thrill of hunting heretics caught on in the community; soon the girls could name almost anyone with impunity. As far as they were concerned, almost anyone was available. To be on their spite list was enough.

One of the interesting sidelights in the Massachusetts Bay Colony witch hunts was how many of the victims were drawn from approximately the range of Mrs. Ann Putnam's acquaintances, whose only child, a twelve-year-old girl, was one of the two most active of the "afflicted girls." She bore many grudges, and young Ann, through her mother, "knew all evil; there was not a scandal or rumor of scandal of the past twenty years of which the child could not speak with authority." [23] The collective fever served the mother's private motives.

Under the rising fever of excitement the circle of candidates was soon extended beyond the range of expendable victims against whom the community could easily be united. John Alden, sea captain and soldier, son of Priscilla and John, was cried out in court after being identified for the girls. "There stands Alden! A bold fellow with his hat on before the judges. He sells powder and shot to the Indians and French and lies with Indian squaws and has Indian papooses." The girls having heard rumors of his immorality thus punished him for tales to which they should not have listened.

Among those cried out because he dared to deny the validity of the girls' accusations was the Reverend Samuel Willard of the Old South Church of Boston, whose critical views on the witchcraft heresy hunts were well known. He was "a thorn in the side of some of the afflicted and their advisers." Common people are said to have quivered and thrilled at the audacity of the accusation. But Willard simply was not psychologically available. Said the presiding judge, in so many words, "You are mistaken." [24]

23. *Ibid.*, p. 19.
24. *Ibid.*, p. 169.

The witch mania thus began to subside when the circle of potential victims widened to include practically anybody. The accusations became a source of serious embarrassment. When even a trial judge could be cried out, there was no longer a clear line demarcating victim and accuser. Doubts about the charges were bound to arise.

How this actually happened is pathetically shown in the rather ludicrous story of the girls' activities in Andover, where sickness was raging. Members of families in which sickness had struck sought the witch responsible for the scourge. The girls "could see a witch spectrally ply her trade but they could seldom positively identify her." [25] It was the misfortune of Andover that the circle of Mrs. Ann Putnam's acquaintances did not extend that far.

The answer was a scientific experiment in the form of a ghostly police line-up. Led before the girls to undergo the test of touch were various men and women, some of them suspects, but others—for the sake of the experiment—completely above suspicion. The hands of the suspect were guided to the hands of the girls. If the latter then drew a sobbing breath and relaxed her struggles, this was evidence that yet another witch had been made to call off her devils. But where the people of Andover had counted on finding, at the most, half a dozen witches, they uncovered by this test an astonishing surfeit of them. The unforeseen and horrible result was that almost everyone of those tested "failed," and some forty people were arrested. For all one knows, the whole town might have been dubbed a nest of witches had not the magistrate in charge refused to sign any more warrants on such evidence.

The wholesale selection of victims finally defeated its ends. What happened at Andover began, in various fashions, to happen all over the colony. As the mania spread, those chosen as victims hardly gave offense to the established order. Their offense was principally to the leaders of the mania. What they dared to challenge was the delusion itself. Moreover, the witches who would not belie themselves by confession, though contributing to their own destruction, spread doubt. Ultimately they served as rallying points in the cause of sanity.

As soon as the circle of guilt widens indiscriminately, it begins to undermine the stability of the community which the selection of the scapegoat is to reinforce. This principle seems to apply to other forms of persecution as well. Once the accusations begin to name figures who should be above suspicion, the witch hunts slows in its tracks. The credibility of the charges can then be challenged. People everywhere become terrified;

25. *Ibid.*, p. 184.

no one is considered safe from accusation. With the distinction between victim and persecutor obscured, the witch hunt no longer meets its main social function: to be a force for solidarity. It creates new schisms and leads to generalized terror.[26]

CRIMINALS AS VICTIMS

Criminals are among the legitimate victims of society. The punitive reaction of which they are the object is said to serve several social functions. Whether rightly or wrongly, the act of punishment is often assumed to have a *deterrent value,* and this assumption often legitimates the penal sanction. For example, the classical theory of criminology held that punishment had to be severe enough to outweigh any possible gain expected from the delinquent act, so that anticipation of similar punishment would deter potential offenders. This theory, though discredited in scientific circles, is still widely held among the public and still more often acted upon in the disciplining of children.

Punishment serves other functions as well—namely, that of *reinforcing social norms.* In stigmatizing offenders and in subjecting them to indignities to which members in good standing are not ordinarily exposed, they are in effect deprived of status and "cast out." But through their punishment they also atone for what they have done and are thereby enabled to make their way back to good grace (*reacceptance*). Finally, as Durkheim has pointed out, the amount of repressive or penal law reflects the degree to which common moral sentiments are violated by transgressions against the norms. Accordingly, in *reaffirming the moral sentiments* of those "wronged," punishment acts as a visible stabilizer of these feelings.

Legal punishment is of course a highly structured and institutionalized collective act. In modern society its administration is governed by a detailed legal code. Nevertheless, the public preoccupation with crime and criminals occasionally results in a collective excitement that is not congruent with the lack of sustained interest in crime prevention. This preoccupation with crime appears to derive from motives other than those generally recognized. Public reactions are usually emotional. Sometimes they are the very opposite of what they appear to be—or should be.

The criminal becomes a collective object of attention largely because

26. In the 1950's inquisitors undoubtedly hurt their own cause when they named as "traitors" such unimpeachables as General George Marshall, the Army leaders, and other high government officials who questioned the procedures as well as the credibility of the charges. Such accusations threaten the whole authority structure as well as strongly entrenched interests (such as the "twenty years of treason" charge leveled against the Democratic party in its entirety). See Bert Andrews, *Washington Witchhunt* (New York: Random House, 1948), and Alan Barth, *The Loyalty of Free Men* (New York: The Viking Press, Inc., 1951).

he answers two psychological needs: (1) He acts out what is generally forbidden. Persons who are close to, as well as far removed from, the criminal and who outwardly conform to the demands of society, often vicariously—and thus guiltlessly—share the enjoyment of his antisocial behavior—and sometimes even its actual rewards. (2) Like the scapegoat on whom others' sins are cast, the criminal is required to atone for this vicarious enjoyment. The persecution of criminals is, after all, a justified outlet for aggression. It can be rationalized on the basis of morality. Society has "need" for criminals just as communities once "needed" their witches. The criminal scapegoat permits the externalization of inner conflicts, while his persecution offers relief.

Much criminal behavior originates in the psychological structure of a family. Sociological literature contains many references to parents who provide poor models of behavior. Often the parent himself is not directly involved or apprehended. He may nevertheless have encouraged theft by his willingness to accept stolen goods—or to purchase them from friends of the child—even if he did not explicitly tell his child to steal.

Of particular interest here is the refusal to perceive the delinquent behavior of a child or, on perceiving it, the denial of its significance or its seriousness. Consider the seven-year-old who has just taken a dollar from the dresser without asking permission. This is not altogether a trivial matter. Yet recurrent minor thefts are frequently rationalized as a bad habit which the youngster, left to himself, will outgrow. Moreover, parents whose inhibitions are so poorly internalized as to allow them to overlook recurrent delinquencies frequently react with sudden guilt when complaints come from school or from outside the home. They suddenly punish the child, who had been led to believe that he could act as he did without being held to account. He may even have inferred tacit approval from home. The parents' attitude of injured innocence in response to these sudden charges relieves them from blame; they excuse themselves by saying "they didn't know" and promise to "watch out" for the boy. The young delinquent stands betrayed by parents who paid no heed to the early warning signals.

The following represents a familiar pattern: The child, quick to sense any parental gratification or interest in his misbehavior, will persist in it, even if punished. Antisocial behavior is first "overlooked." When apprehended on the outside, the boy is blamed and punished at home; yet in public the parents pay back the money stolen, etc. The delinquent behavior is usually ascribed to some accidental disposition or some unique circumstance.

Tacit support for delinquent behavior is manifest also in the parents' refusal to come to grips with its underlying cause. There is the sensational case of William Heirens.

Heirens, a seventeen-year-old University of Chicago freshman, found guilty of killing and dismembering a six-year-old girl, was imprisoned for life. He also confessed to two other murders and to numerous burglaries. When thirteen and about to receive his diploma from the eighth grade, he had already been arrested for, and confessed to, burglarizing at least eleven homes, all in a period of six months. A "model boy" up to that time, he said he stole "to see if he could get away with it." [27] His parents appear not to have known of his delinquencies. While a teen-ager, their son held jobs but gave his parents gifts out of proportion to his earnings. Nor did they ever "find" the loot he kept hidden, though hardly very well, in his room.

Yet remarks attributed to his mother, if true (and they appear to be), indicate that her unawareness of William's criminality was a form of self-deception.[28] When the son was charged with a dollar burglary which ultimately linked him to murder, a police captain telephoned his mother. As he recalled it, she came right over asking, "What's happened to Bill?" Being told, she said to the captain, "You're trying to make it easy for me . . . You want my boy for something far more serious than what you're telling me." [29] According to newspaper reports, when the terrible murder of the small girl was the news of the day, Mrs. Heirens talked to her son, "I said to him I was glad he wasn't mixed up in anything like that. You would not have done such a terrible thing, would you?" [30]

At the time of her son's first arrest, the juvenile court judged the mother "overprotective." She "ranted and raved" at Bill at home, while in public she solicited leading citizens to plead her boy's cause. The judge advised that, unless the parents arranged to place their son under proper supervision, the boy would be committed to the state institution at St. Charles: "The mother was very much opposed to anything of that sort. She wanted him to go to St. Bede's [a boarding school for boys run by Benedictine fathers]. I said I would not consider that. I did not think it a proper place for the boy. *It would merely give him further opportunity to carry on as a burglar* because it did not have the supervision I was determined he should get." [31] The judge managed to get Heirens confined to a first-rate semi-correctional school. Despite his excellent record there, he was once

27. Lucy Freeman, *Catch Me Before I Kill More* (New York: Pocket Books, Inc., 1956), p. 91.
28. Eissler, *op. cit.*, p. 300.
29. Freeman, *op. cit.*, p. 96.
30. A combination quote drawn from Freeman, *op. cit.*, p. 153, and Eissler, *op. cit.*, p. 300.
31. Freeman, *op. cit.*, p. 94; italics ours.

more arrested for burglary soon after his release. This time, "in response to the parent's plea," he was sent to St. Bede's. Had his delinquent record been known, he would never have been admitted, but the parents managed to keep it secret. Heirens' first murder was committed while home on vacation from St. Bede's.

Thus, the seduction of the delinquent seems to involve unconscious approval which is often difficult to detect. For delinquents coming from apparently "normal" homes and families of good reputation, this kind of seduction is typical.[32] Johnson and Szurek state that:

> unwitting sanction or indirect encouragement is a major cause of, and the specific stimulus for, such anti-social behavior as fire-setting, stealing, truancy, and unacceptable sexuality displayed by young delinquents or their adult counterparts, the psychopaths. . . . We have never observed these parental permissions without anti-social behavior in at least one child who had been chosen as a scapegoat.[33]

But the same seduction one observes in the family circle also manifests itself in the larger society. There is the same persistent failure to intervene decisively to remove the conditions that produce delinquents in large numbers, such as slum neighborhoods, crowding, lack of recreational facilities, inadequate educational opportunity, and the resulting family discord. Unless a public scandal breaks, the prevalence of crime is usually overlooked. The ambivalent feelings about crime in general also holds for so-called "white collar" offenses. Most Americans do not have many scruples concerning petty graft. The bonus for an apartment, paid in an underhanded manner, the expense account as a means of tax-exempt income, the entertainment of influential persons as a palatable sort of bribe, etc., are all pretty much taken for granted. Nevertheless, revelations about the public servant or petty official caught with his hand in the till or accepting mink or vicuña are avidly read. There is resignation mixed with glee: that "corruption" should appear so widespread is a justification, and those not without blame themselves are often ready to cast the first stone. Thus, those victimized also serve as rallying points. The criminals are important stabilizers.

32. Negative suggestion can be as effective as exposure to temptation. The parent who constantly expresses unfounded fears about a son who someday may steal usually has half-conscious fantasies of using him as a scapegoat to carry out his own unacknowledged impulse.

33. Adelaide M. Johnson and S. A. Szurek, "Causes of Delinquency," in Grant S. McClellan, *Juvenile Delinquency* (New York: H. W. Wilson Co., 1956), p. 52.

The Criminal as Hero

The American hero, writes Marya Mannes, is still "the private who shows up the general, the boy who fools his professors, the hoodlum who tricks the police." [34] It would be a mistake, however, to consider this condition a peculiarity of the contemporary United States. Almost every country has thieves and bad men whose exploits are idolized in poetry and folklore. During the eighteenth century, Mackay tells us, there were a number of thieves "whose peculiar chivalry formed at once the dread and delight of England . . . [one was Jack Sheppard] as brutal a ruffian as ever disgraced his country, but who has claims upon the popular admiration which are very generally acknowledged." Hanged when he was only twenty-three, "he died much pitied by the crowd. His adventures were the sole topics of conversation for months; the printshops were filled with his effigies, and a fine painting was made by Sir Richard Thornhill." [35]

Sheppard did not, like Robin Hood, steal from the rich to help the poor. Nor did he rob with the courtesy of other well-beloved thieves. His escape from Newgate Prison "with the fetters on his limbs" made him the idol of the people. This achievement in outwitting authority endeared him to the throngs. How he thereby won the admiration of even the champions of morality is delightfully illustrated in the sermon of a street preacher delivered about the time of Jack's execution:

> The orator, after animadverting on the great care men took of their bodies, and the little care they bestowed upon their souls, continued as follows, by way of exemplifying the position:— "We have a remarkable instance of this in a notorious malefactor, well known by the name of Jack Sheppard. What amazing difficulties has he overcome! what astonishing things has he performed! and all for the sake of a stinking, miserable carcase, hardly worth the hanging! How dexterously did he pick the chain of his padlock with a crooked nail! how manfully he burst his fetters asunder, climb [sic] up the chimney, wrench out an iron bar, break his way through a stone wall, make the strong door of a dark entry fly before him, till he got upon the leads of the prison, then, fixing a blanket to the wall with a spike, he stole out of the chapel! How intrepidly did he descend to the top of the turner's house! how cautiously pass down the stair, and make his escape to the streetdoor!
>
> "Oh, that ye were all like Jack Sheppard! Mistake me not, my brethren

34. Marya Mannes, *More in Anger* (Philadelphia: J. B. Lippincott Co., 1958), p. 21f.
35. See Mackay, *op. cit.*, pp. 632–46.

—I don't mean in a carnal, but in a spiritual sense; for I propose to spiritualize these things . . ." [36]

Thus, without making it necessary to acknowledge criminal impulses, society is nevertheless continuously providing opportunities for delinquency. While we refuse to pay for the prevention of crime, we punish those whom we seduce and whom we subconsciously admire, or even openly celebrate, in our television shows, movies, and many of our books.

THE PERSON AS RALLYING POINT

IN A SMALL FACE-TO-FACE GROUP, some particular act evident to all members at the same time may instantaneously give rise to admiration or persecution. A team has its heroes after every game; a school class is ready to join in malicious laughter over the misfortunes of a student who plays the fool. More often such roles, even in small groups, emerge gradually but persist over time.

The rallying point of an unorganized collectivity rarely emerges all at once. Even after a person has been moved into the public limelight, people often disagree about him. Each has a public that cultivates its particular image. Especially in the political arena, names are repeatedly invoked for boos, catcalls, hisses, and other "proper" expressions of derision. For many years the Democrats successfully employed the name of Hoover to symbolize indifference to the suffering of working people during depressions and mass unemployment. Elvis Presley, Louis Armstrong, and Leonard Bernstein have been idolized by different sections of the public. Only over time is consensus attained.

THE NATURAL HISTORY OF A RALLYING POINT

It is possible to outline a natural history of phases by which a person becomes a rallying point: the subject of an accepted legend or the object of an established cult of worship or vilification. The scheme outlined should not be reified. It has only heuristic value, enabling one to single out the important factors in the emergence of a traditional rallying point.

1. *The precondition is some kind of critical situation.* A discrepancy exists between what is acknowledged as reality and the reality—that is, between aspiration and achievement or between impulse and opportunities for its expression. In such a situation any person suitable for the externalization of the conflict is potentially a collective object. For ex-

36. *Ibid.*, p. 637f.

ample, the hero stirs imaginations as he demonstrates that the superhuman is humanly possible. Or through laughter the fool provides an acceptable form for the expression of hostility, otherwise prohibited.

2. *The person gains the attention of a plurality of people.* He does this by some feat or achievement, some stroke of luck or misfortune, some personal failing, or by giving some kind of offense. Thus, the hero earns spontaneous adulation; the fool becomes the butt of a joke, etc. In each case the public displays a common emotion toward the object. It rallies behind him or against him. This initial rallying is often altogether spontaneous, but the central person is nevertheless beginning to be defined as a certain "type"—namely, as hero, tragic hero, *bête noire,* or fool. A special status is thereby conferred upon him. Temporarily a collectivity forms as a result of patterned acts. But it may disintegrate in a matter of seconds (as soon as the laughter has died down or the victim of the mob is destroyed); it may also help to create a more permanent role for the central person.

3. *A more or less definite image of who the central object is and what he has done is disseminated among and accepted by his public.* In the small group this image thrives on rumor, gossip, and spontaneous ridicule. On a larger scale, propaganda, public relations, and the journalistic exploitation of public sentiment help to spell out and fix the image. Legendary reputations are thus made, but also quickly forgotten when the hero of the hour, the current boob, the man of the week, or the villain of the year have served their purpose and are no longer needed. In the interval, however, his story is public property, his name on everyone's lips, and he enjoys considerable notoriety.

4. *Ultimately more permanent forms must displace this spontaneous sentiment.* As the novelty recedes, the legend becomes crystallized, and as such it reaffirms the prevailing norms or itself becomes the norm. Thus the holy man may be elevated to sainthood. The hero after his ticker-tape welcome becomes an elder statesman consulted in times of stress. The name of the villain is invoked whenever treachery is to be illustrated. A traditional rallying point can be dethroned only after time and historical research redefine the image.

THE HEROES OF TRADITION   The image of an idol or a villain as stabilized in legend and myth rarely emerges during his lifetime. Lord Raglan, writing about the hero in traditional narratives, says his feats are of mythological rather than historical origin. The narrative originates in a cult, and in it are reflected ritual practices and beliefs prevalent at the time. The myth, in clarifying the derivations of current practices, contributes to their legitimacy. Before mythical feats can be claimed for a hero, Raglan concludes, sufficient time must elapse for the true facts to have been forgotten. The position of the hero is established only to the degree that the feats attributed to him are plausible and strike the public fancy. By invoking appropriate and valued sentiments, the ritualistic cults of traditional figures serve to fortify social consensus. The hero of a cult is the personification of an ideal.[37]

THE TRADITIONAL VILLAIN Before a person can serve as a proper villain, he must be dehumanized: the human being must be separated from the evil he symbolizes. The response to the villain who is physically present is punitive. But once he is viewed as a human being, sympathy and compassion enter our consideration of him. He may be transformed into an object of pity or even of laughter. It is significant that, although the villain *personifies* evil, the label "villain" is as likely to be attached to a whole group or race as to an individual. The individual is usually treated impersonally, as a representative of some accursed group outside the pale of sympathy and understanding.

CHARACTERISTICS

Both idols and villains are essentially dehumanized; still, there are general characteristics that determine why one contemporary person rather than another is likely to be singled out as a rallying point.

First, physical accessibility is *not* a necessary condition. It suffices that the individual personify some general achievement or represent some accursed group. The capacity of far-away persons to elicit the deepest sympathies and thus serve as rallying points sometimes assumes surprising proportions. Heroes are seldom known directly, and many who most persistently vilify minorities have never had personal contact with individuals in them.

Second, high visibility or a conspicuous personality is a contributory condition. Public imagination fastens more easily on colorful elements in a person's appearance or in his mode of behavior. Klapp suggests that such "color" may have three functions: "(a) to excite attention, interest, imagination, and interpretation; (b) to set a person apart, rendering him unique or peculiar; and (c) to make him unforgettable." [38] The Elvis Presley haircut, General Patton's set of pearl-handled pistols, or President Eisenhower's facial grimacing help to foster the image and to fix it. Such color may be a matter of apparel or strictly a public relations stunt; it may be part of a person's role. The fool's deformity or deviance is fixed through public caricature while the villain can be more effectively portrayed if he has boorish manners and the physical stigmata of criminality (i.e., flattened nose, contorted face, etc.). The more the whole person can

37. Lord Raglan, *The Hero* (New York: Vintage Books, 1956), chap. 11.
38. Orrin E. Klapp, "The Creation of Popular Heroes," *American Journal of Sociology*, LV (September, 1948), pp. 135–41.

be represented by a particular trait or by an aspect of his role, the more readily he can be dramatized as a rallying point.

Third, deviance in some form appears indispensable. The group rallies to the person who "dared" or who met with exceptional tragedy. In general the hero turns the exceptional into a normative standard, while the object of pity is the victim of an uncommon fate. The fool is deftly deprecated for some imagined failing, though others might do the same in his situation. Finally, the villain represents moral failings that we are loathe to admit as our own; often he is the symbolic representative of an outgroup that can be blamed and hissed at but is rarely so corporeal as to be hated and destroyed. In every instance, even the ordinary is made to seem extraordinary.

Fourth, it is necessary that the person conform to a type. The image of the idol or the villain is rarely realistic but a rarefied collective representation built around a real person. In a mass society especially, there are cues learned early in life by which "good guys" can be separated from "bad guys." The hero in the popular horse opera wears a white hat and light-colored clothing; he is shaven, clean, and upright in appearance. The villain is easily distinguished by his black hat and dark clothing. Sometimes he is unshaven and clothed in rags.[39] Latter-day wrestling matches reiterate similar distinctions. The idols fight "clean" and behave politely toward the audience. Villains scowl and growl and raise their fists while the audience boos. The Kefauver Committee crime hearings, one of the most spectacular actuality broadcasts of early television, provided the public with villains who were movie bad guys come to life.[40]

Finally, the traits and deeds of the object that inspire positive emotions or disgust and hatred must be congruent with the dispositions of the public. "In general, personal traits are relatively unimportant," says Klapp about popular heroes, for their emergence is a "matter of popular selection . . . Therefore, we may say that roles rather than traits make heroes and that personal traits are subordinate to roles." [41] This formulation is applicable to other rallying points. The situation must make it possible for the trait or performance to be recognized and acted upon. The status is conferred by a willing public whose imaginations are captured and who act toward the object in the requisite manner. But to say that idols and villains are made rather than born does not deny their own contribution.

Some vested or private interests often stand to gain from public senti-

39. John Steinbeck, "Good Guys and Bad Guys," in Leslie Fiedler (ed.), *The Art of the Essay* (New York: Thomas Y. Crowell Company, 1958), pp. 357–62.

40. Eric Goldman, *The Crucial Decade* (New York: Alfred A. Knopf, Inc., 1956), p. 194.

41. Klapp, *op. cit.*, p. 135.

ment that defines a person positively or negatively. The rise of a popular idol to prominence is, indeed, often planned most carefully, and an appropriate image is deliberately cultivated. In this case the image is not an end in itself; once the person is properly elevated or depicted as loathsome, the image can be used to serve other causes. Movie stars, a modern type of hero, not only sell the films in which they appear; they also sell commercial products, charity, and war bonds. Lindbergh received money from the St. Louis *Post-Dispatch;* his flight was promoted by those who wanted to dramatize the potential of aviation. Fishwick claims that Paul Bunyan was originally a genuine folk hero among lumberjacks. The tales made sense to them alone. This local image of Bunyan was deliberately transformed into a public one by promoters who flooded the market with Bunyan literature in order to sell lumber and gain favorable publicity for the industry.[42] In the same way, a viewpoint saddled with a villain is discredited more easily

IDOLS

It can be said of idol worship, as Santayana said of love, that it is 10 per cent in the beloved and 90 per cent in the lover. But the choice of idols reflects more than individual desires. Each society in each era creates its idols in its own image, and these personify its ideals. The classical era made heroes of mythical figures. The Middle Ages had their saints. The Renaissance nourished the ideal of the cultivated man. The self-made man was enthroned in the nineteenth century. And now the common "ordinary" man is said to be heroic.

In his classic essay, "The Passing of the Saint," John M. Mecklin showed how in every period the ideal of the saint was identified with its objective morality. In early Christianity it developed simultaneously from two sources: the messianic eschatology derived from the Judaic tradition and the uncompromising opposition to pagan morality. The medieval Church formulated an ideal of sainthood that preserved uncompromising idealism and otherworldly attitudes but also made allowance for values embodied in society and its institutions. The ascetic ideal was incorporated in the monastic orders. The saint's cultivation of ascetic moral perfection inspired all others and thus helped to reinforce the spiritual solidarity of the society and bridge its essential dualism. Tales of miracles legitimated his claim to divine grace. Still the Catholic Church demanded that the canonized saint also possess such natural virtues as were commensurate with the special responsibilities of his station in society. "Canonization thus became a most effective instrument for institutionalizing certain

42. Marshall W. Fishwick, *American Heroes: Myth and Reality* (Washington, D.C.: Public Affairs Press, 1954), p. 4.

types of personalities, thereby insuring the perpetuation of group ideals." [43]

The passing of the saint as a viable idol had several causes. The excessive zeal displayed by the members of some monastic orders meant that their ideal became inbred and sectarian. They became a law unto themselves. Hence, in the Protestant version of sainthood, the saint lost his "red-blooded" character. The ideal became essentially theological. The saint represented values that were mostly metaphysical, and his acts, rather than inspiring directly, merely testified to his "predestination." Understanding the Calvinist saint requires an understanding of all its involved theology. To be sure, only an institutionalized church can provide the tradition and discipline to cultivate the saintly character.

> But as the church becomes more and more departmental and the center of gravity for moral and spiritual values is transferred to the community, the saint himself tends to become departmental, traditional, and conventional and ceases to play the role of moral and spiritual leadership characteristic of the saint of the Middle Ages. Here we have the explanation of the growing sense of unreality, not to say antipathy, the modern world associates with the saint. There is apparently no place for him in the modern social order. [44]

For the saint is essentially an aristocrat; only a superior individual can personify the spiritual ideas of a society.

The idol may be a hero who has led his people to some victory, or an artist or a scientist who has sensed and interpreted the values of his age. He may represent a cause or be a rogue who dares to defy authorities no longer held in esteem. But specialization and democracy together have contributed to make extraordinary achievement less easily known and subject to distrust. Hence, public fancy is apt to turn not to "super" or "extraordinary" men but to those who seem "just like us," Mr. Average Man. In politics there is a premium on sincerity. On the other hand, Americans tend to worship people who do extraordinary things that most people cannot do or do not have the opportunity to do but which they nevertheless readily understand. They take as idols sports champions and daredevils: people who fly the ocean first or faster than anyone before; people who swim channels; or people who kill numerous enemies in face-to-face encounter (during war when killing is condoned and honored in society). [45]

43. John M. Mecklin, "The Passing of the Saint," *American Journal of Sociology,* LX (May, 1955), part 2, p. 50.

44. *Ibid.,* p. 53.

45. Dixon Wecter, *The Hero in America: a Chronicle of Hero Worship* (New York: Charles Scribner's Sons, 1941), chap. 18.

Idols may be long remembered, but if their feats concern peripheral areas, they are more apt to be passing fancies. Therefore in periods of quickly shifting attention, hero-making is of a faddish nature. These seem to be periods when society is not especially troubled by political, military, or moral crisis. The "Roaring Twenties" in the United States typify such an era of mass elation. Idols were easily found and swiftly adopted, but they were discarded just as quickly when the bored public shifted attention to more exciting ones. The idols of that period were channel swimmers, flagpole sitters, movie queens, and ballyhooed screen lovers like Rudolf Valentino. Mass sympathy was quickly aroused by personal tragedy but left untouched by misfortune on a large scale. A hillbilly trapped in a cave became the subject of the first on-the-spot radio newscast. The plight of Floyd Collins and the efforts of his rescuers were shared by millions of radio listeners who followed his doomed fight for life.[46]

The mass media, in general, have been able to project their own stereotypes of popular idols. To some extent, they have no doubt reflected changes in attitude among the reading public, but the media themselves have had a hand in this change. A study of popular biographies in magazine fiction showed that the hero of the 1940's came most often from the world of popular entertainment; his precedessor during the first two decades of the century was a successful self-made man from the field of industry.[47] The advent of nation-wide television meant a rapid shift of focus which introduced a whole slew of personalities, including the quiz show idols of the 1950's who got rich overnight and who, to millions of viewers, represented extraordinary intellectual attainments. Great attention was given to movie stars who personified sex and beauty, and tragedies produced their objects of pity; for instance, a girl trapped in a well who, as the victim inexorably doomed by fate, aroused sympathy throughout the nation for a few days.

THE VILLAIN

The rallying point for common grievances, frustrations, and hostile impulses is designated a villain. He usually signifies moral depravity, and his existence sometimes highlights and dramatizes the norms he supposedly has violated. He is needed as an object on whom hatreds, whose open expression would be disruptive, can be displaced. Therefore where

46. Frank Edwards, *My First 10,000,000 Sponsors* (New York: Ballantine Books, Inc., 1956), chap. 4.
47. Leo Lowenthal, "Biographies in Popular Magazines," in B. Berelson and M. Janowitz, *Reader in Public Opinion and Communication* (Glencoe, Ill.: The Free Press, 1950), pp. 289–98.

no natural villains exist, their villainy often has to be invented. These images are often carefully cultivated and preserved, as it is always easier to seize on some villain than to search out the causes for unemployment, inequality, moral failure, or defeat in war. Vilification is a symptom of moral alarm. It can be used to spur on a crowd, whip up public enthusiasm, or reaffirm individual feelings of moral righteousness.

The image of the typical villain, like that of the idol, has undergone change over time. Christianity nourished the image of the devil, and Bolshevism, the capitalist plot. Modern villains are apt to be secular images, like traitors, criminals, or members of out-groups. Modern history is replete with illustrations of the tendency to impute hostile intent and great potency to certain anonymous entities. Among the favored negative rallying points have been Wall Street bankers, Madison Avenue hucksters, communists and their "fellow travelers," "eggheads," and various anonymous political and criminal syndicates.

Every one of these stands for an essentially anonymous category of persons, whose members are assumed to act in perfect unison and in accordance with some preconceived plan. Because the exact nature of their conspiracy is always shrouded in mystery, the group appears all the more dangerous. Its existence helps to explain any number of diverse misfortunes. The anonymous villain serves as a unifying agent of fundamental importance.

The group that collectively serves as villain supplies an inexhaustible supply of potential victims. In view of the natural tendency to wish the villain destroyed, the accursed group proves very useful. A crowd's anger is often assuaged by violence against *any* member of the group who is accessible and visible. For example, the allegation that a particular offense was committed by some Negro or some Jew often produces indiscriminate aggression against every person recognized as a member of that minority. Still, their total destruction would eliminate their usefulness as a symbol.

Some people always stand to gain from violence against some or all members of a particular group. In the Middle Ages, when Jews were frequently under attack as ritual murderers, a decree issued by Pope Gregory X in 1272 made clear some of the more mundane motives.

> Since it happens occasionally [he wrote] that some Christians lose their Christian children, the Jews are accused by their enemies of secretly carrying off and killing these same Christian children and of making sacrifices of the heart and the blood of these very children. It happens, too, that the parents of these children, or some other Christian enemies of the Jews, secretly hide these very children in order that they may be able to injure these Jews, and in order that they may be able to extort

from them a certain amount of money by reducing them from their straits.[48]

Nevertheless, the Jews were seldom so completely bankrupted through extortion that they lost their usefulness as rallying points.

Frequently, though not always, religious dissenters and ethnic minorities who are "outsiders" are singled out. The accusations themselves are usually of a projective nature. The image of each group seems to correspond to some particular function. In the United States the Negro is used largely for projecting anxieties concerning impulsivity—that is, sex, filth, and physical aggression. By contrast, the Jews represent the forces of control, a well-organized group which threatens because it members are depicted as too successful in attaining the very values that the dominant group prizes. It is not, however, their actual financial or political power that makes Jews such natural villains. Because of his ambivalent feelings about his own controlling institutions, the persecutor casts the Jews in the villainous role. He invokes a "specter of power," at once envied and feared, which serves to rationalize and explain his own failure.

Perhaps the most important point to be made concerning the vilification of whole categories of persons is their prior dehumanization. Members of the accursed group often can, however, save themselves from destruction by conforming to an idealized version of the official morality; that is, Jews can accept baptism and publicly denounce their own heresy.

MARTYRDOM: VICTIM, VILLAIN, AND IDOL

In the case of the martyr, the individual dehumanizes himself until he is only the *representative* of a cause or a principle defined as villainous by his persecutors.

The martyr, as the term is employed here, exhibits some degree of subjective identification with a cause he represents. One is the victim *of* persecution or even *of* circumstances. But the martyr's victimization is *on behalf of* something in which both he and some circle of "true believers" have faith. He is not necessarily a person of nobler character. But his dehumanization makes him a rallying point. To this process he consciously contributes. He is vilified or destroyed for a cause and thus may be idolized—or, more properly, idealized. In one sense, then, the martyr is a willing scapegoat, but of course no scapegoat is per se a martyr.

48. James B. Ross and Mary M. McLoughlin, *The Portable Medieval Reader* (New York: The Viking Press, Inc., 1949), p. 1172.

The willingness to undergo suffering—that is, to become a victim—is best illustrated by the Christian martyrs. By denying his faith and substantiating that denial with evidence, a potential martyr could escape his fate. Christian leaders used a variety of methods to maintain control over their followers so that the latter would not deny their faith in court. First, the rewards of confession and the punishments in both this world and the hereafter were vividly outlined to the potential martyr. Second, he was indoctrinated with the importance of maintaining the fellowship of the community and of acting as its representative. Third, he was trained to anticipate and make the appropriate response to every possible incident in his persecution. Finally, wherever possible, other Christians tried to make their moral support apparent to the martyrs on trial. All of these techniques helped to elicit voluntary confessions of faith. Their martyrdom made them rallying points for other Christians.

Dehumanization

Ethel and Julius Rosenberg serve as examples of modern martyrdom. They were the first Americans put to death in peacetime by an American civil court for spying against their own country. Not that the Rosenbergs were in any sense typical martyrs; they were hardly willing victims but instead proclaimed their innocence to the very end. Nor were they, during a painstakingly correct trial, centers of public controversy or of mass hysteria. Nevertheless by the logic of the situation, they were dehumanized to a point where they could not but contribute to their own martyrdom.

The basic charges made at their trial held that they had participated in a conspiracy to transmit military secrets to a foreign power, the Soviet Union, in the period from 1944 to 1950. During part of that period the United States was at war. This fact justified a death sentence but hardly made it mandatory, and many persons not at all in sympathy with their acts were for humanitarian, judicial, and other reasons shocked at the sentence. Consequently great pressure was brought on the presiding judge to reduce its severity. During the trial the basic facts were hardly challenged. The Rosenbergs denied their guilt and their party membership. Even the Communists maintained an official silence; intervention could only have proven embarrassing.

The court case need not interest us here, for it was only in their trial before world opinion that the Rosenbergs emerged as martyrs. In the latter part of 1951 a committee was formed to spearhead a mass campaign to save the victims. In the world-wide campaign that ensued the Rosenberg case was likened to the Dreyfus case. They were portrayed as the victims of anti-Semitism, though sentenced by a Jewish judge. They were compared also with known victims of antilabor hysteria. Like Sacco, Vanzetti, and Tom Mooney, they were portrayed as victims of the class struggle and thus political prisoners rather than apprehended spies. In some parts of Europe the Rosenbergs were seen as innocent scapegoats. Opinion in France was described as "virtually unanimous, reflecting a universal feeling of horror at the drama unfolding at the other side of the Atlantic, and a feeling of consternation when its final outcome became known . . . We believe that they were expiatory victims who were handed over to satisfy a public impatient to be rid of its own anti-Communist fears and a bad conscience. . . ."[49] The French president and three former premiers of France relayed appeals for clemency to the President of the United States. Thousands of British subjects cabled the American courts. Eight Dutch jurists asked for clemency, and eighteen rabbis from Israel (several of whom later withdrew their names) made a similar appeal. Even Pope Pius XII advised the American President of the extraordinary appeals that had reached him on behalf of the Rosenbergs.

The Communists themselves took up the cause only late in 1952, when the campaign was already running under its own steam. It is not unlikely that the Communist press raised the case at this time to keep the Rosenbergs from talking. For until the last minute they were promised clemency on the condition that they confess their guilt. They were also in a position where they could name others involved with them in the espionage. The campaign carried on by the Communist side, Daniel Bell conjectured, "so martyrises them that confession becomes psychologically difficult."[50] Thus, the Rosenbergs were offered spiritual salvation if they passed the test of faith.

Clearly the Rosenbergs enjoyed much sympathy in the United States, though there was almost no one who considered them innocent of the crime of which they were convicted. But notwithstanding their apparently genuine love for each other and for their two young sons, they played the part in which they had been cast. They refused the opportunity to obtain mercy by pleading guilty: they had by now identified themselves fully with the role of martyr. In turning themselves into representatives of a cause, they dehumanized themselves. All the time they spent in prison they wrote letters that seem to have been written for the world and for posterity rather than for each other. In these there are clues to the kind of personality that promotes such self-victimization: "It is as if these two had no internal sense of their own being but could see themselves only from the outside, in whatever postures their 'case' seemed to

49. Robert Barrat, "From France: The Rosenberg Case," *Commonweal,* LVIII (August 14, 1953), p. 465f.
50. Daniel Bell in a letter to the *New Statesman,* XLV (January 31, 1953), pp. 120–21.

demand—as if, one might say, they were only the most devoted of their thousands of sympathizers." [51] Not even their own experiences belonged to them any longer:

> It has been reported that when the United States Marshal came to tell Ethel Rosenberg that the final stay had been rescinded and the execution would take place in a few hours, she said simply, "Well, the Rosenbergs will be the first victims of American fascism." . . . For her, this was a sufficient definition of what was about to happen to her. Perhaps the fact that she could say this, externalizing even her own death—not she was about to die, but a "victim of fascism"—should be for us sufficient definition of what she had made of herself. [52]

Being the objects in a power struggle, they subsequently contributed to making use of themselves. They denied the essence of what they themselves were. This is complete self-alienation. [53]

The question of how persons contribute to their own martyrdom is hardly exhausted by the Rosenberg case. Martyrdom willingly entered often represents a form of indifferentism where doctrinal purity and absolute values matter more than practical consequences. This is a social type. Psychologically it springs from an overidentification with a cause and resulting loss of self: the narcissism of the martyr becomes unlimited as he sees himself honored forever through his association with the cause.

FOOLS

The fool is a special variant of the villain, one who is ridiculed and laughed at rather than hissed or harmed. The typical fool "represents values rejected by the group, causes that are lost, incompetence, failure and fiasco." [54] He is not threatening. On the contrary, the fool's part is ascribed to a person by virtue of some assumed defect in intelligence or

51. Robert Warshow, "Idealism of Julius and Ethel Rosenberg," *Commentary*, XVI (November, 1953), p. 415.

52. *Ibid.*

53. There is a point of bitter irony in this, as Leslie Fiedler, Warshow, and others have pointed out. The appeal the Rosenbergs made was in terms of universally understood human motives—for example, the desire to see their children grow up. They could not actually mention the Communist Party, to which both were dedicated. They could not go down singing the "internationale" and, in true martyr fashion, proclaiming their faith. See Leslie Fiedler, *An End to Innocence* (Boston: Beacon Press, Inc., 1955), chap. 2; see also, for a study of Jewish reaction to the Rosenberg case, Aaron Antonovsky, "Like Everyone Else, Only More So," in M. Stein, A. Vidich, and D. M. White (eds.), *Identity and Anxiety* (Glencoe, Ill.: The Free Press, 1960), pp. 428–34.

54. Orrin E. Klapp, "The Fool as a Social Type," *American Journal of Sociology*, LV (September, 1949), p. 157.

sobriety or competence, to cite Klapp once again.[55] Through the ridicule, moreover, the fool is rendered harmless, for nothing isolates one as quickly and as spontaneously as suddenly being the butt of a joke. This places the fool in an inferior status. He is depreciated but, unlike the villain, not necessarily despised or hated.

Throughout history there have been readily definable types of candidate for the fool's part. In Greek mythology it was the lame and crippled Hephaestus who evoked uproarious laughter from the gods. In medieval days people used to laugh with uninhibited cruelty at idiots, dwarfs, cripples, and so forth. These were legitimate targets of ridicule. The court fool, who was subjected to the most inconsiderate practical jokes, was on a par with the village idiot. In Western culture today, this kind of hilarity is possible only in unusual instances; pity and compassion interfere with the free expression of hostility. Therefore, before the laughter can catch, the hostile impulse must be disguised. The modern fool is laughed at more often for bravado, wastefulness, or foolhardy daring than for deformity. Grotjahn illustrates the current need for the average man to disguise his feelings of superiority toward the cripple.

> As the clown watches, his stupid partner, Dumb August, is walking inside the [circus] arena with one foot on the side wall which fences in the arena and the other on the ground, limping terribly. After watching thoughtfully, the clown finally calls to August: "Hey, come over here," which August does. He no longer limps, of course, on the level ground. His face lights up, he seizes the hands of the clown and thanks him profusely: "And I thought I was lame; you have cured me!" A physical defect is replaced by a mental defect. Aggression is disguised to appear as a good deed.[56]

The fool may play the role expected of him in two basic ways. First, he can be the prankster who refuses to learn, shirks responsibility, and thereby perpetuates his childhood rebellion against authority by refusing to grow up. His indifference to conventions, his frivolous and inept behavior tend to make him a lovable fool who is tolerated for the free ways he represents. Second, he may be dethroned from a position of authority. The fallen idol easily becomes a fool. This is best illustrated by an inclination to make older persons the objects of laughter. Their fall from authority is not only inevitable but quietly enjoyed and thus hardly threatening. Their eccentricity is tolerated since it can be represented as loyalty to outdated ways. Older people often willingly play the role: hav-

55. Orrin E. Klapp, "Heroes, Villains, and Fools, as Agents of Social Control," *American Sociological Review*, XIX (February, 1954), p. 58f.

56. Martin Grotjahn, *Beyond Laughter* (New York: McGraw-Hill Book Co., Inc., 1957), p. 94.

ing long lived within the codes of society, they are apt to resent change and feel that their old age earns them at least a right to take a holiday from restraint. An old folk song expresses the philosophy of a righteous patriarch who, having suffered loss of status, thumbs his nose at the new authorities:

I have led a good life, full of peace and quiet,
I shall have an old age, full of rum and riot;
I have been a good boy, wed to peace and study,
I shall have an old age, ribald, coarse and bloody.
I have never cut throats, even when I yearned to,
Never sang dirty songs that my fancy turned to;
I have been a nice boy and done what was expected,
I shall be an old bum loved but unrespected.[57]

Ridicule as a Weapon

Because of the underlying aggressiveness in ridicule, the fool has been classified as a villain. The process of fool-making masks the hostility and is therefore an admirable weapon. Much as his actions contribute to his emergence as an object of ridicule, a fool is made by the actions of his detractors.

The first person to tell a joke or make a witty remark perceives an idea which he uses to attack a second person, who then becomes the comic butt—that is, his victim. But the motive is cloaked by the cleverness of the remark. Its form (play on words, displacement on irrelevant details, etc.) gives pleasure and overshadows the underlying wish. In order to test the success of the witty disguise, Freud contends, the thought must be conveyed to still another person (not the victim), one who is merely an innocent witness and therefore removed from any possible guilt over the hidden sexual or hostile tendency. When that third person reacts with laughter, it becomes evident that the disguise has succeeded and the first person is freed to join in it. On the other hand, everyone knows how painful to all concerned a misfired joke can be, to the one who tells it as well as to his hearers, and how easily the borderline between a witticism and offensiveness is crossed. The enjoyment of a witticism depends on the quality of the disguise. The point of the joke permits the consummation of a fantasy in an acceptable and socialized manner.

Ridicule and wit together are essentially social. The listeners must be stimulated but protected from guilt, for they are required as allies in the

57. Carl Sandburg, "The Good Boy," in Sigmund Spaeth, *Read 'em and Weep* (New York: Arco, 1959), p. 81.

depreciation of the object. The contagious character of the laughter illustrates how repressions are lifted in the entire group and give way to inaccessible sources of pleasure. This must come as a surprise as people are "tricked" by the witticism. The brevity of the joke thus is one of its main advantages. It creates a nonrational consensus, summing up rather complicated thoughts.

The most primitive forms of ridicule are: "kidding," which justifies hostile depreciation as a jest; practical joking, by which sadistic tendencies are given expression; and aggressive and "risqué" humor which seeks accomplices in a questionable enterprise. There are also the more sophisticated forms. Caricature and satire are established means of unmasking and depreciating authorities. By comparison, the current political joke is a spontaneous expression of hostility. Such humor is especially difficult to suppress because of the pleasure it gives to others, which renders it apparently harmless. Wherever open criticism is stifled, clandestine humor becomes an effective weapon; no one is of such stature that no ludicrous presentations can be made of him. Court jesters sometimes harbored revolutionary ideas. Likewise, in totalitarian regimes, which forbid open criticism, clandestine political humor on forbidden subjects flourishes. The subject matter of such humor concentrates especially on the failings of individual leaders.[58]

One must distinguish the fool, who is victimized by laughter, from the wit and the jester. The jester and the wit, the practical joker and the "kidder" clearly are aggressors rather than victims. The comic and the clown, on the other hand, perform institutionalized roles with consummate skill for the amusement of the audience. But the person who good-humoredly accepts the joke played on him or who becomes the buffoon is different from comic or clown. His part, though accepted, is nevertheless played reluctantly. Because he adopts the viewpoint of the public that laughs at him, the clown protects himself and avoids feeling foolish. The ability to laugh at oneself takes the bite out of the hostility.

The person who offers himself as a victim of ridicule is somewhat analogous to the martyr. The would-be victim who overlooks the seriousness or discomforts of the situation in which he has been placed reacts with good humor. He becomes a rallying point because he spares us sympathetic affect. We gain pleasure from comparing his unconcern with our own probable reaction under the same circumstances. The good-humored fool shows us a way of laughing at misfortune.

Freud supplies a further clue concerning the motives of the self-appointed fool in his incisive discussion of *Galgenhumor* (gallows

---

58. Cf. W. H. Chamberlin, "The 'Anecdote': Unrationed Soviet Humor," *The Russian Review*, XVI (July, 1957), pp. 27–34; and concerning Germany, Eugene Lyons, "Stifled Laughter," *Harper's Magazine*, CLXX (April, 1935), pp. 557–67.

humor)[59] in its coarsest form, akin to the "sick" jokes of the 1950's. He cites the story of the prisoner who, led out to execution on a Monday morning, remarks: "Yes, this week is beginning well." Another, more witty example concerns the imprisoned Oscar Wilde, who protested indignantly about being made to stand in the pouring rain, handcuffed and altogether miserable: "If this is how Her Majesty treats her prisoners, she does not deserve to have any." The humor in these two examples depends on the dispassionate and objective view the subjects take of themselves. "The ego [in Freud's view] adopts the point of view of the superego and from this height looks down upon itself like a kindly parent smiling at the petty concerns and quaint behavior of a little child." [60] The grown-up makes a comparison with his childhood in which intensely painful affects were experienced. He can laugh about these experiences now, because the infantile reaction represented such an unnecessary expenditure of emotion and psychic energy. Besides, the humorous attitudes of the two prisoners introduce a "half-playful assumption that things are much as usual and that normal values therefore still obtain; all of which contribute to the peculiar quality of humour . . . a quality of exaltation. [Sensing his own unimportance] with the consequent indifference to extinction [enables the person to present] a bold, united (we might say heroic) front towards a hostile and menacing reality." [61]

Most fools, though, do not deliberately play their part. Almost any form of deviance, provided it does not arouse pity, can nominate a person as a fool. Psychotic episodes have been acted out in the glare of publicity. A rookie baseball player entertained the sports public with his wacky behavior for an entire season. But after his commitment to a mental institution, he became an object of pity, a tragic hero, and the story he wrote after his release became a best-seller.[62] Nothing interferes with fool-making as quickly as compassion. How easily the boundary between permissible deviation subject to ridicule and the emergence of guilt stimulated by compassion is crossed will be illustrated through the brief career of Marion Zioncheck, United States Representative from the state of Washington, who, in a short span of time, played the parts of hero, villain, fool, and tragic object for a national public.

59. Sigmund Freud, *Basic Writings* (New York: Modern Library, 1938), p. 798.
60. Quoted in Flugel, *op. cit.*, p. 221.
61. Flugel, *op. cit.*, p. 222f.
62. Jim Piersall and Albert Hirschberg, *Fear Strikes Out: The Jim Piersall Story* (Boston: Little, Brown & Co., 1955).

Marion Zioncheck

The case of Marion Zioncheck illustrates how easily the hero who fails to measure up to his public image can be transformed into a fool. From 1932 until January, 1936, Zioncheck was a villain to his opponents and a hero to his followers. In the six months before his death in August, 1936, Zioncheck is said to have received "more attention than any other public figure except the President." [63] His exploits made headlines all over the United States, and people everywhere followed what must have appeared to them as outrageous shenanigans with derision, shock, head-shaking, and laughter. Of the millions amused by his exploits, few knew anything of his opinions or his background. For most he was but an alcoholic gone haywire.

Zioncheck first gained local notoriety in 1928 when, as president of the student body at the University of Washington, he campaigned against certain undemocratic practices in campus fraternities and sororities. He also urged that money spent for athletic equipment be diverted toward erecting a building to serve as a social center for all students on campus. A group of football players, dressed in hooded robes, got together one night, shaved off the crusader's hair, and threw him into Lake Washington, having first seen to it that the press was on hand to photograph the ducking.

So victimized, Zioncheck early in his short life became a controversial figure, a villain to some but a hero to like-minded reformers. As a lawyer, he later argued a number of civil rights cases. He led a successful campaign for the mayoralty of Seattle. In November, 1932, he was elected to the House of Representatives, and he was re-elected in 1934. He appears to have been a sober industrious Representative, too left of the New Deal to please many political pundits but popular with the people who had elected him. To some he continued to be a villain as late as May, 1936. To his opponents he seemed "a new type in American public life, a type thrown to the surface by the depression," one of the radical had-nots.[64]

Until he emerged as public fool, Zioncheck had led a reasonably quiet life. Suddenly in January, 1936, he was arrested for speeding, took two trips to jail, and had a fist-fight with the police. Shortly after, he married a young government employee and then went on a wild, well-publicized Caribbean honeymoon. Upon his return he spent forty-six hours entertaining in New York, when he waded in the Rockefeller Center fountain, kissed night-club girls, and gave out recipes for newfangled highballs.

63. Richard L. Neuberger, "Zioncheck: An American Tragedy," *Nation*, CCVII (August 22, 1936), p. 207.

64. George Creel, "Loudest Radical," *Collier's*, XCVII (May 30, 1936), p. 15.

Back in Washington he was arrested following an argument with his landlady, during which he physically evicted her from his apartment. When his bride, too, fled the apartment, he threw her clothes and other belongings out the window, along with a typewriter. He then went to call on President Roosevelt dressed in a sweater and an old pair of pants. As the President was out of town, Zioncheck left him "a little present," consisting of a briefcase crammed with two empty beer bottles, a ping-pong ball container, and a mothball can. Next he went to swear out a warrant against Vice President Garner for being in "on the deal to take my wife away from me." [65]

This six-month reign in the headlines as a public fool ended only when Zioncheck threw himself out of his office window in August, 1936. Since he destroyed himself, he could no longer be remembered as an object of laughter and derision. The public had quickly to bury its guilt over his destruction, for by his last act he proved himself an object more deserving of pity than ridicule. As late as June 3 a chain-letter movement had been started by his constituents to force the resignation of "Seattle's playboy Congressman." It should have been obvious that Zioncheck had suffered a mental breakdown beginning in January. But even after he had been arrested and committed for mental observation, many people continued to look on his activities as escapades rather than as signs of mental illness. Recognition of their true nature came only after outrage and laughter gave way to compassion.

The fool always walks a tightrope: he must amuse without being offensive and deviating too far from prevalent norms of behavior. The tolerance the fool enjoys extends only to his violations of conventions, not of mores. The mechanisms of fool-making define the deviations as antics and cloak hostile depreciation in laughter. The press reported with glee the trials and tribulations of an ailing septuagenarian Congressman's marriage, and readers apparently chuckled. But at about the same time, the second marriage of an American rock-and-roll singer to his fifteen-year-old cousin so outraged the British that he was soon invited to leave; his career even in the United States was at least temporarily checked. Such deviance offended moral scruples and could not be laughed away. The singer was not a fool but a villain acting out impulses too sternly forbidden. The borderline between ridicule and vilification is crossed as easily as that between ridicule and public pity.

THE SOCIAL OBJECT AS UNIFIER

Spontaneous victimization or vilification, etc., can be considered an effort to affirm social norms. Vilification and ridicule are most effective

65. *Newsweek,* June 6, 1936, p. 11.

forms of *sanction,* and potential targets may go to considerable length to avoid them. Furthermore, vilification and ridicule constitute forms of *collective defense.* Thus, they are somewhat akin to other social safety valves by which inner conflicts are successfully externalized (as in scapegoating) and hostility becomes acceptable (as in fool-making). The behavior toward social objects also operates as a *demonstration of solidarity* by which shared sentiments are visibly affirmed. There are few methods as effective as being in on a secret joke, expressing sympathy or homage toward a hero, or watching justice being done. From the individual viewpoint, such behavior may be competitive as he seeks to share in the glory of the idol, by being closest to him, or demonstrating his superiority to the villain. But such behavior tends to take on conventional forms and may ultimately congeal into a full-fledged ritual in which the initiates share together.

The central person may also be a collective symbol that serves as a rallying point for common sentiments. In this manner a psychological unity is cemented. The social object collectively invested with the label signifying heroic or anti-heroic status dramatizes for the members of a group the ideals aspired to and the pitfalls to be avoided. He personifies a role that can operate as a *normative standard of reference.*[66] In the second place, the ascription of heroic deeds of innocent suffering, or of inferiority both physical and moral, to a particular individual *condenses and crystallizes* complicated ideals. How neatly the fool can summarize a larger dilemma or the idol the aspirations of the populace has been repeatedly commented upon. But the specific behavior or traits that are imputed or ascribed to the rallying point also serve to *legitimate and explain.* Like the traditional myths of oral tradition, they function as a charter which commends and justifies the behavior, except that in the emergence of a social object one deals with the more spontaneous processes of rumor, gossip, and propaganda rather than established tales. Finally, the function of the social object as a *stabilizer* should not be overlooked. The existence of a popular hero means that superhuman achievement is still possible. Through the villain, members of society often act out vicariously their own forbidden and unacknowledged impulses; the fool expresses deviance with a lack of inhibition long lost to us and thereby personifies freedom, whereas through unexplained collective pity, identifications usually dormant are reactivated and reasserted.

66. This point is especially stressed by Klapp.

BIBLIOGRAPHY

DAVIS, KENNETH. *The Hero; Charles A. Lindbergh and the American Dream.* New York: Doubleday, 1959. A biography of the "flying fool" and a serious effort to explain the causes for his popularity.

FRAZER, SIR JAMES G. *The New Golden Bough.* New York: Criterion Books, Inc., 1959. Unsurpassed in the amount of data on scapegoating ceremonies all over the world.

GROTJAHN, MARTIN. *Beyond Laughter.* New York: McGraw-Hill Book Co., 1957. A psychoanalytic interpretation of the comic.

HARVARD UNIVERSITY DEPARTMENT OF PSYCHOLOGY. *ABC's of Scapegoating.* Chicago: Central Y.M.C.A. College, n.d. A simple discussion of what accounts for the persecution of racial, religious, and ethnic minorities.

HIBBERT, CHRISTOPHER. *The Road to Tyburn.* Cleveland: The World Publishing Company, 1957. A study of the criminal as a hero in the eighteenth-century London underworld.

KAHN, E. J., JR. *The Voice: The Story of an American Phenomenon.* New York: Harper & Brothers, 1946. A profile of Frank Sinatra by a *New Yorker* writer.

KLAPP, ORRIN E. "Heroes, Villains, and Fools, as Agents of Social Control," *American Sociological Review,* XIX (February, 1954), pp. 56–62. A brief discussion of the roles and behavior patterns associated with each social type.

VON HENTIG, HANS. *The Criminal and His Victim.* New Haven: Yale University Press, 1948. Part V discusses the victim as a contributory agent in the criminal act.

WARNER, W. LLOYD. *The Living and the Dead; a Study of the Symbolic Life of Americans.* New Haven: Yale University Press, 1959. See Part I for a description of the rise and fall of a local hero, as well as a discussion of various types of social object.

WECTER, DIXON. *The Hero in America: a Chronicle of Hero Worship.* New York: Charles Scribner's Sons, 1941. A series of historical accounts about real as well as legendary heroes.

IV

Collective Processes in the Mass Society

CHAPTER 12

Mass, Mass Behavior,
and Mass Society

T HE TERM "MASS" is widely used as a descriptive epithet, but its meaning is not often fixed with any degree of precision. It has currency in any number of apparently different contexts: *mass* culture, *mass* communications, *mass* education, *mass* production, *mass* movement, to mention but a few. Moreover, the contemporary situation in its entirety is commonly characterized as a *mass* society. J. B. S. Hardman's statement, written some decades ago, still applies today:

> The term masses, an elastic epithet devoid of any precise scientific content, is more likely to reveal the point of view of the person using it than to clarify the phenomena in question. In spite of recent moves, notably among the German critics of Le Bon, in the direction of clarifying the terminology, the older metaphorical connotations persist.[1]

The concept of mass is nevertheless one of the most important sociological categories and, indeed, indispensable in the analysis of large-scale collective dynamics.

SOCIOLOGICAL DEFINITIONS

ANY SOCIOLOGICAL DEFINITION must fix the unique character of the mass as a form of social action in relation to other accepted categories. Gerhard Colm, in a standard sociological reference work,[2] advanced the

---

1. "Masses," *Encyclopedia of the Social Sciences*, X, p. 195.
2. Gerhard Colm, "Die Masse," *Handwörterbuch der Soziologie*, edited by Alfred Vierkandt (Stuttgart: Ferdinand Enke Verlag, 1931), pp. 353ff.

idea that the mass is one among the four basic categories of social "group." The others are the community, the fellowship, and the society (or association).

The *community* (e.g., the village) involves, above all, a common fate; individuals share a course of life together, irrespective of any conception of common interest. In the *fellowship* (i.e., the *Bund*), exemplified by lovers devoted to each other or by true believers devoted to a cause, the ties are affective and give rise to primary identifications with another person or with some abstract ideal. Members join and work together in various kinds of *association* in pursuit of some rationally conceived common goal or interest; the association as such is instrumental in attaining this goal. Finally, the *mass* shares grievances and problems that give rise to a common state of agitation, a common temper or a mood, which becomes shared because every member of the mass experiences within himself the same inner tension. These disconnected individuals are welded into some kind of collectivity, feeling that what each experiences on his own is shared by others.

None of these forms of socialization completely excludes the others; in many groups, Colm maintains, characteristics of the mass are found together with those of the others. For example, a loose association of members, all experiencing the same agitation, might be considered a mass association. Still, any particular grouping can be categorized by its predominant characteristics.

In Colm's scheme any loose and transient grouping, between whose membership there are no structured relations, constitutes a mass. The mass is juxtaposed to other groups which exhibit a more definite structure and by comparison with which it represents a spontaneous formation. Thus, the mass is almost a summary term for any large-scale elementary collective phenomenon. There is no clear distinction between "mass," "crowd," or "public." A crowd merely expresses the concrete form of action of which a mass is capable.

For other sociologists, "mass" has a much more narrow meaning. Most widely accepted among American sociologists has been the formulation offered by Park, Blumer, and Wirth. They consider the mass only one among the three major types of transient, spontaneous, and unorganized collective formation; the crowd and the public are the other two.

The crowd is a collectivity in its own right, forming out of any multitude on the basis of physical contact, circular reaction, and rapport, while the mass, as a noncontact grouping, draws its membership from anywhere. In this mass, the element of discussion, the exchange of ideas characteristic of a public, is absent. Public opinion, the behavior of a public, emerges out of the give-and-take among all persons divided with regard to some issue; the discussion leads to consensus and compromise.

Given the incapacity of the mass to articulate its sentiments in discussion with others, its action as a mass emerges solely from the convergence of the lines of action by separate individuals on a common object—that is, all the people who sing the same song, or read the same newspaper headline, or switch to filter-tip cigarettes.[3] The mass may become a crowd or a public. As a mass, however, it has unique characteristics.

IMAGES OF MASS ACTION

THE NATURE OF THE MASS is revealed most clearly by the way it behaves. By asking *how a mass acts,* instead of what it is, one can partially sidestep the futile dispute over formal definition. There are, in broad outline, three kinds of social phenomenon that have attracted attention as "mass."

The *unqualified mass* interferes with the functioning of elites. Individuals, though unqualified, intervene in cultural affairs and are effective because of their sheer numbers.

The *alienated mass,* cut off from meaningful participation in the social order, gives rise, when activated, to revolutionary crowd action and to mass organizations. Whereas the unqualified mass acts primarily on culture-bearing institutions, the alienated mass acts principally against the political order.

The *aggregate mass* represents the chance convergence of the behavior of many disparate individuals, households, or other atomistic units. Individuals do not act as members of a mass, but the totality of their actions represents collective action with consequences *sui generis.*

Among these three conceptions there are many points of contact. But before a synthesis can be presented, it is first necessary to illustrate the kinds of collective action typified by each.

THE MASS AS UNQUALIFIED

According to this view of the mass, a process of fundamental democratization undermined the exclusiveness, the political monopoly, and ultimately the social homogeneity of the established elites—that is, those who had some corporate identity by virtue of superior wealth, a prestigeful style of life, and, above all, their power. As a result of this process the masses have been elevated to a plane where they have "made"

3. The essential of the views of these three representatives of the Chicago school can be found in Herbert Blumer, "Collective Behavior," in A. M. Lee (ed.), *New Outline of the Principles of Sociology* (New York: Barnes and Noble, Inc., 1951), pp. 178ff.

history. Needless to say, this elevation was a source of disenchantment to the culture-bearing classes, destroying their romantic picture of the universe. Before the onslaught of technology and of newly mobilized populations, the individual, creative, heroic personality had to give ground. At the same time, the mass made up of unqualified persons—politically, intellectually, and morally—comes more and more to set standards of behavior once set by the trained elites, who monopolized administrative expertise, access to the machinery of legislation and administration, the military and police forces, the press and, more recently, the media of mass communication. The traditional social order, based on an established relationship between the classes and the masses, was upset. Personal achievement was replaced by a deindividualized mass, a quantity whose ideal was the "mass man."

This conception of the mass goes back a long way. Among the early prophets of the mass age were: Alexis de Tocqueville, the French chronicler of American life; the Swiss historian Jakob Burckhardt; and the German philosopher Friedrich Nietzsche. While this may appear a European notion, it has not been without its influence on American sociology. In a rather extreme formulation, the division of society into masses and select minorities (i.e., creative elites and disciplined aristocracies) is viewed as a division not between social classes but, as Ortega y Gasset explicitly states, among

> "classes of men." The select minorities are individuals or groups of individuals which are especially qualified. The mass is the assemblage of persons not specifically qualified . . . The mass is the average man. In this way what was mere quantity—the multitude—is converted into a qualitative determination: it becomes the common social quality, man as undifferentiated from other men, but as repeating in himself a generic type . . . In those groups which are characterized by not being multitude and mass, the effective coincidence of its members is based on some desire, idea, or ideal, which of itself excludes the great number.[4]

Strictly speaking, then, the mass is a psychological fact. It includes all those who are content to be exactly like everyone else. Hence, the concept is not identical with the less priviliged classes. Any particular individual, any one opinion, any product may bear the imprint of the mass.

Quantity—sheer numbers and very little else—accounts for this depreciation of individuality. One sees its hypertrophy in the surfeit of material and cultural products modern technology makes available to practically everyone; and in the mass of people whose opinions all count

4. José Ortega y Gasset, *The Revolt of the Masses* (New York: W. W. Norton & Company, Inc., 1932), chap. 1.

equally—as in the plebiscite. Legitimation of taste and opinion by numbers means that everything and everyone is leveled to the lowest common denominator. Thus, the depreciation of values is no mere transitory phenomenon but inherent in the mass.

There is a second side to this linkage between quantity and quality of collective experience. Group size, as a factor in its own right, affects the behavior of group members as much as their individual behavior may affect the group. Therefore, the commonplace qualities of individuals are not what makes the mass commonplace. Nor is it necessarily the superior competence of individuals that make elites superior. When the superior person becomes a member of the mass, he loses some of his individuality, because a large group cannot encompass the total personal existences of its members. On the contrary, it includes but a fragment of their personalities, those parts in which each coincides with all others. "What is common to many must be accessible even to the lowest and most primitive among them. Even nobler and more differentiated personalities in relatively large numbers never meet on complex and highly developed ideas and impulses but only on those that are relatively simple and generally human." [5] The smaller the group, the wider the range given to individuality and the more complex the range of alternatives and ideas that can be considered by it. Individuality is always due to participation in many small groups. The mass as such has no identifying features beyond those that result from the downgrading of individual standards that occurs in any group as it gets larger and brings mass characteristics to the fore.

Nevertheless, even in this view, size alone does not define the mass. The mass, and masses generally, are seen as the antithesis of institutions, as their negation.

On the one hand, the area in which mass standards can hold sway is limited by the persistence of an organized framework. Masses set standards only in those areas not governed by tradition and where institutions do not meet vital needs. Effective integration of a person's interests into a variety of social structures that are linked with each other militates against the independent effects of an object of mass attention. The areas where mass behavior occurs are unlikely to involve deep commitment or to affect the individual in any fundamental way. Individuals in the unqualified mass look toward each other for the validation of their tastes, but their goals are particularistic. Theirs is a retreat from a common responsibility—a kind of collective demoralization—though in seeking to further their own privatized needs, their separate actions converge on common objects.

5. Georg Simmel, *The Sociology of Georg Simmel,* trans. Kurt H. Wolff (Glencoe, Ill.: The Free Press, 1950), p. 93.

When there is no recognition of a respected authority, of objective standards of judgment, or of an organizing principle to offset the regressive tendencies of large numbers, institutions may be modified or undermined by mass behavior. An institution oriented to the mass substitutes size for quality and content. It is unlikely to stress or promote superior and lasting achievements on which the continuity of the culture depends. What is really identified by the term mass, writes Selznick,

> is a social system in which the indispensable function of creative elites cannot be performed. It is not the quality of the individuals which is in point but their roles; it is not so much that the mass is unfit in any literal sense as that the nature of the system prevents the emergence of an effective leadership. In a sense, a mass society is one in which no one is qualified. This is so because the relationships involve a radical cultural leveling, not because no superior individuals exist.[6]

Mass Institutions

The effectiveness with which an institution acts on a mass following can be judged in several different ways:

One measure is its capacity to make contact with and to enlist the support of a potential following. This is made possible by the efficient use of the resources of an institution. For example, the efficiency of Billy Graham's mass revivalism is evidenced by his ability to attract capacity audiences night after night, to keep himself in the limelight, and to reach souls not ordinarily in contact with religion. Effectiveness may also be measured against the goals and purposes of the institution. Hence, the effectiveness of the Graham crusade, quite apart from its efficiency, is measured by the number of new members enlisted in co-operating churches. The efficiency of the Graham revival team is fairly well established, but its *effectiveness* is open to some question.

But effectiveness may also be determined by the impact of the institution on individual attitude and behavior. Neither of the criteria above judges the impact on the individual. Just how, one asks, did the Graham revival influence those who stepped forward to make a decision for Christ? Some may have been on the verge of joining a church; in that case, they seized an opportunity to "sign up," but their religious outlook cannot be said to have been revitalized; it was merely crystallized. The question unanswered is whether the campaign succeeded in affecting deeply and permanently the lives of decision-makers.

6. Philip Selznick, "Institutional Vulnerability in Mass Society," *American Journal of Sociology*, LVI (January, 1951), p. 321.

Mass institutions generally affect the participants only superficially. By their very nature some institutions—such as the mass media of communication and political parties—depend on widespread popular support. Whether they have a mass following depends, however, not so much on size as on how popularity is achieved.

As Gilbert Seldes showed some years ago, the image of the mass audience that dominated the American mass communications industry was of an undifferentiated mass.[7] After careful research into the habits and preferences of the potential audience, broadcasters served up entertainment and views geared to a common denominator of taste bound to appeal to the largest possible number of people. Imagining the great audience as an unqualified mass, they failed to take into consideration the many special interests of people and the so-called "minority taste."

The mass communications industry, in general, works with this image of their clientele as a homogeneous mass seeking *divertissement*. They judge their own effectiveness by how much of some unqualified mass they reach. Audience ratings tend to reassure them in this regard. The effectiveness of television or radio or a large share of the press thus appears greatest in areas that are the least vital. In this concession to mass appeal, basic values are compromised. By appealing primarily to similarities among disparate individuals, the institution demands no new commitments and is not apt to leave any deep impact as a character-defining institution. The communicators act not as a creative elite guiding the mass toward a more creative way of life but as an adjunct and handman of Ortega y Gasset's mass man.

The avoidance of controversy, which often serves in lieu of a positive policy in the mass communications industry, cannot be attributed entirely to the domination of business interests or to the fact that the industry is, as is so often pointed out, just another business. At times, business interests have been fostered by the exploitation of minority tastes and interests, either where these were deemed large enough to cultivate or where their cultivation seemed necessary for protection against vociferous public criticism or governmental intervention.

Institutions that depend on widespread popular support display considerable effectiveness in mobilizing or manipulating a following for some specific end: the mass media constantly deliver their audiences; mass political parties garner votes; some institutions of higher learning satisfy a mass demand for diplomas. Their effectiveness in these matters depends most on the competing influences—that is, on the amount of resistance—which they are rationally organized to overcome. Responses can be molded most easily if issues are so defined as to raise no great resistances.

7. Gilbert Seldes, *The Great Audience* (New York: Viking Press, 1950).

Minimization of resistance means either that there are no strong prior commitments because the issue is a matter of indifference or that the suggestions are in line with existing tendencies.

The approach of the mass institution to the mass is oblique. It makes use of private dispositions and group networks of communication. It seeks not so much to mold opinion as to make use of opinion that is already molded. In this way the impact is somewhat superficial; it mainly concerns matters that are peripheral, where attitudes can be readily changed because they are not held too clearly or dearly. The mass institutions do not remold outlook or develop new insight and consensus. The values communicated are essentially stereotyped versions of conventions.

THE ALIENATED MASS

The alienated mass is best typified by the revolutionary aggregate,[8] by the disaffected middle classes, pensioners, minorities, or returning military veterans who, when aroused, act directly and spontaneously against established institutions. It is made up of "have-nots" who sense themselves victims of a common fate. Its unity is based on the sharing of negative sentiments, like envy and resentment. Though composed of "have-nots," who can be found in every society, the alienated mass is not identical with the underprivileged or the lower classes. For an alienated mass to form, the individuals who compose it must sense themselves a part of a multitude of "have-nots" who share the institutional incapacities inherent in their inferior status. They are alienated from the larger society, but there is a sense of being shut out *together*, instead of alone. Moreover, an alienated mass, though not a unified interest group with common goals and organization, gives the *appearance* to the dominant groups of being such. This definition reinforces the internal sense of solidarity.

Mass action characteristic of the alienated mass differs from that of the unqualified mass, whose major impact on institutions stems not from direct action undertaken together, but from the convergence of unqualified choices to which popular institutions, dedicated to the mass, cater. The alienated mass, driven by a sense of common deprivation and common fate, acts in collective defense against the anxiety bred by futility. As a mass it acts directly against existing institutions and may destroy them. Still, as Marx recognized, the spontaneous mass action of the revolutionary aggregate does not suffice to build new institutions. As

8. Cf. Theodor Geiger, *Die Masse und ihre Aktion* (Stuttgart: 1926); and Karl Mannheim, *Man and Society in an Age of Reconstruction* (New York: Harcourt, Brace & Co., 1951).

far as he was concerned, proletarian mass action was necessary to the destruction of capitalism but incapable in itself of achieving a socialist society. As a mass, individuals can be manipulated by persons who wish to overthrow old institutions; but as soon as they act, the political short-comings of the masses, deliberately kept impotent and ignorant by those in power, become a source of concern. Its explosive potential makes the alienated mass a danger even to those who unleash it. Witness nation-alistic fervor which, let loose in the name of anticolonialism, threatens to thwart the growth of democratic institutions for which the mass clamored. Once the alienated explode into mass action, their energy, to serve constructively, has to be checked and diverted.

The Alienated Mass and the Mass Movement [9]

The alienated mass is a main source of recruitment for leaders of mass movements, but the mass movement is not identical with the alienated mass. The alienated mass is, as noted, often manipulated by the leaders of some mass movement for their own purposes. But when the "have-nots" act as members of a mass movement, they engage in a differ-ent form of action than they do as an alienated mass. As part of the alienated mass, they share a common hopeless fate. When they explode, their anger is directed at the symbols of law and order. The participants feel themselves set apart from the rest of society; any mob they form is a desperate cry against an overwhelming feeling of impotence. The mass movements that recruit followers from the alienated mass appeal to those whose expectations have been aroused but who somehow are blocked in their fulfillment. The mass movement gives them new hope, the promise that they can have a hand in shaping their own fate, and a new feeling of involvement. Undisciplined, spontaneous, explosive ac-tion of the alienated mass is ultimately superseded by revolutionary ac-tivity based on discipline. The organized movement channels the senti-ments of mass man into social action.

An active mass movement can arise out of an alienated mass and is essentially a matter of collective defense against demoralization. This spirit develops most readily among a group that exists separate from the dominant community. Any frustrations are thus likely to be ex-perienced by many people *at the same time,* and any specific grievance or wrong is immediately communicated. When the experiences of such alienated masses are reproduced in many particular localities, when the same sources of discontent make them rather homogeneous, a broader mass movement, hostile to the institutions on which the social order rests, is likely to erupt. Thus, the main threat to these institutions comes

9. The mass or social movement is discussed at length in chapters 16 and 17.

not from demoralized individuals in an unqualified mass, but from alienated masses who are joined together but excluded from participation.

By way of illustration, the anticapitalist spirit that became the norm for many proletarian associations can be traced, according to Michels, to developments that isolated and separated the workers as a whole from the remainder of the community.[10] Peasants, domestic workers, and artisans from the countryside and small communities were assembled in factory towns and afterward, in the metropolitan community, segregated in working-class quarters. Here they were confronted by identical conditions. They learned to collaborate under the discipline of the machine, while the factory whistle, the weekly routine, and the ups and downs of the business cycle homogenized them in entirely unexpected ways. After-work contact with nonworkers, especially their "betters," was hindered by residential segregation. Further, the division of labor and the large industrial plant also meant that workers no longer worked alongside their employers, who delegated more and more of the functions of management to hired supervisory personnel. The owners became remote personalities. They made their presence felt on increasingly rare occasions, and as their direct influence within the shop declined, it waned in other respects as well.

This destruction of the occupational and the residential communities, in which workers participated together with other classes, left them as an alienated mass, with few ties to the remainder of society. Where industrialism was introduced by an alien group from the very beginning, the effects of the proletarian's isolation were greatly aggravated. These can be seen, for example, in the Union of South Africa. The discipline exercised by the dominant white group is based on force and restrictive legislation. With the weakening of tribal organization and the absence of a broader consensus to include both African and white populations, there exist forms of disorganization that have given signs of exploding into a violent mass movement.

THE MASS AS ACCIDENTAL AGGREGATE

A third view of mass is as the chance convergence of the behavior of many disparate individuals, firms, households, or local groups. These atomistic units together form a mass. The individuals in this mass are not bound together by any common purpose; their aggregate pattern of behavior is purely fortuitous. It is the outcome of autonomous decision-making—decisions in connection with purchases and investments,

10. Robert Michels, "Psychologie der antikapitalistischen Massenbewegungen," *Grundriss der Sozialökonomie*, Vol. II, Part 2 (Tübingen: J. C. B. Mohr, 1926), pp. 244–81.

where to locate a plant, where to make one's home, whether to vote yes or no in a referendum, what to watch on television, what games to play, what books to read. Each individual (or unit) is nominally free to make his own choice, and his choice is made with no intent of affecting a collective result or accomplishing a collective task. A man goes to a movie because he wants to see it, not because he wants to make it a smash hit or to express his solidarity with other movie fans. He becomes a participant in a mass simply because his choice coincides with that of many other individuals.

Mass behavior, conceptualized in this way, reveals itself only in its totality. The individual decision has no relevance except insofar as it is repeated simultaneously—or in rapid order—by many others. Thus, it is possible to get at mass action, viewed as an aggregate propensity, only by means of some summary measure which interprets not individual decisions but their total impact. Thus a mass buying spree is the summation of numbers of individual decisions to buy, whatever or however different the individual motivations for buying may be. One speaks of a mass exodus when myriads of individual families desert the city for the surrounding suburbs, whatever their reasons for going. Shifts in individual motivation are reflected in changes in the summary measure.

This quantitative image of the accidental aggregate presupposes a society in which many matters are resolved in accordance with the laissez-faire principle. To speak of a mass pattern is meaningful only if the revelant behavior involves genuine options. This means: (1) that an individual is not restrained from following his own interests or inclinations as he perceives them, and (2) that the collective pattern cannot be explained in terms of some common purpose or rule that takes the behavior out of the realm of choice. Thus the individual is free to choose among alternatives. His voting, viewing, or purchasing decisions are limited by the existing alternatives and by his ability to avail himself of any one of them. One can choose only from the television programs offered by stations within range. Nor is nonviewing, if one's set is out of order, completely voluntary. Income, contractual obligations, etc., set limits to one's freedom of purchase. The second of the two conditions above, the absence of group norms and sanctions which make a decision mandatory, is equally important. If voting is compulsory and open to official scrutiny, the collective decision can scarcely be called a mass decision. Or, school children who must listen to a particular program as part of an educational assignment scarcely constitute a mass.

A lack of common purpose does not, of course, stipulate a mass of isolated individuals completely uprooted from local tradition and from all face-to-face influences. Certainly what relatives, friends, neighbors, and work associates think and do goes a long way toward determining what one buys, what one likes, how one votes, how one views the world and one's position in it. There are also structurally determined similarities in the behavior and opinions of people occupying similar positions in society. But what is true of each decision taken separately need not be true of the totality of decisions. Each decision may be anchored in habits and interests developed in smaller structures; still, the aggregate pattern of behavior in which the individual decisions culminate cannot be explained in terms of common tradition and common purpose. For instance, the decision of a particular family to join a westward movement may be perfectly understandable in terms of local customs and interests; but the westward movement itself constitutes a mass migration representing a break in custom. It is a mass phenomenon only in its totality—that is, as an aggregate propensity.

SYNTHESIS

These, then, are the essential features of mass phenomena, whether the mass is viewed as alienated, as unqualified, or as a chance aggregate.

1. Every mass phenomenon is an aggregate made up of autonomous acts on the part of many individual units. It makes no sense to speak of a mass unless large numbers are involved. The importance of mass phenomena generally and the effectiveness of a specific mass depend on quantitative predominance.

2. The pattern the mass displays as an aggregate is not the outcome of societal regulation. The laissez-faire character of certain areas of decision-making places them outside the realm of organized group decision. Moreover, the mass often acts in direct opposition to, or in flagrant disregard of, standards set by social authorities. Hence, mass behavior arises with regard to those matters where there are no established rules of conduct, where these are ignored or rejected, or where individuals or groups are not fully integrated in social structure.

3. The collective dimension of mass behavior results from needs and sentiments and, above all, expectations that are generated separately in many particular settings. The individual in the mass cannot raise himself above his everyday milieu. There is little two-way communication in the mass as a whole and (at least, while they are participating) even less understanding, on the part of individuals, of the history-making nature of their action. For the participants who make up a mass are usually dispersed over a fairly large area. They are not assembled. Mass action is essentially matched-independent behavior.

4. Though the mass, unlike the crowd, does not mill, participants generally have some vague image of the abstract multitude who make

up the mass. This awareness is no recognition of a structure of generally valid norms of behavior, but it does mean that the participants act by reference to what appears to be the momentarily prevailing sentiment as far as they can recognize it. They sense that the climate of opinion is such that one cannot criticize the government, or they respond to feelings of speculative excitement. This mass perspective explains the cumulative and contagionlike spread of mass behavior over and above what it would be if individuals acted altogether autonomously without any image of what nameless others were doing.

5. The action of the mass is elementary and unorganized. However momentous the impact of mass behavior, the individuals in the mass lack effective influence to determine its course. They do not generally understand the conditions that shape it; nor do they possess the institutional means to control it. The mass may give rise to a collective enterprise, but it has none of the features of one: it has no organization, no leadership, no program, no goal, no articulated policy.

Group Influence and Mass Suggestibility

Mass behavior thus occurs in a context of demoralizing tendencies in the sense that this process was defined in Chapter 4. Such collective incapacity as the mass displays is attributable to historical circumstances that have uprooted individuals from the bonds of tradition and yet left them poorly prepared for the tasks they see themselves called upon to perform in the larger society. Participation in small face-to-face groups is still more meaningful to most individuals, as it can integrate them into society more completely and in many more areas of behavior than can a momentary coincidence of expectations, grievances, and sentiment. Indeed, under the impact of mass sentiments, character-defining institutions, based on long-standing loyalties and particularistic interests, tend to lose their stabilizing influence. The members of the mass begin to act independently of them, and a peculiarly unstable form of leadership arises on every level of the mass. When the various lines of action momentarily converge, their impact can be tremendous. But this convergence is hardly a sign of social integration.

The apparent hypersuggestibility of individuals in the mass is a collective, and not an individual, phenomenon. Taken by themselves, the individuals in the mass are no more subject to influence than people integrated into organized groups. Still, it is easier for a person who wishes to influence the group member to predict the interests to which he is likely to respond; he is likely to be susceptible only to certain arguments or to the appeals of particular prestige figures. The certainty with which one can *predict* not only how the "organization man" can be swayed but also the limits of his susceptibility actually makes him appear less susceptible than the individual who responds to a mass appeal.

Voting studies have repeatedly pointed to the stability of political sentiment that is group-anchored. When one's friends, family, colleagues, etc., all share the same political opinion, it is neither very easy to resist sharing it nor very likely that one has a strong inclination to do so. In modern society political opinions are sustained by group relations. The voter's mind is generally made up early in life and early in every political campaign. Once a stand is taken, it is unlikely to change as long as it is supported and confirmed by everyday contacts.

Uncertainty, on the other hand, results from cross pressures when people are given contradictory advice by others whom they respect or when conflicting group identifications pull them in opposite directions. More often than not, the voter who postpones his decision until election time is the one who has no clear group standards to guide him. He is at loose ends, at least politically. He may be using the time to collect information from speeches and party platforms and to decide, on the basis of what he learns, what he and his country need in the way of government. But the late decider is not usually a really "independent" voter; he is more likely to be a "floating" voter who finally makes up his mind how to vote through some chance conversation or observation, even heard just before he enters the polling booth. Since he represents an element of instability, he appears more susceptible than others to heteronomous influence. Actually, as an individual he is no more so, and perhaps even less so, than the voter who accepts direction from the very outset.

One would not expect to find the same stability and continuity in a nonhomogeneous environment (represented by the mass society) as in the more or less insulated and self-contained community. But when people have to make up their minds for themselves—though not of course completely by themselves—their competence to do so becomes of crucial importance. Seemingly erratic behavior often stems from a lack of appropriate social forms, and individuals, faced with some new choice, tend to act hesitantly at first until support for a particular line of action becomes evident. In a mass, such support usually originates from actions outside the everyday local milieu—from what one hears or reads about what "others" are doing.

THE STUDY OF AGGREGATE PATTERNS

ANY SOCIOLOGY OF THE MASS deals of necessity with aggregate patterns. Though every aggregate pattern is a mass phenomenon, not all mass phenomena fit the category of collective action labeled mass behavior. What then distinguishes mass behavior from other, apparently similar aggregate phenomena?

Mass behavior refers to such phenomena of collective dynamics as entail shifts on the part of many dispersed individuals in response to some external event that, in the absence of a clear framework of shared norms, produces effects that become cumulative. Since many aggregate phenomena are neither made up of responses to external events that intrude on the consciousness of many individuals nor are cumulative in their ramifications, some distinction among several types of aggregate phenomena different in their collective dynamics seems in order.

In the first place, there are certain shifts in aggregate distributions that follow from the way in which local conditions impinge on many individuals. They are deducible from similarities in the way in which circumstances affect the needs or capacities of the individual units that contribute to the trend. They entail no convergence on a common object and will therefore be referred to as *simple aggregates.* Many population movements, many economic fluctuations, and some changes in life styles represent precisely such shifts which, if they do occur *en masse,* produce aggregate changes rather closely related to the status divisions in the society.

Second, shifts that occur in response to the same external event or focalize on a common object as a solution to problems experienced individually are of a somewhat different order. The actions of the units are not only similar but they converge. The *convergent mass,* the focalized action of a dispersed multitude, forms in response to news events, promotional activities, etc., that elicit the same reaction from many persons.

Third, the individual units who respond in a similar fashion are usually oriented, at least in some vague way, to an image of how the mass of others is reacting. Influenced by what they think is the prevailing sentiment of the multitude, they act as if that sentiment actually prevailed and so set in motion a current of *mass sentiment,* to which each contributes.

In any concrete manifestation of mass behavior, all three phenomena are usually present, but in varying degrees.

SIMPLE AGGREGATES

The stability of many aggregate patterns has long been noted. Rates, distributions, relationships, etc., express what individuals will do as a rule and on the average in certain situations. The stability of such summary measures forms the basis of many sociological generalizations on the aggregate level. For example, the suicide rate is higher among Protestants, the middle classes, and the unmarried than among Catholics, workers, and the married. Similarly, the differences observed in the consumer behavior, political preferences, residential mobility, crime rate, and tastes for the arts of people occupying different social positions lend themselves to many meaningful statements about persistent aggregate patterns of behavior.

Aggregate phenomena also exhibit patterns of variation over time. Consumer behavior is not altogether stable; sometimes people embark on a spending spree, after which they hoard their goods and money. There are suicide waves, political upsets, population treks, crime waves, and fashions and fads in which the stable patterns appear to be upset. While focusing on these shifts brings us a little closer to mass behavior, many aggregate changes are adequately explained by changes in a potential that is related to status and role. A baby boom is certainly a mass phenomenon, but it is not necessarily mass behavior: an over-all increase in fertility can occur without any change in the average number of children born to women in specific age groups. A declining death rate, so that more women survive their full childbearing period—usually defined as between the ages of fifteen and forty-four years—suffices to produce the aggregate change in the birth rate. If the average woman continues to give birth to the same number of children in every year of her life-span, "age-specific birth rates," as they are called, remain constant. The baby boom has resulted solely from an enlargement of the population potential reflected in the age structure.

To predict a population change under the above circumstances—a model that assumes no changes in the relationship between the number of births and the factors that determine average fertility—is sufficient. Of course, other more variable factors, such as attitudes toward early marriage, the desirability of large families, and approval of contraceptive practices, may upset these rather gross predictions. Similar models can be employed to predict many other aggregate changes. In politics, one speaks of a "party potential" made up of persons who, in view of their past history, social background, and immediate environment, can be counted on to produce large majorities for that party. The major political turnover that produced the New Deal and the Fair Deal of the 1930's and 40's is in large measure attributable to increases in the population groups that had been for a long time the traditional sources of Democratic strength. A high birth rate, immigration, and urbanization had augmented the voting potential in the Democratic cities. These party loyalties persisted through the 1950's. Notwithstanding the personal popularity of President Eisenhower, the New Deal generation continued to produce major Democratic victories. General political trends and even specific elections can be predicted with reasonable accuracy from an analysis of the political potential. To do this, one needs to know little about the motives of individuals. As long as the general and average relationship between social position and voting remains undisturbed, aggregate predictions can be made from aggregate data.

CONVERGENT MASS

An aggregate change is mass behavior only if it is accounted for by novel factors—an external event—that affect the subjective orientations of large numbers. Even the founding of a family involves conscious choice, and many parallel decisions may thus alter the aggregate pattern established in the past. For example, the passage of a peacetime draft in 1940 raised the marriage rate. This, coupled with an improvement in economic conditions, meant an increase in births the following year. Decisions less dependent on the life-cycle, such as a vote, a purchase, a decision to strike, are affected even more by specific events. They do not result entirely from influences operating on individuals but also from the fact that masses of people are oriented to the same unsettling influences.

A judgment of whether or not aggregate behavior constitutes mass behavior must recognize the peculiar sociological character of the mass. The mass in itself is not organized but results only from many individual autonomous shifts. None of the many individuals who together form the mass can significantly affect the aggregate trend by his own behavior. Power and influence are dispersed throughout the entire mass and are exhibited only when the many autonomous actions happen to coalesce into some general shift. But this coalescence is not a matter of design. For the mass to act according to some plan, it would first have to be organized and would thereby cease to be a mass.

Why Families Move

What subjective orientation accounts for any particular aggregate trend is always a problem to be resolved through investigation. But unless the autonomous decisions arise from perspectives individuals derive from their position in a mass, the accidental aggregate results solely from the sum of individual potentials. A study of four Philadelphia neighborhoods, undertaken when the suburban exodus was already in full swing, tried to discover why families moved. It was found, first of all, that residents did not rate the desirability of their area—that is, its accessibility and suitability for residence—in the same way as did an "objective" observer.[11] Moreover, since the newcomers were not in any way considered by residents to differ from those who were living in the neighborhood, most moves were not efforts to escape from a neighborhood that was in the process of change.[12] In view of this, the aggregate mobility of each area was a simple function of the presence or absence of factors that accounted for dispositions to move, and these varied from household to household.

Each family unit decides for itself when and where it should move. Their decisions rest on a judgment, first about the adequacy and suitability of the present housing, and, second, about the possibility of better meeting their needs elsewhere. Of course, some moves are necessary owing to eviction, forced relocation, or job transfers. But the voluntary moves usually result from changes in the mode of life that occur within the normal family life-cycle.

The aggregate mobility of an area is a summary measure of the number of families who have decided to resolve their personal situation in a similar way. The behavior of these families coincide because a number of them have defined their present housing as unsatisfactory at about the same time. "Mobile areas are mobile," says Rossi, "because they provide housing for households in those life-cycle stages which are particularly unstable"[13]—that is, when marriage, children, and social ascendancy create demands for more space and for new styles of life.

But when one considers, not specific moves, but the pattern of residential movement, it becomes evident that the individual decisions are responsive to the larger ecological structure and to the opportunities presented from the outside. Movement can occur only into areas where new housing is available and such movements often exemplify a convergent mass. After World War II new housing developments at the fringes of cities offered the only real opportunity for escape from overcrowded neighborhoods. Over and above this, the suburban exodus was also something in the way of a mass psychological phenomenon. It represented a shift in mass sentiment toward a new way of life. The virtues of suburban living, the advantages of owning over renting, and the evils of city living were widely proclaimed and believed. Moving to the suburbs, following the path so many others had already taken, became the thing to do. As the problems of suburban living become evident, however, there may well be a mass reaction against it, and it may once more become fashionable to reside in cities. By the late 1950's, cutting

11. Peter H. Rossi. *Why Families Move* (Glencoe, Ill.: The Free Press, 1955), chap. 3.
12. *Ibid.*, chap. 4.
13. *Ibid.*, p. 181.

satirizations of the suburbanite were finding a more ready acceptance than any one would have guessed a few years before. And this coincided with a gradually accelerating rate of return to the cities.

STRIKE WAVES   The importance of subjective attitudes to either local conditions or non-local events can also be illustrated against a background of fluctuating economic conditions. Many aggregate social phenomena stand in some determinate relation with the business cycle. This is especially true of indices of disorganization, like the frequency of crime, suicide, divorce, industrial conflict, etc.[14] Some of these parallel the ups and downs in economic conditions, while others are inversely related to them. The conclusion is inescapable that economic conditions have certain generally similar effects on people everywhere.

Strikes, for example, do not occur most frequently in periods of greatest distress. The number of man-days lost in strikes increases as business conditions improve, apparently because of a greater willingness on the part of individual workers to participate in a walkout. Just what accounts for this increased propensity to strike is not entirely clear. It may be an altogether individual reaction. Perhaps a short strike with strong prospects of victory means a welcome vacation and relief from the drudgery of prolonged employment, while the financial losses suffered during the strike can more easily be borne. But individual unions and their leadership may also be reacting directly to an improved labor market. Armed with economic statistics, they seize a proffered opportunity, aware that employers are reluctant to suffer production losses when an expanding market can readily absorb their products and inventories are declining.

It is also true that many strikes result from a particular grievance rather than from some general cause. But a decision to strike may be deferred until conditions are judged ripe, thus fitting in with the general trend. Hence, the cyclical pattern could be explained as a response to certain non-local events rather than to similar situations. Moreover, strikes often occur in waves. A successful strike triggers similar demands elsewhere. Many factors other than the business cycle affect the timing of strikes. Political events, government policies, and the anticipation of public sympathy help to account for many specific deviations from the normal cyclical pattern.[15] In view of all this, many specific strike waves represent convergent mass behavior but also represent shifts in mass sentiment.

14. Ernest R. Mowrer, "Social Crises and Social Disorganization," *American Sociological Review*, XVI (February, 1950), pp. 60–66.

15. Albert Rees, "Industrial Conflict and Business Fluctuations," in Arthur W. Kornhauser, Robert Dubin, and Arthur M. Ross (eds.), *Industrial Conflict* (New York: McGraw-Hill Book Co., 1954), p. 220.

Mass Sentiment

Some years ago a historian, the late Carl L. Becker, popularized the notion of "climate of opinion" by means of which the underlying thought of an epoch could be characterized. This climate of opinion was deduced from the disciplined thought of the period, from the ideas of the great thinkers. Their ideas about social reality were affected by that reality. Eighteenth-century philosophers thus constructed their "heavenly city"; nineteenth-century economists were overwhelmed by the problem of scarcity, and mid-twentieth-century critics by what to do with so much potential affluence. But the climate of opinion, as revealed in literary works, is a history of intellectual thought and not of mass sentiment. Mass sentiment refers to the general hopes and fears, the broad likes and dislikes, the prevailing outlook of people concerning events that lie outside their community of direct experience and, in view of this, often cannot be substantiated by objectively validated information. Sentiment is to be distinguished from opinion in that the former is not a reasoned view to be defended; it is rarely articulated completely or chronicled into a permanent record. Nevertheless, many opinions and actions are founded largely on general sentiment. The large-scale shifts of sentiment throughout a society in which the autonomous reactions of large masses are important tend to create an atmosphere through which things are judged. To say that something is "in the air" is to imply that it reflects mass sentiment.

When life conditions change very rapidly, shifts in mass sentiment will also occur in rapid succession. A brief summary of four decades suggests that each was marked by some dominant temper: the "Roaring Twenties" are remembered for their exuberant spirit; the Depression decade was a period of intense concern with social and economic issues; during the war years a spirit of optimism prevailed; while the "Fabulous Fifties" seem best characterized in terms of the vague but widely prevalent feeling of uneasiness that things were too good to last.

Such summaries of the general outlook of an entire decade cannot but be of dubious accuracy, since one is forced to overlook whatever does not fit into the dominant pattern. But shifts in mass sentiment can be observed in connection with specific events that affect behavior in limited areas. Such shifts are fairly unpredictable, but a boom, a wave of speculation, a financial panic, etc., are short-run mass psychological phenomena with discernible consequences.

ATTITUDES TOWARD SPENDING: AN ILLUSTRATION   The relationships among a simple aggregate, a convergent mass, and a shift in mass sentiment can be illustrated by tracing several formulations concerning the effect of economic expectations on consumer demand.

1. Keynes defines the propensity to consume as that part of a community's total disposable income that is spent for consumption. The relationship between these two aggregate quantities—total expenditure for consumption and total national income—is predictable according to the following general pattern: As national income increases, Keynes held, consumption will also increase—only not as much as income, and therefore a larger proportion of income will be saved. Conversely, a decline in national income usually results in reduced consumer expenditures, but again not by as much as the reduction in income. Thus, income and consumption always move in the same direction; the size of the inevitable gap between income and consumption depends on income and, in Keynes's view, on income alone.[16] In the form given it by Keynes, this is a near-perfect illustration of a proposition concerning aggregate patterns as determined by two variable quantities—the effect of a change in potential. It is a useful tool in macro-economic analysis provided other, especially volatile, psychological factors remain fairly constant.

But Keynes derives the regularities in the propensity to consume not from experience but from a psychological postulate which, he says, governs the dispositions of men "on the average and as a rule." During short-term changes in income, he asserts, men's habits "are not given time enough to adapt themselves to changed objective circumstances." These habits prevent the immediate adjustment of consumption to a rise in income; adjustment would mean spending the entire increase. The achievement of a higher level of income will likewise have the effect of widening the gap between income and consumption, because a person's immediate and primary needs have the first claim on his income, and other motives, like that of accumulation and security, "only acquire effective sway when a higher margin of comfort has been attained." [17] In other words, his assumption of stability in the aggregate propensity to consume is derived from an assumption as to how that propensity operates in each individual. Individual deviations—that is, spending or saving in excess amounts—tend to cancel each other out and therefore need not be considered separately.

This model permits gross aggregate predictions in the long run, as long as the propensity to consume a certain proportion of one's income

---

16. John Maynard Keynes, *The General Theory of Employment Interest and Money* (London: Macmillan and Co., Ltd., 1936), III. This summary of Keynes's views leaves out the detailed assumptions that allow him to reduce the propensity to consume to such a simple relationship. The definition of income has to be in wage units (eliminating price fluctuations) and measure "disposable income" (eliminating taxation). Many other factors, such as the distribution of income, are considered to change but slowly and therefore are not taken into account. But the detailed economic argument is irrelevant in this context.

17. *Ibid.,* p. 97.

remains a simple function of income, the change in income constituting a change in "potential." Changes in total income thus reflect changes in the proportion of households with given amounts of income, and these changes are assumed to have similar and parallel effects on the propensities of individuals. Aggregate changes are simply functions of conditions confronted by many households which lead each of them, by itself, to increase or curtail expenditures at a certain rate.

2. There are, indeed, considerable differences in the propensity of individual units to consume as well as variability in the behavior of any one household from one year to the next. According to managers at credit centers, the $10,000-to-$20,000 yearly income bracket contains a much higher proportion of reckless spenders and credit risks than the group directly below it. During any one year some units will save a considerable portion of their income, some will save little or nothing, and some will definitely add to their debt (dissave). Income differences do not adequately explain these observations.

A two-wave survey of the behavior of the *same* households was conducted by the Survey Research Center of the University of Michigan for two consecutive years, 1947 and 1948.[18] These were years of steady economic growth, of rising income, and of general optimism concerning business conditions. On the aggregate level, the survey found, the spending-saving performance of this sample of households was substantially the same for both years. But this was not nearly as true in individual households. Fully one third of them had a net deficit (an increase in indebtedness) in one of the two years but a net increase in assets in the other. Unexpected reductions in income, caused by temporary unemployment or emergencies, such as illness, hospitalization, etc., accounted for only a few of these reversals. Moreover, in the face of the over-all stability, the worsening in the financial position of individual families did not represent a trend, and their excess spending was offset by amounts saved in other units or by these same units during alternate years.

The repetitiousness in the individual performances was largely accounted for by contractual forms of savings (e.g., life insurance or installment payments) and by outlays that vary little because they are habitual and obligatory. Variability, by contrast, was due primarily to decisions concerning the allocation of income between certain highly discretionary expenditures and optional forms of saving. Whether a household saved or dissaved during a given

18. George Katona and Janet A. Fisher, *Post-war Income Changes of Identical Consumer Units,* Vol. XIII of *Studies in Income and Wealth* (New York: National Bureau of Economic Research, 1951).

period seemed to depend on the amount of durable goods it had acquired and on such "unusual" expenditures as were incurred for home repairs, trips, etc. Outlays that increased indebtedness were not usually repeated in the two consecutive years, during which objective economic conditions and financial attitudes remained fairly constant. Hence, in this instance, individual shifts could be ignored. They were randomly distributed and did not form a trend.

This does not mean, however, that individual variability is always random. The convergent mass, as it has been defined, consists of persons who, from diverse situations, make the same decision in response to the same events. The over-all outcome of their decisions can only be predicted insofar as one knows what the individual expectations and resources are. The propensity to consume, for example, is not entirely a matter of income. Families whose head was twenty-five to thirty-four years of age reversed their savings behavior most frequently in the two years. These are, of course, years of instability, during which families get settled, often away from their home town, and have their children, all of which create new demands without corresponding increases in income. These years are, however, governed by optimistic expectations. As long as nothing happens to upset many people all at once, the mass will continue to behave in a way that is predictable from individual needs.

3. Variation over time in the manner individuals exercise their discretions is not always due to independent factors which impinge separately on individuals. Sometimes their effects are cumulative. They may result in waves of optimism or pessimism concerning the economic future which, initially, may be justified neither by economic indicators nor by individual experiences. The critical question is: to what extent do broad shifts from optimistic to pessimistic expectations (or vice versa) have an independent causative influence on the over-all pattern of economic behavior? It is answered, but only partially, by another series of surveys by the Survey Research Center. The purpose of these surveys was to "analyse the variations in spending and saving that occurred in the years 1950 to 1952 with the aim of clarifying the role of consumer attitudes in accelerating or retarding the rate of consumer spending in our economy." [19]

19. George Katona and Eva Mueller, *Consumer Attitudes and Demand, 1950–1952* (Ann Arbor, Mich.: Survey Research Center, 1953), p. 1. For a general discussion of the role of expectations, see George Katona, *Psychological Analysis of Economic Behavior* (New York: McGraw-Hill Book Co., 1951). A brief summary of the results of this and the preceding survey can be found in George Katona, "Variability of Consumer Behavior and the Survey Method," in Lawrence R. Klein (ed.), *Contributions of Survey Methods to Economics* (New York: Columbia University Press, 1954).

Two peaks in buying coincided with an American military set-back in Korea in the summer of 1950 and with the retreat caused by the intervention of Chinese troops in the winter of 1951 to 1952. In August, 1950, Americans expected price rises. They were startled by unusual events far away, which they did not fully understand. The great majority concluded that prices would go up, many of them anticipating substantial increases. The buying spree was obviously based on these expectations and, in its turn, played a role in driving prices to a higher level than they might have otherwise reached. The increased demand created inflationary pressure. Furthermore, insofar as demand depended on expectations of price rises and price increases were in part caused by the scare reaction, these expectations, irrespective of whether initially there was any factual basis for them, were confirmed. An added element of instability lies in the "one-way" nature of inflationary expectations. People often interpret even a minor increase in prices (or a slight drop in employment, for that matter) as signaling the beginning of a trend instead of a fulfillment of their expectations. Hence, they do not believe that a minor change will be countered by a movement in the opposite direction. On the contrary, the steeper the price rise at a given moment, the more it is likely to be interpreted as a harbinger of long-run increases.

Actually by the spring of 1951, the predominantly pessimistic mood had given way to uncertainty and caution. As scare buying decreased, price rises came to a halt. It would be important to know, the authors of this report suggest, "how it came about that early in 1951, a large proportion of the American people turned from a feeling that inflation and shortages were ahead to the notion that 'this is a bad time to buy' or turned from fear of war to a notion of 'prolonged stress and feeling of uncertainty.' " [20] To this last question no clear-cut answer can be given. But a sound case can be made for the interpretation that consumer expectations and the attitudes derived from them influenced both the behavior of consumers and the price fluctuations to which they were a response.

A similar explanation is offered by John Kenneth Galbraith, an economist, for the great wave of stock market speculation that collapsed in 1929. In retrospect it has become clear that evaluations of the market and its potentialities were accepted as fact and passed on from person to person, though they bore little relation to the underlying reality. Nevertheless, several million investors—perhaps as many as one out of twenty adults, according to a Senate Investigating Committee in 1934—

20. Katona and Mueller, *op. cit.*, p. 57.

participated in and followed eagerly every move of the market. To them only the increasing monetary values were real; the flimsy substance they represented mattered little. Galbraith writes:

> We do not know why the speculative orgy occurred in 1928 and 1929. The long accepted explanation that credit was easy and so people were impelled to borrow money to buy common stocks on margin [by taking a loan with the stock as security and then selling it to repay the loan plus interest and still realize a profit] is obvious nonsense . . . Money, by the ordinary tests, was tight in the late twenties. Far more important than the rate of interest and the supply of credit is the mood. Speculation on a large scale requires a pervasive sense of confidence and optimism and the conviction that ordinary people were meant to be rich.[21]

The rise and fall of expectations, the swings between extremes of sentiment, the social atmosphere that made speculation commendable, the acceptance and quick discard of a novelty, etc., all constitute genuine mass psychological phenomena on the part of people who participate in something new. The change in mood may be subtle. It does not always cross the threshold of awareness until the inevitable reaction against the trend has set in. Sometimes carefully designed attitude surveys are needed to catch the drift. But there have also been numerous occasions in which masses have been caught up in an epidemic whose beginnings, whose peaks, and whose subsidance can be plotted with some accuracy, because they made news and were talked about everywhere. The effects of such a psychological epidemic on those stricken are most real, and the phenomena appear to be contagious. But if the assumptions behind the excessive excitation and activity are completely unfounded, the mood will not last. A retrenchment, a return to "normalcy," a shocking re-awakening to reality, or even a swing in the opposite direction, caused by disillusionment, is inevitable.

THE NATURAL HISTORY OF MASS PHENOMENA

This movement from the normal and habitual to sudden excess and back to some kind of equilibrium is in the nature of sudden mass psychological phenomena. Participants respond not only to unsettling events, but also to a change in temper. The natural history of mass psychological upswings and their subsequent denouements can be depicted in four phases.

1. *The development of awareness.* Mass sentiment arises in connection with nonroutine circumstances or new objects, which gain the atten-

21. John Kenneth Galbraith, *The Great Crash, 1929* (Boston: Houghton Mifflin Co., 1955), p. 174.

tion of people not effectively restrained by the norms of groups in which they ordinarily participate. At first, the significance of the unsettling experience is not likely to be grasped immediately. People will act hesitantly and self-consciously, seeking support and confirmation from every possible source. In this situation people are susceptible to influence, and any confirmation of their expectations, any "leads," suggesting explanations, are eagerly accepted.

2. *Mobilization*. This is the period in which a particular sentiment gains ground. Whether people are generally inclined to respond in a uniform way depends on how they see themselves affected. If reactions are governed by autonomous decisions, each individual counts only as one in a mass of humanity. In that case the similarity of reactions depends on the presence of broadly similar dispositions toward the event. Initially, only those who respond directly in the same way are mobilized. Hence the "initiators" of new responses during mobilization are those on every level of society and in every locality who are most sensitive to these outside influences. By their response they tend to carry along with them the more hesitant and timid.

3. *Confirmation*. During this phase these reactions are no longer governed solely by dispositions characterizing the individuals by themselves. The changed atmosphere finds general recognition, and people, in turn, react to it. During the height of such a phenomenon, expectations become cumulative and give rise to behavior that once more confirms the expectations. The new mood creates definitions assumed to be valid because no one questions them. As the new fashion appears, people feel compelled to conform and thereby enforce conformity on others. When prices do rise in response to scare buying or successful speculators display their winnings, a strong incentive for others to join is created. In this entirely new reality the things people ordinarily take for granted no longer apply.

4. *Stabilization*. Attitudes and expectations do not operate in a total vacuum. In the long run, some readjustment is therefore inevitable. Either expectations become stabilized at a new level—for example, the expectation of continuing but *slight* price rises in the second year of the Korean War. Or expectations are drastically contradicted once a segment of the population defects. This is what happened during the stock market collapse. The speculative fever depended on a continuing increase in values. As soon as some speculators dropped out and the increase could no longer be sustained, there was a mass flight to pull out of the market. Extreme optimism turned into extreme despair, once it dawned on people that the declines were real. Hence, the unpredictability of the course of such aberrations.

The Florida Land Boom: An Illustration

An excellent illustration of the unpredictability of mass behavior and of the importance of outside events is provided by the Florida land boom in the 1920's. Like other speculative bubbles, it blew up after values inflated by unrealistic expectations were no longer sustained by that "reality."

The boom psychology followed upon what had been indeed a long period of steady advancement in real-estate activity and in the development of the area. The climate also had its very real attractions. The area was a paradise for naturalists, and members of the socially prominent Astor and Vanderbilt families had been yachting and fishing in the surrounding waters for years before the boom. Wealthy men, like James Deering, of International Harvester, and James H. Snowden, the oil millionaire, had built palatial mansions in the Miami area. Close to the Bahamas and to Cuba, Miami also became a center for rum-running. Local authorities practically ignored Prohibition and left its enforcement to federal agencies. During the boom typical advertisements stressed the mild winter climate, inviting Northern tourists to leave behind the cold and their cares. But, despite uninterrupted progress in development since 1918, accommodations were still woefully inadequate to cope with the influx.

The persistent increase in activity reached boom proportions only in 1923. A peak was achieved in the summer of 1925. At that time some Northern experts predicted an inevitable decline. But despite some leveling in the autumn of that year, a really severe reaction set in only the following spring and summer.

The center of the boom activity was concentrated along a strip on the east coast of Florida reaching from Miami to Palm Beach, some sixty miles to the north. Some speculative activity also hit the west coast of Florida and the citrus areas in the center of the state. Jacksonville, an older and more settled city, experienced some rise in activity, but only very late in the boom. Several coast towns in Mississippi and Georgia and the region of Asheville in North Carolina had local booms apparently promoted in imitation of Florida.

On the whole, according to Vanderblue, the course of earlier booms, such as that in California in the late 1880's or in Chicago some ninety years before, "seems to have been followed with striking similarity in Florida." [22] But the true extent of the speculative fever is measured less by the area in which speculative activity was concentrated than by the way it attracted investors from practically all over the United States. There were two important innovations: the free motor transportation to carry people across Florida into the locality and the unprecedentedly extravagant advertising. For the first time skilled professionals employed every conceivable trick to persuade people that their wildest fantasies had a solid basis in Florida. The boom became news as soon as speculation spread. People from all over heard of the latest "gold rush" and how fabulous wealth could be secured in an almost miraculous fashion.

The boom was heavily promoted. But its success was practically guaranteed by unusually easy conditions on the money market. Real-estate bonds were sold to investors, often by mail and for term payments. These bonds were secured by mortgages on apartment houses and on hotels, some of which had not yet been built. In order to aid in the promotion, municipalities permitted the floating of tax-free bonds to undertake "improvements" and to build facilities that were still lacking. The kind of mass psychology generated by these activities on the scene is graphically described by the report of Walter C. Hill, the vice president of the Retail Credit Corporation of Atlanta, on a visit to Miami.

> Lots are bought from blue-prints. They look better that way. Then the buyer gets the promoter's vision, can see the splendid curving boulevards, the yacht basin, the parks lined with leaning coconut trees and flaming hibiscus. The salesman can show the expected lines of heavy travel and help you select a double (two-lot) corner for business or a quiet water-front retreat suitable for a winter home. To go see the lot—well, it isn't done. In fact, often it isn't practicable, for most of the lots are sold "pre-development." The boulevards are yet to be laid, the yacht basins must be pumped out, and the excavated dirt used to raise the proposed lots above water or bog level. Then they will be staked, the planting done, and the owner can find his lot.
>
> Around Miami, subdivisions, except the very large ones, are often sold out the first day of sale. Advertisements appear describing the location, extent, special features and approximate price of the lots. Reservations are accepted. This requires a check for 10% of the price of the lot the buyer expects to select. They are numbered consecutively as they come in. On the first day of sale, at the promoter's office in town, the reservations are called out in their order, and the buyer steps up and, from a beautifully drawn blue-print, with lots and dimensions and prices clearly shown, selects a lot or lots, gets a receipt in the form of a "binder"

22. Homer B. Vanderblue, "The Florida Land Boom," *The Journal of Land and Public Utility Economics*, II (May, 1927), pp. 113–31, and II (August, 1927), pp. 252–69.

describing it, and has the thrill of seeing "Sold" stamped in the blue-lined square which represents his lot, a space usually 50 by 100 feet of Florida soil or swamp. There are instances where these first-day sales have gone into several millions of dollars. And the prices! It takes days to get accustomed to hearing them without experiencing a shock. They will compare favorably with choice building lots in our largest cities. Inside lots from $8000 to $20,000. Water-front lots from $15,000 to $25,-000. Seashores from $20,000 to $75,000. And these are not in Miami. They are miles out, 10 miles out, 15 miles out, and 25 miles out . . .

The buyer's next obligation is to pay one-fourth of the purchase price in 30 days. But here is where the fun comes in. But few plan to pay it; they expect to sell their "binder" contract for a substantial profit over what they paid down. Practically all lots immediately go on resale, marked up by the new owner at a new figure. They may be listed at a dozen or more sales offices. The promoters announce "Sold Out," and individual trading begins. Ordinarily they turn fast. A lot, or a binder for it, may change hands several times before the first down payment is due . . .

Who is in Miami real estate? It would not be regarded there as an exaggeration to say "everybody." . . . But what I shall speak of here are the hordes of men and women, mostly young, many of them very young, who have flocked there from the four corners and are engaged wholly in what is practically a curb market in real estate covering the whole Miami business section and operating over the whole state of Florida.[23]

What brought the wave of speculation to a halt? Essentially, reality eventually caught up with the overoptimistic expectations on which investors' decisions had been so largely based. That the boom was without sound objective foundations was overlooked, and this irrationality is a mass psychological phenomenon per se. Under its influence the small speculator was induced to overextend himself, so that he was driven from the market by the pyramiding of cash commitments. The cash payment on a real-estate binder due after thirty days was considerable. It had to cover 35 per cent of the heavily inflated price of the lot (i.e., the 10 per cent down payment and the additional 25 per cent due thirty days after) plus whatever profits had been made during prior transfers. The new purchaser also had to assume any and all cash obligations still outstanding. Hence, the funds of many persons who had to meet payments on binders in their possession soon became exhausted. They had to sell or withdraw from the active market. When some sections of the market became stagnant and demand slackened, the ramifications were cumulative.

23. Quoted by Vanderblue, *op. cit.*, p. 118f.

Other developments contributed to the timing of the decline which, in itself, seemed inevitable. For one thing, the Florida East Coast Railway intended to lay a second track in 1925 during the normal slow season in the summer. That year there was no slow season, and the track could not be laid. In October the company was forced to declare an embargo on all carload commodities except foodstuffs. Soon building materials piled up at the terminal points, and the congestion could not be fully cleared until the following spring. At this crucial point, when the winter tourist season usually began, an old ship that had served as a floating hotel went aground in the Miami basin where it blocked the entrance. Shiploads of urgently needed building supplies could not be unloaded. To add to the misfortune, two large hotels in Palm Beach burned to the ground.

The rush of newcomers expected as early as November did not materialize. Promoters held unfavorable Northern propaganda responsible for this. In actuality, very little unfavorable information concerning unsanitary conditions in Florida, which had resulted in outbreaks of smallpox and of typhoid, or about the high cost of living there and the difficulty of securing work ever made the newspapers, though by this time substantial citizens everywhere began to be concerned about the transfer of funds to Florida. A stock market decline in early 1926 sent a number of Florida speculators back north. That winter, too, the Tunney-Stribling bout slated for Miami had to be called off because no one could be found to guarantee Tunney a $50,000 share in the takings. Litigations against fraudulent promotions by managers of "developments" also dampened enthusiasm, and the remaining vestiges of confidence were blown to bits by the hurricane that hit Miami in September, 1926. It caused over a hundred deaths and untold destruction. The headlines it received nationally signaled the end of this speculative orgy.

Mass Society

MASS SOCIETY designates the kind of social system in which mass behavior plays an important role. It is not an all-or-nothing concept, but refers to conditions that societies exhibit in varying degrees. The more these conditions prevail, the greater the incidence of mass behavior and the more one is justified in characterizing the society as a whole as a mass society.

The first of these conditions is *functional interdependence*. Mass production and mass communications, both products of an industrial technology, have made people more dependent on others who live at a distance from them without contact. But because the ramifications of unexpected shifts in one area are likely to be felt throughout the society, individuals are forced more and more to develop perspectives toward a nonlocal world and to respond to images of collective action that are not anchored in local norms. Consequently, people feel less bound by tradition; they respond as a mass to new objects that intrude into their experiences.

The second of these conditions is an *acceleration in the tempo of social change*. With the extension of modern industrialism to all corners of the world, the community of experience rooted in common sentiments and primary ties has partially disintegrated before any new faith could fill the void. People have been thrust into the larger world. They have become more mobile; they move more often from place to place, and they feel more strongly impelled to seek out opportunities and lines of action that are not traditional for persons of their status. Where social change has been most rapid, as in the metropolis or in colonial frontiers, the instability of the "masses" has also been most marked.

The third condition is the *exclusion of the masses from meaningful participation*. In this context, the term "masses" has a connotation somewhat different from the mass as a form of social action. It refers to a specific segment of the population: those who, by virtue of their social position, are excluded from meaningful participation in society to which they aspire. These masses are usually lower-class persons, but others, such as intellectuals who are *déclassé*, also swell their ranks. These masses are a source of instability. When their number is large, they constitute a powerful threat. While the advance of industrialism has caused widespread disaffection, it is of course impossible to say with any degree of confidence that dissatisfaction today is greater than, say, two hundred years ago. The point is, however, that the failure to integrate them effectively has produced a new kind of discontent. The alienated masses are functionally integrated into the economic order, while their loyalty to established values often appears tenuous.

Given this situation, consensus can be maintained by increasing rationalization at the top, which harnesses to the regime the primary loyalties and enthusiasm of the uprooted at the bottom. Totalitarian regimes constantly mobilize mass enthusiasm to protect themselves from mass discontent. The masses are repeatedly herded together in crowds.[24] Their emotions are kept at a high pitch and directed against a common enemy by invoking symbols of hate. Propaganda, pageantry, mass forma-

24. Emil Lederer, *State of the Masses* (New York: W. W. Norton & Company, Inc., 1940), chap. 1. Lederer calls the mass a "herd" when incorporated into an institutional framework where it is manipulated and called out whenever it suits a regime.

tion emphasize undying loyalty to a leader. Finally, an apparatus for the perpetuation of terror becomes imperative to allocate concrete rewards and enforce adherence to directives.

Totalitarian regimes are mass institutions because they seek to take over vital primary functions. For example, no loyalty to subleaders is tolerated. The destruction of all other particularistic ties means that once the controls imposed on the mass by rational means lose their effectiveness, the purely private needs of individuals will once again assert themselves with full force. There are no mediating institutions to check individual impulse. Society reverts once again to a demoralized mass with each individual acting autonomously in terms of his local setting. The disintegration of the fascist dictatorships, following their defeat in World War II, seems to bear this out.

Just as the mass institution appeals directly to the individuals in the mass and harnesses them from above, so the mass movement coalesces them from below. The mass ideal remains undiluted by the variety of primary social ties that obligate individuals in many different directions. The mass movement appeals to grievances and appetites and turns them against the *status quo*. It can arise only when polarization is so complete that the mass stands arrayed against all social authorities.

When the mass movement erupts, it often acts with the explosive violence of an alienated mass provoked beyond endurance. The movement is not primarily an association to defend the rationally conceived self-interest of its members. Its "spirit," and not its concrete achievements, is what matters. "When a mass movement begins to attract people who are interested in their individual careers," says Hoffer, "it is a sign that it has passed its vigorous stage; it is no longer engaged in molding a new world but in possessing and preserving the present." [25] It has created an institutional apparatus with vested interests, which must be defended, and has thereby ceased to be a mass movement.

For example, in a strike fomented by a mass movement, concrete bargaining gains will not be as important as the demonstration of solidarity. The highest prospective gain is the release of accumulated tension. Strikes governed by this spirit often account for a substantial portion of man-days lost in a strike wave. Or they may culminate in a large general strike. By contrast, associations are restrained because they represent the interests of their membership in only one respect and must therefore take account of their alternate allegiances. Unions that are limited-purpose associations have very little mass spirit. In joining them, one need not forsake other ties. The strike on the part of a union whose members are integrated into the community is likely to be not a small-scale revolt against the social order, but a carefully fashioned weapon used to attain

25. Eric Hoffer, *The True Believer* (New York: Mentor Books, 1958), p. 22.

specific ends. Thus, an association, however large its membership, will not be a mass movement; it functions as part of a generally recognized framework of order and the mass of its members are restrained by other ties. It is no accident that, in almost every country, miners, sailors, stevedores, loggers, and, to a lesser degree, textile workers have usually been found in the forefront of revolutionary activity. The I.W.W. (International Workers of the World), the only American radical movement to have a trade-union basis, developed out of the Western Federation of Miners. It still has some following among sailors and dock workers. The workers in these industries often live in geographically isolated and highly specialized communities, such as the coal patch, the ship, the logging camp, and the textile town. Or they are socially isolated within the metropolitan community, as in the waterfront district. In these communities the workers have their own code of solidarity, with its myths and heroes. Moreover, the work is usually unpleasant and often dangerous. It attracts hardy personalities and is itself conducive to hardening. Any grievance is broadly similar for all members of the group and therefore is likely to be verbally shared. Mobility out of the industry is difficult and, since a worker's skills are not transferable, must occur early in life, mostly through education. Furthermore, such communities harbor few neutrals capable of mediating a conflict and of diluting the mass that stands opposed to the owners, for the whole community is solidly behind the strikers, even when there are expectations of economic losses never to be made good.[26]

The model of the mass, as depicted through mass institutions and mass movements, is not, of course, an entirely accurate reflection of contemporary society. Neither the hierarchical control of society through bureaucratic institutions nor polarization between the mass and social authorities is as extreme as suggested by the model. Opinions still count, and discussion goes on constantly on many levels of the society. Furthermore, the influence of the agencies of mass propaganda is mitigated by competition among the mass media to gain a share of their audience in a pluralistic universe, consisting of individuals with many different interests.

In the following chapters, our focus will be on the various shifts that occur in the large society, and the fact will be kept in mind that contemporary society exhibits many of the features of a mass society, though not in the extreme and untempered form posited by the theoretical model.

---

26. Clark Kerr and Abraham Siegel, "The Interindustry Propensity to Strike," in Kornhauser, Dubin, and Ross (eds.), *op. cit.*, pp. 189–212.

BIBLIOGRAPHY

BELL, DANIEL. "The Theory of Mass Society," *Commentary*, XXII (July, 1956), pp. 75–83. Bell argues against the usefulness of the concept of mass society, because it fails to describe modern society accurately and therefore cannot explain its pathology.

COLEMAN, JAMES, and MCPHEE, WILLIAM. "A Program of Research in 'Mass Dynamics,'" *Prod*, I (March, 1958), 6–10.

GALBRAITH, JOHN KENNETH. *The Great Crash, 1929*. Boston: Houghton Mifflin Co., 1955. An economist's case study of the stock market crash of 1929.

HOGGART, RICHARD. *The Uses of Literacy*. London: Chatto and Windus, 1957. This discussion of mass culture is based on a vivid account of the use working-class people in Northern England make of its products.

KORNHAUSER, WILLIAM. *The Politics of Mass Society*. Glencoe, Ill.: The Free Press, 1959. The thesis that a mass society, in contrast to a pluralist one, is vulnerable to totalitarian movements.

LEDERER, EMIL. *State of the Masses*. New York: W. W. Norton & Company, Inc., 1940. An analysis of the dynamics of modern dictatorship as an organized or institutionalized mass.

MANNHEIM, KARL. *Man and Society in an Age of Reconstruction*. New York: Harcourt, Brace & Co., 1951. Especially Parts I and II. The implications of recent social developments for the rationality of the mass society.

ROSENBERG, BERNARD, and WHITE, DAVID M. *Mass Culture*. Glencoe, Ill.: The Free Press, 1957. This collection contains many general critiques of modern culture and a number of concrete studies.

SELZNICK, PHILIP. "Institutional Vulnerability in the Mass Society," *American Journal of Sociology*, LVI (January, 1951), pp. 320–31.

CHAPTER 13

Public Opinion: The Achievement
of Popular Consent

POLITICIANS AND REFORMERS, spokesmen for various interests and viewpoints, and the man on the street continually refer to public opinion to back up their claims against vested interests and to legitimate their own specific viewpoints. Newspapers give a big play to public opinion trends, and governments are said to watch them carefully as some kind of public will is considered the keystone of representative government.

THE NATURE OF PUBLIC OPINION

MOST TRADITIONAL doctrines viewing public opinion as the basis for popular government assume that sovereign authority resides with the people. Public opinion, embodying what everyone agrees to, is the expression of their will. But when the concept of sovereignty describes a vague collectivity, like an entire people, it fails to locate the specific agent or agency in which ultimate political authority is vested.[1] The supposed "mandate" the people hand to their government entails nothing more than a willingness to be ruled in accordance with custom and law.

Some doctrines specifically identify public opinion with the decisions of a representative body or executive organ, forcing one to the conclusion that ultimately all government, however despotic, rests on public opinion, a conclusion brilliantly put forth two centuries ago by David Hume. This view extends the concept too far and yet defines it too narrowly. Unless the concept of public opinion is kept distinct from its products—

1. Carl J. Friedrich, *The New Belief in the Common Man* (Boston: Little, Brown & Co., 1942).

[369]

such as the decisions of some constituted authority which supposedly reflect and express it—one tends to overlook the fact that these authorities often make decisions when no public opinion has yet formed. Popular consent is assumed—an assumption usually warranted by persistent attitudes and habits that go much deeper than opinions of the moment. On the other hand, the force that inheres in effective opinions asserts itself not only through the decisions of legislative bodies or other authority but also at times against them. It is then that public opinion "leads" governments, leaving them little choice but to follow.

Our first task, then, is to locate the agents in which the force of public opinion resides.

PUBLIC OPINION AS A FORM OF SOCIAL CONTROL

In setting standards that are accepted and enforced, public opinion takes its place alongside custom and law. The authority inhering in custom is legitimated by the past. The older a practice, the more it is likely to be invested with and sustained by beliefs concerning its necessity for the continued welfare of the community. Custom as such provokes no discussion, and conformity with it is often reinforced by a variety of common moral sentiments. Because customs are deeply ingrained in habit and belief, they change but slowly under the impact of altered circumstances, so slowly in fact that people are often not aware of the change. Law entails a much more rational orientation. It differs from custom in two important respects: in the codification of practices into some consistent body of rules and in the attachment of specific sanctions to violations. The rules embodied in laws are subject to conscious and deliberative modification as the facts to which they are meant to apply change.

Every standard whether imbedded in unreflective custom or rationally formulated has some kind of "objective" validity. Public opinion differs from law and custom in that it operates primarily in those situations where acquiescence to standards cannot be taken for granted and where consent must therefore first be ascertained. The study of public opinion draws attention to those processes by which a standard for collective action is affirmed, modified, or rejected. An image of consent, where none can be taken for granted, emerges only through discussion. This consent refers to the effective and valid opinions by which decision-makers are guided when resolving a problematic issue.

Public opinion, as Lowell [2] pointed out, must be opinion, and opinion always concerns an issue. Not every belief, regardless of how widely held, is opinion. Thus, the beliefs that witches inhabit the night, that a

2. A. Lawrence Lowell, *Public Opinion and Popular Government* (New York: Longmans, Green & Co., Inc., 1913).

cure for the common cold is imminent, or that fluoridation of water is injurious to health become opinion only when they impel the holder to make them prevail over the beliefs of others as valid norms of conduct. Opinion is not a matter of determining what a rule is but, rather, whether it ought to apply or how it should be applied. To say that something is a matter of opinion means that alternative judgments are possible. It is when an issue poses a question that requires conscious deliberation because neither precedent nor valid rule of law are automatically accepted, or one cannot count on unanimity of consent or habits of obedience, or there is a question about whether a course of action will be accepted, that public opinion comes into play. Hence, public opinion is to some extent always unpredictable.

Public opinion, as Lowell also pointed out, refers not only to opinion but also to a public. Of the two elements, "public" is the more difficult to make concrete. One easy way out is to say that public opinion concerns "public" rather than "private" affairs, except that the borderline between the two is often thin and may generally be defined only within the context of a concrete situation. Marriage, for instance, is a private affair between two parties, but when a princess wishes to marry a commoner, the marriage becomes a matter of public concern. A man's health concerns him alone, until he becomes an official entrusted by the nation with public responsibility.

The solution is sometimes sought by defining "public" opinion as the opinion held by the members of a certain collectivity, a public. A *public* consists of all those divided on an issue, who, because they take an interest, are actively thinking and talking about it. The existence of active concern and discussion transforms individual private opinions into some kind of public opinion. This kind of public, however, forms spontaneously; its boundaries are fluid. Hence, the individual opinions that enter public opinion can be separated only with great difficulty from the opinions anyone volunteers to an interviewer.

The important thing is that to be a controlling force, public opinion must be publicized, though not necessarily published. Many a private representation by a pressure group exerts effective influence. But organized interests reflect public opinion only if they operate publicly, whereas the intervention of vested interests behind a shield of secrecy often neutralizes the force of public opinion. The lawmaker or the official who does private favors for his constituents may be responding to pressure; in doing so, he ignores public opinion. This criterion differentiates public opinion from other unpublicized pressures in the influence process.

The force of opinion can also assert itself when there are no articulate expressions. It emanates from "such chance persons as the party in question [the decision-maker] may happen in the course of his life to have concern with, according to each man's spontaneous disposition, and not according to any settled or concerted rules" (Jeremy Bentham). The public opinion to which public figures are oriented acts as a form of social control because at the time the momentary consent or approval of bystanders provides the only standard by which, apart from questions of fact, a decision can be legitimated.

In view of all this, the student of public opinion is induced to pay special attention to situations in which public endorsement is deliberately elicited. Whenever a government is legally required to justify its decisions before an electorate, it forces the decision-makers to look continuously for guidance to some image of consent. Hence, the anticipated public support becomes an important element in day-to-day decisions. This is the *public opinion situation* within which modern democracies function.

It is furthermore important to distinguish between this image of consent and the various group activities in pursuit of specific interests. The *public opinion process* refers to all the activities of individuals and pressure groups as well as the communications on every level of society through which a particular image emerges. The product of this process is *public opinion.* It is the standard by which an act is judged or an issue resolved. It rarely constitutes a clear-cut directive, but its content usually has to be inferred from a variety of data brought to the attention of those sensitive to such opinion. Hence the *public,* the persons whose collective judgment serves as a standard, while not exactly the "phantom" that Lippmann thought it to be, serves as something like a "reference group"—namely, as the imagined others whose consent is seen to govern some particular question.

The Study of Public Opinion

To elucidate the nature and function of public opinion as a form of collective behavior, we have organized the discussion around four problems.

THE STATE OF PUBLIC OPINION   How do we ascertain the objective content of opinions that have some influence at a given moment? This is essentially a problem of measurement. To solve it one needs, first, to develop sensitive instruments which will tap the "real" and true opinions of individuals, and, second, to differentiate between purely personal views and those expressed opinions which "count" because they are constituents of the process by which public opinion crystallizes and makes its weight felt. A measure of the effective public opinion is not obtained solely by an accurate measurement of the content of individual opinions.

OPINION FORMATION   How are opinions formed and maintained, and under what conditions are they reinforced or abandoned? The explanation of how individuals form opinions really deals with one aspect of the socialization process and thus belongs in the realm of social psychology. Both stability and change in the opinions of an individual are to be explained in terms of a convergence of psychological and social influences upon an individual. Much research on the dynamics of public opinion has concentrated on how individuals respond to and cope with pressures from their surroundings.

THE MOVEMENT OF PUBLIC OPINION   What produces shifts in the opinion alignment of a collectivity? These shifts depend only to a limited degree on what happens to the individual and more properly fit into the subject matter of collective dynamics. They can be best understood as changes in the distribution of opinions and in the lines of division with regard to issues. It is possible for both the alignment and the issue to change drastically without any drastic reorientations in the opinions of individuals. This point will be explained.

THE POLITICAL PROCESS   In what ways does public opinion influence the political decision-making process of the large society? Public opinion entails a conception of the influence process; that is, of the way in which opinions, through their weight, affect decisions by those who act in relation to the opinions of a collectivity. Therefore, a sociology of power is implicit in the study of public opinion. Though the power of the public resides in the binding force of an electoral decision, public opinion also operates, sometimes even more forcefully, in the period between elections. On the whole, however, public opinion tends to be somewhat quiescent; it is often unstable and its influence is subtle. We shall be concerned with both the historical emergence of public opinion and the role it has played in specific political decisions of a modern democracy.

The State of Public Opinion

THE OBJECTIVE CONTENT of effective and valid opinion can usually be ascertained only with great difficulty and at considerable expense. The public under whose scrutiny decisions are taken has no voice of its own and is heard only as the various individuals and groups whose opinions are considered important assert their claims. As Sir Henry Maine said in his discussion of popular government,[3] "The devotee of democracy is in much the same position as the Greeks with their oracles. All agreed that the voice of an oracle was the voice of a God; but everybody allowed that when he spoke he was not as intelligible as might be desired." It was to gain more precise measures of the alignment of popular opinion that elec-

3. Sir Henry Maine, *Popular Government* (New York: Henry Holt & Co., Inc., 1886), p. 184f.

tions, referendums on specific questions, and most recently the public opinion poll came into existence.

THE EXPRESSION OF THE ELECTORATE

Individual votes in their totality constitute a definitive judgment backed by the force of both custom and law. After each election, it is said that the people have spoken. Still, public opinion and electoral behavior are by no means identical. The vote is but one element, albeit an important one, in the day-to-day functioning of public opinion.

In the first place, the electorate is called upon to pass a judgment only on certain special occasions, and it may, indeed, be argued that public opinion operates more decisively and influentially between elections than during a campaign, when everything is subordinated to the competition for votes. Few decisions are ever made during a campaign, and the issues "discussed" in it are usually derived from actions taken during the quiescent periods between elections.

Second, an individual's vote is fundamentally an affective response to a party symbol. These responses are established rather early in the lives of most people. They require little deliberation, only familiarity with the symbol, and are not easily changed. Many an election is decided solely on the basis of general party preference. These preferences are group-linked: each region, social class, ethnic and religious group, etc., has a characteristic party alignment that changes only slowly.[4]

Third, even when there is no doubt about the outcome of an election, it is rarely clear on just what grounds the electorate has rendered judgment or what mandate they have given their representatives. The character of a candidate or the existence of some overriding issue at times outweighs party loyalties, so the traditional allegiances of voters cannot always be relied on to produce a given electoral result. For example, the American presidential elections of 1896 and 1920 both turned on one overriding issue: the first, on the question of free silver; the latter, on whether or not the United States should adhere to its traditional policy of isolation.

In 1952 and again in 1956 the University of Michigan Survey Research Center conducted a nation-wide poll to identify the "motivational" variables that underlay an individual's vote and to disentangle them from the vote decision itself. Each of three factors—party identification, candidate

4. See especially the studies on political ecology by André Siegfried, *Tableau politique de la France de l'ouest sous le troisième republique* (Paris: Armand, Colin, 1913); V. O. Key, *Southern Politics in State and Nation* (New York: Alfred A. Knopf, Inc., 1949); and Bernard Berelson *et al.*, *Voting* (Chicago: The University of Chicago Press, 1954).

preference, and issue orientation—were found to have had an independent influence upon the statistical distribution of the vote. On the basis of their analysis the researchers suggest that 1948 (Truman vs. Dewey) was primarily a party year, but that in 1952 (Stevenson vs. Eisenhower) "the more variable factors of issues and candidates assumed an unusual importance." [5] But even in 1948 Truman won primarily because he managed, by his forceful campaign, to reactivate disintegrating loyalties to the Democratic Party, stressing those socioeconomic issues on which the traditional loyalty to his party was based in crucial states.[6] But, in general, what moves voters cannot be determined without a careful analysis of the vote. Usually candidates and partisans advance interpretations of election results based primarily on what they themselves wish to believe. To substantiate these claims one needs poll data and a detailed breakdown of voting patterns or preferably both.

Fourth, only a fraction of the eligible voters exercise their franchise in an electoral contest. In the United States the turnout in national elections has generally ranged between 50 and 70 per cent. The latter proportion has been achieved in more recent contests, but in local elections, especially during an off year, it may be considerably lower.[7] The spread of education and an increasing reliance on the mass media, especially television, to stir up interest may have brought a general and perhaps permanent increase in voting participation. The number of nonvoters in an election is usually a key factor in the outcome. A sufficient turnout of habitual nonvoters can reverse the anticipated results.

Finally, there is the question of how far the electorate acts out of some conception of self-interest and a conviction that they have a stake in election results. It is no secret that voting turnout depends upon effective political organization. The voter who responds to organizational pressure may, of course, have an independent opinion which he is eager to make felt when given the opportunity. Many people measure up in some degree to the ideal of a responsible voter who is interested in politics, engages in discussion about issues, forms his opinions with the objective welfare of the community in mind, and weighs the effects of alternatives. However a high proportion of vote decisions are merely the expressions of traditional loyalties to established symbols, to momentary pressure, or to personal inclinations. Furthermore, the most volatile segment of the electorate—the ones who by their shifts from party to party or by their participation and nonparticipation usually determine the out-

5. Angus Campbell, Gerald Gurin, and Warren E. Miller, *The Voter Decides* (Evanston, Ill.: Row, Peterson & Company, 1954), p. 184.

6. *Ibid.*

7. Cf. R. W. Scammon, *America Votes, A Handbook of Contemporary American Election Statistics* (New York: The Macmillan Co., 1956).

come of an election—tend to be the least interested. Their convictions have the least foundation in knowledge and are for that reason the least stable, and they can hardly be said to render an opinion in the sense that Lowell used this term.[8]

Recall, Initiative, and Referendum

In partial recognition of the number of factors involved in an individual's vote decision, there have been proposals to make the vote a more accurate reflection of "public opinion." These proposals have included an increase in the frequency of elections, as well as the primary, the recall, the initiative, and the referendum.[9] The first three are intended to make the individuals elected more responsive to public opinion. Suffice it to say that only rarely have such measures had the desired effect. They have reduced government efficiency by diverting energy to the fight to stay in office. They have put the burden of expensive campaigns on independent candidates and have hardly succeeded in curbing many of the abuses of machine politics. At the same time, the opinions that govern the vote for a candidate in a primary or a recall remain as elusive as ever.

The essence of the initiative and the referendum lies in the opportunity they offer the electorate to express opinions on a specific question. In the *initiative* voters are required to pass a measure before the legislature can enact it into law, whereas in the *referendum* the people approve or reject a measure already passed by the legislature. Yet many of the same factors that make an election an inaccurate reflection of total opinion continue to operate even when people vote on a specific issue. In the first place, usually a considerably smaller proportion of the electorate votes on a proposition than in a regular election. Much depends also on whether the vote on a proposition occurs at the same time as other electoral contests or as votes on other propositions. There is some tendency for people to vote a straight "yes" or a straight "no" on every proposition listed on a ballot. Consequently issues voted down by clear majorities in one election are often accepted by equally clear majorities in an election shortly afterward. But the greatest difficulty resides in the complicated nature of many propositions. People have little chance to study their merit, to familiarize themselves with the relevant facts, or even to read them fully while in the polling booth. Hence, the decision is often made on the basis

8. See Bernard Berelson, "Democratic Theory and Public Opinion," *Public Opinion Quarterly,* XVI (Fall, 1952), pp. 313–30, for a discussion of the characteristics of the electorate. See also M. Janowitz and D. Marvick, *Competitive Pressure and Democratic Consent* ("Michigan Governmental Studies," No. 32 [Ann Arbor, Mich.: University of Michigan Press, 1956]).

9. Lowell's classic analysis, *op. cit.,* covers most of these measures.

of completely extraneous considerations or solely in response to organizational pressure.

The difficulty of using referendum returns to interpret the state of public opinion can be illustrated by a study undertaken in Dade County (Miami, Florida).[10] An advisory referendum was held in 1953 on whether the school board there should allocate unspent funds for audiovisual aids for an educational television station. The decisive defeat the proposal suffered at the polls was broadly interpreted as the people's voice speaking out against the idea of a channel being set aside for school programs. However, when a representative sample of *voters* was asked on leaving the polling places where they had just voted, "Can you tell me in your own words just what you were asked to vote on in the 'straw poll'?" the majority failed to identify accurately the essential features of the proposition. Few had any opinion on whether or not private stations serving the area were meeting, or potentially could meet, the recognized need for educational materials. When queried about the feasibility of a separate noncommercial channel, however, they expressed a fundamental reservoir of good will toward the idea.

Here were two contradictory measures of public opinion: the definitive *rejection of the proposition* (the sample turned down the proposition in roughly the same proportion as the entire electorate) and the *expression of agreement with the fundamental principle* it embodied by two-thirds of the people queried. In plain words, they appeared to favor an educational television channel but voted against it!

The explanation for this discrepancy was not hard to find. The "yes" voter saw himself passing judgment on the fundamental merits of an educational television channel for the county. But the "no" voters were inclined to define the issue underlying the proposition quite differently: for over 40 per cent of them, it was essentially: "We need better schools, higher pay for teachers, etc., before we can experiment with new-fangled ideas." Resentment against the school board as well as fear of an increased tax burden also entered into the vote against the proposition.

A more dramatic example of the perils of assuming that referendums clearly indicate the state of public opinion concerns the "right to work" amendments placed before voters in some half-dozen states in 1958. It was the purpose of these amendments to outlaw the union shop, which requires new employees in plants where a union is the duly certified bargaining agent to take out union membership within a specified period as a condition of employment. Union dues are often deducted directly by employers. At the time Congressional committees had been exposing corrupt union practices in well-publicized hearings. Some resentment against organized labor had undoubtedly been stirred up. Although the

10. From the files of the authors.

polls were predicting a Democratic year and Democratic candidates were generally opposed to the amendments, it seemed altogether possible that the voters would outlaw union shops.

In most states these laws, nevertheless, were soundly defeated—in many cases the Republican candidates polled more votes than the proposition. The defeats were widely heralded as a vote of confidence in organized labor, particularly in the principle of the union shop. This may even be the "true" sentiment of the people in states where "right to work" laws were defeated, but evidence suggests that the meaning of the vote is less clear-cut. According to Louis Harris,[11] a well-known pollster, it was the sponsorship of the proposition that defeated it in Ohio. In many communities the laws were pushed strongly by industrialists and other powerful figures. This tagged the laws, in spite of the fact that the sponsors, by dubbing the amendments "right to work" laws, were counting on the effect of a favorable symbol. Whatever resentment had accumulated against these persons, due to their past community activities or because of plant shutdowns in the recession, rebounded against the propositions they were sponsoring. Harris has suggested that during the campaign there was a definite turn in the tide against the laws as the machinations of these power-wielders became clear. In brief, many people voted against these *men* as much as they voted against the "right to work" laws.

THE PUBLIC OPINION POLL

After the discussion of electoral decisions, the increasing reliance on polls to interpret the voter's mind should become understandable. Since the 1930's public opinion polls have been used more and more to measure the state of public opinion at any given moment and to provide a record of the fluctuations at frequent intervals.

The logic of the public opinion poll is implicit in its procedures.[12] The idea is to elicit from a representative sample of the population an accurate and complete expression of each respondent's personal views. How accurately a poll measures the division of opinion within an aggregate depends on how well each of three problems is resolved: (1) whom to interview; (2) what to ask and how to phrase the question; and (3) how to elicit the kind of response that can be considered a constituent part of the effective public opinion.

The polls strive to sample a population segment in such a way that

11. Talk by Louis Harris at the Fourteenth Conference on Public Opinion Research of the American Association for Public Opinion Research held at Bolton's Landing, New York, 1959.

12. For an excellent discussion on survey procedures as such, see Herbert Hyman, *Survey Design and Study Analysis* (Glencoe, Ill.: The Free Press, 1955).

every kind of individual and every combination of individuals have an equal chance of being contacted. There are practical obstacles to the achievement of this ideal, but the scientific procedures of selection provide a reasonably close approximation of it. The poll assumes that the opinion of every individual in the population is (a) independent and (b) equally likely to contribute to the formation of an effective public opinion.

Thus, the model that pollsters apply to the problem of public opinion is essentially that of a market. Do specific opinions held by individuals on the basis of personal inclinations and social position result in market decisions that are characteristic of mass behavior? A market decision is one that an individual is in a position to implement for himself. If a persons intends to buy a new house or to cut his front lawn, he is likely to find some way to do so. Whether he buys a house depends on whether he finds a suitable dwelling he can afford; whether he mows the lawn depends on whether he has a lawnmower, the time, and the energy. The same person may have strong opinions about wanting his next-door neighbor to move or about how his neighbor maintains his grounds. Whether he is in a position to do anything about his opinions is not entirely dependent on the firmness of his personal convictions or on the explanation he gives for them. Harassing his neighbor is not likely to have much effect, especially if it creates a swell of sympathy on the part of other neighbors for the one he is annoying. In fact, he may be convinced, regardless of his personal preference, that to say and do nothing, and thereby keep peace, is the best policy. Unlike his buying intent, his opinion about his neighbor may not be implemented at all. It can have an effect only in conjunction with others.

Public opinion, then, is hardly an individual matter, but opinions that set standards affecting the actions of others contribute to its formation. They result in ideological decisions as to how others should act, and when they are expressed they have a certain amount of moral force. How much weight an individual's opinions carry depends on the concrete network of his relationships, his status, and his ability to influence others. The sum of individual marketing decisions may measure market behavior as a convergent mass; but public opinion is different from the sum of individual opinions.[13]

13. Walter Lippmann, *The Phantom Public* (New York: Harcourt, Brace & Co., 1925). See also Herbert Blumer, "Public Opinion and Public Opinion Polling," *American Sociological Review*, XIII (October, 1948), pp. 542–49, for an incisive critique of the use of polls in public opinion research.

The Pre-Election Poll

The best-known public opinion polls are those that seek to predict the outcome of elections. Notwithstanding the fiasco of 1948 (Truman vs. Dewey) in which several pre-election polls showed Governor Dewey [14] clearly ahead in the presidential race, the polling experts have had considerable success in forecasting the outcome of elections.[15] This success stems from their concentration on vote intention and on the factors determining it rather than on "opinion." A vote intention, though influenced by and influencing the opinion of others, is nevertheless more like a market decision that every individual can implement for himself. It consists essentially of an individual response of like or dislike toward a party label or a candidate. The outcome the poll seeks to predict is the sum of responses, as implemented in the polling booths. A successful poll measures with a high degree of accuracy not only intention but the probability that these intentions will be implemented.

Knowledge of factors that determine how and whether an individual will vote increases the accuracy of prediction. For example, there is a clear-cut relationship between various measures of "interest in the electoral campaign" and the determination with which a person expresses his intention to vote. Both of these are strongly correlated with the fact that he *will* vote. Again, when a person is not subjected to cross pressures—that is, when his friends and relatives share his views, when he likes the party's candidates, agrees with its stand on issues, etc.—he is more likely, on election day, to vote the way he "intended" to.

Also the pre-election poll can predict voting with considerable accuracy precisely because the person who intends to vote usually can get to a polling booth. Where people lack the means to implement their individual opinions, the predictive uses of mere "opinion" data are more open to question. The importance of means for implementing opinion will be illustrated by two studies: one concerns the telecasts of Senator Kefauver's investigation into crime and corrupt practices; the other, Southern attitudes toward desegregation.

THE KEFAUVER HEARINGS   According to the first study, the impact of the televised crime hearings, in New York, was considerable.[16] The

14. Other important uses of polls to obtain information on images, latent dispositions, etc., of an audience are discussed in the next chapter. Pre-election polls touch on opinions only peripherally and are designed instead to locate sources of strength and vulnerabilities.

15. Frederick Mosteller, *The Pre-Election Polls of 1948* (New York: Social Science Research Council, 1949).

16. G. D. Wiebe, "Responses to the Televised Kefauver Hearings: Some Social Psychological Implications," *Public Opinion Quarterly,* XVI (Summer, 1952), pp. 179–200.

general reaction was hardly one of apathy, and the majority of persons interviewed expressed considerable intensity of feeling. But this apparently phenomenal impact seemed to dwindle in the light of what these "indignants" did about their opinions and whether what they did made any difference.

Over half the respondents said they "would like to take part in improving conditions." Yet most did nothing beyond talking to other persons of approximately the same influence and deference level. They felt they had no means through which they could exert an effective influence. Some others wrote to a Congressman, to a public official, or to an influential person, or they sought to prevail on others to recognize the importance of the problem. Only 18 per cent of those who took these steps felt that their action might have made some difference.

Had there been a vote on "doing something about crime," the hearings undoubtedly would have had an influence on its outcome. They did later, when Rudolph Halley, chief counsel of the committee, was elected president of the New York City Council and when Senator Kefauver was propelled into a position where he could make a strong play for the Democratic presidential nomination. Beyond that, there was no strong move for reform. A potential for a reform movement existed, but in the absence of an organization through which to give it forcible expression, the indignation people felt could not crystallize into an effective protest.

ATTITUDES TOWARD DESEGREGATION   The state of public opinion cannot be determined solely by asking people about their *intentions* as distinct from their *opinions*. Tumin, studying readiness for desegregation in a North Carolina county,[17] assumed the total attitude toward the Negro and toward desegregation to be made up of several dimensions:

1. The *image*, or mental picture, that the respondent has of the Negro as compared with whites.

2. The *ideological position* concerning the preferable or most desirable kind of social relations between Negroes and whites.

3. The personal *sentiment* of the respondent; that is, how he personally would feel in a number of interracial situations in which legal restrictions against Negroes had been eliminated.

4. The statement of *probable behavior* by the respondent as to what he would do in the circumstances above.

5. The *specific action set*—that is, the respondent's approval or disapproval of various ways to prevent desegregation in the public schools.

As expected, respondents were much more "segregationist" in their private feelings than they were in their willingness to subscribe to or voice approval of certain resistance measures. The reason for the more

17. Melvin M. Tumin, *Desegregation: Resistance and Readiness* (Princeton, N.J.: Princeton University Press, 1958).

moderate publicly expressed opinion was their awareness of the consequences such resistance might entail.

To what extent can the "readiness" to acquisesce in a desegregation policy laid down by the Supreme Court be predicted from stated intentions? For instance, for over two years in Little Rock resistance to school desegregation had kept the issue alive and prevented the schools from opening on the basis of even token integration. In other Arkansas towns, school desegregation had proceeded without major incident. Did Little Rock resistance depend on the amount of private approval given to obstructionist measures? Or is progress in desegregation based on the kind of leadership that emerges and on the amount of open support it can rally? The concrete pressures through which public opinion crystallizes find their reflection in individual opinions usually only after the issue and the apparent consequences of taking sides have become fully defined.

When opinion is forming around some new issue, not every privately expressed opinion or intention, unlike those in a market situation, carries the same weight, because individuals participate in the process with different degrees of influence. As Bryce once said, there are, with respect to public opinion, three kinds of people: those who have no opinions, those who hold opinions, and those who lead opinion.[18] Through methodological refinements, the public opinion poll has been more and more successful in discriminating between those who do not have an opinion and those who do. But these same methods do not ferret out those who "make" opinion and impress their views on others—namely, the opinion leadership.

The Leader Poll

Polling experts, taking into account the distinctive role opinion leaders play in the public opinion process, have begun to gauge opinion from the responses of influentials. Stouffer and his associates, for example, in their nation-wide survey on communism, conformity, and civil liberties, included interviews with a special sample of community leaders in cities whose population ranged from 10,000 to 150,000.[19] They then compared the leaders' views with those of cross-sections of people in these same cities and of the entire national sample.

The basic aim of the survey was to assess the reactions of Americans to dangers arising from the "Communist conspiracy outside and inside the country" and from "those who in thwarting the conspiracy would

18. James Bryce, *The American Commonwealth* (New York: The Macmillan Co., 1910), p. 321f.

19. Samuel A. Stouffer, *Communism, Conformity and Civil Liberties* (Garden City, N.Y.: Doubleday & Company, Inc., 1955).

sacrifice some of the very liberties which the enemy would destroy." A scale designed to get at "willingness to tolerate non-conformity" was the key measure in this assessment. The items of which this scale was constructed inquired about how much leeway and freedom the respondent would be willing to grant to an admitted Communist, to a person whose loyalty had been questioned by a Congressional committee, but who denied under oath ever having been a Communist, to a person who advocated government ownership of railroads and big industries, and to a person who was "against all churches and religion." In each instance the respondent was asked for a statement of what should be done about this nonconformist.

The comparisons based on this scale revealed that "all categories of community leaders, including commanders of the American Legion and regents of the D.A.R., tend on the average to be more respectful of the civil rights of those of whom they disapprove than the average person in the general population." [20]

However in 1953–1954, according to Eric Goldman, McCarthyism

> was permeating every state and every occupation, sometimes ridiculous, sometimes frightening, sometimes bordering on the incredible. Five distinguished ex-diplomats warned that the assaults on the State Department were having "sinister results . . . A premium has been put upon reporting and upon recommendations which are ambiguously stated or so cautiously set forth as to be deceiving . . . The ultimate result is a threat to national security." The major drama publisher, Samuel French, announced a playwriting contest in which one of the conditions was that the sponsor "reserves the right at any time to declare ineligible any author who is, or becomes publicly involved, in a scholastic, political, or moral controversy."

Albert Einstein was privately advising his correspondents that, even if it meant going to jail, they should refuse to testify on personal beliefs before Congressional committees.[21] In Indiana a member of the State Text Book Commission charged that Communists had been directed to stress the Robin Hood story as an account of robbing the rich to give to the poor. Librarians were removing controversial books from their shelves, and a survey of the academic profession revealed widespread anxiety and no great inclination to speak out. Specifically in the early summer of 1954, when the survey was taken, the Army-McCarthy controversy, with the Wisconsin Senator charging the armed forces with sheltering Communists, was at its height.

20. *Ibid.*, p. 27.
21. Eric F. Goldman, *The Crucial Decade* (New York: Alfred A. Knopf, Inc., 1956), p. 257.

Given these circumstances, one assumes that "leaders" were also subject to influence from what appeared to be the dominant opinion. Their relatively greater tolerance, as expressed privately in the poll, did not necessarily indicate their public opposition to the demand for conformity expressed by the general population. Often those favoring tolerance did not speak publicly, and, even when they did, their voices were drowned out in the clamor about conspiracies. Leaders among the intolerants, taking advantage of the widespread fears, were able to gain consent to rather drastic measures. It is in this context that the difference between "leadership" and general opinion was of dubious significance in the situation at the time.

If the opinions of individuals included in the leadership sample actually carried weight in the formation of public opinion, one would expect them to have prevented the many manifestations of intolerance. While they did support the gradual subsiding of the heresy hunt, culminating in the censure of Senator McCarthy by his fellow Senators, there is no evidence that they appreciably affected the image of consent. Neither is there any support for the assumption, widely held, that before McCarthy could be challenged the views of the general public were changed by those more tolerant leaders. On the other hand, during the height of the scare, a deviant leadership, perhaps not recognized in the official power structure, apparently exerted sufficient influence on community leaders to force them to retreat before what appeared a landslide of pro-McCarthy sentiment. Though the survey found that the Communist threat was uppermost in the minds of but few people, and not very many admitted to being worried about it, some informal leadership must have been tapping ordinarily latent views.

One crucial problem in determining the state of public opinion is to locate the informal opinion leaders. This leadership often emerges only as a function of a particular situation, as the momentary alignment of opinions changes. It may not be identical with formal leadership, but persons in formal positions of authority can sometimes be made to submit to it. Especially in fluid situations, the formal criteria of status do not suffice to locate influentials. Numerous studies have shown that opinion leadership operates in every stratum of society and among the different subgroups. The hypothesis that the more tolerant community leaders so influenced public opinion that McCarthy could be deposed can be tested only by comparing the distribution of opinion in specific communities with the degree of tolerance displayed by their leaders. Even were the hypothesis to be substantiated, an explanation is still needed for why—in the light of their tolerance—public opinion acquiesced for so long in the most intolerant measures and practices. The question can only be posed here, not answered.

THE PUBLIC OPINION SITUATION

Specific opinions can be measured, but the image of consent that emerges through discussion can only be inferred from the various concrete expressions of public opinion. Hence, every measure, even when not obtained "scientifically," is a constituent of the public opinion situation, and there is no clear line of demarcation between the various assessments of public opinion and the image of popular consent as it ultimately emerges. But when abstracted from the situation even the most scientific measures of public opinion are not enough to give an indication of how public opinion crystallizes and functions. Knowledge of the state of public opinion—that is, of the distribution of opinions—is nevertheless a prerequisite for analysis.

A public opinion situation exists whenever in a large society, where action requires some implied consent, the decision-makers are guided by some assessment of public opinion before they act. This image is no mere adding up of private opinions. In a mass society, political symbols and political organizations serve as mediating mechanisms by which private opinions are translated into ideological decisions. It is in this connection that Toennies speaks of *a* public opinion as the deliberate expression of some collective interest organized around a symbol.[22] A public opinion of this sort is to be distinguished from specific individual opinions on public matters and from the general opinion which is accepted as governing and thus dubbed "public opinion."

In this total public opinion situation, the decision-makers do not play an altogether passive role. Because consent can neither be relied on nor accurately foretold, it is necessary to reduce uncertainty concerning the popular reaction. For this reason, though not for it alone, decision-makers employ specialists in poll-taking and in propaganda: the former to provide information, the latter to exploit it. Pressure groups operate in much the same way. On the one hand, they claim to represent public opinion; on the other, they arouse and create it. All these activities enter into the public opinion situation in which favorable judgments are to be elicited from relevant publics.

OPINION FORMATION

A PERSON's OPINIONS are often highly personal assessments of situations. Opinions on public matters also entail personal judgments of

22. Ferdinand Toennies, *Kritik der öffentlichen Meinung* (Berlin: J. Springer, 1922).

events, personalities, and policies, but they are refracted through some collective interest. What, then, determines the side a person is likely to take on a public issue?

The opinions people form on specific questions are the outcome of four major influences. (1) The basic ideologies to which specific opinions are linked are transmitted through the main socializing agencies in much the same way as attitudes are generally. (2) The extent to which these ideologies are accepted or rejected and how they are interpreted is affected by idiosyncratic learning experiences. (3) Through the mobilization, in specific situations, of social pressure individual judgments are linked with salient group symbols. (4) An opinion is, among other things, a function of available information.

BASIC SOCIALIZING AGENCIES

It would be difficult to overestimate the importance of the family in the political socialization of the individual. The high degree of intrafamily agreement on political matters has been documented in many studies. Reviewing these, Hyman writes that "the import is clear. While influence might conceivably flow from child to parent, what is much more likely is that the parents are agents who transmit the political relevant attitudes to the children." [23] A person's fundamental political orientation, though it undergoes continuous enlargement and differentiation, provides a frame of reference for judging new issues. The family also determines to a considerable degree one's future participation in groups where more differentiated political attitudes are developed. Nevertheless, college represents for many a period of ideological revaluation. Geographical and social mobility also broaden a person's range of experience and confront him with new issues. Thus, to predict the opinion a person holds about a clearly drawn issue one has to consider many things about his background, social status, and status aspirations. For example, the stands that students at the University of California took on the loyalty oath, required of the faculty as a condition of employment, could be fairly well predicted from the relevant variables describing their background and current affiliations.[24]

IDIOSYNCRATIC LEARNING

The relationship between opinion and personality is much more elusive than that between opinion and social milieu. Many political opin-

23. Herbert Hyman, *Political Socialization* (Glencoe, Ill.: The Free Press, 1959), p. 72.
24. Seymour M. Lipset, "Opinion Formation in a Crisis Situation," *Public Opinion Quarterly,* XVII (Spring, 1953), pp. 20–46.

ions contain at least an element of externalization. The psychodynamic function of political ideology has already been discussed in connection with leaders and followers.[25] But, although opinions are undoubtedly related to personality needs, it must also be recognized that the same set of ideological convictions can be held out of rather different motives and that a variety of ideologies are capable of serving rather similar personalities.

Two specific observations are pertinent. In general, whether rebellion against parents takes the form of "political revolt" depends on the salience of political attitudes in the home. Unless parents have rather strong political convictions, children who rebel are more likely to select some area other than politics in which to do so. In the United States, where the salience of political ideology relative to other attitudes is generally low, the incidence of protest as a factor in political belief can thus be expected to be lower than in countries where political ideologies are more firmly implanted.[26] One might further hypothesize that the neurotic potential plays less of a role in group-related opinions than in those more private ones which are either highly personal or which, like market decisions, can be implemented by the individual.

The importance of personality is much greater in the political leader, who fashions an ideology and forms opinions, than in the follower. The latter's psychodynamic patterns are more likely to shape the "style" of his politics, while the specific ideology he accepts matters much less. For example, the personalities of authoritarians usually incline toward low political interest and activity, inhibition and criticism of political authority, and pessimism concerning the potentialities of social progress. But, given an appropriate leader, these people may find political expression for these attitudes.

THE INTERPERSONAL SITUATION

Opinions depend as much on interchanges in specific situations as they do on basic indoctrination and ego defense. The cognitive framework and basic defensive patterns of early socialization are only a background against which opinion on any particular matter is elicited. It is in the nature of an opinion that it be asserted for something or someone and

25. Cf. chapters 9 and 10; also T. W. Adorno *et al., The Authoritarian Personality* (New York: Harper & Brothers, 1950); and Harold D. Lasswell, *Power and Personality* (New York: W. W. Norton & Company, Inc., 1948).

26. E. E. Maccoby *et al.,* "Youth and Political Change," *Public Opinion Quarterly,* XVIII (Spring, 1954), pp. 23–39; Robert E. Lane, "Father and Sons: Foundations of Political Beliefs," *American Sociological Review,* XXIV (August, 1959), pp. 502–10; and H. E. Krugman, "The Role of Hostility in the Appeal of Communism in the United States," *Psychiatry,* XVI (August, 1953), pp. 253–62.

against something or someone. In the opinion process participants enter into "team alignments" around perceived interests. Discussion sharpens issues and reduces the number of viable solutions. This puts the uncommitted under pressure to declare his solidarity. In this regard, the appeal of the agitator to the potentially rebellious is no different from the persistent efforts of people to influence friends, neighbors, and work associates.

Individual opinions usually crystallize so that there is maximum harmony between them and those of the people around whom important social relations are centered. When the immediate personal environment is "homogeneous" and people generally agree, discussion brings specific perceptions and beliefs into line with the side one has chosen. For instance, the candidate chosen by one's party seems ever more the right choice as the campaign proceeds. Uncertainty about one's basic loyalty results in an unstable opinion. This is the case when face-to-face influences pull a person in contradictory directions as both sides contest for his support. He is then under "cross pressures." This cross-pressure hypothesis can be expanded to embrace not only conflicting primary group influence (Republican wife vs. Democratic co-workers) but other conflicting affiliations (between religion and trade union, or between family tradition and occupational interest).

THE INFORMATION ENVIRONMENT

Opinions are judgments that depend to a large degree on available facts. A news event, such as the explosion of the first hydrogen bomb by the Soviet Union or their launching of Sputnik, certainly affected opinions concerning other Russian capabilities. Furthermore, people are inclined to accept as fact many of the opinions that they hear everywhere around them.

The more puzzling feature about opinions is not, however, that they give way before new facts but that they are held tenaciously even while the "facts" on which they are based change. Most people do not actively seek out information that tends to refute their ideological beliefs. There exists apparently a general tendency to construct one's cognitive environment so that it is consistent with one's opinion. Hence, unsubstantiated rumor first finds credence among those whose opinions it sustains. In their search for cognitive balance, people will primarily seek out information that validates views they already hold, and will tend to misunderstand or forget dissonant items.

The role of mass communication in public opinion will be discussed in greater detail in the next chapter. But the effects of information on opinion can briefly be summed up in this way: When the overwhelming majority of "facts" at hand clearly favors one side and no contrary evidence is available, the opinions implied by the facts will naturally be accepted. Information is also likely to be an important factor in opinion on a new issue, when neither prior commitments nor group interests force individuals to take sides prematurely. Facts are important when judgment can be suspended. Finally, information often helps a person to establish the relevance of some specific objective to his own ideology. Thus, issues that had left him indifferent become a matter of concern. For example, being apprised that a given policy is detrimental to labor may establish a hitherto unrecognized connection with a group interest.

THE MOVEMENT OF PUBLIC OPINION

THE PUBLIC at large is a collectivity with no clear boundaries but those created by the process of controversy itself. It consists of many different persons who take sides on an issue, the side each takes being determined by background, situation, and, to some extent, the available facts. It may be useful to recall here that the public differs from an integrated group, which often postpones a decision or action until a unanimous opinion has been formed.

In a public unanimity is not easily attainable. First of all, every public consists of many groups. Also, a public, by reason of its heterogeneity and the variety of interests it represents, cannot act and need not act. Its members merely pass judgment on the actions of others. In the third place, most members of a public do not have, and cannot get, the kind of information necessary to make technical decisions preliminary to action. Therefore, effective compromises are negotiated and policies are planned on a level and in terms quite different from those that dominate the public debate.

On the esoteric level on which executive decisions are made, "inside" knowledge of a highly technical nature is required; on the exoteric level on which public controversy occurs, information plays less of a role. Perhaps the decision-making process on the esoteric level approximates that in face-to-face groups. But the public at large does little more than legitimate, by its majority vote, the decisions of executive bodies. In the development and shifts of such majorities, one finds one measure of the dynamics of public opinion.

POLARIZATION

The public opinion on the exoteric level—for example, during a nationwide political debate or in an electoral campaign—serves primarily to move into the forefront those symbols and allegiances that attract support. The net effect of discussion on a social aggregate is to increase polarization. The oscillations between varying degrees of polarization conform roughly to the following model: During quiescent times when a collectivity is confronted with no issue and no election, latent cleavages are ignored. The emergence of an issue brings the following sequence of events: (1) It confronts individuals with a problem on which they have to take sides; (2) intensified discussion mobilizes those social pressures that force the individual to align with his peers and reference groups; [27] (3) discussion also provides the information that justifies opinion and makes it internally consistent, and thus produces the ideology necessary for partisan consensus; (4) this crystallization of opinion tends to disrupt social relations that cut across partisan lines, so that polarization is assured. After the issue is resolved, partisanship is no longer relevant, and the pressure on each person to line up on one side or the other is eased.

This model describes an oscillation which appears almost mechanical. New ideas are assimilated; and old ideas reactivated. At best, it describes short-run changes in the alignment of public opinion that are attributable to the rising tenor of discussion. At its worst, the model neglects entirely those forces that, given certain conditions, may produce basic change if the pressures activated in the public debate do not affect all population groups alike.

REALIGNMENT

Political discussion produces, by its temporary increase in polarization and hardening of divisions, some kind of political oscillation from campaign to campaign and from issue to issue. Under what conditions can trendlike changes in the opinion alignment be expected?

One condition is an event or a set of events that links specific opinions to new group allegiances. An excellent example is found in data from surveys taken before and after a radio address by Senator Hugo Black in the fall of 1937,[28] when his appointment to the Supreme Court was up for confirmation. In his speech he explained his attitude toward the Ku Klux Klan, to which he was alleged to have once belonged. Almost 40 per cent of those interviewed after the speech said they had changed their minds

27. If the relevant ideological commitments and group allegiances are known, the direction in which discussion will move the individual can be fairly well predicted. See Paul F. Lazarsfeld, *et al.*, *The People's Choice* (New York: Columbia University Press, 1948); Lipset, *op. cit.*

28. Paul F. Lazarsfeld, "The Change of Opinion During a Political Discussion," *Journal of Applied Psychology*, XXIII (February, 1939), pp. 131–47.

about confirmation of his appointment. Actually many of these people had not made up their minds before the speech, so the speech only crystallized a prior inclination. But 12 per cent switched sides, and another 6 per cent who had had a definite opinion before the speech became "undecided." Although many individuals changed sides, the proportions favoring and opposing the appointment remained pretty much as reported in a survey before the speech. The lines along which opinion was divided, however, had shifted. Before the speech Democrats generally favored Black, who was known as a New Dealer, and Republicans were inclined to oppose him. Opinion divided around the issue of liberalism versus conservatism. Six weeks of discussion, climaxed by Black's explanation, transformed a socioeconomic issue into a racial-religious one.

Here is how the lines shifted: *When the appointment was first announced,* Catholics and Jews split three to one in favor; Protestants were almost evenly divided. The divisions *within* the religious groups were a matter of economic status. So were the differences *between* religious groups; Catholics and Jews tend to be lower in social status and hence Democratic. *After the discussion and the speech* the socioeconomic division along party lines disappeared. Democrats were now split evenly; Republicans were inclined to favor the appointment. The main line of cleavage was religious. Catholics and Jews, previously pro-Black, opposed the appointment two to one, while five out of eight Protestants had come to favor it.

The religious minorities in the Democratic Party and Protestant Republicans were most likely to have changed their opinion. Black admitted that as a young man he had been a member of the anti-Catholic and anti-Semitic Ku Klux Klan, but had long since repudiated and "atoned" for his transgression. This admission was enough to put Democratic minority groups under cross pressures; their political and religious affiliations came into conflict. If opinion became linked to religious affiliation, the individual was likely to shift. In other cases, individuals subject to cross pressures from their socioeconomic ideology and religious ties wound up with "no opinion." They no longer approved the appointment but could not, in view of Black's New Deal record, bring themselves to disapprove it. For many Protestant Republicans, it may be assumed, the discussion activated a latent issue and thereby crystallized opinion along lines made relevant by the discussion. The revelations about Black's past may have made him more acceptable, either because he elicited sympathy or because of any anti-Semitism or anti-Catholicism that existed among some Protestant Republicans.

Two other instances, the Supreme Court controversy and the 1948 Fair Deal rally, illustrate how realignments of opinion may come about within a brief period.

PACKING THE SUPREME COURT   Early in 1937, President Franklin D. Roosevelt proposed a reorganization of the Supreme Court of the United States, which had declared unconstitutional much of the legislation enacted during his first term of office. The President's plan called for an increase in the number of Justices from nine to fifteen and for mandatory retirement at the age of seventy. These "reforms" would allow him to replace some of the "tired old men," holdovers from past Republican administrations, with appointees who would look with greater favor on New Deal legislative measures.

A poll taken shortly after the President announced his plan showed opinion much more crystallized than it ever had been over the Black appointment. The 90 per cent who expressed an opinion split equally between those in favor of and those against the plan. During the next five months, support and opposition rose or fell slightly, more or less in response to major moves by politicians in the debate.

A turning point was apparently caused by a major event: the Supreme Court reversed a former decision and held constitutional the minimum wage law of the state of Washington, thus paving the way for federal minimum wage legislation, a major New Deal objective. Its effect on public opinion was nothing short of profound. Opinion in favor of reorganization began to decline sharply. From March 15, a week before the Supreme Court switch, the proportion favoring reorganization dropped from a high of 45 per cent to a low of 31 per cent by the middle of May.[29] However, those who were estranged from the proposal after the court decision did not immediately oppose it but became instead part of the "no opinion" group. Subsequent events, in particular the announcement that seventy-eight-year-old Justice van Devanter intended to retire, caused a crystallization of opinion that benefited the opposition. Van Devanter's retirement meant a reversal of the five-to-four majorities that had been overturning New Deal measures. Simply by appointing a replacement in sympathy with the New Deal, Roosevelt could bring about a *de facto* reorganization of the court. The main argument in favor of the reorganization plan was thus invalidated by events, and this affected disproportionately the partisans in favor of reorganization. The same thing may happen whenever an issue appealing primarily to adherents of one side is highlighted.

THE 1948 ELECTION   Reactivation of latent issues produced a short-run opinion change in the two months preceding the 1948 presidential election. This so-called Fair Deal rally primarily involved persons who had been for Roosevelt in 1944 but whose loyalties to the Democratic party had withered away by the summer of 1948. Many were undecided;

29. Frank V. Cantwell, "Public and the Legislative Process," *The American Political Science Review*, LV (1946), pp. 924–35.

many others were planning to vote for the Republican candidate. But in the closing weeks of the campaign enough of them rallied to Truman's support to stop what had seemed a sure victory for Thomas Dewey.

Two major factors have been cited to account for this shift: Truman's vigorous whistle-stopping campaign emphasizing socioeconomic issues, and declining farm prices which made farmers look once more to the government for help. If we consider the switchers' political pasts, as well as demographic and social characteristics that made them subject to pro-Democratic pressures, the mid-campaign switches appear to have stemmed from a reactivation of latent Democratic dispositions and not from a change of opinions. Truman's campaign arguments and the price changes were assimilated to the milieu in which these persons moved.[30] Nevertheless, the rally exemplifies a significant short-term shift in the balance of opinion because it undermined an alignment that had begun to develop, based on the predominant issues of military and foreign policy and alleged waste and corruption in government. The reactivation of the socioeconomic issue in this case benefited only one side.

AGGREGATE CHANGE   Changes in the aggregate of opinion, as opposed to mere polarization, are also likely when crises affect all individuals of the public alike. Then the similarity of self-interest de-emphasizes other potential cleavages. Before our entry into World War II, when American involvement began to appear inevitable, people everywhere, regardless of their prior opinions, began to accept involvement as a fact. Views and opinions favorable to high morale developed as the European war came closer. Confronted with the necessity of taking certain measures, people developed the appropriate outlook. In 1939 after Germany invaded Poland, the proportion of Americans who considered involvement in World War I a mistake declined dramatically. Then for two years, while the United States remained officially neutral, there was very little change in this aggregate judgment. Late in October, 1941, when war with Japan became imminent, there was again a drastic change, with 15 per cent more than had previously approving the past action.[31]

How an event or a set of events can unite a divided collectivity is further illustrated by the farm vote, which in recent years has been most restless in its shifts from party to party. Farmers, who stuck with the Republican Party throughout the 1920's, a period of chronic agricultural depression, have come to exhibit quite a different pattern. When farm prices fall below a certain level, so that all farmers are caught in the cost-price squeeze regardless of the crop they raise and of the amount of their

30. Cf. Berelson *et al.*, *op. cit.;* and Angus Campbell and Robert E. Kahn, *The People Elect a President* (Ann Arbor, Mich.: University of Michigan Press, 1952).

31. Hadley Cantril, *Gauging Public Opinion* (Princeton, N.J.: Princeton University Press, 1944), chap. 16.

indebtedness, they tend as a group to turn to the Democratic Party for help. But even a partial improvement in economic conditions means that the price squeeze becomes less general. Those who continue to be hard-hit continue to seek government support, while those whose economic troubles are alleviated are likely to respond to other issues, such as foreign policy, government philosophy, etc. Another emergent division among farmers results from the number employed seasonably in factory work. Attitudes toward such ideological issues as the union shop are becoming much more favorable among this group compared with farmers who have never left the fields.[32] Thus, once the problem affecting all alike declines in acuteness, farmers become less homogeneous in their opinion and divide much like other population groups.

The possibility of short-run shifts depends also upon whether there are hardened and clearly recognizable divisions within the community. If a certain line of cleavage is reinforced by social and class barriers and therefore widely taken for granted, this mitigates against the likelihood of dramatic changes. Because every issue will be interpreted in terms of partisan interest, it will affect differently the opinions already crystallized into stable "parties" or "factions." On the other hand, where homogeneous elements are confronted by the same crisis, drastic shifts of opinion may occur.

For example, Schleswig-Holstein was the only German province where the Nazis, as early as 1932, obtained an absolute majority of valid votes, even though in the past the region had been a stronghold of the Liberal and Socialist parties.[33] Nazi voting strength in the province during the 1920's had varied considerably from area to area, in accordance with its prevailing social characteristics. The *tempo* of change from Liberalism in 1919 to National Socialism in 1932 was fastest in areas containing mostly medium and small family farms usually operated without hired help. Since most of them depended on the same one or two cash crops, they were subject to the same economic instability. These homogeneous village communities were also well integrated; there was not much social differentiation.

The movement toward the Nazi party and its precursors in these homogeneous areas was especially pronounced. By 1932 many of these communities voted for the Nazi party by more than 80 and sometimes nearly 100 per cent. People in these communities, small in size and lacking in economic diversification, reacted alike to the agricultural crisis

32. Samuel Lubell, *Revolt of the Moderates* (New York: Harper & Brothers, 1956), p. 173.

33. Rudolf Heberle, *From Democracy to Nazism; a Regional Case Study on Political Parties in Germany* (Baton Rouge, La.: Louisiana State University Press, 1945).

and to political events; the more passive were carried along. By contrast, other parts of this North German province showed greater resistance to the rise of Nazism. Sharp differences in wealth or class meant a Marxist-Conservative split. Both these parties had been strong, and their leadership posed an obstacle to the Nazis since it meant an interpretation of the crisis along class lines.

BASIC TRANSFORMATIONS

Opinion shifts take place within the few weeks or months of an active campaign; realignments also occur in the decades during which a major issue is resolved. There are realignments and defections so permanent and so significant that one speaks of a change in the general outlook or "climate of opinion." People in any period fasten on certain ideas that are not so much opinions looked upon as right as "inevitable categories" of the human mind. They represent characteristic ways of choosing things, interpreting events, and resolving issues. Every historical era has its abstract ideology in terms of which issues and opinions are formed, and which account for the main lines of division.

Dicey, in his classic work, provides us with an analysis of a transformation of this sort in nineteenth-century England, when the doctrine of uncompromising individualism and complete laissez-faire was abandoned in favor of at least some of the tenets of what he calls "collectivism." [34] This turn away from individualism became marked sometime around 1870.

For some thirty to forty years following the passage of the Reform Act of 1832, Benthamite individualism, according to Dicey, held an uncontested position of supremacy among the leading classes who influenced opinion in England. In those years these people placed much faith in self-help as a remedy for the ills of society. Among their basic articles of faith was the conception that men existed as separate persons who worked out their own happiness and well-being by their own efforts. Each man's self-interest, if correctly recognized, led him to seek his own welfare, which would also mean the welfare of the state. "Collectivists"—Dicey's term for those who tempered the individualist doctrine by acknowledging the need for some public remedies—stressed the social nature of man and derived from it an altogether different principle to guide their legislative action; namely, that promotion of the general welfare was the best way of promoting the welfare of the maximum number of citizens. It is of course clear that the trend toward "collectivism" as defined by Dicey has not yet halted and, furthermore, that many countries besides England have undergone similar transformations.

34. Albert V. Dicey, *Lectures on the Relation Between Law and Public Opinion in England During the Nineteenth Century* (London: Macmillan and Co., Ltd.), 1914.

The same general factors that account for short-run opinion realignments seem also to account for these broader shifts. First, a number of events tended to affect every sector of the society in much the same manner. The realities of economic life—in particular the growth of corporate activities as reflected in the Railway Company Acts, passed between 1856 and 1862, and in the Joint Stock Company Acts—began to undermine the old laissez-faire doctrine. The acts themselves were incontrovertible proof that the nation *had* a vital interest in the conduct of certain businesses. The need to bring monopoly under state regulation, for example, is, of course, in itself consistent with laissez-faire doctrine, but the existence of monopoly forced some modification, at least in application, of that doctrine, even among those who held to it most tenaciously.

A broad opinion trend must also be linked to the specific cleavage underlying it. The Benthamite doctrine, which held such complete sway among the dominant classes of England, had never evoked the same loyalty or served the same purpose among all strata of English society. Among the specific events to which Dicey attributed a significant part in the shift toward collectivism was the definitive defeat in 1848 of the People's Charter, which incorporated the more radical demands of the working masses. "It demanded the immediate transfer of electoral power from the middle-class electorate of 1832 to the numerically superior labouring class through universal franchise, the ballot, annual parliaments, the abolition of the property qualification, payment of members and equal electoral districts." [35] Defeat of the Charter brought the abandonment of the violent agitation that had characterized the Chartist Movement. As a consequence the alienated classes turned to trade unionism. Their prime concern became the improvement not of their political lot but of the social situation of labor. At the same time the dominant classes, once their intense fears of the radicalism of the working movement were allayed, came to look with less disfavor on combinations formed by working men to achieve limited objectives. Meanwhile, the Chartist Movement had also forced attention to the employment of children in coal mines and the horrors of hunger. "So long as . . . rioting continued, worthy and peace-loving folk set their faces resolutely against the rioters. But when it was over they took counsel of their consciences." [36]

Potentialities for a new line of division, nonexistent in the early nineteenth century and later on stifled in the dominant movement toward individualism among the middle classes, moved to the forefront of attention. The humanitarian element, so inseparably bound to the spirit of in-

35. Arthur Bryant, *English Saga: 1840–1940* (London: Collins with Eyre & Spottiswoode, 1940), p. 69.
36. *Ibid.*, p. 76.

dividualism, aided the submerged working classes. It culminated in a movement to improve the conditions of labor in the factories. An alliance between the Tories and British wage earners effectively weakened the Manchester liberalism, against which the two, for somewhat different reasons, made common cause. The ideological basis for this alliance, especially after 1848, lay in an emphasis on the humanitarian, rather than the laissez-faire, elements in the doctrine of individualism. This shift in emphasis was again aided by certain events of great historical significance, especially the victory of the North after the drawn-out civil war in America. The suffering of the Lancastershire hands during the cotton shortage had aroused much sympathy, and disenfranchisement of British wage earners could no longer be justified once the right to vote had been given to Negroes in America. The Tories, educated by Disraeli, seized on this change in opinion. The Reform Act of 1867, passed under Tory sponsorship and followed by that of 1884, gave the vote to artisans. The opinions of the latter now became a factor to be reckoned with in an entirely new way. With the extension of suffrage, Parliament ceased to reflect primarily the views of the middle classes.

This analysis, based on Dicey, uses the acts of Parliament as its major indicators of opinion. Since the change in the principle underlying legislation was effected without violence of any sort, Dicey assumes Parliament to have been responsive to the "predominant convictions of an indefinite number of Englishmen." [37] Who were the carriers of the new opinions? Was the shift primarily a collective response to an altered social milieu, as a result of which latent dispositions among particular segments of the population were activated? Or was it largely a matter of succession and replacement of the carriers of the "old" opinions by the participation of new population groups in the public opinion process?

Long-term opinion changes differ from short-term ones in that they are irreversible. Specific events often bring about short-term realignments, but the original alignment is often re-established by future events. But with the accession of a new political leadership, trained by a philosophical cadre that is responsive to altered circumstances, change becomes irreversible. Dicey deals especially with the emergence of new opinions on an esoteric level among certain social philosophers. Apart from published opinions, which were without a doubt both an influence on and an expression of parliamentary decision, Dicey uses no measure of public opinion. It is now necessary to turn to the problem of "succession" as it affects a whole generation of voters and to disentangle the various factors that account for differences in the opinions of people separated from each other in point of time.

37. Dicey, *op. cit.*, p. 240.

The Succession of Political Generations

Political life is competitive. Groups and parties that are carriers of different opinions compete to achieve dominance for their views. The competition takes place between "generations" as well as between social classes. Membership in a generation is determined by biological age rather than social position, but the sociological concept refers to more than just a cohort of persons within a given age range. *A generation is a collectivity consisting of contemporaries (about the same age) whose outlook and opinions are affected by the historical circumstances prevalent at the time they entered political life.* Under certain conditions the members of a generation may develop a considerable degree of self-consciousness with regard to their interests vis-à-vis other age groups. But since certain political experiences, because of their priority in the lives of a cohort, are crucial in shaping their future orientations, the age factor contributes to the generation's outlook irrespective of any self-consciousness or sense of historical mission. These experiences affect significantly the opinion alignment of the future, because around them a frame of reference is formed through which events are perceived and interpreted.

When social conditions are rapidly changing, these experiences will differ considerably for ten-year and even five-year cohorts. Under such circumstances the concept of a social-psychological generation seems a most useful tool of analysis. Yet in times of political stability, differences in opinions among age groups are much more likely to be affected primarily by differences in actual social position than by historical milieu: one's age is an important criterion for status. We must therefore separate (1) those factors that affect opinion in the sense that they are a collective response to a specific historical milieu from (2) other factors that account for observable differences in opinion among age groups and between historical eras. The latter differences can be traced to any one or combinations of the following four factors: (1) differential recruitment and survival, (2) structural mobility within the society, (3) intrafamily conflict, (4) psychological and social consequences of aging. These do not relate to the succession of generations.

DIFFERENTIAL RECRUITMENT AND SURVIVAL   Net changes in the aggregate distribution of opinion can occur even if political opinions are transmitted more or less intact from parents to children. In his inventory of the research literature on political socialization, Hyman points out that "the overwhelming resemblance between most parents and most children, demonstrated in a variety of studies, despite the fact that the world is ever-changing, patently argues against the significance of the doctrine [of generations]." [38] But if new voters are recruited disproportionately from a particular stratum or if, conversely, the mortality of one side is disproportionately high, the younger age groups may exhibit a significantly different distribution of opinion from their elders. The long-run operation of such trends may easily tip the balance of opinion.

This is illustrated most generally by the mass enfranchisement of the English working classes and the far-reaching political overturn it signified. Similar measures enacted in other European countries had much the same effect, bringing about the rise of labor and socialist parties and creating a political climate favorable to social legislation. In the United States it was primarily population shifts, caused by immigration and reflected in the westward movement, that upset an established political balance. The relocation of population west of the Appalachians made possible the rise of Jacksonian democracy, while the post Civil War upsurge of Republicanism owes much to the growth of the Midwest.

The upset in American voting brought about by the "New Deal generation" is attributed by Lubell in large measure to the "triumph of the birth rates of the poor and underprivileged over those of the rich and well born." [39] Population increased rapidly among those groups who were the important reservoirs of Democratic strength—namely, the urban immigrants and the marginal farm areas in the Appalachians which, after the cut-off of immigrants, replenished the labor supply of the big cities. Throughout the New Deal the preponderance of Democrats among the youngest voters was considerable and derives from the fact that these were the children of parents who had strong Democratic leanings.[40] In the elections after 1948 this trend was reversed. The youngest cohort, the new voters between twenty-one and twenty-four years of age, often voted more heavily Republican than their elders between twenty-five and thirty-four years old. The slowdown of immigration, the Americanization of the children of immigrants now parents themselves, their upward mobility, the move to the suburbs, etc., may very well mean that a higher proportion of youth now coming of age have parents who have been or are shifting toward the Republican Party.

STRUCTURAL MOBILITY   In the formulation above the political opinions of recent new voters are transmitted to them from parents whose opinions, in turn, were a response to the position they had achieved. In

38. Herbert Hyman, *Political Socialization* (Glencoe, Ill.: The Free Press, 1959), p. 124. The following discussion of the problem of generations draws heavily on Hyman.

39. Samuel Lubell, *The Future of American Politics* (Harper & Brothers, 1951), p. 31.

40. Survey data, based on retrospective statements, bear out this contention.

considering political change, one must therefore take into account those changes in status likely to affect outlook. Some political realignments are but translations into opinion changes of structural changes—such as those caused by urbanization, automation, the spread of college education—which affect the status of large masses of people.

Many of these changes affect the young much more than the old. The movement of rural people into the city is most frequent in the younger ages; the tendency of farmers to change their view of the union shop as they take on seasonal factory work has already been cited. Perhaps the greatest change now influencing the young is the increasing proportion of this generation, compared with their elders, who go to college. College education is associated with many attitudes that also differentiate the various age cohorts. Among these are faith in science, internationalism, and willingness to tolerate nonconformity, in all of which the college-educated rate higher than others. Differences between age groups are therefore often a result of other social characteristics, such as education, and only incidentally associated with age.

For example, Stouffer's data on willingness to tolerate nonconformity indicate a continuous diminution in the proportion who are tolerant for every ten-year age group from those in their twenties to those over sixty. Further analysis revealed that these differences were largely due to differences in education. Within every age group, the people with more education were also the more tolerant. Still, the differences due to education tends to become less marked among older age groups. The analysis concludes that a person is likely to be more tolerant at sixty than were his parents at sixty, but at the same time he may be less tolerant than he was in his younger days.[41]

INTRAFAMILY CONFLICT   Intrafamily conflict in the area of political opinion is the exception rather than the rule in the United States. Where such conflict does occur, its effects are essentially idiosyncratic. On the other hand, in a social milieu in which intrafamily conflict is aggravated and where, moreover, young people are excluded from positions of leadership, intrafamily conflict may well be channeled into politics and contribute to a new political climate. For instance, youth movements among the German middle class, in revolt against parental restriction, rebelled against the Weimar Republic ruled by "old men" and rallied to the National Socialist cause.

In the United States, the political effects of intrafamily conflict are probably attenuated by two conditions: the "democratic" nature of family relations and the fact that the broad political environment is typically experienced only after family ties have been broken; that is, when people have gone to college or left home to form their own families. The assimila-

41. Stouffer, *op. cit.*, p. 94.

tion of political attitudes in college has been especially well documented. Here students absorb opinions that may be at variance with those at home and, in turn, as parents pass their new opinions on to their children.

THE CONSEQUENCES OF AGING   Old age is popularly associated with conservatism in general as well as in politics. There are many explanations at hand. The decline in physical strength is expressed in a more pessimistic outlook. People also become more set in their habits and less ready to accept changes. In addition, older age groups—let us say, those over forty —often occupy the higher status positions. Their conservatism, acquired along with rank, continues to serve them as a defense against those who covet their status. This formulation presupposes that differences of outlook between age groups are in large measure a function of position in the life cycle and of position in society as it is influenced by the former. If the influence of the historical process can be ignored, the opinion of the older age groups would be essentially similar to those of their predecessors at the same age. It is difficult, however, to disentangle the age factor from historical influences.

First, on many questions both young and old will react to historical events in much the same way. A series of cross-sectional surveys dealing with responses to a question concerning government ownership of railroads were subjected by Evan to a secondary analysis in terms of corresponding age groups in different periods. Comparison of the distribution of responses in 1937 (a depression year), in 1945 (the year World War II ended), and in 1953 (a year of prosperity) revealed an unmistakable trend toward increasing opposition to government ownership among all age groups.[42] Opinion differences between old and young in the same historical setting were clearly smaller than those between persons of the same age in different periods.

Still, there is no reason to assume that the relative importance of the historical situation vis-à-vis biological age should be the same for all subject areas. Toch's comparison of the "fifty plus group" with younger age groups suggests that psychological hardening and loss of adaptive power occurs primarily in two areas: matters of personal habit and morals, which presumably entail strong psychological commitment, and matters that are "novel" in that persons obtain little guidance from past experience. With regard to smoking, drinking, gambling, birth control, sex education, etc., the "fifty plus" group was clearly more conservative. Moreover, the "fifty pluses" were persistent in their conservatism over the years. In 1952 they were as conservative, and in some respects even more so, than persons in that age group in 1938. Toch used as examples of

42. William Evan, "Cohort Analysis of Survey Data: A Procedure for Studying Long-Term Opinion Change," *Public Opinion Quarterly*, XXIII (Spring, 1959), pp. 63–72.

novel situations the appeal of swing music in 1938 and the reactions to the Korean War in 1952. The older group was definitely more conservative and hostile in regard to both.[43]

Toch interprets these attitudinal differences entirely in terms of psychological aging, but other selective factors associated with age may partially account for them. For example, the negative reaction to swing may be due to the rural background and greater religiosity of the old in 1938. Or, opposition to the Korean War may be a residue of isolationism, which is known to be negatively associated with education. Thus the more internationalist response of the younger group may in large measure be a result of longer schooling.

Two other assumptions about the effects of age are open to question: the assumption that the old are usually more conservative and that their conservatism is of necessity the residue of an ideology formed in response to a social and political environment of the past rather than to current status.

The opinions of both an older and a younger cohort, when compared on how they stood on government ownership in two different periods (in 1937 and in 1953 when both groups were "older"), moved toward greater conservatism in the intervening years. But the older cohort was found to have changed considerably less than the younger one. By 1953 their relative positions were actually reversed. While the younger cohort was initially less opposed to government ownership, the older cohort, though somewhat more opposed in 1953 than it had been in 1937, was actually less opposed and thus more "radical" than the young cohort.[44] This may well be a trend. During the 1950's, in both the United States and Great Britain, persons just coming of age were inclined to vote for parties representing a more conservative philosophy on economic questions, while the old remained committed to liberal ideologies that they developed in response to conditions of extreme social instability. Thus, we may very well be confronted with a situation in which the Western young, coming of age in a period of prosperity and stability, are considerably more conservative politically than their elders.

Again, it must be noted that inclinations toward radical or conservative responses are always related to social status, so that the consequence of age may vary considerably depending on how the historical milieu impinges on that status. Confronted with serious threats to their social status, the old may *turn* to the left. The Townsend Plan of the 1930's, a

43. Hans Toch, "Attitudes of the 'Fifty Plus' Age Group: Preliminary Considerations toward a Longitudinal Survey," *Public Opinion Quarterly,* XVII (Fall, 1953), pp. 391–94.
44. Evan, *op. cit.*

radical scheme for the redistribution of wealth designed to appeal especially to pensioners, found a huge following among the old. Also the generally conservative "fifty plus" group was definitely more "radical" on the issue of social security, which in 1938 was still the subject of heated controversy.

THE IMPACT OF THE HISTORICAL SITUATION   The term "conservatism" in this context is ambiguous. In the light of evidence, the notion that older people usually support the status quo must certainly be qualified. That they tend to cling to ideas developed in the past is probably true, but hard to verify because of the number of social factors other than age that determine opinion. Still, they are conservative in the sense that certain experiences to which they, and not younger age groups, have been exposed, lie in the past. When society is undergoing rapid change, the body of experiences to which members of different generations are exposed is discontinuous, and it is only in the light of such experiences that each age group, as it rises into the ranks of leadership and displaces the old, effects its own innovations. Thus, Mannheim has drawn attention to the fact that belonging to the same class and belonging to the same generation have this in common: they locate the individuals in the social and historical process, and "thereby limit them to a specific range of potential experience, predisposing them for a certain characteristic mode of thought and experience, and a characteristic type of historically relevant action." [45] But the effect of the situation may nevertheless be different for different age groups, because reactions are always refracted through other statuses that are in some ways associated with age.

Hence, the notion of politically relevant experience is difficult to pin down. As pointed out, people born over a rather large span of years may all react to the same experiences (war, depression) so that several age groups often respond to the same experiences. Second, a generation exercises leadership in political life only after it reaches, say, forty. By that time the body of experiences it shares with older incumbents is apt to be considerable. On the other hand, if a young age group has to assert itself against an octogenarian elite, the discontinuities are likely to be considerable. Finally, the experiences that are decisive for the formation of an ideology vary considerably among social groups. Thus among one stratum the contest between generations, based on divergent experiences, may be rather great, while others exhibit little conflict. To the extent, therefore, that one can speak of "decisive politically relevant experience" it would seem to be made up of the following main elements:

1. The prevalent conditions of life during the formative years and the

45. Karl Mannheim, *Essays on the Sociology of Knowledge* (London: Routledge & Kegan Paul, Ltd., 1952), p. 291.

way in which these entered the predominant outlook. Some eras are dominated by a concern with national liberation, depression, war, etc., which pervades the entire political life.

2. The major political issues of the period through which the dominant divisions are defined. The terms of future controversies, the relevant symbols and ideologies, are often set by rather small but active political groups.

3. The specific events, experiences, conflicts, and social movements, which are, of course, differently experienced by the various social strata and partisans—for example, the sitdown strikes and the organizing drive of American labor in the 1930's.[46]

A rather interesting difference in the voting patterns between generations appears to be the decline of "religious" voting. Data from Erie County, Ohio, in 1940 and from Elmira, New York, for 1948 show that young Catholics were less strongly Democratic and that young Protestants were more Democratic than their elders, who exhibited a much more clear-cut tendency to split along religious lines.[47] Especially the Elmira data suggested that younger people (under forty-five) more often resolved a conflict between religious affiliation and class status in favor of the latter, whereas the older group continued to be oriented along primarily religious lines. The Depression apparently left a different mark on the two age groups, perhaps because they suffered in different degrees from prolonged unemployment, perhaps because the young were partially liberated from voting ties based on religion and thus looked to politics as a means of redress for economic ills. Thus, while both groups probably reacted alike to economic deprivation, they entered the Depression with different backgrounds and in different social statuses.

STABILITY AND MODERATION

To this examination of change in opinion, both short-run and long-term, must be added a discussion of factors determining the character of the interaction between the factions in any controversy. *Stability in the alignment*, rather than in the individual opinion, and the *dimension of moderation versus extremism* are two relevant variables. They overlap. Many factors that make for moderation also make for long-run stability. But both some degree of continuity and some restraint on partisanship are necessary if discussion is to be an effective procedure for resolution of controversy.

STABILITY Unequal participation in the opinion process by the

46. Rudolf Heberle, *Social Movements* (New York: Appleton-Century-Crofts, Inc., 1951), p. 122f.
47. Lazarsfeld *et al., op. cit.;* Berelson, *et al., op. cit.*

potential followers of two factions constitutes a constant, though latent, source of instability. If the normally inactive potential is concentrated on one side, the balance in the alignment can be upset without effecting any persuasion. That side needs only to arouse its potential following; thus, political upsets often result from sudden and dramatic increases in voting turnout. A tabulation of the outcomes of fluoridation referendums in different communities shows clearly that proposals—almost always administration-sponsored—were more likely to be defeated when voting turnout was above 30 per cent than when it was minimal—that is, under 10 per cent. It appears that antifluoridation forces often succeeded in mobilizing voters whose participation in community affairs was not continuous.[48] Once these usually inactive citizens were aroused, the defeat of the fluoridation proposal was sometimes followed by a definitive defeat for the administration at the next election.

The sudden mobilization of an ordinarily passive potential seems to occur primarily among those groups who feel cut off from meaningful participation and influence in important matters—where there is, in fact, alienation. Their vague feeling that an administration or a party is not responsive to their needs usually has some basis in reality. The lower classes, for example, do not participate in the formulation of policies to the same degree as do community influentials. Nor are they as a rule consulted. Therefore the apathy they often display is a not altogether unrealistic response to their actual power position. On occasion, their resentments and frustrations crystallize into political expressions that are directed against the "ins," against governments, and against any leadership that can be charged with arbitrariness exceeding its authority.[49]

An analogous factor in instability is the length of time a generation retains power that is not shared with others. The longer a new generation is kept out of positions of influence, the more drastic will be the overturn led by those who are both at once resentful of what has been and responsive to a new set of experiences. The anti-policies of revolutionary leaderships may be a case in point.

The fact that the involvement of new partisans is usually unmediated by their participation in organized groups and thus a direct response to real or imagined frustrations, has other consequences. Interests and ideologies crystallize in organizations. The ordinarily indifferent voter is more likely to become aroused by some overriding issue or moral crusade if his opinion is not sustained by persistent primary group pressures.

48. James Coleman, *Community Conflict* (Glencoe, Ill.: The Free Press, 1957), p. 17.

49. In a paper dealing with local referendums, read at the annual meeting of the American Sociological Society in Seattle, 1958, Wayne E. Thompson has tried to show that the predominantly negative votes of the alienated are not deducible from other social characteristics.

Therefore, active partisans tend to frame an issue so as to attract those with a poorly articulated ideology, relying on demagogic and sensational themes. Thus, the issue tends to become more general. Janowitz and Marvick have shown that among those not under concerted group pressures to vote one way or another, Eisenhower's personality and moral crusade appealed to those who were highly self-confident but lacked a feeling of self-interest in the election outcome.[50]

MODERATION   The generality of an issue, quite apart from the particular interests to which opinions are linked, has an influence on the degree of moderation in the controversy. The content of issues changes over time. In one era people dispute most heatedly over religious matters or over the right of labor to form associations. Currently in the United States schools and education stir much controversy, but even here the focus varies. In the South it is on desegregation; in the North, on curriculums, buildings, and teachers' salaries. But when an issue is limited to some specific measure or policy, it is less likely to disrupt social relations between partisans with different views.[51] On the other hand, the promotion of any kind of radicalism depends on subordinating particular ties to the general issue. Thus, during its periods of radicalism the Communist Party has always forced its members into opposition with the trade-union leadership because party policy included abandoning all agitation for current reforms. Specific issues were entirely subordinated to the conflict with the *status quo*.

Issues linked with basic values are more easily generalized than power struggles between specific interests. How an issue is formulated will depend, therefore, on the kind of stratification within the community or group. A pluralistic universe encompasses individuals with many different values and commitments, and total commitment cannot be expected to any issue that forces people to choose sides. The partisans on either side have too many competing interests. For example, American political parties are recruited from precisely such a pluralistic universe. Each is a coalition of many interests. Hence, on many points of a party program, agreement among the supporters is far from complete. For the majority, support of one party entails a compromise with varying aspects of its ideology. So as not to drive away these compromisers, parties are dissuaded from taking too radical or too uncompromising a position on specific issues.[52] This prevents divisions from being hardened, which

50. Morris Janowitz and Dwaine Marvick, *Competitive Pressure and Democratic Consent*, Michigan Governmental Studies, No. 32 (Ann Arbor: The University of Michigan, 1956), p. 86f.

51. Coleman, *op. cit.*

52. This point is developed by Berelson *et al.*, *op. cit.*; Seymour M. Lipset, *Political Man; the Social Bases of Politics* (New York: Doubleday & Company, Inc., 1960).

would make appeals to the "independents" on the basis of positive self-interest more difficult. The possibility that other issues important to large sections of their following may grow in importance pushes them toward moderation.

The opposite is true if the partisans can capitalize on smouldering resentments that support the emergent division in any specific issue. The fusion of many issues into one overriding issue can split a collective right down the middle and undermine the common framework of consensus necessary for any discussion, as in the violent eruptions of colonial peoples or in one-industry communities under the impetus of an apparently minor provocation. Controversy is heightened by developing animosity. If a political issue is sustained by religious, racial-ethnic, and social class cleavages—all of which split the collectivity along the same axis—the partisans will, as discussion becomes more violent, confront each other as antagonists. Solutions may even have to be enforced against the wishes of large sections of the community.

A collectivity stratified along a single dimension lacks persons who have social ties with both camps and are therefore available as mediators. Their absence is an important obstacle to discussion. In this connection "nonpartisan" associations may help to bridge cleavages. Religious leaders, for example, serve as nonpartisan mediators only where their denomination is not clearly linked with one side. Individuals and groups under cross pressures with regard to an issue may act in response to the general and public, rather than partisan, interest. By providing forums for free discussion, they act as "clarifiers."

THE EFFECT OF PUBLIC OPINION

PUBLIC OPINION enters into public decision either *directly* or *indirectly*. The influence of opinion is felt directly when a show of hands decides the pleasure of the meeting or when an election, with legally binding force, puts officials into office or commits an administrator to a given policy. But its influence is more continuously experienced indirectly insofar as every decision-maker who may have to defend his decisions is oriented to a real or imagined public opinion. It does not much matter whether or not these opinions actually exist; the real power of public opinion lies to a very large degree in the sway it has over the minds of men.[53]

53. Kurt Riezler, "Political Decisions in Modern Society," *Ethics*, LXIV (January, 1954), part II, pp. 1–55.

INDIRECT EXPRESSIONS

Those concerned with the totality of response to a public question always evaluate its constituent expressions before acting upon it. These expressions come to them via the press, direct representations, and the tabulations of pollsters. The opinions contained in press editorials are clearly not identical with public opinion; neither are those many demonstrations conducted by segments of the public to gain publicity. Yet most everybody concerned with public opinion maintains or subscribes to a clipping service to "find out what the public is thinking." The press is useful in other ways. Strategy requires getting and retaining a "good press," and responsible journalists help in launching "trial balloons" by which public response to policies contemplated may be assessed.

Decision-makers must be sensitive to the articulate opinions that reach them in the form of petitions, representations, and especially mail. Generally these are carefully evaluated; most Congressmen have their own sets of criteria to tell them which letters to ignore and which to heed. Those that come from "important" people are carefully considered and answered, as are those in which the writer, however unimportant, concerns himself with the general merits of a legislative proposal or with its effect on himself. The latter type of mail serves as a qualitative gauge of public sentiment. But decision-makers also pay attention to the quantity of mail. Organized "pressure" mail usually is discounted, because it is too easy for almost any interest group to solicit a flood of letters—often from writers who have no sustained concern with the question. The volume of "spontaneous" mail is quite another matter. It gives some picture of what the articulate part of the public may think. Also a favorable ratio of mail can be a telling argument with the public or with other politicians. Franklin D. Roosevelt was especially skillful in eliciting the kind of mail he needed to help him persuade Congress; his fireside chats often brought in sacks of mail. He also relied heavily on mail to get wind of subtle shifts in public sentiment.[54]

Most politicians know that the numerical breakdown of mail may not accurately reflect the division of opinion among the public with which they are concerned. Thus, polls serve legislators, administrative agencies, and prospective candidates as a useful antidote. Senator Kefauver reported that at one point in the 1946 debate over lifting wartime price controls, mail was running 4 to 1 for their removal. The Senator, who favored their extension, was able to point to a Gallup poll which showed

54. Leila A. Sussman, "FDR and the White House Mail," *Public Opinion Quarterly*, XX (Spring, 1956), p. 6f.

70 per cent of the public for continuation. In many instances polls have reversed the picture of public opinion inferred from the mail.[55]

Actually most legislators who employ polls use them in conjunction with other expressions of public sentiment. Even Congressmen who rely heavily on polls seldom alter their stand on proposed legislation as a result. The special utility of polls is in keeping abreast of constituents' views.[56] Strategy, speeches, and other communications can then be designed to educate constituents to the viewpoint held by their representatives.

The interaction between public opinion and legislative decision is illustrated in a comparison of shifts in Senatorial and public opinion on the Supreme Court Reorganization Bill.[57] At the beginning of the debate, 90 per cent of persons polled were ready to declare themselves for or against the President's proposal; only 63 per cent of the Senators were prepared to do so. Obviously the Senators' declaration would have been a matter of public record, whereas the persons polled were merely making their opinions known to an interviewer. The hesitancy of many Senators sprang from a reluctance to declare themselves publicly as long as the ultimate direction of public opinion was uncertain. Those who waited to find out which way the public was going waited in vain. At no point during the debate was there any spontaneous movement on the part of the public to dictate—through mail and other pressures—a particular course of action. Most legislators were not content merely to follow the lead of public opinion. They made an effort to mold and to direct it.

ORGANIZED INTEREST

So far only passing references have been made to the role of interest groups, the organized part of the public. Knowledge about organized interests, political associations, and lobbies is indispensable for an understanding of the political process as such. But our concern here is not with the whole process by which power is wielded and distributed but with the role of opinion as a less-organized and spontaneous form of influence.

These groups cannot be viewed as a force juxtaposed to public opinion, for their influence depends, among other things, on the shifting currents of public opinion. Dexter has pointed to an effect of the dissemination of

55. Philip M. DeVaney, "Congressional Use of Polls: A Symposium," *Public Opinion Quarterly*, XVIII (Summer, 1954), p. 138.

56. *Ibid.*

57. Cantwell, *op. cit.*

poll results that seems more important than the oft-discussed but completely undocumented "bandwagon" effect (i.e., joining up with what appears to be a winning side). The bandwagon effect may be important in integrated groups, when a rapidly rolling bandwagon sets off a rush to show a unanimous decision. But as far as political parties are concerned, Dexter argues, polls showing an even division between them are likely to lead to special effort; polls showing a party far out front are likely to produce "organizational weakening in it," [58] that is, the party organization is likely to slacken in its efforts to get out the vote and to get financial support. Conversely, an apparently certain loser is not likely to attract financial backing; he appears an unsound investment. Overconfidence or despair among party workers is thus partly determined by the prevailing assessment of public opinion.

Most important, organized interests create channels of communication between parts of the public and decision-makers. According to the group view of politics, interests are part of public opinion—namely, its more organized manifestations.

Interest groups differ in their structure. The special interest association (e.g., the National Retail Druggists Association, which was instrumental in promoting "Fair Trade" legislation) usually is formed for the express purpose of representing the common views of its members in the proper places and to the proper persons. Associations with a more heterogeneous membership (e.g., League of Women Voters) address a larger proportion of their communications to their own members than do the special interest groups. These heterogeneous associations educate their following on points of principle. In this sense they can be viewed as creating public opinion—that is, helping it to crystallize.

THE ROLE OF PUBLIC OPINION

Any policy decision is the outcome of three considerations in varying degrees: (1) the exigencies of the situation which policy is to remedy; (2) the realities that determine what is possible; (3) and the desires and ideals indicated by the public. Thus, public opinion is only one element in the decision-making process. Its role will be described in three different situations.

The Peace Settlement with Japan

American "public opinion" in this case imposed few restrictions on the policy-makers in their search for a realistic formula that would be

58. Lewis A. Dexter, "The Use of Public Opinion Polls by Political Party Organizations," *Public Opinion Quarterly*, XVIII (Spring, 1954), p. 53f.

internationally acceptable. During the drafting of the treaty that would officially end the war with Japan, there was little controversy on any level. This enabled the policy-makers to concentrate on what was objectively necessary and to enter into the kind of negotiation that would assure acceptance of the treaty.[59] What contributed to this situation?

To begin with, popular opinions, articulate interests, and press opinion exhibited no strong concern over conditions in Japan. The scant press coverage, justified by the prevailing public indifference, "increased the necessity and the importance of utilizing private contacts for the few persons and groups with special interests in the settlement; but it also meant that the messages relayed in these contacts lacked the political resonance provided by a broad and deep attentive public." [60]

An equally, perhaps more, important element in the outcome was the broad framework of agreement on the desirability of a permissive settlement. The general population reacted largely to a series of events. Despite the antagonism and animosity toward the Japanese people generated by the war, the combined pressures of the Communist military threat in the Far East and the barrage of official praise of Japan's progress under the occupation seemed to have produced a favorable appraisal of Japan. To many Americans, the Japanese people began to look more and more like a people misled into war by their ruling classes. In the winter of 1951–1952, two out of three reported it as their belief that Japan could be counted on to co-operate with the United States. Also most of the broad membership organizations that took a stand on the issue—such as the National Association of Manufacturers, the Chamber of Commerce, the trade unions, the National Council of Churches, etc.—supported a nonpunitive settlement.

Opposition tended to be concentrated in the smaller ideological fringe groups of both the "left" and the "right." Sentiments favoring the peace settlement were most prevalent among the usually political more attentive and alert—namely, men, the college-educated, the upper socioeconomic levels. People in the Far West, more sensitive because of their geographical position to events in the Pacific, were if anything more favorable. The only restrictions the public was inclined to impose on Japan were the continuation of the stationing of American troops in Japan and some assurance that Japan would not trade with China. Both these restrictions received official support in high quarters.

The few letters, telegrams, briefs etc., that did reach Congress and the Executive were not entirely representative of general public opinion as revealed by the polls. The organized interests were usually concerned

59. Bernard J. Cohen, *The Political Process and Foreign Policy; the Making of the Japanese Peace Settlement* (Princeton, N.J.: Princeton University Press, 1957).
60. *Ibid.*, p. 120.

with some specific aspect of the treaty, the most important of these being the protection of West Coast fishing interests. Most of these demands and objections were met in advance. John Foster Dulles, a Republican called into the State Department by a Democratic administration on the treaty assignment, was able to stress those aspects on which there was broad agreement. In this he was aided, first, by his own conception of the treaty as a brief document incorporating only broad principles, thereby deferring specific issues to be negotiated later and, second, by the fact that his Republican affiliation put the peace settlement under the mantle of bipartisanship.

All these factors together gave maximum flexibility for the formulation of the treaty within the broad framework of agreement. Its major goals were realized without much opposition. Its principle had received wide support, and in both the drafting and the ratification divisive issues were avoided. Throughout the period the general level of popular interest remained low.

The Prohibition Issue [61]

The Prohibition Amendment, which forbade the traffic in and the manufacture of alcoholic beverages, was passed apparently in response to a prevailing mood. Yet, quite soon after its passage, "public opinion" effectively undermined the law. The major responsibility for creating the mood that made passage possible must be given to the Anti-Saloon League.

The success of the League lay in its concentration on a single goal to the exclusion of all others—namely, the election of a "dry" Congress which would submit a prohibition amendment. Unlike the Prohibition Party, which shared this goal, the League rarely took sides on other issues. It was never sidetracked in its efforts to build an effective political machine dedicated to a single purpose.

In these efforts the League was aided by an opinion climate—namely, the near universal and highly emotional abhorrence of the oldfashioned saloon and the liquor traffic. It was on this groundwork that the League conducted its campaign. In its propaganda the saloon was presented as responsible for the corruption of children and the breakup of many homes, as the headquarters for crime, vice, and corrupt politics, and as aggravating the poverty of the already underprivileged. The economics of the liquor traffic, which brought profit to those cashing in on these

61. Peter H. Odegard, *Pressure Politics: The Study of the Anti-Saloon League* (New York: Columbia University Press, 1928). The prohibition movement is discussed at great length in Chapter 17, following.

evils, were also invoked as an argument. It stands to reason that the out-lawing of the saloon and the prohibition of the traffic in liquor found acceptance among those concerned with various social ills. But many of these people would not have been willing to support legally enforced abstinence. The arguments of the League were effective with these groups because they avoided as much as possible direct reference to the temperance issue as such.

From what is known—no opinion poll was conducted at the time—the prohibition measure was passed in an atmosphere of general public approval. To be against Prohibition was tantamount to taking the side of the devil. It also meant being unpatriotic, since so many saloonkeepers were German. Another argument held that the grain needed overseas to feed the boys in the AEF was being diverted to manufacture alcoholic spirits for greater profit. And yet, as the subsequent history of the "great experiment" proved, the same public that had endorsed the measure was unwilling to co-operate in assuring its success. The passage of the Eighteenth Amendment was followed by a period of corruption and breakdown of law enforcement unprecedented in American society. It seems that the communications received by policy-makers did not reflect the degree of co-operation required to assure success for a policy that touched closely on the everyday lives of an overwhelming majority of the population. The likelihood of support for such a measure can not be gauged simply from the proportions who might think it a "good idea"; some awareness of the consequences is necessary. Also, a policy in order to be successful requires more nearly unanimous approval when it can be carried out only with the co-operation from an overwhelming majority of the population. The image of public opinion in this instance contradicted the wishes of individuals.

The Fluoridation Controversy

On occasion the public intervenes directly to prevent or to repudi-ate an executive decision taken by its representative. The role of aroused public sentiment in the public opinion process can be illustrated by the series of local referendums on the allocation of funds for artificial fluori-dation of the water supply. The manner in which communities arrived at a decision is almost in direct contrast to the process by which a Japanese peace treaty was drafted and ultimately ratified. One might reason that the difference in the extent of popular participation in the two cases is explained by how directly the public saw itself affected. Yet people in general seem to have had no greater understanding of scientific evidence in support of fluoridation than of the complicated set of events dictating policy vis-à-vis Japan. Still, where medical practices are concerned, deep-seated anxieties about physical harm are easy to arouse. Practically every innovation in the area of public health was initially met with resistance.

It may also be argued that the public intervened in the fluoridation controversies in protest against the "extension" of government into a new area—dental health—while the power to make war and to conclude peace is an established federal prerogative unlikely to raise many questions among the public. Still, the federal government has often been challenged on the conduct of its foreign affairs. The long debate over NATO and the assessment of blame for the Nationalist defeat in China are two recent examples.

Perhaps the crucial difference is that the initiative for fluoridation has usually come from interested private groups who obtained the necessary endorsement for the measure from local authorities. It is true that most petitions of this type are not seriously challenged; the public is usually uninformed or indifferent. But the formation of strong public sentiment against a measure need not be accompanied by knowledge. No government can maintain a policy for long if opposition to it is on the basis of principle rather than on the rational evaluation of facts. This is the more true when a referendum on the issue can be forced by an agitated public, as happened in many communities all over the United States.

ACTIVE EXPRESSION   Public distrust of fluoridation has continued even though in the years after 1950 just about every important public health agency and organization concerned with dental health gave its approval to the measure. By the late fifties, fluoridation was defeated in roughly 60 per cent of the communities where the issue was put to referendum.[62] Moreover, by the middle of 1956, fluoridation had been abandoned *after* it had been in effect, due to public pressure, in about sixty communities.[63] The controversy concerning fluoridation was in many instances the most bitterly contested question in decades; individuals with otherwise divergent viewpoints joined forces with each other and with those normally apathetic regarding community affairs. Debates were liberally sprinkled with references to basic values, and emotions on both sides reached a high pitch. This left little discretion to public officials. They had little opportunity for behind-the-scenes mediation. They were confronted by a mobilized and articulate opinion to which

62. For these and other facts concerning fluoridation controversies, see Donald R. McNeil, *The Fight for Fluoridation* (New York: Oxford University Press, Inc., 1957).

63. *American Communities Reported Adopting, then Rescinding Fluoridation* (Syracuse, N.Y.: New York Reference Library, Bureau of Municipal Research), April 6, 1956, mimeo.

they had to respond and whose judgment, in a majority of instances, was directly contrary to that of the informed scientific community.

THE ESOTERIC LEVEL   One thing must be clearly understood: there was a fluoridation issue within the scientific community, where its feasibility and safety were debated on the basis of evidence long before voters ever asked to pass judgment on its merits. The answers to the questions raised depended on experiments, on research, and on engineering skills. For a small group of enthusiasts, however, the superior dental health observed in communities whose water supply had a high natural fluoride content constituted sufficient proof that other communities could enjoy these same benefits without any ill effect on general health, even before all the scientific evidence had been fully evaluated.

Arrayed against this group of enthusiasts were many other scientists who were disposed to withhold judgment until all the facts were in. But as medical records from communities who had begun fluoridation as well as a large-scale controlled experiment documented the beneficial effects of fluoridation on children's teeth but turned up no evidence that it was a health hazard in other respects, the crusaders won over one by one the major scientific bodies. Endorsement of fluoridation by the U.S. Public Health Service in 1950 was followed by that of the American Dental Association, the American Medical Association, the Dental Section of the American Association for the Advancement of Science, and many others. The American Water Works Association approved the feasibility of fluoridation, leaving the judgment of medical merit to authorities. Subsequently it also urged its members not to participate in any of the public controversies. But at the time that the endorsement by public health organizations took place and when most of the great controversies occurred, the ten-to-fifteen-year period for which experiments had been planned had not yet elapsed. Opponents continued to hold that neither long-run effectiveness nor long-run safety had been fully established. Some toxic effects of artificially fluoridated water, they claimed, would take fifteen to twenty years to show up. Nevertheless, several persons who had spoken against fluoridation in the 1952 Congressional hearings of the Delaney Committee on fluoridation had reversed their opinion when they were called on to testify before another committee in 1954.

THE EXOTERIC DEBATE   Until about 1950 the controversy concerning the advisability of artificial fluoridation took place almost exclusively among scientists. Nevertheless, it was from the very beginning a political matter. Politicians had to generate support, and debate soon involved persons outside of the scientific community, since implementation was in the hands of public officials. The decision to purchase equipment, the fluoride compound, etc., usually required some kind of authorization.

As controversy moved to the exoteric level of public debate, the habitual caution of the scientists became a potent weapon in the hands of those opposed to fluoridation.

Quite evidently on so technical a matter as fluoridation the public is not fully informed. One cannot, however, simply accept Lowell's contention that under these circumstances there can be no real public opinion.[64] Like all decisions of special bodies, this one was subject to scrutiny by all other persons who were or believed themselves affected by it. Most petitions for fluoridation, when first proposed, aroused no unusual amount of interest. As a rule some public health group initiated the proposal. Sometimes public hearings were held on the question; sometimes it was referred to a committee for study and report. At this stage also, the public seemed apathetic and content, as it often is, to leave the decision to those professionally concerned with public health. At the first hearing in Baltimore, for example, not a single person showed up to present testimony in opposition to the proposal. At a subsequent hearing some fourteen months later, following a widely publicized Congressional report, about eighty women appeared in order to attack it on a variety of grounds.[65] Discussions and unanimously favorable decisions taken by the city council of Cambridge, Massachusetts, between February and June, 1951, were fully reported in the Cambridge weekly paper. During this time there was no evidence of popular opposition. But about a year after discussions had begun, a feature story in a Boston paper apparently sparked a letter-writing campaign and petitions asking the Cambridge city council to rescind its decision.[66] Cambridge was not the only community where public interest was aroused months after the initial hearings and discussion. A few communities had actually initiated fluoridation by the time the public became stirred up.

ARTICULATE OPPOSITION   Even public opposition to a proposal requires some leadership before it can become articulate. Apparently opposition on the exoteric level was spearheaded largely by individuals and groups whose discontents found a focus in the fluoridation issue. In many communities the opposition was led by "anti-administration" groups. McNeil reports how at Stevens Point, Wisconsin, (population 15,000), the first open opposition came from a self-appointed long-time "watchdog of the public treasury." [67] The measure went down to defeat. In Coeur d'Alene, Idaho, there was little controversy about either the dental effects or the safety of fluoridation, but fluoridation was rejected just the same.

64. Lowell, *op. cit.*
65. H. Berton McCauley, "How Fluoridation Facts Were Presented to the Citizens of Baltimore," *American Journal of Public Health* (July, 1954), pp. 892–98.
66. Thomas F. A. Plaut, "Analysis of Voting Behavior on a Fluoridation Referendum," *Public Opinion Quarterly*, XXIII (Summer, 1959), pp. 213–22.
67. McNeil, *op. cit.*, p. 86.

People were stirred up by groups . . . ably assisted by a chinchilla breeder and the so-called "pure Water Association." All of these groups combined and incorporated as the "Liberty Party," and since they were able to defeat the fluoridation program, they have been active in resisting school improvements, attempting to defeat the formation of a hospital district and the smearing of individuals in the city administration and other political subdivisions, and these are matters of record.[68]

In Northampton, Massachusetts, the foremost opponent of fluoridation was elected mayor some months after the city council had voted for it, while the leader of the antifluoridation forces in Cambridge was the leader also of those groups who hoped to defeat a referendum on proportional representation, which was to be held concurrently with the fluoridation vote.[69]

Among the leading opponents to fluoridation were certain nativist agitators, such as Gerald Winrod ("Defenders of Christian Faith"), Gerald L. K. Smith, and William D. Herrstrom. In San Diego, California, one of the most extremist agitators, a man named De Aryan whose real name was Constantine Legenopol, tied it to an anti-Jewish campaign. Organized opposition also came from groups basically opposed to conventional medical practices, preferring instead some specific form of healing.

The opposition to fluoridation was soon co-ordinated on the national level in a National Committee Against Fluoridation. One of its leading spokesmen listed thirty-one additional organizations, operating on the state or local level, formed explicitly to support the opposition "movement."[70] These groups distributed literature in which all the arguments against fluoridation were listed.

AGITATION   Public discussion among the population at large was on an entirely different plane from that of the experts. Scientific arguments were employed only to bring about the defeat of fluoridation. To accomplish this, the opposition played upon many understandable fears, which were used to spread distrust about the motives of those supporting fluoridation. The Mausners report that in Northampton they were "struck by the pervasive attitude of suspicion among those who opposed fluoridation. They were suspicious not only of the scientific organizations but of the scientists themselves."[71] In many communities

68. *American Communities Reported Adopting, then Rescinding Fluoridation, op. cit.*

69. Bernard and Judith Mausner, "A Study of the Anti-Scientific Attitude," *Scientific American*, CXCII (1955), p. 36; and Plaut, *op. cit.*

70. F. B. Exner and G. L. Waldblott, *The American Fluoridation Experiment* (New York: The Devin-Adair Co., 1957). This book is a summary of the opposition to fluoridation.

71. Mausner, *op. cit.*, p. 38.

fluoridation was considered analogous to the Nazis' experimentation with human beings. Instead of accepting the recorded and official judgments of scientific bodies, many people relied on the views of unrecognized authorities or of a few scientists who were at odds with the majority of their profession.

The major antifluoridation themes are listed by the Mausners:

1. Fluoridation is an experiment which has not proved its value and may hold unknown dangers.

2. Fluorides are poisons.

3. Treatment by public agencies of the water that everyone must drink is a step in the direction of socialized medicine and an invasion of individual rights.[72] Of the three arguments, the first entails a scientific issue, but quite deliberately only one side was given. The second constitutes an incontrovertible fact, but one that must be viewed in context. The same can be said of chlorine, of ordinary table salts or vitamins, etc., part of the normal water or food supply but clearly harmful unless intake is regulated. The final argument is clearly ideological and one that a public must judge. Let us now see on what the opinion distribution and, consequently, the public decision depended.

DETERMINANTS OF OPINION   The "antis" differed from those in favor of fluoridation in a number of social characteristics as well as in certain general attitudes.

The antis were predominantly older people without children under twelve years of age.[73] Neither they nor any member of their family could possibly benefit by the treatment of the public water supply, for which they were being asked to approve a public expenditure that, however minimal on a per capita basis, was considerable. The aged in the community, commonly faced with the prospect of a stable or declining income, are often reluctant to accept new demands on capital outlay, which the influx of newcomers and younger people often requires. For example, Massachusetts communities that implemented fluoridation generally contained a large proportion of children and were rapidly expanding. Also, the old are more concerned about their health and hence more susceptible to arguments playing on this fear.

The higher the per capita income of a community and the higher the educational level of its population, the more likely it was to accept fluoridation. In Cambridge the upper-middle class (i.e., "educated") precincts produced a higher pro-fluoridation vote. Opposition to fluoridation was most frequent among individuals who had failed to finish high school, were among the lower income brackets, and reported being employed in occupations that would be considered "lower class." [74]

72. Ibid.
73. Ibid.
74. Ibid.; and Plaut, op. cit.

Nonetheless, fluoridation is clearly *not* a class issue but one that concerns the extension of community action to a public health measure from which all children would stand to benefit and which would affect all families alike. Rather, the opinion differences seem to be related to more general attitude clusters.

Susceptibility to the poison theme and the possible health hazards, key themes in the anti arguments, seems related to a failure to understand the reasoning behind the scientific outlook. Surveys indicate that the public as a whole is not very enlightened about the nature of science and scientists, but that the degree of understanding is higher among the more educated and higher income groups who work in closer proximity to scientists. People who confuse science with technology, whose benefits are tangible and easy to recognize, are nevertheless antiscientific in outlook.[75] In the case of fluoridation, many anti voters refused to accept the evidence of large-scale experiments or its evaluation by scientific bodies. A basic obstacle to acceptance lay in this evidence: Under certain circumstances a poisonous substance administered in small quantities can be successfully eliminated from the circulatory system. The evidence appeared to indicate that the toxic effects of fluoride compound could be neutralized by such natural defenses, thus eliminating the health hazard. Interestingly, in the United States no general alarm had crystallized concerning the increase of radioactive substances in the atmosphere and in certain foods, even though their health and genetic effects were already fairly well demonstrated. One may speculate that the fears of fluoridation were a displacement of anxiety over the side effects of nuclear tests, the continuation of which many felt to be in the national interest.[76]

75. Albert B. Wolfe, *Conservatism, Radicalism and Scientific Method* (New York: The Macmillan Co., 1923). In a pioneering work, Wolfe tried to describe the scientific attitude. The real difference between it and an unscientific one, he contended, is its "objectivity" in the sense that a person holding a view believes only what is forced on him by the use of reason and intellect. The unscientific attitude is, by contrast, subjective: the person believes what he is inclined to believe in any event, though his views may be justified by complicated rationalizations. Thus, the "objective" and scientific individual strives for reality, where the "subjective" individual perceives the world as distorted by a projection of his desires and is not motivated by dispassionate inquiry.

76. In a recent article Morris Davis has said he discerned in the opposition to fluoridation a "naturalist" attitude syndrome, according to which everything "unnatural" is considered *artificial* and *perverse*. Cf. "Community Attitudes toward Fluoridation," *Public Opinion Quarterly*, XXIII (Winter, 1959–1960), pp. 474–82. The utility of introducing such a syndrome is questioned, because people who show great concern about food additives and nuclear testing are often pro-fluoridation. It would seem more useful to treat the cluster of "naturalist" attitudes Davis assumes as an expression of projective distrust and to relate the specific objects of distrust to the liberal-conservative dimension.

The mass medication theme is clearly ideological. Consequently opinions on fluoridation, as on many public health measures, may be considered a component of the broader liberal-conservative dimension. A "liberal" viewpoint, whether on the assumption of world responsibilities by the United States or on domestic issues, was associated with voting "yes" on fluoridation. This was true of those in a California community who agreed with isolationist statements or who supported racial integration, while in Cambridge a heavier vote for fluoridation was obtained in precincts that had supported "liberal" propositions and "liberal" candidates in the past.[77] Yet the "liberal" votes in Cambridge correlated much more strongly with each other than with the fluoridation vote, indicating that on a new issue of this sort the liberal-conservative dimension is perhaps not an entirely adequate measure.

The imagery associated with a negative vote on fluoridation suggests that it was in large measure a revolt against authority, scientific as well as political. James Rorty, a free-lance writer who has taken liberal positions on many social questions, frequently spoke for the antifluoridation "movement," maintaining that the earliest advocate of fluoridation was the Sugar Research Foundation. Its motive in mobilizing the dental societies behind fluoridation, Rorty declared, was to ward off criticism of the high sugar intake which, as is widely known, contributes more than any other element in the American diet to dental decay. It was also alleged that the Aluminum Company of America was seeking a market for the fluoride wastes accumulated during the process of refining aluminum.[78] In one community where a survey was taken just after the referendum, 52 per cent of the "no" voters agreed with the statement that "chemical industry is for fluoridation even though it may be dangerous, because it will profit from it," and 85 per cent agreed that "dentists will profit from fluoridation because it mottles teeth." Over one-third also refused to believe that scientific bodies like the American Dental Society and the United States Public Health Service were good judges of the merits of fluoridation, and, the many official assurances notwithstanding, they also feared sabotage of the public water supply.[79] The suspicion of fluoridation as an industry plot was coupled with a belief that it was inspired by the Communists or that it was effort on the part of governmental agencies to expand the scope of their authority. These attitudes may be related to the authoritarian syndrome, with which generalized distrust is fused, but little direct evidence of this has so far been produced.

On the other hand, the "no" votes may have been a response to a

77. Cf. Plaut, *op. cit.*
78. James Rorty in Exner and Waldblott, *op. cit.*
79. Mausner, *op. cit.*

very real assessment of the power position rather than to either social characteristics or attitude clusters. The pro-fluoridation forces could usually count on support from dental societies, P.T.A. groups, and other civic organizations. But those groups that led the campaign for fluoridation did not always wage an effective campaign—probably because they were so convinced of its merits. The failure of the initial hearings to attract attention led them to underestimate the degree of potential opposition. This lack of attention, in turn, became a telling argument in the hands of the antifluoridation forces: asked whether fluoridation was being foisted on the community by a conspiracy and without consultation of the people, 82 per cent of those voting against fluoridation said "yes." Thus, the public often intervened to prevent or repudiate a decision by its representatives.

B I B L I O G R A P H Y

ALMOND, GABRIEL A. *The American People and Foreign Policy.* New York: Harcourt, Brace & Co., 1950. Discusses the impact of public attitudes on foreign policy.

BLUMER, HERBERT. "Public Opinion and Public Opinion Polling," *American Sociological Review,* XIII (October, 1948), pp. 542–49. A critique of polling techniques in the light of a functional theory of public opinion.

BURDICK, EUGENE, and BRODBECK, ARTHUR J. (eds.). *American Voting Behavior.* Glencoe, Ill.: The Free Press, 1959. Comments by political scientists, psychologists, and sociologists on major voting studies and their significance for an understanding of the political process.

DEWEY, JOHN. *The Public and Its Problems.* Chicago: Gateway Books, 1946. A philosophical discussion of what the public really is.

HYMAN, HERBERT. *Political Socialization.* Glencoe, Ill.: The Free Press, 1959. An excellent inventory of research on how political opinions are learned, transmitted, and changed.

LAZARSFELD, PAUL F. "Public Opinion and the Classical Tradition," *Public Opinion Quarterly,* XXI (Spring, 1957), pp. 39–53. A review of the research tasks implied in the classical theories of public opinion.

LIPPMANN, WALTER. *The Phantom Public.* New York: Harcourt, Brace & Co., 1925. Lippmann discounts the role of the public in democratic polity.

LIPSET, SEYMOUR M. *Political Man; The Social Bases of Politics.* New York: Doubleday & Company, Inc., 1960. A discussion of the conditions by which stable political equilibrium can be achieved, with many illustrative references to a number of countries.

RIEZLER, KURT. "Political Decisions in Modern Society," *Ethics*, LXIV (January, 1954), Part II, pp. 1–55. A general discussion of the nature and influence of the public opinion process in political decisions.

TRUMAN, DAVID B. *The Governmental Process.* New York: Alfred A. Knopf, Inc., 1951. Chapter 8 deals especially with public opinion and contains, as does the rest of the book, many interesting illustrations of the influence process.

C H A P T E R 14

Mass Communication

Through mass communication the same content is made uniformly available to a physically dispersed mass. This requires a complicated apparatus run by professionals with special communication skills, which to be employed efficiently must produce an almost continuous stream of messages. The activity of mass communicators makes possible speedy, almost instantaneous, diffusion of images concerning any object or event picked up by them.

That the flow of mass communications is predominantly one way, from professional communicator to mass audience, follows logically. There is no equally efficient channel by which the audience can respond. The much-heralded "feedback," designating the audience response that in reaching the communicator shapes his communication, seldom becomes the genuine two-way interaction typical of most human communication. To ascertain just how an audience is responding demands painstaking research and time. Usually there is a considerable lag before such knowledge can be incorporated into mass communication. Although the audience exists as a collectivity only in the mind of the communicator, he is nevertheless continuously oriented toward some audience image, which continuously influences his activities. He slants the content to fit the inferred interests and needs of certain categories of people, who are assumed to be engaging in some kind of activity. Hence, the communicator, the audience, and his image of that audience are among the elements considered in studying the process of mass communication.

Mass communication, then, refers to the use of a technology by professional specialists to disseminate large amounts of identical content to a physically dispersed mass.

[423]

THE IMPACT OF MASS COMMUNICATION

EVERY COMMUNICATION situation can be broken down into five elements: *communicators* who transmit a given *content* via a *channel* to an *audience* with some kind of *effect*.[1] The definition of mass communication touches only the first four elements. It says absolutely nothing about effects, and yet it is the effects, or impact, of mass communications that most concern people.

"Effect" does not flow automatically from the fact that a given content is disseminated. Rather, to elicit a *particular* response, or effect, at least three conditions must be met: first, the message must gain someone's attention; second, it must be understood as intended; and finally, the response must be within the capacity of the individual, sanctioned by him and by his associates. By observing with increasing care and with ever more refined methods a variety of concrete communication situations, research has placed in proper perspective what was once seen as the unlimited potential, for both enlightenment and propaganda, of mass communications. Many factors in the communication situation, besides the manifest content of the messages, were found to determine their effect. Among these were pre-existing disposition, social orientation, the situation in which a message is received, and the evaluation of its source by the recipient. As a matter of fact, success in isolating noncontent factors affecting responses to communications has been an informal measure of progress in the scientific study of mass communication.[2]

A response is hardly a simple reaction to some item of content. Rather the content elicits only responses that have support from dispositions, habits, norms, and interests which are already present in a total situation and which are thus the *mediators* of those responses. Any incentive toward change coming from the content itself may be neutralized by these mediating factors. The research literature documents how a message may boomerang, eliciting a response directly opposite to that intended by the communicator, how the immediate reaction to a message may be nullified as competing social influences come into play, and how the only visible response to a message may be inattention, cynicism about the communicator's intention, discounting of its credibility, or rejection of its interpretations or directives. Following a survey

1. See, for instance, Harold D. Lasswell, "The Study and Practice of Propaganda" in Lasswell, Ralph D. Casey, and Bruce L. Smith, *Propaganda and Promotional Activities* (Minneapolis: The Minnesota Press, 1935), pp. 3–27.

2. Elihu Katz and Paul F. Lazarsfeld, *Personal Influence* (Glencoe, Ill.: The Free Press, 1955), p. 20.

of mass communication research, Klapper concludes that, except on certain occasions, these mediating factors "typically render mass communications a contributory agent, but not the sole cause, in a process of reinforcing conditions." [3] Furthermore, when communications induce a change in attitude, the change can usually be traced to these mediating factors: either the factors themselves support the change or they are temporarily inoperative.

Since the same message was often found to have widely different effects on different individuals, generalizations about the impact of mass communications have to be evaluated in terms of the unit whose responses are being gauged. Research can thus focus, first, on how the individual in the mass audience responds. Second, in measuring the impact of a campaign or a program, one can focus on the aggregate, that is on the distribution of responses. The impact of mass communications can be considered, third, in its cumulative and society-wide ramifications; that is, how it affects the orientations of crucial persons.

ATOMISTIC RESPONSES

The majority of social science propositions about the impact of mass communication have been generated by research designed to meet the operational needs of communicators and propagandists. In the latter's image of the communication process, the individual occupies a terminal point on which a whole series of influences converges. Atomistic communication events, rather than collective behavior, have occupied the center of research interest, the communicators' concern being primarily to know more about the audience to whom they communicate and the situation in which their communications are received. They have sought especially information about the perceptual and cognitive processes that govern the responses of the individual in the audience—that is, the processes of selection, interpretation, and implementation.

Individual Consistency

Implicit in the study of atomistic responses is an underlying consistency in the behavior of the individual. A good deal of this consistency is accounted for by the socialization process, which establishes basic modes of response to new situations. Both personality and social position lend stability to a person's behavior and to the beliefs by which he sustains them. In order to function, moreover, a person relies on an

3. Joseph T. Klapper, "What We Know About the Effects of Mass Communication: The Brink of Hope," *Public Opinion Quarterly*, XX (Winter, 1957–1958), p. 457.

integrated view of the world. When his beliefs are momentarily upset, there is a tendency to look to one's associates for assurance. Responses to mass communications, too, are governed by an effort to maintain a maximum degree of consistency among all the cognitive elements in a situation.[4] In exposing himself to new information, in evaluating it, or in accepting its implications, a person will usually seek to maintain his habits and beliefs and to reduce dissonance between the new information and his surroundings.

SELECTION AND INTERPRETATION   The particular communications a person pays attention to are largely governed by habit and interest, as exposure to them is only a secondary activity. The morning newspaper is read at breakfast, on the way to work, or during the coffee break. Each person has a newspaper he loyally reads as well as an established manner of skimming through it. During the evening hours the search for diversion and entertainment results in peak television audiences. Most persons have their established favorites. By taking into account these habits and preferences, as far as they are known, the communicators frame their messages to attract, captivate, and capture the attention of as many persons as possible. Whenever possible, communicators supply the mass of readers, listeners, and viewers with the kind of materials they are least likely to reject. In so doing, they also tend to reinforce the habits, tastes, and beliefs of their audience.

Many an information campaign has foundered on the rock-ribbed conservatism of individuals who do not go out of their way to learn anything that might be unsettling. Efforts to publicize the role of the United Nations, for example, have been primarily successful in reaching those already interested in foreign relations and well informed on the subject.[5] The specialized bulletins of the financial world, on agriculture, on intergroup relations appeal to those who actively seek out this information. During a political campaign also, members of the electorate usually look to those sources that present them with arguments likely to resolve any lingering doubts. They find primarily the content that strengthens and bolsters positions toward which they are strongly inclined. This tendency is reinforced by the interpersonal network through which the content is diffused. The importance of certain content is confirmed by the reactions of one's acquaintances. Sometimes an event or information disseminated through the mass media reaches a person only indirectly, by word-of-mouth. Or he goes to a movie or reads about an innovation only after its importance has been indicated to him by influentials. The

4. Leon Festinger, *A Theory of Cognitive Dissonance* (Evanston, Ill.: Row, Peterson and Company, Inc., 1957).

5. Herbert H. Hyman and Paul B. Sheatsley, "Some Reasons Why Information Campaigns Fail," *Public Opinion Quarterly*, XI (Fall, 1947), pp. 412–23.

two-step flow of mass communications—from the mass media to "opinion leaders" and from them to the mass—usually emphasizes the second step. On the whole, attention is centered on sources that are already trusted because they have been useful in the past and because the information they present is congruent with reality as it appears through personal experiences. The most striking direct effects have usually been observed in laboratories or on other "captive" audiences, who in real life, when free to select their own content, are not likely to have exposed themselves to the communication.[6]

But even if a communication reaches an audience, this does not guarantee that it will be understood as intended, because people tend to actively seek new information only when already torn by doubt or confronted by a problem they are seeking to resolve. Hence, selective inattention, selective retention and forgetting, and sometimes even gross perceptual distortion often prevent the main import of a message from coming across in the way intended by the communicator.

The mechanisms by which these occur are too numerous to be described in detail. They include the following: questioning the validity of the information; evaluating the evidence as quite unimportant in comparison with other facts; a shift of attention away from the message to the communicator, so that his motives and his credibility become the main concerns; focusing on a relatively minor detail of the communication which "derails understanding"; refusing to recognize the implications the information has for one's opinion or action; or simply blanket rejection and criticism of the message.[7] In fact, subjecting a person to a continuous flood of "persuasive communications" has sometimes promoted a "deafness" to all arguments. As long as individuals are free to reject the import of a message, there is always the possibility that they may discredit communications as just so much propaganda.

Because the individual's response to a communication tends to be governed by the need to maintain consistency and reduce dissonance, communications strengthen and reinforce more often than they convert. Even in a carefully prepared two-sided presentation of all facts, those that sustain existing inclinations are more likely to be noticed and to be forgotten less quickly. Only when the matter is peripheral to one's inner balance are new suggestions readily accepted and acted upon. As a general rule, at least, this is true.

The conformity of an individual's response to the intent of the communicator may be considered a measure of its efficiency. The most

6. Joseph T. Klapper, *The Effects of Mass Media* (New York: Bureau of Applied Social Research, Columbia University, 1949).

7. Eunice Cooper and Marie Jahoda, "The Evasion of Propaganda," *Journal of Psychology*, XXIII (1947), pp. 15–25.

efficient communications are those that link up with pre-existing tendencies. Therefore, the most efficient communications often have the least impact in the direction of change.

IMPLEMENTATION   Mass communications will affect a person's behavior only if the response suggested is within a person's capacity. Furthermore, it must promise new and unexpected rewards, especially if it goes contrary to prior inclinations. Unless these two conditions are met, reaching an individual and getting him to understand the meaning of a message will not lead to implementation.

The capacity for implementation is of course a relative matter. An advertising campaign for a given product will not succeed if the product is priced too high or not generally available in retail outlets. A campaign to make people aware of the responsibilities of citizenship will produce new responses only if it depicts ways of implementing the pious maxims in everyday situations. In every instance, the behavior to be elicited must be weighed against the effort or price exacted. For this reason, soliciting pledges and contributions personally, before intentions have a chance to erode, is usually more effective than a simple mass media appeal. The latter either has to be followed up with contacts or must use some device (e.g., a telephone pledge) by which the response can be elicited immediately.

Individual Gratification

Mass communications can, however, directly affect the perceived reward structure by making a person aware of new opportunities for gratification. These gratifications are individual and do not depend on support from others.

Most of the time, meaningful and concrete rewards come from an individual's social participation, by comparison with which exposure to mass communications is momentary. The continuous gratifications and possibility of sanctions that come from a person's associations point to the pervasive importance of social support.

Strictly individual reactions to the mass media are most frequently elicited when an individual does not act as a member of a recognized group. There is, for example, some relationship between social isolation and use of media for *gratification*. One study showed that school children who are oriented to their peers but do not have many close friends exhibited the greatest appetite for such offerings on television as adventure, crime, and Western features.[8] Another study showed that the middle-class child who is subjected to strict discipline at home spends

8. Matilda W. Riley and John W. Riley, Jr., "A Sociological Approach to Communications Research," *Public Opinion Quarterly*, XV (Fall, 1951), pp. 444–60.

more of his time watching television alone than do his age mates.[9] Finally, persons from the lower socioeconomic brackets, who are shut off from many forms of social participation and diversion available to those economically better off, are generally more avid and indiscriminate consumers of all types of radio and television entertainment.[10] For these especially, the communication revolution has meant entertainment that is cheap and omnipresent.

In the instances above, the communication content is primarily a substitute for action. The gratification derived from exposure prevents remedial action that may require effort and prove painful or expensive. The content feeds into perspectives that already exist. In fact, Warner and Henry have suggested that the addiction of some housewives to the kind of daytime soap opera that used to be standard radio fare enabled them to sustain unrewarding life styles.[11]

Counter-Norm Inducement

When *counter-norm* suggestions are propagated via the mass media, the individual's degree of integration in the group is crucial. For example, throughout most of World War II, the German infantry soldier seemed immune to Allied propaganda. Allied leaflets argued that Germany had lost the war and, promising "safe conduct" into the Allied lines, exhorted him to desert. Only after casualties had undermined the primary groups on whose protective capacities the individual's faith was based did concern with personal safety again assume great importance. The direct personal controls and social incentives to which the *Landser* had responded throughout the war began to lose their effectiveness. Concern with his family began to supersede loyalty to the army; in this situation, Allied propaganda leaflets offered an acceptable solution.[12] Similarly, during an election the mass media content seems to play a greater role in determining the votes of those for whom primary groups do not project homogeneous preferences. The "marginal" individual— for example, the immigrant seeking integration into the larger community—often finds in the mass communication content knowledge that helps him to act.

9. Eleanor E. Maccoby, "Why Do Children Watch Television?" *Public Opinion Quarterly,* XVIII (Fall, 1954), pp. 239–44.

10. Leo Bogart, *The Age of Television* (New York: Frederick Ungar Publishing Co., 1956), chap. 4.

11. W. Lloyd Warner and William E. Henry, "The Radio Day-Time Serial: A Symbolic Analysis," *Genetic Psychology Monographs,* XXXVII (1948).

12. Edward A. Shils and Morris Janowitz, "Cohesion and Disintegration in the Wehrmacht in World War II," *Public Opinion Quarterly,* XII (Summer, 1948), pp. 280–315.

The impact of mass communications on integrated groups is clearly different than on individuals who act on their own. When an objective dramatized via mass communications links up with the norms of a group, the needed support and sanctions that induce compliance are already present. Otherwise, the group will react to neutralize the suggestion. On the other hand, mass communication messages sometimes facilitate the resolution of conflict when group standards provide no clear indication of how to act.

SUMMARY   An individual's response to any particular mass communication always occurs in a direction to minimize conflict. The response itself is an effort to maintain an image of the world consistent with a person's preferences and consistent in itself and, furthermore, to keep conflict with one's surroundings and associates at a minimum. Since mass communications trigger changes in the individual only if the ground has already been prepared for them, their impact is considered relatively minimal compared with other influences. On the whole, therefore, mass communications strengthen and support patterns of behavior that already exist. The conformity of an individual's response to the intent of the communicator may be considered a measure of its *efficiency*. The most efficient communications are those that link up with pre-existing tendencies. Therefore, the most efficient communications often have the least impact in the direction of change.

THE AGGREGATE LEVEL: DISTRIBUTIONS

An individual's reaction to a given message or set of messages is essentially a function of the meaning and implications the message has for him, how it relates to his personal needs, and how it fits in with his social relationships. Though every member in a collectivity may receive the same message, the collectivity as a whole does not interpret it in the sense that any individual member does. Interpretation differs from person to person. Berelson wrote in 1948—and his finding has been reaffirmed many times since—"some kinds of *communication* on some kinds of *issues*, brought to the attention of some kinds of *people* under some kinds of *conditions*, have some kinds of *effects*." [13] This is about as specific as one can be in generalizing about aggregate impact. As responses of individuals are so diverse, the impact of mass communications on a society is often viewed as the summation of responses observed in individuals. One can speak of it only, according to Schramm,

13. Bernard Berelson, "Communications and Public Opinion," in Berelson and Morris Janowitz (eds.), *Reader in Public Opinion and Communication* (Glencoe, Ill.: The Free Press, 1953), p. 451.

as some kind of average.[14] Nevertheless, self-selection, selective perception, and social barriers, by eliciting different responses, result in certain aggregate distributions.

Effectiveness

Effectiveness is an aggregate measure. If a campaign increases the proportion of people in possession of certain information, it is effective. Yet if this new information is not related to relevant attitudes or behavior, these remain much as they were before the campaign. Similarly, a blood bank drive that brings in the necessary donors, a political campaign that mobilizes the electorate, a bond campaign that steps up sales, or a crusade for souls that attracts new members to the churches is effective. Yet the real impact of such an "effective" mass media campaign, as judged by its ability to effect change in individuals, is often rather minimal. Studies have found, for example, that new bond-subscribers are primarily people who expected to buy bonds anyhow and were looking for an opportunity to do so; that most new church members, attracted by evangelists' appeals, are essentially religious but, for one reason or another, had not taken the step of formally affiliating with a church—and they might not stay long now. To effect basic changes requires social reinforcement. Hence, it is possible to achieve high effectiveness in communication, like high efficiency, without producing any great impact or lasting reorientation.

Polarization

Many mass media campaigns increase polarization, the counterpart on the aggregate level to individual reinforcement. As the discussion on public opinion showed, a mass media campaign can contribute to polarization without directly converting any single individual. Political debate as well as major events lead to a "strain for consistency." They force the undecided to line up. If those who were previously neutral move predominantly to support one side, the aggregate balance may be upset. This happened in Truman's campaign of 1948. Assuming that mass communications do little more than keep old issues alive, the stress on bread-and-butter issues by Truman reactivated the eroding loyalties of enough Democrats to win the election. If reactivation benefits one side more than the other, changes in the balance can occur. The strategy of

14. Wilbur Schramm, *The Process and Effects of Mass Communication* (Urbana, Ill.: University of Illinois Press, 1954), p. 37.

political campaigns is designed primarily to activate the unutilized potential.

Stratification

Mass media audiences are, of course, stratified by regional, cultural, education, class, and professional interests. Failure to recognize this encourages oversimplified generalizations about their aggregate effects. Each medium of communication as well as every source of content has a different impact on its audience. Only certain kinds of content are disseminated to each kind of audience. Thus Robert E. Park and his associates paid special attention to the role of the immigrant press as a socialization agency striving to meet the specific needs of a population not fully assimilated into American life. Their own newspapers provided the immigrants with information not contained in the major papers.[15] Park's conclusions were subsequently reaffirmed with respect to radio programs that dramatized the unique background and contributions to American life of various minority groups. Any program had great resonance among the members of the minority with whom the program dealt, but it was listened to very little by the rest of the population.[16]

Also, the local community press still flourishes in many neighborhoods and caters to specialized needs centering around residence and children. It does not compete with the larger metropolitan press, but has considerable impact on certain issues. Finally, there are a host of specialized professional, political, religious, and esthetic publications that address themselves to the homogeneous needs of some stratum of the population. For their particular audiences, they are most important and influential channels of orientation.

Audiences are also stratified by "taste"—that is, by content preferences. One of the authors analyzed the "overlap" in preferences for certain radio programs. In almost every one of the conventional content classifications, such as drama, music, etc., clusters of preferences linking several programs emerged. But most persons were not simply drama fans; a taste for certain kinds of drama program went with a taste for certain kinds of musical program, and so forth. If a person mentioned one particular program among his favorites, he was likely to mention spontaneously a preference for some particular other program as well. These areas of preference cut to some extent across the conventionally defined socioeconomic groupings. In any event, the kind of stratification in the audience must always be considered when gauging the impact

15. Robert E. Park, *Society* (Glencoe, Ill.: The Free Press, 1955), chap. 13.
16. Paul F. Lazarsfeld, *Radio and the Printed Page* (New York: Duell, Sloan & Pearce, Inc., 1940).

of the mass media on the aggregate level.[17] It is possible to obtain important responses from communications deliberately slanted to appeal to the right segment of the population, irrespective of whether this segment is defined in terms of some recognized social grouping or only as an abstract mass.

Conditions of Diffusion

That mass communications facilitate the diffusion of new objects hardly requires documentation in this day of advertising. When no partisan cleavages are involved and the mass media proclaim something uniformly, saturating every kind of medium, the diffusion is greatly speeded up. To be successful in this, mass communications require support from local influentials and group standards, but in this instance the so-called opinion leaders are really only transmitters of what the mass media content offers and promotes. Studies on the diffusion of fads, song hits, best-sellers, new products, fertilizers, and hygienic practices indicate that persistent plugging does make some difference but cannot overcome every resistance.

A NOTE ON TOTALITARIAN COMMUNICATION   Aggregate effects of the most dramatic proportions are achieved in totalitarian regimes, where the masses appear to be responding constantly anew to appeals, drives, and campaigns on various subjects. The relative success of mass communications under totalitarian regimes seems to rest on two factors: the maintenance of a controlled information environment and supplementation by personal networks to sustain the influence of mass communications.

All the media of mass communication are under central co-ordination: they participate in a saturation campaign; all counter arguments are excluded from official media, and foreign literature is censored, and foreign broadcasts are jammed so that they cannot usually be heard. The mass media campaigns are co-ordinated with local agitational drives. This takes the form of forced attendance at public meetings where major radio addresses are heard, discussions in which the general appeal is translated into local action and specific tasks, and an effective system of rewards, spying, informing, and terror to see that they are implemented. The effectiveness of the media of mass communication expresses the degree of control or regimentation a power group is able to exercise.[18]

17. Kurt Lang, "Areas of Radio Preferences: A Preliminary Inquiry," *Journal of Applied Psychology,* XLI (February, 1957), pp. 7–14.
18. Paul Kecskemeti, "Totalitarian Communications as a Means of Control," *Public Opinion Quarterly,* XIV (Summer, 1950), pp. 224–34; and Alex Inkeles, *Public Opinion in the Soviet Russia* (Cambridge: Harvard University Press, 1950).

When control over the stream of mass communication is complete and local networks are successfully integrated with the campaign, a high degree of effectiveness is assured.

The effectiveness of totalitarian communications is nevertheless subject to some limit, which resides in the rigidity of the system. To reach the entire population, the communicators must constantly appeal to emotions held in common by all. When communications convey an impression of a regime's uninterrupted successes that is too clearly irreconcilable with everyday experiences, it begins to suffer defections, because enthusiasms that rest on this impression cannot be sustained. As privatization progresses, the repeated exposure to dramatic appeals weakens their effectiveness. Such general withdrawal of trust from the official mass communication system occurred in Germany during the latter years of World War II. Declining morale could be measured by the amount of listening to foreign broadcasts, even though heavy penalties were attached to it. Listening became one of the most widespread forms of resistance, and people came to rely increasingly on these broadcasts for information concerning bombing damage and the military situation.

IMPACT ON COLLECTIVE BEHAVIOR

Every society and every specific form of collective action rests on meanings shared through some pattern of communication. Mass communication, like any other communication system, has an impact on collective life. By distributing information and imagery to various parts of a population, it affects perspectives that orient thought and sometimes action. Through mass communication channels, new understandings indispensable for the functioning of the large society, as we know it, are supplied to relevant populations. Almost every aspect of social life today reflects the influence of mass communications in at least some remote way.

The study of how some individuals react to a particular content does not suffice for an understanding of the impact of mass communication on an entire society. That impact can be understood only if the specific decisions of mass communicators, their relation to power holders, and the distribution and withholding of information from communication channels are included in the analysis. One must consider also the "sleeper" effects which become manifest only after the initial responses of people on various levels have had their ramifications. Some of these effects are delayed and some are most indirect.

MASS COMMUNICATION AND COLLECTIVE DYNAMICS

WE SHALL EXAMINE in some detail the following four propositions *re* mass communication effects of particular relevance to collective behavior.

1. *Mobilization.* The increase in communication due to new communication channels changes the pattern of social participation; it contributes to the involvement of new population masses in the political, intellectual, and cultural life of the large society.

2. *Refraction.* Mass communication channels have deficiencies not unlike personal channels in that they do not convey objects and events with absolute fidelity. The image of the larger world transmitted through mass communication entails a certain amount of refraction not entirely mitigated by the existence of multiple channels, since the various media have a tendency to confirm and reinforce each other.

3. *Silhouetting.* The imagery made available through mass communication channels is linked to secondary symbols, through which abstract collectivities, based on similar positions, are silhouetted.

4. *Legitimation.* Individuals on every level of society respond in terms of what they perceive to be the responses of others. Many an action is legitimated by way of reference groups perceived primarily through the media of mass communications.

MOBILIZATION

Developments in the technology of mass communications that make possible more frequent and regular communication with an "outside" world have created the prerequisites for a more intense involvement of population masses in the political, intellectual, and cultural life of the large society. With each presentation of content over an established network, mass audiences are constantly called into being and enabled to share some experiences. Mass media participation alone makes possible the superimposition of a world of vicarious experience on the intuitive knowledge and shared sentiments grounded in the community of direct participation.

The psychic mobilization here attributed to mass communication is related to a number of other developments that have quickened the tempo of life. More frequent contact among people from different local traditions has been brought about by urbanization, by the extension of a market economy, and by industrialization with its attendant specialization and increased geographical mobility. Among all these factors, the initial impetus toward the increasing involvement of individuals in the larger society comes from urbanization. It is in cities that new habits of thought develop and are spread as literacy spreads. The literate first develop the new media of communication and, through the application of industrial skills to a mass communication system, make possible large-scale participation in mass institutions.

Still, once a certain level of urbanization has been reached, mass communication has an independent effect on psychic mobilization. Lerner presents data showing that media participation and literacy then become better indices of participation in political life through voting than urbanization itself or density of population.[19] This is to say that in highly rural and underdeveloped countries, those most sensitive to the world outside their local milieus are the city people, who, because of their literacy, are the original cosmopolitans. But once a society attains a degree of urbanization, mass literacy becomes a necessity, and the development of communication media reaches even the more backward populations, who then become attuned to the world outside as well.

To begin with, it should be noted, only the literate formed a cosmopolitan outlook. But, with the advent of broadcasting, literacy and high usage of media continue to go hand in hand. A person who is strongly interested in a topic will follow it through a variety of media to inform himself. Reading, listening, and viewing supplement each other. The objects served up as news or entertainment penetrate daily routines. They become common property so that some knowledge of their content serves as a background against which interpersonal communication takes place. Participation in the world portrayed by the mass media becomes a necessity for meaningful participation at the local level. Movies, radio, and television cease to be forms of esthetic experience; they present objects that demand some kind of response. The responses to the several media come to depend on each other: without reading the newspapers, one can not understand the jokes of the television or nightclub entertainer.

Radio and television (to a lesser degree the comic strips) account for still another kind of participation in the secondary world. For persons attracted primarily by sensationalism and human interest, radio and television personalities (the Hollywood or Broadway columnists) take on concrete dimensions, and the audience's relationship to them becomes continuous. Wohl and Horton,[20] for example, have designated as "para-

19. Daniel Lerner, "Communication Systems and Social Systems; a Statistical Exploration in History and Policy," *Behavioral Science*, II (October, 1957), pp. 266–75.

20. Donald Horton and R. Richard Wohl, "Mass Communications and Para-Social Interaction," *Psychiatry*, XIX (August, 1956), pp. 215–29.

social" the relation of people to the television personalities who constantly enter their living rooms. It acts as a substitute for an intimate relation.

High consumption of media content is related to participation in activities that are visibly affected by what goes on in the larger community. The politically active pay attention to news from every kind of medium; the businessman receives information about markets and prices from many sources. Hence, consumption of the mass media content is as much a function of social position as it is of literacy, and the two are closely related.

Persons of high status enjoy more contacts with a greater variety of people than those below them. Not only does a member of the lower class lack power, prestige, and wealth, but his contacts, even in present-day America, are much more confined to persons in his immediate neighborhood, and therefore he is less free to deviate from local customs. Nor does he participate as fully in the political, intellectual, and social life of the larger community, feeling that he has no great influence on it. All this is reflected in the communication behavior of the poorer classes and their generally lesser concern with communications about the secondary world.[21]

Exposure to mass communications does tend to liberate people from the narrow perspectives imposed by in-group attitudes. Those exposed become aware of new possibilities. Lerner points out how important images of American or Soviet standards of living were in disenchanting Turkish people with their lot in life.[22] Such exposure also sensitizes people to the different standards prevailing in other groups. For example, Southerners who habitually made use of many different news media were also more ready to accept desegregation. While it had little effect upon belief in the alleged inferiority of Negroes, an image deeply imbedded and reaffirmed by local conventions, exposure to a number of news media (like national magazines, television commentators, etc.) made a considerable difference in the kind of antidesegregation action a person was willing to endorse.[23] It seemed to make people more cognizant of the full consequences of any one of several proposals for resistance. Their awareness of legal complexities, of possible political repercussions, of the effects that the closing of schools would have on the school-age population, etc., resigned them to desegregation, despite the persistence

21. Genevieve Knupfer, "Portrait of the Underdog," *Public Opinion Quarterly,* XI (1947), pp. 103–14; S. N. Eisenstadt, "Conditions of Communicative Receptivity," *Public Opinion Quarterly,* XVII (1953), pp. 363–74, for the communication behavior of immigrants to Israel.

22. Daniel Lerner, *The Passing of Traditional Society* (Glencoe, Ill.: The Free Press, 1958).

23. Melvin M. Tumin, "Exposure to Mass Media and Readiness for Desegregation," *Public Opinion Quarterly,* XXI (Summer, 1959), pp. 237–51.

of their stereotypy of the Negro, which was reaffirmed in day-to-day social experiences.

High media exposure was, of course, related to education and social class, but some residual differences in attitudes toward desegregation remained even after they were allowed for. The high communicants in every social category were generally less prone to take precipitate action based on sentiments embedded in local mores. The fact that media participation and social participation are mutually reinforcing suggests that the further spread of literacy and education among the masses provides an unprecedented opportunity for the mobilization of publics around social issues.

REFRACTION: THE MASS COMMUNICATION SYSTEM

The term "communication system" designates a network. The diffusion of information throughout such a network is far from random. On the contrary, it tends to follow certain regular channels, each of which is adapted to transmit particular information.

Clearly, not all available information is publicly transmitted. The other side of publicity is secrecy. No individual reveals everything he knows; he is, moreover, likely to be more discriminating with some people than with others. Some secrets are not willingly shared with anyone; some are revealed to a closed circle; still other information is willingly disseminated because it is to the interest of the person to have it known; some *cannot* be revealed because we lack the communicative skills to convey the proper impression. What holds for individuals also holds for groups and institutions. Public relations is only a formalized, professionalized aspect of what one might call "information control." The upshot of all these efforts to control—to facilitate as well as to impede— the flow of information throughout a society, is some image of the society its members hold in common and validate in communication with each other.

The image projected is always somewhat out of focus. It contains primarily what a communicator is willing and able to project, though he does not always succeed fully in his aims. Because every communication system is less than perfect in this regard, the content that emerges always bears the imprint of the system. *The influence of the communication system on the content is designated here as refraction.*

Barriers

Though mass communication has increased immeasurably the flow of information, there are always barriers that cannot be crossed and "gatekeepers" who seek to control the flow of information through particular channels. Moreover, every system has its boundaries in the sense that some population groups are inaccessible or otherwise not reached. In general the barriers within any system of communication are due to technological, cultural, and social factors.

TECHNOLOGICAL BARRIERS   There are, to begin with, geographical limits to the range of effective communication. Every network that links people in frequent and intense communication has boundaries beyond which communication, though possible, is difficult and hence less frequent. These boundaries are largely set by technology. Frequent communication requires either spatial proximity or some means of transmitting and receiving coded information over distances. The circulation area of print, for example, is largely a matter of cheap and quick reproduction (through rotary presses) and of physical transport. The development of electronic means of communication made the diffusion of images instantaneous. Still, the availablility of receiving sets plus the necessary signal strength set limits to the area in which images could be diffused. To expand the geographical area within which a signal can be picked up, for example, often requires an investment in transmission lines or relay stations.

The point is easily illustrated. Some time ago Robert E. Park guided a series of studies of the circulation areas of newspapers. The number of subscribers to Chicago newspapers, Park found, declined fairly regularly in direct ratio to their distance from the center of that metropolis.[24] A majority of subscribers in localities within the commutation area took Chicago papers. As the commutation area grows, the metropolitan papers also extend their influence. Consequently, with improvement in transport, more and more people in the region surrounding a city are linked through their consumption of the same news about it. People from the exurban areas surrounding a great metropolitan center may seldom get into the city proper, but they live in it through newspapers—as well as through radio and television news.

Most mass communication systems are national, rather than local, in scope. Most countries have a nationwide railroad system as well as a broadcasting network. The development of national communication systems can be studied in a manner similar to Park's. Deutsch showed that the "natural" boundaries of population groups, speech communities, markets, and transportation facilities, while not exactly identical, were nevertheless reasonably close approximations of each other as well as of the political boundaries of national states.[25] The various networks overlap, forming clusters of areas within which information travels. Special

24. Robert E. Park, "Urbanization and Newspaper Circulation," *American Journal of Sociology,* XXXV (July, 1929), pp. 60–79.

25. Karl W. Deutsch, *Nationalism and Social Communication* (Cambridge: The Technology Press of the Massachusetts Institute of Technology and John Wiley & Sons, Inc., 1953), chap. 2.

agreements between the managers of communication enterprises are necessary before information can be shared across boundaries. On the other hand, the gradual emergence of a European market cutting across national barriers seems to be paralleled by the development of "Eurovision," the linking of several European countries by coaxial cable, which will enable audiences to view the same television picture at the same time. This constitutes another step forward in the enlargement of the area of communication.

NONTECHNOLOGICAL BARRIERS   A consideration of national communication networks makes it quite evident that the harmony of linguistic, cultural, and psychological background on which effective communication depends becomes more significant as improved technology spans geographical barriers and conquers space. What we call the *universe of discourse* also limits the range of effective communication. The universe of discourse includes all those who share the common meanings on which a communicator must depend if he is to get his message across. The susceptible audience consists only of those who are part of the same linguistic community. But more than that: when addressing a mass audience, the communicator will depict events, personalities, and subjects in terms with which his audience is already familiar. Thus, he relies on cultural traditions, a past that is shared, and experiences that are supposedly commonplace. Mass communication means new experiences in common *if* the symbols are understood in the same way by all.

The Flow of Information

The channels employed to widen the range of communication also influence the direction in which it flows. With improvement in communication, the influence of dominant centers is considerably extended. The important news is made in the world's political and commercial centers. Just as the influence of the metropolis is extended through its newspapers, the newspapers, in turn, rely more and more on wire services and syndicated material that is not produced locally. There are also cultural centers in which production facilities, like studios, are concentrated and toward which skilled talent consequently converges. For many years, until high costs and taxes as well as competition from television drove them elsewhere, most celluloid film materials originated in Hollywood, though finances were controlled from New York. New York is also the hub of the book trade and the large broadcasting networks. Both of these derived considerable advantage from the concentration of editorial and theatrical talent in that city.

This concentration of power means that a high proportion of the mass communication content is controlled by relatively few large enterprises. The Associated Press and other syndicated services supply a great deal that local papers cannot afford to gather on their own. For example, a high proportion of all foreign news enters the United States via the AP wire in New York. The programming of television stations is largely supplied and governed by the network with which it contracts. In fact, an independent paper or a local station, unless located in a major market with large populations, has little chance of surviving without syndicated features or network affiliation. Over the decades, both the number of competing newspapers and the competition between various media have declined.[26]

Difficulties encountered in seeking to alter the "natural" direction of flow as determined by geographical and cultural topography are illustrated in the communication policies of the government of Canada. The first national enterprise, after federation in 1867, was to build an east-west railway that would lie exclusively on Canadian territory. In this way, the diverse regions (the West Coast, the Prairie Provinces, the Maritime areas, etc.)—each of which enjoyed trade relations, a similar milieu, and many cultural links with American regions directly across the border— were to be linked. The trans-Canada railway was followed, over the years, by the Trans-Canada radio network, the National Film Board, and a national television system. Each of these has sought to supply Canadians with Canadian content produced by Canadian talent. Nevertheless, Canadians continue to read more foreign periodicals than domestic ones (other than newspapers),[27] and the major population centers, lying within easy reach of American stations, continue to be inundated by American materials, which can draw on larger capital resources and transmit their product to a Canadian market at little additional cost.

Communication systems, then, span natural areas within which communications flow from a center toward outlying areas. Within any network the communicators constitute crucial links. But refraction results from two further factors: inadequacy of "feedback" and the relation of the communicator to his sources.

FEEDBACK Not only do mass communicators talk more to their audience than they listen, but they also listen considerably more to each other than to their audience. They constantly look toward each other for leads. In the field of mass entertainment, as Gilbert Seldes has pointed out, competition for the same large audience leads to standardization of content.[28] A success formula is quickly imitated with only minor variations, quickly creating the fashions to which the communication industry is

26. See, for instance, the section "Communication Media: Structure and Control" in Berelson and Janowitz, *op. cit.*, particularly the article by Raymond B. Nixon, "Concentration and Absenteeism in Daily Newspaper Ownership," pp. 193–207.

27. *Report of the Royal Commission on National Development in the Arts, Letters and Sciences 1949–1951* (Ottawa: Government of Canada, 1951), Section II.

28. Gilbert Seldes, *The Great Audience* (New York: The Viking Press, Inc., 1951).

subject; that is, a successful Western breeds more Westerns, a quiz show with high ratings leads to more quiz shows. The need to build circulation of newspapers places great emphasis on "exclusives." A "scoop" is often blown up beyond its actual importance. The requirement that news always be "new" means that quick vignettes of events just before the deadline are more important than continuous trend reporting of major developments. Newspapers also look to each other for leads. An event that achieves great publicity in one medium becomes, by virtue of that fact, too important to be ignored by the others.

It is of course well known that small newspapers, besides rewriting wire service news, also rewrite stories from larger papers with better news-gathering facilities. Recently Warren Breed called attention to the phe-nomenon of "newspaper opinion leadership," which exercises a kind of informal social control.[29] The editor of the small daily watches the metro-politan prestige papers for ideas about his leads and angles.

SOURCES   The relation between the newspaperman and his source of news is also of interest. Keen competition makes it imperative that each newspaper assure itself of informants who will brief him, confirm leads, and occasionally leak him an exclusive. Here again the prestige papers have a great advantage. They have displayed their "responsibility" by printing only what is fit to print. As a result they are often trusted with information they are pledged not to print, a trust that they do not often violate. At the same time, key newspapermen are often called in to help launch a "trial balloon"—that is, to report a story from an "anonymous" source. If necessary, the story can then be denied. The great dependence of newsmen on official handouts indicates how often the communicator serves only as an extension of what government and business (or sponsors) are willing to have disseminated.

We cannot answer categorically the question of whether the communi-cation content reflects primarily the interests of power holders or the communicator's image of his own role and function or "what the audience wants." Each factor exerts some influence. The audience does seem to act primarily as a negative control: the press and the mass media tend to stay away from what is obviously controversial. For it is in the area of the personal and moral that individuals are least willing to grant the press free expression. This nevertheless leaves the communicators wide latitude in other regards. Their own decisions about how the potentialities of their medium can best be dramatized inject an element of refraction for which they are responsible. Newsmen have, after all, their own pro-fessional standards. Moreover, the working press (and publishers and broadcasters generally) are subject to influence and pressure much more

29. Warren Breed, "Newspapers' 'Opinion Leaders' and Processes of Standardiza-tion," *Journalism Quarterly*, XXXII (Summer, 1955), pp. 277–84.

direct, immediate, and specific than that to which they are subjected by their audiences. As already pointed out, their reliance on sources, on handouts, and on press conferences publicized in advance extends to power holders an open invitation to make news. In this connection the role of public relations must also be mentioned; its efforts are directed at dramatizing particular events at the expense of others. Finally, the influence of advertisers on newspaper content seems to be much less than their influence on the broadcasting materials the American public is allowed to hear and see. They practically dominate the field of television, which certainly amounts to a refracted image of America.[30]

SILHOUETTING

The reality and information conveyed by the media of mass communication refer to events, objects, personalities, etc., that usually lie outside the range of local experience. This makes the refraction introduced by the system incalculably significant. It is impossible, for example, to ascertain with any certainty that a reported news event actually occurred or that a person speaking on television actually feels as he says he does. Yet mass communication audiences are constantly called upon to make such judgments. These are usually based on one of two tests: *congruence* —whether the reality disseminated via the mass media appears authentic in terms of one's own definitions of that reality; *consistency*—whether the various mass media or the content within any one medium forms a consistent image.

The media of mass communication agree more continuously on what events occur than on what these mean. As already pointed out, the common emphasis on events introduces some refraction into a mass communication system in its entirety, putting the images out of focus or in focus according to one's point of view. But mass communication systems are not entirely uniform in what they emphasize. They define certain areas of behavior as non-debatable, while dramatizing particular lines of division within a society. In associating certain events and personalities with certain causes, they create and promote symbols which become associated with private dispositions, dissatisfactions, and grievances. These secondary symbols represent recognized clusters of partisan and special interests, that is, demands and expectations that seem to go together. *The definition*

30. The influence of advertising on the structure of radio and television broadcasting and also on newspapers is documented in Charles A. Siepmann, *Radio, Television and Society* (New York: Oxford University Press, Inc., 1950); also, Gilbert Seldes, *The Public Arts* (New York: Simon and Schuster, Inc., 1956). A more popular version appears in E. S. Turner, *The Shocking History of Advertising!* (New York: E. P. Dutton & Co., Inc., 1953). For empirical studies, see the *Journalism Quarterly* and the *Public Opinion Quarterly*.

by the mass media of these relevant clusters and their delineation from competing clusters is here called silhouetting. The images of interests so silhouetted become collective representations, which may serve as a focus for primary sentiments.

The Silhouetting of Group Unity

The mass media play an indispensable part in presenting the symbols toward which psychic mobilization sensitizes the individual. But not every symbol finds full and equal acceptance among all populations. The symbols most likely to find universal acceptance are those based on "human interest."

In the mass society, "human interest" has largely taken the place of the gossip that characterizes the social circle in intimate contact.[31] The "human interest" value in a story reduces a complex reality to meaningful terms, congruent with the perceptions of reality operating among many different people. Through "human interest," people gain a sense of participation that they may otherwise lack. The fictitious figures of the comic strips, television performers, and screen idols play somewhat the same role. They emerge as real people on whom problems and aspirations can be projected. The "human interest" may be manufactured, but the interest generated in the personalities thus created is natural.

Mass media personalities also emerge as rallying points for causes. This happens when the personality appears as the personification of some collective interest. The role of the leader as a symbol of group unity has been discussed. Many formal leaders are personifications of group ideals. But the rise to official leadership entails, among other skills, the ability for dramatization over the mass media. Consequently, the personality that is congruent with imaginations can emerge spontaneously through the mass media as the representative of collective aspirations.

KATE SMITH: A STUDY IN CONGRUENCE [32]   On September 21, 1943, Kate Smith, a well-known radio singer and entertainer, staged a marathon drive to sell war bonds. Speaking over the radio for a minute or two at a time, sixty-five times over a period of eighteen hours, she urged listeners to buy war bonds. This all-day drive, her third, reportedly netted thirty-nine million dollars in bond pledges.

Merton, Fiske, and Curtis found the public imagery of Kate Smith congruent with the meanings that war bonds held for the public. Re-

31. See Helen MacGill Hughes, *News and the Human Interest Story* (Chicago: The University of Chicago Press, 1940).

32. Robert K. Merton, assisted by Marjorie Fiske and Alberta Curtis, *Mass Persuasion; The Social Psychology of a War Bond Drive* (New York: Harper & Brothers, 1946), particularly chap. 4.

spondents "attributed a symbolic, virtually sacred, character to war bonds," and Kate Smith was judged by them to be particularly fit to sell them. For these respondents, the study points out, she possessed attributes ordinarily reserved for the moral leader. She was looked upon as an incarnation of the American gospel of sincerity, benevolence, and, above all, patriotism.

Radio listeners were familiar with Kate Smith as a radio personality. But they did not think of her primarily as an entertainer. They stressed that she had done "so much for the war effort," that she was a "sincere" and a "real American," who had "done so much good for people." Her appeal in selling war bonds thus appeared as an unselfish, patriotic act, and each specific plea as a spontaneous gesture coming straight from the heart. (Actually, Miss Smith did donate her services but her text was written for her.) Everything about the radio marathon served only to validate the beliefs of those already disposed to consider her sincere, generous, and patriotic.

Having available a personality whose public image was congruent with the purpose of selling bonds, the producers of the radio marathon needed only to see that every element in it was consistent with that image.

To spell out the techniques by which Kate Smith the entertainer emerged as Kate Smith the philanthropist-patriot is not to question her sincerity. The point is that sincerity in itself does not suffice unless it can be dramatically projected via the mass media. These techniques do, of course, permit the building up of a public personality completely at variance with his real self.

The first technique was that of inadvertence:

> As one informant puts it admiringly: "She gives in such an offhand way —doesn't make a fuss about it." . . . The accounts of her benevolence slip out inadvertently, as a by-product of some other discussion and without any manifest concern for the building of a reputation. Casual mention of Smith's latest excursion to army camps and hospitals . . . or a story in a popular magazine supplies inside information about her unostentatious gifts to a poor family or her patriot endeavors.[33]

A second technique aimed to refute an image of Kate Smith as Lady Bountiful while building up an image of a humanitarian. Hence, Kate Smith's direct participation in her humanitarian enterprises was dramatized: she sang to help the poor; she collected toys for orphans; she had been invited to christen a bomber named after her, which led many of her fans to believe that she herself had donated it to the government. But the image of Lady Bountiful was effectively refuted by her insistence on

33. *Ibid.*, p. 98.

being one of the plain folk, her use of simple language, her homey anecdotes, and her simple manner.

Kate Smith's long-standing association with the song "God Bless America," which she helped popularize, now helped to establish the genuineness of her patriotic motives. Indeed, she had a propensity for the word "America." "The words 'America,' 'American,' 'Americans' occur 45 times in 36 broadcasts covering a total of about one hour of her actual speaking time." [34] As one listener said, "When you think of Kate, you think of America." The radio star also promoted the image of a patriot by participation in activities close to the actual experience of most Americans—songs for wounded soldiers in hospitals, excursions to camps, and many charity drives.

The technique of the marathon itself helped validate the image of her sincerity. It dramatized her efforts. Listeners became cued to signs of possible fatigue as the broadcast made frequent reference to the number of hours over which Kate Smith continued her appeals.

By talking a great deal in terms of the appropriate symbols and by partaking in events that dramatized the image already created, Kate Smith thus built a reputation for patriotism as well as benevolence. She emerged unopposed as a symbol of humanitarianism, a "human interest" personality who could become the rallying point for a surge of patriotic buying. Personalities thus dramatized via the mass media can be used in support of a cause. Furthermore, the support a mass media personality commands helps to nominate him as a potential leader. For example, a political leader whose actions receive frequent recognition in the mass media becomes a force to be reckoned with by his peers.

Consensus and Cleavages

The media of mass communication help to delineate more sharply the unity of a mass of people and to silhouette the main lines of division within it. They do this by propagating secondary symbols, such as nation or class, which are linked with specific personalities, objects, or events that are congruent with concrete sentiments. Mass sentiment takes on a more concrete form when the sentiment evoked by "home" becomes attached to the American way of life or when the frustration suffered in a depression is interpreted as the fate of a class. The tie-up with the secondary symbol facilitates the emergence of some kind of collective consciousness out of the shared sentiment, a consciousness that the symbol represents. Thus, admiration for the achievement of some individual comes to represent a collective aspiration, while personal suffering represents a collective fate.

34. *Ibid.*, p. 103.

Dramatization of the unity of a group is aided through the depiction of personalities, objects, and events in terms of unifying symbols that express consensus. The pianist Van Cliburn, after winning an international competition in Moscow, became the personification of American superiority over the Soviet Union. Lindbergh, flying the Atlantic, was not just a hero, but an American hero. The common identification with his achievement helped to define the American nation, while Kate Smith, in her marathon, symbolized American patriotism and self-sacrifice.

Though frequently built around personalities, the representation of an abstract collectivity is as often an impersonal object or event. The development of national consciousness can, as a matter of fact, he gauged from the use of secondary designations of nationality that are attached to communications about "primary" events—that is, communications into which each person is free to read his own meaning. A stirring literary masterpiece comes to be hailed as a piece of Americana, or "being helpful to one's neighbors" becomes the American way. Among subject nationalities, the development of a literature and a press supported in turn by the self-conscious belief in the values and superiority of one's vernacular and culture may lead to separatist or secessionist goals. The contributors become their representative spokesmen.

Consequently, though the media of mass communication define the area of consensus by providing unifying symbols, they also facilitate the coalescing of alienated masses into self-conscious collectivities. Demands for recognition come from minorities and from submerged social strata. When their demands are formulated in terms of class interests, with an ideology to provide the expectations which support the demands (e.g., the demands raised by labor have frequently been rationalized by the millenial hopes of socialist ideology), this marks the beginnings of class consciousness. To attach the divisive symbol of class to every issue is to sharpen the class division. This happens especially when various classes, supported by their own media, develop a literature, a culture, and a community life that everywhere sets them apart from the dominant group. In that instance, every issue becomes a class issue. The symbols of ethnic identity also play an important role in the United States. The development of special mass media addressed to a particular minority forces a recognition of ethnic issues even in the general press.

The secondary symbols of class, ethnic group, religion, region, etc., in terms of which debate is carried on, influences the acrimony of the debate. Linking every issue to the same divisive symbols is apt to weaken consensus, whereas the existence of a variety of issues which cut across class, religious lines, etc., permits conflict without threatening to disrupt the underlying unity. It is important to note that the mass media as a whole both reinforce and change the major terms in which issues may be defined. Thus, an examination of the impact of the Black speech (Chapter 13) showed how the dramatization of personalities and incidents through the mass media can change the main lines of cleavage on an issue. From the viewpoint of the individual, there was no change; people lined up in terms of their prior dispositions. Nor was there any drastic aggregate re-alignment of the opinion. However, the secondary symbols to which the appointment of Black was linked shifted. In this manner, through their projection of important symbols, the media of mass communication set a framework for debate.

The mass media similarly define areas that are beyond controversy. A study of newspapers showed that certain topics were not subject to attack.[35] National interest is one of them. The medical profession seems to enjoy a partial immunity from attack. One of the most phenomenal political events of recent times was the way in which Dwight Eisenhower, as President, remained above criticism. He was not only a hero but an American hero, so that to criticize his actions as President was, for some, to criticize America, to engage in an unpatriotic act. This was especially true in the field of foreign policy.

THE DRAMATIZATION OF TENSION   In a diverse society, tension between groups in some form is usually endemic. The mass media, by presenting appropriate symbols, by selecting certain events, and not others, for coverage, often dramatize tension in relation to a specific issue or incident. Specialists in intergroup relations have given a good deal of attention to the role of the mass media in creating and abetting conflict and to the possibility that a more careful strategy might minimize conflict even more.

Riots that occurred in Los Angeles in 1943 illustrate how the media create symbols for tensions to crystallize around to the point of open intergroup conflict. The so-called "zoot-suit riots" occurred principally between United States Naval personnel (sometimes egged on by civilians of the Anglo community) and members of the Mexican minority. An analysis of the portrayals of Mexicans in the *Los Angeles Times,* the local newspaper with the largest circulation, by Turner and Surace [36] revealed a striking shift in the symbols used during the ten and a half years prior to the riots. The old image of the "Mexican," whose favorable overtones of romance, history, devotion, and artistic creativeness balanced the less favorable images of delinquency, crime, and public-relief burdens had been displaced, prior to the riots, by the unambiguously negative symbol of the "zoot-suiter." There was nothing good about this juvenile in the

35. Warren Breed, "Mass Communication and Socio-Cultural Integration," *Social Forces,* XXXVII (December, 1958), 109–16.

36. Ralph H. Turner and Samuel J. Surace, "Zootsuiters and Mexicans: Symbols in Crowd Behavior," *American Journal of Sociology,* LXII (1956), pp. 14–20.

zoot suit, which was "a badge of delinquency" and stood for crime, sex violence, gang attacks, and Mexicans generally. The zooter theme, once established in the press, seemed to be self-perpetuating. What would have been reported as an adolescent gang attack came to be reported as zoot-suit violence.

No doubt tension existed before the "Mexicans" were turned into zoot-suiters by the newspaper, but the newspaper's label of "zoot-suiters" brought the tension into focus. Most of the unfavorable attitudes toward Mexicans could now be acted out on the zoot-suiter. With their long suit jackets and trousers pegged at the cuff, draping fully around the knees and ending in deep pleats at the waist, zoot-suiters were made visible. They also lacked all good qualities. They came to be defined as not human and thus were available as victims against whom the community could, without guilt, unite in attack.

A second illustration raises the question of the extent to which the mass media, by reporting certain incidents, can create a psychological atmosphere that did not exist.[37] Early Christmas morning, 1959, a synagogue in Cologne, which Chancellor Adenauer had shortly before helped dedicate, was smeared with swastikas and slogans proclaiming: "Germans demand that Jews get out." A memorial to seven Gestapo victims in a near-by park was similarly defaced by black marks covering the inscription: "This Memorial Recalls Germany's Most Shameful Period." Two twenty-five-year-old culprits, quickly apprehended, were both members of the German Reichs Party, which was regarded as the spiritual heir of Nazism and at the time had sixteen thousand members. After the Cologne incident a rash of similar outrages swept through West Germany. Not only synagogues, but three churches—two Roman Catholic and one Evangelical—were desecrated. On January 2, the West German government angrily charged that the wave of swastika-painting and related acts of hooliganism represented a deliberate effort to defame the republic. Meanwhile, similar incidents were reported from England, Scotland, Austria, France, Italy, Denmark, Belgium, Holland, Norway, Greece, and the United States. Over the New Year weekend three synagogues and a public building in and around New York were targets of attack. One of the six young boys judged juvenile delinquents for breaking windows in a Hebrew school and a near-by synagogue in Brooklyn was Jewish.

37. Cf. Nahum Z. Medalia and Otto N. Larsen, "Diffusion and Belief in a Collective Delusion," *American Sociological Review*, XXXIII (April, 1958), pp. 180–86, for an interesting study of an "epidemic" of windshield-pitting in Seattle. The newspapers called the residents' attention to some five thousand windshields having "bubbles in the glass of about the size of a thumbnail." The mayor even appealed to the President for help, saying it was no longer a police matter. After the "epidemic" faded from the newspapers, the pitting was proved to be a normal occurrence incurred in the course of driving over a period of time.

Newspaper, radio, and television treatment of the Cologne incident exploited the shock value of the story. With the new incidents, attention gradually turned to ways of coping with the apparent epidemic of Nazi-like vandalism. Some saw in the incidents the work of organized groups —either neo-Nazis or Communists out to embarrass the Adenauer government. Others attributed the incidents in Germany as well as elsewhere to individual hooligans and crackpots who were reacting to the notoriety such acts had brought to others. Background news stories and editorials pointed up the persistence of racial hatred in Germany, evidenced in recent public opinion surveys, and also reported surveys showing that West German youngsters were learning little of the Hitler period, except that he was a man who built *Autobahns* and wiped out unemployment.

Whether there really was an epidemic of swastikas and, if there was, how much of it was a response to the newspaper publicity will probably never be determined fully. It is common knowledge, however, that since Hitler's defeat desecrations of this kind had been occurring in many places many times. But coming on Christmas Eve, the desecration of a synagogue the German Chancellor had dedicated was a dramatic event which, picked up by news reporters, brought into the light of publicity tensions which had existed all along but were not being talked about. Anti-Semites, supported by some vandals, could not resist the opportunity to get in on the melee. Many others reacted with shock to find that a problem, supposedly solved, simply would not go away. One swastika painting, obviously the work of a child of nursery-school age, also became part of the statistics and contributed to the atmosphere of tension. The "epidemic" was checked once the incidents that made it up were no longer looked upon as news.

LEGITIMATION THROUGH RECOGNITION

The influence a person has in face-to-face communication rests, in the last analysis, on his status. His statements and his commands are accepted because of who he is, because of the recognition he enjoys among others intimately acquainted with him. With the enlargement of the world through mass communication, so that much of it can no longer be experienced directly, directives of local influentials, through whom impressions can be confirmed, are less and less accepted simply on faith. They operate increasingly against a background of secondary symbols through which trust is channeled and the major allegiances are silhouetted. Because of this, the recognition or support a person gains from the mass media overshadows at times any trust he may or may not enjoy by virtue of his status or any trust he may place in somebody in his local milieu.

It is important to note the role of mass communications in informing an actor about the reactions of others to what he does or plans to do. This function develops in two related ways: publicity forces a person to pay attention to the support he receives, and the support he sees himself receiving is largely inferred from the mass media coverage he gets. The inferred approval or support helps to legitimate the action. Legitimation by the mass media is especially important when secondary identifications are unclear or shifting and consent cannot be counted on. The momentary backing of some collectivity serves as a guide for action. Thus a hit, a best-seller, or a political act is legitimated by the support it appears to arouse.

Representative Roles

The importance of the mass media in legitimation derives from their capacity to make public what has been personal and, to some extent, privileged. This capacity inheres in the new technological means and in the audience that mass media systems have built for themselves. Both actors in any dyadic communication—and particularly those who in any way represent the people or depend on their approval—become increasingly sensitized to a category of third persons who watch and scrutinize their action. Once the possibility exists that their personal, privileged, and secret communications may be opened to public scrutiny, the reactions of outside parties, the third persons, must be considered.

The point is an old one, and its validity does not depend solely on historical documentation. Simmel and Freud, in altogether different contexts, have shown how the presence of third persons changes the nature of a dyadic relationship. In wit, Freud said, the originator of a witticism seeks an ally for his aggression against the victim of the joke. If the third person unconsciously harbors the same aggressive intent, which the witticism disguises, and signifies his approval by laughter, then the witticism has been successful. Without the presence of another person, the aggression could not have been successfully disguised.[38] More generally, Simmel has pointed out that the introduction of a third element into a dyadic relationship means a transcendance of its particularistic nature by an objective social framework. There is a disturbance of and distraction from the pure and immediate reciprocity which characterized the two-party group.[39] Thus, the target of the wit is disarmed by the public approval the witticism gains for the aggressor. Or the joke misfires

38. Sigmund Freud, "Wit and its Relation to the Unconscious," in *The Basic Writings of Sigmund Freud* (New York: The Modern Library, 1938), pp. 695f. and 732ff.

39. Georg Simmel, *The Sociology of Georg Simmel* (Glencoe, Ill.: The Free Press, 1950), p. 136.

as the public spontaneously rallies to the defense of the victim. In either event, one of the two parties gains in power from the approving responses of a category of third persons. The dyad may act as one, but in the triad, says Simmel, there is always a division, a pair of two in some kind of relation to the third.

To assure their success in the glaring light of publicity, leaders and persons who serve as social objects are impelled to give greater consideration to the general attitudes and norms that goven their following. Publicity creates audiences for roles reciprocally enacted. The importance of that audience remains even when its reaction is not directly perceived by the actor, but merely anticipated. An "unseen" audience in whose presence a task is performed seems even more threatening to self-status than an audience whose composition is known and to whom it is possible to direct oneself.[40] Presumably to perform under the scrutiny of the mass media or before an "unseen" audience has somewhat similar effects on behavior; the performance takes into consideration the responses of third parties.

In modern society the publicity function is institutionalized in the media of mass communication. A major consequence of such publicity is to close the gap between particularistic norms and public morality.[41] Dyadic relationships, which behind a shield of secrecy could deviate from generally recognized standards, are forced to conform to what a broader public expects. Unless the public at large has access to information about events they cannot personally witness, no participant society is possible. But this impels the public figure to assume the perspective of the population that has been mobilized by the mass media; he must live his life in a goldfish bowl. For instance, the televising of Congressional hearings has tended to make political parties and legislators more susceptible to influence from what they define as the force of public opinion. Trade-union practices, business operations, educational curriculums, etc., are similarly shaped in part in anticipation of the judgment the public may render upon them. A favorable public image must be maintained whatever it costs.

All this tends to place great restraint on decision-makers, who no longer can expect automatic compliance. The "leader" of a large col-

40. An experiment on 120 undergraduate students who were asked to choose the one of two words that fitted most closely a particular phrase, revealed that they performed more slowly and apparently more self-consciously before an "unseen" audience. S. Wapner and T. G. Alper, "The Effect of an Audience on Behavior in a Choice Situation," *Journal of Abnormal and Social Psychology*, XLVII (1952), pp. 222–29.

41. Cf. Paul F. Lazarsfeld and Robert K. Merton, "Communication, Popular Taste and Social Action," in Lyman Bryson (ed.), *The Communication of Ideas* (New York: Harper & Brothers, 1948), p. 103.

lectivity is forced to make himself the "representative" of a category of persons. The following proposition seems to apply to all social systems: the higher the proportion of nonprivileged actions, the more important do representative acts become. Each individual action is judged by broader normative standards. It forces the perspective of the mass on persons occupying special statuses. This has been documented in relation to the conditions that make for successful political negotiation. The presence of the fourth estate has meant excessive caution as well as a stiffening of lines. Several writers have tried to show how the participants in international negotiations react more in terms of domestic problems that are projected on the international sphere than in terms of reaching a workable arrangement.[42] The conditions for effective secret diplomacy in the international game of politics have been destroyed. A recent monograph on the Samoan trusteeship has documented a similar decline in the efficacy of elite negotiations between chiefs of varying tribal groups when the legislative council's proceedings were broadcast over the radio.[43] Strong primary sentiments become involved in the negotiations between representatives of secondary entities.

On the national scene, the nomination of General Eisenhower at the expense of Senator Robert Taft in 1952 has generally been attributed to a failure of Senator Taft's managers to understand the power of television to arouse public sentiment. When, before the convention, the Taft forces refused to open the Credentials Committee hearings to the television cameras, television was said to have destroyed them. In any case it presented the Eisenhower group with an issue on which the majority of the public presumably sided with them. The actual impact of television on political conventions and political parties is a complicated one, in need of further study. Certainly its assumed capacity to let people "see for themselves" an alleged "steal" of delegates forces public figures to recognize that certain practices, however justifiable they appear to politicians, may no longer be condoned by the public.[44]

In general, an image of public support is conveyed in one of three ways: (1) the mass media dramatize an incident that elicits anticipations of support by leaders who are already inclined to take certain actions; (2) public sentiment is defined by the mass media and serves as a cue

42. E. H. Carr, *Nationalism and After* (New York: The Macmillan Co., 1945); Harold Nicolson, *Diplomacy* (London: Thornton, Butterworth, Ltd., 1939).

43. Felix M. Keesing and Marie M. Keesing, *Elite Communication in Samoa: A Study of Leadership* (Stanford, Calif.: Stanford University Press, 1956).

44. Cf. Leo Bogart, *The Age of Television* (New York: Frederick Ungar Publishing Co., 1956). Chapter 11 contains a summary of all the evidence available up to that point on the political impact of television, including empirical studies of the televising of the political conventions undertaken by the authors of this book.

to which leaders are responsive; and (3) recognition of a leader or of some collective political action by the mass media serves as a morale builder because it arouses images of support.

Focalization through Incidents

No social action occurs to remedy many situations simply because the public seems to be apathetic and no reward for action is perceived by those in a position to take action. Some incident may occur that the media of mass communications play up. It may create an issue in itself, or it may change the perception of potential support for some action. The dramatization of the event serves as a cue that the public support the decision-makers require before they are ready to take action will actually be forthcoming. Though a problem is known to exist—be it crime, hit-and-run accidents, inadequate fire inspection, or discrimination—it can often be dealt with only when it seems to assume vivid or epidemic proportions.

One instance is the exposure of Charles Van Doren, quiz idol on the television program *Twenty-One*, who admitted having received answers ahead of time. For several weeks, newspapers were filled with the latest on television practices, the lack of effective regulation, the tyranny of program ratings, the control exercised by sponsors. Polls and studies indicate that Van Doren, as a person, was not heavily censured by the majority of the public but that broadcasting companies, sponsors, and all those connected with the program were condemned for tempting him. There appeared to be little clamor for prosecution of the quiz winners themselves, but Congress, forever sensitive to what it considers public opinion, took courage to embark on some investigations of television programming that it had not previously pressed.

Another example is the impact of Sputnik, the first manmade satellite successfully launched into space. Journalists and professionals, in short the issue-makers, were much more sensitive about the political implications of this Russian achievement than was the general public, whose undeviating faith in the superiority of American technology seemed unshaken. But many people had long been critical of the educational system, of its so-called "frills," though they rarely spoke up. The launching of Sputnik was used to focus attention on the need for speed-up programs in science, on the lack of seriousness about educational shortcomings, on the lack of educational facilities, on low teacher salaries, etc. Whether their dramatization had any effects beyond stirring debate is still to be determined.

Still another case has to do with the downfall of Senator Joseph McCarthy. His fall into disgrace and the decline of his power has been laid in large part to the chance people had to see him in action via television during the Army-McCarthy hearings in 1954. In particular, one incident during the hearings has been singled out for its effect upon the public image of McCarthy. It was said to portray McCarthy for what he actually was. The scene was unstaged. The Senator, who rarely answered a question with a straight "yes" or "no," but used every occasion to launch counterattacks by questioning the integrity of his examiners and their associates, impugned the name of a young man, a lawyer on Joseph Welch's staff, and thereby of Mr. Welch himself. Mr. Welch, the counsel for the Army, stunned by the attack, cried out against McCarthy's sudden attack on the personal honor of a young man who had no conceivable connection with the matters at issue.

The crucial question here involves the reaction of McCarthy the man at this point. According to one prominent radio commentator in Washington, D.C.:

> He appeared, for a moment, astonished that one more thrust at one more helpless, absent victim should arouse any feelings, anywhere; and no less revealing was his immediately succeeding attitude; *clearly* he did not sense that the audience was crying shame upon him; he had no feeling that he had done anything morally wrong; *clearly,* his only feeling was that he had done something tactically wrong, that he had merely lost a point in that particular round; *and what has long been clear to many observers here and what one may surmise became clear to thousands of others in that moment, is this—that these were his only feelings.*[45]

Another veteran journalist interpreted McCarthy's reaction differently:

> When Counsel Welch spoke up in behalf of an unknown lawyer . . . that nationwide jury heard him ask, "At long last have you left no sense of decency?" . . . The camera, at this point, came back to a closeup of Senator McCarthy. In a *curious way, it was a moment that did him credit. He had the grace to look ashamed.*[46]

From different bases both observers projected different feelings onto the scene and thus interpreted McCarthy's reactions differently. What McCarthy's real feelings were at this point only he knew; how it affected the thousands of viewers, each knew only as far as he himself was affected. Surely there were among them those so partisan that they neither cared nor saw what the feelings of the protagonists were, but only hoped that their side—McCarthy or Welch—had scored a point. And there

---

45. Eric Sevareid of the Columbia Broadcasting System, quoted in the appendix of Max Wylie, *Clear Channels* (New York: Funk & Wagnalls Co., 1954); italics ours.

46. Harriet Van Horne, television columnist, quoted in Wylie, *op. cit.;* italics ours.

must have been still others who thought Welch was shielding a Communist or, noting nothing but the histrionics, hoped for an open clash.[47] What is significant, however, is that *the incident was played up by the press and generally interpreted as having hurt McCarthy.* The press itself was a force in that direction. Major figures in Congress and in the administration decided that the moment was propitious. What they had believed they could make clear to the public only with difficulty could now be assumed to have been "seen" by many. Their decision to move against McCarthy was legitimated by the more outspoken criticism of the Senator, by the refusal of the press to make news out of every action in which he participated, as it had previously done. The public, who once supposedly demanded such news, now supposedly demanded it no longer. Thus, the press (including the broadcasting media) was an important factor in the final move for formal censure.

Images of Support: The Landslide Effect

A perceptual correlative of the much-heralded bandwagon effect is the landslide effect. Images of support that predominantly favor one side are projected, and as a result the opposition is quieted because it fears to go against the main stream of sentiment. McCarthyism was for some years supported by such an image of overwhelming public support. In much the same way, Democratic criticism of the Eisenhower administration appears to have foundered on the rocks of the unimpeachable hold of his personality on public imagination. How much, we may inquire, did the assumption of reporters about this unshakable popularity prevent them from featuring less popular images of the Eisenhower personality and thus help to maintain the popular public image as such?

These definitions of overwhelming public sentiment—landslide perceptions—tend to be cumulative. They influence political strategy; they inject a tone into news reporting; they seem to produce a certain reserve in personal discussion, since much conversation revolves around what is assumed to be held in common (like views on the weather). For the communicator, assumptions about the public temper "legitimate" what is communicated to the mass. These assumptions likewise "legitimate" the omissions already mentioned. If the assumption about the unanimity of a public mood is erroneous, omissions of news about dissenting views or dissenting imagery make the apparent unanimity much more marked than it is. It leaves uncriticized what everyone else is believed to approve.

For example, the public reaction to President Truman's summary dismissal of General of the Army Douglas MacArthur as supreme com-

47. G. D. Wiebe, "The Army-McCarthy Hearings and the Public Conscience," *Public Opinion Quarterly*, XXII (Winter, 1958–1959), pp. 490–502.

mander in the Far East in 1951, during the active phase of the Korean War, for his repeated declaration for policies that did not have the support of the White House, appeared, from press reports, to exhibit a striking unanimity in rallying behind MacArthur. In addition to the official hero's welcome for the ousted general, the press reported many minor public demonstrations in sympathy for MacArthur and against the Truman administration. For some months public discussion took its cues from this assumed sentiment; only the brave politician dared to raise his voice publicly against MacArthur and to uphold the principle of civilian supremacy over the military, which fully justified the President's action. Most waited until the storm "blew over," and MacArthur had faded from the headlines as he had promised he would.

Analysis of the television coverage of MacArthur's homecoming reception in Chicago reveals how it contributed to this image of overwhelming public support for MacArthur.[48] Mass observation of the crowd showed that most of them turned out to welcome a general and watch a spectacle, rather than to participate in a political demonstration of support for his policies. The televising of the welcoming parade, however, conveyed the impression of overwhelming pro-MacArthur sentiment. Television, which gives people a chance to "see for themselves," did not correct the images conveyed by the other media; it only reinforced and contributed to the impression of a landslide of public support.

The authors of this analysis explain that the telecast was made to conform to a pattern of viewers' expectations inferred from earlier publicity. In line with this pattern, the drama of MacArthur, notwithstanding its deep political significance, was built around unifying symbols, personalities, and general "human interest" appeals. It deliberately ignored the issues and the possibility of offending anyone. A drama it had to be, even at the expense of reality. The camera, the commentary, and to some extent the television consciousness of parade spectators highlighted the drama. Two characteristics, implicit in the character of television as a medium rather than in the specific preconceptions of the spectators, enhanced the dramatic impact of the telecast and thus contributed to the misevaluation of public sentiment: the depiction of the ceremonies to a mass audience in terms of unifying rather than particularistic symbols, which allowed little room for dissent; and—a general characteristic of television—the enlargement of the viewer's field of vision without supplying a more accurate context for the interpretation of these events. Thus, the camera put the viewer in the center of the entire crowd, but, unlike the person on the scene, he could not interpret the meaning of crowd actions. He was at the mercy of the medium that controlled his

48. K. and G. E. Lang, "The Unique Perspective of Television and Its Effect: A Pilot Study," *American Sociological Review*, XVIII (February, 1953), pp. 3–12.

perceptions. He could not test his impressions—could not shove back the shover, inspect bystanders' views, or attempt in any way to affect the activity. The cameras following the general as he motored through Chicago transmitted a video image of a mass of humanity jostling to cheer him.

The average citizen and the politician, both of whom are sensitive to what they define as the public sentiment, do in fact see only a small segment of it. They nevertheless continuously make estimates of the true reading of public opinion. Actions and campaigns are supported by the support they seem to enjoy from others. If the public is quiescent, these others constitute at least an action potential that can be mobilized. The evaluation of the public temper therefore enters the total political situation as perhaps one of the weightiest factors. The most important single effect of the coverage of MacArthur was the image of support it conveyed to people who responded to it.

Recognition via the Mass Media

Recognition via the mass media changes the implications of an act. When an actor or some action is assumed to be in the purview of millions, this affects its significance even for the participants. Four illustrations of this form of legitimation follow.

THE TRANSFORMATION OF A POLITICAL HERO   Warner's study of Yankee City includes an account of the transformation of a lower-class maverick, pursuing a line of indiscriminate attacks against the "sacred symbols" of the upper-class Hill Street community. This transformation occurred, even in his home town, only after he received national recognition as a hero via the mass media. Biggy Muldoon's fight with Hill Street had earned him some notoriety in Yankee City. The fact that it was played before two audiences—the local citizens of Yankee City and, through the mass media, a national audience—meant that his actions had different meanings for the two audiences. For the local one, Biggy's antics were serious. While many people supported his fight against the snobbery of Hill Street, the future of political life in the city was involved. For the audience beyond Yankee City, he was a clown, ridiculing rigid moral beliefs and defying adult authorities, and thus his antics could be vicariously enjoyed without being taken too seriously.

Biggy, deciding to run for mayor of Yankee City, had placed an ad in a local newspaper, painting himself as a champion of the poor and appealing to their votes. Then, just before the election, the story was published in a Boston paper with Biggy's picture, recounting all the screwball things that had gained him local attention in the past: he had entertained motorists along the Yankee City Turnpike with displays of circus posters, imitation gravestones, and genuine oldfashioned chamber pots;

he had declared that when elected he would commit the police chief to an old men's home and designate the deputy chief official keeper. In all of this, he was carrying on a private feud with Hill Street, whose leaders had sought to prevent commercial use of a mansion he had bought in the upper-class residential neighborhood. With national attention Biggy became a different public symbol.

> Biggy the man remained largely the same, but Biggy the symbol went through mutations and elaborations that made him a national celebrity. Minor aspects of his public personality took new form and grew into dominant themes of the fabricated legend; soon the man Biggy was acting a new role before the new audience the mass authors had created . . . It was no longer easy for Biggy's enemies to ask rhetorical or satirical questions in the local press about his competence and know that the answers from the electorate would always be the ones they wanted . . . The local audience now read about Biggy in the metropolitan press [Half the papers sold in Yankee City came from outside metropolitan areas so that] what people thought and did was now determined somewhat by symbols coming from the outside world as well as from the local group.[49]

The stereotype created by the mass media and the real became one. Facts were fitted in with the stereotype. He was changed from a "bad" person to a "bad boy." The impressions of Biggy gathered at some distance from the mass media were "confirmed" by people's immediate experience. Elected mayor, Biggy continued to be a national figure. But when, later on, the metropolitan press became hostile to him, he suffered defeat at the polls. People's attitudes toward him were only partly determined by what he did locally. The new image was legitimated by the millions who presumably accepted the mass media stereotype.

THE HUNGARIAN REVOLUTION   During the Hungarian uprising against the Communist regime in 1956, statements broadcast by Western radio stations had a considerable influence in persuading Hungarian Freedom Fighters to keep up the fight and in inducing others to join the revolution.

> For the people of little Hungary [wrote Meray] the news that the United Nations might take their case was a powerful stimulant . . . The fact that the leaders and the press of the greatest countries in the West were rendering homage to the people of Hungary had an extraordinary effect on events. The mere possibility that the United Nations might put the

49. W. Lloyd Warner, *The Living and the Dead* (New Haven: Yale University Press, 1959), p. 61f.

Hungarian question on its agenda was taken as an assurance that this international organization would take Hungary under its protection.[50]

This is not to say that Western broadcasts provoked the uprising, which had many other causes. But there is ample evidence that among the various events that transformed a peaceful demonstration into an armed uprising, which was crushed only after the Russians moved in heavy tanks, the altogether mistaken notion that Security Council action meant intervention helped to buoy up Hungarian self-confidence. Whether they would have offered the same resistance against overwhelming odds they faced after the Russian intervention is, of course, a moot question.

THE BERLIN BLOCKADE   The way in which the mass media confer recognition on groups and thus make their action significant is even better documented by survey data obtained in Berlin during the Soviet blockade of 1948–1949. At the end of World War II the city of Berlin had been divided into four sectors, each administered by a different power. In June, 1948, the Russians, seeking to force the three Western powers to abandon Berlin, imposed a full blockade of the land and water routes that were the West's sources of supply to Berlin. According to W. Phillips Davison, who made an extensive study of it, the defeat of Soviet aims was due to two factors: the West succeeded in supplying the necessities of life to the people of Berlin, and the two million people crowded into West Berlin accepted—with very few and insignificant exceptions—the privations and resisted threats and enticements from the Russians, who completely surrounded them. Their conviction that they were making history was one of the major factors that induced the Berliners to hold fast. Largely as a result of exposure to Western-oriented mass media, Berliners came to feel that the whole free world was watching them. Day after day expressions of sympathy for Berlin and admiration for the Berliners were voiced in West Germany and throughout the free world. Throughout the blockade, but especially during its early days, non-Communist newspapers in the city devoted a large share of their space to these tributes.[51] As a consequence of the recognition of their efforts, Berliners felt that they were helping to restore the damaged reputation of Germany before the free world. By the prominence with which they featured a significant reference group, the press and the radio strengthened and reaffirmed the actions people were inclined to take. It does not follow, however, that the mass media necessarily reflected accurately the

50. Tibor Meray, *Thirteen Days That Shook the Kremlin* (New York: Frederick A. Praeger, Inc., 1959), p. 115f.

51. W. Phillips Davison, "Political Significance of Recognition via Mass Media— an Illustration from the Berlin Blockade," *Public Opinion Quarterly,* XX (Spring, 1956), p. 331.

degree of concern of the people in the West with Berlin, nor their willingness to alter their image of Germany.

COLLAPSE OF A STUDENT STRIKE   The mass media similarly speed the collapse of collective actions from which they withhold recognition. This occurred in Washington, D.C., when a segment of the population tried to resist the school desegregation policy enacted in response to the Supreme Court's decision. In October, 1954, groups of students in a number of schools in the nation's capital stayed away from classes, ostensibly to protest the transfer of Negroes into their schools. These demonstrations occurred in the fourth week of the semester after school authorities, encouraged by the complete lack of incidents up to then, had decided to speed the pace of desegregation.| Absenteeism reached an estimated peak of only 2,500, roughly 2.5 per cent of the school population, with most of it concentrated in about half the city's high schools and junior high schools. Classes continued to meet, and by the following week attendance was back to normal. The elementary schools remained completely unaffected.

The participants in the demonstration quite evidently had the approval of their parents. They expected support from their teachers. Furthermore, the students expected their demonstration to elicit support from the community; they believed that it would have some influence on policy.

Actually the Washington community, though a majority of its population continued to support segregation, reacted in a definitely negative manner. When Washington students began to stay away from classes, community leaders urged the local papers not to play up their activities and instead to treat the whole thing as a late summer lark. It was apparently these pleas that led the Washington papers to deglamorize the "strike," to pinpoint the small amount of absentees, to emphasize countermeasures taken to limit its spread, and to publicize the firm attitude of local officials. That the student strikers themselves were aware of the effect of press belittling upon their efforts was revealed in a spot survey. A large percentage of seventy-five students involved in the demonstration regarded the mass media as biased against them.

One can imagine the reaction of the champion of segregation upon returning home from his exploits to find himself portrayed in the evening newspaper as a child taking advantage of the nice weather to play hookey from school. The mass media's deglamorization of the demonstrations and the demonstrators no doubt played an important part in bringing home the futility of their efforts.[52]

52. Harold Mendelsohn, "The 'Student Strike' as a Social Psychological Reaction to Desegregation" (unpublished paper).

B I B L I O G R A P H Y

BERELSON, BERNARD, and JANOWITZ, MORRIS (eds.). *Reader in Public Opinion and Communication.* Glencoe, Ill.: The Free Press, 1953.

KATZ, DANIEL, *et al.* (eds.). *Public Opinion and Propaganda.* New York: The Dryden Press, Inc., 1954.

SCHRAMM, WILBUR (ed.). *Mass Communication.* Urbana, Ill.: The University of Illinois Press, 1960.

The three books above, readily available, contain representative readings about mass communication and mass communication research.

DEUTSCH, KARL W. *Nationalism and Social Communication.* Cambridge, Mass.: The Technology Press of the Massachusetts Institute of Technology and John Wiley & Sons, Inc., 1953. A serious, if not altogether successful, attempt to derive nationalism from the flow and distribution of information.

HOVLAND, CARL I. "Effects of the Media of Mass Communication," in *Handbook of Social Psychology,* ed. GARDNER LINDZEY. Cambridge, Mass.: Addison-Wesley Publishing Co., Inc., 1954, chapter 23. A review of the literature that emphasizes the experimental evidence.

INNIS, HAROLD A. *The Bias of Communication.* Toronto: University of Toronto Press, 1951. Selected papers by the Canadian economist on the relationship between the technology of communication and the forms of dominance.

KELLY, STANLEY. *Professional Public Relations and Political Power.* Baltimore: Johns Hopkins University Press, 1956. Several case studies of the techniques used in and the impact of campaigns on specific questions.

KLAPPER, JOSEPH T. "What We Know About the Effects of Mass Communication: The Brink of Hope," *Public Opinion Quarterly,* XXI (Winter, 1957–58), pp. 453–74. One of the most systematic formulations, based on recent research, about specific short-term effects of mass communication.

LAZARSFELD, PAUL F. "Communication Research and the Social Psychologist," *Current Trends in Social Psychology,* ed. WAYNE DENNIS. Pittsburgh: University of Pittsburgh Press. 1948, pp. 218–73. A summary of mass communication research which pays attention to both specific effects and cumulative impact of the communication system on the society.

Public Opinion Quarterly, XXIII (Spring, 1959). Contains a symposium on the current state of mass communication research by leading scholars in the field.

WIRTH, LOUIS. "Mass Communication and Consensus," *American Sociological Review,* XIII (February, 1948), pp. 1–14. A sociological discussion of the mass in relation to mass communication.

WRIGHT, CHARLES R. "Sociology of Mass Communication," in *Sociology in the United States of America: A Trend Report,* ed. HANS I. ZETTERBERG. Paris: UNESCO, 1956. Another review of the social impact of mass communication.

CHAPTER 15

Fashion: Identification and Differentiation in the Mass Society

WITHIN MODERN SOCIETY there is a segment of behavior and belief generally recognized as being under the sway of fashion. There are fashions in science and education no less than in styles of living; in art no less than in clothes and furnishings. But a definition of what fashion entails is more difficult than such denotative identification. To illustrate particular fashions or fashionable beliefs does not identify the basic nature of fashion per se.

When we call something a fashion, the judgment usually involves a bit of debunking. Pinning the fashion label on a cultural commodity is an effective, if roundabout, way of demoting it. The label suggests, first, that the commodity is *transitory*, not lasting or permanent. Second, its *novelty*—not any intrinsic rationality—governs its acceptance; the value of what is fashionable is independent of its rational utility. Third, the label suggests the *trivial*. Fashion is allowed free sway because it is assumed to move only within the limits of what is culturally approved. Traditional ways of doing things, institutionally accepted attitudes, ideas that matter are not affected, and thus individuals are free to indulge themselves in the marginal, and sometimes bizarre, vagaries that the world of fashion opens to them.

Fashion, then, connotes the transitory, the novel, the trivial. But the label also implies a force beyond individual control. Fashion is a collective creation. It is determined by what *they* say. The world of fashion is not so much available to people as imposed on them. In one way or another it dictates to everyone. It is contagious. Any individual or group may resist a particular fashion, but fashion, as such, cannot be resisted.

There is [according to Sumner] no arguing with fashion. . . . The authority of fashion is imperative as to everything which it touches. The sanctions are ridicule and powerlessness. The dissenter hurts himself; he never affects the fashion.[1]

The Power of Fashion

Fashion is here treated as an elementary form of collective behavior, whose compelling power lies in the implicit judgment of an anonymous multitude. This view is questioned by persons who point to a well-organized industry which, through its advertising campaigns, foists on a gullible public what one critic called "the overwhelming flood of cultural sewage that is manufactured especially for the taste of the lowbrow and middle-brow."[2] There are, of course, fashion industries and formal communication systems which promote the products of these industries. In view of this, can one call the sway of fashion spontaneous?

It is a basic question whether public taste is first manufactured and then disseminated through organized channels and foisted upon the mass *or* whether changes in the moods and life conditions lead to irrational and widespread changes of taste even without promotion. To what extent the tastemakers merely cater to the changing whims of the great public and to what extent they manipulate changes which are thereafter legitimated by mass acceptance will be illustrated by reference to the "New Look."

THE NEW LOOK: AN EXAMPLE

The collective resistance to the New Look in 1947 is often cited as an example of the limits beyond which women will not be dictated to by fashion. Actually the natural history of the New Look provides a first-rate illustration of the compelling nature of fashion innovation.

The Fashion Is Planted

The New Look involved two major changes in women's dress: the shape was to be radically altered, and the skirt noticeably lengthened. According to fashion publicists, after two decades of the "American Look," marked by slim hips, casual appearance, reasonably short skirts, etc., the female was to cloak herself in hourglass fashion: round shoulders

1. William Graham Sumner, *Folkways* (Boston: Ginn & Company, 1906), p. 194.
2. Winthrop Sargeant, *Life,* XXVI (April 11, 1949), p. 102.

(no more exaggerated padding), sucked-in wasp waist, and, most important, very long skirt.

This new round-shouldered, hourglass fashion, like other major style innovations, was planted. "Months ago," wrote *The New York Times* on September 7, 1947, "the Western world learned that skirts this autumn would be full and longer, hips padded, waists waspishly thin, shoulders daintily rounded . . ." Among the style planners or norm creators responsible were "a bunch of Paris and New York designers," the custom designers, like Christian Dior, Sophie Gimbel, and Hardy Amies. The first to adopt the New Look were the chic clientele of these designers. Thereafter the fashion received public legitimation by those who customarily are named best-dressed women by the style planners and the style communicators. It was legitimated also by royalty and Hollywood movie stars, who traditionally have acted as style leaders and thereby give something in the nature of official status to projected fashion innovations. For instance, Princess Elizabeth of England was reported to be ordering her wedding trousseau in calf-length skirts.

The New Look also had to be disseminated to a wider audience. A full-scale, well-organized publicity campaign aimed at familiarizing people everywhere with the New Look well ahead of the time dresses in the style were available for sale in stores catering to the general trade. First, there had to be pictures. Women not only had to hear about the New Look; they had also to see it. The first to wear a new fashion are not necessarily the members of the smart international set who order from the top couturiers. Mass fashions are "tested" by professional *modistes* who appear at racetracks, theaters, parties, and other public gatherings to display newly created apparel. *Vogue* and *Harper's Bazaar* featured the New Look, and by the time it reached other magazines of the fashion press—*Mademoiselle, Seventeen, etc.*—the New Look seemed familiar indeed.

Publicity and production must go hand in hand. Through their advance publicity, volume manufacturers, who had secured models from Paris, assured themselves of a demand for the new models. Newspaper ads for the smarter stores began to feature the change. *Women's Wear Daily*, the garment trade paper, began to talk of the new styling, and style consultants for the small shops and large department stores everywhere catering to mass taste began to order the new dresses.

In other words, the New Look was promoted and sold to the public through certain tested and well-organized channels. These networks of communication existed long before the New Look and would long survive it. Through them, the New Look was planted. The change in styling was the initial result of an idea germinated in the fashion industry and nourished by publicity and organization.

The New Look Meets Resistance

How strong was collective opposition to the proposed change? Newspapers and magazines publicized the advent of the change, but it was dramatized even more by the isolated instances of organized resistance reported concurrently. College students protested to the New York Dress Institute. A rumor had it that the J. Arthur Rank Organization in England would continue to dress its film stars in short skirts. *Time* (September, 1947) said: "The furor over the new fashions rose to a fine, shrill pitch. Across the land, women by the *hundreds* (sic)—and city editors too—flocked to the banners of resistance." Most publicized was the resistance of a group of women in Dallas, Texas, who demonstrated against the new style. According to one report (*Collier's*, October 11, 1947), thirteen hundred women in that city "formed the 'Little Below the Knee Club,' sworn to hold the hemline at that elevation . . ." Meanwhile a legislator in Georgia announced that he would soon introduce a bill banning long skirts. That summer of 1947 the polls showed that a majority of American women disliked the new styles—but would wear them anyway.

The most singular, and certainly the most drastic, effort to halt the New Look occurred in England. In September, 1947, the Labour government was reportedly considering a decree governing the length of women's skirts. The postwar period found Britain continuing some of its rationing restrictions to regulate the use of scarce materials and to fight the black market and inflation. Moreover, England was hoping to promote its export market and achieve a more favorable balance of trade. Behind the opposition to the fashion innovation was the legal force of government.

> Here is a puzzle. Can Sir Stafford Cripps (or anyone else) prevent women's skirts being longer if Fashion decrees that they shall be? That the ruling [Fashion's ruling for the New Look] is idiotic and anti-social at a time when we need to save every yard of material is obvious. Nor does anyone, outside the trade, want skirts longer. Men find short skirts more comely than the half-length style that flops around the woman's calf. Women find the short skirt much more comfortable and women's organizations in America and Paris are protesting against the dictatorship of Paris . . . Anyway, whatever the reason, I find no one bets on Sir Stafford winning this battle if he engages in it. You may plan peace and war, but women's clothes are like the weather—beyond the control of government.[3]

3. Critic (pseudonym), *New Statesman and Nation*, XXXIV (September 20, 1947), p. 225.

What resistance developed outside official government undoubtedly was not a matter of dwindling national dollar reserves. Nor was it a matter of taste or a deliberate effort to resist the crowd. An English girl summed up the dilemma common to women everywhere:

> . . . I know from daily contact with working girls who take a pride in their clothes, that they are thrown into a quandary. I heard one of them saying, "I don't know whether to try to scrounge a lot of coupons [rationing] and sell off my clothes or just appear dowdy." [4]

She went on to cite George Orwell's observation that fashions, by making working girls almost indistinguishable from the wealthy, were helping to break down class barriers. Might not the New Look, she asked, in this period of scarcity and hardship, again widen the gulf between the classes?

While there was some annoyance and concern over the command to change wardrobes and isolated, if well-publicized, instances of deliberate opposition, the New Look caught on and had a lasting effect on women's dress styles. If by the season of 1948, one year after the New Look was "sweeping the country," most skirts did not quite reach the decreed ten or eleven inches from the floor, they were nevertheless considerably nearer the floor than they had been for decades. Also gone were the huge padded, mannish shoulders which had so long seemed natural to women.

We have, then, to account for the success of the New Look by considering two aspects of fashion change: first, why women everywhere conform to a change and, second, why there is any change at all. Consideration of both may clarify what is meant by the "compelling nature of fashion."

The Compelling Nature of Fashion

The fashion world plans and makes available clothes, and, where the major source of supply is ready-made, women must for practical reasons go along. Yet to follow a major change in fashion means for most women a complete turnover in wardrobe. Had women everywhere in 1947 simply replenished their current wardrobes, bought one new dress or one new suit, this would not have constituted a major turnover in fashion. If fashion were a mere caprice in what is available, the styles of yesteryear would not be altogether inappropriate after the change. For instance, when the sack dress, the trapeze, and the chemise were promoted in 1957, many women bought one of the new creations, but the older, more

4. Letter to the Editor, *New Statesman and Nation,* XXXIV (October 4, 1947), p. 270.

closely fitted dresses did not thereby seem inappropriate. It is unlikely that any, save the most modish, felt compelled to discard or alter entire wardrobes. Fashion induces a change in mass taste. The short skirt, which one season seems esthetic and appropriate, comes to look ugly and out of place—somehow improper.

In this context, we are using taste to designate the subjective preference for which there are no objective standards. We are not concerned here with esthetic judgment—that is, with the cultivation in the individual of a standard of beauty and truth which secures the gentleman, the scholar, and the esthete from the influences of the vulgar. Fashion is a collective phenomenon and has an objective existence apart from any individual. It makes attractive what often seems outrageous and bizarre to the preceding generation as well as the next. The standard set by fashion is, according to Sapir, "accepted by average people with little demur and is not so much reconciled with taste as substituted for it." [5] In the mass, most are "average," and taste becomes what fashion is all about. Taste implies a purely subjective judgment with which there is no arguing, but esthetic judgment requires a certain consistency with esthetic principles as well as an evaluation of the functional relevance of an object.

How the fashion process operates to produce a simultaneous change in the personal taste of individuals all over is well illustrated in this letter by an American returning in 1947 to the United States after a year abroad:

> At every airport where we stopped on the way back from China I started watching the women coming the other way. At Calcutta the first long skirt and unpadded shoulders looked like something out of a masquerade party. At the American installations in Frankfurt (also in Vienna) a lot of the newer arrivals were converted and were catching everyone's attention. At the airport in Shannon I had a long wait; I got into a conversation with a lady en route to Europe. She was from San Francisco, and told me that there they still hadn't been completely won over—just as many were wearing the long skirts as not. But as she flew East, she found that just about everybody in New York had gone in for the new styles and she was happy she wasn't staying or her wardrobe would have been dated. By the time I took the train from New York for home, my short skirts felt conspicuous and my shoulders seemed awfully wide! Two weeks now and I am letting down hems, trying to figure out which of all my China-made clothes can be salvaged, and going on a buying spree!

The operations of the bandwagon and the way in which it snowballs are well illustrated. When the first few fashion leaders adopt a new style,

5. Edward Sapir, "Fashion," *Encyclopedia of the Social Sciences* (New York: The Macmillan Co., 1931), VI, pp. 139–44.

they identify themselves as members of an elite apart from the rest of the world. In this age of rapid communication, the news of their adoptions soon spreads and helps to make the new mode familiar. The first few to dress in it are objects of interest and excitement; they are different, strange. A few more follow, impelled to be *à la mode* by the need to assert their difference from those less fashionable. The bandwagon is gradually on and soon it begins to roll. In the end no one can afford to be different. The final blow comes when the woman standing aside appears ridiculous even to herself. "They" are no longer odd; she herself is. Popular taste, even one's own, has changed. But in the meantime the fashion innovators may already be striking out in new directions.

Thus, the collective change in taste—an objective trend—is dictated not by an organized fashion industry but by the nature of fashion itself. The essence of fashion lies in its caprice: the transitory shift in some trivial area toward novelty for the sake of novelty. Fashion, then, is a process by which the taste of a mass of people is collectively redefined.

FASHION, CUSTOM, STYLE

NOT ONLY have the times to suit a change, but the particular change has to meet the demands of the times. Hence, life conditions are not entirely unrelated to fashion changes. In connection with the New Look, it is relevant to note that uniforms and uniformity had been a way of life during the war. In England there had been mass production of one-style utility dresses, utility shoes, and other garments, to be had only in exchange for rationing coupons. This meant that people wore uniforms even as civilians. After the war ended, matériel shortages necessitated continuation of rationing in clothing. There had also been a need to "pull together" during the war. For a brief time after the armistice, the camaraderie gained in air raid shelters, the spirit of mutual effort, the impelling breakdowns in class barriers, and other unifying forces, carried over from the wartime period, continued to exert their influence. But as the sense of danger passed, the spirit of competition and individual aggrandizement began once more to dominate the economy. The New Look, with its accent on "the illusion of being different," fitted the changing temper of the times.

Whenever a fashion has met the mood of the public and fitted its way of life, neither religious or legal decrees against it have succeeded. Indeed, some "fashion" changes are cues that major social changes are occurring. A major fashion change no longer concerns merely the trivial. Its appeal is more lasting and does not rest on novelty alone.

It is the visible sign that a transformation is taking place in the intellect, customs, and business of people . . . Taine wrote this profound sally: "My decided opinion is that the greatest change in history was the advent of trousers . . . It marked the passage of Greek and Roman civilization to the modern . . . Nothing is more difficult to alter than a universal and daily custom. In order to take away man's clothes and dress him up again you must demolish and remodel him.[6]

There is something to fashion besides the subjective judgments of individuals. The movement of fashion marks a trend in the collective definitions of taste, which can be objectively charted, like the ups and downs of hemlines or the use of certain layouts in homes. But certain other objective patterns that are clearly not fashion also affect the design of apparel and homes. It is necessary to distinguish the influence of custom and style from that of fashion.

FASHION AND CUSTOM

What identifies fashion is its novelty value, its seeming departure from custom. Fashion, Sapir tells us, is "the legitimate caprice of custom"; it is custom in the guise of departure from custom.[7] In going along with fashion, we deny the oldfashioned; what counts against the latter is its age. But custom completely lacks novelty value. It is age that legitimates custom. Custom is time-honored rather than fashionable and is passed down from generation to generation.

The word custom is used to apply to the totality of behavior patterns which are carried by tradition and lodged in the group . . . Custom is often used interchangeably with convention, tradition and mores, but the connotations are not quite the same . . . Such terms as custom, institution, convention, tradition and mores are, however, hardly capable of a precise scientific definition. All of them are reducible to *social habit* or, if one prefers the anthropological to the psychological point of view, to *cultural pattern*.[8]

Custom is universal to the group. Everybody conforms to custom, and custom is necessary if a group is to function as a group. It constitutes the body of common understandings that survive the individual members and sets off one group from another in the larger society. Members of any collectivity reassert their in-groupness, or solidarity, each day as they

6. Pierre Clerget, "The Economic and Social Role of Fashion," *The Annual Report of the Smithsonian Institution,* Washington, D.C., 1914, p. 763.

7. Sapir, *op. cit.,* p. 140.

8. Edward Sapir, "Custom," *Encyclopedia of the Social Sciences,* IV, p. 658.

adhere to the ways of doing things that are traditional to their way of life. But in fashion people exercise their personal option in areas that do not fundamentally matter to set themselves apart. However compelling a fashion change appears, it is in the last analysis a matter of taste.

Consider the matter of men's clothing. An officer of the Federal Reserve Bank, asked what was adequate compensation for wearing his wife's hat to the office some morning, first answered, "Fifty thousand dollars." Then, after thinking it over for a moment, he said, "it would have to be as much as he could expect to earn the rest of his life, since afterward he could never expect to hold a position of financial responsibility again; and in the end he concluded that no price would be enough for the loss of prestige entailed." [9] That a man should wear a man's hat rather than a woman's is not a matter of fashion; it is a matter of custom. It is part of the social heritage, and for society at large it is not a trivial or laughing matter. We can be quite certain that the banker never once entertained the thought that he might choose to wear his wife's hat anywhere (save a masquerade party), let alone to his place of work. Were some men to start wearing women's hats, the group would somehow feel threatened. The established order of things would have been questioned; the individual deviant would be punished or quickly diverted.

Fashion operates without disrupting group unity so long as capricious deviation from customary norms occurs *within* the framework of the larger body of mores and does not offend. Through adherence to fashion, individuals legitimate and indulge their need for personal deviation without either risking ostracism or threatening group solidarity. It provides them with the illusion of being different. But fashion differs from custom in that it affects only those areas of life that are both trivial and peripheral. Fashion is not so much significant to our day-to-day experience as functionally irrelevant. Mass deviations from custom are permissible as long as they leave untouched the central ethos of the culture. Sapir tells us that there is a "reconciliation of individual freedom with social conformity which is implicit in the very fact of fashion." [10] We are not fundamentally in revolt from custom but we have a yen to break away just a bit. In fashion there can be found certain accepted ways of revolt.

Many speak of fashions in thought, art, habits of living and morals. It is superficial to dismiss such locutions as metaphorical and unimportant. The usage shows a true intuition of the meaning of fashion, which while it is primarily applied to dress and the exhibition of the human body

9. Agnes B. Young, *Recurring Cycles of Fashion* (New York: Harper & Brothers, 1937), p. 187f.
10. Sapir, "Fashion," *op. cit.*, p. 140.

is not essentially concerned with the fact of dress or ornament but with its symbolism. There is nothing to prevent a thought, a type of morality or an art form from being the psychological equivalent of a costuming of the ego. Certainly one may allow oneself to be converted to Catholicism or Christian Science in exactly the same spirit in which one invests in pewter or follows the latest Parisian models in dress. Beliefs and attitudes are not fashions in their character of mores but neither are dress and ornament. In contemporary society it is not a fashion that men wear trousers; it is the custom. Fashion merely dictates such variations as whether trousers are to be so or so long, what colors they are to have and whether they are to have cuffs or not. In the same way, while adherence to a religious faith is not in itself a fashion, as soon as the individual feels that he can pass easily, out of personal choice, from one belief to another, not because he is led to his choice by necessity but because of a desire to accrete to himself symbols of status, it becomes legitimate to speak of his change of attitude as a change of fashion. *Functional irrelevance* as contrasted with symbolic significance for the expressiveness of the ego is implicit in all fashion.[11]

FASHION AND STYLE

Style, like fashion, refers to matters of taste, except that "style doesn't change every month or every year. It only changes as often as there is a real change in the point of view and the lives of the people for whom it is produced." [12] Style is the characteristic or distinctive mode of expression, the prevailing taste in some field of art or in artifacts, that reflects the outlook either of some person or group of persons. One can define style as the *permanent element in fashion.* Although the actual changes seem to occur rapidly, suddenly, and dramatically, the style of life changes only over longer periods. It reflects a secular change.

Hence, fashions are not really innovations but recurrent deviations. They are not so much born as rediscovered.[13] The cyclical nature of fashion, the tendency of many fashions to repeat themselves at intervals, has been documented in a number of studies of women's apparel, music, and even hog "styles." [14] Among the most careful documentations of the long-term cyclical nature of fashion is Kroeber's work (some of it in

11. *Ibid.,* p. 143f.

12. Elizabeth Hawes, *Fashion Is Spinach* (New York: Grosset & Dunlap, Inc., 1940), p. 5.

13. Rolf Meyersohn and Elihu Katz, "Notes on a Natural History of Fads," *American Journal of Sociology,* LXII (May, 1957), p. 597.

14. *Ibid.,* p. 598. See, in addition to Kroeber cited below, particularly Young, *op. cit.*

collaboration with Richardson).[15] He used the change in the length and width of skirts in full-dress toilette from 1844 to 1919. The duration of any one phase in a cycle was found too long to be attributed to the influence of any one designer. Major changes occurred as social conditions changed and generations succeeded one another. Some fashions (or fads) follow shorter cycles; for example, the reblossoming of fake flowers seems to follow a seven-year cycle.[16] Popular tunes seem to be revived after approximately twenty years. In 1957 many of the "new" popular songs were revivals of popular tunes from the 1930's and some from the 1920's. They were old enough to have a nostalgic, not deadening, effect on the older members of the population and to be really new for young people. When fashions are old enough to be new, they may be born again.

Finally, fashion involves fairly minor changes in taste. Its cyclical movement is confined by the prevailing style. But the concrete relationship between style changes and fashion changes needs study. One may suddenly discover that an accretion of apparently minor alterations has produced a major change in style. For instance, women's dress in the Western world today expresses a style basically different from that fifty years ago, a change that can be traced directly to the "Roaring Twenties." American couturier Norman Norell wrote:

> Women are still wearing, and throughout this century will continue to wear changes that came about in the Twenties: short hair; interesting make-up; red, red lips; the basic black dress (before the Twenties black was worn only for mourning); the color beige; fake jewelry; short skirts; plain pumps for daytime; nude stockings, and gloves that pull on easily. These are just a few of the things that were launched in the Twenties.
>
> Clothes also became easy and comfortable for the first time. They were loose and sexy and a woman could relax, untrammeled by rigid bones, stays and long skirts. What's more, she could go from morning to dinner without changing.[17]

Since the middle and upper as well as the lower classes now go into the world and work, the styling of woman's clothes has to emphasize not

15. The classic work by Alfred L. Kroeber is "On the Principle of Order in Civilization as Exemplified by Changes in Fashion," *American Anthropologist*, XXI (1919), pp. 235–63. Also Jane Richardson and Alfred L. Kroeber, *Three Centuries of Women's Dress Fashions: A Quantitative Analysis*, University of California, Anthropological Records, V, No. 2, 1940.

16. *The New York Times*, March 29, 1957, fashions page.

17. "Four Inside Views of Fashion," *The New York Times Magazine*, June 19, 1960, p. 20.

only esthetic but practical needs. The style limits the fashions that may be reborn; corsets that inhibit breathing, skirts that sweep the floor, hair that requires hours of arranging, etc., can return only when the prevailing style of life changes.[18] At the same time, the prevailing taste for practical clothes, in which women may live from morning through evening, can be attributed to the many small fashion changes that have come through the years—including quick drying, little-iron fabrics, a lack of frou-frou, etc.

THE REALM OF FASHION

The fashion process is the manner in which new fashions are born (or revived) and spread in mass society. What kinds of idea, what ways of doing things, what among the objects we buy, what activities are subject to the whims of fashion? What are the areas in which custom leaves an area of tolerance, and when does this tolerance evolve into a compulsion to conform to a new pattern?

The fashion process operates in many areas where the choices made are not functionally relevant to some goal or purpose to be achieved. Nystrom, discussing the economics of fashion in women's clothes, has talked about *taste* as the "ability to discern and appreciate what is *beautiful* and *appropriate*." [19] But what is beautiful and what is appropriate are always matters of judgment and subject to qualification. One can judge what is beautiful and appropriate at a given time and place only from certain standards. Absolute standards of beauty and fitness, however, are seldom attainable; there can be no objective test for them.

This applies to many areas other than feminine dress. It applies equally, for example, to the feminine face and feminine contours. Over the years the average contestant in the Atlantic City beauty pageant has changed in height, hair style, weight, general facial features, and body contours. Was the standard of 1924 right and is the present one misguided? In international contests does one judge among Miss China, Miss Sweden, and Miss Togoland by Caucasion standards of good looks? Or, to take another example, it may be appropriate to wear a tie when teaching a college class, but how can we demonstrate the wearing of a tie to be really "proper"? As William Graham Sumner pointed out long ago, fashion operates where there can be no proof of validity. Because of this, one can only deprecate but not argue with legitimate fashion.

18. In 1960 elaborate hair styles taking little time were made possible through the popularization of wigs and hairpieces. Women could change their hair style as quickly as they could change from one wig to another.

19. Paul Henry Nystrom, *Economics of Fashion* (New York: The Ronald Press Company, 1928), p. 3.

. . . they [certain rules of conduct] are fashions because they are arbitrary, have no rational grounds, cannot be put to any test, and have no sanction except that everybody submits to them.[20]

Nor do fashion changes depend on manipulation. The fact that wearing apparel, particularly women's, is used so often to illustrate the fashion process has focused attention on the network of communication through which fashions are produced and promoted. Where these networks exist, they do of course permit, within certain limits, manipulation of the mass by organized interests. But control over what is made available on the market and use of the mass media to stimulate consumer demand are not indispensable to the fashion process. Fashion often is in evidence even where there is no organization of this kind, though it probably diffuses more slowly.

We have found no evidence, for example, that fashions in given names are deliberately promoted. Among the names most common to girls born in Boston in the seventeenth century were Hannah, Abigail, Mehitabel, Bethiah, and Dorcas. Also fairly common were the "meaningful" names of abstract qualities: Mercy, Thankful, Desire, and the like.[21] How many Mehitabels and Mercys do we find now? Certainly very few. Names given babies change even from year to year, and one can sometimes mark a man's age by his given name. Nor is this simply a matter of infants bearing names like Franklin D. Roosevelt Jones, as in the popular song.

The suggestion is often made that just as in an earlier period names were strongly influenced by patriotic figures, so they now are influenced by the celebrities of screen, radio, and athletics. Undoubtedly there is some such influence but it is not so strong as to be easily demonstrated statistically. *Gone With the Wind* was the most read book of the nineteen-thirties, and its two chief feminine characters bore the curious names Scarlett and Melanie. One can now find a few girls bearing these names, but they have certainly not seriously affected our name pattern. Since actors and actresses often take stage names, the reasoning, in fact, often has to be reversed. An actress' name may rise to sudden popularity, not because babies are named after her, but because she herself took the name that was becoming fashionable. The same may be said for heroes and heroines of novels and plays.[22]

What makes names in general—not any particular name—subject to fashion? In the matter of names, as in all fashion, one can be different but

20. Sumner, *op. cit.*, p. 195.
21. George Stewart, *American Ways of Life* (Garden City, N.Y.: Doubleday & Company, Inc., 1954), pp. 210–11.
22. *Ibid.*

not too different. Stewart points to a tendency for the total number of given names in circulation to increase. New names are manufactured, while old ones are revived along with the new.

> . . . the commonest way of manufacturing a name is to take elements of established names. Thus there are a number of suffixes that indicate or suggest a feminine ending. Here we have -ie, -etta, -ene, -illa, -elle. Then the name manufacturer may select the first part of some standard name, and thus produce Kathetta, Marilla, or Elizene.[23]

Not all social circles participate equally in this game of invention. At one time it was thought to be a peculiarity among Negroes. By now it has been fairly well established that the practice is most typical of those sometimes called "poor whites" and those slightly above them on the social and economic scale. At the other extreme, the Blue Book circles of New York City also make use of it. Fashion innovation in its most extreme and bizarre forms is usually found among those who can afford to be different and those who have something to gain by it. A fashion, once established, is followed by those in-between, the middle classes, whose sensitivity to the mode makes them the mainstay of most fashion movements.

Even science is not altogether exempt from fashion. Medical practice has its fads. Within the last few decades, science writers have successively hailed as keys to the cure of mental disease electro-shock therapy, brain operations (lobotomies), and tranquilizing drugs. Tranquilizers can become fashionable among noninstitutionalized persons as well as in therapy. Yet, the hold of fashion in science is shaky, for the appropriateness of drugs, operations, or shock treatments is subject to empirical test. Fashion holds sway only in those circles where, instead of relying on evidence, the general taste is followed. Once an objectively validated answer is widely available, a standard set by fashion will no longer be acceptable.

The area subject to fashion, though limited, includes all those market decisions in which individual preferences are reflected and those of others affirmed or rejected. That there are fashions of saving or spending has been shown in a study of war bonds.[24] The injunction to honor thy

---

23. *Ibid.*

24. George Katona, *Psychological Analysis of Economic Behavior* (New York: McGraw-Hill Book Co., 1951), p. 79. ". . . during the war most people knew that other people—their neighbors, friends, and colleagues—were buying war bonds, were saving part of their income, or were abstaining from spending in one or the other respect. There was hardly any such verbal expression as 'spending a lot of money is out of place during the war,' but it appeared that the accepted pattern of behavior, the one which represented climbing on the band wagon, was represented by buying war bonds or putting money in the bank. This was, for most people, not frugality . . . as spending reached record levels."

mother may become unfashionable in some circles as too much honoring induces suspicions of mother-fixation. Modes of expression, even the modulation of one's voice and certainly the whole code of manners, can enter into fashion. Individual preferences may be conscious efforts to satisfy one's own esthetic, intellectual, creative, social, or medical needs; that is, an individual may be deliberately pursuing the taste he has developed. But the choices are not derived from esthetic or scientific principles. They express a need for individuation without the risk of group disapproval. By adopting what is fashionable, one identifies with a group. By being ahead of others in one's adoption, it is possible to succeed in standing out in a group and yet be reaffirming its collective preferences.

FASHION AND SOCIAL STRUCTURE

THE MOTIVES of those who innovate a fashion are quite different from the motives of those who follow. "The essence of fashion consists in that it is practised by only a part of the group, but that the totality should just be on the way to it." [25] Because the appeal of fashion depends primarily on novelty, it must always, as the novelty fades, fasten on new patterns.

A classic picture of the diffusion of a fashion is set forth in the writings of Thorstein Veblen. A fashion, he held, usually begins with the adoption of innovations by members of the leisure class who have money. Some fashions are attractive for no other reason than their great expense. The dresses custom-made in the great fashion houses command exorbitant prices not only because they are in great demand and thus scarce; their fantastic price itself contributes to the demand. The style itself is less important than the need to consume what is dear and therefore a mark of prestige. Only a fresh supply of "Veblenish" models can keep pace with the demand.

This "Veblen" effect [26] is effective only among the fashion leaders, who are then emulated by the socially ambitious middle classes. After being taken up by the latter, the fashion trickles down to the broad masses until cheap imitations bring it within the range of everyone. The diffusion of the fashion immediately means its depreciation as a symbol for invidious comparison. A copy indistinguishable from the original is still not an original. Once machine-made replicas of the latest mode are offered to the mass at reasonable prices, the patterns themselves lose in

25. Georg Simmel, "Die Mode," *Philosophische Kultur. Gesammelte Essais* (Leipzig: Kroner, 1919), p. 41.

26. H. Leibenstein, "Bandwagon, Snob, and Veblen Effects in the Theory of Consumers' Demand," *Quarterly Journal of Economics*, LXIV (1950), pp. 183–207.

value. The upper classes also abandon any area as a means of displaying their status when the status symbols become too popular and too widely available.

> Just as soon as the lower classes begin to copy their style, thereby crossing the line of demarcation the upper classes have drawn and destroying the uniformity of their coherence, the upper classes turn away from this style and adopt a new one, which in its turn differentiates them from the masses: and thus the game goes merrily on.[27]

A "snob" effect works against universal adoption of a fashion and thus counteracts the bandwagon effect which induces women to follow along. Among some groups, demand for a fashion decreases precisely because others share in it. The first to accept a new fashion are therefore also the first to abandon it as soon as too many others have accepted it. An extreme example of this is the deliberate effort on the part of some to be indifferent to fashion.

IDENTIFICATION AND DIFFERENTIATION

Whatever the diverse private motives that induce conformity to fashion, *social* valuations are essential. The movement of fashion exemplifies the basic collective process of definition. Each individual seeks the security that comes from conforming and knowing where he belongs as well as distinction from among his fellow men. Fashion satisfies both. Simmel wrote:

> Two social tendencies are essential to the establishment of fashion, namely the need for union on the one hand, the need for isolation on the other. Should one of these be absent, fashion will not be formed—its sway will abruptly end.[28]

Fashion becomes more significant as a means of identification and differentiation when social contacts are secondary, fleeting, and relatively anonymous, and when individuals are only partially integrated in specific associations but react as part of a larger mass. Hence, individuals are more concerned with the appropriateness of their behavior and, at the same time, less certain of what is appropriate. The styles that become fashions—in dress, in housing, in consumption pattern, in art—are short cuts through which one's place in a large and diffuse status system is easily recognized, even on casual contact.

Where custom rules and the society is clearly stratified, people learn

27. Georg Simmel, "Fashion," *The American Journal of Sociology*, LXII (May, 1957), p. 545.
28. *Ibid.*, p. 546.

how to dress, express themselves, behave, and think as befits their station. A highly regimented society might institutionalize dress (and other areas in which fashion reigns) and freeze class divisions. In such a society, uniforms serve important functions. For some, they are means of binding anxiety as well as testimonials of status. They show that a person belongs and differentiate him from those who do not. The wearing of uniforms is one way of ruling out fashion. Yet where masses of people are forced to wear the same uniform and still seek distinction, fashion has a way of reasserting itself. American soldiers in World War II took to wearing a variety of colored scarves, while members of the British Desert Army adopted corduroy pants, suede shoes, scarves, and fly-switches as their distinguishing apparel.

The individual choices through which individuals seek to identify themselves result in some patterning of public preferences. The fashion movements describe long-run definitions and redefinitions about what is proper and right, whether it be a product, a given name, a magazine, an educational theory, etc. To the individual this choice is a very personal thing. It is a symbol of the ego, the core of the self, his social personality. Even an unimportant individual, by his fashion, becomes the representative of a joint spirit. Hence, broad fashion movements depend on the existence of social democracy in some form. On the other hand, it is sometimes suggested that the increasing emphasis on social conformity and standardization of products will immunize the mass society to fashion. The next section, in particular, takes up the relation of the mass market to fashion.

THE MARKET AND FASHION MOVEMENTS

According to a theory now abandoned, fashion movements were believed to be closely connected with the business cycle. Especially during periods of depression, it was said, lively fashions served to compensate for the drabness of human existence generally. Women's fashions, if nothing else, would at least reintroduce gaiety. Young's study, however, found no consistent relationship between women's dress and the ups and downs of the business cycle,[29] and what the theory claimed for the feminine mode cannot even be claimed for other areas of fashion.

Fashion movements are much better understood in relation to broad changes in the market than to simple fluctuations in business activity. There has been a major change in the American market over the last few decades. Marketing men in the 1920's, according to the editors of *Fortune*,

divided all consumers into two groups, the "class" and the "mass" market. The "class" market consisted of the very wealthy and some-

29. Young, *op. cit.*

what less wealthy, who could buy almost offhandedly all the comforts and luxuries of life, including the time of numerous menials; the "mass" market consisted of the remainder, some of whom were just beginning to buy the durables that are now commonplace.[30]

Today, they continue, the great "mass" has been converted into a new moneyed middle class which seems destined, sooner or later, to become *the* American market. The graduated income tax and excess profits taxes limit "class," while social security, social services, and lack of immigration delimit "mass." Where fashion once served above all to conserve the pre-eminence of class over mass, the various consumption patterns now in fashion help primarily to bring into being and to sort out new groupings who share, not a similar socioeconomic status, but similar taste. The differentiation is not so much in terms of class but from a mass that has been leveled in certain respects.

This growth of the middle-class market in many areas has not altogether negated the "trickle-down" theory of fashion change. Although now differentiated less clearly by their fabulous wealth from the bulk of the middle classes, there are still upper-class fashion leaders. What has changed is the rate at which a new fashion diffuses and this, in turn, has affected the way the fashion game is played. The middle class has always been the true carrier of fashion.[31] Emulation of the upper classes is imperative if the middle classes are to maintain their separateness from the lower classes, out of which many have risen. But the advance of so many into the middle class has put more purchasing power where it can be effectively used to follow fashion by a class ordinarily most susceptible to it. The increase in demand brings about keener competition and hence more rapid dissemination and quicker succession of fashions. To keep up with changing fashion entails great expense.

Still, the increasing cost of fashion has not led to its abandonment, the claims of the popular press notwithstanding. It does mean, however, that differences in class and, to some degree, in income now express themselves somewhat less in novelty than in unique and individual styling, in the quality of workmanship, in the appropriateness of dress for a variety

30. Editors of *Fortune, The Changing American Market* (Garden City, N.Y.: Hanover House, 1955), p. 15.

31. Simmel, *op. cit.* See also Nancy K. Jack and Betty Schiffer, "Limits of Fashion Control," *American Sociological Review*, XIII (December, 1948), pp. 730–38. In this attempt (inspired by the advent of the New Look) to investigate the limits within which fashion designers must remain if they are to be followed, the authors point out that at the "middle level" skirt lengths were more extreme (longer or shorter) than at the "top level" or among "average women." This seems to be empirical corroboration that the middle classes are least resistant to the demands of fashion.

of occasions. The upper classes still differentiate themselves from those below them in many subtle ways. Visitors to the United States comment publicly on how well dressed even the ordinary working girl *appears*.[32] The development of cheap synthetic fibers has further contributed to this trend. Fine materials and workmanship, rather than novelty, have become the true marks of the "fashionable."

The stepped-up pace of communication and the quick adaptation of the clothing industry to any shift have also made fashion more important in other areas of life. To the extent that one cannot readily distinguish the fashion worn by Mrs. Astor from that worn by the girl in the typing pool, novelty in dress has been de-emphasized. But fashions in hair styles, furnishings, music and art, houses, recreation and resorts, have become more important. Some of these are beyond the means of even the new middle-class market. Therefore, the realm in which an individual feels subject to the dictates of fashion now seems a more meaningful hallmark of class in the mass society than do the externals of dress.

Class, Status, and Taste

Stratification—that is, the ranking of individuals in a hierarchical order—may be based on a number of criteria. Following Max Weber, one usually speaks of "class stratification" if the ranking is based on the person's relation to production and determines his potential for acquiring material wealth. One speaks of a "status system" when a society is "stratified according to the principles of their consumption of goods as represented by special 'styles of life.' "[33] Every system of social stratification is related to consumption patterns, but it is possible that either production orientations (class) or consumption orientations (status) predominate. Very little can be said as to the general economic conditions that make for a predominance of stratification by "status."

> When the bases of the acquisition and distribution of goods are relatively stable, stratification by status is favored. Every technological repercussion and economic transformation threatens stratification by status and pushes class situation into the foreground. Epochs and countries in which the naked class situation is of predominant significance are regularly the periods of technical and economic transformations. And every slowing down of the shifting of economic stratification leads, in

32. "There goes an American . . . The classless way they dress. Filing clerk and company president's wife. The same nylons, little hats, tweed suits, navy-blue dress." *Vogue* (February 1, 1950), p. 125.

33. H. H. Gerth and C. Wright Mills (eds.), *From Max Weber: Essays in Sociology* (New York: Oxford University Press, Inc., 1946), p. 194.

due course, to the growth of status structures and makes for a resuscitation of the important role of social honor . . .[34]

Thus, in prosperous and economically stable periods, status predominates. A number of well-known writers see a major change in the underlying principle of stratification.[35] A system of valuation based on what a man produces is being replaced with one that is based on what a man chooses to do with his money and time. What is relevant in this thesis is the assumption that where once occupation identified class, and class, through the style of life that grew up around it, dictated taste, we have come to a point where taste alone is sufficient to endow a person with high status. Hence, competition revolves around the symbols of status, which rather than expressing status, now come to determine it. Fashion leadership supposedly guarantees a position of prestige, whereas once it was only position already acquired that enabled a person to act as a fashion leader.

Whether the middle masses of the affluent society have really acquired life "styles" is a very real question, though the consumption orientation—especially where there is a high degree of residential mobility and fleeting contact—is beyond dispute. To illustrate this consumption orientation, McLuhan cites an advertisement for Lord Calvert whisky, showing the "Man of Distinction" holding a glass of whisky in his hand.

> What really emerges from this item is the notion of distinction and culture as being a matter of consumption rather than the possession of discriminating perception and judgment . . . This whiskey ad bristles with techniques of persuasion. It is a blatant proclamation on culture as understood today. Consumers of expensive and refined clothes and whiskey, as pictured here, are cultured. They are distinct from the herd.[36]

Here is another ad typifying the same trend, titled "Without a Word Being Spoken":

> . . . a new Cadillac car states the case for its owner with remarkable clarity and eloquence. For people everywhere have come to know and accept the "car of cars" as the dwelling place of America's front-rank citizens—and wherever highways lead, the man who sits at its wheel is accorded the courtesy that goes with respect.

34. *Ibid.*
35. Among them, David Riesman, Russell Lynes, and Vance Packard.
36. Marshall McLuhan, *The Mechanical Bride* (New York: Vanguard Press, 1951), pp. 57–8.

But whereas fashions and other symbols of economic achievement can be bought, style of life cannot. Russell Lynes has depicted with some insight how one can discern from a person's choice of clothes, furniture, salads, games, reading, entertainment, and even the "causes" he endorses whether he is highbrow, middlebrow, or lowbrow.[37] Whatever the tastes by which people may be distinguished, one critic reasons that:

> What culture and civilized living we have today is provided by the interaction of two groups—the esthetically radical highbrows and the somewhat more conservative and stable upper-middlebrows. Beneath the upper-middlebrows there yawns an awful chasm peopled by masses whose cultural life is so close to that of backward children that the difference is not worth arguing about. Lower-middlebrows and low-brows may be bank presidents, pillars of the church, nice fellows, good providers or otherwise decent citizens, but, culturally speaking they are oafs . . .[38]

Fads and Fashion

From one point of view a fad is only a special variation of fashion. Nystrom, for example, calls a fad "a miniature fashion in some unimportant matter or detail"; anything more important and far-reaching is fashion.[39] Accordingly, since any difference in effect is only a matter of degree, it can safely be disregarded. Some patterns, like men's wristwatches, bobbed hair, lawn tennis, and crossword puzzles, which are now accepted as part of culture have indeed arisen as fads. But on the whole, fads are the highly transitory and somewhat bizzarre behavior in which people, from time to time, seem to indulge themselves when on something of a rampage. Most fads last less than a year. In many instances, to make a hard and fast distinction is difficult, and in the preceding pages no attention was paid to whether something was fashionable or faddish.

It is nevertheless possible, and often productive, to distinguish between the two. Faddish behavior involves fewer people, is more personal, shorter in duration, and tends to be socially disapproved. There is "something unexpected, irresponsible or bizzarre" about many fads (or crazes).[40] Among the more widely publicized have been the swallowing

37. Russell Lynes, *Life,* XXVI (April 11, 1949), pp. 99–102. See also Lynes, *The Tastemakers* (New York: Harper & Brothers, 1954).
38. Sargeant, *op. cit.,* pp. 102ff.
39. Nystrom, *op. cit.,* p. 3.
40. Sapir, *op. cit.*

of goldfish, sitting on flagpoles, wearing one earring at a time, shaving the top of one's head, crowding into telephone booths, etc. The persons who engage in wild fads are not necessarily under great personal stress or abnormally isolated from the main current of society.[41]

Fads and fashions serve somewhat different societal functions. In following fads, people set themselves apart, so that faddish behavior is a countervailing fashion movement that, within very restricted limits, challenges the *status quo*. Moreover, fads disseminate very rapidly and thus cut across class lines, whereas fashion reinforces the prevailing class structure. Fads afford an opportunity for quick recognition and momentary notoriety. By following fads, dissatisfied and restless individuals manage to express in a mild and harmless way their protest against the boredom they experience in their normal way of life.

Both fashion and fad are alike, however, in that they involve the dual attempt at "identification with" and "differentiation from" others in the mass society. The persons whom one copies are often one's intimate associates, but the collectivity from which one sets himself apart is vaguely conceived and abstract, sometimes designated as "square." In empirical research, some distinction in terms of duration, numbers involved, triviality, etc., may be useful. But limiting the term "fad" to definitions that are less important and universal but nevertheless rapidly and widely adopted raises a number of interesting questions: What makes some innovations of the fad type, even though they diffuse widely, less compelling? How does one account for the occasional fad that becomes fashion? Do fads flourish when the dominant stratification is by class or by status? The difference in the societal functions of fad and fashion especially needs clarification and development. For example, the scion of an upper-class family *may* wear leather patches on the elbows of his suit jacket, pepper his speech with ain'ts and mispronunciations, and belch at the table. Is this faddish behavior and, if so, does it help to obliterate the *status quo?* Is faddish behavior most typical of those who feel alienated from the society, or of the unqualified mass, or of those, like this upper-class youth, so assured of their status that they can afford to adopt the mannerisms and inventions of lower classes—such as jazz— and so give impetus to new fads?

The most significant aspects of fashion and faddish behavior are those that relate them to social structure. What does fashion mean for the group, and how important is the group for fashion? If fashion is the caprice of custom, how capricious can different individuals, groups, and societies be? What areas of deviation from custom are permissible at various times? Under what circumstances is it fashionable to be in

41. Ralph Turner and Lewis Killian, *Collective Behavior* (Englewood Cliffs, N.J.: Prentice-Hall, Inc., 1957), p. 208.

fashion? And in what groups is it most fashionable not to follow fashion? Above all, is fashion inevitable in any mass society, and under what conditions may its influence be minimized and maximized?

Fashion also needs to be related to social change. While fashion changes often appear irrelevant or trivial, they are generally related to more significant behavior. Both fashions and fads serve as weathervanes indicating changes in the social structure and in the style of life.

B I B L I O G R A P H Y

These four works, available in English, are basic to an understanding of fashion:

SAPIR, EDWARD. "Fashion," *Encyclopedia of the Social Sciences,* Vol. VI, pp. 139–41. New York: The Macmillan Co., 1931. A brilliant, succinct, but comprehensive statement by the anthropologist of the function of fashion in society.

SIMMEL, GEORG. "Fashion," *The American Journal of Sociology,* LXII (May, 1957), pp. 541–58. A reprint of his 1904 article containing the classic treatment of fashion, as a form of collective imitation and differentiation.

SUMNER, WILLIAM GRAHAM. *Folkways.* Boston: Ginn & Company, 1906. Available in various editions, including paperback. The well-known statement that there is "no arguing with fashion," backed by many examples.

VEBLEN, THORSTEIN. *The Theory of the Leisure Class.* New York: The Macmillan Co., 1899. Available in many editions. The classic work of the great social economist, inquiring into the mode of life, views, and habits of expenditure of the leisure class.

The following are also good background books to the more empirical studies mentioned in the text.

BARBER, BERNARD, and LOBEL, LYLE S. " 'Fashion' in Women's Clothes and the American System," *Class, Status and Power,* ed. REINHARD BENDIX and SEYMOUR M. LIPSET, pp. 323–32. Glencoe, Ill.: The Free Press, 1953. Concerning the manifest and latent functions of fashion for different aspects of the American social system.

HAWES, ELIZABETH. *Fashion is Spinach.* New York: Grosset & Dunlap, Inc., 1940. A best-seller written by a successful designer with a social conscience. An introduction to the organized aspects of the fashion industry.

HURLOCK, ELIZABETH. *Motivation in Fashion.* New York: Archives in Psychology, 1929. This monograph contains an excellent summary of what other writers—Ross, Bernard, Tarde, etc.—have had to say about motivation in fashion and what generally is referred to as fashion theory and definitions.

NYSTROM, PAUL HENRY. *Economics of Fashion.* New York: The Ronald Press Company, 1928. Written by a professor of marketing, the book has a good statement in its first sections of what fashion is, how it operates, and what factors influence its operations.

The American Journal of Sociology, LXII (May, 1957). A special issue on "The Uses of Leisure." Contains the Simmel essay, articles by John Johnstone, Elihu Katz, Donald Horton, Anselm Strauss, Rolf Meyersohn, and Murray Wax, having to do with fads and the sociology of taste. The bibliography by Reuel Denney and Mary Lea Meyersohn contains a number of popular studies of fads.

CHAPTER **16**

An Introduction to Social Movements

T HE CATEGORY "SOCIAL MOVEMENT" has come to designate a wide range of phenomena that span the entire continuum from the tightly knit secret organization to some of the most amorphous forms of mass behavior. A similar vagueness exists when it comes to defining the boundaries of a single social movement. Everything is included from the most time-bound agitation for a specific measure to the never-ceasing efforts of people all over the world to effect a better way of life. The following list will give an indication of the variety of phenomena referred to, discussed, and analyzed as social movements in sociological literature: the Abbey Theater, an enterprise to establish a national theater in Ireland; African nationalism; the American Revolution; the Anti-Saloon League, which spearheaded the final drive for prohibition of the liquor traffic; the birth control movement for the dissemination of advice on contraception; calendar reform; the Canadian Commonwealth Federation, a socialist party with a largely agrarian base in Canada's Prairie Provinces; Castro's 26th of July Movement, which wrested political power from the Batista dictatorship in Cuba; Christian Science; communism in its various international and national manifestations; the Co-operative Movement to set up enterprises jointly owned and run in the interests of all participants; fascism; fashion movements; Father Divine's Peace Mission; the feminist movement for general recognition of women's rights; the French Revolution; the rise of the Grange to represent the interests of American farmers; the Ku Klux Klan; the little theater movement; the Lucy Stone League of women determined to continue using their maiden name after marriage; a lynch mob; the Great Revival on the American frontier, which won many adherents to the new Methodist and Baptist churches; McCarthyism as the collective designation for post-World War II antisubversive agitation in the United States; the modern art movement; Mormonism; National Socialism; the Oxford Movement (later renamed Moral Rearmament and also known as Buchmanism) which won converts to the idea that major world problems could be solved through "inner" reform of the individual; the Pentecostal Church (one of the "Holy-Rollers"); Populism, the widespread political protest in the American Midwest and West in the 1880's and 1890's; prison reform; the prohibition movement; the Risorgimento, one of the Italian secret societies that contributed to unification; the Russian Revolution; the terrorist Irish Sinn Fein; international socialism; the United African Nationalist Movement of American Negroes; vegetarianism; the European *Wandervogel,* which proclaimed a program for youth early in the twentieth-century; the youth movement generally; and Zionism, which aimed at the re-establishment of a homeland for Jews in Palestine.

This partial list should indicate that we are dealing with a rather diffuse category. It includes, first, certain broad social changes that occur when many social currents and specific grievances crystallize into a major upheaval, such as the French Revolution or African nationalism. It includes, second, specific innovations carried by widespread agitation from a popular base, as in Prohibition or the struggle for recognition of collective bargaining. In the third place, many specific phenomena expressive of social unrest are included as well, though they are as different in scope and effectiveness as a lynch mob, a religious revival, and McCarthyism. Fourth, many movements are defined by a broadly similar ideology; the many socialist groups together form the socialist movement, even if organizationally they are badly split. Still a fifth variety consists of cultish phenomena, like the Oxford Movement, with a rather broad following, and more short-lived fashions and fads, such as Bloomerism. Finally, there are the little movements, usually made up of small groups that crystallize in many localities and unite for certain specific purposes; the theater and arts movements are prime examples.

SOCIAL MOVEMENTS AS CRUSADES

A SOCIAL MOVEMENT is here taken to mean *large-scale, widespread, and continuing, elementary collective action in pursuit of an objective that affects and shapes the social order in some fundamental aspect.* The "social" in "social movement" refers to the objective, and not to the people working for the objective. There are changes in specific realms—fashion, opinion, politics, religion, art, etc.—that are not social movements though they affect the entire fabric of society and are aspects of larger transformations and unrest. The changes effected by social movements do not grow out of a series of minor but cumulative shifts; on the contrary, they are consciously worked for. Organized effort, though necessary for any enterprise of such magnitude, is not, however, its essence. A social movement is a more elementary collective phenomenon. Its spirit counts. The collective enterprise resembles somewhat a crusade for a cause that "moves" people.

The definition above requires us to clarify, first, the kind of change that is at issue and, second, the nature of the collective enterprise and of the organization that is its agent.

THE SCOPE OF OBJECTIVES

Social movements are directed toward objectives that are the deep and vital concern of society as a whole or of sizable and powerful segments of that society. They lie in areas closely related to the mores and to basic social values. Because they affect basic interests, strong affects either in support or in opposition of a movement are likely to be generated. By this criterion, trends in popular or esoteric taste (the whole world of fashion) are not in and of themselves social movements, even though a change in the mores may be the consequence of the cumulative impact of innumerable fashion changes. The significance of fashion is primarily for the individual: he differentiates himself within a class system. It affects individual preferences and tastes in areas that are essentially unrelated to the more fundamental values of the community.

Moreover, social movements seek changes in behavior or belief that are to be enforced by sanction, where conformity is not optional. This explains why so many social movements have sought political power that would enable them to achieve their objectives through legislation. The behavior to be changed is considered important enough to the participants to become legally prescribed.

The objectives of many social movements are so far-reaching, the conflict in values so drastic, that action to achieve them cannot take place *within* the framework of the social order. In that case the participants in the social movement must radically break with the rest of society. Furthermore, since its values often conflict with those supported by social authorities, it often meets with strong opposition. Individual participants attract the disdain, the hostility, and often the active persecution of representatives of the official order. This confronts many social movements with two alternatives: either to retreat from this-worldly pursuits, fleeing into the wilderness, or somehow to isolate themselves in separate communities or to operate illegally, using forbidden tactics, spreading their ideas through clandestine channels. Success of the movement in gaining its objectives necessitates a change in power, which grants either full recognition to its goals and the movement itself or immunity from persecution, or it involves the seizure of power by the aspiring movement, which can be achieved only through extra-legal methods.

Many social movements are definitely not revolutionary. But the objectives of every movement have this in common: the interests it represents have failed to find full recognition and representation in the existing power system. The spontaneity and other characteristics of social movements flow from this fact. Notwithstanding their spontaneity, the activities of many social movements have left enduring marks on their society. It is by the relative permanence of their effects that social movements can be distinguished from the more transitory manifestations of social unrest, such as shifts in public sentiment, crazes, fads, and psychic epidemics.

Nevertheless, the more ephemeral innovations carried by mass psychology are not irrelevant to the study of social movements. They are indicative of underlying unrest but characterize at best only one phase of a social movement. Fads and crazes and shifts in public moods may signal the start of a social revolution or may provide superficial but symbolic activities into which emotions stirred up by social movements may be channeled. Thus, the "Turkish costume," a pair of trousers gathered at the ankle and worn under a shortened skirt and referred to by scoffers as "bloomers," was originally worn for outdoor work by women at the Oneida Community of John Humphrey Noyes' Perfectionists in 1848. While bloomers were at first a fad, picked up from the Perfectionists, they became a symbol of woman's emancipation, rousing the suffragettes but evoking cries of derision and ridicule from the antifeminists. By way of another example, the beards grown by Fidel Castro's small band of Cuban revolutionaries in the late 1950's were a symbol of defiance. Immediately after the Castro victory they were a badge of pride and a symbol of status. About the same time in the United States growing a beard was a fad among young men everywhere. For the so-called "beats" it was a symbol of rebellion, perhaps marking the stirrings of some yet unborn social movement.

NATURE OF THE COLLECTIVE ACTION

There are two rather distinct aspects to the systematic study of social movements. David Sills pointed, in his study of the March of Dimes Campaign, to the *unorganized* social movement whose participants have in common some interest or frustration that affects them all and the "activities on the part of *organized* groups to affect some change in society."[1] Though Sills was concerned only with the latter aspect, many students of social movements have especially stressed the unstructured one.

Stressing the organized aspect, Wendell King, for example, defines a social movement as a "group venture extending beyond a local community or a single event and involving a systematic effort to inaugurate changes in thought, behavior, and social relationships."[2] In line with this definition, he treats social movements as those dynamic aspects of larger social systems that are the effects of group activities, mostly of voluntary organizations. Those, on the other hand, who emphasize the unstructured aspect of social movements look upon them as a form of elementary collective behavior, distinct from such other forms as the crowd, the public, and the mass. Herbert Blumer, for example, defines the social movement as a "collective enterprise to establish a new order of life,"[3] a definition that Turner and Killian refine to include not only a collectivity that promotes change in a society or group but also one that resists it, as long as it acts with some continuity.[4] Rudolph Heberle, though limiting himself to movements seeking fundamental *political* change, distinguishes them from organized political parties and pressure groups by their broad collective basis—namely, the unrest, the commotion, the stirring, and the agitation associated with political upheaval.[5] Actually the elementary and organized aspects must be considered together when dealing with any specific social movement. A phenomenon that is purely elementary and lacks all organization would be mass behavior, while spontaneity and contagion serve to distinguish the social movement from more highly organized associations and interest groups.

Elementary Processes: Spontaneous Aspects

Like social movements, the associations, such as pressure groups or political parties, are agents of enacted social change. But their differences go beyond the difference in the scope of their objective. The es-

1. David L. Sills, *The Volunteers* (Glencoe, Ill.: The Free Press, 1957), p. 244.
2. C. Wendell King, *Social Movements in the United States* (New York: Random House, 1956), p. 27.
3. Herbert Blumer, "Collective Behavior," in A. M. Lee (ed.), *Principles of Sociology* (New York: Barnes & Noble, Inc., 1951), p. 199.
4. Ralph Turner and Lewis Killian, *Collective Behavior* (Englewood Cliffs, N.J.: Prentice-Hall, Inc., 1957).
5. Rudolph Heberle, *Social Movements: An Introduction to Political Sociology* (New York: Appleton-Century-Crofts, Inc., 1951).

sential difference is in the degree of organization, in the way in which the activities of the association are adapted and co-ordinated to achieve some clearly defined goal. Usually the activities of associations are confined to the joint pursuit of interests that members as individuals have in common and that constitute the reason for forming the organization in the first place. The pursuit is highly organized, and special tasks are relegated to representative spokesmen and a staff of specialists. Sometimes when it furthers the aims of the association, mass support is carefully elicited, but it is never permitted to dominate the organization. Hence, established political parties, though forced to appeal to the mass of voters at election time, are not social movements. Neither are, in this view, the Anti-Saloon League, which played such an important part in the passage of the prohibition amendment, or the National Association for the Advancement of Colored People, which confines itself to the achievement of specific objectives by means of deliberate pressure tactics. Social movements have certain dynamic qualities. Thus, the leadership of a social movement may have rational plans, but since their objectives are not recognized, extra-legal means are often used. If outlawed, the leadership may operate as a conspiratorial group; if they have no press, they communicate by word of mouth. The masses who become involved under these conditions make a stable leadership difficult. They often force upon the leadership tactics and objectives that go beyond limited objectives. Thus, they subject the organization to sudden changes.

Another distinguishing feature of the social movement is that the interests accounting for "participation from below" are often vague compared to those represented by the association seeking a specific objective. For example, the supporters of a pressure group, while committed to some limited goal, are hardly "involved" in the venture in the way in which the participants in a social movement are stirred by zeal and enthusiasm. The sentiment and enthusiasm, the sense of mission, is a much stronger bond in the social movement than the specific interest to be worked for.

In the third place, it is easy to distinguish between the social movement and associations that may appear similar by the clarity of their boundaries. Pressure groups seldom involve persons who are not members of their organization, or if they do, it is as a tactic to gain support. The social movement, by contrast, is in flux, involving at different times and for different maneuvers people who have no formal relation to it except their participation in it. This tendency to spill over is lacking in the well-ordered and self-contained interest group. The social movement's character manifests itself especially at moments of crisis and during intensive drives.

Finally, it is possible for a voluntary association to take on the characteristics of a social movement. The hope of victory stirs up emotions and draws recruits to a cause as orderly channels of communication give way to confusion, rumor, panic, or the rule of crowds. The history of strikes often reveals such a pattern. A strike begins with the specific demands of an organized association, but as it drags out, arousing public sympathy or inspiring others with similar grievances, it can become a strike movement. The desegregation efforts of the Congress on Racial Equality were carried on for years by well-disciplined small groups of supporters, until in 1959 and 1960 they erupted into the sit-in strike movement in the South and other parts of the country.

The spread of influence is not, however, enough to transform an interest group into a social movement. A Greek letter society may come to have chapters everywhere without changing its essential character. Pressure groups remain pressure groups so long as they operate through organized channels of communication. Only when such an association begins to "spread the gospel" does the original group serve as a core for a social movement. One speaks of Mormonism (in its formative stage) and Moral Rearmament (the Oxford Movement) as social movements because, though organized into chapters, each depends on a sense of mission, which involves new followers even before they have formally joined up. The reservoir of a social movement resides in supporters, whose grievances make them responsive to any appeal.

The Imperative of Organization

To understand the success or failure of a social movement, it is often necessary to study the activities of some conspiratorial society, pressure group, sectarian nucleus, etc., which, though often mistaken for the movement itself, operates as its organized core. The organized aspects of a social movement never entirely encompass it; they reside in a core group whose role in relation to the social movement is, in itself, never planned. There is no completely organized social movement.

A core group serves to mobilize, define, and channel emotions and grievances that have not yet been self-consciously put in the service of some larger cause. Its function emerges in a number of ways. (1) The originating spark, the inspiration, goes from the core group to other groups who become dedicated to the same cause. In this instance, the core group has no power to direct the activities of other groups, except insofar as its advice continues to be honored and its personalities continue to serve as inspiration—for example, Moral Rearmament. (2) The core group supplies the directing cadre around which vague unrest crystallizes. Such a group will be highly organized, disciplined, and exclusive. It directs the activities of members everywhere and, in case of success, will wield power in the name of the entire movement—for example, Bolshevism. (3) The core group heads up the movement by claiming to be its legitimate spokesman. For example, the Anti-Saloon League, a pressure group, was largely responsible for translating into a concrete plan of action the less-organized efforts and more amorphous goals of groups who made up the prohibition movement. But the League, though its activities brought it a degree of organization, never saw itself as primarily part of a larger movement.

Many social movements arise from the parallel activities of groups dispersed through space. The groups themselves are often highly organized. In other cases, their actions are largely spontaneous. Moreover, participation in the movement occurs often only through the particular group with which individuals are affiliated. One group working for a cause, such as women's suffrage, may appear to be so involved in its quarrels with another group sharing its objective that members of both groups hardly seem to be participants in the same movement. Yet, however ridden by factional disputes a movement may be, the knowledge that other groups are working toward the same ends gives each unit a sense of participation in it. They compete to see which is the purest representative of its doctrine.

The literature on social movements has emphasized the organized aspects. Indeed, most of the empirical studies are essentially studies of core groups. That this should be so is understandable. The social movements with which we are most familiar are "successful," and their histories are generally written by or for the core groups that finally brought them to a successful conclusion. Thus, to read of the women's rights movement is mainly to read the history of leadership succession and organizational development. The colorful temperance movement resolves itself into a history of the Woman's Christian Temperance Union. In this emphasis on leadership, intraorganizational squabbles, specific changes in tactics and strategy, etc., there is a tendency to overlook the zeal stirred up among the larger following which distinguishes a social movement from other kinds of organized efforts after change— that is, from established political parties, lobbies, etc.—and gives any social movement the character of a crusade for a historic cause.

SUMMARY

A social movement always refers to elementary collective behavior on a large scale. The scope and durability of the activity as well as of its objectives help to differentiate the social movement from waves of public sentiment, fashions, and faddish behavior. The dual imperative of spontaneity and organization, characteristic of social movements, sets them apart from pressure groups and other types of voluntary association, which lack their spontaneity, and from mass behavior, which is altogether devoid of even the rudiments of organization.

Every social movement (1) seeks recognition of interests that have repercussions on fundamental norms and values and that therefore concern the whole society or community and (2) leaves changes that are apt to endure. The activities of the movement are (3) largely spontaneous and characterized by contagion but are (4) co-ordinated by some core group. Unless we are able to distinguish between the core group and a larger mass of supporters not formally joined, we are not dealing with a social movement.

Types of Social Movement

The variety of social movements that have arisen in the most diverse circumstances make some kind of classification imperative. Unfortunately the many classification schemes proposed have not promoted agreement on taxonomy. There have been, of course, a number of purposes in classifying social movements.

One has been the need to link a number of historical occurrences by some guiding thread that makes understandable what happened in history and facilitates lucid presentation of massive arrays of historical and empirical data. Most of these have resulted in *ad hoc*, though interesting, classifications. Another is to achieve practical guidance. Accordingly, one may wish to know which movements are to be considered harmful and bear watching: the Western world, for instance, seeks explanations of the methods and vulnerability of pro-communist movements. Likewise, those seeking reform might wish to study the tactics of similar movements in order to gauge their effectiveness and to learn about the conditions that promote success. Many lessons are to be learned from this kind of comparison. Sociological classifications are distinguished from the above, however, by the fact that they are consciously framed to be logically consistent and to lead to analytical generalizations. Differentiation turns about such factors as origins, patterns of development, type of leadership, nature of the objective, and type of appeal.

Broadly speaking, typologies of social movements have been based on four different attributes: (1) some external criterion, such as the area of activity, the interest represented, or the content of its ideology (phenomenistic); (2) the type of value orientation; (3) the nature of the goals; and (4) the growth pattern.

PHENOMENISTIC TYPOLOGIES

Classifications by some external and visible criterion are essentially descriptive. They nevertheless offer a starting point for more refined categorization. The most common kind of classification is according to the area of activity. One finds typologies that divide social movements into political, religious, economic, esthetic, literary, intellectual, etc., according to the realm in which their objectives lie. Classification often makes use also of the group whose interests are professedly being represented: youth, women, labor, minority, national, peasants, etc. Still other classifications involve some aspect of an ideology, like collectivism or messianism. Yet all of the movements above could be either collectivist or messianic in the context of what they proclaim. Obviously many combinations are possible; some labor movements are political while others confine their activity entirely to economic issues; literary movements have nationalistic overtones or they express the spirit of rebellion on the part of youth. The difficulty with these classifications, useful for specific purposes as they are, is that no satisfactory system can be evolved. The same movement can be classified in many different contexts, depending on the interests of the analyst, and any number of categories can be developed, again depending on the interests of the analyst.

VALUE ORIENTATIONS

Most interesting has been the distinction, made by Sighele and emphasized by Park and Burgess in their pioneer work in collective behavior, between movements directed *inward* and those directed *outward*.[6] These terms refer not to the goal but to an ethical orientation that dominates the behavior of participants. *Inward* movements aim at renovating and renewing the life of the community from within by remolding individuals and getting them to concern themselves with absolute values. The values these movements proclaim are good or bad in themselves. Their goals are to be realized only through the moral regeneration of the people who comprise them. Inward movements are moral crusades. *Outward* movements seek to recast the social order from without, through a change in laws and in the institutional structure. The values they live by "fit the times." The realization of some absolute value appears only

6. Scipio Sighele, *Psychologie des Sectes* (Paris, 1894), p. 46; cited in R. E. Park and E. W. Burgess, *Introduction to the Science of Sociology* (2nd ed.; Chicago: University of Chicago Press, 1924), p. 873f. Max Weber made a similar distinction.

as a remote possibility *after* the social and political structure has been modified by pressure and force.

The use of value or ethical orientation as a classificatory criterion runs into certain difficulties. Moral crusades that start out as inward movements have a way of evolving into a crusade for institutional reform—that is, outward movements—whereas most reform or revolutionary movements aimed specifically at institutional change have overtones of a moral crusade. For instance, the movement for temperance that arose in nineteenth-century America gave way in the twentieth to a crusade for legislative reform known as the "prohibition movement." Early American crusades against slavery, moral in form, helped spark a moral crusade for the recognition of women as human beings; the latter, in turn, evolved into a crusade for suffrage employing not moral suasion but every form of political pressure. Revivalistic movements and nationalist-patriotic movements may at one stage of development be moral crusades, reaching the individual, while at a later stage they stress the concrete objectives of institutional reform or the usurpation of power. The moral crusader, failing to change men's minds through "suasion," often turns toward legislative reform. If people stay away from church on Sunday, he tries to get them there by limiting their choice; he enacts blue laws, closing stores, bars, and theaters and forbidding ballgames on the Sabbath. The effort to produce outer change through inner reform turns into a direct assault on some obstacle in the structure of society. Vice versa, men, despairing at legislative and diplomatic efforts to effect changes they deem necessary, may launch moral crusades to effect the renovation. Moral Rearmament, against war, thrived in the 1930's and was revived in the 1950's, overtly as a moral crusade to reduce international tension. Pacifists and believers in the principle of nonviolence everywhere believe that wars will end forever when men refuse to fight. The tactics of passive resistance and hunger strikes constitute an effective form of pressure, to be applied under the guise of moral suasion, when more open demonstrations are under a ban that can be enforced by superior power. In this instance the moral crusade achieves tangible objectives, but on other occasions, the participants have isolated themselves and eschewed worldly concerns.

Many movements at some point in their careers pass through a phase in which their orientation is predominantly inward and moral. Nevertheless, the distinction between inward and outward orientations remains a source of fruitful hypotheses. For instance, there appears to have been a considerable amount of duplication in "membership" between the temperance and the human rights movements in America. The amount of overlap was greater than that between the temperance and prohibition movements, superficially ideological kin. The divergence in value orientation between these two deserves explanation. Before temperance could become Prohibition, the leadership had to pass into new hands and the masses of followers had to be succeeded by a different type to whom the new outward orientation appealed. The general hypothesis emerges that the leaders and followers of social movements with the same value orientation will be more interchangeable and their tactics exhibit greater similarities than those of two social movements, one of which is inward-oriented and the other outward-oriented.

GOALS

A useful formal criterion of classification, whose application appears tricky at times, concerns the importance of goals versus sentiments in integrating a movement as well as several differences in the nature of the goals.

Expressive and Institutional Movements

A number of writers have translated Sighele's distinction between outward and inward orientation into the presence or absence of a common goal—namely, into movements that are institutional and movements that are expressive. Accordingly, institutional movements pursue some objective that entails a change in the laws or the institutions of society. Expressive movements, by contrast, are said to develop no collective goal whatsoever.[7] In many moral crusades (revivals, messianic movements, etc.) participation in the movement is viewed as an end in itself; the forms of activity it develops exhaust the purposes of the movement, so that no goal beyond it serves as a unifying factor. Those who engage in a moral crusade against drunkenness form a society for reformed drunkards; they concern themselves exclusively with their personal salvation. The Indian Ghost Dance that swept the western plains in the 1890's channeled the despair and hate the defeated Indians felt into ritualistic activities by which they prepared themselves for the promised redemption.

The contention that the expressive movement is not held together by some objective or ideology is difficult to maintain in practice. The withdrawal of action from the external world to a concern with insular

7. Park and Burgess used a three-fold distinction: revolutionary, reform, and expressive, of which the first two correspond to Sighele's "outward" and the last one to his "inward." They are followed in this by Blumer. The trichotomy is preserved by Turner and Killian, who fasten on the "aspects emphasized." The inward-expressive movement is "participation-oriented"; the outward movement is either "value-oriented" (governed by an ideology) or "power-oriented."

forms of participation appears essentially an adaptation to circumstances. A movement thwarted in its worldly ambitions will turn inward and preserve its own purity. This is, nevertheless, a form of protest, though the means used are largely symbolic.

To distinguish between social movements according to the motives for participation is equally difficult. The camaraderie of those united in a cause is often as effective as the official goal. Hence "true believers" easily move from one movement to another, even though the avowed aims of the second movement have no apparent similarity to those of the first.[8] The importance of the participation and fellowship a movement offers reveals itself also in the tenacity with which remnants of movements survive, once their manifest purpose has been accomplished or superseded. They often find new causes to embrace.

Gusfield cites the case of the Woman's Christian Temperance Union, once the core of the larger cause, which, having lost that cause, continued to work for it as an organized group, seeking to preserve and propagate the ideal of temperance.[9]

Content of Goals

On the assumption that every movement has some goal, one can make some useful distinctions in terms of its goals. Traditionally one differentiates between movements according to the relationship of programs to the *status quo*. Hence, social movements traverse the entire continuum from reactionary to radically progressive. But since all movements represent goals not fully acknowledged and incorporated in the social order, a picture of historical progress really underlies this distinction. There are radical movements of the "right" as well as of the "left." Whether it is called reactionary or progressive seems to depend largely on the kind of social order it idealizes. The distinction is somewhat like that Mannheim had in mind when he coined the terms "ideology," designating the philosophy in defense of the interest of some class entrenched in power, and "utopia," [10] the picture of the future society in which the aspirations of a class still excluded from power were realized.[11] Consequently, this distinction relates a movement to the class interests it supposedly represents. In recent historical transition, the aspirations

8. Eric Hoffer, *The True Believer* (New York: Mentor Books, 1958), chap. 3.

9. Joseph R. Gusfield, "Social Structure and Moral Reform: A Study of the Woman's Christian Temperance Union," *American Journal of Sociology*, LXI (1955), pp. 221–32.

10. Karl Mannheim, *Ideology and Utopia* (New York: Harcourt, Brace & Co., 1946).

11. Louis Wirth, *Community Life and Social Policy; Selected Papers* (Chicago: University of Chicago Press, 1956), pp. 237–60.

of the independent entrepreneur and professional classes and of peasants against aristocratic interests based on landed property have been considered progressive. So have the demands of the industrial working classes and urban populations when asserted against large industrial corporations.

In the past the demands of each rising group have typically served to extend rights that only the privileged class had enjoyed. The movement of the "left" usually made common cause with other suppressed groups. They incorporated the demands of the majorities. But the judgment about the progressive or reactionary character of a social movement of the underprivileged was complicated whenever its goals served to exclude other groups. American organized labor in the early 1900's widely supported anti-immigration movements, which were generally regarded as reactionary and nativist. During the Civil War, Irish immigrants, then a definitely underprivileged group, fought emancipation of Negroes, which they defined as aimed against labor. Since the consequences of a movement can be judged only after it has run its course, the assessment had best be made in terms of its class base rather than in terms of whether it is reactionary, conservative, liberal, or progressive.

The totalitarian-democratic dimension becomes increasingly important for distinguishing among the goals of social movements. Totalitarianism cuts across the typical reactionary-progressive dimension. It refers to the willingness to recognize and incorporate the interests of groups other than one's own. Totalitarian features can be found in the ideologies of movements on both the "right" and the "left."

Movements on the part of national minorities are often categorized in terms of their willingness to adapt themselves to, live with, or radically alter the *status quo*. Louis Wirth defined the various types by how they sought to regulate their relations with the dominant group in society.[12] Pluralistic movements seek recognition of their own ways and tolerance to pursue them within the framework of the dominant society; they are willing to live and let live. Assimilationist movements raise demands for equal opportunity and full participation in the dominant society. Secessionist movements espouse complete separation from the dominant group, either through independence or joining another nation. Militant movements seek to make a minority group dominant through conquest or other means. The messianic movement among primitive nations, a variant of the militant type, which exhalts the "old" or "golden" way of life of the ancestors and seeks a return to it through the complete eradication or expulsion of the dominant group, represents an extreme totalitarian minority movement.

The variable, "willingness to adapt to, live with, or radically alter the

12. *Ibid.*

status quo," can also be used to type various movements in such areas as youth, labor, religion.

Specificity and Comprehensiveness of Goals

The specificity or comprehensiveness of the objective a movement pursues has been used as a formal criterion to distinguish between reform and revolutionary movements. There are objectives that involve limited change and that one could designate *reform* goals. *Revolutionary* goals, by contrast, involve a fundamental alteration and a radical break with the existing way of life. But the goals themselves do not suffice to distinguish between social movements. The difference is more a matter of general outlook. The atmosphere of the reform movement is less hostile. It leans heavily on persuasion and education, avoiding a complete break with the past. Consequently, the membership it attracts is rather different from the following of a revolutionary movement. Because the latter is essentially utopian in its aims and its members believe the future belongs to them anyhow, they are willing to employ any tactics that seem to bring them within reach of their objective.

Revolutionary movements are always general protests against some social order. They may, however, from tactical considerations, focus attention on some limited goal. The so-called transitional program of a revolutionary movement is usually carefully framed to channel the general discontent of alienated masses into demands that cannot be met within the framework of existing power relationships, while giving the impression of seeking only limited objectives. On occasion, movements in pursuit of specific objectives turn revolutionary, once the impossibility of realizing even limited demands becomes apparent. Something like this happened in the Soviet Union in the years just preceding the 1917 uprising.

Some revolutionary movements, such as the Anarchists, have refused all support to reform measures, viewing the latter as opiates that inure the injured to their hardships and impede the radical alienation of the masses. Others have been more opportunistic. The Communist movement in the United States and in other parts of the world has sometimes supported reform and sometimes refused to support it altogether. But, in either case, the question of reform involved a tactical maneuver, with the concrete objectives supported never being the ends of the movement.

One can, however, use the specificity or comprehensiveness of goal in classifying certain types of movements. As examples of specific social movements, there are the many crusades to obtain redress for some specific ill. Much of what is today taken for granted was achieved only after widespread and enthusiastic agitation. The antivivisection statutes and blue laws of some states, safety regulations in factories, shortening of the work week, the right of women to vote, etc., are directly or indirectly the products of specific reform movements. The wave of sitdown or stay-in strikes that swept the United States in 1935–1937 took on the semblance of a genuine social movement and culminated in the defection of industrial trade unions from the American Federation of Labor to form the C.I.O.

Often the specific objectives toward which some movement is aiming serve only to channel into support for some tangible measure the energies building up for a generalized protest against an existing religious, political, moral, or social order. Moreover, participation in one movement can be instrumental in gaining the broader objectives of another. Slavery was the specific evil that the movement for abolition sought to eradicate; some women active in the agitation for women's rights worked for abolition hoping to solicit support for their cause in return. But the women's movement in the United States at that time was something more than a simple demand for suffrage. It represented a general protest against a social order in which the "tyranny of man" had been institutionalized. The belief that women were inferior—physically, mentally, and morally—and therefore condemned to bear the burden of original sin, permeated intrafamily relations that were regulated by custom as well as by law.

GROWTH PATTERN

A fourth formal criterion for differentiating among social movements is the pattern by which they grow. The relation between the larger movement and its core group(s) is of crucial significance for this, for some degree of organization as well as some spontaneous resonance are essential for the emergence of a social movement.

Social movements either fan out from a center or coalesce from a number of smaller cells of unrest.

The movements that fan out exhibit a *centrifugal* career pattern. They originate in a small active nucleus, a single core group, which, by its energy, its conviction, the charismatic appeal of its leader, manages to win a larger following. As the movement grows, new cells and new chapters are formed to guide the activities of persons in different localities. Religious movements built around a prophecy, like Jehovah's Witnesses, or on the evangelical appeal of a single leader, like the Methodists or the Mormons, often follow a centrifugal pattern of development. The religious revival and ultimately the denomination made successful by widespread proselytizing grows out of the small sect of original believers.

But besides moral crusades, revolutionary movements also may begin with the plotting of a group whose small size is made necessary by the secrecy of their enterprise.

Any core group, if it is to be successful, must be able to link up with other groups pursuing similar objectives. When no central core group exists but, on the contrary, the movement develops out of many small independent groups, separated from each other, which then join in a common enterprise, we call the movement *centripetal.* A central directorate coalesces gradually out of the many cells of unrest. Their unity lies in a shared sense of mission, and often their efforts seem hardly co-ordinated with so many cells feuding among each other. This latter growth pattern is more likely when cells grow out of and must deal with rather similar conditions. In time, the various forms of action taken to remedy these conditions coalesce, either through usurpation, as was true of the Bolsheviks, or through some kind of loose working agreement to lend moral, financial, or tactical support to each other, as was generally true of the American labor and the women's movements.

The Study of Social Movements

The attributes used to construct typologies of social movements are numerous. The preceding discussion does not exhaust the subject. Its main purpose, other than a general introduction to the field, is to indicate the attributes to be considered in selecting movements for study. If one wishes to select a sample that will encompass a variety of analytically useful types, one should include movements of both major types of value-orientation, movements directed at specific objectives and movements encompassing general protest, as well as movements exhibiting both centripetal and centrifugal patterns of growth. To repeat, the purpose of the typology is not to classify each movement. Such classification in itself is of little use.

Three other approaches to the study of social movements seem fruitful. The first focuses on the natural history of social movements.[13] By viewing a particular social movement over a period of time, one may discern a typical sequence pattern: its crystallization out of social unrest, its phase of active agitation and proselytization, its organized phase, and the achievement of its objectives. It may be supposed that leader-

13. Rex. D. Hopper, "The Revolutionary Process: A Frame of Reference for the Study of Revolutionary Movements," *Social Forces,* XXVIII (March, 1950), pp. 270–79; also Carl A. Dawson and Warner E. Gettys, *An Introduction to Sociology* (rev. ed.; New York: The Ronald Press Company, 1935), chap. 19.

ship, tactics, psychological fabric, its following, and the degree of recognition accorded to it differ from phase to phase, but are more or less the same for all movements in the same phase.

A second approach could be called cross-sectional, to distinguish it from the natural history approach. The idea is to study the various currents of agitation and unrest that come together at one point in time. Accordingly, one would study not only the inner dynamics of a specific collectivity but the way the social movement appears from a variety of perspectives. In studying a revolution, for example, it would be important to consider not only the sequence pattern but how various individuals who are participants, bystanders, and opponents of the revolutionary change contribute to the historical development. Such an approach is essentially historical and idiographic, but the application of sociological principles allows one to discern the part that leaders, followers, mass media, indecision of those in power, the degree of cohesiveness of the movement, etc., play in its development.[14]

The third approach is comparative. One examines a variety of situations which are similar in certain aspects but different in others and through which one seeks out the factors accounting for the different degrees of "success" in a given social movement. Thus, some social movements achieve their objective completely and maintain their existence as an organized group even afterward, while others completely disappear and disintegrate once their objective is achieved. Moreover, many movements, despite fabulous success in achieving prominence quickly, disappear from the scene as suddenly as they arose without leaving any permanent mark on the society.[15] Still others collect a loyal following, but they never blossom forth to reach the dimension necessary to realize their objective.

The approach taken in the following chapter is closest to the last. Through examples principally drawn from the American scene—on the assumption that readers will be more familiar with them—the conditions, the formation, the leadership, the characteristics of followers, the organization, the ideology, strategy, and tactics, and finally the psychological fabric of various movements are examined in order to gain some understanding of what accounts for different degrees of success.

14. See Chapter 18 for further discussion of the cross-sectional approach in the empirical study of social movements.

15. Howard Scott's Technocracy, which flourished in 1933, is a good example. See Frank Arkright, *The ABC of Technocracy*, (New York: Harper & Brothers, 1933). Gilbert Seldes, *Years of the Locust; America 1929–1932* (Boston: Little, Brown, & Co., 1933) is a little known but valuable source of information on incipient left-wing and right-wing movements that flourished in the Depression and died out just before Franklin D. Roosevelt came to office.

CHAPTER 17

The Dynamics of Social Movements

THE SOCIAL MOVEMENT, while itself a collective enterprise to effect changes in the social order, is also a response to changes in social conditions that have occurred independently of its efforts. Social movements, therefore, are more likely to arise in a society undergoing rapid social change than in a stable one. A revolution in technology, for example, creates new conditions requiring adaptation. Also, the more heterogeneous the elements making up a society, the more likely it is that the various subgroups will be affected in different ways by changes; sudden crises may sharpen cleavages already present. Unless mechanisms exist for the adaptation and incorporation into the social order of the demands of dissatisfied groups, these segments of the population, finding their aspirations unrecognized, will provide a fertile field for the growth of sectarian associations.

PSYCHOLOGICAL PREREQUISITES

EVERY SOCIAL MOVEMENT also depends on shared perspectives. Mass communication offers the opportunity for a quick focalization of unrest on a comman objective among people who share the same frustration. Therefore, one can assume that the use of mass communication for propaganda facilitates the rapid spread of a movement. Still, mass communication probably moderates the degree of conflict generated by a movement. Through the mass media the masses share common experiences and are integrated into the larger society. If the followers of a social movement thus continue to participate—however vicariously— in the life of the larger community, they are not likely to be involved in the movement as completely as they would be if such links were lacking.

[507]

Since a mass-communication system can either dramatize or play down cleavage, it certainly affects the character of any social movement.

The formula that best sums up the psychological, as contrasted to the social, prerequisites for the emergence of an active social movement consists of two terms: widespread *discontent* plus *faith* in the mission of the movement. Although in a heterogeneous mass society an underlying potential for social movements always exists, we can nevertheless identify certain periods in which the psychological factors are present to an unusual degree. Eruptions of unrest into active social movements seem to run in cycles. The notion of a natural oscillation is sometimes used to explain the alteration of periods in which social movements proliferate with periods of apparent quiescence. The 1930's in the United States were certainly a decade of activity, whereas the 1920's and the years following World War II, though years of excitement, were marked by sporadic fads, crazes, and sometimes bursts of mass indignation and hero worship. Movements for social reform or moral regeneration were relatively few and confined in scope. The lack of agitational fervor that marked the 1920's and 1950's has been popularly interpreted as proof that after years of crisis people need a period of calm, a breather, a time to rest and to indulge their individual whims in escapist ventures. Having recuperated, people are psychologically ready once more for crusading.

The existence of such cycles seems undeniable. Though one can find many expressions of unrest even in the quiescent periods, the occasional agitation for religious and moral panaceas, even crusades to raise the moral tone of politics, are usually abandoned as suddenly as they erupt. The zeal they attract is only transitory. Still, these periods of seeming quiescence are sometimes decisive for future social movements. A backlog of discontent guarantees receptivity for a movement which, once it arises, directs that discontent to specific targets and holds promise of change. Core groups develop and unrest accumulates during these periods of calm. In periods of dramatic change, new collective solutions emerge while old ones are abandoned with alacrity.

Changes in Life Conditions

Here we shall speak of turning points rather than of oscillations in activity. A revolutionary period represents a turning point in which a number of minor and sporadic movements coalesce into one major upheaval. Revolutions and other turning points are the outgrowth of tensions accumulated by changes in life conditions and by the changes in perspectives that are related to altered circumstances. Given these changes in life circumstances, there is usually some realignment. Some movements disappear, their energies being absorbed into others. Others, successful in adapting themselves to changed circumstances, are radically transformed. Finally, new movements in keeping with the psychological temper of the times become dominant.

Any crisis that assumes catastrophic proportions in the eyes of large segments of the population can become a turning point in the development of a social movement. Among these are natural disasters, economic depressions, and wars. It should be pointed out, however, that it is not only the change in conditions but the perspective from which they are viewed that account for the cycles of activity. For the emergence of social movements, the psychological prerequisites are as important as the social changes that underlie them.

THE CIVIL WAR

Wars often correlate with basic psychological realignments. The importance of war as a turning point in the history of social movements can be illustrated by examining the American Civil War. The fortunes of many social movements were deeply affected. In the first place, some saw in the war itself a realization of their objective. Either they were absorbed in the war effort or their cause no longer seemed important after the war. At the same time, the character of other movements was radically transformed by the social changes and realignments the war brought about. Finally, the origins of new social movements that came to dominate the Reconstruction Period can be traced to unrest stirred up during the war and to new objectives that emerged as a consequence.

With the outbreak of the war, the antiforeign, anti-Catholic, but pre-eminently anti-Irish nativist movement, which had flourished in the 1850's and was personified by the infamous Know-Nothings (among other groups), came to a temporary halt.[1] Abolition, because it was joined to the cause of preserving the Union, became the more important issue, and some of the agitation, on each side of the Civil War, turned to objectives concerned with the moral justifications for abolishing or retaining slavery as an institution. The antiforeign movement thus found itself outside the mainstream of activity. We do not know whether its followers were entirely absorbed in agitation for the Union or the Southern cause. At the very least, however, the advent of the war forced a reconsideration of what, in view of the fundamental cleavage between

1. Carl N. Degler, *Out of Our Past; the Forces that Shaped Modern America* (New York: Harper & Brothers, 1959), chap. 10.

the two, was most worth agitating for. The antiforeign crusade was put aside to erupt again as a major concern only in the last decades of the nineteenth century.

The more potent enemies that emerged during the war itself provided targets on whom those susceptible to hate appeals could spend their venom, be it the "Yankees" or the "Rebs." Even after the war was over, and for some years thereafter, the venom that might have spilled back into a new nativist movement was, according to Gustavus Myers, diverted into the campaign to extirpate the Mormon practice of polygamy.[2] Thus bigots joined with the members of many churches in a new crusade against a common enemy. Only when the threat of polygamy had been effectively countered did a new nativist movement attract considerable support.

The increasing political and economic power of the Irish, major target of the pre-Civil War nativist movement, was undoubtedly another major factor in its cessation. Once the Irish became a force to be reckoned with, they were less vulnerable. The wartime riots of 1863, in which the Irish protested the inequities of the draft law, seemed to have left the impression that the Irish were not putting their full weight behind the common effort. But many served with great distinction, proving the patriotism of these "foreigners." The contribution a minority group makes in wartime often helps to stem the agitation against it.[3] The military feats of Americans of Japanese ancestry in World War II, for example, helped to gain them recognition as Americans.

Besides bringing a halt to several movements, the Civil War changed the character of many others—for instance, Abolition. This did not simply disappear as its major goal, the abolition of slavery, was realized. Energies were mobilized on behalf of early abolition in the name of humanitarianism. Some of these energies, supplemented by new passions stirred up by Abolition as a patriotic cause, were redirected to feed a movement for revenge and to exact tribute from the defeated South.

Also, speaking broadly, the Civil War transformed some predominantly moral crusades into movements for social reform. For example, the temperance movement was, by the time of the Civil War, already giving way to the prohibition movement.[4] The war helped to make

2. Gustavus Myers, *History of Bigotry in the United States* (New York: Random House, 1943), p. 214.

3. Leonard Wibberly, *The Coming of the Green* (New York: Henry Holt & Co., Inc., 1958).

4. See Roy A. Haynes, *Prohibition Inside Out* (Garden City, N.Y.: Doubleday, Page & Co., 1932); John Allen Krout, *The Origins of Prohibition* (Alfred A. Knopf, Inc., 1925); or Raymond W. Cooper, *The Drama of Drink* (New York: Cornwall Press, 1932) for a history of the early temperance movements and the origins of Prohibition.

temperance seem too slow and wasteful a process. The advocates of temperance sought personal salvation from the evil of drink through spiritual guidance; to begin with, they urged self-restraint, not abstinence. The advocates of prohibition sought institutional and legal measures to control the liquor traffic and remove temptation, thus saving the alcoholic from himself. The decline of this and other moral crusades reflects the same process of diversion of energy that marks the decline of nativism. Although a war calls for individual sacrifice and heroism, the objective is achieved within the framework of formal institutions. In the collective enterprise to win the war, the patience required to achieve individual conversion appears wasteful. Thus, a wartime decline in civilian neuroses is accounted for, in part, by the substitution of a collective madness that diverts from individual ailments and makes them seem trivial. Neuroses simply can't be tolerated. Whatever the explanation, the fact is that after the war the movement against the evils of drink became alienated from the humanitarian spirit, its hallmark in the days before the war. Drink was the evil to be eradicated through prohibition; the attempts at mass conversion of drinkers were too wasteful.

Similar transformations occurred in other movements. The movement for women's rights had received its initial inspiration from female crusaders dedicated to securing from men of influence recognition of woman's rights in all spheres of life.[5] Many feminist leaders had supported Abolition, a support for which they were never rewarded. The freedom won by former slaves as a result of the war received recognition in the extension of suffrage to Negro adult males. But women, regardless of color, remained inferior to men. After the war the women's movement became less and less of a moral crusade and focused instead on institutional reform, dominated by one single issue—achieving the right to vote. As the war had given women more economic power, because of their participation in war work, the movement gained an impetus.

This was true to some extent of the labor movement as well. In pre-Civil War days it was very closely tied to the demand for universal public education. Especially during the fifties, it came under the influence of various humanitarian and utopian philosophies. It became more nearly identical with practical trade-union demands in the years after the war.[6]

New movements were also an aftermath of the war. As a social movement, the Ku Klux Klan, directed against the Negro as its specific villain,

5. A colorful, if somewhat colored, introduction to leaders of the feminist movement can be found in Oliver Jensen, *The Revolt of American Women; A Pictorial History of the Century of Change from Bloomers to Bikinis—from Feminism to Freud* (New York: Harcourt, Brace & Co., 1952), chap. 11.

6. The classic work on the early American labor movement is John R. Commons *et al.*, *The History of Labor in the United States* (New York: The Macmillan Co., 1918), I and II.

was a direct outgrowth of the new political realities. Moreover, industrial growth and the new conditions it produced stirred up the first currents of agitation for what was later to become the eight-hour-day movement. Antecedents for this movement can of course be found in the demands for a shortened work-day which were raised by local Workingmen's Associations in the administration of Andrew Jackson and were briefly revived in the 1850's. Still, the agitation in the various localities never quite coalesced into a movement on a national scale. The new labor movement that culminated in the trade-unionism of today developed only after the Civil War.

CHANGING PERSPECTIVES

As IMPORTANT as the changes in life conditions are the social perspectives from which these changes are viewed. These perspectives are, of course, governed largely by the way individuals occupying similar statuses feel themselves affected by any change. But the particular set of statuses that emerges as relevant to a problem faced by many is a collective process in its own right. It is a matter of collective definition. Consequently changes in perspective, while not exactly independent of social structure, may affect the fortunes of a social movement, speeding its rise, facilitating its success, and hastening its decline. Thus, a cause that appears at one time as a specific issue may become linked with broader national or class interests. A general humanitarian goal is redefined as a class interest, or vice versa. The transformation of the prohibition question from a class issue into a general moral issue over a period of years illustrates how changed perspectives account for the success or demise of a movement.

THE PROHIBITION MOVEMENT

Prior to World War I the controversy over legal prohibition of the transport and sale of alcoholic beverages was implicitly a class issue. Predominantly rural or of rural origin, the middle classes were as strongly for prohibition as the urban working classes were against it. But as a class issue the prohibition amendment could never have obtained enough popular support for ratification by three-quarters of the states. Actually the issue was so redefined and the perspectives on alcohol were so changed that, with the passage of time, the issue ceased to be one that involved contrasting class perspectives—or, at least, it involved them to a lesser extent.

In its latter stages in the decades before World War I, the focal target of the prohibition movement was the saloon.[7] It was made the symbol of all the evils attributed to drink. Many humanitarians who had supported temperance but were opposed to prohibition, because it meant an abridgment of personal rights, were strongly in favor of outlawing the saloon. It was in relation to the saloon, much more than to drinking, that persons were divided along class lines.

Middle-class reformers saw the workingman seduced by the avaricious saloonkeeper into drinking up his pay while his family went hungry.[8] When liquor is not available, they argued, people don't get used to it. The liquor traffic had to be halted if for no other reason than to spare those still too young to learn to drink. Entrepreneurs and factory owners saw in the saloon a threat to productivity. Many employers had once paid part of their employees' wages in grog and thus helped to make the latter's laborious lot bearable. With increasing mechanization, efficiency on the job became more important. Hence, employers came to view liquor (and those who dispensed it) as productive of inefficiency. The saloon became a threat to the economy. Meanwhile, the middle and upper classes had no need to patronize the saloon since private clubs served highballs, Scotch, cocktails, and good wines in much more pleasant surroundings.

The saloon was, however, the poor man's club.[9] It provided fellowship; it was the meeting place for organizations; men met there to exchange information and political gossip, to engage in philosophical talk. For some, it was a refuge from exhaustion and depression; it was, for example, the only place where a stranger to a city could go for a bit of warmth and a helping hand, where, if in need, he might get a loan from the saloonkeeper to tide him over. Their employers might look upon drinking as a threat to the economy, but workers knew that the jobs in the liquor and brewing industries that were providing many a livelihood would disappear with prohibition. Some of the most militant and successful unions were connected with the brewery industry, so that the stand by organized labor against prohibition was dictated in part by self-interest.[10] When Terence Vincent Powderly, Grand Master Workman of

7. For a first-rate account of how the saloon served as a symbol of evil, see Peter Odegard, *Pressure Politics; the Story of the Anti-Saloon League* (New York: Columbia University Press, 1928).

8. Charles Stelzle, *Why Prohibition?* (New York: George H. Doran Company, 1918).

9. Jack London, *John Barleycorn* (New York: The Century Company, 1913).

10. Haynes, *op. cit.*, p. 118, mentions the Bartenders League of America, The International Union of Brewery Workmen, and the Glassblowers, Cigarmakers, and Coopers unions which, with others, formed the Trade Union Personal Liberty League to fight the dry movement.

the Knights of Labor, took a stand for prohibition, it helped trigger the demise of his organization.

Defections from the solid front of labor presaged the future turn. Many individuals active in the labor and socialist movements came out for prohibition—that is, against the saloon.[11] In a tract called *John Barleycorn,* Jack London, himself a long-standing alcoholic, detailed his early addiction to liquor and through it the larger evils. But it was only the advance of the war that made a significant proportion of voters shift their view on prohibition. The movement for prohibition was successful because its propaganda was able to sensitize voters to aspects of the situation that had not been important before. In the wake of anti-German sentiment unleashed by the war, the German origin of the major brewers assumed new significance. The saloonkeeper as the German saloonkeeper, the brewer as the German brewer, became real devils. Especially the latter were said to be diverting into the manufacture of alcoholic beverages grains that should have been used to feed American armies overseas.[12] Moreover, the workingmen were asked to sacrifice for the war effort some of the pleasure the saloon afforded. Doing well under war conditions that provided full employment, they could do no less. Once it was no longer viewed as a class issue, prohibition of the liquor traffic became a feasible measure. Support from the working classes was obtained largely because the objective was appealed to in the name of the common good.

HISTORICAL EVENTS: 1886

A social movement is carried by the amount of enthusiasm and support it attracts among a wider public. Support for its objective depends on many specific and unique circumstances and not just on broad social changes. Specific events shape the collective definition of a movement. If the resulting image changes, an objective can become quickly and completely discredited even though a potential for broad support exists. Consequently, the fortunes of a social movement cannot be predicted solely from the underlying social trends that appear to favor or discourage it. The Haymarket Affair of 1886 provides an example of the role of specific events. Public support for the eight-hour day was undermined so effectively and so decisively that the demand, even though clearly consistent with the aspirations of labor, did not again come to the fore as a

11. *Ibid;* see also, Upton Sinclair, *The Cup of Fury* (Great Neck, N.Y.: The Channel Press, 1956).
12. Stelzle, *op. cit.*

major objective until the public temper changed radically during the great depression of the 1930's.[13]

The unrest that fed the eight-hour movement stemmed from several general and specific frustrations. An average working day of fourteen to eighteen hours meant that workers in some industries actually lived in the shop, falling asleep from exhaustion after work and waking to begin work again the next day. The labor movement, in its infancy at the time, was still smarting from the crushing defeat it had suffered in the unsuccessful railroad strikes of 1877. Their bargaining power was minimal, since the rapid introduction of new machinery had increased the number of unskilled and semiskilled in their ranks. There was a surplus of labor, due to the peak wave of European immigration, rural migration to the cities, the exhaustion of the supply of free public lands, and the new pools of manufacturers. Finally, the depression of 1884–1885 made conditions of labor even worse. Workers throughout the country responded enthusiastically to the eight-hour movement; they expected an easier working day which would spread work, creating jobs for the unemployed.

Grand Eight-Hour Leagues were formed in the principal cities and manufacturing centers of the North. The new Federation of Organized Trades and Labor Unions (forerunner of the American Federation of Labor) called in 1884 for an eight-hour day by May 1, 1886. As a result of rank-and-file agitation, the Knights of Labor, notwithstanding the reluctance of their leadership, who considered the demand too radical, found themselves spearheading a movement they had neither created nor approved. Powderly, their Grand Master, called the demands premature. He insisted that public sentiment was not yet ready to support the demand and that a hostile press, feeding on general ignorance of the movement, was successfully tying the demand to socialism, anarchism, and revolution. Nevertheless, the popularity of the demand was reflected in the membership figures of the Knights of Labor. It rose from 104,066 in July, 1885, to 702,924 in July, 1886, with the bulk of the increase occurring in 1886 as the target day neared.

Optimism concerning the chances of success ran high, especially in the first days of May as a series of strikes gained momentum. According to one report, altogether three hundred thousand workers struck. Then on the night of May 4, 1886, a bomb thrown in Haymarket Square in Chicago exploded, killing seven policemen and wounding sixty more.

13. Data on the eight-hour movement and the effects of the Haymarket Affair were drawn primarily from Samuel Yellen, *American Labor Struggles* (New York: Harcourt, Brace & Co., 1936), and George Brooks, "Historical Background," in A.F.L.-C.I.O., *The Shorter Work Week* (Washington, D.C.: Public Affairs Press, 1957), pp. 7–19.

With them was blown up any hope that the eight-hour demands would be realized. This unforeseen event had a certain shock effect. Mass agitation for an eight-hour day ceased abruptly, and the subsequent history of the American labor movement was certainly shaped by it.

Several anarchists were tried and convicted for throwing the bomb. Whether they actually did or whether the bombing itself was a "frame-up" is for the historian to decide. The police, claiming to have discovered evidence of anarchist plots, broke up gatherings of strikers. A disordered surrender began. There was much confusion among the rank and file; workers enthusiastic about shortening working hours were not necessarily enthusiastic about bomb-throwing anarchists imported from abroad. Indeed, it was the following year that a revived nativist movement got under way. Meanwhile with the connection between eight-hourism and anarchism already planted in the public mind by the press, much of the just indignation against the bombing naturally turned against the strikes then in progress. In these circumstances, employers were able to retract even the promises they had already given.

What happened in Chicago was that two movements crossed paths. The revolutionary goals of the one adversely affected the possibility of the other's gaining its reform demands. As a mass movement, eight-hour agitation was stopped in its tracks. One of the ironies of history is that the reluctant Knights of Labor, which at one point even tried to withdraw secretly from the target date, suffered most from the disappointment and confusion, and that the American Federation of Labor gained ascendancy over the old organization after the Haymarket Affair. The shorter working day, which had stirred so many, did not thereafter emerge again as a predominant objective. Instead, it becomes one of many demands raised within the framework of collective bargaining, designed to gain improved working conditions in the organized trades. It was finally embodied into law when the economic depression of the 1930's led people once more to define the reduction of working hours as a method of spreading work and creating jobs.

It can be concluded, then, that the fortunes of social movements are determined by social conditions that create unrest, by the way in which these social conditions are viewed and interpreted, and by events that trigger or discredit the flow of sentiment toward an objective around which new hopes crystallize. We shall turn now to the way in which definitions necessary to a social movement develop out of unrest.

LEADERSHIP IN SOCIAL MOVEMENTS

THE HISTORIAN usually finds the beginnings of a social movement in some specific event: the prophet who had a vision; the meeting of a small group to launch a sectarian association; or some spontaneous collective action, such as the challenge of a mob to constituted authority. The sociologist explaining a movement is more likely to point to the general social unrest and to seek underlying causes in the social structure. Neither of the two constitutes a full explanation of how a *movement* itself was launched. A movement arises when the general situation is favorable, and at the same time it gets its impetus from some specific person or event. There are several ways in which the diffuse unrest comes to congeal into a collective enterprise that promises remedy for a widely recognized social ill.

EARLY LEADERS

To say how a social movement began is often difficult, since the original instigators become known only through the successful groups. Furthermore, what is known about them is usually distilled in the glorification of early struggles by those who inherit the movement and lay claim to its tradition. The early leaders best remembered are most likely to be those who, canonized as martyrs and heroes, served best to unify the followers. It does not follow that they played the most significant role in the formation of the movement or that the deeds recorded about them were typical for those early activists who sparked the movement. For example, people remember Carry A. Nation for her saloon-smashing fame. Mrs. Nation's career has been chronicled and we are told that the death of her husband, a physician, from acute alcoholism accounts for her participation in the crusade.[14] It is much more difficult to track down the background of such early temperance workers as Mrs. Eliza Jane Trimble Thompson, of Hillsboro, Ohio, known as "Mother" Thompson, first leader of the Crusade Movement, which later became the Woman's Christian Temperance Union. Published sources do tell us that she felt herself called to duty through a conversion experience.[15]

This holds true of many other movements. The importance of the role played by Louis Fraina in the foundation of the American Communist Party was until 1957 almost undocumented and his life shrouded in

14. Stewart H. Holbrook, *Dreamers of the Dream* (Garden City, N.Y.: Doubleday and Company, Inc., 1957), p. 99f.; Jensen, *op. cit.*

15. Haynes, *op. cit.*

mystery.[16] Much work has been done on the life of Hitler, but little is known of other leaders with whom he joined in the very early days of the movement. Martov, leader of the Russian Menshiviks and an important figure in the early history of Russian socialism, also remains obscure because he did not participate in the successful uprising that culminated in the Russian Revolution.

Speaking generally, social movements get their impetus from instigators or initiators who supply examples, from the active direction of a recognized leader or core group, from a small group or leader who offers a solution (ideology or plan) for their unfocused sentiments, or from any combination of these.

Where the initial impetus comes from an *example*, the behavior imitated must appear to be a solution to the problem the mass following shares. The instigator setting the example may be either an individual or a collectivity. In either case, the example set is followed because it holds promise of success.

Leadership differs from instigation by example inasmuch as the leader initiates group action for a following. His *directives* are accepted as solutions because of the faith, trust, and authority he enjoys.

The impetus to a social movement may come from the way *the situation is defined*. An ideology that explains the sources of frustration and offers a plan promising relief is congruent with the dispositions of the potential following. Under conditions of extreme discontent, many solutions, however illogical, may be accepted because they seem to define the situation in a plausible manner.

Impetus by Example

A moral crusade often rests on individual example. The Washington revival, which focused attention on a way of dealing with insobriety

> . . . originated, so far as any complex movement may be said to have a single origin, among a group of tipplers in Chase's Tavern, Baltimore, Maryland. On the evening of April 2, 1840, six convivial friends, long accustomed to while away their evenings in gaming and drinking, met at the tavern with no thought of changing the usual program. In a spirit of fun, however, one of their number suggested that they send a committee to hear a temperance lecturer who was announced to speak in a near-by church. The committee returned from the lecture with an enthusiastic report of what they had heard, which started a spirited discussion of the total abstinence principle and its power to change men's

16. Theodore Draper, *The Roots of American Communism* (New York: The Viking Press, Inc., 1957), I.

habits. This interchange of views resulted in a decision to form a society that would commit them to abstinence from the use of all intoxicants. William K. Mitchell, who was delegated to put their resolution into writing, presented the following pledge for their approval: "We, whose names are annexed, desirous of forming a society for our mutual benefit, and to safeguard against a pernicious practice which is injurious to our health, standing and families, do pledge ourselves as gentlemen, that we will not drink any spiritous or malt liquors, wine or cider." Having signed this comprehensive pledge, the six charter members turned their attention to the election of officers, the method of obtaining revenue and the problem of securing new members. . . .

Labelling themselves as reformed drunkards, the founders of the new movement were immediately successful in persuading others to join them. . . . As the society grew, the problem of making the meetings interesting demanded solution. President Mitchell, quick to sense that which would be popular, suggested that the program of stated meetings be limited to a narration of personal experiences by members who had felt the saving influence of the pledge. . . . Thus, the standard for other Washingtonian societies was set, and the chief characteristic of the movement became the reformation of drunkards by reformed drunkards.[17]

The six tipplers in the Baltimore pub set themselves up as examples. They were also able to redefine the problem of liquor as a problem of temptation. The example they offered showed how by the mobilization of inner and moral resources temptation could be resisted. Out of the active core who set out to proselytize other drunkards, the so-called "Cold Water Army" was born.

Movements aimed at institutional reform may gain their impetus in a similar manner. Partisan and resistance movements seize on tactics that have met with success, even if carried out by a small group or a few persons. The movement that culminated in the C.I.O. in the 1930's gained its mass support when the sitdown strike tactics succeeded in closing a plant by barring scabs. A social movement evolves from example when the behavior imitated offers not just an individual solution, as in mass behavior, but becomes part of a collective enterprise.

Impetus by Direction

No social movement is more spontaneous than that which spreads solely by example. But in most instances, leadership, which directs attention and validates it, is needed to supplement the example. Thus, the successful example is likely to put the individual at the head of a group of followers who from here on obey his directives. Such movements often

17. Krout, *op. cit.*, p. 23.

bear the name of their leader because they are built around his image. The 26th of July movement, officially inspired by an act of rebellion, is most widely identified as Castro's Movement.[18] Indeed, there was no well-thought-out program for reform after victory. Many supporters of the Cuban revolution were satisfied to put their trust in Fidel Castro and to follow wherever he led them.

Persons successful in their solution generally find it relatively easy to seize leadership. The Russian Bolsheviks, rather than the more sophisticated German Marxists from whom the Bolsheviks had learned, assumed leadership and shaped the international communist movement from 1919 on. According to Theodore Draper, Russian-born leaders actually exercised a dominant influence on the formation of the American Communist party, when in its early days it crystallized out of a number of other movements.[19] Because Russians had succeeded in making a revolution in Russia, a revolution in which the Russians themselves had never expected to succeed and whose success they could not clearly understand themselves, they became oracles of knowledge on successful revolution.

Impetus from Definition

The most organized impetus comes from a group which sets out to propagate a specific solution to a problem. In many instances, sectarian associations which hatch conspiratorial plans or cultivate a specific ideology do not succeed in redefining the problem for a larger following. But given the proper circumstances and successful agitation and propaganda, a message may be spread. Groups have succeeded in obtaining support for "share the work" plans as an answer to depression. The problem of old age became redefined into an unwillingness of politicians to sponsor a plan that would ensure each senior citizen a fabulous monthly pension (i.e., the Townsend Plan). Every movement has a tendency to develop, as it becomes more organized, an intricate ideology through which the major social problems with which it is concerned are defined and solutions spelled out.

LEADERS

As a movement changes, the kind of leadership demanded also changes. At the beginning, a movement requires agitators—that is, persons who are able to "stir things up." But the agitator is not enough. A move-

18. Fidel Castro, *History Will Absolve Me,* plea before the Emergency Session of the Court of Santiago de Cuba, October 16, 1953 (pamphlet published by Liberal Press, Inc., 1959).
19. Draper, *op. cit.*

ment needs a man of vision to show the way, a prophet. The prophet is in a sense still an agitator, but he is above all capable of painting a utopia from which the hope for the movement derives. The administrator becomes more important as the movement grows and spreads. His major function is to co-ordinate the movement and supervise its apparatus. Finally, the statesman is the politician who adroitly moves within the realm of the possible and helps the movement gain its objective.[20]

Leadership Roles

Although the kinds of tasks required of each leader vary as the movement passes through different phases, it seems incorrect to identify a specific type of leader with each phase. In many religious or quasi-religious movements—for example, the Muslims, a black supremacy movement—the leader during its agitational phase is a charismatic prophet to whom almost mystical qualities are imputed. But in another very similar movement, the United African Nationalist Movement, the head of the movement acts as a statesman, making contact with other groups in the United States and the Middle East. The agitational function is taken over by professional agitators who go out on the street and stir up the people on Harlem streetcorners from soap boxes.[21] A division of labor makes possible the cultivation of an image that may be out of line with the major activity of the movement.

If a social movement built essentially around one person is to survive his death or fall from grace, provision must be made for an heir apparent. The continuing success of the movement represented by Father Divine depends largely on a belief in his immortality. A cult, based on myths concerning his survival, has been built up.[22] By contrast, the Jehovah's Witnesses, brought into being by the persuasive preaching of Charles Taze Russell, never focused all attention on a single personality. The International Bible Students, formed in response to the message of this lay preacher, could be transformed from a sect into a full-scale religious movement only because the personal charisma of its leader was played down. Russell's successor, J. F. Rutherford, a lawyer who in 1931 gave

20. Dawson and Gettys saw the agitator as typical of the period of social unrest, the prophet-reformer characteristic of the stage of popular excitement, the administrator leading in the period of formal organization, and the statesman leading in the final phase when a movement becomes institutionalized. This typology is often cited. C. A. Dawson and W. E. Gettys, *Introduction to Sociology*, (rev. ed.; New York: The Ronald Press Company, 1935), chap. 19.

21. From a television script, "The Hate That Hate Produced," produced by Mike Wallace (WNTA–TV, New York City, July 22, 1959, 8:00–10:00 p.m., E.D.T.).

22. Rumors keep springing up that Father Divine is actually dead. Whether or not he is, and whenever he is, it seems likely that the believers will carry on since, dead or alive, he is immortal.

the society the name by which it is now known, also stayed very much in the background. Stroup claims that he was almost a secret personality, much as Father Divine has become for his followers. But unlike Father Divine, Rutherford was an excellent administrator, with a good head for finance. When the scandal of his divorce rocked the movement, it survived because hate for the devil was a more important unifying force than faith in and attachment to a personal prophet. Nathan H. Knorr, Rutherford's successor, also sought anonymity, directing the attention of the followers to Jehovah God.[23]

It is a rare for a single individual to survive the transformation of a social movement through its active agitational phase and its more organized phase. To be able to do so requires unusual adaptability. Margaret Sanger's birth-control movement seems to have been guided throughout by the person who initiated it. Mrs. Sanger's role as leader changed through the years, but she continued to remain as its head. Under her guidance, the movement has coalesced into an organization, so that its fortunes no longer depend on her survival.[24] Many one-man movements, especially those of unclear origin built around the message of a particular prophet, do not survive the death of the leader unless they develop an effective apparatus.

An analogous phenomenon is the co-optation of leaders trained in one movement by another movement that succeeds and displaces it, provided the leadership roles are similar. The history of the women's rights movement is replete with women who were "trained" in the Abolition and temperance movements. Lucretia Coffin Mott began as a crusader for Abolition; Amelia Jenks Bloomer had agitated for temperance as had Susan B. Anthony and the Reverend Antoinette Brown. Others had been leaders of socialist and religious sects. Similarly, many American leaders of the communist movement were trained in the 1912–1913 strikes of the Paterson and Lawrence mills, protests led by the International Workers of the World. Among them were John Reed, Louis C. Fraina, and Elizabeth Gurley Flynn.

The Involvement of Leaders

A typology of leadership roles in social movements must consider not only necessary skills but also the degree of involvement demanded.

23. Herbert H. Stroup, *Jehovah's Witnesses* (New York: Columbia University Press, 1945); Marcus Bach, "The Startling Witnesses," *Christian Century*, LXXIV (February 13, 1957), pp. 197–99.

24. There were a number of movements sponsoring birth-control. Mrs. Sanger's, in the United States, became Planned Parenthood. See Lawrence Lader, *The Margaret Sanger Story and the Fight for Birth Control* (Garden City, N.Y.: Doubleday & Company, Inc., 1955).

Some movements demand complete dedication, but even those concerned only with limited objectives frequently expose the leader to friction and irritations from former associates. Many speak of the sacrifices that leaders make for a movement. According to Eric Hoffer, the leader is motivated to make the sacrifices required of him because he believes in the inevitability of his cause. The Reverend H. H. Russell of Berea, Ohio, sometimes referred to as the "father of the Anti-Saloon League," saw his as a sacrifice demanded by his creator. Speaking in 1913, he said:

> The Anti-Saloon League movement was begun by Almighty God. . . .
> Often I have been asked how I came to suggest this plan of organiza-
> tion to my Oberlin friends and to enlist as the first organizer and leader.
> I have answered, "I could not help it. There was nothing else I could
> do." . . . Whenever I passed a saloon, I sent up a prayer, "O, God,
> stop this!" At length God said to me, "You know how to do it; go and
> help answer your own prayers!" [25]

The assumption is that the leader undergoes some kind of conversion that ties him to a cause.

But commitment to the movement offers rewards for the sacrifices demanded. In some cases leadership is little more than a career gamble, promising great returns if it succeeds. On the other hand, a reformer like Susan B. Anthony, the famous crusader for women's rights, suffered general ridicule and ostracism. She gained in exchange the applause and fellowship of a dedicated group of crusaders. In reading about her life, one senses that the social movement was not only a means to a goal but her whole life.[26] The price of involvement must be measured against the security and comradeship offered by the circle of the select. Total involvement promotes undeviating dedication to a single cause. In general, total dedication has been seen as most typical of movements with extremist goals, but the deep involvement of a Susan B. Anthony is characteristic of leaders in many reform movements. In many ways the proportion of sacrifices asked to rewards gained may be greater in the case of a reformer who takes to the hustings for a limited goal than for the dedicated revolutionary or sectarian. The sporadic fellowship the reformer receives in return for his espousal of an unpopular cause rarely compensates for the rupture of social relations it requires. Of all the leaders of social movements, the reformer appears by this formula the most lonely and therefore the most dedicated to his goal.

25. Odegard, *op. cit.*, p. 8.
26. Florence H. Bryan, *Susan B. Anthony: Champion of Women's Rights* (New York: Julian Messner, Inc., 1947); A. Lutz, *Susan B. Anthony* (Boston: Beacon Press, Inc., 1958).

Recruitment

Many reform leaders are persons whose social position provides a certain amount of leisure time and whose training stresses humanitarian ideals and an aristocratic sense of responsibility as their brother's keeper. Leaders of this sort have seldom been recruited from among the persons who stand to benefit directly from the reform. Convicted criminals are not likely to head movements for penal reform; the wives of habitués of the workingmen's saloons did not spearhead the prohibition movement. Nor was a destitute mother of fifteen children likely to spark the birth-control movement. On the contrary, women of better-and-average education, secure in economic status, and seeking a socially useful outlet for their energies, have provided a high proportion of the leaders in American reform movements.

Movements seeking to attain revolutionary goals by mobilizing mass support have often recruited leaders from among the young and discontented "intellectuals" of a society—the students and professionals—and, to some extent, from among the self-schooled underprivileged. The dissatisfied intelligentsia have been the traditional reservoir of "revolutionary" leadership. Blind and fanatical dedication seems most typical of the social categories whose intellectual discontent and rebelliousness find support in sectarian associations that provide the ideology for or become the core group of revolutionary mass movements.

Consequently, the leadership potential for social movements depends on the social structure. An increase in education without a corresponding increase in opportunities for the educated fosters a revolutionary leadership—for example, observe the radical movements led by students in many underdeveloped countries. Similarly, where economic development swells the ranks of the middle classes but fails to inculcate the newly risen with a humanitarianism typical of the oldfashioned Tory, few leaders will arise to launch new moral and social crusades. Redress will be sought from private institutions and government agencies already established rather than by agitating for new causes.

THE FOLLOWING

THE "MOVEMENT" characteristic of a collective enterprise hinges on its capacity to inspire support from a large following. Still, generalization about the follower as a unitary type is difficult and probably unwarranted. Several distinctions among followers are suggestive, including:

the phase of the movement in which they join; their proximity to the core group; and the degree of involvement and commitment to the cause.

ORDER OF AFFILIATION

The following of any social movement can be differentiated by the phase during which they join. There are, first, the *early converts,* won over to the movement when it is still small and sectarian. They are followed by the *active reinforcements,* "old fighters" all, through whose support the movement begins to attain some significance even though the odds are still against it. The *joiners* constitute the mass of supporters who climb on as the bandwagon begins to roll and the movement becomes, so to speak, respectable. A last category, the *resisters,* consists of potential followers, persons who might be expected to display some affinity toward a movement which they strongly resist.

Informal rankings based on order of affiliation are recognized in almost every movement. Among the Nazis, the "old fighters" who participated in the 1923 beer-hall *Putsch* became a near-official club, while for the Russian Communist the designation "Old Bolshevik" was a badge of merit.

The character of the membership changes as the movement progresses. Such a change has been documented, for example, among the Jehovah's Witnesses. As the movement has gradually become institutionalized, its increasing respectability has attracted more professional people and a smaller proportion from among the misfits and outcasts of society. Such a change in membership usually accompanies the transformation of a sect into a church. But the Jehovah's Witnesses continue to attract converts. Yet, where for many years they attracted mostly delinquents from the traditional churches, today's converts, according to Bach, are often from accredited churches.[27] Joseph Gusfield traced the changing composition of the Woman's Christian Temperance Union after its success in getting prohibition ratified; there was a steady decrease in the proportion of professionals, proprietors, managers, etc., and an increase in the proportion of working-class people.[28] Other illustrations, especially the differences between active Nazis and non-Nazis, were presented in Chapter 10.

27. Bach, *op. cit.,* and Stroup, *op. cit.,* both document this change. Joseph Zygmunt's M.A. thesis, "Social Estrangement and the Recruitment Process in a Chiliastic Sectarian Movement" (Chicago, 1953), is a valuable source of information on the Witnesses.

28. Joseph R. Gusfield, "Social Structure and Moral Reform: A Study of the Woman's Christian Temperance Union," *American Journal of Sociology,* LXI (1955), pp. 221–32.

The motivations of different categories of members need study. How do the motivations of early converts and active reinforcements differ from those of late joiners? What is each willing to sacrifice and what does each stand to gain in case of success? How important is personal contact and social pressure as opposed to ideology and objective in each phase? To study the influence of different orders of membership upon the character of a movement is equally important. When the old guard is replaced by late comers, the leadership is likely to adapt itself to the new motivations.

ACTIVE CORE VERSUS PERIPHERY

There is a "division" of labor among the followers of every social movement. A central core of followers, the true believers about whom Hoffer writes, perform the routine work and dedicate what spare time they have to the movement. Some of them consider themselves leaders, but in fact they only do the work. Opposed to this cadre is the larger rank and file of the movement, who "march" along. The majority of them are loyal; they attend meetings, participate in activities, believe its ideology, and learn its songs and slogans. Beyond them is a much larger periphery of individuals, not clearly either in or outside the movement. They act as a "cheering" section, whose support can be mobilized on occasion. Although their connection to the movement is tenuous, they are crucial to its success.

Because no clear criteria of membership exist to identify them, the mass following has often been overlooked in favor of the core membership. Among the most useful studies of the mass following is Selznick's study of the fellow-travelers in the American Communist Party.[29] The loyalty of more peripheral followers can be great, although psychological commitment probably declines with distance from the core. Thus, one may infer that of all followers the most strongly committed to a movement are its paid workers, however menial their task. Because their livelihood is tied to the movement, and sometimes because they literally live in it, these "functionaries" find it hardest to get out.

THE DEGREE OF INVOLVEMENT

Involvement is itself a variable tied to psychological commitment. There are objective indices by which involvement can be determined. The degree of involvement helps to distinguish among followers, while

29. Philip Selznick, *The Organizational Weapon; A Study of Bolshevik Strategy and Tactics* (Santa Monica, Calif.: Rand Corporation, 1952).

movements as such can be distinguished by the degree to which followers are involved.

Participation that entails a complete rupture of previous associations means total commitment. The "totalitarian" character, irrespective of its ideology, of a movement is revealed when the recruit must give up and radically break with his prior life to dedicate himself to the cause. The more totalitarian a movement in this sense, the more does the act of affiliation constitute a conversion.

Inward movements (moral crusades) seem to effect this total commitment in a manner somewhat different from outward movements (crusades for institutional reform). The inward movement structures the relationship of its members with outsiders in terms of some tenet of morality. Only the small sects (e.g., the various utopian communities) withdraw their followers entirely from normal social relations. Those that seek to proselytize shape their relations in terms of their need to contact outsiders. A central core of full-time workers may give up their worldly goods to the movement in exchange for comradeship and room and board. The outward movement is more likely to require a complete commitment on the part of all but the most peripheral followers. In an underground movement, such demands are made for the sake of security. But the right of a movement to regulate friendships and employment and to demand severance of family ties, if they contradict its objectives, is unquestioned if complete dedication is a criterion for active participation.

Reform movements rarely attract the completely dedicated true believer. Though a movement successfully pursuing reform goals must have its share of full-time workers, some of whom spend their entire life working for its cause, they are not required to give up contact with the "outside." The fellowship they find in the movement does not require sacrificing other friendships, and often they are induced to join a movement only by friends who are already in it. An exception to this rule of limited commitment is found in some movements with reform goals that many consider a threat to the social order—for example, movements to eliminate discrimination in the South or the reforms advocated by the early labor movement. Participants in such movements, finding themselves socially ostracized, singled out for rough treatment, and even threatened with physical violence, etc., must choose between full commitment or dropping out entirely. Where such opposition tactics fail to destroy a movement, the members who remain will be a select group displaying exceptional morale. The history of the labor movement, in particular, upholds the validity of this proposition.

Both the degree of involvement and the number from whom complete dedication is demanded change as a movement passes through various phases. The degree of involvement is probably highest during the early phases. Early converts are often people fired by enthusiasm who, because of their zeal, are willing to pay the price of ostracism. At the same time, the fellowship developed in a movement during its active phase, when it attracts true believers, makes a break easier. The support a movement promises the perpetual "outsider" makes him want to belong and thereby escape frustrations experienced in his previous life. But as movements lose their spontaneous quality and a division of labor evolves, the involvement demanded from the majority of members can be expected to decline. Similarly, when objectives, once considered radical, become respectable, high commitment is no longer instrumental in achieving them.

The size of a movement is also likely to affect the involvement demanded. As it grows, control of all participants becomes less possible. As it reaches out for mass support it requires at crucial moments, the criteria of membership are often watered down. The mobilized masses cannot be controlled. With success, the motives of followers also change.

A strategic adaptation to a specific situation sometimes radically transforms the hold a movement has on its membership. A movement dedicated to the achievement of revolutionary goals may, as a temporary tactic, seek mass support by emphasizing specific reform goals. To do this, it will have to reduce its demands on potential followers. An interesting example is the transformation of the Communist Party in the United States during World War II into a movement dedicated simply to Soviet-American friendship. Since it demanded little from new recruits, save dedication to co-operation in the Allied war effort, membership in the C.P.U.S. between 1941 and 1944 approximately doubled.[30] Initiation into the now respectable movement entailed no break with one's circle of intimates. The new recruit was expected to be neither a dedicated revolutionist nor a political activist but had only the vaguest of political responsibilities. He was required only to "agree with the platform" and apply it wherever he was active, to participate in some phase of war, not party, work, to read the party press, and to pay dues to some branch. Attendance at meetings was not compulsory.[31]

The low degree of involvement exacted from the new recruit had a profound effect on the commitment of long-term party members.

Gone were the days when the members were bound by the closest fraternal and ideological bonds into a community of the elect (or as some almost seemed to feel, a consecrated family). . . . Instead as a . . . Communist leader would recall, "The rank and file were once again tast-

30. Irving Howe and Lewis Coser, *The American Communist Party: A Critical History, 1919–1957* (Boston: Beacon Press, Inc., 1957), p. 407.
31. *Ibid.*, pp. 420ff.

ing the joy of being accepted by all groups. The party line made it possible during this period for ordinary members to be merely human beings and to act naturally, for their neighbors were now less frightened, and even listened to Communists explain how they were on the side of the American people." [32]

After the war the thousands of new members recruited in the name of Soviet-American friendship dropped out. As members, they had never left the "outside world," their involvement in the movement having been so negligible. But long-time active and dedicated Communists were similarly softened by the minimal demands made upon them. In the war years they had once more known respectability and the compensations it brought. Many of them defected once outside pressures again built up against the party; psychologically they could no longer take total involvement.[33]

THE RECRUITMENT BASE

The recruitment base, from which a social movement attracts its following, varies considerably from movement to movement.

The inward movement usually directs its appeals to those whose anxieties and problems it promises to solve. Thus, the nineteenth century Societies for Reformed Drunkards or today's Alcoholics Anonymous offer moral regeneration to those in need of it. The crusade for women's rights in its early days appealed primarily to women willing to carry the moral message to men. Conviction that the moral message is personally meaningful is essential.

In the case of outward movements the delineation of recruitment bases is slightly more complicated. As already pointed out, many movements in support of specific reforms, such as the abolition of capital punishment or prison reform, recruit primarily among those in the upper or upper-middle classes who have a sense of responsibility toward those less fortunate and have leisure time to devote to reform activities. Still, when a specific reform goal is pursued with mass support, the humanitarian spirit behind it often disappears. It gets lost in the quest for assurance of moral support or becomes hostile in tone as it seeks to mobilize the mass demonstration of sympathy at critical moments. To be sure, every movement seeks moral support for its objectives, but not all do so if it entails the sacrifice of basic values. A movement with ostensibly humanitarian but far-reaching goals may count on mass demonstrations for its objectives when, so to speak, the time is ripe. For this reason, it must

32. *Ibid.*
33. *Ibid.*, p. 431.

promote its image as a movement not only *for* but *of* the people its program ostensibly seeks to aid. As it mobilizes the disaffected, its appeals become more extreme and their tone more hostile. The disciplined core of followers is rarely recruited primarily from among those most directly affected.

The participation of these masses confronts the core group with the problem of control. How much the movement depends upon discipline to gain its objective should be evident. For example, emotions aroused by nativist agitation fanned a riot in the course of which New York City's Astor Place opera house burned down, a loss that could only discredit the nativist leadership. In the strike movements of the Great Depression which had at times the appearance of a social revolution, organizers were hard put to head off the wildcat walkouts which employers actively provoked. It is well known that crowds go berserk in almost every social revolution, destroying property and participating in pointless violence, contributing little to and often impeding the achievement of concrete objectives. Strictly speaking, there can be no successful movement unless the masses themselves are disciplined by a cadre. This cadre is always recruited from a limited group.

Demographic Analysis

Much can be learned from an examination of the demographic base from which the social movement recruits its active members. Thus, movements can be compared in terms of the social class, age, sex, educational background, occupation, economic status, religion, etc., of their members. Deviant case analysis seems rewarding when characteristics of participants differ from those expected on the basis of ideology or by comparison to similar movements.

For example, hate movements are recruited predominantly from among the lower-middle and the lower classes. Intolerance goes together with limited educational achievement. Yet Degler shows two main sources of support for Know-Nothingism in Massachusetts: (1) old-line Whigs and (2) liberal Whigs and disaffected Democrats. The old-line Whigs were conservative, but they saw a threat to their political power in the growing number of Massachusetts Irish. The second group was opposed to the Irish because they were the mainstay of a dominant Democratic Party which they considered too conservative. The Know-Nothings are largely remembered as a nativist "hate" movement. But the Massachusetts Know-Nothings, though clearly anti-Irish, revealed their progressive spirit when elected in 1855. They passed a series of reform laws, including one for runaway slaves and free Negroes and another expanding the rights of women.[34]

34. Degler, *op. cit.*, chap. 10.

A study of demographic composition also enables one to define the potential universe from which followers are recruited. One may assume that movements recruited from the same universe are broadly similar. For example, in the period just prior to the American Civil War, there were movements for temperance, for women's rights, for the abolition of slavery, for human rights generally, as well as others to establish utopian settlements and test out various panaceas, all of which were supported mainly by the "aristocratic intellectuals" and the better-off socioeconomic classes.[35] Gusfield points to the affinity among all these movements. Temperance supporters, he states, formed larger segments of such other movements as sabbatarianism, abolition, women's rights, agrarianism, and humanitarian attempts to improve the lot of the poor.[36]

Similarly, there may be considerable overlap in the followings of various small sects that promise personal salvation. Cantril indicates that the followers of Father Divine had previously been Baptists, "Holy Rollers," Christian Scientists, and Theosophists.[37] Although the potential universe among these sects overlaps with that of various minority and labor movements, one would not expect to find any overlap between the movements that direct effort into political reform and those that build small heavens by reforming the inner man.

ORGANIZATION, STRATEGY, AND TACTICS

THOUGH A MOVEMENT as such is not organized, it faces structural problems that must be solved if it is to survive. The manner in which these problems are met usually entails some organization and rules in terms of which to meet future contingencies. The major structural problems are:

1. Regularizing the relations between leaders and followers.
2. Developing an appropriate type of leadership.
3. Determining the hierarchy of leaders and functionaries.
4. Organizing of a staff.
5. Co-ordinating the relations among various groups within the movement.

35. At a meeting called by the Friends of Universal Reform in the 1840's, there were present, among others: Grahamites (religious vegetarians), Thomsonians (a medical cult anti-Epsom Salts, bleeding, calomel, etc.), and representatives of such community experiments in living as Brook Farm, Fruitlands, Hopedale, Northampton, Shirley, and the North American Phalanx. Among the many interesting sources of materials on Nineteenth-century utopian communities in the United States are: Gilbert Seldes, *The Stammering Century* (New York: The John Day Co., 1928), and Holbrook, *op. cit.*, especially Part 1 on the Perfectionists.

36. Gusfield, *op. cit.*

37. Hadley Cantril, *The Psychology of Social Movements* (New York: John Wiley & Sons, Inc., 1941), p. 141.

6. Setting the criteria for full membership in the core group, including the duties and obligations of such membership.
7. Co-ordinating the activities of the movement in its dealings with other groups and outsiders in general—that is, developing an executing a strategy and tactics.[38]

Since social movements pass through several phases in the course of their development, the problems as well as the characteristic ways of dealing with them differ from phase to phase.

THE CAREERS OF SOCIAL MOVEMENTS

Several characteristic sequence patterns have been used to depict the career of a social movement. They have in common the notion that every movement passes through an incipient phase, a phase in which it organizes, and finally a stable phase when the forms have become fixed. The scheme of Dawson and Gettys is probably best known.

1. A period of social unrest with the agitator as the typical leader.
2. The period of popular excitement in which the vision of the prophet or the objective defined by the reformer spreads by contagion.
3. The stage of formal organization, headed by an administrator, with the beginnings of a division of labor, formal criteria of membership, etc.
4. The stage of institutionalization, when the movement, now bureaucratized, is represented by a statesman.[39]

If at any point in its career leadership fails to measure up to the contingencies confronting it, a movement will fail. Actually the study of abortive social movements may bolster our understanding of their mechanics considerably more than the concern with sequence patterns. One such abortive movement was Coxey's Army of the Unemployed (the Commonwealth Movement) which marched toward Washington, D.C., in 1894 to demand relief but never got beyond its popular phase. Technocracy, a mushrooming doctrine during the depression of the 1930's, disappeared as suddenly as it rose to prominence. With regard to many fascist and nativist groups in the United States in the same period, Shils suggests that they never got off the ground because their leaders, though reflecting the collective paranoia of their followers, lacked the requisite organizational skills to launch a larger movement.[40]

38. Adapted from Rudolph Heberle, *Social Movements* (New York: Appleton-Century-Crofts, Inc., 1951), p. 273f.
39. Dawson and Gettys, *op. cit.*, Hopper, *op. cit.*, in his study of revolutionary movements, indicated the form of collective behavior characteristic of each of Dawson and Gettys' stages.
40. Edward A. Shils, "Authoritarianism—Right and Left," in R. Christie and Marie Jahoda (eds.), *Studies in the Scope and Method of the Authoritarian Personality* (Glencoe, Ill. The Free Press, 1954).

OLIGARCHY AND FACTIONALISM

Some kind of administrative superstructure is undoubtedly necessary if a movement is to survive and enlarge its following. With this in mind, Robert Michels, observing the socialist parties of Europe as they evolved from the socialist movement, formulated his "iron law of oligarchy." He reasons that leadership will always treat the organization—that is, the administrative apparatus, the party press, the electoral system, etc.—as instruments for perpetuating their power, notwithstanding the democratic ideology of the movement. According to Michels, "it is organization which gives birth to the dominion of the elected over the electors, of the mandataries over the mandators, of the delegates over the delegators. Who says organization says oligarchy." [41]

In a study of the Canadian Commonwealth Federation, an agrarian socialist movement in the Canadian prairies during the great depression, Lipset noted an extremely high degree of membership participation and few oligarchal tendencies.[42] The geographic dispersal of members in the agrarian region necessitated a decentralization of activities. The movement had to rely heavily on local initiative, and a high proportion of the members were functionaries in its various activities. Mediating organizations serve as bases from which to oppose the encroachments of central oligarchy. A lack of bureaucratized leadership is also claimed for the Moral Rearmament movement; perhaps the explanation lies in the same tendency to seek "guidance" in local groups.

The reverse of oligarchy is factionalism, a problem responsible for the demise of many movements. Factionalism is most likely to develop when there are many bases of power while a central apparatus through which control can be exercised has not yet fully developed. Operating under conditions of illegality in small groups, the Bolsheviks developed many divergent factions, notwithstanding an official ideology that called for democratic centralism. Many of the leaders carried their private following into the new Soviet apparatus. But as long as the personality of Lenin was dominant, factionalism was held in check. The bitterness of the struggle that followed his death was enhanced by the inability of secondary leaders to step down and accept Stalin's control of the party apparatus. It can be hypothesized that factional, as opposed to oligarchic, tendencies will be more pronounced when there are (a) many private and personal bases of power and (b) no approved institutional means for gracefully surrendering positions of power.

41. Robert Michels, *Political Parties* (Glencoe, Ill.: The Free Press, 1949).

42. Seymour M. Lipset, *Agrarian Socialism* (Berkeley, Calif.: University of California Press, 1950).

THE STYLE OF ORGANIZATION

What is called, for lack of a better term, the "style of organization" refers to the general mode of regulating relations within a movement, resolving its conflicts, and meeting external contingencies. Among the factors that affect the style of organization are:

1. The *degree of opposition* the movement encounters. A movement operating under strong threat is likely to develop a quasi-military style of organization. This is imperative for a movement that wishes to survive illegality. But even a religious movement, like the Jehovah's Witnesses, confronted by a hostile world and threatened with suppression because of refusal to recognize state authority, adopts both a military type of organization and military terminology.

2. The *social position of its followers*. The style of organization tends to be adapted to what followers expect. For example, a movement based on the middle classes will generally tend to rely on parliamentary procedure in the conduct of its internal business and on official channels of communication to effect its ends. On the other hand, European workers liked use the intimate form of address provided by their native tongues and the appellation of "comrade."

3. The *aims of the movement*. An inward movement that aims at moral regeneration is likely to involve every one of its members. Since active proselytizing is required of every convert, the movement will be organized in such a way as to give each follower some kind of task, to let him know just what his role is. By contrast, a movement working toward a highly specific objective rarely involves its followers as deeply in its activities. Its organization may be so haphazard that members, recruited and anxious to contribute, cannot find out how to go about doing so.

4. The *cultural ethos* of the society. Styles of organization reflect the country and the period in which a movement emerges. Messianic movements of the nativist variety, aimed at extirpating Western influence, usually adopt the old tribal forms of organization in every detail. Or, if a tradition for democratic organization exists, the leadership of the movement is likely to offer opportunities for participation at the grassroots level.

5. The *type of leader*. A charismatic leader is more likely to have an appointed staff. Where the movement is headed by a statesman or an administrative type of leader—that is, in its later phases—both the leader and his lieutenants are likely to be elected. As the charismatic element in leadership declines, the staff is bound primarily to the organization; its loyalty can be readily transferred to new leaders.

STRATEGY AND TACTICS

Strategy and tactics refer to the manner in which a social movement goes about achieving its objective. The over-all design for action represents its strategy. Tactics, on the other hand, have to do with the manner of meeting day-to-day contingencies, such as attracting and holding members, exerting pressure on the opposition, choosing one's propaganda targets, etc. Strategy and tactics not only are interdependent but in fact often fuse.

Strategies are often classified according to the means favored for action. Inward movements place their greatest reliance on education and on individual proselytizing, although they have often reinforced their conversion efforts with threats and force. The strategy of outward movements is usually designed to move large masses, not individuals. The manner in which pressure is applied varies among these movements. Some rely primarily on negotiation and pressure carefully applied; some make extensive use of mass propaganda and demonstrations; finally, some use various degrees of "force," such as mass boycotts, strikes, and other pressure tactics, as their strategy. The distinction among strategies based predominantly on education, on mobilizing mass support through propaganda, and on force seems meaningful.

Some movements are specifically identified by their strategy. The strategy of passive resistance, utilized against the British by the Indian nationalists under Gandhi, has since been exported to South Africa and to the American South. Its aim is to solicit moral support when open resistance would be immediately suppressed. It has also been repeatedly adopted by movements with pacifist overtones. On occasion, the hunger strike, popularized by Gandhi's religious fastings to wrest concessions from the British, has also been used as a tactic by individuals belonging to movements fundamentally different in spirit from Gandhi's. Its great advantage, as recognized for example by the Zionists in Israel, lies in the way it fixes public attention on the moral struggle, in which the person fasting represents a rallying point for the movement.

Still other distinctions among strategies make use of the degree of "gradualism." One speaks not only of revolutionary versus reform goals but also of two types of strategy. The strategy that aims to achieve its objective by means of some dramatic uprising (e.g., a general strike, a march on Washington) not only appears revolutionary but may actually, because of its implications, be so. The reformist strategy aims to achieve its goals by the constant pyramiding of specific achievements, however trivial each in itself may seem. To each strategy there usually corresponds some particular set of tactics. But a movement relying on a revolutionary strategy often finds it useful to hide its true intent and make extensive use of "reform" tactics. Sometimes a given set of tactics becomes divorced from its end and becomes an end in itself, but, on the whole, tactics are more subject to change than strategy; they must be constantly adapted to meet the demands of new situations.

The dramatic success of some social movements is attributed primarily to their tactics. For example, the phenomenal growth of the Jehovah's Witnesses indicates the success of the tactic of door-to-door visiting. Each Witness is a minister, and as such he acts as a house-to-house visitor, convinced that he is a trained servant of God, in possession of an absolute and final truth that must be accepted on invincible and divine authority. The movement's success at persuasion, rather than its high morale in response to persecution from outside, best explains its success. Another example of success due to superior tactics was the successful political lobbying of the Anti-Saloon League (see Chapter 16).

Tactics used successfully by one movement are frequently taken over by others. Once the sitdown strike had met with success in the Auto-Lite plant in Toledo, Ohio, it was quickly adopted by rubber, automobile, and steel workers in 1936, whence it spread to France as a favored tactic in the Popular Front days.[43] Sometimes tactics spread by imitation, because of their past success, even when local circumstances seem altogether unfitting. As we have pointed out, after 1917 the American communist movement modeled its strategy on the Russian Revolution. The wonderment was how the Bolsheviks, numbering only eleven thousand members in all Russia as late as May, 1917, were able to seize power five months later. The answer, it seemed, must be found in their tactics. "If great numbers were not necessary, the revolution in every country [they reasoned] was much closer than anyone had dared to hope," leaving out of account all the particular circumstances that made Russia different from the United States.[44]

In comparing movements, one finds few tactical innovations, except those that rely on modern technological means, such as the media of mass communication. For example, the idea that converts could be held only if organized into small prayer groups was already known to and widely applied by John Wesley over two hundred years ago. It is a tactic essentially similar to that employed by Moral Rearmament to gain converts and by Alcoholics Anonymous to regenerate alcoholics. Likewise, one

43. Among many useful studies of the sitdown strike movement are: Edward Levinson, *Labor on the March* (New York: Harper & Brothers, 1938); Irving Howe and B. J. Widick, *The UAW and Walter Reuther* (New York: Random House, 1949), especially chap. 2; Rose Pesotta, *Bread Upon the Waters* (New York: Dodd, Mead & Co., 1945), especially chaps. 19–23.

44. Draper, *op. cit.*, p. 104.

finds that Billy Graham's only major addition to the tactics used by Billy Sunday in his revival some forty years earlier was the widespread use of television, not available to his predecessor. Billy Sunday, in his turn, had served a successful apprenticeship under the Reverend Dwight Moody, a famed revivalist in the preceding generation.[45]

Finally, it must be recognized that tactics are directed as much to maintaining the internal stability of a movement as to the achievement of its concrete objective. Demonstrations, strikes, efforts to seek out converts, etc., are often necessary if morale and faith in the movement's mission is to be maintained. Because of the ideology and psychological fabric that hold a movement together, its leadership often has little choice as to means. Trade-unionists, trained in a tradition of militancy, will agree to strike even if economic conditions are unfavorable and public resentment seems likely to result in punitive action.

IDEOLOGY

THE CONTENT of the official doctrines for which a movement stands are collectively designated as its ideology. Included in the ideology of a social movement would be the following:

1. A *statement of purpose* defining the general objective of the movement and giving the premise on which it is based.
2. A *doctrine of defense*—that is, the body of beliefs that serves as a justification for the movement and its activities.
3. An *indictment,* a criticism, and a condemnation of existing social arrangements.
4. A general *design for action* as to how the objective is to be achieved.
5. Certain *myths* that embody the emotional appeals, a promise of success (based on a revolution or an "objective" law of history), its heroes, and the many folk arguments that are taken seriously.[46]

Attention to the structural aspects of a movement should never lead one to ignore its ideology. The sociological significance of ideology lies in the clues it provides for linking a specific group to a more general ideological current. Such connections are sometimes established by tracing the ideological antecedents of a core group. Furthermore, the study of ideology—that is, the targets at which criticism is aimed and the ultimate goals espoused—helps to identify the class whose interests the

45. William G. McLoughlin, *Billy Sunday Was His Real Name* (Chicago: The University of Chicago Press, 1955).

46. Adapted from Herbert Blumer, "Social Movements," in A. M. Lee (ed.), *New Outline of the Principles of Sociology* (New York: Barnes & Noble, Inc., 1946), chap. 22.

ideology reflects. For example, in studying any socialist group, one needs to relate it to the broader socialist movement as well as to identify the groups it most strongly idealizes. Similarly, the Populist revolt in the West, the Wisconsin Progressive movement, and McCarthyism had their roots in the same geographic area; to some extent they also attacked the same targets, an affinity that analysis of ideology is able to reveal.

Ideology is not only more than the specific program of a movement but also something different. A program is the official face a movement presents to the outside, a platform on the basis of which it seeks support. During periods of active agitation, many people join in support of a movement solely because they agree with some part of its program, without being fully aware of its ideology. Moreover, just as a social movement has various categories of follower, it also may have more than one ideology. The existence of several sets of ideologies side by side in the same movement is due to these factors:

1. One ideology is, as Blumer suggests, for the inner circle, especially the erudite and scholarly intellectuals, and the other, a more simplified version, is for popular consumption. The latter is slanted toward a large body of followers who are judged incompetent to comprehend the complex social philosophies, theologies, economic theories, or scientific evidence that underly the exoteric doctrine. Could the Single-Taxer be expected to understand, or even have first-hand acquaintance with, the economic theories of Henry George? or the rank-and-file Communist to master Marxian economics? or the opponent of nuclear testing to comprehend fully the scientific basis on which an evaluation of the harmful effects of fallout must be made? The more complex the esoteric doctrine of the inner circle, the more will its popularized version differ from it. But in these instances we are really dealing with different presentations or versions of the same ideology.

2. The exoteric doctrine often hides the diversity of interests that underly the movement. Hence the "official" doctrine may serve to provide a semblance of the unity required for common action. The ideology of the Massachusetts Know-Nothings, already mentioned, helped a movement consisting of several core groups to maintain a common front, even though several interests were represented, each seeking the same goal for different reasons. The abortive movement (the Progressive Party) that in 1948 sought to elect Henry Wallace President of the United States was made up of many diverse elements. Among them were many liberals and New Dealers of the moderate "left," who had never favored Truman over Wallace as a running mate for Roosevelt in 1944 and wished for a third party to represent the interests of liberals and labor. A second element consisted of persons with pacifist inclinations, concerned over worsening relations with the Soviet Union. A third core of followers consisted of Communists and their fellow-travelers who sought a forum

for their pro-Soviet policy. The ideology espoused by the group covered these divergent interests, but once the degree of control achieved by the Communists became evident, the "movement" fell apart.

3. The ideology presented to the mass of followers is a "mask" for the real beliefs of the inner core. Its "real" ideology is hidden from all but the initiated. Almond discusses in some detail the esoteric and the exoteric doctrines as they apply to Communist followers.[47] But fascist, Nazi, and other movements seeking mass support for a conspiracy, no less than the Communists, have used two ideologies as well as many front organizations. For instance, the real intent and ideology of the Coughlinite movement was successfully hidden from the mass of its followers for some time. Father Charles E. Coughlin's radio talks at first gained him a considerable following among working people, including Negroes and Jews. Through his National Union for Social Justice, he campaigned against the gold standard and depicted the World Court as the fountainhead of evil. Both his headquarters and greatest source of strength was the auto capital, Detroit, and he also had a sizable following in other industrial cities. When in 1936 the United Auto Workers launched an organizing drive in Flint, Michigan, their organizers found that many of their new recruits were ardent Coughlinites. Also a number of auto locals had endorsed the radio priest's sixteen-point program and were contributing funds to him. They continued to receive advice from him on union tactics and organizing strategy. It was only after the violent strike against General Motors in the fall of 1936 that union members began to discern his real intent. Coughlin, despite repeated requests from strikers, failed to raise his voice to support them.[48] The anti-Semitic nature of the movement became clear only when he began to preach driving the "money changers" from the temple. His National Union was not publicly exposed as pro-fascist and pro-Nazi in ideology until some time later.

Unifying Forces

SYMBOLS AND ACTIONS supplement ideology as unifying forces binding the participants together. Bonds that develop out of common emotions toward a social object, whether common love or common hate,

47. Gabriel Almond, *The Appeals of Communism* (Princeton, N.J.: Princeton University Press, 1954).

48. Discussion of the Coughlin loyalties of auto workers is found in Henry Kraus, *The Many and the Few* (Los Angeles, Calif.: The Planten Press, 1947). In their book Howe and Coser, *op. cit.*, refer to Kraus's interpretation of the Flint strike as highly biased and suspect. Whatever conflicts there may be among various writers in their interpretations of leadership—the role of the Reuther boys, etc.—Kraus's remarks on Coughlinism seem valid.

are as important as belief in a principle. Every movement has its heroes as well as its villains.

The sense of positive identification with a movement, pride in belonging and in its accomplishments, which are so essential to its persistence, constitute the *esprit de corps* of a movement. A movement develops the proper spirit by directing all positive emotions into group-relevant symbols. Largely this is a function of experiences shared over time. But *esprit de corps* also is developed through practices that increase the involvement of members in the movement. Its fellowship is advanced by initiation rites, designed to enhance the superiority of insiders, by various kinds of ceremonial behavior, by opportunities for informal fellowship, by cultivating special forms of expressive behavior. Songs in particular have been effective unifying agents. The Cold Water Army advanced the temperance cause immeasurably by the way it employed both songs and the kind of oratory that was a substitute for vaudeville. Referring to the temperance orator, Jensen wrote,[49]

> Generally this Demosthenes was a reformed old soak, and one of them was famous for the child he planted in the audience. When he reached his peroration: "As for the rum seller, my friends, what name black enough shall we call him?" the shrill voice would shriek, "Devil! Devil!" and the audience would sob its amens.

Some movements, such as the I.W.W., the colorful "Wobblies," have been "singing" movements. Their songs (e.g., "Joe Hill," "Solidarity Forever," "Casey Jones") are now part of trade-union tradition throughout the English-speaking world.

The effect of the villain on the unity of a mass movement seems fundamentally different from that of the idol. Whereas the latter evokes sentiments that become attached to the movement, the invocation of the devil serves primarily to move the collectivity to action. Hoffer has insisted that mass movements can rise and spread without a belief in a God but never without a belief in a devil.[50] Actually, hate suffices to unite a group of followers in outbursts of violence, but hate alone does not enable a movement to develop a permanent identity and a positive program, once the accumulated emotion has spent itself, unless new devils are found. An enemy promotes unity within a movement torn by inner dissension, but only when the internal forces that hold it together are present. Hence, the typical follower of mass movements about whom Hoffer writes quickly abandons one movement for another when it fails.

The crystallization of permanent nuclei that survive the particular

49. Jensen, *op. cit.*, p. 49.
50. Eric Hoffer, *The True Believer* (New York: The New American Library of World Literature, Inc., 1958), p. 86.

eruption of unrest requires the development of a lore, which includes saints, heroes, legends of successful action, forms of expressing fellowship, as well as villains against whom to unite. The lore of a movement includes more than rumors about conspiracies and immorality on the part of the enemy. The morale of a movement depends on a belief in one's rightness, invincibility, and a willingness to sacrifice. *Esprit de corps* and morale are intimately connected, but whether *esprit de corps* is actually translatable into morale can be established only during periods of adversity. High morale enables a movement to weather a setback. Hate, though necessary, never accounts for the *persistence* of a *collective* enterprise when it encounters obstacles.

Social movements effect conversions because they assimilate their followers into a compact body, which offers at once fellowship and rallying points. In the inward movement, the hostility is internalized, leading the participant to make strict demands on himself but to fight a devil with love. This permits a movement to accept converts; the ability to win sinners from the enemy is a mark of one's own superiority. By implanting in its members a deprecating attitude toward outsiders, a focus on the future, and an unquestioning belief in the movement (e.g., fanaticism), movements are able to rally followers.

To understand a social movement it is always necessary to refer to the opposition it encounters. By definition a social movement always represents some unrecognized interest. Unless there is some degree of opposition, the mass of potential followers will not develop the zeal, the opposition, the conviction, and the fanaticism necessary for the success of a social movement. In this case, there is no need to combine with others in a collective effort toward fundamental change in the social order, since aspirations can be channeled into private goals.

B I B L I O G R A P H Y [51]

BELL, DANIEL (ed.). *The New American Right.* New York: Criterion Books, Inc., 1955. A series of careful interpretative essays on the stirrings of right-wing sentiment in the early 1950's.

BLUMER, HERBERT. "Social Movements," *New Outline of the Principles of Sociology*, ed. A. M. LEE, chap. 22. New York. Barnes & Noble, Inc., 1946. A definition of the major categories of social movements, which was the first introduction to the field for a generation of students.

51. Suggested bibliographic references on specific movements are given in footnotes in the two chapters on social movements.

BRINTON, CRANE. *The Anatomy of Revolution*. Englewood Cliffs, N.J.: Prentice-Hall, Inc., 1952. This comparative study of the English, American, French, and Russian revolutions looks for a common underlying pattern.

CANTRIL, HADLEY. *The Psychology of Social Movements*. New York: John Wiley & Sons, Inc., 1941. Written from a psychological orientation, this book places its emphasis on the motivations for participation in social movements.

GREER, THOMAS H. *American Social Reform Movements; Their Pattern Since 1865*. Englewood Cliffs, N.J.: Prentice-Hall, Inc., 1949. A good source for historical materials on some American social movements.

HEBERLE, RUDOLPH. *Social Movements*. New York: Appleton-Century-Crofts, 1951. A general sociological theory, based on comparative case materials, on the relation between social movements and political parties.

HOFFER, ERIC. *The True Believer; Thoughts on the Nature of Mass Movements*. New York: Mentor Books, 1958. This off-beat, but very provocative, book by a longshoreman concentrates on the inner core of followers and their leaders.

KING, C. WENDELL. *Social Movements in the United States*. New York: Random House, 1956. The Grange, Christian Science, and the Ku Klux Klan especially are used to summarize major principles, especially on the organized aspects of social movements.

LAIDLER, HARRY W. *Social-Economic Movements*. New York: Thomas Y. Crowell Company, 1944. A standard treatise on the major movements.

SOREL, GEORGES. *Reflections on Violence*. Glencoe, Ill.: The Free Press, 1950. The classic study, first published at the turn of the century, on the role of "myth" in social movements.

V

Research in
Collective Dynamics

Research in Collective Dynamics

C OLLECTIVE BEHAVIOR is one of the oldest of the conventional divisions of sociology. Yet professional sociologists, it is fair to say, have never regarded the empirical investigation of the collective dynamics of mass society as either especially rich or promising in results. Anselm Strauss, summing up the state of knowledge immediately after World War II, referred to collective behavior as

> one of the most unworked of our research areas. . . . Collective behavior phenomena have been almost wholly neglected as objects for serious investigation. . . . Anyone who attempts to teach a course in collective behavior finds abundant descriptive and illustrative material for teaching purposes, but finds also a scarcity of generalizations dealing with each collective behavior phenomenon. . . . It can be said, furthermore, that except in perhaps three or four areas (public opinion, propaganda, revolutionary movements, and perhaps the ideology of social movements) we are little more advanced in our knowledge of the general field than we were a decade or two ago.[1]

While this assessment would require some qualification today, it still seems fundamentally valid.

Most students of collective behavior would agree that further progress in their field calls, first of all, for a remapping of its boundaries, its subdivisions, and the major problems in need of study. An up-to-date inventory of what we now know and still need to know, a presentation of propositions that are fairly well confirmed and propositions that can be put to test has high priority. This book, in modest degree, attempts such an inventory even though in some problem areas the number of

1. Anselm Strauss, "Research in Collective Behavior: Neglect and Need," *American Sociological Review*, XII (June, 1947), p. 352.

propositions appears pitifully limited and the evidence for them very thin. Consequently, like others, we have been forced to rely heavily on illustrations.

But having taken a groping first step in the direction of reviewing the body of available knowledge, we find ourselves less inclined to share the pessimistic assessment of the field. One major promise—mostly unrealized—lies in the systematic exploitation of research from related fields to derive theoretical formulations about collective behavior phenomena. Anything from the study of hypnosis, psychoanalysis, and small groups to research in public opinion, intergroup relations, political science, military sociology, and history can be useful in the formulation of testable hypotheses.

WHY THE NEGLECT?

SOCIOLOGISTS as a group have seen it necessary neither to sponsor such an inventory nor to conduct extensive empirical investigations into collective behavior. As pointed out in Chapter 1, they have been much more concerned with the study of social structure. One reason for this neglect of a field first staked out by them lies in the subject matter itself; the other, in the sociologist's commitment to research tools that, although adapted to the study of social structure, are not wholly suitable for investigation in this area.

The nature of the subject matter makes observation difficult. The phenomena, as repeatedly noted, are generally transitory, as well as characterized by an element of unpredictability which is not entirely reducible to social structure. Structure persists, but breaks in pattern have always to be tracked down. Often only a lucky accident puts an observer in a position to make significant observations on how a gang forms or to trace the career of a crowd, whereas recurrent interaction patterns are always on hand to be studied.

Moreover, many of the phenomena can only be understood in their natural context, a context that often includes the entire society. In fact, to speak of a crowd or public opinion or a social movement is rather meaningless unless one is dealing with phenomena of some magnitude. But because of their magnitude and complexity, these phenomena are not directly amenable to observation under the kind of rigorously controlled conditions most sociologists would choose. Simple observations of rather strictly delineated phenomena are therefore preferred.

The sociologist seeking recognition for his discipline as a science dealing only with hard facts finds that the collective dynamics of mass society are not particularly amenable to research, so that results of his work may not justify the effort and the expenditure. Sound research is generally thought to require careful and time-consuming planning in advance. The investigator wants to pre-test his instruments and to anticipate with some degree of confidence the range and shadings of the responses he can expect. He wants to train his interviewers and observers, minimize interviewer "effect" or observer bias, and above all carefully sample the phenomena to be observed. These goals are accomplished only by a certain amount of routine. Yet many elementary collective phenomena disappear while researchers are still preparing to move into the field; others have a habit of undergoing unexpected metamorphoses even as they are being studied.

More open-ended and, therefore, more flexible research tools seem better suited to research in this area. Yet their utility is also limited. They are employed primarily in exploratory or pilot studies, to get hunches which may be followed up in more systematic inquiry. It is evident that the focused interview, the open-ended query, the interview in depth, and participant observation, considered as alternatives to more restrictive research tools, are most useful for obtaining data on the individual respondent. The use of respondents, instead of trained observers, as informants on the behavior of others always raises serious questions about (1) the reliability and accuracy of their observations—that is, observer bias—and (2) the representativeness of the entire group of respondents and their observations, however accurate individual reports may be. Most sociologists have not found it desirable to rely on unsystematic data from observers who are likely to have been influenced by personal bias and by their perspectives. Because of the sociologist's insistence on a representative description, he uses with caution generalizations based on journalistic accounts, personal documents, and historical studies of unique events.

PROGRESS AND PROSPECT

TO PERSIST IN EMPIRICAL RESEARCH, the student of collective behavior has either to compromise somewhat his commitment to systematic techniques or to run the risk of missing the most intriguing features of the phenomena under study. Whether he chooses to follow traditional procedures or to venture into new paths, he faces the problem of generalizing from incomplete observation: in the first case, from observations concerned with only one aspect of the phenomena; in the latter, from data whose representativeness and objectivity are open to question. In coping with this problem, the answer seems to reside less in technical refinements than in more painstaking interpretation of data obtainable through techniques already in use. This task has to be faced squarely; it is not to be confused with the problem of reliability or validity of any specific research technique.

SURVEY DESIGNS

A technique favored for the study of organization has been carried over into the study of collective dynamics; that is, the survey that solicits information from a representative sample of respondents about themselves. To mention the survey is to think of the public opinion poll, but it is as feasible to conduct surveys among participants in a crowd, members of a gang, followers in a social movement, or transmitter-recipients in the rumor process. The sample survey can provide the investigator with comparable data on a large number of persons, which can then be subjected to rigorous, especially statistical analysis. For this advantage, a price is exacted.

In the first place, as illustrated in the discussion of the opinion poll (Chapter 13), survey data tend to put the emphasis on the determinants of the individual response. One learns primarily how different categories of individuals respond to danger, who are the instigators or followers in a crowd, what distinguishes various types of leadership, who joins a sect, etc. Second, the survey tends to focus not on the emergent behavior but only on some particular aspect of the behavior. Understanding who does what and why does not necessarily allow one to reconstruct either the collective processes by which the behavior spreads or the general conditions conducive to this spread. To know that young women are listened to for advice on "fashion" leaves most of the fashion process still unexplained. Finally, this kind of analysis favors the recurrent patterns in the behavior of *individuals*, the essence of structural analysis. Thus, one learns about the way leadership in a social movement is exercised, what is the typical pattern of interaction in the gang, etc. The survey fosters the tendency to concentrate on the most organized aspects of collective behavior.

This predilection for recurrent patterns applies even to the panel interview design, in which the same respondents are interviewed on several occasions, permitting the observation of changes and some analysis of processes. Panels have been used most extensively for the study of consumer behavior and election campaigns, both involving forms of collective behavior with a strongly conventional element. To set up a panel in an unpredictable area of behavior would involve great effort and expense which might not be warranted by results. Still, the possibility of using existing panels to collect data on reactions to unexpected occurrences and shifts of behavior in areas they were not designed to cover has not yet been adequately explored.

EXPERIMENTAL DESIGNS

The laboratory has two unique advantages: it permits the kind of manipulation and control of individuals and of specific factors in the total situation necessary for the testing of a hypothesis; it reduces a complex phenomenon to proportions that make possible its observation in its entirety. It makes possible also training of observers, crosschecking their reliability, and developing procedures for observation. But the translation of collective definition, demoralization, etc., into laboratory situations is not exactly easy. Many experimental designs have failed to produce reasonable facsimiles of real life conditions. The effects observed in the laboratory seem trivial when compared with the widespread and basic transformations outside the laboratory. There is a tendency to seize on minor differences and to repeat essentially similar designs, varying factors that are controlled rather easily, even though their theoretical relevance remains questionable. Laboratory designs seem most promising when it comes to pinning down hypotheses that have already been refined and spelled out on the basis of real-life data.

Experimental studies in actual institutions can be valuable. Though some control is sacrificed, the researcher retains the natural context of the miniature phenomenon. Also a staff of trained observers is usually available, making it possible to trace the progress of a planted rumor or fad or to trace gang formation under artificially created conditions of conflict. Even when manipulation is not possible or desirable, riots within prisons or grapevines within institutions usually involve few enough people to allow one to identify with reasonable accuracy the roles played by participants, the crystallization of patterns, the twists and turns in sentiment or definition and to relate them to antecedent conditions.

THE CASE STUDY

Those doing empirical research in collective dynamics have favored the case study as a means of clarifying concepts and putting to the test models hypothesized by theory. The case study method, more than others just discussed, preserves a full view of the phenomenon in its qualitative richness. It is possible to use almost any type of datum. But because the vagaries of collective behavior phenomena cannot be fully anticipated, the researcher depends on such data as chance has made available. This means, first of all, a bias in the phenomenon subject to detailed study. The investigator is most likely to find data on (a) the more structured and enduring phenomena in their more organized phases (e.g., an officially validated legend, the core group of a social movement, a sect or a gang well past its first beginnings), and (b) the more successful and dramatic phenomena (e.g., fads that were successfully promoted, a sect with especially colorful leaders, etc.).

Most available case studies provide mainly vivid descriptions of a single incident or collectivity, often stressing its more curious and bizarre aspects. This is exactly the kind of investigation that has resulted in innumerable critiques as well as a proliferation of typologies. Beyond identifying and typing phenomena, there is usually little analysis. But to type a phenomenon is not to explain what accounts for the development of one type rather than another. Still, the various case materials, whatever their limitations, offer a rich source of comparative data which can be exploited to develop a broad set of propositions about collective dynamics.

ANALYSIS OF AGGREGATE TREND DATA

For analysis in collective behavior, sociologists make use of certain aggregate trend data initially collected for other purposes. Basic census data, economic indicators, election statistics, data on consumer behavior, indices of social disorganization, and recurrent public opinion questions are just about the only information available on a continuing basis. Identical data systematically obtained from a large number of people permit one to locate even minor changes. Although they offer many clues about the type of person who accounts for the trend, these data supply no measure of change or turnover in the individual, as do data from panel studies. The specific processes still have to be inferred. Nevertheless, even relatively crude indices, when subjected to careful analysis, often yield interesting interpretations. Thus, the number of lynchings and the proportion of the two-party vote in favor of the Democrats have been correlated with certain economic indicators. Long-term studies of voting statistics indicate the effect of a specific campaign, and long-term trends in church membership, the impact of mass revival campaigns.

The major obstacle to the exploitation of such aggregate trend data is the lack of a clearing house in which relevant information can be sifted and filed. The center set up at Williams College for storing survey data collected by individual polling agencies is a step toward rectifying this. A number of recent studies have shown how useful trend data are in reducing the area of speculation.[2]

2. Herbert Hyman and Paul B. Sheatsley, "The Political Appeal of President Eisenhower," *Public Opinion Quarterly*, XVII (Winter, 1953–1954), pp. 443–60.

MASS OBSERVATION

A panel of observers can be employed to record both routine occurrences and events of special interest—a method pioneered in England before World War II by an organization called Mass-Observation. Mass-Observation "started life as a 'movement' aimed in somewhat shrill protest against the inactivity of social science. . . ." [3] Through its army of participant observers, it was to provide what Malinowski called a "nationwide intelligence service." Unfortunately this approach never really got beyond the boundaries of Britain.

The techniques of Mass-Observation make use of the city, in the sense in which Robert E. Park spoke of it, as a laboratory for the investigation of collective behavior; for example, strikes, minor revolutionary movements, intergroup warfare, fads, and new sects are almost daily occurrences. Especially useful in the study of collective dynamics is the "overheard," a study of chance conversations unobtrusively collected. "Systematic listening to unprompted conversations," comments Madge, "gets as near as the outsider can to the 'frank' level of opinion, and especially to spontaneous interest and intensity of feeling." On the other hand, "the chanciness of overhearing and the natural tendency of the observer to select, memorize, and record the more bizarre conversations make it rather rash to use such material as the basis of generalizations about current public interest or public attitudes." [4]

Most of the observers retained by Mass-Observation were unpaid volunteers recruited through advertisements in newspapers; for some more intensive studies, full-time observers were employed. In 1939 fifteen hundred eager amateur observers from all over England were sending in reports, on request, about what had happened to them and what they saw on any particular day. From their reports were compiled analyses that included reactions to the political crises and the spread in 1938 of the dance craze called the Lambeth Walk. Another obvious shortcoming was the unrepresentativeness of the sample of observers as well as their lack of training. The least literate segments of the population could hardly be expected to report.

Still, these shortcomings are not inherent in mass observation as an approach. Greater resources than Mass-Observation had at the time would permit the use of trained observers, more carefully briefed, working with a clear idea of the information they need, and applying themselves systematically to obtain it. Some kind of mass observation setup,

3. John Madge, *The Tools of Social Science* (London: Longmans, Green & Co., Ltd., 1951), p. 135f.
4. *Ibid.*, p. 138.

based in university towns, could easily be recruited and used to undertake studies on given occasions. Indeed the Tavistock Institute of Human Relations in England has used a modified version of this design. The American Political Science Association used it in 1952 to observe the nominating process in American political parties. Nor can one leave unmentioned the mobile teams organized by the National Opinion Research Center, set up under a grant from the National Research Council, to study reactions to disasters as soon as they occurred. The purpose of these teams was to obtain information as soon as possible and on the spot, even if something in the way of sampling and pre-testing had to be sacrificed. In a somewhat similar fashion Margaret Mead and her associates obtained the initial reactions to the launching of the first man-made satellite, before responses were structured as a result of social support or recognition via the mass media and before they had become crystallized into public opinion around the issues of public education and the national defense effort. Such data make possible the observation of the collective process from its points of origin.

RECONSTRUCTING THE UNORGANIZED PATTERN

BY SUBSTITUTING the term "collective *dynamics*" for the more conventional "collective behavior," we meant to emphasize that the interactions to be studied were in process and that the relationships revealed in these interactions had not yet congealed into some kind of recurrent pattern or, if they had, that they were temporarily disrupted or transformed. But we also stressed that it was not with the particularistic aspect of the relationships that collective behavior was primarily concerned. The passing along of *a* rumor or the relationship between *a* leader and *a* follower was not our chief interest. What does interest us are the dynamic patterns in which these particular acts result. Since these patterns as well as when they will occur are somewhat unpredictable, their study in real life has to be adapted to the chameleonlike nature of collective behavior. Many of the most interesting aspects have never been subjected to systematic inquiry, because too many studies have exclusively relied on a design allowing them to draw on data from only one source. A flexible research design is much to be preferred.

Thus, the investigator in the field of collective dynamics is something of a detective-reporter, forever keeping his eyes open and his ears to the ground, while at the same time he constantly keeps in mind the over-all pattern which has to be constructed out of many small items of information. Though concerned with unstructured behavior, collective dynamics is not exactly chaotic or random behavior. In fact, the assumption of some kind of pattern is indispensable. The units that account for this pattern are perspectives, and the researcher has to reconstruct the underlying pattern out of the partial and divergent perspectives of a multiplicity of observers. The reconstruction of such a pattern is much easier when one deals with organized structures; the persistent perspectives of every person can be deduced from his status. But where behavior is not governed by status, it is imperative to get data about the perspectives themselves.

For example, the analysis of social structure is governed by the assumption that the participants in any role-relationship share some kind of common definition. Because this is so, one need not study in detail *each* individual's definition of a situation. Likewise, people occupying similar positions share perspectives. In collective dynamics, on the other hand, one must begin by sampling the various perspectives from which a phenomenon can be experienced. Thus, the individual perceptions growing out of one perspective will be modified and "corrected" by those stemming from another. Out of all these perspectives emerges a collective definition, and the process through which it emerges is what has to be reconstructed.

In studying all the other processes, such as demoralization, collective defense, crystallization, conversion, it is equally necessary to consider all the perspectives that enter the situation. Not only does the crowd consist of an active core, but timid followers, passive bystanders, the actions of possible victims, even the impressions gained by a mass medium audience, etc., all contribute to what the crowd is all about. To be able to command data of such complexity, the investigator needs, above all, something that one might call a sensitivity to the group atmosphere. It consists of at least two completely different elements: (1) theoretical sophistication, which sensitizes the investigator to significant clues he might otherwise ignore, and (2) trained imagination, which enables him to discern and imaginatively reconstruct out of these clues the total situation in which the various direct and indirect participants interact.

B I B L I O G R A P H Y

BLUMER, HERBERT. "Collective Behavior," *Review of Sociology: Analysis of a Decade,* ed. J. B. GITTLER. New York: John Wiley & Sons, Inc., 1957. Summarizes and evaluates the major research during the decade 1947–1957.

FOOTE, NELSON N., and HART, CLYDE W. "Public Opinion and Collective Behavior," *Group Relations at the Crossroads,* ed. M. SHERIF and M. O. WILSON, chap. 13. New York: Harper & Brothers, 1953. An argument for studying the collective process by which new attitudes crystallize out of pre-verbal behavior before it is well under way.

MADGE, CHARLES, and HARRISON, TOM. *Britain by Mass-Observation.* Harmondsworth, England: Penguin Books, Ltd., 1939. Vivid accounts, illustrating the use of planned observation to assess public reactions.

STRAUSS, ANSELM. "Collective Behavior: Neglect and Need," *American Sociological Review,* XII (June, 1947), pp. 352–54. A pessimistic assessment of research done in collective behavior up to and including World War II.

Author Index

Subject Index